Basic Issues in Econometrics

Arnold Zellner

Basic Issues in Econometrics

The University of Chicago Press
Chicago and London

Arnold Zellner is the H. G. B. Alexander Professor of Economics and Statistics at the University of Chicago Graduate School of Business. He is the founding editor of the *Journal of Business and Economic Statistics* and director of the H. G. B. Alexander Research Foundation.

The University of Chicago Press, Chicago 60637
The University of Chicago Press, Ltd., London

Printed in the United States of America

93 92 91 90 89 88 87 86 85 84 54321

Library of Congress Cataloging in Publication Data

Zellner, Arnold
Basic issues in econometrics.

Includes bibliographies and indexes.
1. Econometrics. I. Title.
HB139.Z44 1984 330'.028 83-24285
ISBN 0-226-97983-0

Contents

Preface vii
Introduction ix

1 Philosophical and General Issues

1.1 Philosophy and Objectives of Econometrics 3
1.2 Perspectives on Mathematical Models in the Social Sciences 12
1.3 Basic Issues in Econometrics, Past and Present 26
1.4 Causality and Econometrics 35
1.5 Is Jeffreys a "Necessarist"? 75

2 Aspects of Econometric Models and Model Construction

2.1 Statistical Analysis of Econometric Models 83
2.2 Time Series Analysis and Econometric Model Construction 120
2.3 Simulation Experiments with a Quarterly Macroeconometric Model of the U.S. Economy, *with S. C. Peck* 141
2.4 Retrospect and Prospect: Summarization of the 1976 NBER-Census Conference on Seasonal Analysis of Economic Time Series 158
2.5 The Quality of Quantitative Economic Policymaking When Targets and Costs of Change Are Misspecified 169

3 Bayesian Econometrics and Statistics

3.1 The Bayesian Approach and Alternatives in Econometrics 187
3.2 Maximal Data Information Prior Distributions 201
3.3 Bayesian and Non-Bayesian Analysis of the Log-Normal Distribution and Log-Normal Regression 216
3.4 Bayesian and Non-Bayesian Analysis of the Regression Model with Multivariate Student-*t* Error Terms 225
3.5 Estimation of Functions of Population Means and Regression Coefficients Including Structural Coefficients: A Minimum Expected Loss (MELO) Approach 238
3.6 Jeffreys-Bayes Posterior Odds Ratio and the Akaike Information Criterion for Discriminating between Models 269
3.7 Posterior Odds Ratios for Regression Hypotheses: General Considerations and Some Specific Results 275
3.8 The Current State of Bayesian Econometrics 306

Author Index 323
Subject Index 329

Preface

The papers published in this volume reflect some of the research in econometrics that I have carried forward since the mid-1950s. Much of this research was performed while I held appointments at the University of Washington, the University of Wisconsin, and the University of Chicago. The freedom and support provided by these institutions are much appreciated. In addition, colleagues and students, too numerous to list by name, have been very stimulating and helpful. At the University of Chicago, participants in the Econometrics and Statistics Colloquium have given me much constructive advice, as have members of the NBER-NSF Seminar on Bayesian Inference in Econometrics.

Much of the research reported herein was supported by funds from the H. G. B. Alexander Endowment Fund, Graduate School of Business, University of Chicago, and by grants from the National Science Foundation, for which I am most grateful.

Kind permission to reprint published papers was provided by the American Statistical Association, Croom Helm, Ltd., Macmillan Publishing Company, Marcel Dekker, MIT Press, and North-Holland Publishing Company.

Finally, I thank my secretary, Pamela Eckert, for her valuable assistance in preparing this manuscript.

Introduction

The essays included in this volume are presented in three parts, entitled Philosophical and General Issues, Aspects of Econometric Models and Model Construction, and Bayesian Econometrics and Statistics. Many basic issues of concern to economists, econometricians, and statisticians are considered. Since these issues are important in relation to the progress of econometrics, I hope that the essays included in this volume will contribute to enhanced understanding of them and to improvements in theoretical and applied econometrics.

Part I, Philosophical and General Issues, is included in this volume because philosophy is important in all areas of life and work, including econometrics. I believe that a good understanding of the philosophy of science as it relates to econometrics provides invaluble guidance in research and teaching. Unfortunately, many econometrics textbooks do not discuss basic philosophical issues such as alternative definitions of probability, the nature of induction and reduction, alternative systems of statistical inference, the meaning of causality, and many other important topics. The discussions of these topics in the papers included in this section have been presented to students in my graduate econometrics courses for many years with very favorable reactions. On the other hand, I recognize the danger that students may become enmeshed in endless methodological discussions and be diverted from creative work in econometrics. Thus, in my lectures I emphasize the following words of Henry Moore:

> It is a mistake for a sculptor or a painter to speak or write very often about his job. It releases tension needed for his work. By trying to express his aims with rounded-off logical exactness, he can easily become a theorist whose actual work is only a caged-in exposition of conceptions evolved in terms of logic and words.[1]

1. Henry Moore, "Notes on Sculpture," in B. Ghiselin, ed., *The Creative Process* (New York: Mentor Books, 1952), p. 73.

What Moore has said about work in art applies to work in econometrics. However, as stated above, an understanding of methodological issues is important for students, researchers, and teachers. Indeed years ago in my undergraduate work in physics, I was required to take a course in the philosophy of science and had the good fortune to listen to lectures by Philipp Frank. Since views on methodological issues knowingly or unknowingly guide our work, it is valuable on occasion to reflect on them and it is in this spirit that the essays in this section are presented.

The first essay in this section, "Philosophy and Objectives of Econometrics," is a written version of my invited Association Lecture presented at the 1980 meeting of the British Association of University Teachers of Economics. It was a pleasure to discuss the roles of description, induction, and reduction in econometric research with British colleagues. In the paper, deductive, inductive, and reductive inference are defined, discussed, and related to work in econometrics. The implications of this discussion for the basic issues of econometric model size and complexity are detailed. In particular, the complexity of operating macroeconometric models is criticized with the constructive suggestion that research should be directed toward simplifying them. It is noted that leading researchers in many fields of science exhibit a preference for sophisticatedly simple models that are understandable, explain past data, and predict well. Further, it is observed that unusual facts often play a key role in the production of new economic models and theories. While making this point in a lecture several years ago, it occurred to me that more thought should be given to procedures for producing unusual facts in economics. In the paper, eight procedures for producing unusual facts are described that are thought to be useful in econometric research. I suggest that economic theorists and others often make substantial research contributions by constructing explanations of unusual empirical findings. This is an example of the interaction between theoretical and empirical research that has been very fruitful in econometrics and other sciences.

The second paper in Part I, "Perspectives on Mathematical Models in the Social Sciences," was written in connection with consulting work on a Battelle Memorial Institute project to determine how proposed dam construction on the Susquehanna River by the U.S. Army Corps of Engineers might affect regional growth.[2] A detailed model of the Susquehanna River basin economy was built and used in simulation experiments to appraise the economic effects of proposed dam construction. Since many top Battelle

2. See H. R. Hamilton, S. E. Goldstone, J. W. Milliman, A. L. Pugh, E. R. Roberts, and A. Zellner, *Systems Simulation for Regional Analysis: An Application to River-Basin Planning* (Cambridge: MIT Press, 1969) for a report of this project.

administrators were engineers and physicists, it was necessary to provide them with perspectives on modeling social systems that are described in the paper.

In the Susquehanna modeling work, which extended over approximately a five-year period, a key issue was whether to pursue a Forrester "industrial dynamics" approach or an econometric modeling approach. After long discussions, it was decided to attempt to synthesize elements of both approaches in producing the Susquehanna model. Forrester and his colleagues, including Pugh and Roberts, who were engaged in our project, were correct in criticizing econometricians for their relative lack of attention to determining functional forms of relations, lag structures, and dynamic properties of models. On the other hand, the industrial dynamics approach in the mid-1960s did not involve much economic theory and use of data to estimate and test models with appropriate statistical procedures.[3] In our modeling work, we attempted to use the best elements of both approaches to the extent that data constraints permitted.

The third paper in Part I, "Basic Issues in Econometrics, Past and Present," is a written version of my John R. Commons Award Lecture presented at the Allied Social Science Associations meeting in December, 1981. In the paper, I provide an overview of some salient past and present issues in econometrics. From a current reading of my paper, I am struck with how similar the basic issues that concerned Keynes and Tinbergen in the late 1930s and early 1940s are to those that face econometricians today. Indeed they appear to be issues that are present in science generally, namely measurement problems, inference issues, fruitful interaction between measurement and theory, and the role of theory and prediction in science. There is no doubt but that much progress has been made in econometrics during the past half century with respect to these issues. That is, the data bases in economics today are much improved realtive to those of the 1930s. Economic and statistical analyses are much more sophisticated now than in past decades. Computer techniques are now much more powerful than in the past. Yet, there is room for improvement as pointed out in my paper. A more pronounced interaction between economic theory and applications seems to be desirable. More economic theories that take proper account of stochastic elements in behavior and that yield empirically verifiable predictions would be welcome. Continued work on producing better measurements of economic variables is certainly needed, as is proper attention to the quality of measurements in econometric analyses. Finally, it is pointed out

3. For a more recent discussion of these issues, see J. Forrester, "Information Sources for Modeling the National Economy," and my discussion of Forrester's paper in *Journal of the American Statistical Association*, 75 (1980): 555–69.

that good strategies for formulating and investigating the forms of econometric models are needed, an area that is currently being investigated quite vigorously. Given that many economists and econometricians are aware of these problems and are working hard to provide better solutions to them, I am fundamentally optimistic about the future of econometrics.

"Causality and Econometrics," the fourth paper in Part I, was written at the invitation of Karl Brunner and Allan H. Meltzer, two distinguished monetary economists. They were very concerned about the appropriate interpretation of various statistical "tests of causality" reported in the economic literature. Not only did these tests have important implications for monetary economic theory but also for practical policy problems. To complicate matters further, the results of some of the tests are contradictory. It took a lot of work during a cold Chicago winter to hit upon an appropriate approach for my paper. Rather than try to formulate a new concept of causality, as some econometricians have attempted to do in the past, I decided to consider the philosophers' definition of causality and to contrast it with those put forward by econometricians. From these considerations, I concluded that the philosophical definition, "predictability according to a law or set of laws" is adequate for work in econometrics and preferable to several other definitions published in the econometric literature. Discussions with my good friend Clive Granger reveal that he is sympathetic to the philosophers' definition and now regards his proposed "tests of causality" as tests of the suitability of models' formulation or of model identification rather than of causality. In this paper several applied "tests of causality" are also critically reviewed with the conclusion that for a variety of reasons they are defective and not tests of causality as defined by philosophers.[4]

To establish causality, it is necessary to have well-thought-out economic theories or laws that provide understanding of economic behavior and that have been shown to predict well in many actual applications. Successful prediction alone without economic theory and laws that provide understanding is not an adequate basis for asserting causality, a restatement of the old adage that correlation does not necessarily imply causation. Considerations such as these are basic for an understanding of econometric results but unfortunately are not discussed in many econometrics textbooks, perhaps because there has been some confusion about the meaning of causality that my paper attempts to dispel.[5]

4. See C. Hernández-Iglesias and F. Hernández-Iglesias, "Causality and the Independence Phenomenon: The Case of the Demand for Money," *Journal of Econometrics*, 15 (1981): 247–63, for an illuminating analysis and reinterpretation of some of these conflicting results.

5. For another useful discussion of these issues, see H. A. Simon, "Causation," in W. H. Kruskal and J. M. Tanur (eds.), *International Encyclopedia of Statistics*, vol. 1 (New York: Free Press, 1978), pp. 35–41.

The last paper in Part I, "Is Jeffreys a 'Necessarist'?" discusses definitions of probability, the meaning of the word "necessarist," and the issue of whether Jeffreys is a necessarist. It was written with the objectives not only of addressing the necessarist issue but also of bringing to the attention of econometricians and statisticians some basic issues in the philosophy of knowledge. These relate to how an individual researcher interprets his data and the connections among individuals in interpreting a particular investigator's data and results. Jeffreys's discussions[6] of these issues, which are reviewed in the paper, bring to the fore the relation of empirical work to philosophical views of the world including realism, idealism, and solipsism. Most important is the view that there is no logical necessity involved in accepting results of researchers. Each individual researcher must convince others of the validity of his conclusions by presenting sound results and arguing the empirical validity of them. In view of these and other considerations, it is concluded that Jeffreys is not a necessarist.

On concepts of probability used in applied econometric and statistical work, Jeffreys states that while many applied workers assert that they utilize a frequency or "objective" definition of probability, in their actual work they use a "reasonable degree of belief" concept of probability. Since probability is used extensively in applied work, use of an appropriate and fruitful concept of probability is a basic issue that deserves much thought and analysis on the part of econometricians so that they can interpret their empirical results in a satisfactory fashion.

Part II, Aspects of Econometric Models and Model Construction, begins with a paper, "Statistical Analysis of Econometric Models," that deals with many issues that arise in formulating and analyzing econometric models. After reviewing the remarkable progress that has been made in measuring economic variables, developing concepts needed in econometric modeling, and producing statistical estimation, testing, and prediction techniques, some additional issues requiring more research are discussed in the paper.

In the first part of the paper, econometric model construction is viewed as a sequential, iterative process involving use of economic theory and other outside information, data, statistical inference techniques, data evaluation, diagnostic checks of model adequacy, mathematical and computer simulation analyses, and forecasting and prediction tests employing new data. While this sequential, iterative approach seems reasonable and in fact is utilized by many model builders, it is the case that most model builders use it in an informal way since, unfortunately, formal procedures are as yet not available. In a later part of the paper, a structural-econometric-modeling-

6. H. Jeffreys, *Theory of Probability*, 3d ed. (London: Oxford University Press, 1967; 1st ed., 1939) and *Scientific Inference*, 3d ed. (Cambridge: University Press, 1973; 1st ed., 1931).

time-series analysis (SEMTSA) approach, developed jointly with Franz Palm, is described that may be helpful in this connection. In the SEMTSA approach, it is suggested that a synthesis of structural modeling and time series analysis concepts and procedures will probably be fruitful in producing econometric models that perform better in forecasting and policy analysis. Earlier, many econometricians believed that time series models were naive, mechanical models completely unrelated to structural economic models. The SEMTSA approach emphasizes that structural econometric models are multiple time series models and hence are intimately related to various time series models, including Box-Jenkins models[7] studied intensively by statisticians. One basic problem in the pure time series approach to modeling is the fact that multivariate time series models, be they in multivariate autoregressive-moving-average form or in vector autoregressive form, have many parameters in them. In practice this means that it is difficult to estimate them precisely and that tests have low power against important alternative hypotheses. In the SEMTSA approach, additional information coming from economic theory and other subject matter considerations is utilized to augment the information in the data and will probably contribute to the production of better econometric models.

With respect to a given variant of an econometric model, current econometric estimation, testing, and prediction methods are reviewed. It is suggested that Bayesian inference procedures will be very useful in estimation, testing, and prediction.[8] The paper was published in the *Journal of the American Statistical Association* followed by the remarks of invited discussants and the author's response.[9]

In the second paper of Part II, "Time Series Analysis and Econometric Model Construction," the SEMTSA approach is discussed further and simple examples are presented to illustrate it. In this work, much of it joint with Franz Palm, simple monetary models of the type put forward by Milton Friedman are analyzed. Also a hog-market supply and demand model is considered. The results contained in the paper indicate that much can be learned about models' inadequacies by pursuing the SEMTSA approach

7. G. E. P. Box and G. M. Jenkins, *Time Series Analysis, Forecasting, and Control*, rev. ed. (San Francisco: Holden-Day, 1976; 1st ed., 1970).

8. An example of the fruitfulness of Bayesian forecasting methods is given in R. Litterman, "A Bayesian Procedure for Forecasting with Vector Autoregressions" (Department of Economics, MIT, Cambridge, Mass., 1980).

9. My paper was written at the request of S. James Press, formerly invited papers editor of the *Journal of the American Statistical Association*, who invited D. A. Belsley, E. Kuh, C. F. Christ, P. M. Robinson, and T. J. Rothenberg to comment on my paper; see *Journal of the American Statistical Association*, 74 (1979): 628–51 for my paper, the discussants' comments, and my rejoinder.

and that what is so learned can be useful in improving models in the sequential, iterative, model-building approach described in the paper.

The following paper, "Simulation Experiments with a Quarterly Macroeconometric Model of the U.S. Economy," co-authored with Stephen C. Peck, illustrates another aspect of the sequential, iterative, model-building approach. It was written at the time when I was a consultant to a group building the Federal Reserve–MIT–Penn quarterly macroeconometric model of the U.S. economy. I urged the group to simplify the structure of the model so that it would become more easily understood both conceptually and in practical use. To emphasize the importance of this point, Peck and I performed simulation experiments to appraise properties of the model just as aeronautical engineers subject airplane models to wind-tunnel tests. The results of simulation experiments are presented in our paper and I leave it up to the reader's judgment as to whether he (or she) would be willing to "fly" this model under actual operating conditions. On the positive side, I believe that our experiments brought to light features of the model that are worthy of note in appraising its adequacy. Peck, who is currently a project manager at the Electric Power Research Institute has remarked to me that the discussions and procedures in our paper are very relevant in his current work that involves evaluation of electricity demand, pricing, and capacity expansion models. It is our firm belief that econometric models' local and global properties should be thoroughly evaluated and understood before they are used in actual forecasting and policy analysis.

The paper "Retrospect and Prospect: Summarization of the 1976 NBER-Census Conference on Seasonal Analysis of Economic Time Series" presents in broad outline the major research results and problems discussed at the 1976 conference sponsored by the U.S. Bureau of the Census and the National Bureau of Economic Research. The conference was held at a time when major developments in applied time series analysis were appearing that had important implications for practical seasonal analysis and adjustment. Applied statistical workers in many governmental agencies and businesses in the U.S., Canada, England, Germany, the Netherlands, and several other countries as well as leading statisticians and econometricians participated in the conference. This interaction between theoretical and applied workers in the time series area proved most effective. Many of the procedures discussed at the conference including the X-11–ARIMA procedure of Estela Dagum, the signal-extraction ARIMA approach of George Box, Stephen Hillmer, and George Tiao, the deterministic-stochastic approach of David Pierce, and the Bell Labs seasonal adjustment techniques (SABL) developed by William Cleveland, Douglas Dunn, Irma Terpenning, and others have come into use since the time of the conference.

Most important, the 1976 conference provided an in-depth discussion of the conceptual issues involved in seasonal analysis and adjustment, important topics since many economic time series exhibit considerable seasonal variation. Three approaches to seasonal analysis and adjustment were distinguished, (1) descriptive, (2) statistical modeling, and (3) structural econometric or causal statistical modeling. Issues associated with each of these three basic approaches were discussed at the conference and are presented in my paper.[10] Many applied workers including Julius Shiskin and Shirley Kallek, who based their work mainly on a descriptive statistical approach, such as X-11, were fascinated by descriptions of statistical and econometric modeling approaches. It is to their credit that they have encouraged research on these newer approaches that are currently in use or coming into use.

A major issue in the seasonal analysis area is the economic analysis and modeling of seasonality. I first encountered this problem while at the University of Washington when James Crutchfield and I were involved in a two-year study of the economic effects of the world famous Pacific halibut conservation program. One part of our study dealt with the effects of the conservation program on the seasonal pattern of pricing. We showed that changes in conservation policies, along with other variables, had an effect on the seasonal pattern of pricing. Similarly, changes in monetary and fiscal policies have effects on the seasonal variation of interest rates, unemployment, output, and many other important variables. It is surprising that relatively little econometric analysis has been devoted to the theory and modeling of seasonal variation, optimal (or just good) seasonal economic policies, and appropriate seasonal adjustment. As noted in my paper, Charles Plosser and Kenneth Wallis made contributions in this area. However, much more work remains to be done.

The last paper in Part II, "The Quality of Quantitative Economic Policymaking When Targets and Costs of Change Are Misspecified," appeared in a volume honoring Jan Tinbergen, who is regarded by many as the father of modern macroeconometric modeling and use of models for policy analysis. I wrote the paper in 1971 when I was visiting Ford research professor in the Department of Economics, University of California at Berkeley, where I did my graduate work in economics. In part, the paper reflects the traditional Berkeley concern with policy problems and in part my own curiosity about whether better policy results are obtained when policy targets are set

10. See also *Seasonal Adjustment of the Monetary Aggregates: Report of the Committee of Experts on Seasonal Adjustment Techniques*, G. H. Moore, G. E. P. Box, H. B. Kaitz, D. A. Pierce, J. A. Stephenson, and A. Zellner, (Washington, D.C.: Board of Governors of the Federal Reserve System, 1981).

too high and costs of change are mistakenly assumed to be low, as is the case for some radicals, or are mistakenly assumed to be high, as is the case for some conservatives. In the examples analyzed, it is found that overstating target values and understating costs of change can lead to very serious departures from good economic policies. This area, robustness of policymaking with respect to errors in formulating social welfare and other criterion functions, is an important topic that deserves much more analysis. It is the case that Tinbergen recognized the problem years ago and presented cogent discussions of it in his work.

Part III, Bayesian Econometrics and Statistics begins with a paper, "The Bayesian Approach and Alternatives in Econometrics," that I wrote at the invitation of Michael Intrilligator for an Econometric Society meeting and was published in a book that he edited. The topic is of great importance since procedures for learning from data are central in all sciences, including econometrics. In the early 1960s, I commenced a research program[11] to investigate the relative performance of Bayesian and alternative approaches to inference problems in econometrics. While philosophical considerations are relevant for judging alternative approaches to inference and are discussed extensively in the literature, I decided to adopt a pragmatic approach, namely, to get evidence on the relative performance of Bayesian and alternative approaches in solving specific econometric problems. I found that colleagues in econometrics and economics were generally very interested in the results that I obtained and appreciated the pragmatic approach that I adopted. Contrary to some views on how science progresses, I found colleagues very eager to learn about new Bayesian procedures. In my paper, I make many explicit comparisons of Bayesian and non-Bayesian solutions to a variety of practical econometric problems. It is concluded that the Bayesian approach produces solutions that compare very favorably with those yielded by alternative approaches. It is the case that the Bayesian approach can reproduce many non-Bayesian results and produce other solutions that are difficult, if not impossible to obtain by non-Bayesian methods. Thus it is concluded on pragmatic as well as on philosophical grounds that there is much to commend the use of the Bayesian approach in econometrics. Indeed, the number of studies in econometrics and statistics employing Bayesian methods has been increasing rapidly in the last fifteen years.[12]

11. Much of this work was financed by grants from the National Science Foundation, for which I am most grateful.

12. For example, the *Current Index to Statistics: Applications, Methods, and Theory*, vol. 4 (Washington, D.C.: American Statistical Association and Institute of Mathematical Statistics, 1978), lists about 195 papers treating Bayesian methods and applications.

The second paper of Part III, "Maximal Data Information Prior Distributions" describes a procedure for generating both "noninformative" and "informative" prior distributions for use in Bayesian analysis. Having good procedures for representing prior information is critical since much prior information is used, many times informally in analyzing applied econometric problems. In this paper, an information theory measure subject to side conditions is maximized by calculus of variations techniques to yield a maximal data information prior (MDIP) probability density function (pdf). Several alternative interpretations of the procedure are discussed in the paper.[13] The simplest is that the MDIP is the prior pdf that maximizes the average value of $\log[\ell(\theta \mid y)/p(\theta)]$, subject to side conditions where $\ell(\theta \mid y)$ is the likelihood function and $p(\theta)$ is the prior pdf. The side conditions include the condition that $p(\theta)$ be a proper pdf, that is, $\int p(\theta)\, d\theta = 1$, and possibly other restrictions on the moments of the prior pdf. It is shown in the paper that the procedure readily yields MDIP's for many important problems and that a number of them are similar to or exactly the same as prior pdf's that are currently being employed in practice. Thus the procedure that yields MDIP's and extensions of it will be useful in providing prior pdf's that both reflect prior information and permit the data to have a maximal impact on posterior distributions.

The following three papers on estimation of log-normal models, multiple regression models with multivariate Student-*t* errors, and functions of means and regression coefficients, including coefficients of linear structural econometric models, illustrate Bayesian analyses of difficult, central econometric estimation problems. That they all yield to relatively simple Bayesian solutions is noteworthy.

My work on Bayesian analysis of log-normal distributions and log-normal regressions was prompted some years ago by Yair Mundlak's excellent report on sampling theory techniques for analyzing log-normal regressions presented at a University of Chicago research workshop. The Finney-like sampling theory techniques that Mundlak described seemed complicated to me and thus I decided to analyze the problem from the Bayesian point of view with results that are amazingly simple. It is straightforward to compute posterior pdf's of interest using usual Bayesian methods. Also, I discovered sampling theory minimal mean square error estimators for the median and mean of the log-normal distribution and parameters of log-normal regressions. For a long time, I had difficulty finding a Bayesian interpretation of these results. After much pointless effort, I finally hit on the result that they could be produced from a Bayesian point of view by use of relative squared

13. One of them briefly mentioned at the end of the paper was kindly suggested by the physicist Edwin T. Jaynes on one of his visits to the University of Chicago.

error loss functions that are many times more reasonable than simple squared error loss functions.

The idea to consider the regression model with multivariate Student-*t* error terms arose in part out of a curiosity about how nonnormality affects inferences about regression parameters. The multivariate Student-*t* pdf includes the multivariate Cauchy and normal pdf's as limiting cases. It was found that use of the Student-*t* assumption permits easy determination of the effects of nonnormality on inferences. For example, the variances of least squares estimators are readily obtained and easily compared with those based on a normality assumption. Also certain posterior and sampling theory inferences based on the Student-*t* pdf surprisingly remain the same as those based on an assumed normal pdf for the error vector. That we can analyze nonnormal cases is extremely important since not everything is normal in the world.

The paper on minimum expected loss (MELO) estimates of functions of parameters including those of linear structural econometric models originated from discussions with David Ranson, a former doctoral student at Chicago. In his dissertation work, he had the problem of estimating the ratio of two regression coefficents. He produced the maximum likelihood estimate without a standard error. I insisted that he at least compute an asymptotic standard error, asymptotic because the maximum likelihood estimator of the ratio of regression coefficients does not possess finite sample moments of any order. This exchange caused me to think about the nonexistent mean square error of such an estimator and ways to improve it. The problem is important since maximum likelihood and other estimators for structural coefficients often do not possess finite moments and hence have unbounded risk for quadratic and many other loss functions. As George Barnard pointed out to me when I first presented some of my results, it is possible to bound loss functions and thus to have finite risk for estimators without moments. However, with a bounded loss function, it is not clear that usual estimators are optimal. It should also be appreciated that under some conditions, posterior pdf's do not possess moments and thus, for example the posterior mean, which is optimal for a quadratic loss function, does not exist. With issues such as these in mind, I decided to analyze the simplest cases first, namely, estimation of the reciprocal of a mean or of a reduced form regression coefficient as in the simple Haavelmo two-equation Keynesian consumption model. In this case, $\theta = 1/\mu$, where μ is a population mean (or regression coefficient), and then $1 - \theta\mu = 0$ appeared as a restriction. If $\hat{\theta}$ is an estimate, $\epsilon = 1 - \hat{\theta}\mu$ measures the extent to which the restriction fails to be satisfied. By taking the loss function to be $L = \epsilon^2 = (1 - \hat{\theta}\mu)^2 = (\theta - \hat{\theta})^2/\theta^2$, it is seen to be a generalized quadratic loss function. This simple insight led to explicit MELO estimates for this and more complicated problems including MELO structural coefficient estimates. In later work, further properties of MELO estimates and applications of them have been reported in the literature.[14]

In the next two papers, various aspects of the analysis of hypotheses from Bayesian and non-Bayesian points of view are discussed. Evaluation of alternative hypotheses or models is extremely important as noted above in connection with the sequential, iterative process of model-building. However, current methodology for analysis of hypotheses is woefully inadequate and in need of extension. At a meeting in Valencia, Spain, in 1979, Akaike mentioned to me that this was the reason that he developed his information criterion for choosing between or among models. His criterion, usually referred to as AIC, was discussed at a seminar meeting at Bell Labs in June, 1977. When I saw the expression for Akaike's criterion function, I stated that it looked like a posterior odds ratio. My good friend Seymour Geisser asked me to provide analysis supporting my statement. That very evening I derived the result and showed it to Geisser the next morning at the seminar breakfast. The result, included in the paper in the present volume, indicated that the posterior odds ratio does indeed resemble the AIC but includes additional information that is important in evaluating alternative models.

In the second paper dealing with hypotheses, "Posterior Odds Ratios for Regression Hypotheses: General Considerations and Some Specific Results," evidence from a survey of the 1978 economic and econometric literature is presented to show that hypotheses are not being analyzed satisfactorily in empirical studies. Mechanical testing at the 5% level with no consideration given to tests' power and sample size is prevalent. Important hypotheses are thus being evaluated quite carelessly as was also the case in regard to statistical tests of "causality," mentioned earlier. With this sorry state of affairs established, the next part of the paper deals with basic issues in the methodology of evaluating hypotheses. They are described and analyzed. It is concluded that use of Bayesian techniques, developed in Jeffreys's pioneering work and since extended by other researchers will be of value in improving analyses of hypotheses in econometrics and other areas. Some examples of Bayesian methods for accomplishing this goal are provided in the remaining sections of the paper.

14. A. Zellner and S. B. Park, "Minimum Expected Loss (MELO) Estimators for Functions of Parameters and Structural Coefficients of Econometric Models," *Journal of the American Statistical Association*, 74 (1979): 185–93, and S. B. Park, "Some Sampling Properties of Minimum Expected Loss (MELO) Estimators of Structural Coefficients," *Journal of Econometrics*, 18 (1982): 295–311.

The last paper in this part of the volume, "The Current State of Bayesian Econometrics," an invited paper delivered at the 1981 Canadian Conference on Applied Statistics held in Montreal, provides an account of the development of Bayesian econometrics since its beginnings in about the early 1960s. The interaction between econometricians and statisticians is emphasized as an important element in the rapid growth of Bayesian econometrics. A survey of methodological and applied Bayesian econometric studies is given in the paper. The volume of such work has been growing rapidly since the 1960s. Important in this regard is work on Bayesian computer programs and on procedures for formulating prior distributions, particularly in multiparameter models. It is fortunate that much research is in progress on these and other topics that will help to promote many more applications of Bayesian econometric methodology in the future.

In summary, a number of basic issues in econometrics are discussed in the papers in this volume. Of course, there are other issues that are not discussed, for example, the role of mathematical economic theory in econometrics, field experimentation and econometrics, survey methods and econometrics, robust statistical techniques and econometrics, and so on. While this is recognized, it is thought that the selected issues considered in this volume will probably be of interest to econometricians and others and are relevant for understanding some fundamental aspects of econometrics.

Part 1

Philosophical and General Issues

1.1 Philosophy and Objectives of Econometrics

It is a great pleasure and honor to be invited to present the first Association Lecture. I say that it is a pleasure because this occasion affords me the opportunity to record publicly my appreciation for the outstanding British contributions to economics and statistics by Smith, Ricardo, Marshall, Edgeworth, Keynes, Ramsey, and others in economics and by Bayes, Edgeworth, Pearson, Fisher, Jeffreys, and others in statistics. On the philosophy of science, I have been most strongly influenced by the writings of Sir Harold Jeffreys, of your Cambridge University, who was born here in Durham on April 22, 1891, and in honor of whom I have edited a recently published volume, *Bayesian Analysis in Econometrics and Statistics: Essays in Honor of Harold Jeffreys*. Thus, my present lecture and economics and statistics in general have a major "made-in-Britain" component.

Thc first point that I shall make is that unless we have a good grasp of the philosophy and objectives of econometrics, a term which I use almost synonymously with modern quantitative economics, we really do not know what we are doing in economic research and in teaching economics. The same can be said about philosophy and objectives in any area of knowledge. By thinking seriously about the foundations of econometrics, a topic unfortunately not well treated in textbooks of econometrics, we may possibly obtain a clearer understanding of what it is we are doing and trying to accomplish in econometrics and with these insights become more effective in research and teaching.

On the relation of science and econometrics, I have for long emphasized the unity of science principle, which Karl Pearson put forward as follows: The unity of science is a unity of methods employed in analyzing and learning from experience and data. The subject matter discipline may be economics, history, physics, or the like, but the methods employed in

Reprinted from *Macroeconomic Analysis: Essays in Macroeconomics and Econometrics*, D. Currie, R. Nobay, and D. Peel, eds. (London: Croom Helm, 1981), pp. 24–34, with the kind permission of Croom Helm, Ltd.

analyzing and learning from data are basically the same. As Jeffreys expresses the idea, "There must be a uniform standard of validity for all hypotheses, irrespective of the subject. Different laws may hold in different subjects, but they must be tested by the same criteria; otherwise we have no guarantee that our decisions will be those warranted by the data and not merely the result of inadequate analysis or of believing what we want to believe." Thus the unity of science principle sets the *same* standards for work in the natural and social sciences. For example, this range of considerations is particularly relevant for those in economics who cross-correlate variables and assert causation on the basis of such correlations alone or those who carelessly test all hypotheses in the "5% accept-reject syndrome." Also, we must emphasize the importance of a general unified set of methods for use in science and the undesirability of unnecessary jargon and ad hoc methods.

Given that we take the unity of science principle seriously, we may next ask what are the main objectives of science. As Karl Pearson, Harold Jeffreys, and others state, one of the main objectives of science, and I add of econometrics, is that of learning from our experience and data. Knowledge so obtained may be sought for its own sake, for example, to satisfy our curiosity about economic phenomena and/or for practical policy and other decision purposes. One part of our knowledge is merely *description* of what we have observed; the more important part is *generalization* or *induction*, that is that part which ". . . consists of making inferences from past experience to predict future [or as yet unobserved] experience," as Jeffreys puts it.

Thus there are at least two components to our knowledge, *description* and *generalization* or *induction*. While generalization or induction is usually considered to be more important, description plays a significant role in science, including economics. For example, Burns and Mitchell's monumental NBER study *Measuring Business Cycles* is mainly descriptive but valuable in providing general features of business cycles about which others can generalize. While some have damned this work as "measurement without theory," the opposite sin of "theory without measurement" seems much more serious. In fact there are too many mathematical economic theories which explain no past data and which are incapable of making predictions about future or as yet unobserved experience. Such economic theories are mathematical *denk-spielen* and not inductive generalizations to which I referred above. Further, I shall later mention another important role for description in connection with reductive inference.

In learning from our experience and data, it is critical that we understand the roles and nature of three kinds of inference, namely, deductive inference, inductive inference, and reductive inference.

As regards deductive inference, Reichenbach explains, "Logical proof is called *deduction*; the conclusion is obtained by deducing it from other statements, called the premises of the argument. The argument is so constructed that if the premises are true the conclusions must also be true. . . . It unwraps, so to speak, the conclusion that was wrapped up in the premises." Clearly, much economic theory is an exercise in deductive inference. However, the inadequacies of deductive inference for scientific work must be noted. First, traditional deductive inference leads just to the extreme attitudes of *proof, disproof*, or *ignorance* with respect to propositions. There is no provision for a statement like "A proposition is probably true" in deductive inference or logic. This is a deficiency of deduction for scientific work wherein such statements are very widely employed and found to be useful.

Second, deduction or deductive inference alone provides no guide for choice among logically correct alternative explanations or theories. As is well known, for any given set of data, there is an infinity of models which fit the data exactly. Deduction provides no guide for selection among this infinity of models.

Thus there is a need for a type of inference which is broader than deductive inference and which yields statements less extreme than deductive inference. This type of inference is called inductive inference by Jeffreys. It enables us to associate probabilities with propositions and to manipulate them in a consistent, logical way to take account of new information. Deductive statements of proof and disproof are then viewed as limiting cases of inductive logic wherein probabilities approach one or zero, respectively.

Jeffreys, who has made major contributions to the development of inductive logic in his book *Theory of Probability* states that inductive inference involves "making inferences from past experience to predict future experience" by use of inductive generalizations or laws. And given actual outcomes, the procedures of inductive inference allow us to revise probabilities associated with inductive generalizations or laws to reflect the information contained in new data.

Note that for Jeffreys induction is not an economical description of past data, as Mach suggested since Mach omitted the all-important predictive aspect of induction. Further, predictive inductive inferences have an unavoidable uncertainty associated with them, as Hume pointed out many years ago. For example, it is impossible to *prove*, deductively or inductively that generalizations or laws, even the Chicago quantity theory of money, are absolutely true. Even Newton's laws, which were considered "absolutely true" by many physicists in the nineteenth century, have been replaced by

Einstein's laws. Thus there is an unavoidable uncertainty associated with laws in all areas of science, including economics. Inductive logic provides a quantification of this uncertainty by associating probabilities with laws and providing logically consistent procedures for changing these probabilities as new evidence arises. In this regard, probability is viewed as representing a degree of reasonable belief with the limiting values of zero being complete disbelief or disproof and of one being complete belief of proof.

For Jeffreys, Bayesian statistics is implied by his theory of scientific method. Thus Bayesian statistics is the technology of inductive inference. The operations of Bayesian statistics enable us to make probability statements about parameters' values and future values of variables. Also, optimal point estimates and point predictions can be readily obtained by Bayesian methods. Probabilities and/or odds ratios relating to competing hypotheses or models can be evaluated which reflect initial information and sample information. Thus many inference problems encountered in induction can be solved by Bayesian methods and these solutions are compatible with Jeffreys's theory of scientific method.

To illustrate inductive inference in econometrics, consider Milton Friedman's *Theory of the Consumption Function*. In his book Friedman set forth a bold inductive generalization which, he showed, explained variation in much past data, a fact which increased most individuals' degree of reasonable belief in his theory. Further, Friedman proposed a number of additional tests of his model and predicted their outcomes, an example of what we referred to above as inductive inference. Many of these tests have been performed with results compatible with Friedman's predictions. Such results enhance the degree of reasonable belief which we have in Friedman's theory. This is the kind of research in economics and econometrics which illustrates well the nature of inductive inference and is, in my opinion, most productive.

As regards inductive generalizations, there are a few points which deserve to be emphasized. First, a useful starting point for inductive generalization in many instances is the proposition that all variation is considered random or nonsystematic unless shown otherwise. A good example of the fruitfulness of such a starting point is given by the random walk hypothesis for stock prices in stock market research. Many researchers have put forward models to forecast stock prices by use of variables such as auto sales, changes in money, and the like only to find that their forecasts are no better than those yielded by a random walk model. In other areas, when a researcher proposes a new effect, the burden is on him to show that data support the new effect. The initial hypothesis is thus, "No effect unless shown otherwise."

A second most important guiding principle in the selection of inductive generalizations is the Jeffreys-Wrinch simplicity postulate, namely, "The simplest law is chosen because it is the most likely to give correct predictions," and "simpler laws have the greater prior probabilities. This is what Wrinch and I called the *simplicity postulate*." Jeffreys provides much evidence for the simplicity postulate in his book *Scientific Inference*, in which he shows that scientists in many fields generally have found simple models to be most fruitful. Also, it should be noted that in addition to Jeffreys, R. A. Fisher, J. W. Tukey, G. E. P. Box, M. Friedman, and many others emphasize the virtues of sophisticated simplicity in choice among models, a point of view that is sometimes supported by an appeal to Ockham's razor, the principle of parsimony or the simplicity postulate.

The concept of sophisticated simplicity in model-building does not stand in one-to-one correspondence with the number of equations of a model. For example, it is possible to have a horribly complicated, single nonlinear mixed differential-difference equation. Thus I believe that we must have at least a two-way classification of econometric models, namely, small/simple, small/complicated, large/simple, and large/complicated. The objectives of an analysis and the nature of the available data will often be important in determining the size of a model, for example, whether it need and can be large to capture much detail. In any event, whether models are small or large, I maintain that they should be sophisticatedly simple. Input-output models are examples of large, simple models; however the main problem with them is that they are not *sophisticatedly* simple. Marshallian supply and demand models are examples of relatively simple models which have been of great practical value. On the other hand, there are a number of complicated multiequation macroeconometric models on the scene which violate the simplicity postulate. Some of these involve hundreds of nonlinear stochastic difference equations. I ask builders of such models if their models have a unique solution. Generally, they are unable to answer this question. Further, when I ask them why they build such complicated models, some respond that reality is complicated and therefore models have to be complicated. This response involves an a priori view of nature and a major non sequitur. How do we know that reality (whatever that is) is complicated and not simple? I believe that when we say that something is complicated, it is equivalent to saying that we have something which is not understood. In my view understanding involves simplification not complication and thus I am unhappy with these complicated, little understood models which don't forecast very well relative to simpler models and which are unreliable guides to policy. For example, our simulation experiments with a major U.S.

macroeconometric model have led me to conclude that at best it is to be considered as a very local, not entirely satisfactory approximation to some underlying model and very unreliable for analyses of major recessions, depressions, and inflationary periods. Also, its use as a policy instrument leaves much to be desired. In fact, I believe that this large model, and others like it, should be labelled, "Dangerous, Users Beware."

Very important in improving old inductive generalizations and creating new ones is the third kind of inference, reductive inference, sometimes referred to as abductive or retroductive inference, which dates back to Aristotle. C. S. Pierce states, "Abduction or reduction suggests that something may be. It involves studying facts and devising generalizations to explain them." While many features of reductive inference are not very well understood, Jacques Hadamard's book *The Psychology of Invention in the Mathematical Field* does provide some useful insights. Hadamard surveyed his fellow mathematicians to learn how they made their major discoveries. Almost invariably the responses which he obtained emphasized surprising and unusual facts that played a key role in the production of major discoveries or breakthroughs. That is, rather than solving a given problem, it appears that leading mathematicians' recognition of unusual and surprising facts caused them to think about possible explanations. This thinking involved forming many combinations of ideas with both the conscious and unconscious mind playing a role. Usually a good deal of hard preparatory work is required before one generates a scientifically, aesthetically pleasing combination of ideas which explains the unusual fact and is capable of making additional verifiable predictions. Thus hard work appears to be a necessary, though unfortunately not a sufficient, condition for the production of fruitful new combinations of ideas.

Examples of unusual or surprising facts leading to major developments in economics are not hard to find. For example, Kuznets's finding of the constancy of the savings-income ratio in time series data contrasted with its nonconstancy in cross-section data caused many, including Duesenberry, Modigliani, Brumberg, Ando, and Friedman, to produce new theories of consumption. The surprising linear relation between the logarithm of output per worker and the logarithm of the wage rate across countries prompted Arrow, Chenery, Minhas, and Solow to discover the CES production function. Many other examples of surprising and unusual facts leading to new theories could be provided. In view of the potential importance of unusual and surprising data, it is troubling to see how often outlying observations are discarded without thought or averaged with usual observations by means of "robust" techniques.

Since unusual and surprising facts are considered important in reductive inference, I suggested some years ago that we give a good deal of thought about how to produce unusual facts in economics and econometrics. I shall mention some procedures and hope that you will add to the list.

1. Study of incorrect predictions and forecasts of models can be quite jarring and induce new thoughts on how to reformulate models to explain them. The incorrect econometric models' forecasts of a post–World War II depression in the U.S. prompted a good deal of such model reformulation.

2. Close study of the equations of current macroeconometric models can yield surprising and startling facts. For example, some models' dividend, investment, and consumer durable goods expenditure equations have unbelievably long lags. Studies of micropanel data by several of my doctoral students have convinced me that these long lags are spurious, the result of aggregation over buyers and nonbuyers and firms that change and those that do not change dividend rates. In each of these areas, new models for the micropanel data were formulated, fitted, and compared with macroformulations. The results were most illuminating.

3. Looking for regularities such as constancy of labor's share or of saving-income ratios is a good source of unusual and surprising facts requiring explanation.

4. Strenuous simulation experiments with current econometric models can produce unusual facts about models' properties which require explanations. For example, putting a model through a major depression may reveal many unusual features. Or simulating a model over long periods may indicate unusual fluctuations (or lack of them).

5. Pushing theories to extremes generally produces unusual results. For example, in terms of Friedman's proportionality hypothesis for permanent consumption and permanent income, some years ago I suggested that as permanent income approaches zero, the consumption-income ratio would rise toward one in order to keep body and soul together. Recent analysis of data for low income Indian consumers bears out this contention. Similarly for consumers with very great wealth, it should be the case that the consumption-income ratio is lower than for consumers of just average wealth. If Rockefeller's wealth is 2.5 billion dollars, with a 10% annual rate of return his permanent income is $250 million a year. It is doubtful that he consumes nine-tenths of $250 million. Thus it is probably the case that the consumption-income ratio is near one at low income levels, about .9 over the mid-range and below .9 for high incomes. By pushing other theories to their extremes, similar departures may be discovered which require explanations, a process which resembles what is done in physics by studying systems under extreme conditions of high pressures, low temperatures, and the like.

6. Observing behavior in unusual historical periods, for example, periods

of hyperinflation or great depression, and in very different cultures can yield a number of unusual and surprising facts.

7. Surveys can be designed to produce unusual rather than usual facts by considering measurement of the behavior of unusual groups.

8. Experimental economics, that is, experiments with animals and/or humans, has produced a number of very intriguing and unusual facts which have as yet not been explained. There is fertile ground here for much reductive inference activity.

In the way of conclusion, let me stress the following points.

First, deduction, induction, and reduction deserve to be studied more thoroughly by econometricians and economists in order to achieve a better understanding of their roles in research.

Second, a much heavier emphasis on sophisticated simplicity in econometrics is needed with respect to both models and methods.

Third, the sophisticatedly simple Bayesian learning model and decision-making techniques have been incorporated in econometric textbooks. Further use of them will lead to better analyses of data and decision problems.

Fourth, much greater emphasis on reductive inference in teaching econometrics, statistics, and economics would be desirable. To a certain extent, recent emphasis on exploratory data analysis techniques in statistics is a step in the right direction and would be worth instituting in econometrics.

Finally, I hope that this lecture has provided you with a number of surprising ideas and facts which will stimulate you to reconsider your thoughts about the philosophy and objectives of econometrics.

Selected References

Bhalla, S. S. (1979). "Measurement Errors and the Permanent Income Hypothesis: Evidence from Rural India." *American Economic Review*, 69:295–307.

Box, G. E. P., and G. C. Tiao (1973). *Bayesian Inference in Statistical Analysis*. Reading, Mass.: Addison-Wesley.

DeGroot, M. H. (1970). *Optimal Statistical Decisions*. New York: McGraw-Hill Book Co.

Fienberg, S. E., and A. Zellner, eds. (1975). *Studies in Bayesian Econometrics and Statistics in Honor of Leonard J. Savage*. Amsterdam: North-Holland Publishing Co.

Friedman, M. (1957). *A Theory of the Consumption Function*. Princeton, N.J.: Princeton University Press.

Hadamard, J. (1945). *The Psychology of Invention in the Mathematical Field*. New York: Dover Publications.

Hanson, N. R. (1958). *Patterns of Discovery*. Cambridge: Cambridge University Press.

Jeffreys, H. (1957). *Scientific Inference*. 2d ed. Cambridge: Cambridge University Press.

———. (1967). *Theory of Probability*. 3d rev. ed. London: Oxford University Press.

Pearson, K. (1938). *The Grammar of Science*. London: Everyman Edition.

Reichenbach, H. (1958). *The Rise of Scientific Philosophy*. Berkeley: University of California Press.

Zellner, A. (1971). *An Introduction to Bayesian Inference in Econometrics*. New York: John Wiley & Sons.

———. (1979*a*). "Causality and Econometrics." In K. Brunner and A. H. Meltzer, eds., *Three Aspects of Policy and Policymaking: Knowledge, Data, and Institutions*, pp. 9–54. Carnegie-Rochester Conference Series, vol. 10. Amsterdam: North-Holland Publishing Co.

———. (1979*b*). "Statistical Analysis of Econometric Models" (invited paper with discussion). *Journal of the American Statistical Association*, 74:628–43.

Zellner, A. ed. (1980). *Bayesian Analysis in Econometrics and Statistics: Essays in Honor of Harold Jeffreys*. Amsterdam: North-Holland Publishing Co.

Zellner, A., and S. C. Peck (1973). "Simulation Experiments with a Quarterly Macroeconometric Model of the U.S. Economy." In A. A. Powell and R. A. Williams, eds., *Econometric Studies of Macro and Monetary Relations*, pp. 149–68. Amsterdam: North-Holland Publishing Co.

1.2 Perspectives on Mathematical Models in the Social Sciences

The purpose of this chapter is to give readers some insight into the problems and issues surrounding the role of mathematical models in the social sciences. By having these problems and issues explicitly stated, it will be possible to appreciate and assess the work on the development of the Susquehanna model in a broader perspective and to relate it to the general, continuing research on the problems of producing useful models of social systems. Although special attention will be given to developments in economics, many of the issues and problems that have arisen in economics and are mentioned below have important implications for work in other areas.

The Role of Mathematical Models in the Social Sciences

The role of mathematical models in the social sciences is practically the same as the role of mathematical models in the natural sciences. That is, in the social sciences we have a number of social phenomena that we desire to understand and explain, for example, why certain regional economies grow while others stagnate or why individuals migrate from a given region to other regions. Usually, we have data pertaining to these social phenomena, such as data relating to regional economies or to past migration. Mathematical models are then constructed in an effort to explain and understand the variation in our data. As in the physical sciences, it is assumed that if our models are useful in explaining variation in our given data, then we shall be better able to predict as yet unobserved data and to institute changes which will affect as yet unobserved phenomena, say future regional economic growth, in a predictable manner. Of course, the inference from past given data to as yet unobserved data may not turn out to be correct; however, this eventuality is not peculiar to inferences about social phenomena since the possibility for error in making inferences about as yet unobserved data is present in all of science. For example, Newtonian physics was found wanting

Chapter 2 of *Systems Simulation for Regional Analysis: An Application to River-basin Planning*, H. R. Hamilton, D. E. Goldstone, J. W. Milliman, A. L. Pugh, E. R. Roberts, and A. Zellner, eds., (Cambridge: MIT Press, 1969), reprinted with the kind permission of MIT Press.

regarding its predictions about many phenomena studied in modern atomic physics. Thus, while the possibility for error in our predictions is always with us, it is not necessarily uniquely associated with mathematical models in the social sciences. The usefulness of mathematical models in the social sciences is pretty much an empirical issue which can only be settled by experience with the construction and use of mathematical models.

In the preceding paragraph, the position was taken that the role of mathematical models in the social sciences is not much different from that in the physical sciences. A similar position on the unity of scientific method was eloquently expressed by Karl Pearson many years ago as follows:

> Now this is the peculiarity of scientific method, that when once it has become a habit of mind, that mind converts all facts whatsoever into science. The field of science is unlimited; its material is endless, every group of natural phenomena, every phase of social life, every stage of past or present development is material for science. *The unity of all science consists alone in its method, not in its material.* The man who classifies facts of any kind whatever, who sees their mutual relation, and describes their sequences, is applying the scientific method and is a man of science. The facts may belong to the past history of mankind, to the social statistics of our great cities, to the atmosphere of the most distant stars, to the digestive organs of a worm, or to the life of a scarcely visible bacillus. It is not the facts themselves which form science, but the methods by which they are dealt with.[1]

Thus for Pearson, as well as others, the simple fact that social and economic phenomena constitute an investigator's subject matter does not preclude his being scientific if this term is understood as meaning using scientific methods in dealing with the analysis of observational data. The position taken here, and it is thought to be far from revolutionary or novel, is that the use of mathematical models, particularly probabilistic mathematical models, is a key element in scientific method and thus the use of mathematical models in the analysis of social phenomena is part and parcel of the scientific approach to the analysis of social phenomena.

The last remark may seem trite or obvious. However, this may be *at present*, it is the case that many heated discussions regarding the appropriateness of the use of mathematical methods in the social sciences have appeared in the literature.[2] While no attempt will be made here to analyze all the issues that have been raised in these discussions, a few of fundamental importance will be considered briefly.

1. K. Pearson, *The Grammar of Science* (London: Everyman Edition, 1938), p. 16.

2. See, e.g., D. Novick, "Mathematics: Logic, Quality, and Method," *Review of Economics and Statistics*, 36 (1954): 357–58, and the discussion following his paper.

First, it is obvious that mathematical formulation is no insurance that a model will necessarily be a good one. Clearly, it is possible that a mathematically formulated model may be at variance with known facts and may also yield predictions far from the mark. The same can be said about nonmathematical models. However, mathematically formulated models do have the advantage that in general their logical consistency can be checked using the available operations of mathematics. While this task is not always easy, it does appear easier than that associated with checking the logical consistency of many nonmathematical models.

Second, it is sometimes argued that mathematical models in the social sciences involve precisely defined mathematical variables which have no counterpart in the "real world." This is undoubtedly true of a wide range of mathematical models in the social sciences which have been put forward with little or no emphasis on empirical implementation and use and thus depart from general scientific method which lays great emphasis on the relation of mathematical models to observed data. In cases in which mathematical models have been formulated in such a way as to be empirically implemented, there can be no question that important conceptual measurement problems arise, as, for example, in the case of measuring human skills or regional income. Similar problems arise in nonmathematical discussions of variables of this kind. The very process of having to define and measure these variables, as required in a serious mathematical approach, is a fundamental source of progress in scientific work in the social sciences as well as in other sciences. In the former case, the development of very useful systems of national income accounts was in part prompted by efforts of researchers to implement empirically mathematical models involving such variables as national income, gross national product, unemployment, consumption, and the like. In the physical sciences, attempts to measure illusive quantities such as the "ether wind," the electric charge of an electron, the velocity of light, and other such complex quantities were important steps in the development of science. Similarly, it is to be expected that continuing to face up to similarly difficult measurement problems in the social sciences is the way to make progress rather than by bypassing them as "hopeless." In fact, some of the most promising and important research in economics has recently been aimed at measuring such difficult variables as permanent income, human capital, technological change, the rate of return on education, and so forth.

Third, it is sometimes argued that mathematical models in the social sciences are not likely to be successful because the social scientist cannot perform controlled experiments. There can be no question but that experimentation in the social sciences is difficult and expensive, particularly since such experiments generally involve human beings in a fundamental way. In some areas of social science, extensive experimentation with animals has been carried forward. There is, of course, the problem of relating the results of such experiments to human behavior just as there is in medical experiments with animals. Still, the fact that limited experimentation with humans has been and probably will be the case for some time does not preclude success in applying scientific principles to the nonexperimental data that are and will be available. There are other areas of science, namely, astronomy, geophysics, meteorology, and cosmology, which are faced with difficulties in generating controlled experimental data but which have progressed considerably in spite of this difficulty. It does not seem overly optimistic to predict that similar progress will be experienced in the social sciences. Further, a more important role for controlled experimentation in the social sciences in the near future seems likely.

Fourth, some point to the complexity of social systems as a reason for not being optimistic about the success of a scientific approach in the social sciences. It seems pertinent to point out that similar complexity is a feature of many physical and biological systems. In recent decades, nuclear physics has delved into the complexities of matter producing a large number of new particles including pi, kappa, and tau mesons, netrinos, positrons, and so on, which have not been very well integrated into any general theory of matter. Couple this with the well-known dual wave-particle view of matter, and it appears that the situation in nuclear physics is every bit as complex and unsettled as it is in areas of the social sciences. Moreover, with respect to biological systems, particularly human systems, it is the case that the complexity extends even to include the problem of what life is itself in some areas. These problems, too, are far from simple and appear to be complex. To a certain extent, saying that a problem is complex is saying nothing more than that ignorance exists. More observational evidence and additional thought leading to appropriate concepts and models are what is needed. Hopefully in the social sciences, as in other sciences, such an attack on complex problems will provide a payoff. This has been true in the past and is likely to be true in the future.

Fifth, there is the problem that the social scientist interacts with the social system and may thus be unable to apply the scientific method in the study of social phenomena. At the technical level, it is also true that the atomic or nuclear physicist interacts with the systems which he studies, the fundamental point of the famous Heisenberg uncertainty principle. This interaction sets limits on the accuracy with which certain physical quantities can be determined but does not preclude production of generally useful results. It may be argued in a similar vein that while the social scientist interacts with the systems he studies, this does not logically imply that he will be unable to produce useful scientific results. Perhaps it *may be* more difficult to separate an investigator's value judgments from his scientific work in the social sciences than in the physical sciences and on many occasions this mixture is still encountered. However, more and more in the social sciences, the distinction is sharply made between "positive" social science, that is, the question of "what is," and "normative" social science, the question of "what ought to be," and recognition of this distinction has resulted in there being fewer obstacles to progress in the social sciences.[3]

Lastly, in connection with applying mathematical models in the analysis of social phenomena, it is sometimes asserted that this is a hopeless task because human behavior is random and unpredictable. In this regard, the same remark may and has been made with respect to the weather. Yet, remarkable progress has been made in predicting future weather. This is not to say that weather predictions are deterministic or one hundred percent accurate. In fact current weather forecasts are couched in probabilistic terms. Here intensive observation and analysis of past observations, coupled with theories of meteorological systems, have produced very useful results. Similarly with respect to voting behavior, business conditions, and consumers' behavior, a similar approach seems to be leading to very encouraging results. Naturally, random elements, just as with the weather, can lead to poor predictions of social phenomena. Still, the prospect of being "right" in a high proportion of predictions is a goal which does not seem out of the reach of social scientists in a number of areas.

These considerations provide some basis for thinking that a scientific approach to the analysis of social phenomena using mathematical models and empirical data is possible and potentially valuable. To show that this proposition is not merely speculative and to delve into other issues and problems, a brief account of the development and use of mathematical models in the area of economics will now be presented. This account will feature developments which have a close connection with a number of the methodological underpinnings of the Susquehanna regional economic model.

Mathematical Models in Economics

Mathematics and mathematical models have been used in economics for a long time. For example, among others, Cournot, Marshall, Edgeworth,

3. In economics, M. Friedman's important essay "The Methodology of Positive Economics," in his book *Essays in Positive Economics* (Chicago: University of Chicago Press, 1953), helped to emphasize the difference between "positive economics" and "normative economics" and to suggest that progress in the area of positive economics would be of great value in resolving problems in normative economics.

Walras, and Keynes all relied heavily on mathematical models of economic systems in their works.[4] However, what distinguishes this early work with mathematical models from more recent work is the fact that observational evidence was not systematically and formally brought to bear on the earlier models. The reasons for this are that good economic data were not generally available and, further, even if they were, the statistical techniques and concepts required to analyze observational evidence within the context of mathematical models of economic systems were not available. Also, the computational facilities available to the early mathematical economists were rather inadequate. Thus, even if they had large bodies of good economic data and modern multivariate statistical techniques, these would have been of little value without adequate computing facilities. In addition, the lack of good computing facilities meant that the earlier workers were precluded from exploring many properties of the mathematical models which they developed.

It was not until the twentieth century that the movement toward developing empirically implemented mathematical economic models acquired considerable momentum. The reasons for the recency of this movement are not hard to discover. The movement had to wait for the appearance of such pioneers as H. Moore, H. Schultz, and J. Tinbergen, among others, as well as for the development of appropriate methodological tools, before it could assume major proportions. It is no accident that the major movement toward the use of empirically implemented economic models took place at just about the time that substantial progress was being made in the field of statistics on problems of statistical estimation and testing procedures for multivariate models.[5] These developments, coupled with a growing availability of data, better computing facilities, and a distinct tendency on the part of economists to formulate their models so that they can be empirically implemented are the main elements in the movement toward more widespread use of empirically implemented mathematical models in the field of economics.

J. Tinbergen is often regarded as the father of the movement toward the use of empirically implemented mathematical models for the analysis of economies. His pioneering work,[6] prompted to some extent by the de-

4. In some of these works, particularly Marshall's, the exposition is in large part nonmathematical. However, it appears that many important results were obtained using mathematics and then verbalized with the mathematics sometimes presented in appendixes.

5. Note that much of the path-breaking work in statistics was done in the 1920s, 1930s, and 1940s by R. A. Fisher, J. Neyman, E. S. Pearson, A. Wald, H. Jeffreys, and others.

6. J. Tinbergen, *An Econometric Approach to Business Cycle Problems* (Paris: Herman et Cie, 1937), and *Statistical Testing of Business Cycle Theories* (2 vols.; Geneva: League of Nations, 1939).

pressed conditions of the 1930s, involved construction of multiequation dynamic models of the Dutch, U.S., and British economies which were designed to be useful in furthering our understanding of and possibly in controlling an important economic phenomenon, fluctuations in the general level of economic activity. His model for the U.S., a 50-equation linear stochastic difference equation model, included 32 behavioral, technological, and institutional equations and 18 definitional equations. Among the former group, Tinbergen included equations purporting to explain how consumers and investors behave. In addition, he formulated and estimated equations representing the operation of banks, corporations, and several important markets including the bond, stock, and labor markets, among others. Remembering that this work was done in the 1930s, it is indeed a remarkable achievement, one that showed that modelling economies was possible.

As is to be expected, Tinbergen's pioneering work raised many important issues, many of which are still with us today. In Keynes's review[7] of Tinbergen's work and Tinbergen's reply,[8] a good deal of attention is devoted to the role of economic theory in model-building, the conditions required for statistical methods to be applicable to economic data, the causal interpretation of Tinbergen's model, determination of functional forms and lag structures for economic relationships, appraisal of the economic implications of certain of Tinbergen's results, and so on. These are indeed relevant issues and much work in economics has appeared since the 1930s dealing with them.

Particularly noteworthy in this respect was the work of Haavelmo[9] and of the group at the Cowles Commission at the University of Chicago in the 1940s and 1950s.[10] This work covered a wide variety of important topics and produced many fundamental concepts and techniques. On the side of model construction, Anderson, Haavelmo, Hurwicz, Koopmans, Rubin, and others refined the concept of a complete model, provided basic results on the identification problem, and developed new statistical techniques for estimating coefficients and other parameters of economic models and for testing hypotheses. Much of this research was performed in connection with

7. J. M. Keynes, "Professor Tinbergen's Method," *Economic Journal*, 49 (1939): 558–68.

8. J. Tinbergen, "On a Method of Statistical Business-Cycle Research: A Reply," *Economic Journal*, 50 (1940): 141–54.

9. T. Haavelmo, "The Probability Approach in Econometrics," *Econometrica*, 12, Supplement (1944): 1–118.

10. Some of the main work of the Cowles Commission group appears in T. C. Koopmans, ed., *Statistical Inference in Dynamic Economic Models* (New York: John Wiley & Sons, 1950), and W. C. Hood and T. C. Koopmans, eds., *Studies in Econometric Method* (New York: John Wiley & Sons, 1953).

analyses of the "simultaneous equation" economic model, a special multivariate model which is flexible and general enough to permit lagged and unlagged or instantaneous feedback effects. Simon provided an interesting causal interpretation of simultaneous equation models while Klein, building on the work of Tinbergen, constructed and estimated multiequation dynamic models of the American economy, models in the "simultaneous equation" or "interdependent" form. Klein's early work represented an interesting example of an effort to use existing economic theories to derive the relations of his models of the American economy. Since Klein's early contributions, he and others have continued work on the development of models of economies.[11]

The reaction of the economics profession to the work of Tinbergen, Haavelmo, and the Cowles Commission group was mixed. As usual with a new movement, there was a group of enthusiastic supporters who, in varying degrees, began work on the task of filling in and extending this line of research. However, a much more numerous group expressed skepticism and pointed to serious problems. In this group there were many who lacked the mathematical and statistical background needed to understand and appraise the highly technical and complex contributions of Tinbergen, Haavelmo, and the Cowles Commission group. Their skepticism appears to have been founded on feelings of insecurity and/or a feeling that in general very complicated methods and models were probably not going to work very well. However, some others who had the required technical background to appraise this body of work were also skeptical. A review of some of the main critical points, as they appear to the author, follows.

First, and foremost, there was a feeling that economists did not know enough about the workings of the overall economic system to produce serious and useful dynamic models of national economies. In this connection, it has to be remembered that Keynes's contribution[12] to macroeconomics involved formulation of a comparative *static* model, a model which was not completely understood or accepted by many. The dynamics of consumer and investor behavior as well as the dynamic behavior of markets were relatively unexplored areas in the 1940s and early 1950s. The role of money and prices in influencing economic activity was not well understood.

11. H. A. Simon, "Causal Ordering and Identifiability," in W. C. Hood and T. C. Koopmans, eds., *Studies in Econometric Method*, pp. 49–74; L. R. Klein, *Economic Fluctuations in the United States, 1921–1941* (New York: John Wiley & Sons, 1950); and see M. Nerlove, "A Tabular Survey of Macro-Econometric Models," *International Economic Review*, 7 (1966): 127–75, where models of a number of national economies are described.

12. J. M. Keynes, *The General Theory of Employment Interest and Money* (New York: Harcourt, Brace & Co., 1935).

Many other lacunae in economic knowledge could be mentioned. Given these deficiencies, it was difficult for many to see how the early economic model-building efforts could be successful.

Second, even in terms of the models which were put forward, many felt uneasy because they could not understand how they worked and what they implied. It is, of course, no easy matter to understand the mathematical and economic implications of multiequation dynamic models involving many variables and relationships whose functional forms were often chosen with an eye toward ease of mathematical and statistical analysis and not on solidly based subject matter considerations. And the producers of the early models rarely provided the mathematical analysis or the results of simulation experiments which would aid in understanding the properties of their models. Thus, it is accurate to say that many who produced large-scale models did not know very much about their properties. In fact, this important aspect of model analysis was relatively slighted in favor of a heavy emphasis on the problems of statistical estimation.

Third, with respect to statistical problems, it was pointed out that models containing literally hundreds of parameters had been estimated from very small samples of highly autocorrelated observations using complicated techniques which have only a *large sample* justification *given that the models were correctly formulated and that the data contained no measurement error.* Clearly, there was uneasiness on these technical grounds alone.

Fourth, there were serious aggregation problems connected with these economic models. For example, many of the early models designed for business cycle analysis were formulated and empirically implemented with the unit of time being a year. Clearly, many dynamic responses are of much shorter duration than a year and it was not apparent to what extent these were appropriately represented in models in which the unit of time was taken to be one year. Other aggregation problems arose from the fact that aggregate relationships were used which were supposed to represent the behavior of groups of individuals who were not very similar. Also, aggregate variables included many different components. For example, the consumption expenditure variable in many models included auto expenditures, food expenditures, educational expenditures, and the like. Many felt that work at this level of aggregation was not satisfactory.

Fifth, some of the early models omitted entirely or dealt inadequately with sectors of the economy which some considered to be extremely important. For example, some models neglected to treat money markets. Others gave no attention to the agricultural sector, the housing market, the stock market, and the foreign trade sector. Needless to say, these deficiencies served as another basis for criticism.

Sixth, it was not clear how the early models were to be used in formulating economic policies designed to achieve such objectives as economic stabilization, full employment, and adequate economic growth. To some extent this problem arose because the early economic models did not incorporate a well-developed governmental sector. No allowance was made for the operation of state and local governmental units and even the federal government's activities were not adequately represented in the early models. Perhaps more fundamentally, however, the basic methodology of control theory was not available. Therefore, it is no surprise that the important problem of how models were to be used in controlling economic activity was not dealt with adequately.

While some of the early model-builders were overly enthusiastic and claimed too much, many were acutely aware of the many vexing problems raised by the critics. And, in fact, much of the work since the discussions of the 1940s and early 1950s has contributed toward making progress on these issues and problems. In this connection, the following developments should be noted.

Since the early 1950s, there has been a tremendous growth in the volume and quality of empirical work in economics. In large part this is the result of having more economists who have training in mathematics and statistics, the growing availability of more and better data, and the widespread use of high-speed electronic computers, which facilitates the application of statistical techniques in the analysis of data. The experience and knowledge gained from these empirical studies, coupled with advances in economic theory, have resulted in a fuller understanding of economic phenomena, a precondition for the construction of good economic models.

The importance of the appearance of more and better economic data cannot be overemphasized. Among other things, this has helped enormously in connection with problems of aggregation. Recently, dynamic economic models using quarterly and monthly data have been constructed. This means that the problem of temporal aggregation may not be as serious as with annual data. Thus the dynamic responses of the economic system can be better approximated. Further, a greater richness in our data permits a greater degree of disaggreation with respect to commodities and economic groups and sectors, thereby avoiding to some extent other aggregation problems. Finally, having data pertaining to shorter time periods and formulating models with shorter time periods in mind resulted in simplified forms for the structure of economic models. That is, instead of having to deal with models incorporating instantaneous feedback effects, it becomes possible to have large parts of models or even entire models in a form involving just lagged feedback effects rather than unlagged feedback effects.[13] Since this is a somewhat simpler form, it is easier to understand how such models work and to perform mathematical and computer operations with them.

Since the early 1950s, continuing research on statistical methods for analyzing economic data has yielded a whole new set of techniques for estimating parameters of economic models. Such new techniques as two-stage least squares[14] and three-stage least squares[15] are much simpler than the Cowles Commission maximum likelihood estimation techniques and yet yield estimators with the same large sample properties. Many Monte Carlo experiments have been performed in an effort to establish the small-sample properties of these estimation techniques.[16] Further progress has been made on obtaining analytical results for this problem.[17] More recently, considerable progress has been made in developing and applying Bayesian techniques in the statistical analysis of economic models.[18] Since these techniques provide finite-sample results and provide a means for introducing prior information conveniently, it is thought that their use will contribute to obtaining better results in work with economic models.

13. T. C. Liu has formulated a monthly model having just lagged feedback effects, which he discussed at a seminar at the University of Chicago in 1967.

14. This method of estimation appeared first in H. Theil, *Estimation and Simultaneous Correlation in Complete Equation Systems*, (The Hague: Centraal Planbureau, 1953), and has been and is frequently used in econometric work. It is clearly described in A. S. Goldberger, *Econometric Theory* (New York: John Wiley & Sons, 1964), pp. 329 ff.

15. A. Zellner and H. Theil, "Three-Stage Least Squares: Simultaneous Estimation of Simultaneous Equations," *Econometrica*, 30 (1962): 54–78.

16. See J. Johnston, *Econometric Methods* (New York: McGraw-Hill Book Co., 1963), pp. 275–95, for a review of the results of several Monte Carlo experiments designed to investigate the finite-sample properties of alternative estimators.

17. See, e.g., R. L. Basmann, "A Note on the Exact Finite Sample Frequency Functions of Generalized Classical Linear Estimators in Two Leading Overidentified Cases," *Journal of the American Statistical Association*, 56 (1961): 619–36, and D. G. Kabe, "On the Exact Distributions of the GCL Estimators in a Leading Three-Equation Case," *Journal of the American Statistical Association*, 59 (1964): 881–94.

18. For general treatments of Bayesian methods and principles, see, e.g., Jeffreys, *Theory of Probability* (3d rev. ed.; London: Oxford University Press, 1967), and D. V. Lindley, *Introduction to Probability and Statistics from a Bayesian Viewpoint*, Part 2: *Inference* (Cambridge, England: University Press, 1965). Quite a few papers have appeared since about 1961 in which Bayesian methods have been developed for the analysis of statistical models used in economics. A few of these are J. Drèze, "The Bayesian Approach to Simultaneous Equations Estimation," ONR Research Memo no. 67, the Technological Institute, Northwestern University, 1962; T. J. Rothenberg, "A Bayesian Analysis of Simultaneous Equation Systems," Report 6315, Econometric Institute, Rotterdam, 1963; and A. Zellner and G. C. Tiao, "Bayesian Analysis of the Regression Model with Autocorrelated Errors," *Journal of the American Statistical Association*, 59 (1964): 763–78.

On the problems associated with the use of models for policy purposes, there have been some significant contributions. The problem of maximizing the mathematical expectation of a criterion function involving variables of an economic model, with the equations of the model as constraints, has received a good deal of attention.[19] Results, obtained for the case of quadratic criterion functions, have been used in several very interesting applications.[20] While problems exist with respect to formulation of appropriate criterion functions and how to handle uncertainty about the values of parameters and other features of economic models, it is the case that the fundamental methodology has been created and work is underway to improve and extend it. Further, given that quite a few countries employ economic models as an aid in formulating economic policies, considerable practical experience has accumulated with respect to the use of economic models for policy purposes.

In recent years, that is, since about 1969, under the impact of the implications of Muth's rational expectations hypothesis, it has come to be recognized that changes in economic policies will probably alter the forms of econometric models. For example, Crutchfield and I discovered in the late 1950s that changes in the policies of the International Pacific Halibut Conservation Commission produced substantial changes in the seasonal pattern of pricing in the Pacific halibut industry. Thus controlling a social system is in some vital respects different from controlling a physical system which is assumed to be invariant to changes in control policies. Since the early 1970s, this important point has been emphasized by my colleague at the University of Chicago Robert Lucas. It is having a substantial impact on research on econometric modeling and uses of models in policy analyses.

Another important development is work on checking the accuracy of forecasts yielded by economic models.[21] Since models are modified from

19. Some interesting references are: J. Tinbergen, *On the Theory of Economic Policy* (Amsterdam: North-Holland Publishing Co., 1952); H. A. Simon, "Dynamic Programming under Uncertainty with a Quadratic Criterion Function," *Econometrica*, 24 (1956): 74–81; H. Theil, "A Note on Certainty Equivalence in Dynamic Planning," *Econometrica*, 25 (1957): 346–49; C. J. van Eijk and J. Sandee, "Quantitative Determination of an Optimum Economic Policy," *Econometrica*, 27 (1959): 1–13; H. Theil, *Optimal Decision Rules for Government and Industry* (Chicago: Rand McNally & Co., 1964); and K. A. Fox, J. K. Sengupta, and E. Thorbecke, *The Theory of Quantitative Economic Policy* (Chicago: Rand McNally & Co., 1966).

20. One example is P. J. M. van den Bogaard and H. Theil, "Macrodynamic Policy-Making: An Application of Strategy and Certainty Equivalence Concepts to the Economy of the United States, 1933–1936," *Metroeconomica*, 11 (1959): 149–67.

21. See D. B. Suits, "Forecasting and Analysis with an Econometric Model," *American Economic Review*, 52 (1962): 104–32, and H. Theil, *Economic Forecasts and Policy* (2d ed.;

time to time, data are revised and hopefully improved, and forecasts often are made which incorporate judgmental elements, it is indeed difficult to separate out the contribution of the economic model in evaluating forecasting performance. While this is a problem in interpreting forecasting records, the very fact that these records are being kept and analyzed is indeed a significant step forward in the methodology of model verification and contributes to efforts to improve economic models.

Finally, some progress has been made in the study of the dynamic properties of economic models. Mathematical tecnhniques for analyzing models' dynamic properties have been developed and applied in certain instances.[22] In some cases, simulation techniques have been used to study dynamic properties of economic models.[23] However, this appears to be one of the underdeveloped areas in the analysis of economic models. This is indeed unfortunate since knowing the dynamic properties of an economic model is essential for understanding what the model implies about dynamic economic phenomena. Moreover, it is extremely important that the dynamic responses of a model to changes in policy variables be appreciated before a model is used as an aid in formulating and evaluating alternative policies. To some extent, the failure to study dynamic properties of models has arisen because large complex models are difficult, if not impossible, to analyze mathematically. In view of this, it is to be expected that simulation techniques will be used much more extensively in the future. In this connection, however, the complexity of certain economic models appears to put severe demands on some currently available simulation computer programs. Further work on the planning and design of simulation experiments would also be valuable.

In closing this review of some of the current and recent trends in research on economic models, it must be pointed out that an extremely difficult, but most important, area is receiving very little attention. This is the area of model-formulation and the organization of model-building efforts. The methodology for finding and developing good models is hardly existent

---

Amsterdam: North-Holland Publishing Co., 1961), for some comparisons of predictions with actual outcomes. Suits considers some results for the U.S. economy while Theil reviews results for European economies.

22. Two good examples are A. S. Goldberger, *Impact Multipliers and Dynamic Properties of the Klein-Goldberger Model* (Amsterdam: North-Holland Publishing Co., 1959), and H. Theil and J. C. G. Boot, "The Final Form of Econometric Equation Systems," *Review of the International Statistical Institute*, 30 (1962): 136–52.

23. See, e.g., I. Adelman and F. L. Adelman, "The Dynamic Properties of the Klein-Goldberger Model," *Econometrica*, 27 (1959): 569–625, and T. C. Liu, "An Exploratory Quarterly Model of Effective Demand in the Postwar U.S. Economy," *Econometrica*, 31 (1963): 301–48.

except, perhaps, in the form of an art at which some individuals seem particularly gifted. Such general prescriptions as "use economic theory in constructing models," or "keep models simple," while useful as guides, hardly seem completely adequate in view of the multidimensional activities involved in formulating and developing a serious economic model. Therefore in the next chapter, attention will be devoted to explaining some elements of the approach employed in the Battelle model-building effort and to contrasting it with approaches used in other model-building efforts. This will represent an explicit statement of one approach to model-building which may possibly be of interest and use to others.

1.3 Basic Issues in Econometrics, Past and Present

It is indeed a great honor to be invited to present the John R. Commons Award Lecture. While I was never personally acquainted with John R. Commons, I did learn much about him and his work when I was a member of the Department of Economics, University of Wisconsin, 1961–66 from colleagues who had studied and worked with him. It appears that Commons emphasized a strong interaction between institutional analysis and theory and applications. I was told that he frequently challenged those who sought to change and hopefully improve institutions to draft laws embodying proposed changes and to predict the effects of these proposed, new laws. Thus in Commons's work, he emphasized a fruitful interaction between institutional analysis (descriptive and theoretical), application, and prediction. In econometrics, I believe that a past and present basic issue is the relationship between economic and statistical theory and methods and applied analyses. In teaching and research, many, including myself, have emphasized that a strong interaction between theory and application is most beneficial for the progress of economic science. In what follows, I shall discuss some past and present aspects of the interaction between theory and application and provide some suggestions that may make this interaction even more fruitful in the future.

The relationship between economic and statistical theory and applied, empirical analyses has been a basic issue in econometrics for many years. In the 1920s, demand analysts argued about whether to regress price on quantity or quantity on price in estimating theoretical demand relationships. This fruitful interaction between theory and application was an important factor leading to development of the concepts of parameter identification and specification of complete econometric models. In the 1930s, the valuable exchange between Keynes and Tinbergen on the latter's applied econometric work brought to the fore some basic issues that are still very

Reprinted from *The American Economist*, 26, no. 2 (1982): 5–10, with the kind permission of the International Honor Society in Economics, Omicron Delta Epsilon.

relevant.[1] Among these are the appropriateness of applying statistical methods to nonexperimental economic time series data, possible incorrect specifications of relationships (left-out variables, e.g., psychological variables, incorrect lag structures, etc.) and possible inappropriate measurement of variables. Also, it was not clear to Keynes whether Tinbergen's models were just purely descriptive or could be employed for successful prediction and policymaking. In Tinbergen's cogent response, he emphasized the important role of his empirical results in appraising alternative theories of the business cycle and the merits of his approach in furthering business cycle analysis. In Keynes's rejoinder, he expressed continued skepticism but was willing to have Tinbergen continue his research, research that subsequently inspired the work of Klein and others on macroeconometric modeling of national economies. In the post–World War II period, the empirical implementation of such macroeconometric models raised similar basic issues that are still with us today. Are these large, complex models dependable for forecasting and policy analysis?[2] Do they embody appropriate, sound economic theory?[3] Are they free of major specification errors? Have satisfactory statistical methods been utilized for estimation, testing, prediction, and policy analysis?[4] Current econometric research is much concerned with these issues that have been with us for decades.

The 1946 book *Measuring Business Cycles*, by A. R. Burns and W. C. Mitchell, raised some vital issues regarding the appropriate roles of measurement and theory in economic science. Some damned this work as being an example of "measurement without theory" while others, including myself, aware of the sin of "theory without measurement" were surprised that Burns's and Mitchell's useful descriptions of various features of busi-

1. J. M. Keynes, "Professor Tinbergen's Method," *Economic Journal*, 49 (1939): 558–68; J. Tinbergen, "On a Method of Statistical Business-Cycle Research: A Reply," *Economic Journal*, 50 (1940): 141–54; and J. M. Keynes, "Comment," *Economic Journal*, 50 (1940): 154–56, reprinted in A. H. Hansen and R. V. Clemence, eds., *Readings in Business Cycles and National Income* (New York: W. W. Norton & Co., 1953), pp. 330–56. See also J. Tinbergen, "Critical Remarks on Some Business Cycle Theories," *Econometrica*, 10 (1942): 129–46, reprinted in Hansen and Clemence, eds., *Readings*, pp. 357–75.

2. See C. F. Christ, "Judging the Performance of Econometric Models of the U.S. Economy," *International Economic Review*, 16 (1975): 54–74, for evidence regarding the quality of a number of macroeconometric models.

3. Discussions of these issues appear in E. Malinvaud, "Econometrics Faced with the Needs of Macroeconomic Policy," *Econometrica*, 49 (1981): 1363–75, and C. Sims, "Macroeconomics and Reality," *Econometrica*, 48 (1980): 1–48.

4. Discussion of statistical and other issues appears in A. Zellner, "Statistical Analysis of Econometric Models," *Journal of the American Statistical Association*, 74 (1979): 628–43, followed by invited comments by D. A. Belsley, E. Kuh, C. F. Christ, P. M. Robinson, T. J. Rothenberg, and the author's rejoinder.

ness fluctuations provoked such strong criticism. Obviously, a basic issue in these discussions was (and still is) the appropriate roles of description and economic theory in economic science.

A further set of basic issues arose in connection with the causal interpretation of econometric models in the work of Simon, Wold, Strotz, Basmann, Orcutt, Granger, Sims, and others. Currently, results of many "tests of causality" are reported in the literature that have important implications for economic science and policy.[5] In a recent paper, I have reviewed alternative concepts of causality and some "tests of causality" that have appeared in the literature and concluded that most of them are defective.[6] On the constructive side, I suggested that the philosophers' definition of causality, as summarized in an article by H. Feigl, namely, "predictability according to a law or set of laws," seems adequate for work in econometrics and economics. Note that this definition emphasizes confirmed predictability based on dependable and well-understood economic laws and not just predictability alone. Thus, as is almost obvious, to establish causality in economics, it is necessary to consider *both* economic theory and laws and empirical, statistical prediction, an important interaction between theory and application.

A most basic issue that has been and still is present in econometrics (and statistics) is the appropriate concept of probability to employ in applied econometric work. Without an appropriate concept of probability, the many probability statements made in econometric analyses in connection with tests of hypotheses, confidence and prediction intervals, and the like are unintelligible. Given Jeffreys's devastating critique of frequency and axiomatic concepts of probability,[7] it appears that the most appropriate view of probability is that it is a "degree of reasonable belief." Acceptance of this definition has profound implications for the interpretation of statistical results obtained in econometric analyses, particularly in connection with nonexperimental time series data, for example, macroeconometric data.

Finally, there is the issue of whether to use Bayesian or non-Bayesian techniques in econometrics.[8] Modern econometric and statistical research

5. For an interesting theoretical and applied analysis of some surprising results of "tests of causality," see C. Hernández-Iglesias and F. Hernández-Iglesias, "Causality and the Independence Phenomenon: The Case of the Demand for Money," *Journal of Econometrics*, 15 (1981): 247–63.

6. A. Zellner, "Causality and Econometrics," in K. Brunner and A. H. Meltzer, eds., *Three Aspects of Policy and Policymaking: Knowledge, Data, and Institutions* (Carnegie-Rochester Conference Series, vol. 10; Amsterdam: North-Holland Publishing Co.), pp. 9–54.

7. H. Jeffreys, *Theory of Probability* (3d rev. ed.; London: Oxford University Press, 1967), chap. 7.

8. For discussions of some of the issues in this area, see T. J. Rothenberg's and A. Zellner's essays on "Bayesian and Alternative Approaches in Econometrics," in S. E. Fienberg and A.

has been directed at this basic issue. The results of this research and actual trends in econometric work point toward a growing use of Bayesian techniques in econometrics.[9]

With this said about some general basic issues in econometrics that have been with us over the decades, I shall now turn to consider some of them in relation to present econometric work. Currently econometricians and quantitative economists are engaged in learning from their data and past experience. The knowledge so obtained may be useful in satisfying investigators' curiosity about economic phenomena and behavior and/or in practical forecasting and policymaking. In the process of learning, description and generalization both play significant roles. Description in economics, as in other sciences, plays a key role in bringing to the fore what is to be explained by theory. For example, Kuznets's empirical finding of the very different behavior of the average propensity to save in time series and cross-section data set the stage for significant new theories of consumption and saving. Similarly, the striking empirical result that the logarithm of output per worker and the logarithm of the wage rate are linearly related led Arrow, Chenery, Minhas, and Solow to formulate the CES production function. There are many other examples of surprising facts that have led to major breakthroughs in economics and econometrics. In recognition of the key, triggerlike role of surprising facts in producing new economic generalizations or theories, I have suggested several ways of producing unusual facts in a recent paper.[10] Thus, description, guided by implicit or explicit economic theory and intuition plays an important role in econometric research. Good statistical procedures are required to describe the information in a collection of time series and in cross-section or panel data involving measurements on many different individuals and variables. Recent results in the exploratory

---

Zellner, eds., *Studies in Bayesian Econometrics and Statistics in Honor of Leonard J. Savage* (Amsterdam: North-Holland Publishing Co., 1975).

9. In A. Zellner, "The Current State of Bayesian Econometrics," invited paper presented at the Canadian Conference on Applied Statistics, Montreal, 1981, and to be published in T. D. Dwivedi, ed., *Topics in Applied Statistics* (New York: Marcel Dekker), past and present developments in Bayesian Econometrics are described. See R. Litterman, "A Bayesian Procedure for Forecasting with Vector Autoregressions" (Department of Economics, MIT, Cambridge, Mass., 1980), for a useful application of Bayesian techniques in forecasting U.S. quarterly macroeconomic variables.

10. A. Zellner, "Philosophy and Objectives of Econometrics," invited lecture for the British Association of University Teachers of Economics Meeting, Durham, England, 28 March 1980, and published in D. Currie, R. Nobay, and D. Peel, eds., *Macroeconomic Analysis: Essays in Macroeconomics and Econometrics* (London: Croom Helm Publishing Co., 1981).

data analysis, cluster analysis, and time series analysis areas appear useful for making descriptive analyses more effective.[11]

While description is important in econometric work, the development and use of economic generalizations or models to explain variation in past data and past behavior and, most important, to predict as yet unobserved data and behavior are central and most important activities in past and current econometric research. Some very significant research has resulted in a melding of economic and statistical features of problems in economic models, as in Friedman's theory of the consumption function, Muth's rational expectations hypothesis and efficient market models. These models are to be contrasted with many others that involve only a loose link between static, deterministic economic theory and stochastic statistical models that are employed to analyze data. A coherent relationship between economic and statistical aspects of models seems very desirable in order to reduce the possibility of inconsistent and unclear implications of analyses. For example, the nature of price adjustments in a simple, static, deterministic Marshallian market is difficult to rationalize and explain in terms of rational, disequilibrium behavior of economic actors. Similar considerations apply to disequilibrium behavior in comparative, static macroeconomic models. When stochastic elements are present, as they usually are, traditional, deterministic economic theory has to be broadened to accommodate them in a satisfactory manner, a basic problem in much current econometric work.[12]

On the nature of economic generalizations and theories, it is critical that they be capable of yielding testable implications and predictions. For example, in Friedman's book *A Theory of the Consumption Function*, he listed a number of tests of his theory that could be performed and predicted their outcomes.[13] Since the book was published, many of these tests have been performed with most of them yielding results in accord with Friedman's predictions. Prediction is thus a vital aspect of fruitful economic theorizing

11. Some references are J. W. Tukey, *Exploratory Data Analysis* (Reading, Mass.: Addison-Wesley Publishing Co., 1977); J. A. Hartigan, *Clustering Algorithms* (New York: John Wiley & Sons, 1975); G.E.P. Box and G. M. Jenkins, *Time Series Analysis, Forecasting and Control* (2d ed.; San Francisco: Holden-Day, 1976), and G. C. Tiao and G. E. P. Box, "Modeling Multiple Time Series with Applications," *Journal of the American Statistical Association*, 76 (1981), 802–16.

12. A valuable overview of some work in this area is provided in E. C. Prescott and R. M. Townsend, "Equilibrium under Uncertainty: Multiagent Statistical Decision Theory," in A. Zellner, ed., *Bayesian Analysis in Econometrics and Statistics: Essays in Honor of Harold Jeffreys* (Amsterdam: North-Holland Publishing Co., 1980), pp. 169–94.

13. M. Friedman, *A Theory of the Consumption Function* (Princeton, N.J.: Princeton University Press, 1957), pp. 214–19.

and, as pointed out above, of causality. These points are recognized in many sciences and deserve to be emphasized more in work in economic theory and econometrics. Elaborate mathematical economic theories that yield no verifiable predictions may be contributions to mathematics but are not generally useful contributions to economic science. Similarly, elaborate econometric models that fit data closely (R^2's = .99, and so on) but do not predict well are most likely examples of statistical overfitting and not very useful contributions to economic science. Having econometric models that explain variation in past data in accord with generally accepted principles of economic theory and that predict well is an objective of current econometric research whose accomplishment would constitute a great research contribution whether in the micro or macro areas. To a certain extent, a heavy emphasis on estimation techniques and results has diverted attention of many econometricians away from the fundamentally important activity of prediction. Geisser has made a similar argument with respect to statisticians's activities.[14]

Further on the nature of economic theories and econometric models, there have been extensive discussions of the relative merits of simplicity and complexity.[15] A leading econometrician has stated in public that economic reality is complex and therefore econometric models must be complex. This view of "economic reality" as well as the conclusion drawn from it are, to say the least, debatable. Economic reality, whatever that is, may seem to be complicated because it is not understood. Understanding in my view involves simplification not complication. There are many examples of sophisticatedly simple models that provide understanding and predictions that have been found to be useful. These include Newton's laws, Einstein's laws, quantum theory, laws of supply and demand, and Friedman's theory of consumer behavior. On the other hand, it is difficult to find complicated models that explain past variation well and also predict accurately. Thus when a speaker asserts that a "true model" is a complicated model with an infinite number of parameters, I usually stop him (or her) and request evidence and justification for this view. The Jeffreys-Wrinch simplicity postulate, Ockham's razor and the principle of parsimony all point in the direction of developing sophisticatedly simple models and evaluating predictions derived from them.

14. S. Geisser, "A Predictivistic Primer," in A. Zellner, ed., *Bayesian Analysis in Econometrics and Statistics*, pp. 363–81.

15. See H. Jeffreys, *Theory of Probability*, pp. 47 ff., for a suggested index of the complexity of differential equations. Further work to provide operational and useful measures of simplicity and complexity would be useful.

On the issue of model size and simplicity, it is important to recognize that the objectives of econometric modeling often determine the size of a model. Thus there has to be at least a two-way classification of models, namely, small/large and simple/complicated, as shown below.

	Simple	Complicated
Small	Good	Bad
Large	Good	Bad

Given that the objectives of a modeling project imply that a small model will probably be adequate, I and, I believe, many others would prefer a small simple model to a small complicated model. That is, I would formulate and investigate small, simple models and complicate them only if it were shown that superior performance is obtained by doing so. If the objectives of a modeling project involve capturing much detail, for example, modeling many activities, sectors, and variables, then one has to entertain a large model, but it can be sophisticatedly simple and not complicated. One basic problem with many current large econometric models is that they are very complicated, usually involving hundreds of nonlinear stochastic equations. I often ask builders of such models whether their models have a unique solution and find that they have difficulty in answering this question. Also, the local and global dynamic properties of many of these models are poorly understood. Thus I believe that work to simplify these large, complicated models would be very fruitful.

In terms of econometric model construction, another basic issue is whether a "bottom-up" or "top-down" approach is probably more fruitful. In the "top-down" approach a general, broad model is first formulated (the so-called maintained hypothesis) and then tested to determine whether it specializes to a simpler variant. While this approach may be fruitful in some cases, there is a great danger that the complicated maintained hypothesis may not nest the appropriate, simpler variant. Further, if data are limited, it may not be possible to estimate and test the complicated, general model very well. For example, if the general model is an unrestricted vector autoregression, $\mathbf{z}_t = A_1\mathbf{z}_{t-1} + A_2\mathbf{z}_{t-2} + \ldots + A_q\mathbf{z}_{t-q} + \boldsymbol{\epsilon}_t$, where $\mathbf{z}_t$ is a $p \times 1$ vector of variables, the A's are $p \times p$ coefficient matrices, and $\boldsymbol{\epsilon}_t$ is a white noise $p \times 1$ error vector with zero mean vector and $p \times p$ covariance matrix Σ; then there are $q \times p^2$ elements in the Σ-matrices and $p(p + 1)/2$ distinct elements in Σ. In a "small" system with $p = 6$ and $q = 10$, $q \times p^2 + p(p + 1)/2 = 381$ parameters. Further, if 20 years of quarterly data are available, there are $20 \times 4 \times 6 = 480$ observations and the observation/

parameter ratio, 480/381, is abysmally low. In such a case, estimation and prediction will be imprecise and tests not very powerful. There is a need for model simplification, say by resort to a vector autoregressive-moving average model that is usually a more parsimonious parameterization[16] and by use of economic theory and other information. In fact, unrestricted VAR's performance in forecasting U.S. quarterly data has been evaluated by Litterman and found to be not nearly as satisfactory as that provided by other approaches.[17]

I prefer a "bottom-up" approach that I have called a structural-econometric-modeling-time-series-analysis (SEMTSA) approach.[18] In the SEMTSA approach, an initial variant of an econometric model is formulated that incorporates results from economic theory and other relevant information. The initial variant of the model should be as simple as possible given the objectives of the modeling project. Among many model checks, for example, data checks and mathematical and simulation experiment analyses to determine the model's properties, and so on, it is useful to deduce the implied properties of transfer functions (TF's) and final equations (FE's) associated with an initial variant of a model. These are in the nature of predictions about the properties of TF's and FE's (often in the form of Box-Jenkins's univariate ARIMA schemes for individual variables). Then data are brought to bear on these predictions of the model, that is, the forms of FE's and of TF's are determined from the data using time series methods and checked against the model's predicted forms for these relationships. These operations provide researchers with an intimate knowledge of their data as well as statistical models for forecasting and policy analysis, the fitted FE's and TF's. If the structural model's properties are found to be consistent with the data, it can be estimated and put into use. If not, then the initial variant must be reformulated and its properties reexamined. Further discussion of this approach and analyses illustrating its application can be found in the literature.

Among important results emerging from the "bottom-up" approach that involves intensive examination of individual time series' properties is the fact that many individual series can be modeled by relatively simple processes, for example, random walks, near-random walks, or low-order Box-

16. See, e.g., G. C. Tiao and G. E. P. Box, "Modeling Multiple Time Series with Applications," where this and related issues are discussed.

17. See Litterman's paper, "A Bayesian Procedure for Forecasting with Vector Autoregressions."

18. See my "Statistical Analysis of Econometric Models" and references in it for further information on the SEMTSA approach.

Jenkins ARIMA schemes.[19] Thus relatively simple schemes for time series variables seem to be the case rather than the exception. In some cases economic theory has rationalized these findings.[20] Where they have not been so explained, there is an important challenge to economic theorists and others to do so. The finding of simple time series models for individual economic variables has motivated at least one researcher to incorporate such simple processes in a forecasting model that has produced rather good forecasts relative to those produced by large complicated models.[21] Last, the research findings of relatively simple time series processes for individual economic variables poses another challenge. What structural econometric models imply random walk or relatively simple stochastic models for variables that have been found empirically from analyses of data? While some work bearing on this problem has appeared in the literature, much more needs to be done in order to obtain econometric models that accurately reflect the information in data, are in accord with dependable economic principles, forecast well and are dependable in policymaking. This important research involves significant interaction between theory and application that Commons and many others have emphasized is an important element in the progress of economic science.

19. Empirical results are given in C. R. Nelson, "The Predictive Performance of the FRB–MIT–Penn Model of the U.S. Economy," *American Economic Review*, 62 (1972): 902–17, and J. McDonald, "Modeling Demographic Relationships: An Analysis of Forecast Functions for Australian Births," *Journal of the American Statistical Association*, 76 (1981): 782–91.

20. Some works dealing with these issues are E. F. Fama, "Efficient Capital Markets: A Review of Theory and Empirical Work," *Journal of Finance*, 25 (1970): 383–417; J. Muth, "Rational Expectations and the Theory of Price Movements," *Econometrica*, 29 (1961): 315–35; and P. A. Samuelson, "Proof That Properly Discounted Present Values of Assets Vibrate Randomly," *Bell Journal of Economics and Management Science*, 4 (1973): 368–74.

21. These results are given in R. Litterman's paper, "A Bayesian Procedure for Forecasting with Vector Autoregressions."

1.4 Causality and Econometrics

1 Introduction

Although the concept of causality has been treated extensively in the philosophical literature and used extensively in interpreting data in many sciences including econometrics, almost all, if not all, textbooks treating the methodology of econometrics, that is, econometric theory and/or principles, exclude terms like *causality* and *cause* from their subject indexes. Indeed these econometrics textbooks also say little, if anything, even about the age-old issue of the relationship between the concepts of correlation and causality.

The glaring failure of econometrics texts to treat the fundamental concept of causality could be excused if this concept were irrelevant to or unimportant for economics and econometrics. That such is not the case is easily established by taking note of the following observations:

1. On the opening page of Stigler's (1949, p. 3) influential textbook on price theory, he writes, "The important purpose of a scientific law is to permit prediction, and prediction is in turn sought because it permits control over phenomena. That control requires prediction is self-evident, for unless one knows what 'causes' a particular phenomenon, one cannot effect or prevent its occurrence." Although the word *causes* in this quotation is central, it is not defined, perhaps because its meaning is thought to be self-evident or, more likely, because its meaning is rather controversial, hence the use of quotation marks. Be that as it may, causation is clearly a central concept in Stigler's discussion of the purpose of scientific laws that appear in price theory and econometrics.

2. Cowles Commission Monograph no. 14, *Studies in Econometric*

Reprinted from *Three Aspects of Policy and Policymaking: Knowledge, Data, and Institutions*, K. Brunner and A. H. Meltzer, eds. (Carnegie-Rochester Conference Series on Public Policy [a supplementary series to the *Journal of Monetary Economics*], vol. 10; Amsterdam: North-Holland Publishing Co., 1979), pp. 9–54, with the kind permission of North-Holland Publishing Co.

Method, edited by T. C. Koopmans and W. C. Hood, a key contribution to the development of econometrics, includes a paper by H. Simon (1953) on the nature of causal orderings.

3. In the 1950s and 1960s, controversies regarding the causal interpretation of econometric models involving H. A. O. Wold, R. L. Basmann, R. H. Strotz, and others raged in the literature, giving evidence of much concern and no little confusion regarding the causal interpretation of fully recursive and interdependent or simultaneous econometric models. Given confusion about the causal interpretation of econometric models, there was also confusion regarding the relation of these models to the scientific laws that they were supposed to represent.

4. The more recent economic and econometric literature abounds with papers in which the Wiener-Granger concept of causality appears. In addition, various tests of causality have been formulated and applied, sometimes with startling results.

The few observations listed above, and many more that could be added, testify to the importance of the concept of causality in economics and econometrics. The fact that many textbooks have little or nothing to say about causality is thus considered to be an important omission, one that may be in large part responsible for the difficulties that some have in understanding the results of recent analyses that purport to be tests of causality.

Further difficulties in understanding recent analyses of causality are produced by statements like that of T. Sargent (1977, p. 216):

> It is true that Granger's definition of a causal relation does *not*, in general, coincide with the economist's usual definition of one: namely, a relation that is invariant with respect to interventions in the form of imposed changes in the process governing the causing variables.

The statement is accompanied by the following footnote:

> Sims suggests to me that it is not really so clear that economists' use of the word *cause* typically coincides with "invariance under an intervention" rather than "a one-sided relation with a strictly exogenous variable on the right-hand side." Certainly in the mathematics and engineering literature the concept of a causal relation coincides with the latter one.

From these statements, it seems apparent that the man in the street may not be the only one who is at a loss to understand the nature of causality and causal relations.

Further, in his "Report on the NBER-NSF Seminar on Time Series" (1977), C. F. Ansley states:

> Granger said that he wanted to clarify the notion of causality. Causality is defined as a reduction in forecasting variance with respect to a given information set; this idea dated back to Wiener. The various tests that had been proposed were equivalent only in the population, not in the sample. Given a stationary series, one should use postsample forecasting as a test. Cross-correlation methods are tests of identification [in the time series analyst's sense] only. [P. 20]

While Ansley's statement may provide clarification for some, it is pertinent to note that Granger and Newbold (1977) write:

> It is doubtful that philosophers would completely accept this definition [their definition of causality], and possibly *cause* is too strong a term, or one too emotionally laden, to be used. A better term might be *temporally related*, but since cause is such a simple term we shall continue to use it. [P. 225]

While the five-letter word *cause* is indeed a simple word, Granger's and Newbold's remarks attest to the fact, long appreciated by philosophers, that cause is a rather subtle and difficult concept, which is not completely synonymous with *temporally related* or with *a reduction in forecasting variance with respect to a given information set.*

The discussion presented above reveals that concepts of causation, causality, cause, causal relations, and the like have been important in economics and econometrics. Indeed, Simon (1953) writes, "The most orthodox of empiricists and antideterminists can use the term 'cause,' as we shall define it, with a clear conscience"(p. 51). As this statement implies, a satisfactory definition of cause is relevant for many. However, as is clear from the above discussion, many different definitions of cause, causation, causal relation, and so on, have appeared in the literature, some of them inconsistent with each other and inconsistent with definitions provided by philosophers. There is, thus, a need to reconsider these definitions and try to arrive at a better understanding of the issues involved and how they relate to current econometric practice.

In what follows, I shall attempt to arrive at a better understanding of causation and associated concepts. I shall begin by reviewing a philosophical definition of causation and its implications in section 2. In section 3, the discussion in section 2 will be brought to bear on some major definitions of causation that have appeared in the econometric literature. In section 4, the implications of the preceding sections for tests of causality will be explored. Finally, in section 5, a summary of findings and some concluding remarks will be presented.

2 Review of a Philosophical Definition of Causality and Its Implications

At the end of the last section, we recognized a need for a clear-cut definition of causation. Fortunately, a sophisticatedly simple and deep definition of causation is available in a paper by H. Feigl (1953), which "was written with the purpose of summarizing succinctly some results of the logical and methodological analyses of the concept of causation" (n., p. 408). According to Feigl: "The clarified (purified) concept of causation is defined in terms of *predictability according to a law* (or more adequately, according to a set of laws)" (p. 408). This deceptively simple definition is noteworthy both for what it includes and what it excludes. Most important, it links causation *not just to predictability* but to *predictability according to a law or set of laws*. According to this philosophical definition, predictability without a law or set of laws, or as econometricians might put it, without theory, is *not* causation. As will be seen, linking predictability to a law or set of laws is critical in appraising various tests of causality that have appeared in the econometric literature. This view also coincides with that of Jeffreys (1967), who remarks that the most important part of our knowledge "consists of making inferences from past experience to predict future experience. This part may be called generalization or induction" (p. 1). Jeffreys emphasizes the important role of laws, such as Newton's or Einstein's laws, in efforts to predict future experience or as yet unobserved outcomes. With respect to causality, Jeffreys (1957) writes, "If we can say with high probability that a set of circumstances would be followed by another set, that is enough for our purposes" (p. 190). Since, for Jeffreys, the process of prediction is identified with generalization, his concept of causality is very close to that presented above. Note, however, that Jeffreys mentions "a high probability," while Feigl does not similarly qualify his use of the term *predictability*. Consideration will be given to this point below.

In his definition of causation, Feigl speaks of the "clarified (purified) concept of causation." By *clarified* or *purified*, he means a concept of causation that is purged of "metaphysical, i.e., in principle unconfirmable, connotations that had traditionally obscured, if not eclipsed, the only meaning of causation that is logically tenable and methodologically adequate and fruitful" (p. 408).

What are some of these so-called unconfirmable connotations? First, there is the teleological conception (final cause or causes, considered by Aristotle and others). According to Feigl, final cause is eliminated from the modern concept of causation. In this connection, it is interesting to consider J. M. Keynes's (1921) analysis of the issue of final causes. Keynes writes:

> The discussion of *final* causes and of the argument from design has suffered confusion from its supposed connection with theology. But the logical problem is plain and can be determined upon formal and abstract considerations. The argument is in all cases simply this—an event has occurred and has been observed which would be very improbable *a priori* if we did not know that it had actually happened; on the other hand, the event is of such a character that it might have been not unreasonably predicted if we had assumed the existence of a conscious agent whose motives are of a certain kind and whose powers are sufficient [P. 297].

Keynes provides the following analysis of the problem:

> Let h be our original *data*, a the occurrence of the event, b the existence of the supposed conscious agent. Then a/h [the probability of a given h] is assumed very small in comparison with a/bh [the probability of a given b and h]; and we require b/ah [the probability of b given a and h], the probability, that is to say, of b after a is known. The inverse principle of probability [Bayes's theorem] . . . shows that $b/ah = a/bh \cdot \frac{b/h}{a/h}$, *and* b/ah is therefore not determinate in terms of a/bh and a/h alone. Thus we cannot measure the probability of the conscious agent's existence *after* the event, unless we can measure its probability *before* the event. . . . The argument tells us that the existence of the hypothetical agent is more likely after the event than before it; but, . . . unless there is an appreciable probability first, there cannot be an appreciable probability afterwards. No conclusion, therefore, which is worth having, can be based on the argument from design *alone*; like induction, this type of argument can only strengthen the probability of conclusions, for which there is something to be said on *other* grounds. [P. 298]

Keynes has thus shown that the hypothesis of final causes can be subjected to scientific logical analysis and that the critical result that emerges is one of degree of confirmation; that is, if the initial or prior probability (b/h in Keynes's notation) is very small, the posterior probability (b/ah) will also be very small under Keynes's conditions. This does not lead to a "conclusion worth having." This analysis has relevance for those who argue that an unusual event, for example, World War I or the Great Depression of the 1930s, is the result of some final cause or grand design. Unless there are other grounds or evidence leading to enhancing the value of our prior probability, the result of Keynes's analysis will be an inconclusive result regarding the hypothesis that the supposed conscious agent or grand design exists.

In closing this discussion of final causes or grand design, it is important to point out that Keynes's analysis indicates that these concepts are not to be ruled out a priori. The concepts, according to Keynes, are amenable to scientific deductive and inductive analysis. This important finding is in accord with one of Jeffreys's rules governing any theory of scientific learning or induction, namely, Jeffreys's (1967) rule 5, which states, "The theory must not deny any empirical proposition *a priori*; any precisely stated empirical proposition must be formally capable of being accepted . . . given a moderate amount of relevant evidence" (p. 9).

A second conception of causation that Feigl has purged from his modern definition is the animistic conception. He explains that the animistic conception of causation implies that:

> there is an internal (but unconfirmable) compulsion (conceived anthropomorphically in analogy to coercion as experienced on the human level when forced against our own impulses), which supposedly accounts for the invariable connection of causes with their effects. One fallacious inference from this conception is the doctrine of *fatalism*. [P. 408]

Taking a cue from Keynes's treatment of final causes, I think it may be possible to sharpen and explicate the animistic concept to render it in the form of a clear-cut empirical proposition. If this were done, it seems that an analysis similar to Keynes's analysis of final causes would apply. In this case, however, the hypothesis of the existence of an internal compulsion would replace the hypothesis of the existence of a final cause. The proposition would then become susceptible to empirical investigation in accord with Jeffreys's theory of scientific induction, and the application of Keynes's analysis would lead to a conclusion similar to that reached in the case of his analysis of final causes. Since the animistic concept of causation is sometimes encountered in the economic and historical literature in the guise of "*A* is the inevitable consequence of *B* by the very nature of the circumstances," having an explicit analysis of the nature of such statements is valuable.

The third concept of causation eliminated by Feigl is "the *rationalistic* conception which identifies (I should say, confuses) the causal relation with the logical relation of implication (or entailment)" (p. 408). Feigl says that this conception of causation was repudiated by Hume and that attempts by Kant and others to revive a conception of causation based on conceptions of logical identity, entailment, or necessity "may be said to have failed (for diverse reasons such as mistaken conceptions of logical identity or necessity, . . .)" (p. 408).

The rationalistic conception of causality is rejected, because it conflicts with basic principles of scientific methodology that distinguish the rules of induction and deduction in scientific work. As Jeffreys (1967) puts it:

> Traditional or deductive logic admits only three attitudes to any proposition: definite proof, disproof, or blank ignorance. But no number of previous instances of a rule [or law] will provide a deductive proof that the rule [or law] will hold in a new instance. There is always the formal possibility of an exception. [Pp. 1–2]

This statement embodies the negative findings of Hume's analysis of the nature of causality, namely, that there is no logically necessary relationship connecting cause and effect. Jeffreys (1967) comments further that in much writing on scientific method there is a "tendency to claim that scientific method can be reduced in some way to deductive logic, which is the most fundamental fallacy of all: it can be done only by rejecting its chief feature, induction" (p. 2). Jeffreys (1957) also states, "inference from past observations to future ones is not deductive. The observations not yet made may concern events either in the future or simply at places not yet inspected. It is technically called induction. . . . There is an element of uncertainty in all inferences of the kind considered" (p. 13).

The unavoidable uncertainty involved in making inferences from past data to as yet unobserved data is a basic reason for rejecting the rationalistic conception of causality, which involves the concept of deductive logical necessity, or entailment. Thus, using deduction to prove that, according to economic theory, event A must produce or cause event B obviously does not imply that there is a logical necessity that event B will actually be observed given the occurrence of A. What is needed in such a case is an application of inductive logic that would produce a statement like "Given the occurrence of A, B will *probably* occur." Most important, there is no element of deductive logical necessity in this last statement. The appropriate concept of probability to be utilized in such a statement yielded by inductive logic and the quantification of the phrase *will probably occur* are issues treated at length by Jeffreys (1957, 1967) in his development of a theory of scientific induction. He states, "*the essence of the present theory* is that no probability . . . is simply a frequency. The fundamental idea is that of a reasonable degree of belief, which satisfies certain rules of consistency and can in consequence of these rules be formally expressed by numbers" (1967, p. 401).

Thus, Jeffreys, along with Hume, provides compelling arguments against the rationalistic conception of causality. Further, while perhaps more controversial, Jeffreys's theory of scientific induction requires a particular concept of probability, and in his work he provides many applied analyses illustrating how his concept of probability can be employed to obtain numerical probabilities associated with alternative laws, models, or hypotheses, many of which are frequently encountered in econometrics. In summary, the deductive, rationalistic conception of causality is considered inappropriate and can be replaced by one grounded in inductive rather than deductive logic.

Returning to Feigl's definition of causality, we see that it involves the concept of "laws." It is relevant to consider the types and forms of laws and the domains and levels of their application. Feigl (1953) presents the following list of characteristics:

A. Types of Laws
   1. Deterministic
   2. Statistical

B. Forms of Laws
   1. Qualitative
   2. Semiquantitative (topological)
   3. Fully quantitative (metrical)

C. Domains of Laws
   1. Temporal (sequential)
   2. Coexistential (simultaneous)

D. Levels of Laws
   1. Macro
   2. Micro

In addition, he recognizes that certain laws may have combinations of these characteristics.

Although the above list may not be all inclusive, it does contain many of the characteristics of laws. A brief discussion of these characteristics is worth undertaking. With respect to deterministic laws and determinism, Feigl writes:

> The principle of determinism [i.e., ideally complete and precise predictability, given the momentary conditions, the pertinent laws, and the required mathematical techniques] may therefore be interpreted as a—to be sure, very bold and hence extremely problematic—hypothesis concerning the order of nature. [P. 412]

He goes on to say that most of the younger-generation physicists have definitely abandoned determinism. Jeffreys (1967) also writes, "We must also reject what is variously called the principle of causality, determinism, or the uniformity of nature, in any such form as 'Precisely similar antecedents lead to precisely similar consequences'" (p. 11). He explains that no two sets of antecedents are ever identical. He even rejects a looser form of determinism such as "In precisely the same circumstances very similar things can be observed, or very similar things can usually be observed," with the observations that "If 'precisely the same' is intended to be a matter of absolute truth, we cannot achieve it" (pp. 11–12). He also states:

> The most that can be done is to make those conditions the same that we believe to be relevant—"the same" can never in practice mean more than "the same as far as we know", and usually means a great deal less. The question then arises, How do we know that the neglected variables are irrelevant? Only by actually allowing them to vary and verifying that there is no associated variation in the result; but this requires the use of significance tests, a theory of which must therefore be given before there is any application of the principle, and when it is given it is found that the principle is no longer needed [P. 12]

While the existence of quantum theory, a probabilistic theory, is often cited as evidence against determinism, Jeffreys's critique of determinism goes much deeper and relates to the operational uses of systems, not just their deductive logical structure. Thus, Burks's (1977) observations that "John von Neumann argues that quantum mechanical systems are inherently probabilistic and cannot be embedded in deterministic systems" (p. 589), and that "Einstein believed that when a complete theory of quantum phenomena is developed, it will be deterministic" (p. 590), while interesting, do not have much bearing on the issues raised by Jeffreys's critique of determinism. It is thus concluded that laws to which Feigl's definition of causality relates are in the main, if not exclusively, nondeterministic, statistical, or probabilistic laws.

Next, we take up the forms of laws. There does not appear to be any compelling reason to limit the concept of causality to laws that are "fully quantitative (metrical)." Qualitative laws that yield predictions about the presence or absence of qualities or characteristics and semiquantitative laws involving, as Feigl puts it, "only the relations of 'equal' or 'greater than'" (1953, p. 409) are just as relevant as fully quantitative laws in defining causality.

As regards the forms of mathematical functions appearing in laws, it is sometimes convenient to assume them, and perhaps their first and second derivatives, to be continuous. However, other representations are not precluded. In fact at various stages of the development of a subject, two alternative formulations may coexist. For example, Jeffreys (1967) remarks that:

> The quantum theory and the continuous emission theory both accounted for one set of facts, but each, in its existing form, was inconsistent with the facts explained by the other. The proper conclu-

> sion was that both explanations were wrong and that . . . some new explanation must be sought. . . . But meanwhile, physicists based their predictions on the laws; in types of phenomena that had been found predictable by quantum methods; in phenomena of interference they made predictions by assuming continuous wave trains. [Pp. 411–12]

Another point about forms of laws is that they be capable of yielding verifiable predictions about as yet unobserved data. This requirement does not place overly severe restrictions on the forms of laws or of mathematical functions appearing in them. However, many, including G. E. P. Box, R. A. Fisher, M. Friedman, H. Jeffreys, the present writer, and a number of others, do emphasize the virtues of simplicity in formulating laws. Some exhibit a preference for simplicity by appealing to Ockham's razor, the principle of parsimony, or the Jeffreys-Wrinch simplicity postulate. With respect to the simplicity postulate, Jeffreys (1967) states that contrary to the widespread belief that the choice of the simplest law is merely a convention, "the simplest law is chosen because it is the most likely to give correct predictions; . . . the choice is based on a reasonable degree of belief" (pp. 4–5). Further Jeffreys (1967) writes:

> Precise statement of the prior probabilities of the laws in accordance with the condition of convergence requires that they should actually be put in an order of decreasing prior probability. . . . All we have to say is that the simpler laws have the greater prior probabilities. This is what Wrinch and I called the *Simplicity Postulate*. [P. 47]

He goes on to suggest a tentative numerical rule for assessing the complexity of laws expressible by differential equations. Jeffreys (1957) also presents an analysis of developments in the history of science that provides support for the simplicity postulate. Thus, if the simplicity postulate is accepted as probably valid, it involves a most important ordering of causal laws.

We now consider several aspects of the domains of laws involved in Feigl's definition of causation. The domains of many laws are temporal or temporal-spatial. In regard to the temporal-spatial aspects of laws, Feigl (1953) writes:

> This principle [the homogeneity and isotropy of space, and homogeneity of time], clearly formulated by Maxwell, states the irrelevance of absolute space or time co-ordinates, and in this sense the purely relational character of space and time as seen already by Leibniz and re-emphasized in Einstein's theory of relativity. The place and time at which events occur do not by themselves have any modifying effect on these events. [P. 412]

He goes on to say, "Differences in effects must always be accounted for in terms of differences in the *conditions*, not in terms of purely spatio-temporal location" (p. 412). These considerations and considerations of the reversibility (symmetry) of the cause-effect relation in molecular processes that is assumed in the work of Gibbs and Boltzmann and empirically observed in the case of Brownian motion lead Feigl to state:

> Since the basic laws of classical mechanics and electrodynamics as well as those of modern quantum mechanics are temporally symmetrical, it would seem that the direction of causality may indeed be reducible to Boltzmann's explanation [the probabilities for a transition from a more highly ordered state to one of lower order (greater disorder) are always higher than those for the process in the opposite direction]. Once this is assumed, such statements as "earlier actions can influence later events but not vice versa" are recognized as sheer tautologies. [P. 414]

These considerations of time and space as they relate to physical laws indicate an important probabilistic reversibility of laws in time. As regards laws in the social sciences, it has been customary to think in terms of chronological time and to require that laws be such that causes precede their effects in chronological time. From what has been presented above, it is clear that such a requirement is at odds with important physical laws. In addition, if Allais's (1966) concept of psychological time is considered, then there is no assurance that laws stated in a psychological time frame will necessarily meet the requirement that cause precede effect in chronological time.

Another issue regarding the temporal domain of laws is whether laws relate to continuous or discrete time. There does not seem to be any compelling reason to favor either continuous or discrete time formulations of laws, and, in fact, mixed difference-differential equation formulations of laws are not only possible but have been employed.

Finally, with respect to temporal matters, there is the problem of laws that involve "simultaneity" or "instantaneous causality." As Feigl notes, "an equally well established usage [of the crude concepts of cause and effect] seems to prevail even if the two events (factors, processes) are contemporaneous" (p. 417). In terms of the discussion of temporal ordering presented above, it seems clear that simultaneous or instantaneous formulations of laws cannot be ruled out, provided that these laws are capable of yielding predictions about as yet unobserved data. If they can, then such laws are causal laws according to Feigl's definition.

As regards the levels, macro or micro, to which laws relate, it is, of course, possible to have laws relating specifically to macro phenomena, specifically to micro phenomena, or to combined micro and macro phenomena. While there is a natural desire to have a consistent law applicable to both micro and macro phenomena, the fact that in some areas such a law does not exist does not preclude the use of laws relating to one level until an improved, more general law is formulated.

In the above discussion of some characteristics of a philosopher's definition of causation, namely, "predictability according to a law" (or, more adequately, "according to a set of laws"), not much has been said about the deductive, logical nature of causal laws; rather, more emphasis has been placed on the inductive logical nature of causation, since this aspect seems very relevant to the tasks of working scientists. Also, it must be mentioned that the calculus of inductive logic plays a central role in comparing and testing alternative laws' predictions. Jeffreys (1967, chaps. 5–6) and Burks (1977, pp. 65–91) describe the theory and some applications of this use of inductive logic that involves Bayes's theorem to compute probabilities associated with alternative laws or hypotheses. This inductive logical analysis is needed to provide information about the quality of the predictability of various laws.

In the next section attention is directed to reviewing and discussing several works dealing with causation that have appeared in the econometric literature.

3 Review of Selected Discussions of Causation in the Econometric Literature

The objectives of this review are to establish the extent to which concepts of causation in the econometric literature coincide with or differ from those considered in section 2 and to provide a basis for approaching the tests of causality to be considered in the next section. Because not all discussions of causality that have appeared in the econometric literature can be covered, I have selected several leading works that appear important and relevant for assessing the meaningfulness of tests of causality.

3.1 Simon's "Causal Ordering and Identifiability"

H. Simon's essay "Causal Ordering and Identifiability" (1953) was published as chapter 3 in one of the most influential monographs on econometric methodology, *Studies in Econometric Method*. For this reason and because some recent work by Sims (1977) builds on Simon's contribution, it is worthwhile to review Simon's analysis.

Simon agrees with Feigl that the concept of causation is in need of purification and clarification. In fact, Simon mentions "objectionable ontological and epistemological overtones that have attached themselves to the causal concept" (p. 49). He also notes:

> In view of the generally unsavory epistemological status of the notion of causality, it is somewhat surprising to find the term in rather common use in scientific writing (when the scientist is writing about his science, not about its methodology). Moreover, it is not easy to explain this usage as metaphorical, or even as a carry-over of outmoded language. [P. 50]

Thus Simon is in agreement with the view, expressed above, that the notion of causality is in widespread use in science.

In view of the impure connotations associated with the term *causation* and of "Hume's critique that necessary connections among events cannot be perceived (and hence can have no empirical basis)" (p. 49), Simon opts for a narrower concept of causality. Simon's narrower notion of causality is "that causal orderings are simply properties of the scientist's model, properties that are subject to change as the model is altered to fit new observations" (p. 50). He rightly points out that such a notion of causality can be applied to probabilistic as well as deterministic models. Applicability to probabilistic models is important, since Simon believes that "the viewpoint is becoming more and more prevalent that the appropriate model of the world is not a deterministic model but a probabilistic one" (p. 50).

Whether this last statement is true or not, it is evident that Simon's notion of causality is a deductive logical concept relating to models' characteristics, not to empirical features of the world that require statements of inductive logic. Indeed, Simon (p. 51) states, "It is the aim of this chapter . . . to provide a clear and rigorous basis for determining when a causal ordering can be said to hold between two variables or groups of variables in a model" (and not the "real" world), and "the concepts to be defined all refer to a model—a system of equations—and not to the 'real' world the model purports to describe." Thus, Simon's narrower notion of causality or causation is radically different from Feigl's concept of causation, that is, predictability according to a law or set of laws. For Feigl predictability means predictability of empirically observable outcomes, certainly not just a deductive logical property of a model or of a law. While Simon's notion of causality can be used to describe logically the laws that Feigl mentions, it involves no necessary relation to the prediction of "real" world outcomes. Obviously a law that is causal in Simon's sense need not be causal in Feigl's; that is, the law may be incapable of predicting "real-world" outcomes. Such a law would not be termed causal in an inductive, empirical sense.

In addition to this important distinction between Simon's and Feigl's concepts of causation, it is relevant to note that even within his narrower concept of causality Simon explains that:

> We might say that if A and B are functionally related and if A precedes B in time, then A causes B. There is no logical obstacle to this procedure. Nevertheless, we shall not adopt it. We shall argue that time sequence does, indeed, sometimes provide a basis for asymmetry between A and B, but that asymmetry is the important thing, not the sequence. By putting asymmetry, without necessarily implying a time sequence, at the basis of our definition we shall admit causal orderings where no time sequence appears (and sometimes exclude them even where there is a time sequence). By so doing we shall find ourselves in closer accord with actual usage, and with a better understanding of the meaning of the concept than if we had adopted the other, and easier, course. We shall discover that causation (as we shall define it) does not imply time sequence, nor does time sequence imply causation. [P. 51]

Thus, Simon is in agreement with the discussion in the previous section regarding the nonnecessity of a chronological time ordering between cause and effect. While Simon agrees with this position in the early part of his essay, in his concluding section he remarks,

> There is no necessary connection between the asymmetry of this relation [among certain variables] and asymmetry in time, although an analysis of the causal structure of dynamical systems in econometrics and physics will show that lagged relations can generally be interpreted as causal relations. [Pp. 73–74]

Since it is not clear what specific lagged relations Simon is referring to, it is difficult to evaluate this last remark. Suffice it to say that there are many examples of empirically fitted dynamical systems in econometrics in which a lagged relation cannot be regarded as causal in Feigl's sense.

To illustrate the nature of Simon's analysis of causal orderings, we will review the simplest example presented in his paper. In this example, he considers the following three-equation, linear, deterministic system (p. 58):

$$(1) \qquad a_{11}x_1 = a_{10},$$

$$(2) \qquad a_{21}x_1 + a_{22}x_2 = a_{20},$$

$$(3) \qquad a_{32}x_2 + a_{33}x_3 = a_{30},$$

where x_1 is an index measuring the favorableness of weather for growing wheat; x_2 is the size of the wheat crop; x_3 is the price of wheat; and the a's are parameters. Simon writes: "We suppose the weather to depend only on a parameter; the wheat crop, upon the weather (we ignore a possible dependence of supply on price); and the price of wheat, on the wheat crop" (p. 58).

Since the value of x_1 can be determined from (1) alone, it is possible to substitute this value in equations (2) and (3) to get a reduced system involving x_2 and x_3. The substitution from (1) into (2) yields a relation determining the value of x_2, which when substituted in (3) along with the value of x_1 from (1), determines the value of x_3. This ordering of the algebraic solution of the system in (1)–(3) results in Simon's writing:

$$(1) \longrightarrow (2) \longrightarrow (3),$$

which Simon interprets as "(1) has direct precedence over (2), and (2) over (3)," (p. 58) and

$$x_1 \longrightarrow x_2 \longrightarrow x_3,$$

which he interprets as "x_1 is the direct cause of x_2, and x_2 of x_3" (p. 58).

While Simon analyzes systems more complicated than that shown above, this simple system reveals well the nature of his notions of causality and causal orderings, which are, as he emphasizes, just logical properties of the model considered. He leaves the inductive relevance of the model aside, probably on purpose; yet, it is the inductive aspect of this and other models that is critical for appraising the degree to which the model is causal.[1] In discussing a concept of causality close to Simon's, Jeffreys (1967) expresses a similar point of view:

> Causality, as used in applied mathematics, has a more general form, such as: "Physical laws are expressible by mathematical equations, possibly connecting continuous variables, such that in any case, given a finite number of parameters, some variable or set of variables that appears in the equations is uniquely determined in terms of the others.". . . The equations, which we call laws, are inferred from previous instances and then applied to instances where the relevant quantities are different. This form permits astronomical prediction. But it still leaves the questions "How do we know that no other parameters than those stated are needed?" "How do we know that we need consider no variables as relevant other than those mentioned explicitly in the laws?" and "Why do we believe the laws themselves?" It is only after these questions have been answered that we can make any actual application of the principle, and the principle is useless until we have attended to the epistemological problems. [P. 12]

1. In a letter to the author dated 2 May 1978, Simon emphasizes that while in earlier work he "neglected to emphasize the correspondence principle that connects the syntactic with the semantic dimensions of any theory," in more recent work he does recognize this important link.

3.2 The Basmann-Strotz-Wold Discussion of Causality

In three papers published together as "a triptych on causal chain systems" (R. H. Strotz and H. O. A. Wold 1960, R. H. Strotz 1960, and H. O. A. Wold 1960), Strotz and Wold bring together and extend earlier work of Wold (see references in Strotz and Wold 1960), attempting to clarify the causal nature and properties of econometric models, including entire models and particular equations and parameters appearing in models. In a paper dealing with the Strotz and Wold papers, Basmann (1963) writes:

> Wold and Strotz have not stated from what specific definition of causality they argue to the conclusion that only *triangular* recursive systems are causal. Their own view lacks several essential features of the classical notion of causality; the classical notion . . . is not mentioned by them as a possible alternative to their own. It is the purpose of this note to show constructively, by an example, that, contrary to the Wold-Strotz assertion, the hypothetical structural equations which underlie "interdependent," i.e., non-triangular, systems can be validly given a straightforward causal interpretation, at least in the classical sense. [Pp.441–42]

As the quotation reveals, two of the basic issues in this discussion are (*a*) the definitions of causality employed by the participants in this discussion and (*b*) the relationship between concepts of causality and the forms of econometric models. These two aspects of the Strotz-Wold and Basmann discussion are considered below.

With respect to the definition, or definitions, of causality, Strotz and Wold (1960) are rather eclectic. They write, "No one has monopoly rights in defining 'causality.' The term is in common parlance and the only meaningful challenge is that of providing an explication of it. No explication need be unique, and some may prefer never to use the word at all" (p. 418). Also, Wold (1960) states that "in the treatment of the models at issue, problems come up for which the natural sciences give no guidance, an unusual situation in the social sciences. This is in particular so with regard to the causal interpretation of econometric models" (p. 461). These comments raise the issue of whether a single definition of causality, such as Feigl's, is adequate for work in both the natural and social sciences. While it is recognized that improvements in a definition of causality are possible, it would have to be shown that entertaining different concepts of causality in the natural and social sciences is necessary and empirically fruitful. Since this has not been done, as far as the present writer is aware, the proposition that different concepts of causality are required is purely speculative. It is also noteworthy that Strotz and Wold adopt a definition of causality that they believe is in agreement with "common scientific and statistical-inference usage." Strotz and Wold write,

> For us, however, the word [causality] in common scientific and statistical-inference usage has the following general meaning. z is a cause of y if, by hypothesis, it is or "would be" possible by *controlling z* indirectly to control y, at least stochastically. But it may or may not be possible by controlling y indirectly to control z. A causal relation is therefore in essence asymmetric, in that in any instance of its realization it is asymmetric. Only in special cases may it be reversible and symmetric in a causal sense. These are the cases in which sometimes a controlled change in z may cause a change in y and at other times a controlled change in y may cause a change in z, but y and z cannot both be subjected to simultaneous controlled changes independently of one another without the causal relationship between them being violated. [P. 418]

The Strotz-Wold definition, presented above, differs from Feigl's most markedly by bringing in the concept of controlled changes in variables. Feigl's definition of causality or causation can be fruitfully applied to areas of science in which no variables are under control. In addition, the Feigl definition can also apply in cases in which laws or models contain one or more variables that can actually be controlled. Note, too, that Strotz and Wold say, "it is or 'would be' possible by *controlling z . . .*" What do they mean by *would be*? If they mean that z cannot actually be controlled but that they are considering a hypothetical controlled variation of z, then they appear to be admitting impossible experiments into their definition of causality. Whether impossible experiments are admissible in an operational theory of scientific induction incorporating a consistent definition of causality is a controversial issue. Jeffreys (1967), for example, takes the position that "the existence of a thing [e.g., causality] or the estimate of a quantity must not involve an impossible experiment" (p. 8). While the issue of the admissibility of impossible experiments may be relevant to the Strotz-Wold definition, it is still the case that their definition is subsumed under Feigl's more general definition of causation and causal laws.

In his comment on the Strotz-Wold papers, Basmann (1963) presents the following definition of causality:

> The classical scientific notion of causality to which we shall appeal can be expressed satisfactorily as follows: *Assume that* [the] *mechanism under investigation can be isolated from all systematic*, i.e., *nonrandom external influences*; *assume that the mechanism can be started over repeatedly from any definite initial condition. If every time the mechanism is started up from approximately the same initial condition,*

> *it tends to run through approximately the same sequence of events, then the mechanism is said to be causal.* [P. 442]

Also, directly following his definition, Basmann writes,

> Any model that (1) represents a mechanism in *isolation* from non-random external influences and (2) asserts that, when started up from approximately the same initial conditions, the mechanism always tends to run through approximately the same sequence of states is a causal model expressing a causal hypothesis about the mechanism under investigation. [P. 442]

In a footnote to this last sentence, he remarks, "It is not necessary that such experiments be feasible; it is sufficient that they are not ruled out in principle" (p. 442).

If we equate Feigl's concept of "law or set of laws" with Basmann's concept of a "model that represents a mechanism," and Feigl's concept of "predictability" with Basmann's requirement that a model assert that "when started up from approximately the same initial conditions, the mechanism always tends to run through approximately the same sequence of states," we see that Feigl's and Basmann's concepts of causality or causation and causal laws or models are similar from a logical point of view. There may, however, be some question as to whether Feigl's concept of predictability is precisely the same as Basmann's, a point considered below.

Feigl does not rule out the concept of causation, that is, predictability according to a law or set of laws in cases in which, as is common in mainly nonexperimental sciences, a single realization of a process is the rule rather than the exception. Indeed, Feigl (1953) writes,

> In the case of unrepeatable (unique) events, as described in the historical disciplines (as in the history of the inorganic, organic, mental, social, cultural or individual-biographical occurrences), the assertion of causal relations (as in statements regarding who or what influenced events to what degree and in which direction) is often methodologically precarious, i.e., only very weakly confirmable. But it is not meaningless. [P. 410]

Similarly Jeffreys (1967), who has applied his causal concept to much nonexperimental data from astronomy and geophysics, remarks,

> There must be a uniform standard of validity for all hypotheses, irrespective of the subject. Different laws may hold in different subjects, but they must be tested by the same criteria; otherwise we have no guarantee that our decisions will be those warranted by the data and not merely the result of inadequate analysis or of believing what we want to believe. [P. 7]

Thus, predictability and confirmation of predictability are relevant in situations in which repetition of outcomes is impossible. Thus, Basmann's requirement that the experiment mentioned in his definition "not be ruled out in principle" appears to be superfluous. Of course, however, repetition of experiments, when possible, is usually highly desirable, since it provides a greater degree of confirmation, or lack thereof, for a particular model.

On the issue of the forms of econometric models or laws and causality, it is apparent that Feigl's, Jeffreys's, and Basmann's definitions of causality apply to complete econometric models, whether the models are formulated in fully recursive, triangular, or interdependent forms. Models in any of these forms can embody economic laws and are capable of providing predictions about as yet unobserved phenomena. Thus, they are all causal in a logical, deductive sense. Whether particular parts or single equations of such models are capable of yielding predictions and thus can, in isolation, be interpreted causally is a separate issue that can be decided by a careful examination of the structures of particular models as, for example, carried through by Simon (1953) and Basmann (1963). That models be built so as to have *each* equation capable of a causal interpretation in the above sense is an a priori restriction on the forms of models that cannot be justified methodologically. This requirement could be justified if it were found empirically that models so constructed performed better in prediction than models not so constructed. Since this empirical issue has not been settled, or perhaps cannot be settled in view of Basmann's (1965) demonstration of the observational equivalence of fully recursive and interdependent models, it is inappropriate to require that econometric models necessarily be of one form or another simply on a priori grounds.

A similar conclusion applies to the Strotz-Wold view, expressed in Strotz (1960):

> If a causal interpretation of an interdependent system is possible, it is to be provided in terms of a recursive system. The interdependent system is then either an approximation to the recursive system or a description of its equilibrium state. This was the conclusion of the preceding paper, written jointly with Professor Wold. [P. 428]

This statement is an a priori view about the forms of causal laws and, as indicated above, it is methodologically unsound to rule out, on a priori grounds alone, logically consistent laws that assume particular forms. Aside from the observational equivalence of fully recursive and interdependent systems, discrimination among different laws is an inductive issue involving empirical confirmation procedures. Thus, the Strotz-Wold position that interdependent systems are in some sense approximations of "true" underlying recursive systems and that the former systems involve, as Strotz puts it, "some form of specification error" (p. 428) is unacceptable as a general proposition.

3.3 The Wiener-Granger Concept of Causality

Granger (1969) considers a theory of causality that he views as an alternative to those of Simon, Strotz, Wold, and Basmann reviewed above. Granger writes,

> In the alternative theory to be discussed here, the stochastic nature of the variables and the direction of the flow of time will be central features. The theory is, in fact, not relevant for nonstochastic variables and will rely entirely on the assumption that the future cannot cause the past. This theory will not, of course, be contradictory to previous work but there appears to be little common ground. Its origins may be found in a suggestion by Wiener. [P. 428]

Contrary to what Granger says, it is apparent that his theory is contradictory to previous work on causality in at least two important respects. First, in the previous work of Feigl, Jeffreys, Simon, Strotz, Wold, Basmann, and others, *both* stochastic and nonstochastic variables are considered. The analysis is not limited to stochastic variables, and such limitation is certainly not warranted on either methodological or subject matter considerations. Second, Granger, in contrast to Feigl, Simon, and Basmann, embeds the notion of temporal asymmetry in his theory of causality. Feigl and Simon, as explicitly pointed out above, do not identify causal asymmetry with succession of "cause" and "effect" in chronological time. These requirements of the Granger concept of causality that appear contrary to previous concepts of causality are stated explicitly in Granger and Newbold (1977) as follows: "(i) The future cannot cause the past. Strict causality can occur only with the past causing the present or future." "(ii) It is sensible to discuss causality only for a group of stochastic processes. It is not possible to detect causality between two deterministic processes" (pp. 224–25). As stated above, these restrictions, which do not appear in other concepts of causality, definitely restrict the range of applicability of the Granger concept. If an inductive case could be made that such restrictions are required, then they would be acceptable. Because, as far as the present writer is aware, no such convincing case has been made, it is questionable that the restrictions are required for a fruitful definition of causality. In fact, Granger's restrictions appear to rule out economic laws which state that *nonstochastic* variation in one variable causes variation in a second variable or that a nonstochastic trend in one variable causes a nonstochastic trend in a second variable. As discussed above, such a priori restrictions on the forms of economic laws have to be justified on inductive grounds.

Despite the restrictiveness of his theory of causality, Granger (1969) regards his definition as "very general in nature" (p. 428). In developing this definition, Granger considers a stationary stochastic process, A_t. He lets $\bar{A}_t$ represent the set of *past* values of A_t, and $\bar{\bar{A}}_t$ the set of *past and present* values of A_t. Further, he lets $\bar{A}(k)$ represent the set $\{A_{t-j}, j = k, k+1, \ldots, \infty\}$. He also denotes the optimum, unbiased least squares predictor of A_t using the set of values B_t by $P_t(A \mid B)$, the predictive error series by $\epsilon_t(A \mid B) = A_t - P_t(A \mid B)$, and the variance of $\epsilon_t(A \mid B)$ by $\sigma^2(A \mid B)$. Then Granger (1969) writes,

> Let U_t be all the information in the universe accumulated since time $t-1$ and let $U_t - Y_t$ denote all this information *apart* from the specified series Y_t. We then have the following definitions.
>
> Definition 1: *Causality*. If $\sigma^2(X|U) < \sigma^2(X|\overline{U-Y})$, we say that Y is causing X, denoted by $Y_t \Rightarrow X_t$. We say that Y_t is causing X_t if we are better able to predict X_t using all available information than if the information apart from Y_t had been used.
>
> Definition 2: *Feedback*. If
>
> $$\sigma^2(X|\bar{U}) < \sigma^2(X|\overline{U-Y}),$$
> $$\sigma^2(Y|\bar{U}) < \sigma^2(Y|\overline{U-X}),$$
>
> we say that feedback is occurring, which is denoted $Y_t \Leftrightarrow X_t$, i.e., feedback is said to occur when X_t is causing Y_t and also Y_t is causing X_t.
>
> Definition 3: *Instantaneous Causality*. If $\sigma^2(X|\bar{U}, \bar{\bar{Y}}) < \sigma^2(X|\bar{U})$, we say that instantaneous causality $Y_t \Leftrightarrow X_t$ is occurring. In other words, the current value of X_t is better "predicted" if the present value of Y_t is included in the "prediction" than if it is not.
>
> Definition 4: *Causality Lag*. If $Y_t \Rightarrow X_t$, we define the (integer) causality lag m to be the least value of k such that $\sigma^2(X|U - Y(k)) < \sigma^2(x|U - Y(k+1))$. Thus, knowing the values of Y_{t-j}, $j = 0, 1, \ldots, m-1$, will be of no help in improving the prediction of X_t. [Pp. 428–29]

Granger's definition of causality, his definition 1 above, states that if the variance of the forecast error of an unbiased least squares predictor of a stationary stochastic variable X_t, based on all the information in the universe accumulated since time $t-1$, is smaller than the variance of the forecast error of an unbiased least squares predictor of X_t, based on all the information in the universe since time $t-1$ except for the past values of Y_t, then "Y is causing X." Several important characteristics of this definition follow. First, as recognized by Granger (1969), "The one completely unreal aspect of the above definitions is the use of the series U_t, representing *all* available information" (p. 429). In fact, this requirement makes the Granger definition nonoperational and in violation of one of Jeffreys's (1967) rules for theories of scientific induction, namely, "Any rule given must be applicable in practice. A definition is useless unless the thing defined can be recognized in terms of the definition when it occurs. The existence of a thing or the estimate of a quantity must not involve an impossible experiment" (p. 8). In dealing with this problem, Granger suggests replacing "all the information in the universe" with the concept of "all relevant information" (p. 429). While this modification is a step in the direction of making his definition operational, Granger does not explicitly mention the important role of economic laws in defining the set of "all relevant information." By not mentioning the role of economic laws or theory, Granger gives the impression that purely statistical criteria can be employed in defining causality.

Second, Granger's definition of causality is unusual in that embedded in it is a particular confirmatory criterion, the variance of the forecast error of an unbiased least squares predictor. This confirmatory criterion is not applicable to processes that do not possess finite moments. Also, for most processes, even just stationary processes, which involve parameters whose values must be estimated from finite sets of data, an unbiased least squares "optimum" predictor is often not available. Recognizing some of these difficulties, Granger (1969) writes,

> In practice it will not usually be possible to use completely optimum predictors, unless all sets of series are assumed to be normally distributed, since such optimum predictors may be nonlinear in complicated ways. It seems natural to use only linear predictors and the above definitions may again be used under this assumption of linearity. [P. 429]

Even in the case of linear systems with parameters that must be estimated from finite sets of data, an "optimum" (in finite samples) linear unbiased predictor will not always be available. In fact, the restriction that a predictor be linear and unbiased can result in an inadmissible predictor relative to a quadratic loss function even in linear normal models, given the results of Stein. Thus, it is not clear that the confirmatory procedures embedded in the Granger definition of causality are entirely satisfactory.

Third, as regards the implied quadratic criterion involved in the use of unbiased predictors and variance of forecast or prediction errors, Granger (1969) writes:

> It can be argued that the variance is not the proper criterion to use to measure the closeness of a predictor P_t to the true value X_t. Certainly if some other criteria were used it may be possible to reach different conclusions about whether one series is causing another. The variance does seem to be a natural criterion to use in connection with linear

> predictors as it is mathematically easy to handle and simple to interpret. If one uses this criterion, a better name might be "causality in mean." [P. 430]

Thus linking the confirmatory procedure to comparisons of variances is viewed as a matter of convenience. However, as Granger notes, it is not applicable in general. Further, Granger's confirmation procedures depart from those based on posterior probabilities associated with laws that are adopted by Jeffreys (1967), Burks (1977), and others. The posterior probability concept of confirmation is much more general than Granger's; however, it must be recognized that not all technical problems of applying it to a number of cases encountered in practice have been solved.

Fourth, in commenting on the general concept of causality, Granger and Newbold (1977) write,

> The definition as it stands is far too general to be testable. It is possible to reach a testable definition only by imposing considerable simplification and particularization to this definition. It must be recognized that, in so doing, the definition will become less intuitively acceptable and more error-prone. [P. 225]

Some of the simplifications and particularizations have been mentioned above. Most important, though, is the failure of Granger and Newbold to recognize explicitly the role of economic laws or theories in defining causality. They give the impression, perhaps inadvertently, that the concept of causality can be defined entirely in terms of statistical considerations, a point of view that is contrary to the views of Feigl, Jeffreys, Basmann, and others. The simplifications and particularizations that Granger and Newbold discuss appear to be statistical in nature and not of the kind involved in the Jeffreys-Wrinch simplicity postulate that deals with the forms of laws.

Fifth, Granger's definitions 2–4 are also subject to the criticisms brought up in connection with his definition 1. In addition, since the two processes X and Y are not considered within the context of particular economic laws, it is hard to determine whether the modified, operational Granger concepts are indeed applicable and lead to unambiguous results. On this latter point, Granger (1969) himself points out, "Even for stochastic series, the definitions introduced above may give apparently silly answers" (p. 430). After analyzing a case illustrating this point, he goes on to say, "It will often be found that constructed examples which seem to produce results contrary to common sense can be resolved by widening the set of data within which causality is defined" (p. 431). Perhaps a more satisfactory position would be to define causality, as Feigl and others have, in terms of predictability according to well-thought-out economic laws.

Last, while Granger (1969) does not completely rule out the concept of instantaneous causality, he does remark that in some cases,

> although there is no real instantaneous causality, the definitions will appear to suggest that such causality is occurring. This is because certain relevant information, the missing readings in the data, have not been used. Due to this effect, one might suggest that in many economic situations an apparent instantaneous causality would disappear if the economic variables were recorded at more frequent time intervals. [P. 430]

This statement and what has been presented above reveal that Granger generally adopts a temporal asymmetrical view of cause and effect. As mentioned earlier, such a view is not compatible with certain physical science considerations and is not a necesary component of a definition of causality.

In summary, Granger's definition of causality, his definition 1 above, is a nonoperational definition involving consideration of predictability in a very special confirmatory setting. The definition does not involve mention of laws, economic or otherwise. In fact, the conditions surrounding the definition and the suggestions for making the definition operational have important implications for the forms of laws. For example, nonstochastic variables are excluded, and forms of laws for which least squares unbiased predictors are not at least approximately optimal are not covered. Perhaps in principle such variables could be covered if definition 1 were broadened. However, if definition 1 is so broadened, it appears to the present writer that it may as well be broadened to coincide with Feigl's definition of causality, namely, predictability according to a law or set of laws. Given careful attention to the formulation of such laws, confirmatory procedures that are appropriate for them can be applied. Indeed, this last approach seems very similar to that employed traditionally in econometrics.

4 Empirical Tests of Causality

In this section several empirical studies involving issues discussed in the preceding sections will be analyzed. First, consideration will be given to studies that employ what has been referred to above as the "traditional econometric approach." Then recent studies employing the Granger-Wiener concept of causality will be reviewed. In the discussion, it will be assumed that readers are familiar with standard econometric terminology.

Haavelmo's (1947) early paper, reprinted in Cowles Commission Monograph no. 14, involves an econometric formulation and estimation of a simple Keynesian macroeconomic model that appears in many introductory economics textbooks. The simple model that Haavelmo considered is given by:

$$c_t = \beta + ay_t + u_t \qquad (4)$$

$$t = 1, 2, \ldots, T$$

$$y_t = c_t + z_t. \qquad (5)$$

Equation (4) is a consumption function relating two endogenous variables, (*a*) consumption in period t, c_t and (*b*) income in period t, y_t. β and a are parameters with unknown values, and u_t is an unobservable random disturbance. In Haavelmo's empirical work, he employs U.S. Department of Commerce data on consumers' expenditures in constant dollars per capita to measure c_t, and disposable income in constant dollars per capita, to measure y_t. No attention will be given here to the adequacy of these empirical measures. If they are adopted, then equation (5) is an identity satisfied by the data with z_t equal to "investment expenditures, in constant dollars," the difference between disposable income and consumers' expenditure, which Haavelmo points out is equal to private net investment minus corporate savings plus government deficits. While much more could be said about the interpretation of (5) in terms of an equilibrium condition involving aggregate demand and supply with special assumptions regarding aggregate supply, this matter will not be pursued. Haavelmo then completes his model by assuming (*a*) that the u_t's have zero means, constant common variance, and are serially uncorrelated and (*b*) that the time series z_t is autonomous in relation to u_t and y_t, a condition that is fulfilled if the sequence z_t is a sequence of given numbers, or if each z_t is a random variable which is stochastically independent of u_t. Further, he assumes that sample variance of the z_t's converges, either mathematically in the case of nonstochastic z_t's or in a weak probability sense in the case of stochastic z_t's, to a positive, finite constant. In a deductive logical sense, Haavelmo's model is a causal model, since it allows us to obtain predictions of future values of c_t and y_t given parameter estimates and future values of z_t. In an inductive sense, the model may not yield good predictions if it is difficult to obtain (in the case of nonstochastic z_t's) future values of the z_t's or to predict (in the case of stochastic z_t's) the future z_t's very well. Also, the model may not predict very well if there are errors in specifying the consumption function's form or the disturbance term's properties, or if it is assumed that z_t is autonomous. Thus, the autonomous or exogenous assumption regarding z_t is just one of several possible reasons for the model's possible poor performance in actual prediction.

In his paper, Haavelmo gives special attention to the assumption that z_t is autonomous or exogenous. His approach involves elaborating his simple model to provide two alternative models in which z_t is no longer autonomous. His third model involves the following equations:

$$c_t = \beta + ay_t + u_t, \tag{6}$$

$$r_t = \nu + \mu(c_t + x_t) + w_t, \tag{7}$$

$$y_t = c_t + x_t - r_t, \tag{8}$$

$$x_t = \text{an autonomous variable} \tag{9}$$

in which c_t, y_t, and r_t are endogenous variables, (7) is a business saving equation, and u_t and w_t are disturbance terms, not necessarily uncorrelated but with zero means, constant covariance matrix, and serially uncorrelated. Note from (5) and (8) that $z_t = x_t - r_t$ so that if r_t is endogenous, z_t will be also. Given future values of x_t and parameter estimates, it is clear that the expanded model in (6)–(9) can be employed to generate predictions of corresponding future values of c_t, y_t, and r_t.

In his analysis of Haavelmo's expanded model, (6)–(9), Chetty (1966, 1968) points out that if the parameter μ in (7) has a zero value and if the covariance between the disturbance terms u_t and w_t is zero, then the expanded model collapses to become the original model shown in (4)–(5) with z_t autonomous or exogenous. Thus a test of the joint hypothesis $\mu = 0$ and $\text{cov}(u_t, w_t) = 0$ is a test of the hypothesis that z_t is autonomous or exogenous and that the original model (4)–(5) may be adequate if it is not defective in other respects.

The review of Haavelmo's models provides some elements of what might be called the traditional econometric approach to building causal econometric models. In this approach, one uses economic theory and other outside information to formulate a tentative model. If the simplicity postulate is taken seriously, the initial formulation will be sophisticatedly simple. Such simplicity does not necessarily stand in a one-to-one relationship with the size (number of equations) of a model. Clearly, it is possible to have complicated single-equation models. Given the initially entertained model, it is subjected to a number of diagnostic and prediction checks. In this connection, economic considerations, as in Haavelmo's case, may suggest certain broader formulations. After diagnostic and prediction checks have been performed, the model may have to be reformulated. Then the reformulated version is subjected to diagnostic and prediction checks, and so on. Various aspects of this approach to model-building have been discussed both in the econometric and in the statistical literature. For present purposes, it is most important to emphasize the central role of economic considerations, including economic theory, in developing causal economic models. To state this point more generally, subject matter considerations, including theory, play an important role in developing causal models in science. While some may regard this point as obvious, as several empirical tests of causality considered below will show, adequate account is not taken of this "obvious" point.

Since it is impossible to consider all reported tests of causality that employ the Granger concept of causality, attention will be given to just three leading examples, namely, Sims (1972), Feige and Pearce (1976), and Pierce (1977). Sims (1972) writes, "The main empirical finding is that the hypothesis that causality is unidirectional from money to income agrees with the postwar U.S. data, whereas the hypothesis that causality is unidirectional from income to money is rejected" (p. 540). On the other hand, Pierce (1977), who analyzed similar data for the U.S., concludes, "Results of this type [independence or lack of causal relations between important economic variables] have also been obtained in several other studies. Using a similar methodology, Feige and Pearce . . . have found little or no association between the money supply (or the monetary base) and gross national product, using quarterly data" (p. 19). Thus, it appears that the findings of Sims (1972), on the one hand, and of Feige and Pearce (1976) and Pierce (1977), on the other hand, are diametrically opposite. This and other features of these tests of causality are considered in what follows.

First, on the issue of whether the three empirical tests of causality cited above embody anything resembling what Feigl would call a law or set of laws, Pierce (1977) is most explicit when he writes, "The present study centers around an empirical specification of relations between economic time series. The data themselves are permitted, insofar as feasible, to suggest, at least in general terms, the patterns of interrelationships that do or do not exist" (p. 11). Thus, Pierce's approach is described quite frankly as one that involves "measurement without [economic] theory." The phrase "measurement without theory" is not used to condemn Pierce's approach as useless; his approach may be capable of generating important empirical results that can then, perhaps, be explained by old or new economic theories. Until this latter task is accomplished, however, by not incorporating economic law or laws, his analysis is not causal according to Feigl's definition, presented in section 2. Similarly, Sims (1972) and Feige and Pearce (1976), while not as explicit about the omission of theory as Pierce (1977), do not develop the relationships that they examine in the context of a detailed specification of economic laws or theories. As is well known, if relevant economic theory is not considered, incorrect forms of variables, for example, nominal variables rather than real variables, may be included, or relevant economic variables may be excluded. Failure to include more than two variables in these analyses has been recognized as a serious problem by Pierce (1977, p. 18) and by Sims (1977, p. 40). In a conversation with the author, Newbold[2] described the problem as simply analogous to the problem of left-out variables in regression models. Because they do not pay attention to subject matter theory, the studies considered offer little assurance that, in each case, the two variables examined are appropriate and/or the only two relevant for the analyses performed. Thus, the attempt to establish causality without use of economic theory or economic laws is a departure from investigation of causal laws in the sense of Feigl. Sims (1972) appears to realize this fact when he writes, "The method of identifying causal direction employed here does rest on a sophisticated version of the *post hoc ergo propter hoc* principle" (p. 543). Whether the version is "sophisticated" or just "obscure" will not be argued here.

Second, in order to make Granger's definition of causality operational, all three studies introduce specific statistical operations and assumptions that have implications for the forms of economic laws and, probably, for the particular results of these and similar studies. Sims (1972) states some of these assumptions quite cryptically, "We will give content to Granger's definitions by assuming all time-series to be jointly covariance-stationary, by considering only linear predictors, and by taking expected squared forecast error as our criterion for predictive accuracy" (p. 544). Some implications of these assumptions have already been discussed in section 3. Here it is relevant to emphasize that most economic time series are nonstationary, not, as Sims assumes, covariance-stationary. Sims may mean that he will consider filtered series that are stationary. In fact, he mentions that

> all variables used in [his] regressions were measured as natural *logs* and prefiltered using the filter $1 - 1.5L + 0.5625L^2$ [where L is the lag operator]. . . . This filter approximately flattens the spectral density of most economic time-series, and the hope was that regression residuals would be very nearly white noise with this prefiltering. [P. 545]

It is very questionable that this specific filter does what Sims claims (or should do what he claims in terms of producing flat spectra). Further, if his regression error terms were generated by a particular AR(2) process, $u_t - 1.5u_{t-1} + 0.5625\, u_{t-2} = \epsilon_t$, where ϵ_t is white noise, his procedure would produce white noise errors. The results of his empirical tests for disturbance autocorrelation throw considerable doubt on the adequacy of his filtering procedure. However, there may be some filter or filters that, when applied to highly nonstationary variables, render them stationary. Feige and Pearce

2. Newbold (1978), personal communication.

(1976) and Pierce (1977), following Box and Jenkins, employ differencing to render series approximately stationary; that is, their filters are $(1 - L)^a$, where a assumes an integer value, usually 1 or 2, and need not be the same for different variables. Then relationships to be studied are formulated in terms of the transformed or filtered variables, certainly an important restriction on the forms of economic laws. It might be asked, "Why filter?" And "What are the possible effects of filtering?"

On the question "Why filter?" it appears that forms of laws are being thereby restricted so that stationary, *statistical* theory can be applied. In terms of stationary variables, one can employ autocorrelation functions, cross-correlation functions, and the like. However, if it makes economic sense to formulate a law or model in terms of nonstationary variables, for example, nonstochastic variables or trending stochastic variables, it is not necessary to filter variables in order to estimate parameters' values and to predict from such estimated models. Thus, it can be seen that the filtering of variables to produce variables that are covariance-stationary is not necessary in general and is inapplicable to nonstochastic variables. This is not to say, however, that use of prefiltered, stationary variables is never appropriate. Rather, it is to say that subject matter considerations are very relevant in this regard. An excellent example illustrating some of these considerations is provided by Hendry (1977, p. 196). In addition, in terms of analyses using a money variable, it is obvious that controlled nonstochastic changes in the rate of growth of money can produce a series that is difficult, if not impossible, to be made covariance stationary by filtering.

On the question "What are the possible effects of filtering?" it must be remarked that the effects of filtering, whether by differencing or by use of more general filters, can be drastic enough in some circumstances to justify Friedman's phrase "throwing the baby out with the bath water."[3] Also, Friedman's remarks in his letter regarding an earlier draft of the Pierce (1977) paper led me to formulate the following example to dramatize the effects of filtering on tests of causality of the type carried through in the papers under consideration. Consider the nonstationary processes $\ln C_t$ and $\ln Y_t$, where C_t and Y_t are measured real consumption and income, respectively. Assume that

$$\ln C_t = \ln C_t^p + u_t,$$
$$\ln Y_t = \ln Y_t^p + v_t,$$

where C_t^p and Y_t^p are real permanent consumption and real permanent income, respectively. Further, assume that $\ln C_t$ and $\ln Y_t$ are each filtered (if

3. Friedman (1975), personal communication.

$C_t^p = kY_t^p$, with k assumed constant, the same filter can be employed) to produce the stationary innovations, u_t and v_t. If u_t and v_t are cross-correlated or subjected to the Sims regression techniques and found to be totally uncorrelated, what is being obtained is a confirmation of one form of Friedman's theory of the consumption function; the conclusion that filtered ln C_t and filtered ln Y_t are uncorrelated or independent says nothing about the causal relation between C_t^p and Y_t^p and/or the causal relation between C_t and Y_t. The nature of the underlying economic theory is critical in interpreting results based on prefiltering. In addition, measurement considerations are relevant, since u_t and v_t contain errors in measuring consumption and income. It is also the case that filtering is not required in a "nonstationary" version of the Granger (1969, p. 429) definition of causality. This consumption-income example illustrates how important economic laws are in defining causality. While Pierce (1977) recognizes in a special case that "the deterministic detrending/deseasonalization procedure possibly took too much out of the series" (p. 19), he does not link up this possibility with any economic theory. Thus, it is difficult to interpret what is "too much" or "too little."

In general, then, it has to be recognized that filtering economic time series is not usually a mechanical, neutral procedure that necessarily produces satisfactory results. The issues of whether to filter and what kinds of filters to employ, for example, seasonal filtering (Sims [1972] uses seasonally adjusted data), are most fruitfully resolved in relation to specific economic laws or theories and other serious subject matter considerations.

In terms of analyses involving money and either GNP or the rate of inflation, there is the issue of monetary policy and its possible impact on the results of tests of causality. Sims (1972) and Pierce (1977) mention this complication, but Feige and Pearce (1976) do not seem to appreciate it adequately. Pierce (1977) writes, "Thus if the money supply grows by exactly 5 percent over the sample period, it will show up as unrelated to anything else, despite what its actual relationship to interest rates, reserves, income, etc., might be" (p. 18). He also explains:

> The data may be even worse than happenstance [in terms of experimental design considerations] insofar as closed-loop control has probably been operative over the sample period for many macroeconomic series, including such instruments as money, interest rates and government spending and such targets as inflation, unemployment and income. If in the context of the dynamic regression model . . . , suppose x [the input variable] has been adjusted to keep y [the output or dependent variable] on a desired path according to a control strategy $x_t = C(B)y_t$ [where $C(B)$ is a polynomial in the backshift or lag oper-

ator B]. Then it can be shown that not only is the lag distribution [$V(B)$ in $y_t = V(B)x_t + u_t$] unidentifiable, but that identical residuals and model forecasts can result from

i. a model with $V(B)$ chosen so that the disturbances [the u_t's] will be white noise;

ii. a "model" with $V(B) = 0$ so that y is formally related only to its own past;

iii. an infinite number of intermediate models.

Perhaps this is not surprising; if x is determined from present and past y then, knowing y, knowing x in addition tells us nothing new. Certainly control strategies over the past 30 years have been imprecise in the short run and shifting in the long run; but certainly they have existed. [P. 20]

Pierce's thoughtful and insightful remarks regarding the possible effects of monetary control policies on the results of causality tests highlight the importance of serious study of what monetary policies have been pursued in the particular sample period being analyzed. Without such study, as Pierce's remarks indicate, the results of mechanical tests of causality cannot be unambiguously interpreted. Irritating as it may be to those who seek purely statistical panaceas, the nature of policy control requires detailed consideration in formulating causal economic laws and testing their performance in prediction, a problem appreciated, if not completely solved, in the traditional econometric approach.

To return to some other aspects of how "operationalizing" Granger's nonoperational definition of causality leads to restrictions, some of them severe, on the nature of economic laws and some specific test results, consider Sims's (1972) analysis of money, X_t, and income, Y_t, variables. Since these variables are nonstationary, as mentioned above, Sims prefilters the natural logarithms of these variables to obtain x_t and y_t, assumed stationary. He then considers the following linear autoregressive representation of the assumed stationary variables x_t and y_t:

$$\begin{bmatrix} b_{11}(L) & b_{12}(L) \\ b_{21}(L) & b_{22}(L) \end{bmatrix} \begin{pmatrix} x_t \\ y_t \end{pmatrix} = \begin{pmatrix} u_t \\ v_t \end{pmatrix}, \tag{10}$$

where $b_{ij}(L)$ is a polynomial in the lag operator L, $i, j = 1, 2$, and u_t and v_t are mutually uncorrelated white noise errors.

As Sims (1972, p. 544) mentions, Granger has shown that if there is an autoregressive representation as given in (10), then the *absence* of causality, in the Granger sense, running from y_t to x_t is equivalent to the condition that $b_{12}(L) \equiv 0$. Given this condition, (10) reduces to

$$\text{(11a)} \qquad b_{11}(L)x_t = u_t,$$

$$\text{(11b)} \qquad b_{22}(L)y_t + b_{21}(L)x_t = v_t,$$

Since u_t and v_t are mutually uncorrelated and nonserially correlated disturbance terms, (11) is an extreme form of a fully recursive model, extreme since no lagged values of y_t appear in (11a), *an added restriction* to the usual definition of a fully recursive model. From (11b), it is possible to write the dynamic regression for y_t as

$$\text{(12)} \qquad y_t = -\frac{b_{21}(L)}{b_{22}(L)}x_t + \frac{1}{b_{22}(L)}v_t,$$

$$= V(L)x_t + \frac{1}{b_{22}(L)}v_t,$$

with $V(L) \equiv -b_{21}(L)/b_{22}(L)$. As can be seen from (12), the disturbance term is in the form of an infinite moving average, $b_{22}^{-1}(L)v_t$, and hence will in general be autocorrelated. Under the special assumption that $b_{22}(L)$ is of degree zero in L, the disturbance term will not be autocorrelated. On the other hand, if nonstationary variables Y_t and X_t are related by $Y_t = V(L)X_t + w_t$, and a common filter, $C(L)$, is applied to both sides, $C(L)Y_t = V(L)C(L)X_t + C(L)w_t$, or $y_t = V(L)x_t + C(L)w_t$. Then if $w_t = v_t/C(L)$, $y_t = V(L)x_t + v_t$. The disturbance term, v_t, in this last equation differs from that in (12), namely, $b_{22}^{-1}(L)v_t$. Thus, in terms of the system (11) with $x_t = C(L)Y_t$ and $y_t = C(L)Y_t$, the result in (12) indicates that disturbance terms will generally be autocorrelated. If the relationship $Y_t = V(L)X_t + w_t$ is viewed as a starting point, it is clearly not derived from (11), and on filtering both sides using $C(L)$, it will generally have autocorrelated disturbances, except in very special cases. Indeed, Sims (1972) reports results of tests for serial correlation of disturbance terms in (11) and concludes, "The conclusion from this list of approximate or inconclusive tests can only be that there is room for doubt about the accuracy of the F-tests on regression coefficients" (p. 549). Also, Quenouille (1957, pp. 43–44) has pointed out explicitly that serial correlation in the error terms in (10) can be produced by the omission of relevant variables.

For the empirical implementation of (12), it is necessary to make assumptions regarding the form of $V(L)x_t$, an *infinite* distributed lag. Sims (1972) chooses to approximate this infinite distributed lag term by a finite distributed lag term and explains: "the length of the estimated lag distributions was kept generous" (p. 545). Keeping the length "generous" is understandable in terms of avoiding a misspecification of the lag pattern. However, this approach does involve a finite truncation of the lag and introduction of many lag parameters, an important consideration when only 78 degrees of freedom are available in his data. A basic result of this approach is evident from the reported standard errors associated with the estimates of the distributed lag coefficients in Sims's table 4 (p. 547). In his regression of quarterly filtered GNP on eight past, current and four future quarterly values of filtered monetary base, his largest standard error is 0.338, while his smallest is 0.276. The absolute values of his coefficient estimates for the four future values of the monetary base range from 0.088 to 0.65. In the case of GNP on M1, his coefficient standard errors range from 0.294 to 0.318, while the future coefficient estimates range from 0.105 to 0.300 in absolute value. These results indicate that the precision of estimation is quite low even when possible autocorrelation of disturbance terms is overlooked. The same can be said of his other two-sided regressions. This lack of precision in estimation is noted as a statistical caveat by Sims (1972) in about the middle of his paper:

> Though the estimated distribution looks like what we expect from a one-sided true distribution, the standard errors on the future coefficients are relatively high. These results are just what a unidirectional causality believer would expect, but they are not such as to necessarily force a believer in bidirectional causality to change his mind. [P. 547]

In other words, Sims is saying that his analyses, viewed from an estimation point of view, *have yielded inconclusive results*. The results would be even more inconclusive if one were to do a detailed analysis of the validity and power of the *F*-tests employed in the paper. In view of these considerations, it must be stated that Sims's strong conclusions about the exogeneity of money, stated at the opening and end of his paper, are not convincingly supported by his empirical analyses. As pointed out above, his estimates are imprecise and his tests are not very powerful, even when no consideration is given to autocorrelated errors, seasonal complications, effects of filtering, left-out variables, and forms of monetary policies. When these latter points are considered, Sims's conclusion becomes even more uncertain.

Unlike Sims, Feige and Pearce (1976) and Pierce (1977) do not directly estimate a dynamic regression. Instead, they (*a*) use differencing to make their variables stationary, (*b*) construct autoregressive moving average (ARMA) models for their differenced variables, and (*c*) then compute contemporaneous and lagged cross-correlations from the estimated innovations of their ARMA schemes for the pairs of variables under consideration and test their significance. Enough has been said above about the possible important effects of differencing or other filtering techniques on results of analyses as well as complications associated with policy control, errors of measurement, and the like. As regards step (*b*) of the process, there is often some difficulty in determining the forms of ARMA schemes from data. Any errors in this operation would be carried over to affect the operation in (*c*). Finally, in step (*c*), a large sample χ^2 test is employed to test the hypothesis that population cross-correlations are all zero. As lucidly explained by Pierce (1977, p. 15), step (*c*) is closely related to, but not exactly the same as, analyzing a dynamic regression directly, as Sims (1972) does.

In the one explicitly reported example in Pierce's (1977, p. 15) paper, he investigates the relationship between weekly retail sales and currency in circulation. After completing steps (*a*)–(*c*) above he obtains a sample test statistics' value, $n\Sigma\hat{r}_k^2 = 39.1 > \chi^2_{0.01}(21) = 38.1$. Thus at the 1 percent level of significance, his large sample χ^2 test, using the estimated cross-correlations of the innovations, the $\hat{r}_k$'s, $k = -10$ to $k = 10$, yields a "significant" result. Pierce comments,

> One could tentatively conclude that there is unidirectional causality from retail sales to currency (although the situation concerning feedback is somewhat unclear): evidently a rise in retail sales results in a somewhat greater demand for currency. . . The explanatory power of this relationship is quite small, however, as the cross correlations are not large. [P. 16]

These remarks are quite confusing to the uninitiated reader. Pierce's statistical test yields "significant" results at the 1 percent level of significance; yet, he has doubts about the results of the test. A similar methodological statement is made by Sims (1972):

> In applying the F-tests for causal direction suggested in the preceding section, one should bear in mind that the absolute size of the coefficients is important regardless of the F value. It is a truism too often ignored that coefficients which are "large" from the economic point of view should not be casually set to zero no matter how statistically "insignificant" they are. [P. 545]

Apparently, Pierce and Sims are pointing to a defect of mechanical significance tests. The informtion in the testing procedures does not reflect all the relevant information. Nowhere is what Sims suggests is reasonable done by Pierce or by Feige and Pearce; that is, Pierce and Feige and Pearce do not look at the absolute sizes of the individual dynamic regression coefficients and/or their sum. In a simple regression of y on x, the regression coefficient is $\beta = \sigma_{xy}/\sigma_x^2$, while the correlation coefficient is $\rho = \sigma_{xy}/\sigma_x\sigma_y = (\sigma_x/\sigma_y)\beta$. Clearly, a small ρ need not necessarily imply a small β. Similar considerations carry over to apply to cross-correlations and dynamic regression coefficients. Thus, there is an element of uncertainty regarding an analysis of causality that relies only on the estimated cross-correlations and standard significance tests, as employed by Pierce and Feige and Pearce, without adequate concern for the power of these tests relative to precisely specified alternative hypothesis. This point was raised by the author in connection with the Feige-Pearce analysis several years ago in a meeting of the University of Chicago Money Workshop.

From this review of three papers in which tests of causality have been applied, it is concluded that for a variety of reasons the tests' results are inconclusive with respect to the basic issues considered. The inconclusive nature of the results may be due, in part, to technical problems discussed quite extensively by the authors, particularly Pierce and Sims. However, the problem goes deeper than just "technical issues." The fundamental lack of subject matter considerations and theory exhibited in these studies is probably at the heart of the inconclusive nature of the results. Instead of formulating sophisticated models, which take account of subject matter considerations and relevant economic theory, the authors attempted to operationalize a nonoperational definition of causality. This operation led to consideration of an extreme form of a fully recursive model as the null hypothesis with little or no attention paid to economically motivated, *specific* alternatives. The very special null hypothesis appears to have been tested against a very wide range of loosely specified, from an economic point of view, alternatives. Given such a broad range of alternatives, it is no wonder that results are as inconclusive as they are. Further, with little in the way of economic laws and other subject matter considerations involved in the testing, it is questionable that the analyses are properly termed "tests of causality," according to Feigl's definition.

It is indeed surprising that, of the authors considered, only the statistician Pierce appears sensitive to the important role of economic laws or theory mentioned in the previous paragraph. Pierce (1977) writes in his concluding paragraph,

> Considering all of these problems, it is perhaps small wonder that incompatible propositions can often be "confirmed" by the same data, including in particular the proposition that a variable is not related to any of a number of other variables. If future research bears out this type of result, we might justifiably conclude that econometric [i.e., statistical] analysis is of rather limited use in ascertaining certain economic relationships. Economic theory is in such situations all the more important: since we cannot assume that the mathematical rela-

> tionships contained within this theory can be established as valid statistical relationships—that is, as more valid than statistical "relationships" where a variable is related only to its own past—it is imperative that prior information be available concerning these relationships. [P. 21]

Recognizing the failure of "measurement without theory" and the failure of "theory without measurement," Pierce offers the hope that intelligent use of sophisticated economic theory and relevant statistical techniques may be successful. This approach is in line with Feigl's definition of causation and with what has been preached, if not always practiced, in the traditional econometric approach.

5 Summary and Conclusions

In the preceding sections, a philosophical definition of causation, which reflects philosophers' thinking and clarification of the concept of causation, has been reviewed and compared with several definitions of causation that have been published in the econometric literature. In addition, consideration was given to several applications of "causality tests" that have appeared in the literature. From this review and comparison of definitions of causation and analysis of causality tests, the following major conclusions have been reached:

1. The philosophical definition of causality, reviewed above, is adequate for work in econometrics and other areas of science, a conclusion considered to be fortunate, given the importance that the present writer attaches to the unity of science principle.
2. The philosophical definition of causality, reviewed above, is an operational definition in contrast to the Wiener-Granger "population" definition of causality, a fact that would lead some to dismiss the latter definition on methodological grounds alone.
3. Basmann's definition of causality is very close to the philosophical definition provided by Feigl. The former differs from the latter slightly in certain respects in cases in which only data relating to a single realization of a process are available.
4. The Strotz-Wold definition of causality is subsumed in Feigl's and is rather narrow. Insofar as Strotz and Wold require that the world be "truly" recursive, they are placing an a priori restriction on the forms of economic models and laws that cannot be justified on purely *deductive* methodological grounds and is not required by Feigl's, Jeffreys's, Basmann's, and Simon's definitions of causality.
5. Simon's definition of causality is a formal, deductive property of models, not an inductive property involving the quality of models' predict-

ability, a consideration embedded in Feigl's, Jeffreys's, and others' definitions. By narrowing the concept of causality, Simon and others have omitted a fundamental part of what is meant by causation or causality, namely, the quality of predictions. Thus, a model can be causal in Simon's sense and yet yield worthless predictions.

6. Simon's definition of casuality does not require temporal asymmetry between cause and effect in chronological time. Simon's definition is in agreement with Feigl's point of view, but in conflict with the "true recursive model" view of Strotz and Wold and with views expressed by Granger.

7. The Wiener-Granger definition of causality is unusual in that in it is embedded a particular confirmatory criterion that is not very general and is inapplicable in a variety of circumstances. In contrast, Feigl's definition does not mention any particular confirmatory procedure.

8. The Wiener-Granger definition involves a special form of predictability but no mention of economic laws. In this regard it is devoid of subject matter considerations, including subject matter theory, and thus is in conflict with others' definitions, including Feigl's, that do mention both predictability and laws.

9. In "operationalizing" the Wiener-Granger definition of causality, various a priori restrictions are imposed on the class of economic laws covered by the definition. It is concluded that it is preferable to employ a more general definition of causality, such as Feigl's, which imposes only the restriction of predictability on forms of economic laws.

10. From the review of applied "causality tests," it is concluded that results of these tests are inconclusive. The specific reasons for this conclusion can perhaps be summarized by saying that there was inadequate attention to subject matter considerations, or to put it slightly differently, the studies represent examples of measurement without much economic theory and other subject matter considerations. Where subject matter considerations were brought to bear, they were not satisfactorily integrated with the statistical analyses.

11. In the tests of causality involving linear stationary processes, a particularly extreme form of a fully recursive model is regarded as defining the condition under which "one variable causes another" in the Wiener-Granger sense. This extreme restriction on the form of models is not required by a broader definition of a causal model linking the two variables.

12. Sims's use of "forward and backward" regressions and Feige, Pearce, and Pierce's use of cross-correlations of estimated innovations involve consideration of forms of stationary single-equation models involving many, many parameters. This is in violation of the principle of parsimony and the simplicity postulate. Practically, the result of such a violation

in the present instance is consideration of regressions with many free parameters, which when analyzed with limited data resulted in rather imprecise estimates and tests with low power relative to alternative hypotheses involving serious departures from independence.

13. Mechanical filtering of series can exert a substantial influence on causality tests of the kind considered above.

In summary, it can be said that an adequate definition of causality is available. Departures from this definition have produced problems, while offering little in the way of dependable and convincing results. The mechanical application of causality tests is an extreme form of "measurement without theory," perhaps motivated by the hope that application of statistical techniques without the delicate and difficult work of integrating statistical techniques and subject matter considerations will be able to produce useful and dependable results. That this hope is generally naive and misguided has been recognized by econometricians for a long time and is a reason that reference is made to laws in Feigl's definition of causation. In establishing and using these laws in econometrics, there seems to be little doubt but that economic theory, data, and other subject matter considerations as well as econometric techniques, including modern time series analysis, will all play a role. "Theory without measurement" and "measurement without theory" are extremes to be avoided.

References

Allais, M. (1966). "A Restatement of the Quantity Theory of Money." *American Economic Review*, 56:1123–57.

Ansley, C. F. (1977). "Report on the NBER-NSF Seminar on Time Series." Graduate School of Business, University of Chicago. Mimeographed.

Basmann, R. L. (1963). "The Causal Interpretation of Non-Triangular Systems of Economic Relations." *Econometrica*, 31:439–48.

———. (1965). "A Note on the Statistical Testability of 'Explicit Causal Chains' against the Class of 'Interdependent' Models." *Journal of the American Statistical Association*, 60:1080–93.

Burks, A. W. (1977). *Chance, Cause, Reason: An Inquiry into the Nature of Scientific Evidence*. Chicago: University of Chicago Press.

Chetty, V. K. (1966). "Bayesian Analysis of Some Simultaneous Econometric Models." Ph.D. diss., Department of Economics, University of Wisconsin at Madison.

———. (1968). "Bayesian Analysis of Haavelmo's Models." *Econometrica*,

36:538–602. Reprinted in S. E. Fienberg and A. Zellner, eds., *Studies in Bayesian Econometrics and Statistics in Honor of Leonard J. Savage*, pp. 359–81. Amsterdam: North-Holland Publishing Co., 1975.

Feige, E. L., and D. K. Pearce (1976). "Economically Rational Expectations: Are Innovations in the Rate of Inflation Independent of Innovations in Measures of Monetary and Fiscal Policy?" *Journal of Political Economy*, 84:499–552.

Feigl, H. (1953). "Notes on Causality." In H. Feigl and M. Brodbeck, eds., *Readings in the Philosophy of Science*, pp. 408–18. New York: Appleton-Century-Crofts.

Friedman, M. (1975). Personal communication.

Granger, C. W. J. (1969). "Investigating Causal Relations by Econometric Models and Cross-spectral Methods." *Econometrica*, 37:424–38.

Granger, C. W. J., and P. Newbold (1977). *Forecasting Economic Time Series*. New York: Academic Press.

Haavelmo, T. (1947). "Methods of Measuring the Marginal Propensity to Consume." *Journal of the American Statistical Association*, 42:105–22. Reprinted in W. C. Hood and T. C. Koopmans, eds., *Studies in Econometric Method*, pp. 75–91. Cowles Commission Monograph no. 14. New York: John Wiley & Sons, 1953.

Hendry, D. F. (1977). "Comments on Granger-Newbold's 'Time Series Approach to Econometric Model Building' and Sargent-Sims' 'Business Cycle Modeling Without Pretending to Have Too Much A Priori Economic Theory.'" In C. A. Sims, ed., *New Methods in Business Cycle Research: Proceedings from a Conference*, pp. 183–202. Minneapolis: Federal Reserve Bank of Minneapolis.

Jeffreys, H. (1957). *Scientific Inference*. 2d ed. Cambridge: Cambridge University Press.

———. (1967). *Theory of Probability*. 3d rev. ed. London: Oxford University Press.

Keynes, J. M. (1921). *A Treatise on Probability*. London: Macmillan & Co.

Newbold, P. (1978). Personal communication.

Pierce, D. A. (1977). "Relationships—and the Lack Thereof—between Economic Time Series, with Special Reference to Money and Interest Rates." *Journal of the American Statistical Association*, 72:11–21.

Quenouille, M. H. (1957). *The Analysis of Multiple Time Series*. New York: Hafner Publishing Co.

Sargent, T. J. (1977). "Response to Gordon and Ando." In C. A. Sims, ed., *New Methods in Business Cycle Research: Proceedings from a Conference*, pp. 213–17. Minneapolis: Federal Reserve Bank of Minneapolis.

Simon, H. (1953). "Causal Ordering and Identifiability." In W. C. Hood and T. C. Koopmans, eds., *Studies in Econometric Method*, pp. 49–74. Cowles Commission Monograph no. 14. New York: John Wiley & Sons.

———. (1978). Personal communication.

Sims, C. A. (1972). "Money, Income, and Causality." *American Economic Review*, 62:540–52.

———. (1977). "Exogeneity and Causal Ordering in Macroeconomic Models." In C. A. Sims, ed., *New Methods in Business Cycle Research: Proceedings from a Conference*, pp. 23–43. Minneapolis: Federal Reserve Bank of Minneapolis.

Stigler, G. J. (1949). *The Theory of Price*. New York: Macmillan Co.

Strotz, R. H. (1960). "Interdependence as a Specification Error." *Econometrica*, 28:428–42.

Strotz, R. H., and H. O. A. Wold (1960). "Recursive vs. Nonrecursive Systems: An Attempt at Synthesis." *Econometrica*, 28:417–27.

Wold, H. O. A. (1960). "A Generalization of Causal Chain Models." *Econometrica*, 28:443–63.

1.5 Is Jeffreys a "Necessarist"?

In this note, Jeffreys's concept of probability is reviewed and compared with the personal or subjective concept of probability put forward by Savage. Examination of Jeffreys's work[1] indicates that it is incorrect to view his theory of probability as a "necessary" theory according to Savage's definition of this term.

With respect to definitions of probability, in chapter 7 of Jeffreys's *Theory of Probability* (1967), he analyzes and rejects the classical or axiomatic, the Venn limiting frequency, and the Fisher hypothetical infinite population definitions of probability. His criticisms of these "objective" or "frequency" definitions are devastating and, to the best of my knowledge, have been unanswered, perhaps because, as some have observed, they are unanswerable. Jeffreys (1967, p. 369) states,

> In practice no statistician ever uses a frequency definition, but . . . all use the notion of degree of reasonable belief, usually without even noticing that they are using it and that by using it they are contradicting the principles they have laid down at the outset. I do not offer this as criticism of their results. Their practice, when they come to specific applications, is mostly very good; the fault is in the precepts.

On Jeffreys's concepts of probability, he writes, "there is a valid primitive idea expressing the degree of confidence that we may reasonably have in a proposition, even though we may not be able to give either a deductive proof or a disproof of it."(Jeffreys 1976, p. 15). This degree of confidence that an individual has in a proposition, denoted by q, is regarded by Jeffreys to be the probability that the individual associates with the proposition q given his initial information, denoted by p. He writes,

Reprinted from *The American Statistician*, 36 (1982): 28–30, with the kind permission of the American Statistical Association.

1. See Geisser (1980), Good (1980), and Lindley (1980) for insightful discussions of Jeffreys's work.

> We can now introduce the formal notation $P(q|p)$ for the number associated with the probability of the proposition q on data p; it may be read "the probability of q given p" provided that we remember that the number is not in fact the probability, but merely a representation of it. . . . The probability, strictly, is the reasonable degree of confidence and is not identical with the number used to express it. [P. 20]

This is certainly a "personal" or "subjective" view of probability for a single individual.[2]

Jeffreys (1967, pp. 30–33) explicitly discusses and shows the relation of this theory to those of Bayes and Ramsey that define probability in terms of "mathematical" or "moral" expectation. He explains:

> In my method expectation would be defined in terms of value [or utility] and probability; in theirs probability is defined in terms of values [or utilities] and expectations. The actual propositions [of probability theory] are of course identical.[3]

What of the relation of Jeffreys' probability theory for a specific individual and other individuals? This issue is considered explicitly in Jeffreys (1967, pp. 53–56). Very important in linking the views and beliefs of one individual to those of others is the view of the world that is adopted. On this matter, Jeffreys recognizes several philosophical positions:

> In philosophy realism is the belief that there is an external world, which would exist if we were not available to make observations, and that the function of scientific method is to find out properties of this world. Idealism is the belief that the external world is merely a mental construct, imagined to give ourselves a convenient way of describing our experience. The extreme form of idealism is solipsism, which for any individual asserts that only his mind and his sensations exist, other people's minds also being inventions of his own. [P. 54]

2. A referee has remarked, "In Savage, de Finetti doctrine, there is no such thing as reasonable degree of confidence, there is merely degree of confidence constrained by coherence. Thus one should not simplistically lump Jeffreys in with the personalists either." Whether "constrained by coherence" is identical in meaning to "reasonable" is a moot issue. For Jeffreys (1967), "reasonable" probably means probabilities reached in accord with his rules for theories of induction that involve important elements of coherence.

3. This short quotation brings out a fundamental difference between personalists' and Jeffreys's definitions of probability. The former define it in terms of utility considerations, while Jeffreys defines it in terms of past data or experience as a basis for a reasonable degree of confidence. Since the forms of utility functions reflect past experience and data from which tastes and preferences are formed, the distinction between the two views is not as sharp as some claim.

He points out that "The methods developed in this [his] book are consistent with some forms of both realism and idealism, but not with solipsism" (p. 54). After giving reasons for rejecting solipsism, he adds,

> Nevertheless, solipsism does contain an important principle, recognized by Karl Pearson, that any person's data consist of his own individual experiences and that his opinions are the result of his own individual thought in relation to those experiences. Any form of realism that denies this is simply false. A hypothesis does not exist till some one person has thought of it; an inference does not exist until one person has made it. We must and do, in fact, begin with the individual. [Pp. 54–55]

On relations between or among individuals, Jeffreys (1967) writes,

> The situation is that one person makes an observation or inference; this is an individual act. If he reports it to anybody else, the second person must himself make an individual act of acceptance or rejection. All that the first can say is that, from observed similarities between himself and other people, he would expect the second to accept it. The fact that organized society is possible and that scientific disagreements tend to disappear when new data accumulate are confirmation of this generalization. Regarded in this way the resemblance between individuals is a legitimate induction, and *to make universal agreements as a primary requisite for belief is a superfluous postulate.* [P. 55; my emphasis]

These then are the views of Jeffreys concerning definitions of probability and the relation of different individuals' beliefs. His concept of probability is a personal, subjective one. Further, there is no "logical necessity" governing the beliefs of different individuals, as is brought out clearly in the previous paragraph.

In view of what has been presented, it is the case that Jeffreys is not a "necessarist" as defined by Savage (1962). Savage explains that the necessary (or logical) concept of probability "is much like a personal probability, except that here it is argued or postulated that there is one and only one opinion justified by any body of evidence, so that probability is an objective logical relationship between an event A and the evidence B . . . Harold Jeffreys is best described as a necessarist" (Savage, 1962, p. 168). Jeffreys, on the other hand, writes,

> However, I still cannot understand what is meant by "necessarian" . . . . I think that the only things that are necessary are the addition and product rules, and the fact that we need ways of saying "I don't know" in applications to estimation and significance. Nearly necessary

> are, for estimation, Huzurbazar's invariants for distributions having sufficient statistics; somewhat less necessary are my adaptations for tests of significance for additional parameters in such distributions.[4]

From what has been presented above, Savage is correct in saying that Jeffreys's concept of probability is much like a personal one that Savage (1962) defines as follows, "Personal probability is a certain kind of numerical measure of the opinions of somebody about something" (p. 163). However, the quotations from Jeffreys's writings, presented above, indicate clearly that he is not a "necessarist" as Savage has defined this term.[5]

Given that Jeffreys is not a necessarist, how can his theory of probability be described? First, I would term it an individualistic, pragmatic solution to epistemological problems. I have written earlier,

> As regards Popper's statement of the infinite regress argument, namely, that to justify an inductive approach an inductive argument is required which itself needs inductive justification and so on, it seems clear that a deductive approach is open to the same kind of criticism. The best that can be done now, it seems, is to follow Jeffreys by adopting a pragmatic solution, that is, not to prove that induction is valid—since if this could be done deductively induction would be reduced to deduction, which is impossible—nor to show that induction is valid by empirical generalizations—since in this case the argument would be circular—but to state a priori rules governing inductive logic. Then [Jeffreys, 1967, p. 8, states] "induction is the application of rules to observational data." [Zellner 1971, p. 4]

This is certainly a pragmatic and not a necessary approach to epistemological problems.

Second, one of Jeffreys's (1967) rules for theories of induction is "The theory must not deny any precisely stated empirical proposition a priori" (p. 9). Thus empirical researchers can use whatever kinds of personal and other information they have in formulating empirical propositions to be tested with data. Indeed, Jeffreys's theory of significance testing provides the methodology for appraising alternative hypotheses by use of posterior odds

4. Personal communication, dated 5 May 1981.

5. In a personal communication, dated 31 March 1981, I. J. Good provides the following quotation from the 1939 edition of Jeffreys's *Theory of Probability*, "The Theory . . . will give the same results whoever applies it to the same set of hypotheses and the same data" (p. 36). Interpreting "the same data" to mean the same sample and prior information, Jeffreys does not dogmatically state that everyone will always have the same prior information. Further, if "the same data" is broadly interpreted to mean the same utility functions, as well as prior and sample information, then personalists will apparently reach the same conclusions, too; but, of course, this does not imply that their utility functions are in fact always identical.

ratios that incorporate the information in proper informative prior distributions and prior odds ratios.

Third, on "uninformative" prior distributions for estimation problems, Jeffreys has provided well-known procedures for formulating them because he believes that on occasion investigators may know little about parameters' values and that it is important to be able to represent such a state of information. The situation is similar to the need to formulate the concept of a vacuum in physics. For a variety of purposes the concept of a vacuum is useful. In problems for which it is inappropriate to assume the existence of a vacuum, of course, it should not be done. This is very similar to Jeffreys's position on the use of his "uninformative" prior distributions.

Last, Jeffreys's theory is pragmatic in the sense that he emphasizes the predictive aspect of induction.[6] His posterior odds ratios for testing alternative hypotheses and models are well known to be proportional to a ratio of predictive probability densities with the factor of proportionality being the prior odds ratio that can be selected to reflect initial prior information. The predictive implications of alternative hypotheses or models, incorporating prior information are thus pragmatically evaluated by a comparison of predictions with actual outcomes.

For the above reasons, it appears appropriate to regard Jeffreys's theory of probability as an individualistic, pragmatic theory.

References

Geisser, S. (1980). "The Contributions of Sir Harold Jeffreys to Bayesian Inference." In A. Zellner, ed., *Bayesian Analysis in Econometrics and Statistics: Essays in Honor of Harold Jeffreys*, pp. 13–20. Amsterdam: North-Holland Publishing Co.

Good, I. J. (1980). "The Contributions of Jeffreys to Bayesian Statistics." In A. Zellner, ed., *Bayesian Analysis in Econometrics and Statistics: Essays in Honor of Harold Jeffreys*, pp. 21–34. Amsterdam: North-Holland Publishing Co.

Jeffreys, H. (1967). *Theory of Probability*. 3d rev. ed. London: Oxford University Press.

Lindley, D. V. (1980). "Jeffreys's Contribution to Modern Statistical Thought." In A. Zellner, ed., *Bayesian Analysis in Econometrics and Statistics: Essays in Honor of Harold Jeffreys*, pp. 35–39. Amsterdam: North-Holland Publishing Co.

6. In contrast to Mach, Jeffreys (1967, p. 1) defines induction to be the process "of making inferences from past experience to predict future experience."

Savage, L. J. (1962). "Bayesian Statistics." In R. F. Machol and P. Gray, eds., *Recent Developments in Information and Decision Theory*, pp. 161–94. New York: Macmillan Co. Reprinted in *The Writings of Leonard Jimmie Savage—A Memorial Selection*. Washington, D.C.: American Statistical Association and Institute of Mathematical Statistics, 1981.

Zellner, A. (1971). *An Introduction to Bayesian Inference in Econometrics*. New York: John Wiley & Sons.

Part 2

Aspects of Econometric Models and Model Construction

2.1 Statistical Analysis of Econometric Models

1 Introduction

Substantial progress has been made in developing data, concepts, and techniques for the construction and statistical analysis of econometric models. Comprehensive data systems, including national income and product accounts, price, wage and interest rate data, monetary data, and many other measures, have been developed for almost all countries. In many cases, annual measurements have been augmented by quarterly and monthly measurements of a broad array of economic variables. In recent years, scientifically designed sample surveys have been employed to expand data bases of a number of countries. While research continues to improve data bases, we must recognize that the work that produced our current, extensive data bases is a major accomplishment in the field of scientific measurement and enables economic analysts to avoid the charge of "theory without measurement."

In reviewing the development of concepts for the statistical analysis of econometric models, it is very easy to forget that in the opening decades of this century a major issue was whether a statistical approach is appropriate for the analysis of economic phenomena. Fortunately, the recognition of the scientific value of sophisticated statistical methods in economics and business has buried this issue. To use statistics in a sophisticated way required much research on basic concepts of econometric modeling that we take for granted today. It was necessary to develop fundamental concepts such as complete model, identification, autonomous structural relationships, exogeneity, dynamic multipliers, and stochastic equilibrium, to name a few, that play an important role in linking statistical analyses and economic theory.

Many statistical estimation, testing, and prediction techniques have been developed for use in connection with many different kinds of econometric

Invited paper reprinted from the *Journal of the American Statistical Association*, 74, (1979): 628–51, with the kind permission of the American Statistical Association.

models, including linear and nonlinear interdependent structural models, models involving qualitative and quantitative variables, models with time series complications, models for combined time series and cross-section data, and models with random parameters. This research on statistical techniques and computer programs implementing them, a joint product of statisticians and econometricians, has been extremely important in the development of modern econometric modeling techniques.

Given this past record of solid achievement in the areas of measurement, concepts, and statistical techniques, it is relevant to ask how current statistical analyses of econometric models can be improved so as to yield models with better forecasting and policy analysis performance. To answer this question, I shall first try, in section 2, to summarize the main features of current or traditional econometric modeling techniques. Traditional econometric analyses, like many statistical analyses, tend to concentrate attention mainly on given models and not on procedures for discovering and repairing defects of proposed models. Section 3 describes an approach that emphasizes the latter aspect of econometric model construction and is a blend of traditional econometric techniques and modern time series techniques. While this approach, called structural econometric modeling time series analysis (SEMTSA), is not a panacea for all problems, it probably will be helpful in improving the quality of econometric models. A concluding section considers prospects for the future.

2 The Traditional Econometric Modeling Approach

In this section, I shall attempt to characterize traditional econometric modeling techniques, to provide a summary of statistical procedures used in econometric modeling, and to describe some of the statistical needs of traditional econometric model builders.

2.1 Overview of the Traditional Approach

The schematic diagram in figure 1 represents, in broad outline, the activities of many econometric modelers. Whatever the problem, there is usually a statement of objectives, although, at times, the statement may not be so clear-cut and specific as could be desired. Sometimes, objectives are so ambitious that, given our present knowledge, data, and techniques, they may be practically unattainable. The next steps in traditional econometric modeling involve a review of the theoretical and empirical literature bearing on the objectives of a modeling project, preparation of a data base, and preliminary data analysis. The objective of these activities is the formulation of an initial variant of an econometric model. Unfortunately, most econometrics and statistics texts are woefully silent on the basic methodology of

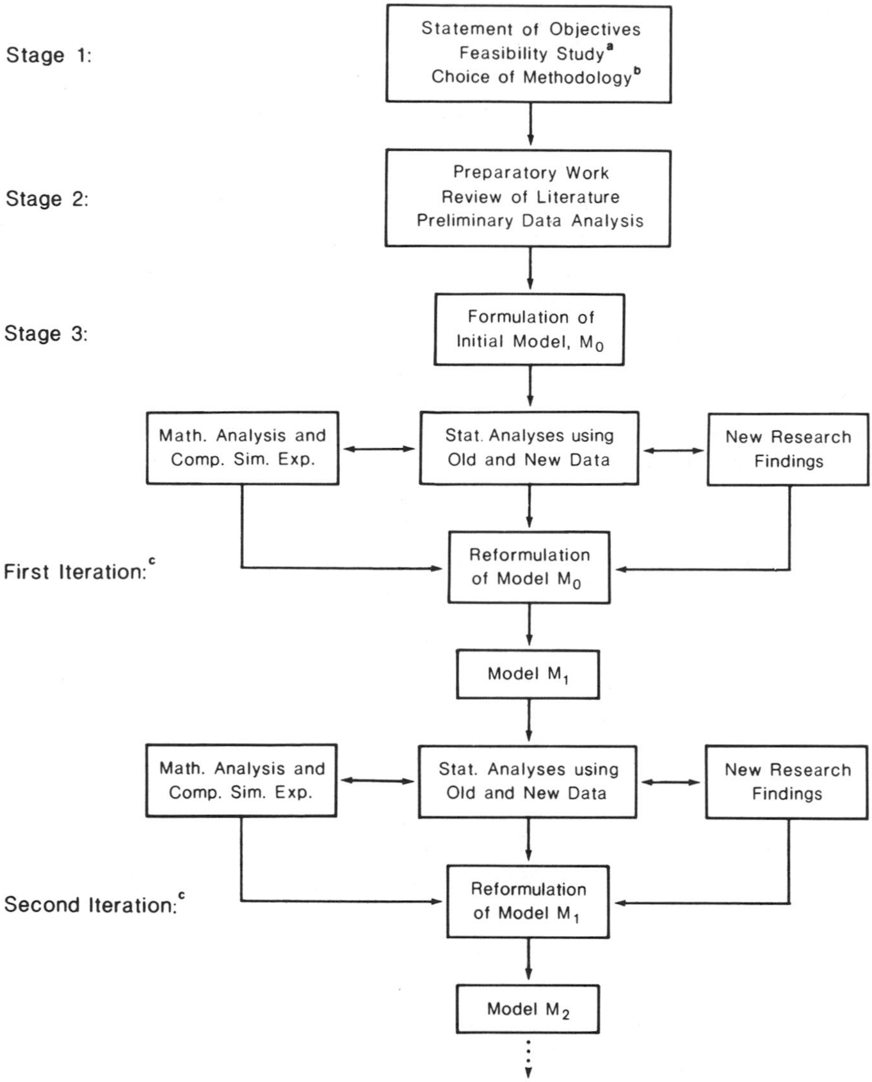

Figure 1 Model-Building Activities: A Schematic Representation

NOTE: For further discussion of this approach to modeling, see Hamilton et al. (1969) and Zellner (1970).

[a]It is assumed that this study shows the project to be feasible.

[b]It is assumed that a modeling approach is selected.

[c]The iterative procedure may disclose problems in the original formulation of goals, feasibility, and methodology so that refining and reformulation of the effort may not be confined solely to the model itself. Also, it is possible that other feedback loops, not shown in the figure, may be important in the process of converging on a satisfactory variant of a model.

how to formulate an initial variant of a model. General prescriptions, such as "use relevant economic theory" and "formulate as simple a model as possible," are valuable guidelines. Often the relevant economic theory does not yield precise information regarding functional forms of relationships, lag structures, and other elements involved in a stochastic specification of a model. Further, model simplicity has yet to be defined in a completely satisfactory manner. Still, it is worthwhile to emphasize the importance of using elements of economic theory, other outside information, and simplicity in formulating an initial variant of a model. For example, models that imply unexploited profit opportunities probably will be unsatisfactory because exploitation of such profit opportunities will generally upset properties of the proposed model that contains them.

Once an initial variant of a model, denoted by M_0, has been formulated, it is traditionally subjected to a number of mathematical, statistical, computer simulation, and judgmental checks. These include simple mathematical checks on the number of equations and number of endogenous variables, consistency of variables' units of measurement, conditions for parameter identification, and compatability with results from mathematical economic theory. Computer simulation experiments are often employed to gain information about local and global dynamic and other properties of M_0. Statistical checks involve formal hypothesis testing procedures, forecasting tests, residual analysis, data evaluation, and other diagnostic checks. In evaluating the adequacy of M_0, a good deal of judgment or prior information is employed, usually informally. For example, the algebraic signs and magnitudes of parameter estimates are reviewed to ascertain whether they are compatible with results provided by economic theory, by previous studies, and by judgmental information.

If M_0 is found to be inadequate in certain respects, work is undertaken to reformulate M_0 and to produce a new variant of the model, M_1. Then M_1 is subjected to the battery of checks mentioned previously. This process of checks and reformulation continues, using as much new data as possible, until a satisfactory version of the model is obtained, satisfactory in the senses that it passes diagnostic checks satisfactorily and accomplishes the objectives of the model-building project.

In connection with realizing the objectives of a model-building project, it is useful to have formulated as simple a model as possible. If the objectives require the model builder to capture much detail, the model probably will be large, but with care in model building it can still be sophisticatedly simple. Large and simple models seem preferable to large and complicated models. In fact, a very disturbing feature of some large, complicated models in the literature is that it is not known whether they have a unique solution or many solutions.

In the past, model builders have used some or sometimes all the elements of the approach described before, but generally have not been vigorous enough in applying the various checks. Mathematical analyses have often been superficial and incomplete. Simulation experiments have not been very extensive or well designed in general. Statistical checks on the quality of data and on specifying assumptions have not been pursued vigorously enough. The relationship of models' properties to relevant economic theory has not been examined thoroughly in a number of instances. Finally, many econometric model builders have not stressed simplicity enough. Some currently operating econometric models are highly complex systems of a hundred or more nonlinear stochastic difference equations with hundreds of parameters that have to be estimated from highly aggregated time series data. Failure to take account of Ockham's razor, the Jeffreys-Wrinch simplicity postulate, and the principle of parsimony in formulating econometric models has had very serious consequences in much traditional econometric model building. (See Jeffreys 1957, 1967 for evidence of the importance of simplicity in science.)

These criticisms of traditional econometric models have to be tempered, however, because many methodological techniques needed in a sensible model-building process are not yet available. Good formal sequential testing procedures for model construction remain to be developed. Even for a given structural econometric model, exact finite-sample tests and optimal finite-sample estimates and predictors have not been available. Good or optimal designs for simulation experiments remain to be derived. The problems of missing and imperfect data have not been completely solved. Tried and tested economic theory dealing with stochastic markets, dynamic reactions, and a number of other important issues has not been available. Thus econometric model building has been a mixture of economic and statistical theory and empirical practice. It is probable that such interaction between theory and practice will produce improvements in both.

To illustrate elements of recent statistical practice in traditional econometric model building, I next review some estimation, testing, and prediction techniques and provide some indications of current developments and open problems.

2.2 *Statistical Estimation Problems*

Learning the values of parameters appearing in structural econometric models (SEM's) is important in checking the implications of alternative economic theories and in using SEM's for prediction, forecasting, and policymaking. Thus, econometric research has placed a heavy emphasis on statistical estimation problems.

2.2.1 Asymptotically Justified Estimation Procedures. Research since the 1940s has resulted in a greatly enhanced understanding of estimation problems associated with SEM's and a relatively large number of operational procedures for obtaining consistent, asymptotically normally distributed, and efficient parameter estimates for some or all parameters of linear and nonlinear, static, and dynamic SEM's with serially uncorrelated or serially correlated errors. These procedures, which are discussed at length in econometric textbooks and the econometric literature, include maximum likelihood, two- and three-stage least squares, $\mathcal{K}$-class, double $\mathcal{K}$-class, instrumental-variable, nonlinear maximum likelihood, nonlinear two- and three-stage least squares, and other procedures. Further, many of the parameter estimates produced by such procedures approximate Bayesian posterior means of parameters in large samples. A most important result of this research, aside from providing asymptotically justified estimation procedures, has been to rule out a number of proposed inconsistent and/or asymptotically inefficient estimation procedures. For example, it is well known by now that misapplication of the classical least squares (CLS)[1] estimation procedure to estimate structural parameters produces inconsistent estimates except in the very special case of a fully recursive SEM.

Choice among alternative asymptotically justified estimates has often been made on the basis of ease of computation. For example, with systems linear in the parameters, calculation of two- and three-stage least squares estimates involves just simple algebraic operations, whereas computation of maximum likelihood estimates involves more complex numerical procedures. Some current computer packages compute a number of asymptotically justified estimates and leave the difficult choice among them to the user. Of course, in truly large samples, asymptotically equivalent estimates should not be very far different. If in practice such estimates, based on a given large sample of data, are radically different, this may be interpreted as indicating that the asymptotic properties of different estimates take hold at different sample sizes or, more likely, that specification errors are present and affect alternative estimates differently. Unfortunately, not much analysis is available on the sensitivity of alternative asymptotically justified estimates to various kinds of specification errors; one recent paper in this area is

1. Some use the phrase "ordinary least squares" (OLS); I prefer "classical least squares" (CLS), since the least squares principle is not ordinary.

Hale, Mariano, and Ramage (1978). More systematic analysis of this range of problems and production of asymptotically justified estimates that are relatively robust to specification errors would be welcome and would serve as a useful additional guide to users in selecting estimates when the sample size is truly large. On the other hand, if the sample size is not truly large, even if a SEM is correctly specified, various asymptotically justified estimates of the same parameter can assume quite different values.

Students and others invariably ask for a definition of what constitutes a truly large sample. An easy answer to this question is hard to give. The sample size alone is not usually all that is relevant. Values of the parameters and features of input or exogenous variables also must be considered. Because parameter values usually are unknown and the object of estimation, prior information about them is needed before one can say with any confidence what is a truly large sample in connection with the estimation of a specific SEM. Needless to say, if the sample size is not truly large, the asymptotic justifications for estimation and other large-sample inference procedures become dubious. In a Bayesian context, one can compute the posterior distribution for a parameter and check to see that it is approximately normal with posterior mean equal to the maximum likelihood estimate and posterior variance equal to the relevant element of the inverse of the estimated Fisher information matrix. If so, large-sample conditions have been encountered. These considerations do not give a justification for using the large-sample normal approximation to the posterior distribution without computing the exact finite-sample posterior distribution.

2.2.2 Finite-Sample Problems and Procedures. Recognition that large-sample justifications for estimation procedures do not contain explicit information on how large a sample must be for them to hold and that practical workers often must deal with limited data has prompted considerable research on the finite-sample properties of estimation procedures. A good deal of research has been concentrated on obtaining analytically the exact finite-sample distributions of certain asymptotically justified estimators, for example, maximum likelihood (ML), two-stage least squares (2SLS), and other estimators for parameters in relatively simple models. This ingenious and difficult distributional work unfortunately has shown that the finite-sample distributions of estimators, derived in the main from an underlying noncentral Wishart distribution, are rather complicated and involve a number of parameters with unknown values. The latter fact makes the application of these distributional results to concrete problems difficult. This research has shown that asymptotically equivalent estimators have very different finite-sample properties. For example, the (limited-information)

ML estimator does not possess finite moments of any order, and in certain frequently encountered cases the 2SLS estimator does not possess a mean or higher moments. Also, certain asymptotically unbiased estimators can have serious finite-sample biases. Further, and perhaps surprising, under some conditions, the inconsistent CLS or OLS estimator has a smaller mean squared error (MSE) than consistent estimators that possess a finite-sample second moment. Of course, if an estimator fails to possess a second moment, it has infinite MSE and is clearly inadmissible. This is not to say that MSE is the only criterion for judging estimators, but it has received considerable attention in this area of research. As stated before, these results have been surprising to many, particularly those who narrowly emphasize unbiasedness, or minimum MSE, or minimum-variance unbiasedness as criteria for judging estimators or who uncritically accept asymptotic justifications. To illustrate that these criteria are inadequate even for the simple case in which a structural parameter θ is equal to the reciprocal of a reduced-form regression coefficient, π, that is, $\theta = 1/\pi$, the ML and almost all other asymptotically justified estimation procedures would recommend estimating θ by $\hat{\theta} = 1/\hat{\pi}$, where $\hat{\pi}$ is the least squares estimator of the regression coefficient π. Because $\hat{\pi}$ is normally distributed, $\hat{\theta}$ is the reciprocal of a normally distributed variable and hence does not possess finite moments of any order. Thus $\hat{\theta}$ has infinite risk and is inadmissible relative to quadratic and many other loss functions.

In addition to exact distributional work on the finite-sample properties of asymptotically justified estimators, research has provided approximations to the moments of these estimators, surprisingly even sometimes when moments do not exist. As Anderson (1977) has pointed out, these moment expressions approximate moments of truncated Taylor or other series approximations to the estimators and not moments of the estimators. How important this distinction is remains to be seen. Further, very fruitful work that uses Edgeworth-Charlier series approximations to the moments and distributions of estimators has been reported by Sargan (1976).

Monte Carlo studies also have been employed in an effort to determine the finite-sample properties of alternative estimators (see Sowey 1973). Generally, these studies have been marred by an inadequate coverage of the high-dimensional parameter spaces associated with models, even simple two-equation supply and demand models that usually contain about 10 or more parameters. Because risk functions of estimators usually intersect, failure to examine the entire parameter space can yield misleading and confusing results regarding the dominance of one estimator relative to another in terms of, for example, MSE. Thus, the results of Monte Carlo experiments that investigate the behavior of estimators over a limited number of points in the parameter space must be considered very cautiously. (See Thornber 1967 for a valuable illustration of this point.)

While much effort has been directed at determining the finite-sample properties of given, asymptotically justified estimators, relatively little work has been done on the problem of producing estimates that have a small-sample justification. Using approximate moment expressions, Nagar (1959) attempted to define an approximate minimal-MSE estimator for structural coefficients within the $\mathcal{K}$-class. Unfortunately, his "estimator" depends on parameters with unknown values that have to be estimated to operationalize his estimator. When these parameters are estimated, it appears that the "optimal" properties of his estimator are vitally affected. His work provides some evidence that use of a value of $\mathcal{K}$ less than one, the value that produces the 2SLS estimate, is probably better than the value of one. Analysis by Sawa (1972) provides the approximate MSE of a $\mathcal{K}$-class estimator for a structural parameter of a simple model and points in the same direction, namely, that finite-sample MSE usually is lower, and sometimes much lower, when a value of $\mathcal{K} < 1$ is employed. Sawa (1972) also has reported properties of estimators that are a linear combination of the 2SLS and the inconsistent CLS estimators. By appropriate choice of the weights, he has obtained approximately unbiased and approximate minimal-MSE estimators. These results do not appear relevant for cases in which the second moment of the 2SLS estimator does not exist, and the justification for considering a linear combination of a consistent and an inconsistent estimator is not apparent.

Recently, Fuller (1977) has presented modified limited-information ML and modified fixed $\mathcal{K}$-class estimators that have finite moments. Restricting these modified estimators to have the same, but arbitrary, bias, he shows that to order T^{-2}, where T is the sample size, the modified ML estimator dominates in terms of approximate MSE.

In almost all the analytical finite-sample work on the sampling properties of estimates, problems with time series complications have not been analyzed, for example, estimates of parameters of models with lagged endogenous variables and/or serially correlated error terms. Relatively little effort has been devoted to obtaining good finite-sample estimates of error terms' covariance matrices. Recent statistical work by Perlman, Eaton, and others certainly seems relevant. It is highly probable that all, or almost all, the asymptotically justified estimators mentioned are inadmissible under quadratic loss and other loss functions over a wide range of conditions. This range of "Steinian" issues has received very little attention in connection with finite-sample work on structural parameter estimators' properties. The impact of pretesting on the finite-sample properties of the usual structural coefficient estimators is relatively unexplored. For example, I have conjectured that the limited-information ML estimator's distribution subject to a favorable outcome of the rank test for identifiability will possess finite moments. In the simple case in which a structural parameter is the reciprocal of a reduced-form regression coefficient, $\theta = 1/\pi$, it is easy to establish that the ML estimator $\hat{\theta} = 1/\hat{\pi}$, subject to the outcome of a t test that rejects $\pi = 0$, possesses finite moments, where $\hat{\pi}$ is the least squares (ML) estimate of π. Last and most basic, the relevance of sampling theory criteria, such as unbiasedness, admissibility, and minimal MSE of estimators for the analysis of a given sample of data has not been considered adequately in the econometric literature. Sampling properties of procedures seem relevant before we take the data in connection with design problems or in characterizing average properties of estimation procedures. The relevance of these average properties in analyzing a particular set of data is not clear. Further, as many, including Tiao and Box (1973), have emphasized, the computed value of an optimal point estimator can be a very bad representation of the information in a given set of data. Likelihood advocates emphasize the importance of studying properties of likelihood functions, while Bayesians emphasize the desirability of studying both likelihood functions and posterior distributions to understand the information content of a given sample for possible values of parameters of a model. For both likelihood advocates and Bayesians, a point estimate is just a summary measure that does not necessarily convey all or most of the information in a sample regarding parameters' probable values.

2.2.3 Bayesian Estimation Results. In the past fifteen years, there has been a growing amount of research concerned with developing and applying the Bayesian approach to the problems of estimating values of parameters in SEM's and other econometric models, and elements of the Bayesian approach have appeared in econometric textbooks. As is well known, inferences about parameters' values, for example, elements of a parameter vector $\boldsymbol{\theta}$, are based on the posterior probability density function (pdf) for $\boldsymbol{\theta}$,

$$p(\boldsymbol{\theta}|D, I) = cp(\boldsymbol{\theta}|I)\ell(\boldsymbol{\theta}|D), \tag{2.1}$$

where $c = [\int p(\boldsymbol{\theta}|I)\ell(\boldsymbol{\theta}|D)d\boldsymbol{\theta}]^{-1}$ is a normalizing constant, D denotes the data, I denotes the prior information, $p(\boldsymbol{\theta}|I)$ is the prior pdf, and $\ell(\boldsymbol{\theta}|D)$ is the likelihood function. The following points are relevant particularly for analyses of SEM's.

1. The posterior pdf in (2.1) is an exact finite-sample pdf, and, hence, large-sample approximations, while sometimes convenient and useful, are,

in principle, not needed. This statement applies to the analysis of all kinds of models, including static and dynamic SEM's.

2. Use of the prior pdf, $p(\boldsymbol{\theta}|I)$, enables an investigator to incorporate prior information in an analysis, as much or as little as he sees fit. Of course, if no sample information were available, as is the case in some low-income countries, prior information would be the only kind of information available. In connection with SEM's, prior information must be introduced in some form to identify structural parameters. In sampling theory approaches, the identifying information almost always has been introduced as exact restrictions on parameter values (e.g., setting certain coefficients equal to zero, equivalent to using a degenerate or dogmatic prior pdf for these parameters in a Bayesian setting). Use of prior pdf's enables investigators to represent this required prior information more flexibly (see Drèze 1975 and Kadane 1975).

3. Use of Bayes's theorem provides the complete posterior pdf for parameters of interest and not just a summary point estimate. If a point estimate is desired, however, it usually can be obtained readily. For example, for quadratic loss functions, it is well known that the mean of the posterior pdf, if it exists, is an optimal point estimate in the sense of minimizing posterior expected loss.

4. Generally, Bayesian estimates have very good sampling properties, because they minimize average risk when average risk is finite and are admissible.

5. In large samples under general conditions, the posterior pdf, $p(\boldsymbol{\theta}|D, I)$, assumes a normal form with mean vector equal to the ML estimate of $\boldsymbol{\theta}$ and covariance matrix equal to the inverse of the estimated Fisher information matrix. Thus, in large samples there is a dovetailing of Bayesian and sampling theory numerical results; however, their interpretation is quite different.

I now turn from the general features of the Bayesian approach to a brief review of some Bayesian estimation results for the SEM. A representation of the linear (in the parameters) SEM is

$$\underset{n\times g}{Y}\ \underset{g\times g}{\Gamma} = \underset{n\times k}{X}\ \underset{k\times g}{B} + \underset{n\times g}{U}, \tag{2.2}$$

where Y is an $n \times g$ matrix of observations on g endogenous (or dependent) variables and X is an $n \times k$ matrix of observations on k predetermined variables, assumed of rank k. Predetermined variables include both exogenous (independent) and lagged endogenous variables. Γ is a $g \times g$ structural parameter matrix, assumed nonsingular, and B is a $k \times g$ matrix of structural parameters. U is an $n \times g$ matrix of disturbance or error terms. It will be assumed that the rows of U have been independently drawn from a g-dimensional normal distribution with zero mean vector and $g \times g$ positive definite symmetric (pds) covariance matrix Σ. Note that if $\Gamma = I_g$, the system in (2.2) is in the form of a multivariate regression model when X contains no lagged endogenous variables or in the form of a multivariate autoregressive system with input variables when X contains both exogenous (or independent) and lagged endogenous variables. In the special case $\Gamma = I_g$, analysis of (2.2) from the Bayesian point of view would proceed pretty much along multivariate regression lines if initial values for the lagged endogenous variables are taken as given (see Zellner 1971 and the references cited there).

The unrestricted reduced-form (URF) system associated with the SEM in (2.2) is given by postmultiplying both sides of (2.2) by Γ^{-1} to yield:

$$Y = XB\Gamma^{-1} + U\Gamma^{-1}, \tag{2.3}$$

or

$$\underset{n\times g}{Y} = \underset{n\times k}{X}\ \underset{k\times g}{\Pi} + \underset{n\times g}{V}, \tag{2.4}$$

where

$$\Pi = B\Gamma^{-1} \text{ and } V = U\Gamma^{-1}, \tag{2.5}$$

with the $k \times g$ matrix Π being the (URF) coefficient matrix and the $n \times g$ matrix V the URF disturbance or error matrix. The assumptions about the rows of U imply that the rows of V can be considered independently drawn from a g-dimensional normal distribution with zero mean vector and $g \times g$ pds covariance matrix $\Omega_g = (\Gamma^{-1})'\Sigma\Gamma^{-1}$.

Under the assumptions made earlier, the parameters Π and Ω_g of the URF system in (2.4) are identified and can be estimated by using Bayesian or non-Bayesian techniques whether or not the structural parameters in Γ, B, and Σ are identified. It has long been recognized that, under the assumptions made before, Γ, B, and Σ are not identified and that additional prior information must be added in order to identify these structural parameters. Identifying prior information can take various forms. Here we discuss only the case in which it involves restrictions that subsets of structural parameters assume zero values. In addition, it is necessary to adopt a normalization rule for elements of the Γ matrix. Here we let all diagonal elements of Γ be equal to 1. We shall write the system in (2.2) with identifying restrictions and normalization rule imposed as

$$Y\Gamma_r = XB_r + U. \tag{2.6}$$

Then the restricted reduced-form system is given by

$$Y = XB_r\Gamma_r^{-1} + U\Gamma_r^{-1} \tag{2.7}$$

$$(2.8) \qquad = X\Pi_r + V_r.$$

Obviously, the fundamental function of the restrictions is to reduce the number of free structural parameters and, by so doing, to provide a model in which the remaining free structural parameters in Γ_r and B_r are identified. Explicit statements of the conditions for identification of structural parameters are given in econometrics textbooks and other works. Since the free parameters in Γ_r, B_r, and Σ are identified, their number cannot exceed the number of parameters in the URF system in (2.4), namely, kg parameters in Π and $g(g + 1)/2$ distinct parameters in the $g \times g$ RF covariance matrix Ω_g.

The likelihood function for the restricted structural system in (2.6) is

$$(2.9) \qquad \ell(\Gamma_r, B_r, \Sigma \mid D) \propto \{\text{mod}\,|\Gamma_r|\}^n |\Sigma|^{-n/2} \cdot \exp\{-\tfrac{1}{2}\,\text{tr}(Y\Gamma_r - XB_r)'(Y\Gamma_r - XB_r)\Sigma^{-1}\},$$

where $\propto$ denotes proportionality, D denotes the data, and mod $|\Gamma_r|$ denotes the absolute value of the Jacobian determinant, $|\Gamma_r|$, for the transformation from the n rows of U to the n rows of Y in (2.6). If the system in (2.6) is autoregressive, (2.9) is the likelihood function conditional upon initial values (assumed given). Then, from (2.1), the posterior pdf for the free parameters in Γ_r, B_r, and Σ is given by

$$(2.10) \qquad p(\Gamma_r, B_r, \Sigma \mid D, I) \propto p(\Gamma_r, B_r, \Sigma \mid I)\ell(\Gamma_r, B_r, \Sigma \mid D),$$

where $p(\Gamma_r, B_r, \Sigma \mid I)$ is the prior distribution and the prior information is denoted by I. Given a prior distribution and the likelihood function, the technical problems of analyzing properties of the posterior distribution, that is, obtaining its normalizing constant, its marginal distributions, and its moments, remain.

In the special case of a fully recursive SEM, Γ_r is in triangular form, implying that $|\Gamma_r| = 1$, and Σ is assumed to have a diagonal form. These assumptions simplify the likelihood function in (2.9) considerably and also simplify the analysis of the posterior pdf in (2.10) (see Zellner 1971 for details). The fully recursive case, however, is a very special case of a SEM. In the general case, work has concentrated on the analysis of (2.10) using the likelihood function in (2.9). In several studies, the posterior distribution in (2.10) has been computed for a few simple models. Drèze and Morales (1976), Harkema (1971), Morales (1971), and Richard (1973) have analyzed it by using several different informative prior distributions. Except for some approximate results provided by Zellner (1971) and Zellner and Vandaele (1975), it is necessary to use numerical integration techniques to analyze features of the posterior distribution. These approximate results have been used by Mehta and Swamy (1978) to provide a ridgelike Bayesian estimate.

Kloek and van Dijk (1976) have studied the application of Monte Carlo numerical integration techniques in analyzing posterior distributions. Although more experience with applications, assessing and using various prior distributions, and computational procedures would be useful, past research has yielded results that will be valuable in obtaining better analyses of given SEM's, particularly in small-sample cases.

Bayesian research also has focused on limited-information analyses, that is, estimation of parameters of a single equation or of a subset of equations of a SEM. Complete posterior distributions for these problems have been obtained and analyzed by Drèze (1972, 1976), Morales (1971), Reynolds (1982), Rothenberg (1975), and Zellner (1971). A single equation of the system in (2.6), say the first, is given by

$$\text{(2.11)} \qquad \underset{n\times 1}{\mathbf{y}_1} = \underset{n\times m_1}{Y_1}\;\underset{m_1\times 1}{\boldsymbol{\gamma}_1} + \underset{n\times k_1}{X_1}\;\underset{k_1\times 1}{\boldsymbol{\beta}_1} + \underset{n\times 1}{\mathbf{u}_1},$$

where $\mathbf{y}_1$ and Y_1 are components of Y, that is, $Y = (\mathbf{y}_1 \vdots Y_1 \vdots Y_0)$ with the variables in Y_0 not appearing in (2.11), X_1 is a submatrix of X, $X = (X_1 \vdots X_0)$ with the variables in X_0 not appearing in (2.11), and $\mathbf{u}_1$ is a subvector of U, $U = (\mathbf{u}_1 \vdots U_0)$ and $\boldsymbol{\gamma}_1$ and $\boldsymbol{\beta}_1$ are parameter vectors to be estimated. The assumptions introduced about the rows of U imply that the elements of $\mathbf{u}_1$ have been independently drawn from a normal distribution with zero mean and variance σ_{11}. The URF equations for $\mathbf{y}_1$ and Y_1, a subset of the equations in (2.4), are

$$\text{(2.12)} \qquad (\mathbf{y}_1 \vdots Y_1) = X(\boldsymbol{\pi}_1 \vdots \Pi_1) + (\mathbf{v}_1 \vdots V_1).$$

On postmultiplying both sides of (2.12) by $(1 \vdots -\boldsymbol{\gamma}_1')'$ and comparing the result with (2.11), we achieve compatibility, given that

$$\text{(2.13)} \qquad \boldsymbol{\pi}_1 = \Pi_1\boldsymbol{\gamma}_1 + \begin{pmatrix}\boldsymbol{\beta}_1 \\ \mathbf{0}\end{pmatrix},$$

where the zero vector on the right side of (2.13) is $(k - k_1) \times 1$, and $\mathbf{u}_1 = \mathbf{v}_1 - V_1\boldsymbol{\gamma}_1$. From (2.12) and (2.13), the estimation problem can be viewed as a restricted multivariate regression problem with the structural parameters $\boldsymbol{\gamma}_1$ and $\boldsymbol{\beta}_1$ involved in the restrictions on the elements of $\boldsymbol{\pi}_1$ and Π_1. A necessary condition for the identification of $\boldsymbol{\gamma}_1$, $\boldsymbol{\beta}_1$, and σ_{11} is that $k - k_1 \geq m_1$. Note that (2.13) reflects restrictions arising from just the first equation (2.11) of a system. The information in restrictions similar to (2.13) associated with other structural equations is not taken into account in estimating $\boldsymbol{\gamma}_1$, $\boldsymbol{\beta}_1$, and σ_{11} and hence the nomenclature, *limited-information* or *single-equation* analysis.

Previous research has shown that ML, 2SLS, and 3SLS estimates are approximate means of posterior pdf's for structural parameters under special conditions. Of course, given complete posterior pdf's for parameters, optimal point estimates can be computed, that is, posterior means for quadratic loss functions and medians for absolute error loss functions. A particularly simple optimal point estimate under a generalized quadratic loss function can be derived as follows. Upon multiplying both sides of (2.13) on the left by $X = (X_1 \vdots X_0)$, we obtain

$$X\boldsymbol{\pi}_1 = X\Pi_1\boldsymbol{\gamma}_1 + X_1\boldsymbol{\beta}_1 = \bar{Z}_1\boldsymbol{\delta}_1, \tag{2.14}$$

where $\bar{Z}_1 = (X\Pi_1 \vdots X_1)$ and $\boldsymbol{\delta}_1' = (\boldsymbol{\gamma}_1' \vdots \boldsymbol{\beta}_1')$. Take as loss function,

$$\begin{aligned} L &= (X\boldsymbol{\pi}_1 - \bar{Z}_1\mathbf{d}_1)'(X\boldsymbol{\pi}_1 - \bar{Z}_1\mathbf{d}_1) \\ &= (\boldsymbol{\delta}_1 - \mathbf{d}_1)'\bar{Z}_1'\bar{Z}_1(\boldsymbol{\delta}_1 - \mathbf{d}_1), \end{aligned} \tag{2.15}$$

a generalized quadratic loss function. Given a posterior pdf for the reduced form parameters $\boldsymbol{\pi}_1$ and Π_1, the posterior expectation of L in the first line of (2.15) can be evaluated yielding $EL = E\boldsymbol{\pi}_1'X'X\boldsymbol{\pi}_1 - 2\mathbf{d}_1'E\bar{Z}_1'X\boldsymbol{\pi}_1 + \mathbf{d}_1'E\bar{Z}_1'\bar{Z}_1\mathbf{d}_1$, where E is the posterior expectation operator. Then the value of $\mathbf{d}_1$ that minimizes expected loss, $\mathbf{d}_1^*$, termed a minimum expected loss (MELO) estimate, is given by Zellner (1978):

$$\mathbf{d}_1^* = (E\bar{Z}_1'\bar{Z}_1)^{-1}E\bar{Z}_1'X\boldsymbol{\pi}_1. \tag{2.16}$$

When the system in (2.12) is analyzed under a diffuse prior for the regression coefficients $\boldsymbol{\pi}_1$ and Π_1 and for the error covariance matrix, the marginal posterior pdf for $(\boldsymbol{\pi}_1 \vdots \Pi_1)$ is in the matrix Student-t form, and, hence, the expectations in (2.16) are readily available. In this case, Zellner (1978) has shown that $\mathbf{d}_1^*$ is in the form of a $\mathcal{K}$-class estimate with a value of $\mathcal{K}$ that depends on the sample size and is less than one in finite samples. Also, $\mathbf{d}_1^*$ possesses at least first and second sampling moments (Zellner and Park 1979). Further, the optimal estimate of $\boldsymbol{\gamma}_1$ is a matrix-weighted average of the 2SLS and CLS estimates with the weight on the CLS estimate going to zero as the sample size increases (Zellner 1980). In small samples, however, the optimal estimate of $\boldsymbol{\gamma}_1$ and $\boldsymbol{\beta}_1$ can be very close to or exactly equal to the CLS estimate. Thus, empirical workers who have persisted in their use of CLS estimates may not be very far from an optimal estimate in small samples. Further, this averaging of 2SLS and CLS estimates bears some resemblance to the work of Sawa, mentioned previously; however, the weights that Sawa uses and those that associated with (2.16) are different. Last, this point estimation approach has been applied to yield a MELO estimate of parameters appearing in all equations of a system, that is, $\boldsymbol{\delta}_1$, $\boldsymbol{\delta}_2, \ldots, \boldsymbol{\delta}_g$, where $\boldsymbol{\delta}_i' = (\boldsymbol{\gamma}_i' \vdots \boldsymbol{\beta}_i')$. (Also see Mehta and Swamy 1978 for some useful Bayesian results for obtaining point estimates of the $\boldsymbol{\delta}_i$'s that are related to ridge-regression results.)

Some additional issues regarding the Bayesian approach have been aptly summarized in the following remarks by Tukey (1976):

> It is my impression that rather generally, not just in econometrics, it is considered decent to use judgment in choosing a functional form, but indecent to use judgment in choosing a coefficient. If judgment about important things is quite all right, why should it not be used for less important ones as well? Perhaps the real purpose of Bayesian techniques is to let us do the indecent thing while modestly concealed behind a formal apparatus. If so, this would not be a precedent. When Fisher introduced the formalities of the analysis of variance in the early 1920's, its most important function was to conceal the fact that the data was being adjusted for block means, an important step forward which if openly visible would have been considered by too many wiseacres of the time to be "cooking the data." If so, let us hope the day will soon come when the role of "decent concealment" can be freely admitted.

2.3 Hypothesis Testing and SEM's

Sampling-theory procedures used for testing hypotheses relating to structural coefficients' values have in the main been large-sample procedures, usually large-sample likelihood ratio tests or large-sample tests based on the Wald criterion, that is, for testing the rank condition for identifiability, overidentifying restrictions on structural parameters, and general linear hypotheses regarding structural parameters' values. Recent research (Berndt and Savin 1975, Savin 1976) has emphasized that asymptotically equivalent testing procedures can produce conflicting results when used in finite-sample situations with a given nominal significance level. Analysis of asymptotic power functions by Morgan and Vandaele (1974) has demonstrated that certain ad hoc testing procedures are dominated by standard large-sample testing procedures. Also, finite-sample approximations to the sampling distribution of the likelihood ratio test statistic have received little, if any, attention in the econometric literature.

In special cases, the exact finite-sample distribution of a test statistic is available. In one such case the null hypothesis specifies the values of all coefficients of endogenous variables in an equation, for example, $\boldsymbol{\gamma}_1 = \boldsymbol{\gamma}_1^0$ and $\beta_{1i} = 0$ in $\mathbf{y}_1 + Y_1\boldsymbol{\gamma}_1 + X_1\boldsymbol{\beta}_1 + \mathbf{u}_1$. Conditional on $\boldsymbol{\gamma}_1 = \boldsymbol{\gamma}_1^0$, it is seen that $\mathbf{y}_1 - Y_1\boldsymbol{\gamma}_1^0 = X_1\boldsymbol{\beta}_1 + \mathbf{u}_1$ is in the form of a multiple regression given that X_1 does not contain lagged endogenous variables. In this special situation, test statistics that have exact t or F distributions are available; however, the requirement that the null hypothesis specify values for all elements of $\boldsymbol{\gamma}_1$ is quite restrictive. Also, when the system is dynamic, that is, when X_1 contains lagged endogenous variables, only approximate large-sample test procedures are available. The quality of the approximation and finite-sample power functions for widely used large-sample approximate tests are relatively unexplored topics in econometric research.

Another topic that has received very little attention in econometric research is the effects of pretests on the properties of subsequent tests and on estimators' and predictors' properties. That pretesting can vitally affect properties of estimators is evident from consideration of simple cases, for example, $y_{1t} = \gamma y_{2t} + u_{1t}$ and $y_{2t} = \pi_2 x_t + u_{2t}$. The RF equations for this simple system are $y_{1t} = \pi_1 x_t + v_{1t}$ and $y_{2t} = \pi_2 x_t + v_{2t}$ with $\gamma = \pi_1/\pi_2$. The ML estimator for γ is $\hat{\gamma} = \hat{\pi}_1/\hat{\pi}_2$, where $\hat{\pi}_i = \Sigma x_t y_{it}/\Sigma x_t^2$, $i = 1, 2$. $\hat{\gamma}$ does not possess finite moments; however, the distribution of $\hat{\gamma}$ subject to the outcome of a pretest that rejects $\pi_2 = 0$, namely, $|\hat{\pi}_2| > cs_{\hat{\pi}_2} > 0$, where c is a critical value and $s_{\hat{\pi}_2}$ is the standard error associated with $\hat{\pi}_2$, does possess finite moments.

Work on Bayesian posterior odds ratios for selected hypotheses relating to SEM's parameters' values is reported in Reynolds (1982). The posterior odds ratio, K_{12}, for two mutually exclusive hypotheses, H_1 and H_2, is given by

$$K_{12} = 0_{12} \times \int p_1(\boldsymbol{\theta})\ell_1(\boldsymbol{\theta}\,|\,\mathbf{y})d\boldsymbol{\theta} \Big/ \int p_2(\boldsymbol{\theta})\ell_2(\boldsymbol{\theta}\,|\,\mathbf{y})d\boldsymbol{\theta}, \tag{2.17}$$

where 0_{12} is the prior odds ratio, and for $i = 1, 2$, $p_i(\boldsymbol{\theta})$ is the prior pdf, and $\ell_i(\boldsymbol{\theta}\,|\,\mathbf{y})$ is the likelihood function. If H_1 and H_2 are mutually exclusive and exhaustive, and H_1 is $\boldsymbol{\theta} = \boldsymbol{\theta}^0$, while H_2 is $\boldsymbol{\theta} \neq \boldsymbol{\theta}^0$, a pretest estimate that is optimal relative to quadratic loss is given by

$$\begin{aligned} \hat{\boldsymbol{\theta}} &= p_1\boldsymbol{\theta}^0 + p_2\hat{\boldsymbol{\theta}}_2 \\ &= \boldsymbol{\theta}^0 + (\hat{\boldsymbol{\theta}}_2 - \boldsymbol{\theta}^0)/(K_{12} + 1), \end{aligned} \tag{2.18}$$

where $K_{12} = p_1/p_2 = p_1/(1 - p_1)$, where p_1 and p_2 are the posterior probabilities on H_1 and H_2, respectively, and $\hat{\boldsymbol{\theta}}_2$ is the posterior mean for $\boldsymbol{\theta}$ under H_2. The Bayesian pretest estimate, which also can be computed for other kinds of hypotheses, is a neat solution to the pretesting problem as it relates to estimation. Similar considerations apply in obtaining combined, optimal predictions from two or more alternative models.

2.4 *Prediction Procedures for SEM's*

Several alternative methods for generating predictions from SEM's have been discussed in the literature. First, it has been recognized that the URF system $Y = X\Pi + V$ can be fitted by least squares and used to generate unrestricted reduced-form predictions (URFP's). Such predictions will not generally be efficient because restrictions on structural coefficients that imply restrictions on the elements of Π are not reflected in URFP's. Second, from the restricted SEM, $Y\Gamma_r = XB_r + U$, we can obtain the restricted reduced-form system $Y = XB_r\Gamma_r^{-1} + V_r$, and restricted reduced-form predictions (RRFP's) can be obtained from $\hat{\mathbf{y}}'_f = \mathbf{x}'_f\hat{B}_r\hat{\Gamma}_r^{-1}$, where $\mathbf{x}'_f$ is a given vector and $\hat{B}_r$ and $\hat{\Gamma}_r$ are estimated restricted structural coefficient estimates. Such predictions will be asymptotically efficient if $\hat{B}_r$ and $\hat{\Gamma}_r$ are asymptotically efficient estimates and if, of course, there are no specification errors. If B_r and Γ_r are estimated by inefficient but consistent methods, it is not always the case that a predictor based on them will be better in large samples than an URFP (Dhrymes 1973). Last, the partially restricted reduced-form (PRRF) equations can be used to generate predictions, namely, $\mathbf{y}_i = X\Pi_i\boldsymbol{\gamma}_i + X_i\boldsymbol{\beta}_i + \mathbf{v}_i$, $i = 1, 2, \ldots, g$. Estimates of Π_i, $\boldsymbol{\gamma}_i$, and $\boldsymbol{\beta}_i$ along with given vectors $\mathbf{x}'_f$ and $\mathbf{x}'_{if}$ yield the PRRFP's $\hat{y}_i = \mathbf{x}'_f\tilde{\Pi}_i\tilde{\boldsymbol{\gamma}}_i + \mathbf{x}'_{if}\tilde{\boldsymbol{\beta}}_i$, $i = 1, 2, \ldots, g$. Since the PRRFP's use more prior information than the URFP's in overidentified SEM's, they will have higher precision in large samples than URFP's. On the other hand, they will not generally be as precise as RRFP's in large samples when no specification errors are present in the SEM. Approximate expressions for the variance-covariance matrix of forecast error vectors are available in the literature for the prediction procedures mentioned previously. Further, it is apparent that specification errors can vitally affect relative large-sample properties of these predictors. Then, too, only limited attention has been given to the problems of predicting future values of the exogenous variables in X.

It has been pointed out in the literature that the RRF predictor, $\hat{\mathbf{y}}'_f = \mathbf{x}'_f\hat{B}_r\hat{\Gamma}_r^{-1}$, will not in general possess finite moments, whereas the other predictors mentioned will have finite moments in general for the URF predictor and in most situations for the PRRF predictor (Knight 1977). More thorough analyses of alternative predictors' finite-sample properties would be most valuable (see Schmidt 1977 for Monte Carlo experimental evidence that led him to conclude that "The first main conclusion . . . is that inferences about forecasts are not terribly reliable, unless one's sample is fairly large" [p. 1004]).

From the Bayesian point of view, the predictive probability function for the URF system, $Y = X\Pi + V$, is available. Its mean vector is an optimal point prediction relative to a quadratic loss function. Optimal multistep predictions for the URF when it has autoregressive complications have been obtained by Chow (1973). Richard (1973) has studied predictive pdf's for the SEM and has applied some of his results that incorporate restrictions on structural coefficients in the analysis of small models. Further work to enlarge the range of prior pdf's used in these analyses and to provide computer programs to perform calculations conveniently would be worthwhile.

Some other issues that arise in use of econometric models for forecasting are (*a*) procedures for using judgmental information and econometric models in making forecasts; (*b*) ways of combining forecasts from alternative models (Nelson 1972; Granger and Newbold 1977*b*); (*c*) criteria for the evaluation of the accuracy of forecasts (Granger and Newbold 1973, 1977*b*); (*d*) data quality and forecasting (Zellner 1958); and (*e*) seasonal adjustment and forecasting (Plosser 1976*a*, *b*). Further, the relative forecasting performance of univariate autoregressive-integrated-moving-average (ARIMA) time series and econometric models has been the subject of much research (Leuthold et al. 1970; Cooper 1972; Nelson 1972; Christ 1975; also see section 3).

3 The SEMTSA Approach

As mentioned before, much past econometric research has concentrated on the analysis of given models and yielded relatively little on formal methods for checking whether formulated models are consistent with information in sample data and for improving models. In addition, many time series aspects of econometric modeling have not been adequately treated. This is not to say that time series considerations were totally absent from econometric research, but rather that there was no systematic synthesis of econometric modeling and time series analysis.

Most important in stimulating some econometricians' interest in time series techniques was the good forecasting performance of simple, univariate time series models relative to that of large econometric models in the work of Cooper (1972) and Nelson (1972). Much earlier, Milton Friedman suggested that econometric models' forecasts be compared with those of simple, univariate "naive" models, a suggestion implemented by Christ (1951). The relatively good forecasting performance of simple univariate autoregressive (AR) or Box-Jenkins's ARIMA models surprised econometric model builders. In theory, a properly specified multiequation econometric model should yield more precise forecasts than a univariate time series model, since the former incorporates much more sample and prior information. The reasonable conclusion, drawn by many from these forecasting studies, is that the econometric models considered in these studies probably contain serious specification errors (e.g., see Hickman 1972). For example, the econometric models may contain incorrect functional forms for relations, inappropriate lag structures, incorrect assumptions about the exogeneity of variables, incorrect assumptions about error terms' properties, and so forth. Because the relationship between econometric models and univariate ARIMA processes was not clearly understood, many econometricians considered simple time series models to be ad hoc, mechanical, alternative models. Further, it was not apparent how time series analysis could be used to improve properties of SEM's. These issues were taken up in an article by Zellner and Palm (1974) and have since been pursued in a number of other works such as Evans (1975, 1976, 1978), Palm (1976, 1977), Plosser (1976*a*, *b*), Prothero and Wallis (1976), Trivedi (1975), Wallis (1976, 1977), and Zellner and Palm (1975).

This research on the SEMTSA approach has, first, emphasized that dynamic, linear (in the parameters) SEM's are a special case of multivariate or multiple time series processes, such as studied by Quenouille (1957) and others. Second, it has been shown that assuming variables to be exogenous places important restrictions on the parameters of a multiple time series process. Third, the transfer function (TF) equation system associated with a dynamic linear SEM has been derived and shown to be strongly restricted by structural assumptions. While the TF equation system had appeared in the econometric literature earlier under other names, its role in econometric model building had not been emphasized. Fourth, in the case of random exogenous variables generated by a multiple time series process, it is possible to derive the final equations (FE's), associated with the SEM, and individual FE's are in the form of ARIMA processes of the type studied by Box and Jenkins (1970) and others. Thus, as emphasized in the SEMTSA approach, the Box-Jenkins ARIMA processes are not ad hoc, alternative (to SEM's), mechanical models but are, in fact, implied by SEM's (see the studies cited previously for explicit examples). In addition, assumptions about structural equations' properties have strong implications for the forms of FE's and TF's that can be tested.

To make some of these considerations explicit, a multiple time series process for a $p \times 1$ vector of random variables z_t (assumed mean-corrected for convenience) is represented as follows (Quenouille 1957):

$$\text{(3.1)} \qquad \underset{p\times p}{H(L)}\ \underset{p\times 1}{\mathbf{z}_t} = \underset{p\times p}{F(L)}\ \underset{p\times 1}{\mathbf{e}_t} \qquad t = 1, 2, \ldots, T,$$

where $H(L)$ and $F(L)$ are finite-order matrix polynomials (assumed of full rank) in the lag operator L, and $\mathbf{e}_t$ is a vector of serially uncorrelated errors with zero mean vector and identity covariance matrix. If, for example, $F(L)$ is of degree zero in L, that is, $F(L) = F_0$, with F_0 of full rank, then the error vector in (3.1) is $F_0\mathbf{e}_t$ with zero mean and only a nonzero contemporaneous covariance matrix, $EF_0\mathbf{e}_t\mathbf{e}_t'F_0' = F_0F_0'$. Other specifications of $F(L)$ allow for moving-average error terms. For stationarity $|H(L)| = 0$ must have all its roots outside the unit circle, while for invertibility the roots of $|F(L)| = 0$ must lie outside the unit circle.

Upon multiplying both sides of (3.1) by the adjoint matrix associated with $H(L)$, denoted by $H^*(L)$, we obtain

$$|H(L)|\mathbf{z}_t = H^*(L)F(L)\mathbf{e}_t, \tag{3.2}$$

a set of FE's for the elements of $\mathbf{z}_t$. Each of the FE's in (3.2) is in autoregressive-moving-average (ARMA) form, that is, $|H(L)|z_{it} = \boldsymbol{\alpha}_i'\mathbf{e}_t$, where $|H(L)|$ is an autoregressive polynomial, and $\boldsymbol{\alpha}_i'$, a $1 \times p$ vector of polynomial operators, is the ith row of $H^*(L)F(L)$. That $\boldsymbol{\alpha}_i'\mathbf{e}_t$, a sum of moving-average processes, can be represented as a moving-average process in a single random variable has been proved in the literature. Thus, even with the general multiple time series process in (3.1), processes on individual variables will be in the Box-Jenkins form.

In structural econometric modeling it is usually assumed that some of the variables in $\mathbf{z}_t$ are exogenous. Let $\mathbf{z}_t' = (\mathbf{y}_t' \vdots \mathbf{x}_t')$, where $\mathbf{y}_t$, a $p_1 \times 1$ vector, denotes the vector of endogenous variables and $\mathbf{x}_t$, a $p_2 \times 1$ vector, denotes the exogenous variables. Then (3.1) can be written as

$$\begin{pmatrix} H_{11} & H_{12} \\ H_{21} & H_{22} \end{pmatrix} \begin{pmatrix} \mathbf{y}_t \\ \mathbf{x}_t \end{pmatrix} = \begin{pmatrix} F_{11} & F_{12} \\ F_{21} & F_{22} \end{pmatrix} \begin{pmatrix} \mathbf{e}_{1t} \\ \mathbf{e}_{2t} \end{pmatrix}, \tag{3.3}$$

where the partitioning of $H(L) = \{H_{ij}\}$, $F(L) = \{F_{ij}\}$, and $\mathbf{e}_t$ has been made to conform to that for $\mathbf{z}_t' = (\mathbf{y}_t' \vdots \mathbf{x}_t')$. The assumption that $\mathbf{x}_t$ is exogenous places the following restrictions on the matrix lag operators in (3.3):

$$H_{21} \equiv 0, \; F_{12} \equiv 0, \text{ and } F_{21} \equiv 0. \tag{3.4}$$

On inserting (3.4) in (3.3), we have

$$H_{11}\mathbf{y}_t + H_{12}\mathbf{x}_t = F_{11}\mathbf{e}_{1t}, \tag{3.5}$$

and

$$H_{22}\mathbf{x}_t = F_{22}\mathbf{e}_{2t}. \tag{3.6}$$

The equation system in (3.5) is the dynamic structural equation system, while that in (3.6) is the multivariate ARMA process generating the exogenous variables in $\mathbf{x}_t$.

By multiplying both sides of (3.5) on the left by the adjoint matrix associated with H_{11}, denoted by H_{11}^*, we obtain the TF system,

$$|H_{11}|\mathbf{y}_t + H_{11}^* H_{12}\mathbf{x}_t = H_{11}^* F_{11}\mathbf{e}_{1t}. \tag{3.7}$$

Last, the FE's associated with (3.5) to (3.6) are obtained by multiplying both sides of (3.6) on the left by H_{22}^*, the adjoint matrix associated with H_{22}, to obtain

$$(3.8) \qquad |H_{22}|\mathbf{x}_t = H_{22}^* F_{22} \mathbf{e}_{2t},$$

and substituting for $\mathbf{x}_t$ in (3.7) from (3.8) to yield

$$(3.9) \qquad |H_{11}|\,|H_{22}|\mathbf{y}_t = -H_{11}^* H_{12} H_{22}^* F_{22} \mathbf{e}_{2t} + |H_{22}| H_{11}^* F_{11} \mathbf{e}_{1t}.$$

Equations (3.8) and (3.9) are the FE's for the variables in $\mathbf{x}_t$ and $\mathbf{y}_t$, respectively. Each variable has an ARMA process, as mentioned before. Simple modifications of the analysis presented previously to take account of nonstochastic exogenous variables, such as time trends, and seasonal or other "dummy" variables, can easily be made.

In structural econometric modeling in the past, workers have concentrated attention on the SEM given in (3.5). Economic and other considerations have been employed to justify the classification of variables into the two categories, endogenous and exogenous. Further special assumptions regarding the matrices H_{11}, H_{12}, and F_{11} are required to achieve identification (e.g., see Hannan 1971). These assumptions place restrictions on lag patterns in equations, serial correlation properties of error terms, and on which variables appear with nonzero coefficients in equations of the system. If the resultant system is appropriately specified and estimated, it, of course, can be used for forecasting, control, and structural analysis, the traditional objectives of SEM's. It must be recognized, however, that a large number of specifying assumptions have to be made to implement the SEM in (3.5), and the probability that errors will be made in specifying an initial variant of (3.5) generally will be high. The solution to this problem is not to discard the initial variant of (3.5), which may contain much valuable information, but to pursue complementary analyses that can help to identify problems in the formulation of the initial variant and to suggest appropriate reformulation of specifying assumptions. Also, it is important that these complementary analyses yield useful results along the way toward obtaining a good SEM.

In the SEMTSA approach, it is suggested that workers use economic theory and other outside information to formulate an initial, tentative form for (3.5). The next step involves deducing algebraically the forms of the TF system in (3.7) and the FE's in (3.9). As is obvious from the forms of the TF and FE systems, assumptions regarding the SEM in (3.5) will result in a number of important restrictions on TF's and FE's that can be checked empirically. For example, from (3.7), (3.8), and (3.9), it is seen that the AR parts of the FE's and TF's will be identical when lag operators do not contain common factors. As pointed out in Zellner and Palm (1974), systems with special features, that is, fully recursive systems or systems in which H_{11} is block-diagonal, will lead to cancellation, and thus the AR parts of FE's and TF's will not be identical. Also, other special assumptions about the forms of H_{11} and H_{12} in (3.5) will result in TF's and FE's with different AR lag polynomials (see Zellner and Palm 1975 for an example). Work on examining the implications of specific SEM's for the forms of FE's and TF's is extremely important in enhancing understanding of SEM's. For example, the effect of changing a variable's classification from exogenous to endogenous on the forms of the TF's and FE's can be easily determined. Also, structural assumptions about lag structures, properties of structural error terms, and forms of policymakers' control policies all result in strong restrictions on TF's and FE's. In addition, Quenouille (1957, chap. 5) has provided valuable analysis of the effects of incorrect inclusion or exclusion of variables, measurement errors, parameters varying with time, nonlinearities, and so on.

When the forms of TF's and FE's associated with a SEM have been derived, the next step in the SEMTSA approach is to analyze data to determine or identify the forms of FE's and TF's to check that the empirically determined FE's and TF's are compatible with those implied by the tentatively formulated SEM. Of course this work not only provides checks on a SEM but also estimates FE's that can be used for prediction and TF's that can be used for prediction and control. If the analysis of the FE's and TF's provides results compatible with the implications of the SEM, the SEM's parameters can be estimated, and it can be used for prediction, control, and structural analysis. If, as is usually the case, the results of FE and TF analysis do not confirm the implications of an initial variant of a SEM, the SEM must be reformulated. This reformulation process is facilitated considerably by knowing the results of TF and FE analyses. That is, the latter analyses usually indicate specific deficiencies of the initial variant of a SEM, and many times recognition of these deficiencies is an important first step in finding remedies for them. When the initial variant of a SEM has been reformulated, its implications for the forms of FE's and TF's can be checked empirically. Also, the roots of FE's and TF's can be calculated, estimated, and examined for reasonableness.

The SEMTSA approach provides an operational and useful synthesis of traditional econometric and time series analysis techniques that can produce SEM's with fewer specification errors and better forecasting performance. As with traditional SEM's, however, some statistical problems associated with the SEMTSA approach require further research. First, there is the problem of determining the forms of the FE's from sample data. Box's and Jenkins's well-known suggested techniques based on properties of estimated autocorrelation and partial autocorrelation functions are helpful in ruling out a number of forms for FE's; however, these techniques are rather informal. For nested FE models, large-sample likelihood ratio tests can be employed to aid in discriminating among alternative FE models. For nested and nonnested models, Bayesian posterior odds ratios also are useful. For example, in discriminating between a white noise process and a first-order moving-average process, Evans (1978) has shown that the posterior odds ratio is a function not only of the first-order sample serial correlation coefficient, r_1, but also of higher-order sample serial correlation coefficients, $r_2, r_3, \ldots$, the latter having weights that decline as the sample size increases. Because r_1 is not a sufficient statistic and because the r_i's are highly correlated in small samples, a large-sample test using just r_1 does not use all the sample information and can lead to erroneous inferences. Posterior odds ratios also are useful in situations in which roots of AR polynomials lie on the unit circle, a situation in which it is known that usual large-sample likelihood ratio tests based on χ^2 statistics are invalid. Geisel (1976) has reported work indicating that Bayesian posterior odds ratios performed better than variants of Box-Jenkins procedures in discriminating among alternative ARIMA schemes. Extensions of this work and the early work of Whittle (1951) on Bayesian hypothesis testing in time series analysis would be very valuable. This work also can shed light on the problem of determining the degree, if any, of differencing required to induce stationarity. Note that in formulating a posterior odds ratio, stationarity is not required. Stationarity is required for most uses of sample autocorrelation and partial autocorrelation functions.

Second, there is the problem of determining the forms of TF's. Important work on this problem for simple TF's has been reported by Box and Jenkins (1970, 1976), Haugh and Box (1977), Haugh (1972), Granger and Newbold (1977*b*), and others. Also, the econometric work on distributed lag models is relevant (e.g., see Aigner 1971, Dhrymes 1971, Griliches 1967, and Nicholls, Pagan, and Terrell 1975). Recent work of Sims (1972, 1977), Pierce and Haugh (1977), Skoog (1976), Wu (1978), and others on tests for special recursive structures, along with procedures suggested by Box, Jenkins, Haugh, Granger, Newbold, and others, may be useful in checking the assumptions about input variables' properties. In TF's with several input variables, it may be advisable to reduce the number of free parameters by using some of the assumptions in the distributed lag literature regarding coefficients of current and lagged input variables (e.g., see Shiller 1973). As with determining the forms of FE's, it is probable that posterior odds ratios will be found useful in discriminating among alternative forms for TF's and in obtaining posterior probabilities associated with alternative variants of TF's.

Third, there is the problem of obtaining good estimates of parameters in FE's, TF's and SEM's. Currently, various asymptotically justified estimates are available, and some of these take account of random initial conditions and restrictions implied by the assumptions of stationarity and invertibility. The small-sample properties of these asymptotically justified estimates require much further investigation, a point also emphasized by Newbold (1976), who writes, "As regards estimation, I am not sure that uncritical use of maximum likelihood estimates is justified in small samples without some investigation of their sampling properties." As pointed out in section 2, ML estimators do not in general possess good finite-sample properties. These comments imply that more work to obtain good finite-sample estimates is required. Extensions of the valuable work of Box and Jenkins (1970, 1976), Newbold (1973), Tiao and Hillmer (1976), and others on Bayesian estimation of time series models seem to be possible and can provide additional good finite-sample estimation results.

Fourth, the problems associated with seasonality are important in formulating and analyzing SEM's and yet have received relatively little attention. Because seasonal variation accounts for a large fraction of the variation of many economic variables, a proper treatment of seasonality is critical. In much econometric work, seasonally adjusted variables are used with little or no attention to the procedures employed for seasonal adjustment and their possible effects on determination of lag structures and other features of SEM's. In the SEMTSA approach, Plosser (1976 *a*, *b*) and Wallis (1976) have provided valuable analyses of seasonality in SEM's.

Fifth, the problem of measurement errors in economic time series requires much more attention. It is well known that a number of economic series are derived wholly or in part from sample surveys. Many statistical analyses of such data are based on the usually erroneous assumption of simple random sampling. Analyses that take proper account of the designs of sample surveys, their sampling errors, and possible biases would be most welcome. Further work to consider SEM's subject to measurement error would also be valuable. For example, (3.5) could be formulated in terms of the true values of variables, $\mathbf{z}_t' = (\mathbf{y}_t' \vdots \mathbf{x}_t')$. The measured values of variables $\mathbf{z}_t^{m'} = (\mathbf{y}_t^{m'}, \mathbf{x}_t^{m'})$ could be assumed given by $\mathbf{z}_t^m = R\mathbf{z}_t + \xi_t$, where R is a matrix of coefficients reflecting systematic measurement errors and ξ_t is a vector of random measurement errors. In this form, the SEM becomes what engineers call a state-variable model. Perhaps results in the engineering literature would be useful in work with SEM's. Measurement problems are not insignificant: Initial and subsequently revised figures for GNP and other important quarterly economic series differ considerably, in some cases systematically, and provide different information regarding cyclical turning points (see Zellner 1958). Similar results have been obtained in current work with preliminary and revised figures for quarterly nominal GNP. Revisions in the preliminary estimates of quarterly GNP amounting to 5 to 10 billion dollars are common. For example, the first and subsequently revised figures (in billions of current dollars) for GNP in the fourth quarter of 1954 are 361.0, 362.0, 367.1, 367.7, and 373.4; for the fourth quarter of 1965, the preliminary and subsequently revised figures are 694.6, 697.2, 704.4, 708.4, 710.0, and 710.0. These figures illustrate an important measurement problem confronting econometric model builders and forecasters that has not been adequately treated in the literature.

Sixth, aggregation problems have received increased attention in recent work. Articles by Geweke (1976), Rose (1977), Tiao and Wei (1976), and Wei (1976) provide valuable results on temporal and other kinds of aggregation in the context of time series models. In work by Laub (1971, 1972), Peck (1973, 1974) and Levedahl (1976), attention has been focused on economic models for individual firms and consumers using panel data and the implications of these microanalyses for aggregate dividend, investment, and automobile expenditure functions. At the microlevel, discrete decisions, such as buy/don't buy or change/don't change the dividend rate, are extremely important. Yet macroformulations of behavioral relationships that are incorporated in many SEM's do not properly take account of this discrete microbehavior and as a result are misspecified. Many estimated investment, dividend, and automobile expenditure functions that are based on partial adjustment models show long response lags that are spurious and are the result of aggregation over buyers and nonbuyers or corporations that change and those that do not change the dividend rate in a particular quarter. Levedahl (1976) has shown analytically and empirically that the adjustment coefficient in a partial adjustment model for automobile expenditures is related to the proportion of consumers purchasing a car in a particular period. Because this proportion varies considerably over time, the adjustment coefficient is an unstable parameter, and models fitted under the assumption that it is stable have obvious problems in forecasting. These findings relating to defects of widely used partial adjustment equations have serious implications for SEM's that incorporate such equations. Further work on formulating macro-SEM's that takes better account of discrete elements in economic behavior seems very important in obtaining better models.

Seventh, forms of policymakers' control may change and thus cause instability in lag parameters and other features of a model, a point emphasized by Lucas (1973). Analyses using subsamples of data may indicate the empirical importance of this problem.

Last, time series analysts have identified relatively simple, low-order

ARIMA processes for economic variables appearing in SEM's. On the other hand, the ARIMA processes or FE's associated with most SEM's usually are complicated, high-order schemes. To illustrate, Leuthold et al. (1970) formulated and estimated a SEM for analysis of hog markets with daily data. They also identified and fitted ARIMA processes for the daily price and quantity variables. Their time series model for price was found to be a simple random walk. As shown in Zellner (1975), the form of their SEM implies FE's for price and quantity with AR parts of at least third order, quite at variance with their random walk finding for the price variable. It seems that they forced a misspecified SEM on the data, one that involves the implicit assumption of unexploited profit opportunities in the hog markets. Indeed Muth (1961, p. 327, n. 11), in his pathbreaking paper on rational expectation models (i.e., models that do not imply unexploited profit opportunities), writes in connection with a general supply and demand model, "If the production and consumption flows are negligible compared with the speculative inventory level, the process [on price] approaches a random walk. This would apply to daily or weekly price movements of a commodity whose production lag is a year." Thus, economic theory provides some support for the empirical finding that daily hog prices follow a random walk and that the SEM for the hog markets is probably misspecified.

Similar considerations apply to the Hendry (1974) model of the UK analyzed in Prothero and Wallis (1976). The latter workers identified rather simple ARIMA processes for variables appearing in Hendry's SEM. The FE's associated with Hendry's estimated model have ninth-order AR parts. Prothero and Wallis (1976, p. 483) apparently take this finding of a ninth-order AR part of the FE's of Hendry's model seriously and attribute the relatively low orders of the empirically identified FE's to "relatively small coefficients of higher powers of L [the lag operator], which proved difficult to detect in our univariate analyses." Also, they state that "the size of the available sample [42 quarterly observations] has clearly restricted our ability to detect subtle higher-order effects." Whether these subtle higher-order effects are real or are results of specification errors present in the eight-equation Hendry model is a point that deserves further attention. In addition, the burgeoning literature on rational expectation economic models has important implications for the formulation and analysis of SEM's (for some examples, see Evans 1975, Grossman 1975, McCallum 1977, Nelson 1975, Ranson 1974, Sargent and Wallace 1975, Wickens 1976, and Flood and Garber 1978).

4 Conclusions

This review of some of the research on SEM's has emphasized the following major points:

1. Substantial progress has been made in research on statistical methods for constructing, analyzing, and using econometric models.

2. There is a serious need for developing and vigorously applying additional statistical, mathematical, computer simulation, and economic diagnostic checks of properties of the SEM's.

3. For given SEM's, more work has to be done to develop and apply estimation, testing, and prediction procedures that have finite-sample justifications. In this connection, the present author and others believe that Bayesian procedures offer good solutions for many finite-sample problems.

4. More formal procedures for using prior information in the analysis of given SEM's are required, a problem area that can be approached most satisfactorily at present by use of the Bayesian approach.

5. Most serious is the need for formal, sequential statistical procedures for constructing SEM's.

6. The synthesis of traditional econometric model-building techniques and modern time series analysis techniques, called the SEMTSA approach previously, probably will lead to improved SEM's, a view of the present writer, Granger and Newbold (1977*a*), and others.

7. Further use of existing economic theory, such as the theory of efficient markets (see Fama 1970 for a review of this theory), and rational expectations theory probably will yield better SEM's. Having SEM's consistent with elements of sound economic theory has long been emphasized in the econometric literature, and further attention to this point in current work with SEM's is critical.

So that this listing of research needs not be construed as misrepresenting the quality of current U.S. macro-SEM's that are used to generate quarterly forecasts of important economic variables, such as GNP, unemployment, prices, and interest rates, it is relevant to consider Christ's (1975) thoughtful and relatively favorable review of the forecasting properties of such models. In the opening sentence of his article, he writes, "Econometric models of the U.S. economy have been developed to the point where forecasters who use them can forecast real and nominal GNP two or three quarters ahead with root mean square errors of less than one percent, and six quarters ahead with RMS errors of one to two percent." This rather optimistic summary statement fails to take account of the fact that population RMS errors have been estimated from rather small samples of forecast errors and hence are not very precise. A confidence interval at a reasonable level for the population RMS error would probably be rather broad. Also, the implication of a 1 to 2 percent error for nominal GNP that now exceeds 1.5 trillion (1,000 billion) dollars, is about a 15 to 30 billion dollar or greater error, which would be considered substantial by most analysts.

Further with respect to the very same models that yield RMS errors of 1 percent or 2, Christ (1975) in the second paragraph of his article writes, "though the models forecast well over horizons of four to six quarters, they disagree so strongly about the effects of important monetary and fiscal policies that they cannot be considered reliable guides to such policy effects, until it can be determined which of them are wrong in this respect and which (if any) are right." This statement clearly indicates that at least some, or perhaps all, of the models that Christ considered (Wharton; Data Resources Inc.; Bureau of Economic Analysis; St. Louis; Fair; Liu-Hwa; Hickman-Coen; and University of Michigan) probably contain serious specification errors.

Next, Christ (1975, p. 59) writes,

> In general, it appears that *subjectively adjusted* forecasts using *ex ante* exogenous values are better than the others. It is no surprise that subjective adjustment helps. It may surprise some that the use of actual exogenous values does not help, and sometimes hinders. But there is likely to be some interaction, in the sense that if a forecaster feels that the preliminary forecast turned out by his model is unreasonable, he may both adjust the model and change his ex ante forecast of the exogenous variables, in order to obtain a final forecast that he thinks is more reasonable.

Christ's conclusion that "*subjectively adjusted* forecasts . . . are better than the others" (emphasis his) underlines the importance of using prior information carefully in preparing forecasts. His statement that use of the actual values, rather than the anticipated values, of exogenous variables "does not help" is indeed surprising. In this connection, it should be appreciated that the subjective adjustments often take the form of adjusting the values of intercept terms in equations of a model. Because equations often are formulated in terms of nonstationary variables and may be considered as local approximations, adjustments to intercept terms and slope coefficients will be needed when values of the variables move away from sample values. In such situations, thoughtful adjustment of intercept terms is a partial step in the direction of obtaining better results; but, because it is partial, there is no assurance that use of actual rather than anticipated values of exogenous variables will produce better results in general.

Last, from the information on models' forecast errors that Christ has assembled, it appears that SEM's for both nominal and real GNP outperform univariate ARIMA schemes for these variables in terms of estimated RMS errors. As pointed out before, many have recognized, implicitly or explicitly, that a correctly specified multiequation SEM should, in theory, perform better in forecasting than a univariate ARIMA process. For example, Box and Jenkins (1976, p. 493) comment,

> If the question is whether a set of univariate [ARIMA] models of this kind which takes no account of relationships between the series describes a set of related time series better than the corresponding multivariate [econometric] model then predictably the answer must be "No." It is a sobering commentary on lack of expertise in the practical aspects of modelling that instances have occurred where well-built univariate models have done better than poorly built multivariate "econometric" ones.

In closing, it must be concluded from what has been presented and from Christ's remarks, that, while considerable progress has been made in work with SEM's, an econometric model as satisfactory as the Ford Model T has not as yet appeared.

References

Aigner, D. J. (1971). "A Compendium on Estimation of the Autoregressive Moving Average Model from Time Series Data." *International Economic Review*, 12:348–69.

Anderson, T. W. (1977). "Asymptotic Expansions of the Distributions of Estimates in Simulataneous Equations for Alternative Parameter Sequences." *Econometrica*, 45:509–18.

Berndt, E. and N. E. Savin (1975). "Conflict among Criteria for Testing Hypotheses in the Multivariate Linear Regression Model." *Econometrica*, 45:1263–72.

Box, G. E. P., and G. M. Jenkins (1970). *Time Series Analysis, Forecasting, and Control*. Rev. ed., 1976. San Francisco: Holden-Day.

———. (1976). "Discussion of the Paper by Dr. Prothero and Dr. Wallis." *Journal of the Royal Statistical Society*, Ser. A., 139:493–94.

Chow, G. C. (1973). "Multiperiod Predictions from Stochastic Difference Equations by Bayesian Methods." *Econometrica*, 41:109–18. Reprinted in S. E. Fienberg and A. Zellner, eds., *Studies in Bayesian Econometrics and Statistics in Honor of Leonard J. Savage*, pp. 313–24. Amsterdam: North-Holland Publishing Co., 1975.

Christ, C. F. (1951). "A Test of an Econometric Model for the United States, 1921–1947." In *Conference on Business Cycles*, pp. 35–107. New York: National Bureau of Economic Research.

———. (1975). "Judging the Performance of Econometric Models of the U.S. Economy." *International Economic Review*, 16:54–74.

Cooper, R. L. (1972). "The Predictive Performance of Quarterly Econometric Models of the United States." In B. G. Hickman, ed., *Econometric Models of Cyclical Behavior*, 2:813–926. New York: Columbia University Press.

Dhrymes, P. J. (1971). *Distributed Lags: Problems of Estimation and Formulation*. San Francisco: Holden-Day.

———. (1973). "Restricted and Unrestricted Reduced Forms: Asymptotic Distribution and Relative Efficiency." *Econometrica*, 41:119–34.

Drèze, J. H. (1972). "Econometrics and Decision Theory." *Econometrica*, 40:1–17.

———. (1975). "Bayesian Theory of Identification in Simultaneous Equation Models." In S. E. Fienberg and A. Zellner, eds., *Studies in Bayesian Econometrics and Statistics in Honor of Leonard J. Savage*, pp. 159–74. Amsterdam: North-Holland Publishing Co.

———. (1976). "Bayesian Limited Information Analysis of the Simultaneous Equations Model." *Econometrica*, 44:1045–76.

Drèze, J. H., and J. A. Morales (1976). "Bayesian Full Information Analysis of Simultaneous Equations." *Journal of the American Statistical Association*, 71:919–23.

Evans, P. (1975). "Time Series Analysis of a Macromodel of the U.S. Economy, 1880–1915." H. G. B. Alexander Research Foundation, Graduate School of Business, University of Chicago.

———. (1976). "A Time Series Test of the Natural-Rate Hypothesis." H. G. B. Alexander Research Foundation, Graduate School of Business, University of Chicago.

———. (1978). "Time-Series Analysis of the German Hyperinflation." *International Economic Review*, 19:195–209.

Fama, E. F. (1970). "Efficient Capital Markets: A Review of Theory and Empirical Work." *Journal of Finance*, 25:383–417.

Flood, R. P., and P. M. Garber (1978). "An Economic Theory of Monetary Reform." Department of Economics, University of Virginia.

Fuller, W. A. (1977). "Some Properties of a Modification of the Limited Information Estimator." *Econometrica*, 45:939–53.

Geisel, M. S. (1976). "Box-Jenkins or Bayes?" Report of research to the Econometrics and Statistics Colloquium, University of Chicago.

Geweke, J. (1976). "The Temporal and Sectoral Aggregation of Seasonally Adjusted Time Series." Paper presented at the NBER-Census Conference on Seasonal Analysis of Economic Time Series, September 1976. In A. Zellner, ed., *Seasonal Analysis of Economic Time Series*, pp. 411–27. Washington, D.C.: U.S. Government Printing Office, 1978.

Granger, C. W. J., and P. Newbold (1973). "Some Comments on the Evaluation of Economic Forecasts." *Applied Economics*, 5:35–47.

———. (1977*a*). "The Time Series Approach to Econometric Model Building." In C. A. Sims, ed., *New Methods in Business Cycle Research: Proceedings from a Conference*, pp. 7–21. Minneapolis: Federal Reserve Bank of Minneapolis.

———. (1977*b*). *Forecasting Economic Time Series*. New York: Academic Press.

Griliches, Z. (1967). "Distributed Lags—A Survey." *Econometrica*, 35:16–49.

Grossman, S. (1975). "Rational Expectations and the Econometric Modeling of Markets Subject to Uncertainty: A Bayesian Approach." *Journal of Econometrics*, 3:255–72.

Hale, C., R. S. Mariano, and J. G. Ramage (1978). "Finite Sample Analysis of Misspecification in Simultaneous Equation Models." Discussion Paper no. 357. Department of Economics, University of Pennsylvania.

Hamilton, H. R., S. E. Goldstone, J. W. Milliman, A. L. Pugh III, E. R. Roberts, and A. Zellner (1969). *Systems Simulation for Regional Analysis: An Application to River-Basin Planning*. Cambridge, Mass.: MIT Press.

Hannan, E. J. (1971). "The Identification Problem for Multiple Equation Systems with Moving Average Errors." *Econometrica*, 39:751–65.

Harkema, R. (1971). *Simultaneous Equations: A Bayesian Approach*. Rotterdam: Rotterdam University Press.

Haugh, L. D. (1972). "The Identification of Time Series Interrelationships with Special Reference to Dynamic Regression." Ph.D. diss., Department of Statistics, University of Wisconsin, Madison.

Haugh, L. D., and G. E. P. Box (1977). "Identification of Dynamic Regression (Distributed Lag) Models Connecting Two Time Series." *Journal of the American Statistical Association*, 72:121–30.

Hendry, D. F. (1974). "Stochastic Specification in an Aggregate Demand Model of the United Kingdom." *Econometrica*, 42:559–78.

Hickman, B. F., ed. (1972). *Econometric Models of Cyclical Behavior*, vols. 1 and 2. New York: Columbia University Press.

Jeffreys, H. (1957). *Scientific Inference*. 2d ed. Cambridge: Cambridge University Press.

———. (1967). *Theory of Probability*. 3d rev. ed. London: Oxford University Press.

Kadane, J. B. (1975). "The Role of Identification in Bayesian Theory." In S. E. Fienberg and A. Zellner, eds., *Studies in Bayesian Econometrics and Statistics in Honor of Leonard J. Savage*, pp. 175–91. Amsterdam: North-Holland Publishing Co.

Kloek, T., and H. K. van Dijk (1976). "Bayesian Estimates of Equation System Parameters: An Application of Integration by Monte Carlo." Report 7622/E, Econometric Institute, Erasmus University, Rotterdam.

Knight, J. L. (1977). "On the Existence of Moments of the Partially Restricted Reduced-Form Estimators from a Simultaneous-Equation Model." *Journal of Econometrics*, 5:315–21.

Laub, P. M. (1971). "The Dividend-Earning Relationship: A Study of Corporate Quarterly Panel Data, 1947–65." Ph.D. diss., Graduate School of Business, University of Chicago.

———. (1972). "Some Aspects of the Aggregation Problem in the Dividend-Earning Relationship." *Journal of the American Statistical Association*, 67:552–59.

Leuthold, R. M., A. J. A. MacCormick, A. Schmitz, and D. G. Watts (1970). "Forecasting Daily Hog Prices and Quantities: A Study of Alternative Forecasting Techniques." *Journal of the American Statistical Association*, 65:90–107.

Levedahl, J. W. (1976). "Predictive Error of the Stock Adjustment Model." H. G. B. Alexander Research Foundation, Graduate School of Business, University of Chicago.

Lucas, R. E. (1973). "Econometric Policy Evaluation: A Critique." Graduate School of Industrial Administration, Carnegie-Mellon University.

McCallum, B. T. (1977). "Price-Level Stickiness and the Feasibility of Monetary Stabilization Policy with Rational Expectations." *Journal of Political Economy*, 85:627–34.

Mehta, J. S., and P. A. V. B. Swamy (1978). "The Existence of Moments of Some Simple Bayes Estimators of Coefficients in a Simultaneous Equation Model." *Journal of Econometrics*, 7:1–13.

Morales, J. A. (1971). *Bayesian Full Information Structural Analysis*. New York: Springer-Verlag.

Morgan, A., and W. Vandaele (1974). "On Testing Hypotheses in Simultaneous Equation Models." *Journal of Econometrics*, 2:55–66.

Muth, J. F. (1961). "Rational Expectations and the Theory of Price Movements," *Econometrica*, 29:315–35.

Nagar, A. L. (1959). "The Bias and Moment Matrix of the General $\mathcal{K}$-Class Estimators of the Parameters in Simultaneous Equations and Their Small Sample Properties." *Econometrica*, 27:575–95.

Nelson, C. R. (1972). "The Prediction Performance of the FRB-MIT-Penn Model of the U.S. Economy." *American Economic Review*, 62:902–17.

———. (1975). "Rational Expectations and the Estimation of Econometric Models." *International Economic Review*, 16:555–61.

Newbold, P. (1973). "Bayesian Estimation of Box-Jenkins Transfer Function–Noise Models." *Journal of the Royal Statistical Society*, Ser. B, 35:323–36.

———. (1976). "Discussion of the Paper by Dr. Prothero and Dr. Wallis." *Journal of the Royal Statistical Society*, Ser. A, 139:490–91.

Nicholls, D. F., A. R. Pagan, and R. D. Terrell (1975). "The Estimation and Use of Models with Moving Average Disturbance Terms: A Survey." *International Economic Review*, 16:113–34.

Palm, F. (1976). "Testing the Dynamic Specification of an Econometric Model with an Application to Belgian Data." *European Economic Review*, 8:269–89.

———. (1977). "On Univariate Time Series Methods and Simultaneous Equation Econometric Models." *Journal of Econometrics*, 5:379–88.

Peck, S. C. (1973). "A Test of Alternative Theories of Investment Using Data from the Electric Utilities Industry." Ph.D. diss., Graduate School of Business, University of Chicago.

———. (1974). "Alternative Investment Models for Firms in the Electric Utilities Industry." *Bell Journal of Economics and Management Science*, 5:420–58.

Pierce, D. A., and L. D. Haugh (1977). "Causality in Temporal Systems: Characterizations and a Survey." *Journal of Econometrics*, 5:265–94.

Plosser, C. F. (1976*a*). "A Time Series Analysis of Seasonality in Econometric Models with Application to a Monetary Model." Ph.D. diss., Graduate School of Business, University of Chicago.

———. (1976*b*). "Time Series Analysis and Seasonality in Econometric Models." Paper presented at the NBER-Census Conference on Seasonal Analysis of Economic Time Series, September 1976. In A. Zellner, (ed., *Seasonal Analysis of Economic Time Series*, pp. 365–93. Washington, D.C.: U.S. Government Printing Office, 1978.

Prothero, D. L., and K. F. Wallis (1976). "Modelling Macroeconomic Time Series." *Journal of the Royal Statistical Society*, Ser. A, 139:468–86.

Quenouille, M. H. (1957). *The Analysis of Multiple Time-Series*. New York: Hafner Publishing Co.

Ranson, R. D. (1974). "Money, Capital, and the Stochastic Nature of Business Fluctuations." Ph.D. diss., Graduate School of Business, University of Chicago.

Reynolds, R. A. (1982). "Posterior Odds for the Hypothesis of Independence between Stochastic Regressors and Disturbances." *International Economic Review*, 23:479–90.

Richard, J. F. (1973). *Posterior and Predictive Densities for Simultaneous Equations Model*. New York: Springer-Verlag.

Rose, D. E. (1977). "Forecasting Aggregates of Independent ARIMA Processes." *Journal of Econometrics*, 5:323–46.

Rothenberg, T. (1975). "Bayesian Analysis of Simultaneous Equations Models." In S. E. Fienberg and A. Zellner, eds., *Studies in Bayesian Econometrics and Statistics in Honor of Leonard J. Savage*, pp. 405–24. Amsterdam: North-Holland Publishing Co.

Sargan, J. D. (1976). "Econometric Estimators and the Edgeworth Approximation." *Econometrica*, 44:421–48.

Sargent, T. J., and N. Wallace (1975). "Rational Expectations, the Optimal Monetary Instrument, and the Optimal Money Supply Rule." *Journal of Political Economy*, 83:241–54.

Savin, N. E. (1976). "Conflict among Testing Procedures in a Linear Regression Model with Autoregressive Disturbances." *Econometrica*, 44:1303–15.

Sawa, T. (1972). "Finite-Sample Properties of the $\mathcal{K}$-Class Estimators." *Econometrica*, 40:653–80.

———. (1973). "The Mean Square Error of a Combined Estimator and Numerical Comparison with the TSLS Estimator." *Journal of Econometrics*, 1:115–32.

Schmidt, P. (1977). "Some Small Sample Evidence on the Distribution of Dynamic Simulation Forecasts." *Econometrica*, 45:997–1005.

Shiller, R. J. (1973). "A Distributed Lag Estimator Derived from Smoothness Priors." *Econometrica*, 41:775–88.

Sims, C. A. (1972). "Money, Income, and Causality." *American Economic Review*, 62:540–52.

———. (1977). "Exogeneity and Causal Ordering in Macroeconomic Models." In C. A. Sims, ed., *New Methods in Business Cycle Research: Proceedings from a Conference*, pp. 23–43. Minneapolis: Federal Reserve Bank of Minneapolis.

Skoog, G. R. (1976). "Causality Characterizations: Bivariate, Trivariate, and Multivariate Propositions." Staff Report no. 14, Federal Reserve Bank of Minneapolis.

Sowey, E. R. (1973). "A Classified Bibliography of Monte Carlo Studies in Econometrics." *Journal of Econometrics*, 1:377–95.

Thornber, H. (1967). "Finite Sample Monte Carlo Studies: An Autoregressive Illustration." *Journal of the American Statistical Association*, 62: 801–8.

Tiao, G. C., and G. E. P. Box (1973). "Some Comments on 'Bayes' Estimators." *American Statistician*, 27:12–14. Reprinted in S. E. Fienberg and A. Zellner, eds., *Studies in Bayesian Econometrics and Statistics in Honor of Leonard J. Savage*, pp. 620–26. Amsterdam: North-Holland Publishing Co.

Tiao, G. C., and S. Hillmer (1976). "Seasonal Adjustment: A Bayesian View." Paper presented at the 13th Meeting of the NBER-NSF Seminar on Bayesian Inference in Econometrics, November 1976.

Tiao, G. C., and W. S. Wei (1976). "Effect of Temporal Aggregation on the Dynamic Relationship of Two Time Series Variables." *Biometrika*, 63:513–23.

Trivedi, P. K. (1975). "Time Series Analysis Versus Structural Models: A Case Study of Canadian Manufacturing Behavior." *International Economic Review*, 16:587–608.

Tukey, J. W. (1976). "Discussion of Granger on Seasonality." Paper presented at the NBER-Census Conference on Seasonal Analysis of Economic Time Series, September 1976. In A. Zellner, ed., *Seasonal Analysis of Economic Time Series*, pp. 50–53. Washington, D.C.: U.S. Government Printing Office, 1978.

Wallis, K. F. (1976). "Seasonal Adjustment and Multiple Time Series Analysis." Paper presented at the NBER-Census Conference on Seasonal Analysis of Economic Time Series, September 1976. In A. Zellner, ed., *Seasonal Analysis of Economic Time Series*, pp. 347–57. Washington, D.C.: U.S. Government Printing Office, 1978.

———. (1977). "Multiple Time Series Analysis and the Final Form of Econometric Models." *Econometrica*, 45:1481–97.

Wei, W. S. (1976). "Effects of Temporal Aggregation in Seasonal Time Series Models." Paper presented at the NBER-Census Conference on Seasonal Analysis of Economic Time Series, September 1976. In A. Zellner, ed., *Seasonal Analysis of Economic Time Series*, pp. 433–44. Washington, D.C.: U.S. Government Printing Office, 1978.

Whittle, P. (1951). *Hypothesis Testing in Time Series Analysis*. Uppsala: Almqvist and Wiksells Boktryckeri AB.

Wickens, M. R. (1976). "Rational Expectations and the Efficient Estimation of Econometric Models." Working Paper no. 35, Faculty of Economics, Australian National University.

Wu, D. M. (1978). "Causality Test and Exogeneity Test." Department of Economics, University of Kansas.

Zellner, A. (1958). "A Statistical Analysis of Provisional Estimates of Gross National Product and Its Components, of Selected National Income

Components, and of Personal Saving." *Journal of the American Statistical Association*, 53:54–65.
———. (1970). "The Care and Feeding of Econometric Models." Selected Paper no. 35, Graduate School of Business, University of Chicago.
———. (1971). *An Introduction to Bayesian Inference in Econometrics*. New York: John Wiley & Sons.
———. (1974). "Time Series Analysis and Econometric Model Construction." Invited paper presented at the Conference on Applied Statistics, Dalhousie University, Halifax, Nova Scotia, 1974. In R. P. Gupta, ed., *Applied Statistics*, pp. 373–98. Amsterdam: North-Holland Publishing Co., 1975.
———. (1978). "Estimation of Functions of Population Means and Regression Coefficients Including Structural Coefficients: A Minimum Expected Loss (MELO) Approach." *Journal of Econometrics*, 8:127–58.
———. (1980). "A Note on the Relationship of Minimum Expected Loss (MELO) and Other Structural Coefficient Estimates." *Review of Economics and Statistics*, 62:482–84.
Zellner, A., and F. Palm (1974). "Time Series Analysis and Simultaneous Equation Econometric Models" (paper presented at the Oslo Econometric Society Meeting, 1972). *Journal of Econometrics*, 2:17–54.
———. (1975). "Time Series and Structural Analysis of Monetary Models of the U.S. Economy." *Sankhyā*, Ser. C, 37:12–56.
Zellner, A., and S. B. Park (1979). "Minimum Expected Loss (MELO) Estimators for Functions of Parameters and Structural Coefficients of Econometric Models." *Journal of the American Statistical Association*, 74:185–93.
Zellner, A., and W. Vandaele (1975). "Bayes-Stein Estimators for $\mathcal{K}$-Means, Regression, and Simultaneous Equation Models." In S. E. Fienberg and A. Zellner, eds., *Studies in Bayesian Econometrics and Statistics in Honor of Leonard J. Savage*, pp. 317–43. Amsterdam: North-Holland Publishing Co.

2.2 Time Series Analysis and Econometric Model Construction

1 Introduction

Since the 1920s, econometricians have produced a large number of econometric models. In fact it is probably accurate to state that an econometric model-building industry has emerged. Workers have built models of consuming units, firms, banks, markets, urban economies, transport systems, educational systems, regional economies, national economies, and so on.[1] These modeling efforts have as one objective the production of results that will be useful in understanding the operation of the particular entity being modeled. In the process of achieving understanding, it is, of course, the case that propositions derived from economic theory are often utilized in models. A second objective of most modeling efforts is that of prediction. For example, several models of the U.S. economy are in operation that yield quarterly forecasts of such variables as gross national product, employment, unemployment, the price level, and the like. Third, models are often employed to analyze the probable effects of alternative policies and/or to provide a basis for implementing good control policies. In the case of a model of a national economy, it is important to be able to predict the effects of a proposed tax cut or an increase in government spending. In some cases, experiments with optimal control policies are being studied. Finally, models

Reprinted from *Applied Statistics*, R. P. Gupta, ed. (Amsterdam: North-Holland Publishing Co., 1975), pp. 373–98, with the kind permission of North-Holland Publishing Co.

1. See Nerlove (1966) for a description of early models of national economies. Hickman (1972) provides information regarding properties of several U.S. national models that are currently in operation. In Hamilton et al. (1969), a review of several regional models is provided. Econometric models of various agricultural markets have been developed and reported in technical bulletins of the Agricultural Marketing Service, U.S. Department of Agriculture. Other models have been reported in economic journals including *Econometrica, Journal of Econometrics, International Economic Review, Review of Economics and Statistics, American Economic Review, Journal of Political Economy*, etc. The *Journal of Economic Literature* provides abstracts and listings of papers appearing in a wide range of economic journals.

can be employed in attempts to assess the probable effects of changes in parameter values, lag structures, and so forth, an area that is called "structural analysis." In summary, econometric models can contribute to (*a*) achieving the scientific objective of understanding economic behavior, (*b*) obtaining better predictions and forecasts and (*c*) improving policymakers' attempts to control economic systems so as to achieve better performance.

Whether, econometric models will in the future make more substantial contributions in the areas mentioned above, obviously depends critically on the quality of econometric models. The quality of econometric models depends not only on the state of our economic knowledge and the quality of our data but also on the methodology of econometric model construction. While much progress has been made in mathematical, statistical, and computer methodology, it is the main point of this paper that much more has to be done in order to produce econometric models that are of high quality, that is, that predict reasonably well and that can be used with a reasonable degree of confidence in analyzing policy problems and in obtaining good control policies.

The schematic diagram in chapter 2.1 illustrates some of the activities involved in econometric model construction. With respect to any project, including an econometric modeling project, it is important to develop an initial statement of the project's objectives. A clear-cut statement of objectives will be helpful in planning and executing a project. The next step is a feasibility study to determine whether the project is "doable" given the state of our knowledge, data, methodology, and time, personnel, and budgetary constraints. Also, the feasibility study should appraise alternative approaches for realizing the objectives of a project. If an econometric modeling approach is selected, it will usually be necessary to review past studies relating to the project's objectives and to engage in some preliminary data gathering and analysis. The purpose of these activities is to produce an initial model, M_0 in the diagram. Generally speaking, it is thought that the initial formulation of a model should be as simple as possible but potentially adequate to realize the objectives of the project. Once M_0 has been formulated, it can be subjected to mathematical and computer simulation analysis to determine that it is logically consistent and to establish its properties. In this work, that resembles what an engineer does with a model of a new airplane in wind-tunnel experiments, a model-builder will often use crude estimates of parameters and experiment with alternative functional forms for relationships. In this way, he builds up a familiarity with the properties of M_0. Further, data can be brought to bear on the initial variant M_0 to check that the implications of the model are in agreement with the information in the data. The results of these mathematical analyses, computer simulation experiments, and statistical analyses may suggest that M_0 is deficient in certain respects. On discovering the nature of the deficiencies of M_0, it will be necessary to reformulate M_0 to provide a new variant, denoted M_1 in the diagram. Then M_1 is subjected to mathematical, computer, and statistical analyses to determine if it is an adequate formulation. Often additional "iterations" will be necessary in order to obtain a variant that is satisfactory. In fact, model improvements usually continue to be made even after a model is in operation just as with yearly model improvements in the automobile industry.

In the present paper, attention will be directed toward one part of the modeling problem, namely, that of using data to "check out" the implications of linear dynamic econometric models. The approach, described and applied earlier, involves drawing out the logical implications of a linear dynamic econometric model for the forms and parameter values of processes on individual variables and for the transfer functions associated with the model (see Zellner and Palm 1974, 1975). Given that these implications are clearly set forth, data and statistical methods can be employed to assess whether the implications are consistent with the information in the data. If a model's implications are consistent with the information in the data, then our confidence in the model is enhanced. If, however, a model's implications are not consistent with information in the data, then reformulation is necessary.

In what follows, we shall specify a multiple time series process (MTSP) in section 2. Processes for individual variables, that we call the final equations (FE's), implied by the MTSP will then be derived. Further, it will be shown how a MTSP can be specialized to assume the form of a linear dynamic simultaneous equation model (SEM). The transfer functions (TF's) associated with the SEM will be derived and their relation to the SEM's FE's will be established. Testable implications of the SEM's TF's and FE's will be indicated. In section 3, some illustrative examples will be provided while in section 4 some issues and problems in statistical methodology will be considered. Last, in section 5, some concluding remarks are presented.

2 Analysis of Linear Dynamic Econometric Models

In approaching the problem of constructing a dynamic econometric model, it is possible to incorporate little or much prior information in an initial formulation. In what follows, we shall begin by considering an approach that initially uses relatively little prior information and then proceed to variants that incorporate more prior information. If our data are extensive, are of good quality, and contain much information, then it is possible to rely more on the information in the data and less on prior information in formulating a model. However, when the information in our data is limited, there will generally be a greater dependence on prior information gleaned from economic theory and other sources in formulating a model.

If we are able to specify the observable variables $\mathbf{z}_t' = (z_{1t}, z_{2t}, \ldots, z_{pt})$ that probably appear in a model and are willing to assume that a linear multiple time series model or multivariate autoregressive-moving-average (ARMA) process is an adequate approximation, we can follow Quenouille (1957) and Zellner and Palm (1974) by writing

$$(2.1) \qquad \underset{p\times p}{H(L)}\ \underset{p\times 1}{\mathbf{z}_t} = \underset{p\times p}{\bar{\boldsymbol{\theta}}} + \underset{p\times p}{F(L)}\ \underset{p\times 1}{\mathbf{e}_t} \qquad t = 1,2,\ldots,T$$

as the process that may be generating the $p \times 1$ vector $\mathbf{z}_t$.[2] In (2.1), L denotes a lag operator such that $L^n \mathbf{z}_t \equiv \mathbf{z}_{t-n}$, $\bar{\boldsymbol{\theta}}' = (\bar{\theta}_1, \bar{\theta}_2, \ldots, \bar{\theta}_p)$ is a vector of constants, $\mathbf{e}_t$ is a $p \times 1$ vector of unobservable random errors, and $H(L)$ and $F(L)$ are each $p \times p$ matrix lag operators with elements that are finite polynomials in the lag operator L. That is, $H(L) = \{h_{ij}(L)\}$ and $F(L) = \{f_{ij}(L)\}$, where the typical elements are given by $h_{ij}(L) = \sum_{\ell=0}^{r_{ij}} h_{ij}^{(\ell)} L^\ell$ and $f_{ij}(L) = \sum_{\ell=0}^{q_{ij}} f_{ij}^{(\ell)} L^\ell$, where r_{ij} and q_{ij} denote the degrees of $h_{ij}(L)$ and $f_{ij}(L)$, respectively. With respect to the $p \times 1$ error vector, $\mathbf{e}_t$, it is assumed that

$$(2.2) \qquad \begin{aligned} E\mathbf{e}_t &= \mathbf{0} \\ E\mathbf{e}_t\mathbf{e}_{t'}' &= \delta_{tt'} I_p \end{aligned} \qquad \text{for all} \quad t, t',$$

where $\delta_{tt'}$ is the Kronecker delta and I_p is a $p \times p$ unit matrix. Possible contemporaneous and serial correlations and differing variances of the elements of the error process can be introduced via appropriate specification of the matrix $F(L)$.

If the matrix $F(L)$ has elements of degree zero in L, (2.1) is a pure AR process. If $H(L)$ has all elements of degree zero in L, the process in (2.1) is a pure MA process. When both $H(L)$ and $F(L)$ contain polynomials not all of degree zero, (2.1) represents a mixed ARMA process. In general, if $H(L)$ is invertible, that is $|H(L)| = 0$ has roots with values outside the unit circle, we can multiply both sides of (2.1) by the adjoint matrix $H^*(L)$ associated with $H(L)$ to obtain:

2. In many applications, it may be that the elements of $\mathbf{z}_t$ will be differences of original variables. As Box and Jenkins (1970) point out, differencing will often be useful for inducing stationarity.

$$(2.3a)\qquad |H(L)|\mathbf{z}_t = \boldsymbol{\theta} + H^*(L)F(L)\mathbf{e}_t,$$

where $|H(L)|$ is the determinant of $H(L)$, a polynomial of finite degree in L, and $\boldsymbol{\theta}' = (\theta_1, \theta_2, \ldots, \theta_p)$ is a vector of constant parameters. Explicitly, the equations of the system in (2.3a), that we call the *final equations* (FE's), are given by:

$$(2.3b)\qquad |H(L)|z_{it} = \theta_i + \boldsymbol{\alpha}_i'\mathbf{e}_t, \qquad i = 1,2,\ldots,p,$$

where $\boldsymbol{\alpha}_i'$ denotes the i'th row of $H^*(L)F(L)$. It is seen from (2.3b) that the processes for individual elements of $\mathbf{z}_t$ are in the ARMA form. If there are no common factors in the terms on both sides of (2.3a), then the order and parameters of the AR parts of the processes in (2.3b) should be *identical*, a point that can be checked in empirical analyses. If empirical analyses yield the result that the order and parameters of the AR parts of the FE's are identical, then the vector $\mathbf{z}_t$ may have been generated by the process in (2.1) without any additional restrictions on $H(L)$. If, however, the order and parameters of the AR parts of the FE's are found to be different for different elements of $\mathbf{z}_t$, then it is possible that $H(L)$ has a special form, for example, $H(L)$ might be a triangular or block diagonal matrix. By study of the empirical results for the FE's it may be possible to infer some possible properties of the matrix $H(L)$. In particular, for large systems if $H(L)$ were completely unrestricted, the processes in (2.3a) would have high-order AR parts, an implication that is not in agreement with empirical findings that point to relatively low-order AR parts of FE's for many economic variables.[3] Whether or not it is possible to infer properties of $H(L)$ from empirical findings relating to the FE's, it is important to note that when FEs' forms have been determined from the data and their parameters have been estimated, these equations can be used to generate predictions.

One assumption, usually employed in econometric work, that specializes the forms of the matrices $H(L)$ and $F(L)$, is that some of the variables in $\mathbf{z}_t$ are exogenously determined, that is, generated by processes that are independent of the processes generating the remaining variables. If we partition $\mathbf{z}_t$ as follows, $\mathbf{z}_t' = (\mathbf{y}_t'\mathbf{x}_t')$, where $\mathbf{y}_t$ is a $p_1 \times 1$ vector of endogenous variables and $\mathbf{x}_t$ is a $p_2 \times 1$ vector of exogenous variables, with $p = p_1 + p_2$, then we can write the system in (2.1) as:

$$(2.4)\qquad \begin{bmatrix} H_{11}(L) & H_{12}(L) \\ H_{21}(L) & H_{22}(L) \end{bmatrix} \begin{bmatrix} \mathbf{y}_t \\ \mathbf{x}_t \end{bmatrix} = \begin{bmatrix} \boldsymbol{\theta}_1 \\ \boldsymbol{\theta}_2 \end{bmatrix} + \begin{bmatrix} F_{11}(L) & F_{12}(L) \\ F_{21}(L) & F_{22}(L) \end{bmatrix} \begin{bmatrix} \mathbf{e}_{1t} \\ \mathbf{e}_{2t} \end{bmatrix},$$

3. See Nelson (1972) and Zellner and Palm (1974, 1975) for examples of FE's that have been determined and estimated from quarterly and monthly economic data.

where $H(L)$, $F(L)$, $\bar{\boldsymbol{\theta}}$, and $\mathbf{e}_t$ have been partitioned to correspond to the partitioning of $\mathbf{z}_t$. The assumption that $\mathbf{x}_t$ is exogenous gives rise to the following restrictions:

$$H_{21}(L) \equiv 0;\ F_{12}(L) \equiv 0;\ \text{and } F_{21}(L) \equiv 0. \tag{2.5}$$

With these restrictions imposed on (2.4), we have:

$$\underset{p_1 \times p_1}{H_{11}(L)}\ \underset{p_1 \times 1}{\mathbf{y}_t} + \underset{p_1 \times p_2}{H_{12}(L)}\ \underset{p_2 \times 1}{\mathbf{x}_t} = \underset{p_1 \times 1}{\bar{\boldsymbol{\theta}}_1} + \underset{p_1 \times p_1}{F_{11}(L)}\ \underset{p_1 \times 1}{\mathbf{e}_{1t}} \tag{2.5a}$$

and

$$\underset{p_2 \times p_2}{H_{22}(L)}\ \underset{p_2 \times 1}{\mathbf{x}_t} = \underset{p_2 \times 1}{\bar{\boldsymbol{\theta}}_2} + \underset{p_2 \times p_2}{F_{22}(L)}\ \underset{p_2 \times 1}{\mathbf{e}_{2t}} \tag{2.5b}$$

The equations in (2.5a) are referred to as the *structural equations* while those in (2.5b) are processes generating the random exogenous vector of variables, $\mathbf{x}_t$.[4]

The assumption that $\mathbf{x}_t$ is exogenous, leading to the restrictions in (2.5), has important implications for the forms of the FE's. Given that $H_{22}(L)$ in (2.5b) is invertible, the FE's for the elements of $\mathbf{x}_t$ are:

$$|H_{22}(L)|\mathbf{x}_t = \bar{\bar{\boldsymbol{\theta}}}_2 + H_{22}^*(L)F_{22}(L)\mathbf{e}_{2t}, \tag{2.6}$$

where $|H_{22}(L)|$ and $H_{22}^*(L)$ are the determinant and adjoint matrix of $H_{22}(L)$, respectively. On substituting for $\mathbf{x}_t$ in (2.5a) from (2.6) and multiplying both sides by the adjoint matrix of $H_{11}(L)$, namely, $H_{11}^*(L)$, the FE's for the elements of $\mathbf{y}_t$ are:

$$\begin{aligned} |H_{11}(L)||H_{22}(L)|\mathbf{y}_t = \bar{\bar{\bar{\boldsymbol{\theta}}}}_1 &- H_{11}^*(L)H_{12}(L)H_{22}^*(L)F_{22}(L)\mathbf{e}_{2t} \\ &+ |H_{22}(L)|H_{11}^*(L)F_{11}(L)\mathbf{e}_{1t}, \end{aligned} \tag{2.7}$$

where $\bar{\bar{\bar{\boldsymbol{\theta}}}}_1$ is a vector of constants. On comparing (2.6) and (2.7), it is seen that the FE's for the elements of $\mathbf{y}_t$, the vector of endogenous variables, have AR parts that have orders equal to or greater than those of the FE's for the elements of $\mathbf{x}_t$ given in (2.6). If $|H_{22}(L)|$ is a polynomial of degree zero in L, the AR parts of (2.6) and (2.7) are of the same order. Usually, the order of the AR part of (2.7) will exceed that of (2.6), a point that can be checked empirically. Further the order of the MA errors in (2.7) will usually be larger than those of (2.6), another point that can be checked empirically. Last, if as is usually the case, more is assumed about the elements of $H(L)$ and $F(L)$,

4. If some of the exogenous variables are nonrandom, (2.5b) should be interpreted as relating just to the random exogenous variables.

then the implications of such assumptions for the forms of the FE's can be deduced and checked empirically.

Another set of equations that is important in analyzing econometric and other models is the set of *transfer functions* (TF's).[5] The TF's can be obtained from the structural equations in (2.5a) by multiplying both sides by $H_{11}^*(L)$, the adjoint matrix associated with $H_{11}(L)$. This operation yields the following set of TF's:

$$(2.8) \qquad |H_{11}(L)|\mathbf{y}_t = \boldsymbol{\theta}_1^* - H_{11}^*(L)H_{12}(L)\mathbf{x}_t + H_{11}^*(L)F_{11}(L)\mathbf{e}_{1t}.$$

As Pierce and Mason have noted, the AR parts of the TF's, $|H_{11}(L)|y_{it}$, $i = 1,2,\ldots,p_1$, are of the same order and have identical parameters if no cancelling occurs in (2.8), a point that can be checked empirically. On the other hand, should $H_{11}(L)$ be given a particular structure (for example, it might be assumed block-diagonal), then the AR parts of (2.8) could differ. By using data to investigate the forms of the TF's, it is possible to check the empirical implications of specific assumptions regarding the form of $H_{11}(L)$. In addition, assumptions regarding $H_{11}(L)$, $H_{12}(L)$, and $F_{11}(L)$ generally imply testable propositions about the lags and parameter values in the terms of (2.8) involving current and lagged elements of $\mathbf{x}_t$ and $\mathbf{e}_{1t}$.

Given that data have been employed to determine the forms of the FE's for the elements of $\mathbf{x}_t$ in (2.6) and the TF's in (2.8), it is possible to substitute the estimated FE's for $\mathbf{x}_t$ in (2.8) to obtain the implied FE's for the elements of $\mathbf{y}_t$. These can be compared with the FE's for the elements of $\mathbf{y}_t$ determined directly from the data. If the two sets of results are in agreement, this provides a further consistency check on results. If, however, some of the elements of $\mathbf{x}_t$ are not exogenous or some other specification errors are present, it is probable that the two sets of results for the FE's for elements of $\mathbf{y}_t$ will not be compatible.

Given that the results of FE and TF analyses are compatible with what has been assumed about the matrices $H(L)$ and $F(L)$ in (2.1) and other assumptions and if sufficient identifying information is present, the parameters of the structural equations in (2.5a) can be estimated.[6] Given that the structural equations are available, they can be used for analyzing the possible effects of changes in structural parameters a problem that cannot generally be analyzed with just FE's and/or TF's. However, these latter equation systems are extremely valuable in the process of checking the implications of given

5. For a valuable discussion of transfer functions, see Box and Jenkins (1970) and Pierce and Mason (1971).

6. Hannan (1971) has provided results relating to the identification of parameters of linear dynamic structural equations with moving-average error terms.

structural equations against the information in the data. That is, since the forms of FE's and TF's can often be determined from information in the data, these empirical results can play an important role in ruling out many variants of the structural equations, an important consideration in efforts to formulate structural equations that are consistent with the information in a set of data. Last, while the role of the FE's and TF's in model building has been emphasized, their uses in approaching the problems of prediction and control should not be overlooked.

3 Examples Illustrating General Approach

In this section we present some examples illustrating the general points made in the preceding section. In this connection, it should be remarked that very few econometricians emphasize or are aware of the implications of linear dynamic structural equations for TF's and FE's. In fact, many econometricians view the ARMA FE's as being naive, alternative, mechanical models.[7] Thus it is thought useful to analyze some special cases to illustrate the points made in section 2.

The first example that we analyze is a supply and demand model constructed to explain the variation in the daily price (P_t) and quantity (Q_t) of hogs at eight large terminal markets in the U.S.[8] The two relations in the model, a demand equation and a supply equation are shown below:

Demand Equation:

$$(3.1)\quad \Delta\log P_t = \beta_{10t} + \beta_{11}\Delta\log Q_t + \beta_{12}\Delta\log Q_{t-1} + \beta_{13}\Delta\log Q_{t-2} + \beta_{14}\Delta\log Wh_{t-1} + u_{1t} \qquad t = 1,2,\ldots,T$$

Supply Equation:

$$(3.2)\quad \Delta\log Q_t = \beta_{20t} + \beta_{21}\Delta\log P_{t-1} + u_{2t} \qquad t = 1,2,\ldots,T$$

where

P_t = average price in \$/hundred wt. of all barrows and gilts sold.

Q_t = total number of head of barrows and gilts sold on day t.

Wh_{t-1} = price of output on day $t-1$ measured as a weighted average of the prices of major wholesale pork cuts in \$/hundred wt. at Chicago.

u_{1t}, u_{2t} = error terms.

β_{10t}, β_{20t} = intercept terms plus dummy variables for different days of the week in both relations and a seasonal dummy in the supply relation.

7. See, e.g., the discussion of Cooper's paper in Hickman (1972) and Nelson (1972).

8. The model considered was formulated and estimated by Leuthold et al. (1970).

The two endogenous variables in (3.1)–(3.2) are $\Delta\log P_t$ and $\Delta\log Q_t$. If we write $\mathbf{y}_t' = (y_{1t}, y_{2t}) = (\Delta\log P_t, \Delta\log Q_t)$, we can express (3.1)–(3.2) as

$$(3.3) \quad \begin{bmatrix} 1 & -\beta_1(L) \\ -\beta_2(L) & 1 \end{bmatrix} \begin{bmatrix} y_{1t} \\ y_{2t} \end{bmatrix} = \begin{bmatrix} \beta_{10t} \\ \beta_{20t} \end{bmatrix} + \begin{bmatrix} \beta_{14} \\ 0 \end{bmatrix} x_t + \begin{bmatrix} u_{1t} \\ u_{2t} \end{bmatrix},$$

where $x_t = \Delta\log Wh_{t-1}$ is assumed exogenous, $\beta_1(L) = \beta_{11} + \beta_{12}L + \beta_{13}L^2$ and $\beta_2(L) = \beta_{21}L$. The determinant and adjoint matrix of the matrix lag operator on the l.h.s. of (3.3) are $1 - \beta_1(L)\beta_2(L)$, a third degree polynomial in L, and

$$\text{Adj} \begin{bmatrix} 1 & -\beta_1(L) \\ -\beta_2(L) & 1 \end{bmatrix} = \begin{bmatrix} 1 & \beta_1(L) \\ \beta_2(L) & 1 \end{bmatrix},$$

respectively. Thus the TF's associated with (3.3) are:

$$(3.4a) \quad [1 - \beta_1(L)\beta_2(L)]y_{1t} = \beta_{10t} + \beta_1(L)\beta_{20t} + \beta_{14}x_t + u_{1t} + \beta_1(L)u_{2t}$$

$$(3.4b) \quad [1 - \beta_1(L)\beta_2(L)]y_{2t} = \beta_{20t} + \beta_2(L)\beta_{10t} + \beta_{14}\beta_2(L)x_t + u_{2t} + \beta_2(L)u_{1t}.$$

It is seen that the AR parts of the TF's are identical, each of order 3. Further in (3.4b), the lag polynomial hitting $x_t = \Delta\log Wh_{t-1}$ is of degree one while in (3.4a) x_t appears with no lag. If u_{1t} and u_{2t} are assumed nonautocorrelated, the error in (3.4a) is in the form of a second-order MA process while that in (3.4b) is in the form of a first-order MA process. These are some of the testable implications of the structural equations in (3.3) that can be checked by analyzing the TF system in (3.4). In addition, if the process generating x_t is assumed to be

$$(3.5) \quad \emptyset_a(L)x_t = \theta_o + \theta_b(L)\epsilon_t \qquad t = 1, 2, \ldots, T$$

where $\emptyset_a(L)$ and $\theta_b(L)$ denote finite lag polynomials of degrees a and b, respectively, ϵ_t is a nonautocorrelated error with zero mean and constant finite variance, and θ_o is a constant and if $\emptyset_a(L)$ is invertible, we have $x_t = \theta_o' + \emptyset_a^{-1}(L)\theta_b(L)\epsilon_t$. If we substitute this last expression into (3.4), we obtain the following FE's for y_{1t} and y_{2t}:

$$(3.6a) \quad \emptyset_a(L)[1 - \beta_1(L)\beta_2(L)]y_{1t} = \theta_o'' + \emptyset_a(L)[\beta_{10t} + \beta_1(L)\beta_{20t}] + \beta_{14}\theta_b(L)\epsilon_t + \emptyset_a(L)u_{1t} + \emptyset_a(L)\beta_1(L)u_{2t}$$

$$(3.6b) \quad \emptyset_a(L)[1 - \beta_1(L)\beta_2(L)]y_{2t} = \theta_o''' + \emptyset_a(L)[\beta_{20t} + \beta_2(L)\beta_{10t}] + \beta_{14}\beta_2(L)\theta_b(L)\epsilon_t + \emptyset_a(L)u_{2t} + \emptyset_a(L)\beta_2(L)u_{1t}.$$

In table 1 the degrees of the lag polynomials appearing in (3.6a–b) are indicated. From the information in table 1, we see that the AR parts of both (3.6a) and (3.6b) are of order $3 + a$, with $a \geq 0$. The error terms of (3.6a) are in a MA form with order equal to $\max\{b, 2 + a\}$ while the order of the MA errors in (3.6b) is equal to $\max\{2 + b, 1 + a\}$. Thus, if the econometric model in (3.1)–(3.2) is correctly specified, the final equations in (3.6) should exhibit AR parts of order $3 + a$, $a \geq 0$, and autocorrelated MA error terms.

It is interesting to note that the workers who formulated and estimated the model in (3.1)–(3.2) analyzed the data for daily prices using Box-Jenkins techniques to identify the underlying process. Their analysis yielded the result that daily price in the eight markets studied follows a random walk, $P_t = P_{t-1} + \eta_t$, a result which they failed to note is apparently in conflict with the implications of their econometric model, in particular equation (3.6a) above. Moreover, the model that they determined for quantity, Q_t, using Box-Jenkins techniques is:

$$(3.7) \qquad (1 - 0.90L^5)(1 - 1.44L + 0.47L^2)Q_t = (1 - 0.70L^5)(1 - 1.52L + .66L^2)a_t,$$

where a_t is a nonautocorrelated error term with zero mean and constant variance. The finding in (3.7) coupled with the finding of a random walk for price seems at variance with the implications of the econometric model in (3.1)–(3.2), particularly those shown in table 1. It is possible that reformulation of (3.1)–(3.2) could result in FE's and TF's in accord with the information in the data.

In concluding discussion of this published example, it is important to note that econometric analysis and time series analysis are viewed as alternative approaches for analyzing data by many econometricians at present. However, from what has been presented above, it is clear that it is possible to synthesize the econometric and time series approaches, a synthesis that provides a number of new ways to check the implications of structural econometric models, to discover errors in model formulation, and to suggest ways in which a model's formulation can be improved.

Table 1 Degrees of Lag Polynomials in (3.5)–(3.6)

		Polynomial for:		
Equation	AR Polynomial	ϵ_t	u_{1t}	u_{2t}
(3.5)	a	b	—	—
(3.6a)	$3+a$	b	a	$2+a$
(3.6b)	$3+a$	$2+b$	$1+a$	a

NOTE: It is assumed that u_{1t}, u_{2t}, and ϵ_t are serially uncorrelated. Thus the degrees of the error term polynomials shown in the table are lower bounds given no cancelling.

The second example that we take up is the analysis of a simple monetary model formulated along lines suggested by Friedman.[9] The equations of the model are:

(3.8)	Money Demand:	$Y_t = Ae^{\gamma_1 i_t} M_t^D$	$A, \gamma_1 > 0$
(3.9)	Money Supply:	$M_t^S = Be^{\gamma_2 i_t} H_t$	$B, \gamma_2 > 0$
(3.10)	Market Clearing:	$M_t^D = M_t^S = M_t$	
(3.11)	Fisher Equation:	$i_t = c_t + r_{Yt}^*$	
(3.12)	Anticipations Equation:	$r_{Yt}^* - r_{Yt-1}^* = \beta(r_{Yt-1} - r_{Yt-1}^*)$	$\beta > 0$

The money demand equation (3.8) links nominal money demanded M_t^D to nominal income Y_t and the nominal interest rate i_t. The money supply equation (3.9) relates money supply M_t^S to the nominal interest rate i_t and "high-powered" money, H_t. Equation (3.10) states that the variables adjust to equate M_t^D and M_t^S to the observed money supply M_t. The Fisher equation relates the nominal interest rate i_t to the anticipated proportionate rate of change of nominal income, $r_{Yt}^* = \log Y_t^* - \log Y_{t-1}^*$, where Y_t^* is the anticipated value of nominal income for period t as of period $t-1$. The quantity $c_t = \rho_t - q_t^*$, the real rate of interest ρ_t minus the anticipated proportionate rate of growth of real income. Initially it is assumed that $c_t = c$, a constant. Last, equation (3.12) is a widely used assumption about how anticipations are formed wherein r_{Yt-1} is the actual proportionate rate of growth of nominal income in period $t-1$.

In (3.8)–(3.12), M_t^D, M_t^S, r_{Yt}^*, and r_{Yt-1}^* are not measured in our data. Thus we substitute from (3.10) in (3.8) and (3.9), take the logs of both sides, and first difference the resulting equations and (3.11) to obtain:

$$r_{Yt} = \gamma_1 \Delta i_t + r_{Mt} \tag{3.13}$$

$$r_{Mt} = \gamma_2 \Delta i_t + r_{Ht} \tag{3.14}$$

$$\Delta i_t = \Delta r_{Yt}^* \tag{3.15}$$

$$\Delta r_{Yt}^* = \beta(r_{Yt-1} - r_{Yt-1}^*), \tag{3.16}$$

where $\Delta \equiv 1 - L$, $r_{Yt} = \Delta \log Y_t$, $r_{Mt} = \Delta \log M_t$, and $r_{Ht} = \Delta \log H_t$. Since (3.16) can be expressed as $[1-(1-\beta)L]r_{Yt}^* = \beta L r_{Yt}$, we have $[1-(1-\beta)L]\Delta r_{Yt}^* = \beta L \Delta r_{Yt}$. Then using $\Delta i_t = \Delta r_{Yt}^*$, from (3.15), we can replace (3.15) and (3.16) by

$$[1-(1-\beta)L]\Delta i_t = \beta L \Delta r_{Yt}. \tag{3.17}$$

9. See Friedman (1970, 1971). This model and several variants of it have been analyzed using monthly data for the U.S. in Zellner and Palm (1974).

Thus the three equations of the model involving the three observable endogenous variables r_{Yt}, Δi_t, and r_{Mt} and the observable exogenous variable r_{Ht} are given by (3.13), (3.14), and (3.17). We can express these three equations, with error terms added, as follows:

$$\text{(3.18a)} \quad \begin{bmatrix} 1 & -1 & -\gamma_1 \\ 0 & 1 & -\gamma_2 \\ -\beta L(1-L) & 0 & 1-(1-\beta)L \end{bmatrix} \begin{bmatrix} r_{Yt} \\ r_{Mt} \\ \Delta i_t \end{bmatrix} = \begin{bmatrix} 0 \\ 1 \\ 0 \end{bmatrix} r_{Ht} + \begin{bmatrix} u_{1t} \\ u_{2t} \\ u_{3t} \end{bmatrix},$$

or in more general form,

$$\text{(3.18b)} \qquad H_{11}\mathbf{y}_t = \boldsymbol{\alpha} r_{Ht} + \mathbf{u}_t,$$

where H_{11} denotes the matrix on the l.h.s. of (3.18a), $\mathbf{y}_t' = (r_{Yt}, r_{Mt}, \Delta i_t)$, $\boldsymbol{\alpha}' = (0,1,0)$, and $\mathbf{u}_t' = (u_{1t}, u_{2t}, u_{3t})$, a vector of error terms.

The TF's associated with (3.18) are obtained by premultiplying (3.18) by the adjoint matrix H_{11}^* associated with H_{11}, namely,

$$\text{(3.19)} \qquad |H_{11}|\mathbf{y}_t = H_{11}^*\boldsymbol{\alpha} r_{Ht} + H_{11}^*\mathbf{u}_t,$$

where $|H_{11}| = 1-(1-\beta)L - \beta(\gamma_1+\gamma_2)L(1-L)$, a second-degree polynomial in L, and

$$\text{(3.20)} \quad H_{11}^* = \begin{bmatrix} 1-(1-\beta)L & 1-(1-\beta)L & \gamma_1+\gamma_2 \\ \gamma_2\beta L(1-L) & 1-(1-\beta)L-\gamma_1\beta L(1-L) & \gamma_2 \\ \beta L(1-L) & \beta L(1-L) & 1 \end{bmatrix}.$$

Explicitly, the TF system in (3.19) is:

$$\text{(3.21a)} \quad [1-(1-\beta)L - \beta(\gamma_1+\gamma_2)L(1-L)] \begin{bmatrix} r_{Yt} \\ r_{Mt} \\ \Delta i_t \end{bmatrix} = \begin{bmatrix} 1-(1-\beta)L \\ 1-(1-\beta)L - \gamma_1\beta L(1-L) \\ \beta L(1-L) \end{bmatrix} r_{Ht} + \begin{bmatrix} v_{1t} \\ v_{2t} \\ v_{3t} \end{bmatrix}$$

with $\mathbf{v}_t = H_{11}^*\mathbf{u}_t$, where $\mathbf{v}_t' = (v_{1t}, v_{2t}, v_{3t})$.

On examination of the l.h.s. of (3.21), it is seen that the structural equations of the monetary model imply that the three TF's have AR parts of order two with identical parameters. In addition, the implied lags on r_{Ht}, the rate of growth of high-powered money, in the TF's are shown below:

TF for	Order of Lag on r_{Ht}
r_{Yt}	1
r_{Mt}	2
Δi_t	2

It should also be noted that (3.21a) involves some additional strong restrictions on the parameters of the TF's that can be appreciated by rewriting (3.21a) as

$$\text{(3.21b)}\quad [1-(1-\beta+\eta)L + \eta L^2]\begin{bmatrix} r_{Yt} \\ r_{Mt} \\ \Delta i_t \end{bmatrix} = \begin{bmatrix} 1-(1-\beta)L \\ 1-(1-\beta+\eta_1) L + \eta_1 L^2 \\ \beta L - \beta L^2 \end{bmatrix} r_{Ht} + \begin{bmatrix} v_{1t} \\ v_{2t} \\ v_{3t} \end{bmatrix},$$

where $\eta = (\gamma_1 + \gamma_2)\beta$ and $\eta_1 = \gamma_1\beta$. The following are the restrictions on the parameters of (3.21b):

(i) The sum of the coefficients of r_{Yt-1} and r_{Yt-2} equals the coefficient of r_{Ht-1} in the TF for r_{Yt}.

(ii) The coefficient of r_{Ht} should equal one in the TF for r_{Yt} and r_{Mt} and be equal to zero in the TF for Δi_t.

(iii) In each of the three TF's, the sum of the AR parameters is equal to β, the coefficient of $r_{Ht-1} - r_{Ht-2}$ in the TF for Δi_t.

(iv) In the TF for Δi_t, the sum of the coefficients of r_{Ht-1} and r_{Ht-2} is zero.

(v) The sum of the coefficients of r_{Ht-1} and r_{Ht-2} in the TF for r_{Mt} equals the coefficient of r_{Ht-1} in the TF for r_{Yt}.

Given data on the variables and assumptions regarding the error terms, the above restrictions can be tested.

With respect to the error vector $\mathbf{v}_t$ in (3.21), given by $\mathbf{v}_t = H_{11}^* \mathbf{u}_t$, it is the case that assumptions about the properties of $\mathbf{u}_t$ imply testable implications about the properties of $\mathbf{v}_t$. For example, if $\mathbf{u}_t$ is assumed to be serially uncorrelated, then the elements of $\mathbf{v}_t$, given by

$$\text{(3.22)}\quad \mathbf{v}_t = \begin{bmatrix} v_{1t} \\ v_{2t} \\ v_{3t} \end{bmatrix} = \begin{pmatrix} [1-(1-\beta)L]u_{1t} + [1-(1-\beta)Lu_{2t} + (\gamma_1+\gamma_2)u_{3t} \\ \gamma_2\beta L(1-L)u_{1t} + [1-(1-\beta)L - \gamma_1\beta L(1-L)]u_{2t} + \gamma_2 u_{3t} \\ \beta L(1-L)u_{1t} + \beta L(1-L)u_{2t} + u_{3t} \end{pmatrix},$$

will be autocorrelated. In fact, under the assumption that the u_{it}'s are serially uncorrelated, the MA processes on the v_{it}'s will have the following properties given that $\gamma_1, \gamma_2 \neq 0$ and $0 < |\beta| < 1$:

Error Term	Order of MA Process
v_{1t}	1
v_{2t}	2
v_{3t}	2

In empirical analyses, these implications regarding the orders of the MA error processes, that are lower bounds, can be tested empirically.

If the process for r_{Ht} is given by

$$\emptyset_p(L)r_{Ht} = \theta_q(L)u_{4t}, \tag{3.23}$$

where $\emptyset_p(L)$ and $\theta_q(L)$ are polynomials in L of finite degrees, p and q, respectively, and u_{4t} is a nonautocorrelated error term with zero mean, and constant variance, that is distributed independently of the structural error terms, we can determine properties of (3.23), including the values of p and q, from analysis of data on r_{Ht}. Further, if we premultiply the TF system in (3.21a) by $\emptyset_p(L)$ and substitute $\emptyset_p(L)r_{Ht} = \theta_q(L)u_{4t}$ from (3.23) we obtain the following FE's:

$$|H_{11}(L)|\emptyset_p(L)\begin{bmatrix} r_{Yt} \\ r_{Mt} \\ \Delta i_t \end{bmatrix} = \begin{bmatrix} 1-(1-\beta)L \\ 1-(1-\beta)L \\ \quad -\gamma_1\beta L(1-L) \\ \beta L(1-L) \end{bmatrix} \begin{matrix} \theta_q(L)u_{4t} \\ +\emptyset_p(L) \end{matrix} \begin{bmatrix} v_{1t} \\ v_{2t} \\ v_{3t} \end{bmatrix}, \tag{3.24}$$

where $|H_{11}(L)| = 1-(1-\beta)L-\beta(\gamma_1+\gamma_2)L(1-L)$. It is seen that the AR parts of (3.24) are identical. Further properties of the FE's are indicated in table 2.

Given that we determine the forms of the FE's and estimate them, it is possible to check whether the information in a sample of data is consistent with the implications of the model. If inconsistencies are encountered, the structural equations can be reformulated as shown in Zellner and Palm (1975). For example, the assumption of unitary income elasticity of real balances can be relaxed. Anticipations can be modeled in accord with Muth's rational expectations hypothesis, etc.

Empirical analyses of monthly data for the U.S., 1953–72, led to the following findings using large-sample likelihood ratio tests and Box-Jenkins techniques to discriminate among alternative ARMA processes.

Table 2 Selected Properties of FE's in (3.23)–(3.24)

Variable	Order of AR	Order of MA Error[a]
r_{Yt}	$2+p$	$\max(1+q,\ p+n_1)$
r_{Mt}	$2+p$	$\max(2+q,\ p+n_2)$
Δi_t	$2+p$	$\max(2+q,\ p+n_3)$
r_{Ht}	p	q

[a] n_i, $i=1,2,3$, denotes the order of the MA process for v_{it}, $i=1,2,3$, respectively. Since, as shown above, the $n_i>0$, $i=1,2,3$, the orders of the MA errors in the FE's are bounded from below.

Table 3 Empirical Findings for Final Equations

	Period of Analysis		
Variable[a]	1953–72	1953–62	1963–72
i_t: (3MTB)	(2,1,3) or (3,1,3)	(2,1,3) or (3,1,3)	(2,1,3) or (3,1,3)
i_t: (4–6MPCP)	(2,1,3) or (3,1,2)	(2,1,3) or (3,1,2)	(2,1,3) or (3,1,2)
$\ell n\ M_{1t}$	(3,1,3)	(2,1,2) or (3,1,3)	(2,1,3) or (3,1,3)
$\ell n\ Y_t$	(0,1,4)	(0,1,4)	(0,1,4)
$\ell n\ H_t$	(0,1,0)	(0,1,0) or (2,1,0)	(0,1,0)

NOTE: Entries in the table in the form (p,d,q) denote a pth order AR and qth order MA process for the dth difference of a variable, notation employed by Box and Jenkins.

[a]3MTB ≡ 3 month Treasury Bill interest rate

4–6MPCP ≡ 4–6 month Prime Commercial Paper interest rate

M_{1t} ≡ currency plus demand deposits

Y_t ≡ personal income

H_t ≡ high-powered money

It is seen from table 3 that the processes identified from 240 monthly observations, 1953–72, are all relatively low-order schemes. In fact, that for $\ell n\ H_t$ is a random walk. Also, the identification of processes for the sub-periods 1953–62 and 1963–72 produced results not far different from those obtained for the full period 1953–72.

Upon comparing the empirical results in table 3 for the 1953–72 period with the model's implications set forth in table 2, the empirical finding for $\ell n\ H_t$, a (0, 1, 0) process indicates that $p = 0$ and $q = 0$ in table 2. Given $p = 0$, the model implies that the AR parts of the FE's for i_t, $\ell n\ M_t$, and $\ell n\ Y_t$ should all be second order (see table 2). The empirical findings in table 3 contradict this implication in that the AR part of the FE for $\Delta \ell n\ Y_t = r_{yt}$ is of zero'th order, that for $\Delta \ell n\ M_{1t} = r_{M_{1}t}$ is of order 3 and that for Δi_t is of order 2 or 3. Since these empirical results are not in accord with the model's implications, other variants of the model were formulated and checked against the empirical findings for FE's. A reasonable variant of the structural model that is consistent with the properties of the empirically determined FE's has been formulated. (see Zellner and Palm 1975). Its TF's are currently being analyzed.

4 Issues and Problems in Statistical Methodology

The issues and problems of statistical methodology that arise in the present context are similar to those arising in many other contexts although here time series considerations are central. With respect to formulation of an initial model, it is the case that subject matter knowledge, data availability, and the objectives of a model builder will be important. Also, the availability of mathematical, computer, and statistical techniques often conditions the formulation of an initial variant of a model. Given that an initial variant of a structural model has been formulated, its FE's and TF's can be derived. Statistical problems arise in checking whether the implied FE's, TF's, and other assumed properties of the structural equations are consistent with the information in the data. This range of issues has been called the problem of model identification by Box and Jenkins. Given that a model has been identified, problems of parameter identification, estimation, and prediction arise. Below a brief review of some aspects of these problems in relation to the procedures described in section 2 is provided.

4.1 Identification of Models

As mentioned above, the problem of identifying models from the data is an important part of model construction. In connection with FE's, we have employed estimated autocorrelation and partial autocorrelation functions in the well-known manner suggested by Box and Jenkins (1970). These procedures have been very helpful in determining forms of individual FE's. While useful, the Box-Jenkins procedures are somewhat informal. To be more formal, we have employed large-sample likelihood ratio tests to discriminate among nested models. That is, given alternative values of p, d, and q, one can formulate associated likelihood functions, evaluate them at maximum likelihood estimates, and form $2 \ell n\lambda$, where λ is the ratio of maximized likelihood functions, that will have a large sample χ^2 distribution. As shown earlier, this procedure is quite operational.[10] However, it is a large-sample procedure that works just for nested pairs of FE's. To handle the problem of both nested and nonnested FE's, we have suggested the use of large-sample approximate Bayesian posterior odds ratios using an approach essentially similar to that put forward by Jeffreys and Lindley for approximating posterior odds ratios.[11] Further, it may be that spectral techniques can also be useful in identifying individual FE's.

Since error terms in different FE's are generally not independent, it would be desirable to have multivariate identification procedures for the set of FE's. This is somewhat complicated since the range of alternative models is often broad. However, work is in progress to get large-sample likelihood ratio tests and approximate Bayesian posterior odds ratios relating to sets of FE's.

As regards identification of individual TF's, the Box-Jenkins suggested

10. Large-sample likelihood ratio tests have been employed in Zellner and Palm (1974, 1975) to aid in identifying FE's and TF's.

11. See Jeffreys (1967), Lindley (1961), Palm (1973), and Zellner and Palm (1974).

procedures have not been too helpful in our work. We have employed large-sample likelihood ratio tests and indicated how to obtain large-sample approximate posterior odds ratios. As with the FE's, multivariate generalizations of these procedures would be extremely valuable.

With respect to the structural equations, it may be that some of the identification procedures suggested by Quenouille (1957) and Tse (1973) that utilize estimated serial correlation matrices will be found helpful. In addition, multivariate spectral techniques may be useful. To date, we have little information about the application and fruitfulness of these methods for identifying structural equation systems or classes of structural equation systems that are consistent with the information in a set of data.[12]

4.2 Estimation of Equation Systems

In the process of identifying FE's and TF's using large-sample likelihood ratio tests or Bayesian posterior odds ratios, parameter estimates are needed. Furthermore, investigators are usually interested in inferring the values of parameters appearing in FE's, TF's, and structural equations. Thus there is a need for good procedures for estimating the values of parameters appearing in these equation systems. To date work has been concentrated on obtaining estimates that have good large-sample properties, either by sampling theory or Bayesian procedures. In large samples, it should be appreciated that maximum likelihood estimates are generally good approximations to Bayesian posterior means for any nondogmatic prior distribution for the parameters. Thus, as Jeffreys has pointed out, maximum likelihood estimates have a large-sample Bayesian justification relative to quadratic loss functions. Some work on estimating parameters of time series models employing "diffuse" and "informative" prior distributions for the parameters has appeared in the literature.[13] At present, we shall briefly review some operational large sample methods that we have employed in our past work and that we are developing.

With respect to individual FE's and individual TF's, we have been employing the Box-Jenkins (1970) nonlinear least squares approach to estimate parameters' values. In their approach, which they have given a Bayesian interpretation, the nonlinear least squares problem is solved using Marquardt's algorithm.[14] In using this approach, we have found that it is necessary to be parsimonious with respect to introducing parameters. When "too

12. As Quenouille (1957) pointed out, different structural equation systems can have identical associated serial correlation matrices.

13. See, e.g., Box and Jenkins (1970), Newbold (1973), Shiller (1973), and Zellner (1971).

14. We have employed a computer program developed by C. R. Nelson and S. Beveridge, Graduate School of Business, University of Chicago.

many" parameters are employed, the likelihood function is often found to be rather flat and imprecise parameter estimates are obtained. Regarding TF's, use of "too many" input variables can cause similar problems.

Just as with sets of "seemingly unrelated" regression equations with correlated error terms, it is possible to get improvements in the efficiency of estimation by joint estimation of a set of FE's or a set of TF's.[15] The approach that we (Palm and Zellner 1980, 1981) developed for estimating sets of FE's involves the following steps: (1) Estimate each equation using the Box-Jenkins procedure and obtain estimates of the error terms, the residuals; (2) use the residuals so obtained to get a consistent estimate of the contemporaneous variance-covariance matrix of the error terms, denoted by $\hat{\Sigma}$; (3) insert lagged residuals in place of lagged error terms; and (4) apply generalized least squares, based on $\Sigma = \hat{\Sigma}$, to obtain estimates of the AR and MA parameters in the same way that "seemingly unrelated" regression coefficient estimates are obtained. Step (4) is a linear operation that can be performed readily using existing computer programs. A similar approach is being developed for application to estimation of sets of TF's. Since part (4) of the procedure involves work with a linear system, estimation with linear restrictions cutting across equations can be readily performed. Also, large-sample tests of linear hypotheses can be carried through as with regression systems. That it is possible to test linear hypotheses cutting across equations and to impose linear restrictions across equations is important since, as shown above, FE's and TF's associated with structural models will often have identical AR parameters.

Estimation of parameters in the structural equations is possible if the structural parameters are identified. Hannan (1971) has provided identification conditions for parameters of AR structural equations with MA error terms. Given that these conditions are met, parameters of individual structural equations can be estimated consistently by an approach described and applied in recent work (see Zellner and Palm 1974). This approach is currently being extended to provide an operational method for jointly estimating parameters in a set of structural equations that resembles in broad outline the three-stage least squares estimation technique.

4.3 Problems of Prediction

How one obtains predictions depends on which equation systems have been satisfactorily identified. First, if just the FE's have been identified, they

15. "Seemingly unrelated" regression systems have been considered in Zellner (1962, 1963), Zellner and Huang (1962), Telser (1964), and Parks (1967) from the sampling theory point of view and in Tiao and Zellner (1965), Zellner (1971), and Box and Tiao (1973) from the Bayesian point of view.

can be used to generate predictions of the future values of variables. Second, if TF's have been identified, they too can be used to obtain predictions given values of the input variables (the elements of $\mathbf{x}_t$) in future periods. When input variables' values in future periods are not known, it will be necessary to predict them using the FE's for the input variables or outside information. Third, if the structural equations' forms have been determined and estimated, it is possible to derive the associated FE's and TF's from the *estimated* structural equations that we refer to as the restricted FE's (RFE's) and restricted TF's (RTF's). The RFE's and RTF's can be employed to generate predictions. Further work is needed to appraise the relative properties of predictions yielded by the procedures indicated above.[16]

5 Concluding Remarks

Elements of an approach to econometric model-building have been described above. It is recognized that many problems that arise in model-building have not been considered, for example, missing and poor data, nonlinearities, seasonality, possible changes in parameters' values, aggregation problems, etc. While much could be said about each of these problems, it was thought worthwhile to abstract from them in this paper. In terms of what has been presented, further work on methods of model identification, estimation, and prediction would be valuable. Experience in applying the modeling approach described above to actual problems and assessing the quality of the resulting models in various dimensions is beginning to accumulate.

References

Box, G. E. P., and G. M. Jenkins (1970). *Time Series Analysis, Forecasting, and Control*. San Francisco: Holden-Day.

Box, G. E. P., and G. C. Tiao (1973). *Bayesian Inference in Statistical Analysis*. Reading, Mass.: Addison-Wesley Publishing Co.

Dhrymes, P. J. (1973). "Restricted and Unrestricted Reduced Forms: Asymptotic Distribution and Relative Efficiency." *Econometrica*, 41:119–34.

Friedman, M. (1970). "A Theoretical Framework for Monetary Analysis." *Journal of Political Economy*. 78:193–238.

16. See Dhrymes (1973) for an interesting analysis of large-sample properties of predictions yielded by "restricted" and "unrestricted" equation systems. McCarthy (1972) presents some finite sample results relating to "restricted" predictors for a static simultaneous equation model.

———. (1971). "A Monetary Theory of Nominal Income." *Journal of Political Economy*. 79:323–37.

Hamilton, H. R., S. E. Goldstone, J. W. Milliman, A. L. Pugh III, E. R. Roberts, and A. Zellner (1969). *Systems Simulation for Regional Analysis: An Application to River-Basin Planning*. Cambridge, Mass.: MIT Press.

Hannan, E. J. (1971). "The Identification Problem for Multiple Equation Systems with Moving Average Error Terms." *Econometrica*, 39:715–65.

Hickman, G. B., ed. (1972). *Econometric Models of Cyclical Behavior*. 2 vols. New York: National Bureau of Economic Research.

Jeffreys, H. (1967). *Theory of Probability*. 3d rev. ed. London: Clarendon Press.

Leuthold, R. M., A. J. A. MacCormick, A. Schmitz, and D. G. Watts (1970). "Forecasting Daily Hog Prices and Quantities: A Study of Alternative Forecasting Techniques." *Journal of the American Statistical Association*, 65:90–107.

Lindley, D. V. (1961). "The Use of Prior Probability Distributions in Statistical Inference and Decisions." In J. Neyman, ed., *Proceedings of the Fourth Berkeley Symposium on Mathematical Statistics and Probability*, 1:453–68. Berkeley: University of California.

McCarthy, M. D. (1972). "A Note on the Forecasting Properties of Two Stage Least Squares Restricted Reduced Forms—The Finite Sample Case." *International Economic Review*, 13:757–61.

Nelson, C. R. (1972). "The Predictive Performance of the FRB-MIT-Penn Model of the U.S. Economy." *American Economic Review*, 62:902–17.

Nerlove, M. (1966). "A Tabular Survey of Macro-Econometric Models." *International Economic Review*, 7:127–75.

Newbold, P. (1973). "Bayesian Estimation of Box-Jenkins Transfer Function-Noise Models." *Journal of the Royal Statistical Society*, Ser. B, 35:323–36.

Palm, F. (1973). "On the Bayesian Approach to Comparing and Testing Hypotheses When 'Knowing Little,'" H. G. B. Alexander Research Foundation, Graduate School of Business, University of Chicago.

Palm, F., and A. Zellner (1980). "Large Sample Estimation and Testing Procedures for Dynamic Equation Systems." *Journal of Econometrics*, 12:251–83.

———. (1981). "Rejoinder: Large Sample Estimation and Testing Procedures for Dynamic Equation Systems." *Journal of Econometrics*, 17:131–38.

Parks, R. W. (1967). "Efficient Estimation of a System of Regression Equations When Disturbances Are Both Serially and Contemporane-

ously Correlated." *Journal of the American Statistical Association*, 62:500–509.
Pierce, D. A., and J. M. Mason (1971). "On Estimating the Fundamental Dynamic Equations of Structural Econometric Models." Paper presented to the Econometric Society Meeting in New Orleans.
Quenouille, M. H. (1957). *The Analysis of Multiple Time Series*. London: C. Griffin & Co.
Shiller, R. J. (1973). "A Distributed Lag Estimator Derived from Smoothness Priors." *Econometrica*, 41:775–88.
Telser, L. G. (1964). "Iterative Estimation of a Set of Linear Regression Equations." *Journal of the American Statistical Association*, 59:845–62.
Tiao, G. C., and A. Zellner (1965). "On the Bayesian Estimation of Multivariate Regression." *Journal of the Royal Statistical Society*, Ser. B, 26:277–85.
Tse, E. (1973). "Report of Work in Progress." Paper presented to a special seminar, Graduate School of Business, University of Chicago.
Zellner, A. (1962). "An Efficient Method of Estimating Seemingly Unrelated Regressions and Tests for Aggregation Bias." *Journal of the American Statistical Association*, 57:348–68.
———. (1963). "Estimators for Seemingly Unrelated Regression Equations: Some Exact Finite Sample Results." *Journal of the American Statistical Association*, 58:977–92.
———. (1971). *An Introduction to Bayesian Inference in Econometrics*. New York: John Wiley & Sons.
Zellner, A., and D. S. Huang (1962). "Further Properties of Efficient Estimators for Seemingly Unrelated Regression Equations." *International Economic Review*, 3:300–313.
Zellner, A., and F. Palm (1974). "Time Series Analysis and Simultaneous Equation Econometric Models" (paper presented to the Oslo Econometric Society Meeting, 1972). *Journal of Econometrics*, 2:17–54.
———. (1975). "Time Series and Structural Analysis of Monetary Models of the U.S. Economy." *Sankhyā*, Ser. C, 37:12–56.

2.3 Simulation Experiments with a Quarterly Macroeconometric Model of the U.S. Economy

1 Introduction

The Econometric Model-Building Industry has produced a number of econometric models purporting (*a*) to represent the operation of national economies, (*b*) to help with the problem of forecasting, and (*c*) to assist in appraisal of proposed alternative economic policies. Unfortunately, few of these models have been subjected to strenuous testing. In fact many models have been presented to the economics profession and to others with relatively little known about their economic and statistical properties. In view of this unfortunate circumstance, it is not surprising that many have been somewhat bearish in their attitudes toward large-scale econometric models (see, e.g., Gordon 1971, Griliches 1968, and Meiselman 1969).

Let us review some of the criteria that have been employed in an effort to check the properties and performance of econometric models. First, most are in agreement that econometric models should reflect sound and tested economic principles. While it is true that many models do reflect some economic principles, it is often the case that model-builders do not provide a clear enough exposition of the theoretical principles and the support for them so as to convince users of their merits. In addition, it must be noted that there are serious deficiencies in theory concerning economic dynamics, expectations, the role of money, speculative behavior, and other topics. Thus it seems fair to conclude that econometric model-building is not simply the application of tested and secure economic principles in the analysis of the behavior of national economies. Rather econometric model-building activities represent in part additional exploration and testing of a conjunction of economic hypotheses relating to the behavior of consumers, investors, government officials, and markets.

Co-authored with Stephen C. Peck and reprinted from *Econometric Studies of Macro and Monetary Relations*, A. A. Powell and R. A. Williams, eds. (Amsterdam: North-Holland Publishing Co., 1973), pp. 149–68, with the kind permission of North-Holland Publishing Co.

Second, the statistical procedures employed to check the properties and performance of models usually leave much to be desired for a variety of reasons. It is the case that models containing literally hundreds of parameters or more are implemented with relatively small samples of aggregated data. Since large-sample procedures are used for estimation and testing, it is practically impossible at present to appraise small-sample properties of statistical procedures that have been applied. Further complications arise from the fact that the same body of data is used for screening alternative versions of equations as well as for estimation of "final" versions. This "pretesting" at present results in final estimates with unknown properties. The same can be said of estimates which reflect an informal use of a priori information. Add to these complications the fact that not much is known about the appropriate quantities to compute in comparing alternative versions of an equation and the fact that tests of one equation's formulation are not independent of those for other equations and the conclusion which emerges is that not much is known about the statistical properties of the "final" estimates of any macroeconometric model.

Third, the forecasting abilities of some econometric models have been studied (see, e.g., Zarnowitz 1970). While this is indeed important, it must be realized that often econometric models are checked in this dimension under the assumption that exogenous variables' values in the forecast periods are known without error. Also the number of forecasts that have been compared with actual outcomes has been small in many cases. Thus, it is the case that few, if any, econometric models have been subjected to thorough tests of forecasting ability.

Last, simulation techniques can be employed to study the properties of econometric models. While this approach is quite straightforward for linear models, its application to nonlinear models requires special solution algorithms which have only recently been programmed for use and which still have relatively unexplored convergence properties. In the past, many models presented to the profession have dynamic properties which were and still are unknown. Aside from possible computational problems, the fact that a model's dynamic properties are unknown means that it is nothing more than a black box that probably should be marked "unsafe for use."

The above points are indeed depressing. Ideally, we would like to have a set of formal, well-tested techniques for model-building and model-evaluation. Since such formal techniques are currently not available, the best we can do at present, it seems, is to use an *informal*, judgmental approach which some have described as an iterative research strategy.[1] Such a strategy

1. A fuller description of such a model-building strategy is presented in Hamilton et al. (1969).

involves use of economic theory and whatever other information is available to formulate an initial model. The initial model should be subjected to statistical testing, mathematical analysis, strenuous simulation analysis, and forecasting tests. Given the results of such analyses, unsatisfactory parts of the model can often be pinpointed and reformulated. Then again statistical, mathematical, and simulation analyses, along with additional forecasting tests, can be performed in an effort to attain an improved version of the model. In these analyses, it is desirable to employ as much new data and information as possible. Again reformulation may be necessary followed by additional analyses. While this iterative approach seems to be an obvious one, it appears that few model-building efforts to date have incorporated it.

In the present paper, we report results of two sets of simulation experiments with a version of the Federal Reserve–MIT–Penn Quarterly Econometric Model of the U.S. Economy.[2] This model features the final demand and financial sectors of the U.S. economy and incorporates several important policy control variables. Our simulation experiments can be viewed as a contribution to the ongoing work of enhancing understanding of the model and of effecting improvements in it. In the first set of experiments, we subject the model to symmetric increases and decreases in an important monetary and then a fiscal policy control variable. Our objectives are to determine the extent to which induced changes in the model's endogenous variables are symmetric and/or linear. Symmetry is of interest for its own sake while a finding of linearity or near linearity may be useful in efforts to simplify the model's structure. Also, since the effects of both relatively small and large changes are reported, we gain information on both the local and global properties of the model. We believe that it is very important to understand local and global properties of a model before it is used for serious policy analysis.

In the second set of experiments, we set up conditions such as to make the model produce a major depression. Again our objective is to provide a check on the global properties of the model and to discover possible weaknesses in its formulation. In particular, we shall be concerned about whether the movements of the model's important variables during the course of the depression are reasonable.

Before turning to the results of our simulation experiments, we provide a brief overview of the version of the Federal Reserve–MIT–Penn model that we employed.

2. Some earlier experiments are reported in Ando and Modigliani (1969) and in de Leeuw and Gramlich (1969).

Table 1 Classification of Equations of Version 4.1 by Sector and Type

Sector	Number of equations	Behav- ioral	Tech- nical	Empir- ical	Defini- tional
I. Final demand	44	17	5	2	20
II. Income distribution	26	2	1	2	21
III. Tax and transfer	21	0	11	1	9
IV. Labor market	13	2	0	1	10
V. Prices	32	2	0	8	22
VI. Financial	35	19	0	2	14
Totals	171	42	17	16	96

2 Brief Overview of the Model

The variant of the Federal Reserve–MIT–Penn model[3] used in our experiments, denoted version 4.1 and dated 15 April 1969, incorporates 171 equations that are classified by type and by sector in table 1. From the information in table 1, we see that a large number of equations, 96 out of a total of 171, fall in the definitional category which includes accounting identities, mathematical transformations of variables, and equations defining variables. With respect to the 16 empirical relations, 8 appear in the price sector incorporating the assumption that price indexes for components of GNP are proportional to the implicit deflator for GNP. Of the 17 technical relations, 11 are institutional relations in the tax and transfer sector, while 6 are depreciation and capital consumption equations. The remaining 42 equations are behavioral equations, most of which are in the final demand and financial sectors.

The final demand sector's 17 behavioral equations relate to the following categories: consumption(2); investment in plant and equipment (7); housing (3); state and local government (3); inventory investment (1); and imports (1). Consumption and consumer durable goods expenditures (ex housing) are treated separately as are also producers' expenditures on plant and on equipment.

The 19 behavioral equations in the financial sector include separate demand equations for currency, demand deposits, and free reserves. In addition, there are relations that generate a treasury bill rate, a corporate bond rate, life insurance reserves, a municipal bond rate, a mortgage rate, and a dividend–stock-price ratio. These and other equations attempt to

3. A listing of the model's equations appears in a document titled "Version 4.1," dated 15 April 1969, accompanied by a document titled "Alphabetical Listing of Variables." The summary presented in this section is a condensation of Zellner (1969).

portray certain aspects of the operation of commercial loan markets, commercial banks, savings and loan associations, and mutual savings banks. It is probably the case that this is the most detailed financial sector of any macroeconometric model currently in operation.

Three important policy control variables in the model are unborrowed reserves plus currency in the hands of the public (M), the federal personal income tax rate (T), and federal government expenditures (G). These are the policy control variables that play a key role in our simulation experiments described below.

3 Linearity and Symmetry Experiments

The objective of this set of experiments is to determine the extent to which the model's responses are linear and/or symmetric. With respect to linearity of responses, if responses are found to be approximately linear over a relevant region of the variable space, then it may be useful to consider working with a linearized version of the model that would represent a significant simplification of the model. On the other hand, if important, reasonable, nonlinear responses are encountered, then, of course, linearization of the model may involve intolerable errors. With respect to symmetry of responses, it is of interest from an economic point of view to discover asymmetric responses of the model. For example, does a two percentage point increase in the federal personal income tax rate produce the same absolute change in the unemployment rate as does a two percentage point decrease? Are there downward rigidities present in the model which make for asymmetric responses? Or are there floors and/or ceilings which produce asymmetries? These are interesting questions that we think should be considered in relation to any econometric model. Our experiments throw some light on these issues in connection with the FRB–MIT–Penn econometric model.

Our experimental conditions are as follows. The model, with parameters estimated with quarterly data, was run out for the period 1964I–1966II, 10 quarters, using historically observed values for initial conditions and exogenous variables. The model's outputs for this run, called the *base run*, are compared with outputs of other runs in which certain of the exogenous policy variables are changed from their actually observed values. In our experiments we introduced the following changes in exogenous policy control variables: unborrowed reserves plus currency in the hands of the public, M, was changed by ± 1, ± 3, and ± 5 billions of dollars and the federal personal income tax rate, T, was changed by ± 2 and ± 5 percentage points. In the case of each change in M and T, the 1964I value and subsequent historically observed values were changed by the indicated amounts. For example, with respect to a 2 percentage point increase in the federal personal income tax rate, the historically observed rates for every quarter in the period 1964I–1966II were increased by 2 percentage points and fed into the model, along with other historically given inputs, to yield the model's outputs. To give the reader an indication of the relative sizes of the above changes, we note that unborrowed reserves plus currency varied from about 53 billion in 1964I to about 60 billion in 1966II while the federal personal income tax rate's value is given in our data as 20.59% in 1964I and 19.53% in 1966II.

In figure 1, the base run input for M and base run output for selected major variables are plotted. Also shown in figure 1 are plots of deviations from the base run for experiments in which M was increased by 1 billion dollars and in which M was decreased by 1 billion dollars. A deviation from the base run for a variable y in quarter t is defined by

$$\delta y_{t,\Delta} = y_{t,\Delta} - y_{t,b} \tag{3.1}$$

where $y_{t,b}$ = value of y in the tth quarter for the base run, and $y_{t,\Delta}$ = value of y in the tth quarter for a simulation experiment in which a policy control variable was changed by Δ units.

Below we shall use the deviations defined in (3.1) to construct descriptive measures of symmetry and linearity. In figure 2, we present base run input for T, the federal personal income tax rate, base run output for the same varibles as in figure 1, and deviations from the base run associated with experiments in which T was changed ± 5 percentage points. The information in figures 1 and 2 provides the reader with a visual display of the paths of the output variables given the historically observed input variables, the base run, and for selected changes in the variables M and T.

Figure 1 shows a remarkable degree of symmetry in the model's output responses to symmetric one billion dollar changes in M. For example, the upward and downward deviations of GNP in constant dollars from the base run are almost identical in magnitude. The variable displaying the greatest asymmetry is the general price level variable (implicit deflator for GNP). In 1966II, this variable's value is about 1.2 percentage points above the base run value given $\Delta M = +1$, while its value in 1966II is -0.61 percentage points below the base run value given $\Delta M = -1$. Thus the model appears to incorporate assumptions producing greater upward than downward price flexibility. This property of the model apparently reflects the nonlinear asymmetric dependence of the employee compensation variable on the unemployment rate. Since the general price level is related to the employee compensation variable in a "mark-up" equation, the effects of the aforementioned asymmetric nonlinearity are reflected in the behavior of the general price level.

In figure 2, the model's responses to very large changes in the federal personal income tax rate, namely $\Delta T = \pm 5$ percentage points, are displayed. For these very large changes, the model's outputs display more asymmetry than was the case in figure 1. The results indicate that a tax cut of 5 percentage points, $\Delta T = -5$, produces larger deviations from the base run than does a tax increase of the same magnitude for all variables included in figure 2. However, the amount of asymmetry is not large in many cases, a surprising result in view of the large size of the tax rate changes, $\Delta T = \pm 5$. Again the variable displaying a good deal of asymmetry is the general price level. For $\Delta T = -5$, its deviation from the base run in 1966II is about 1.9 percentage points, while for $\Delta T = 5$, it is about -1.0 percentage points.

To characterize the degree of symmetry of the model's responses to symmetric changes in input variables, such as M and T, we first define a deviation from symmetry in output of a variable, say y, as

$$\gamma_t = \delta y_{t,\Delta} + \delta y_{t,-\Delta} \tag{3.2}$$

where $\delta y_{t,\Delta}$ and $\delta y_{t,-\Delta}$ are deviations from the base run defined in (3.1). The mean absolute deviation from symmetry is then simply given as the arithmetic average of the $|\gamma_t|$'s, $t = 1, 2, \ldots, 10$, that is,

$$\bar{\gamma} = \sum_{t=1}^{10} |\gamma_t/10|. \tag{3.3}$$

To provide a relative measure of symmetry, we introduce the following absolute deviation from the base run

$$\phi_t = [|\delta y_{t,\Delta}| + |\delta y_{t,-\Delta}|]/2. \tag{3.4}$$

Then the mean absolute distance from the base run, called *DIST*, is given by

$$DIST = \sum_{t=1}^{10} \phi_t/10. \tag{3.5}$$

Finally, our relative measure of symmetry, called *SYM*, is

$$SYM = \bar{\gamma}/DIST. \tag{3.6}$$

Note that

$$SYM = \sum_{t=1}^{10} |\gamma_t| / \sum_{t=1}^{10} \phi_t = \sum_{t=1}^{10} |\gamma_t/\phi_t| \phi_t / \sum_{t=1}^{10} \phi_t,$$

a weighted average of the ratios $|\gamma_t/\phi_t|$ with the ϕ_t's serving as weights. A value of *SYM* close to zero denotes symmetry in the response of an output variable while a large value indicates a lack of symmetry.

In table 2, we present calculated values of *SYM* and *DIST* for changes in T of ± 2 and ± 5 percentage points and for changes in M of ± 1 billion dollars. The results associated with $\Delta T = \pm 2$ indicate a remarkable degree of

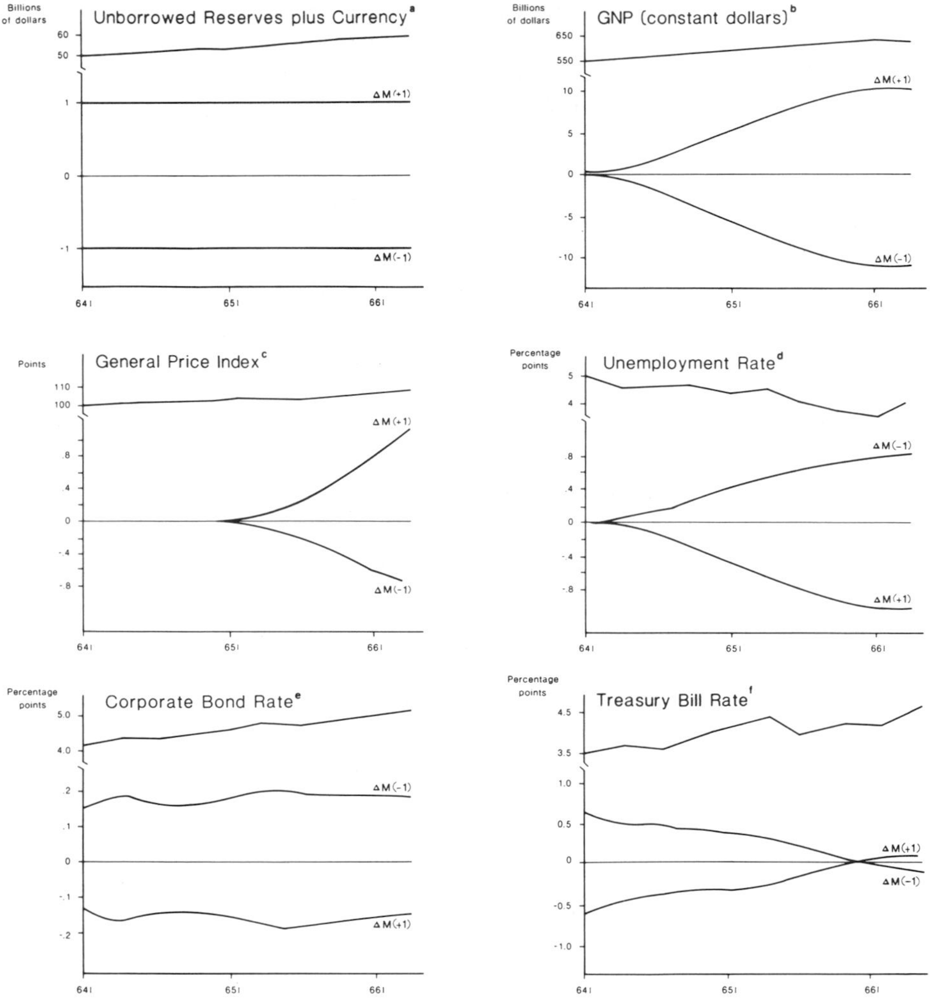

Figure 1 Base run and deviations from base run outputs for selected variables for the period 1964I–1966II for money changes of ±1 billion dollars. At the top of each panel is plotted the behavior of the variables during the base run and in the bottom of each panel the deviations from the base run. [a]Unborrowed reserves at member banks plus currency outside of banks (ZMS). [b]GNP (O.B.E. definition) (XOBE). [c]Price deflator for nonfarm business product (PXB or PNF). [d]Unemployment rate (ULU). [e]Corporate bond rate (RCB). [f]Treasury bill rate (RTB). [g]Effective rate of federal personal income tax (UTPF).

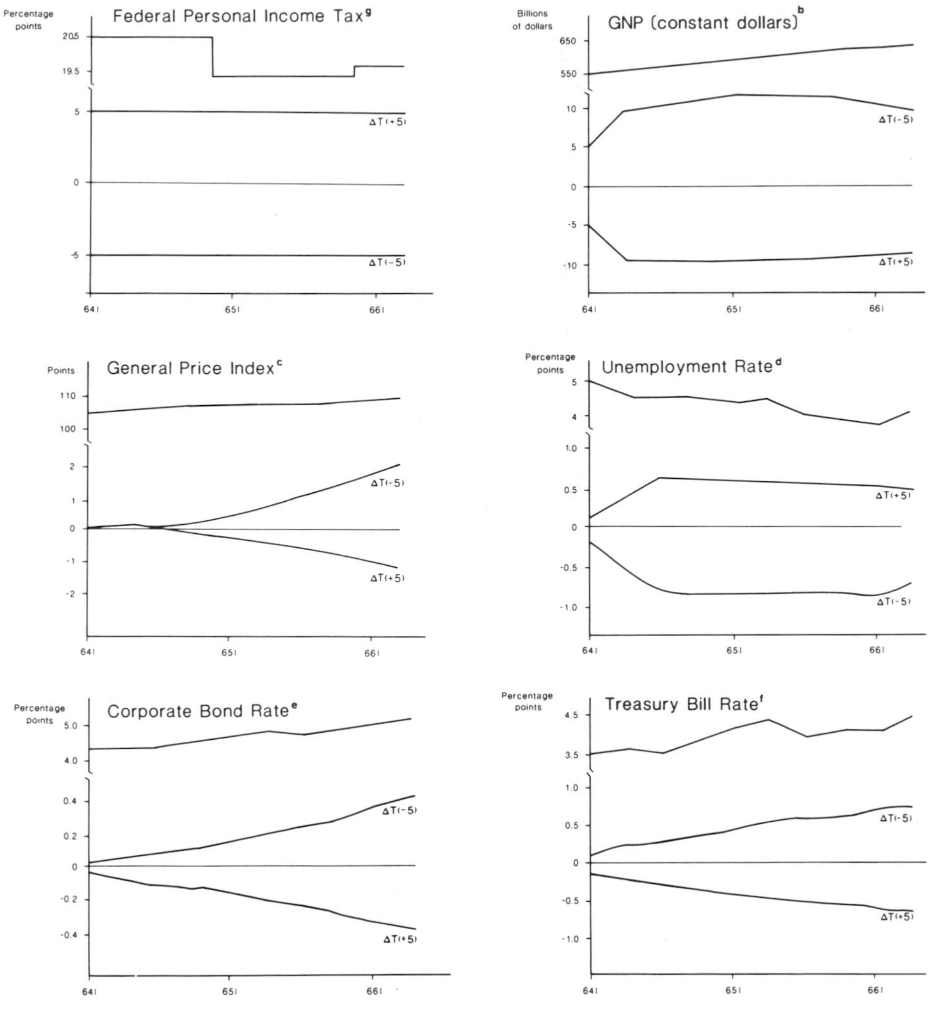

Figure 2 Base run and deviations from base run outputs for selected variables for the period 1964I–1966II for tax rate changes of ±5 percentage points.
[a–g]See notes to figure 1.

Table 2 Calculated Values of Symmetry and Distance Measures for Selected Endogenous Variables

		Endogenous variables[b]					
Changes in *T* and *M*	Measure[a]	Price-deflated GNP	Current GNP	Implicit deflator for GNP	AAA corp. bond rate	Treasury bill rate	Unemployment rate
$\Delta T = \pm 2$	*SYM*	0.075	0.110	0.241	0.066	0.072	0.098
	DIST	4.113	5.537	0.194	0.069	0.181	0.264
$\Delta T = \pm 5$	*SYM*	0.188	0.281	0.604	0.156	0.185	0.247
	DIST	10.206	13.983	0.522	0.175	0.456	0.664
$\Delta M = \pm 1$	*SYM*	0.061	0.128	0.492	0.078	0.120	0.137
	DIST	7.022	8.812	0.219	0.169	0.320	0.460

NOTE: See text for explanation of conditions employed in simulation experiments.
[a]*SYM* and *DIST* are explained in the text.
[b]The symbols employed in the model for the variables shown below are: XOBE, XOBE$, PXB, RCB, TRB, and ULU, respectively. The Office of Business Economics definition of GNP is the one employed. The treasury bill rate is the rate on 90 day bills while the unemployment rate is the percentage of the civilian labor force unemployed.

symmetry for all variables except the implicit price deflator for GNP. For example, $SYM = 0.075$ for price-deflated GNP, indicating that the mean deviation from symmetry, $\bar{\gamma}$, is 7.5% of *DIST*, which for this variable is about 4.1 billion dollars. For the implicit price deflator for GNP, $SYM = 0.241$, indicating that the mean deviation from symmetry, $\bar{\gamma}$, is 24.1% of *DIST*, which for this variable is 0.194 index points. For the larger changes, $\Delta T = \pm 5$, we note a general increase in the values computed for *SYM* with that for the GNP price deflator again being the largest. Its value is also largest in the experiments for which $\Delta M = \pm 1$. The conclusion that emerges from the plots in figures 1 and 2 and the measures in table 2 is that for changes $\Delta T = \pm 2$ and $\Delta M = \pm 1$, the model's outputs for the variables studied are quite symmetric with the exception of those for the implicit price deflator for GNP. For the large changes, $\Delta T = \pm 5$, the degree of asymmetry is large for the implicit price deflator for GNP and increased somewhat for the other variables considered.

With respect to symmetry of outputs and in other respects, it is important to report the results of experiments in which the following changes in *M* were tried: $\Delta M = \pm 3$ and $\Delta M = \pm 5$ billions of dollars. For experiments with $\Delta M = 3$ and $\Delta M = 5$, both fairly substantial quarterly changes, the model failed to converge to a solution. While we can speculate about the reasons for this failure to converge, at present this is still an open problem.[4] Thus these experiments revealed an extremely important asymmetry in the model's performance, one that deserves further attention in our opinion.

We next take up the problem of appraising the extent to which the responses of the model to changes in T and in M are linear. To illustrate our approach to this problem, consider the responses of a variable, say y, to changes in M, namely, $\Delta M = 1$ and $\Delta M = 3$ billion dollars. We computed the deviations from the base run, defined in (3.1), that is $\delta y_{t,1}$ and $\delta y_{t,3}$. Then

$$\eta_t = \delta y_{t,3} - 3\delta y_{t,1} \tag{3.7}$$

was computed for each of the 10 quarters of our output, $t = 1, 2, \ldots, 10$. The η_t's are measures of departures from linearity. To obtain a relative measure of linearity, we compared $\bar{\eta} = \Sigma_{t=1}^{10} |\eta_t|/10$ with the following distance measure:

$$DIST = \sum_{t=1}^{10} \frac{1}{2} [|\delta y_{t,3}| + 3|\delta y_{t,1}|]/10. \tag{3.8}$$

Thus, our relative measure of linearity (or nonlinearity) is:

$$LIN = \bar{\eta}/DIST \tag{3.9}$$

with $DIST$ defined in (3.8). Note that if responses are perfectly linear, $LIN = 0$. Calculated values of LIN and $DIST$ for selected changes in T and M and for selected output variables are shown in table 3.

With respect to the changes in T shown in table 3, we see that the responses of the general price level (implicit deflator for GNP) depart most from linearity as measured by LIN. For other variables, the values of LIN are rather small, ranging from about 0.04 to 0.09. As regards the changes in M, again the general price level's responses are found to be quite nonlinear with values of LIN equal to 0.606 for $\Delta M = -5, -1$, 0.277 for $\Delta M = -5, -3$, and 0.345 for $\Delta M = -3, -1$. For $\Delta M = -5, -3$ and $\Delta M = -3, -1$, values of LIN for other variables are quite small, indicating that the model's responses for these variables are approximately linear. Thus we may conclude that for changes of 3 points or less in T and downward changes of about 2 or 3 billion in M, the variables that we studied responded almost linearly with the exception of the general price level variable.

4. From intensive study of the simulation program's output, we tentatively concluded that an interest rate was forced to be negative on these runs and that the program refused to compute the logarithm of a negative number.

Table 3 Calculated Values of Linearity and Distance Measures for Selected Endogenous Variables

		Endogenous variables[b]					
Changes in T and M	Measure[a]	Price-deflated GNP	Current GNP	Implicit deflator for GNP	AAA corp. bond rate	Treasury bill rate	Unemployment rate
$\Delta T = -5, -2$	*LIN*	0.046	0.088	0.223	0.049	0.062	0.074
	DIST	10.917	15.274	0.610	0.184	0.483	0.720
$\Delta T = 5, 2$	*LIN*	0.068	0.085	0.157	0.041	0.052	0.077
	DIST	9.572	12.531	0.396	0.164	0.425	0.606
$\Delta M = -5, -1$	*LIN*	0.131	0.180	0.606	0.108	0.163	0.180
	DIST	31.947	37.849	0.636	0.929	1.740	1.967
$\Delta M = -5, -3$	*LIN*	0.068	0.086	0.277	0.048	0.073	0.085
	DIST	30.910	36.001	0.516	0.956	1.789	1.870
$\Delta M = -3, -1$	*LIN*	0.065	0.096	0.345	0.058	0.090	0.097
	DIST	19.778	23.619	0.424	0.543	1.004	1.227

NOTE: See text for explanation of conditions employed in simulation experiments.
[a]*LIN* and *DIST* are explained in the text.
[b]See table 2.

4 Major Depression Experiments

As in the experiments reported in section 3, the model was run out beginning in 1964I. The input variable M, unborrowed reserves plus currency in the hands of the public, a major policy control variable, was fed into the model in such a way as to create a major depression. The assumed path for M is shown in figure 3. M remains fairly constant for 6 quarters and then is moved downward by 5% per quarter for 5 quarters. For the remaining 10 quarters, M was kept constant in value. In our first experiment, other exogenous variables were given their historically observed values for the period 1964I–1969I.

The behavior of M, described in the preceding paragraph, did indeed produce a major depression. As can be seen from the plots in figure 3, price-deflated GNP falls considerably. The unemployment rate jumps from about 5% to about 12%. In broad outline, these variables' behavior seems reasonable given the strong downward movement in M. However, the behavior of other variables (see figure 3) seems unusual in the following respects:

(1) The implicit deflator for GNP barely turns down, and at no time is the level of the deflator lower than its level in 1964I, even though the model has produced a 12% unemployment rate, and a substantial decline in real GNP.

(2) The AAA corporate bond rate and the treasury bill rate both move up to extremely high levels, to about 15% in each case. In addition we note that the differential between these two rates changes drastically during the course of the major depression.

(3) The federal government deficit moves up to astronomical levels, about 50 billion dollars; also the net deficit of the state and local governments increases to about 11 billion dollars.

To investigate the possibility that the huge deficits that appeared in our first experiment might have been responsible for the strange behavior of interest rates and the price level, we reduced federal government expenditures and increased grants in aid to state and local governments. Two experiments were performed along these lines; in one the previously described downturn in the money series was combined with a large fiscal downturn (*DLF* in fig. 3), and in the other with a smaller fiscal downturn (*DSF* in fig. 3). The paths of the fiscal variables are shown in the second panel of figure 3; the paths of the other variables are shown in the other panels of figure 3. Even though federal government expenditures were reduced enormously in these two experiments, we note that the behavior of interest rates is still very similar to that encountered in the first depression experiment. Also the path of the price level is not changed very much relative to the depression run, and the change that does occur runs contrary to our intuition; GNP in constant dollars falls more than in the depression run, and yet the price level does not fall as much. Last we note that even with a large reduction in government spending, the deficits are still rather large. It may be that the tax revenue functions of the model are producing too large a decline in tax revenues given the large fall in output and income.

We do not claim to have full explanations of the anomalies reported above. However, the heuristic "*IS-LM* curve analysis" illustrated in figure 4 may be relevant. Given the initial schedules, LM_0 and IS_0, equilibrium income and the interest rate are Y_0 and r_0, respectively. With our drastic decline in M, the *LM* curve shifts upward to the left to LM_1, producing a high interest rate r_1 and a substantially lower level of income Y_1 *under the assumption that the IS curve does not shift*. Possibly, the *IS* curve associated with the model shifts downward to the left but not enough to offset the upward shift in the *LM* curve with the result that the interest rate rises while income falls. Such an effect may be due to the fact that changes in anticipations of consumers and investors are not adequately incorporated in the model's consumption and investment equations. If such factors are important, and many believe that they are, and had they been incorporated in the consumption and investment equations, it may be that the *IS* curve would show a greater downward shift to the left producing a lower rather than a

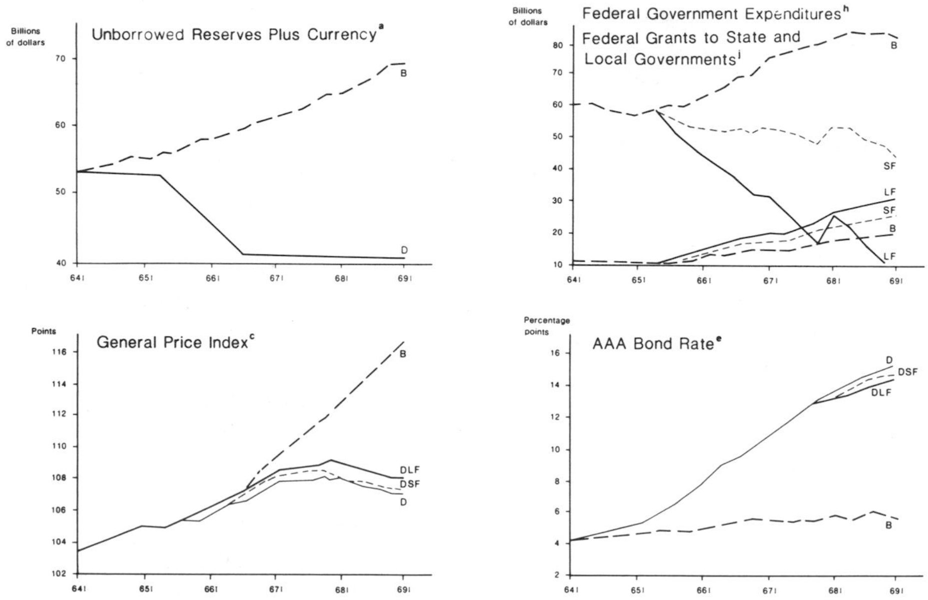

Figure 3 Base and depression runs' outputs for selected variables for the period 1964I–1969I. The first two panels indicate the behavior of the policy variables in the experiments. Each curve is referenced by a letter. *B* refers to the behavior of the money and fiscal variables during the base run. *D* refers to the behavior of the money series during the depression run. *SF* and *LF* refer to the behavior of the fiscal variables in the runs to reduce the budget deficits. *SF* stands for a small fiscal downturn and *LF* for a large fiscal downturn. In the remaining seven panels are plotted the endogenous variables in which we are particularly interested. If a series is referenced by a *B*, it is the behavior of the variable during the base run. If a series is referenced by a *D*, it is the behavior of the variable during the depression run when the money variable is constrained to follow the path indicated by *D* in the first panel. If a series is referenced by a *DSF*, it is the behavior of the variable when the money variable follows the path indicated by *D* in the first panel, and the fiscal variables follow the path indicated by *SF* in the second panel; hence *DSF* refers to the behavior of endogenous variables in the "depression and small fiscal downturn run." *DLF* is to be interpreted similarly.

[a–g]See notes to figure 1.

[h]Federal government expenditures on goods and services (EGF).

[j]Federal grants-in-aid to state and local governments (GFS).

[k]Net deficit of federal government (GDSF).

[l]Net deficit of state and local governments (GDSS).

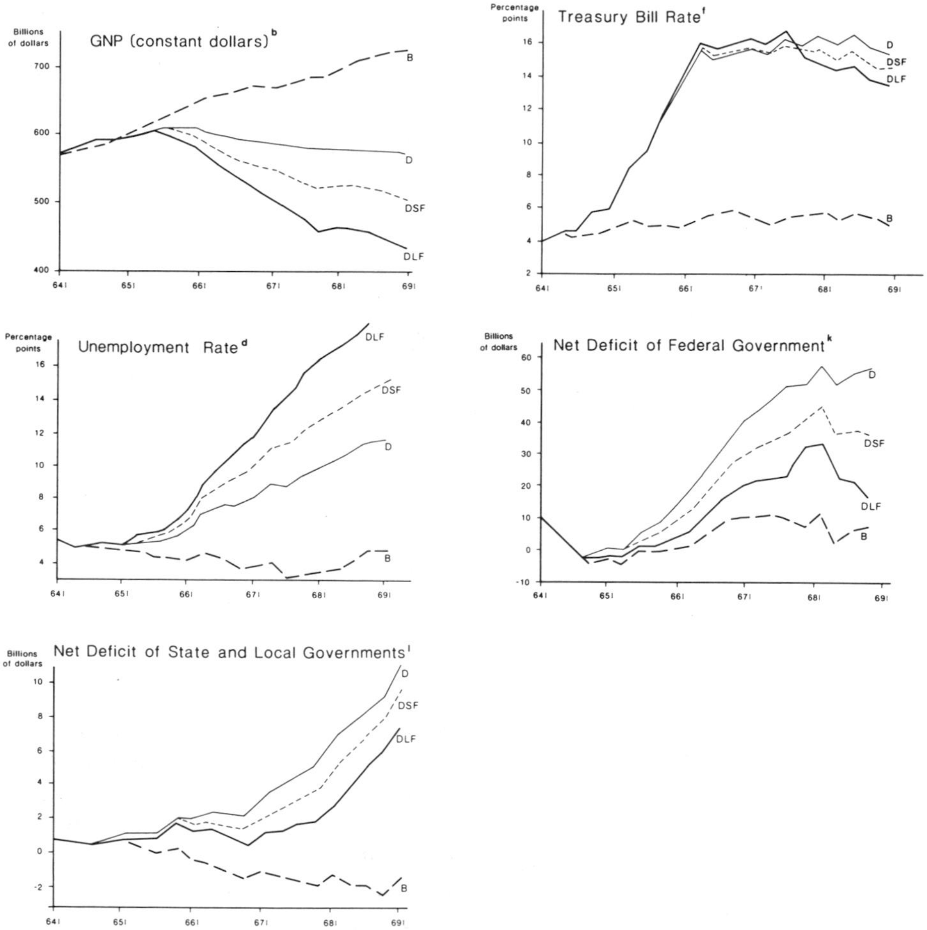
Billions of dollars
GNP (constant dollars)[b]
700
600
500
400
641
651
661
671
681
691
B
D
DSF
DLF
Percentage points
Treasury Bill Rate[f]
16
14
12
10
8
6
4
2
641
651
661
671
681
691
D
DSF
DLF
B
Percentage points
Unemployment Rate[d]
16
14
12
10
8
6
4
641
651
661
671
681
691
DLF
DSF
D
B
Billions of dollars
Net Deficit of Federal Government[k]
60
50
40
30
20
10
0
-10
641
651
661
671
681
691
D
DSF
DLF
B
Billions of dollars
Net Deficit of State and Local Governments[l]
10
8
6
4
2
0
-2
641
651
661
671
681
691
D
DSF
DLF
B

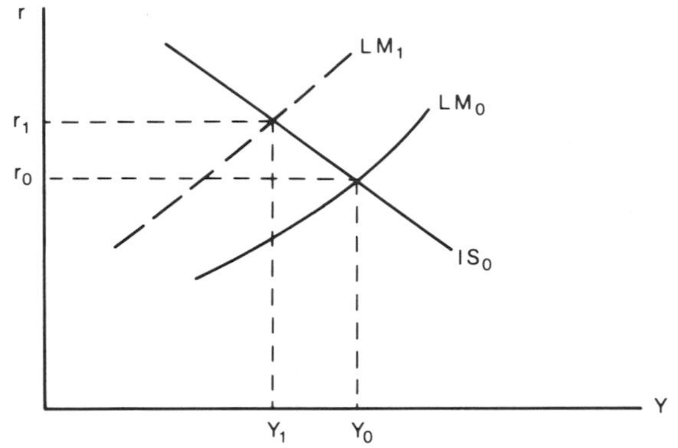

Figure 4 *IS-LM* Analysis

higher interest rate and an even lower level of income. Further work with the model is needed to check out the reasonableness of the above tentative explanation for some of the anomalies encountered in our major depression experiments with the model.

5 Summary and Conclusions

In this paper we have presented the view that understanding the local and global properties of econometric models is extremely important. Further, we have provided some measures of symmetry and linearity that may be useful in characterizing properties of models' responses. In addition, we have stressed the importance of exercising a model strenuously in simulation experiments in order to discover possible model defects. To illustrate application of these methods and principles, we reported results of experiments with the Federal Reserve–MIT–Penn quarterly econometric model of the U.S. economy. For the conditions we employed and for the output variables considered, we found that the model's local responses were quite symmetric and fairly linear with the exception of the responses of the general price level. From our major depression experiments, that bear on certain global properties of the model, we found that the model can indeed yield a major depression. However, the depression behavior of the price level and interest rates yielded by the model appears to us to be rather strange. We suggest that this problem be studied further and that more attention be given to incorporating changes in expectations in the equations of the model. Finally, we hope that our results will be of use to those who are continuing work to improve the Federal Reserve–MIT–Penn quarterly model of the U.S. economy.

References

Ando, A., and F. Modigliani (1969). "Econometric Analysis of Stabilization Policies." *American Economic Review*, 59:296–314.

de Leeuw, F., and E. M. Gramlich (1969). "The Channels of Monetary Policy." *Federal Reserve Bulletin*, June.

Gordon, R. J. (1971). "Short and Long Term Simulations with the Brookings Model: A Comment." In B. Hickman, ed., *Econometric Models of Cyclical Behavior*, pp. 298–310. New York: National Bureau of Economic Research.

Griliches, Z. (1968). "The Brookings Model Volume: A Review Article." *Review of Economics and Statistics*, 1:215–34.

Hamilton, H. R., S. E. Goldstone, J. W. Milliman, A. L. Pugh III, E. R. Roberts, and A. Zellner (1969). *Systems Simulation for Regional Analysis: An Application to River Basin Planning*. Cambridge, Mass.: MIT Press.

Meiselman, D. (1969). "Comment on 'Econometric Analysis of Stabilization Policies' by Albert Ando and Franco Modigliani." *American Economic Review*, 59:318–21.

Zarnowitz, V. (1970). "Econometric Model Simulations and the Cyclical Characteristics of the U.S. Economy." Paper prepared for presentation to the Second World Congress of the Econometric Society, Cambridge, England, September, 1970.

Zellner, A. (1969). "General Description of the Federal Reserve–MIT–Penn Quarterly Econometric Model of the U.S. Economy." Version 4.1, 4/15/69, University of Chicago.

2.4 Retrospect and Prospect: Summarization of the 1976 NBER-Census Conference on Seasonal Analysis of Economic Time Series

At this point, many of us feel overwhelmed by the wealth of material that has been hurled at us during this conference. It calls to mind the story that the economic historian M. M. Knight used to tell. Some of us looking for answers regarding seasonal analysis may feel as if we're in a dark room looking for a black cat. That's bad, but it's not as bad as it could be. Pity the philosophers who are in a dark room looking for a black cat that isn't there.

The conference on seasonal analysis of economic time series comes at a most propitious time for several reasons. First, the Census Bureau is eager to improve its methodology in the seasonal area that includes seasonal adjustment, seasonal analysis, and other topics. Second, there have been major developments in theoretical and applied time series analysis in the last few years, and I believe that the seasonal area is a very good testing ground for these new theoretical and applied time series analysis techniques. Third, there have been tremendous advances in econometric modeling techniques and applications over the years. In fact, I have often suggested that we recognize the econometric modeling industry, provide it with an SIC number, and, above all, institute an annual model show. Fourth, you are well aware of the many advances in computer technology that made possible the processing of large numbers of series, produced multipurpose computer programs, such as the X-11 program, and facilitated applications of advanced statistical techniques. We can expect to see more advances in computer techniques that will be extremely helpful in the seasonal analysis area. Fifth, we are getting more and better data, a development that is of the first order of importance. Of course, in science, generally, measurement plays an extremely important role. In economics, my view is that we are getting more hard boiled about the quality of data, and this changed attitude is having an impact on the quality of all sorts of analyses including seasonal analyses. The last point that makes the timing of this conference very satisfactory is that we

Reprinted from *Seasonal Analysis of Economic Time Series*, A. Zellner, ed. (Washington, D.C.: U.S. Government Printing Office, 1978), pp. 451–56.

are getting many, many more sophisticated users of government data in industry, government, academia, and elsewhere. From personal observations, I believe that the level of sophistication in the business community has risen tremendously over the last decade. I believe the same can be said about users of data in government and in academia. The congruence of the major developments alluded to earlier sets the stage for the conference that has been characterized by a most constructive attitude among the participants and sponsors. This constructive attitude will help to insure that the steady progress in seasonal analysis during the last few decades, outlined in Shirley Kallek's paper and described in the keynote address by Julius Shiskin, will continue in the future at an even more rapid rate than in the past.

Now, let me turn to consider the conference program, since I am to be retrospective in the first part of this talk. The program for the conference was formulated, as follows, by the Steering Committee: The program started with discussion and analysis of the objectives, philosophy, and overview of the problems of seasonal analysis and adjustment. Next, attention was brought to bear on a review and analysis of procedures currently in use and then to improvements in procedures currently being used. From this topic, we went on to new methods of seasonal analysis and to econometric modeling and seasonality. Last, a session was devoted to the analysis of special problems, in particular, aggregation problems and seasonal analysis.

From this review of the program, it is clear that we planned to move from the general framework to a consideration of the older, better-known procedures, possibilities for improving these procedures, newer statistical and econometric methods, and then on to some very troublesome aggravation problems, I mean aggregation problems. Thus, the older approaches were considered in the context of newer approaches; this is very fine and in line with John Tukey's remarks about the desirability of viewing particular procedures in broader contexts. Also, concerning newer approaches, we all realize that some of them are still experimental, particularly from the point of view of those who are on line, have to produce the numbers, and must face the public. Some of this newer experimental work can be regarded as similar to what engineers do with their experimental models in wind-tunnel experiments. That is, some of the experimental seasonal models have been put into a wind tunnel and tested a bit with one, two, or a few economic time series. Wind-tunnel experiments are very helpful and can lead to interesting insights concerning how procedures will probably work in practice. The next stage is to get a real model built, put a test pilot up in the model, and have him take the model plane through strenuous test flights. The problem of some of the developers of new seasonal models and methods will be to find test pilots who are willing to fly these experimental models. On the other hand, I do believe that some of the new modeling techniques described at the conference will be found extremely valuable in practice.

Retrospectively, again, it is almost impossible to summarize all the contributions that were made in our conference program. There are so many "goodies" that it is hard to mention them all. However, what I'll try to do is to describe, using my personal filter, what I consider to be some of the main themes developed for us at the conference. Further, I shall try to put them together in such a way that we can obtain some guidelines about what might happen in the future.

We started with the very important problems of the definition of seasonality and the objectives of seasonal analysis. The thoughtful papers by Kallek and Granger, comments by Fromm, Klein, Sims, and Tukey, and remarks of many others covered aspects of the definition of seasonality and the many-sided question of the objectives of seasonal analysis. Shirley Kallek's paper has a very fine list of objectives, and others have contributed thoughts on this subject. One of the major points that emerged is that the objectives are multidimensional and interrelated. We have to keep this point in mind in discussing particular contributions and techniques. The objectives of seasonal analyses have to be considered very seriously in evaluating techniques. Some objectives I would group under the general heading of scientific understanding of seasonal phenomena. Scientific understanding is often desired for the purpose of getting better predictions, which is very important, since there are many people in the world who have to make forecasts and predictions. Improved understanding of seasonal phenomena can undoubtedly help in producing better predictions. Second, in many areas, for example, labor markets, the housing industry, money markets, agricultural markets, etc., seasonality poses serious policy problems. Thus, there is a link between the formulation of good seasonal policies and scientific understanding of seasonal phenomena.

There is also a strong interest, on the part of many, in isolating and measuring different components of economic time series. The nonseasonal changes in economic series are of great interest to many, as Shirley Kallek pointed out in her paper, and measuring them may be a very basic goal in the efforts of some in analyzing economic time series data. A second point, here, is that the seasonal patterns in economic time series, in and of themselves, are of great interest from the point of view of scientific understanding and seasonal policymaking on the part of firms, households, and governmental units. On this point, I like to think back to my friends in the fishing industry in Seattle, where I spent two years studying their seasonal pricing patterns and how conservation measures possibly affected them. Industry personnel and conservation authorities were certainly concerned about whether one season differed from another, how prices varied from day to day during the season, and related seasonal matters.

Scientific understanding involves approaches at different levels, as many have emphasized. At one level, there is the process of description that involves a descriptive or empirical approach. In this approach, the objectives are to describe, measure, and categorize seasonal effects and fluctuations and to classify series according to the processes underlying them, much in the spirit of the Burns's and Mitchell's NBER research on measuring the properties of business cycles and of Kuznets's early work on seasonal movements in industry.

A second, more ambitious approach, that emerged at the conference, is a statistical modeling approach. Here we have a model for the observations, and, with a formal statistical model for the observations, as many commented, one can do much more in terms of drawing inferences from the data, of deriving optimum predictions, and in estimating seasonal and other components. Of course, it is assumed that the model is an appropriate model that is not too badly misspecified. As long as one has a reasonably satisfactory model, you can do all these things that are harder, or impossible, to do in an empirical or descriptive approach.

At a still more ambitious level, we encountered the econometric-statistical or causal modeling approach in several of the conference papers. Here I mention, in passing, the well-known uses of econometric models, namely, prediction, control, and structural analysis that become possible with a structural, causal, econometric model. Of course, this is a more ambitious level of modeling than is involved in a purely statistical modeling approach.

Many, including Box, Hillmer, and Tiao, have emphasized the interaction of work, at all levels, as being very fruitful, a point that will serve as a focal point for some of my retrospective review of other major themes at the conference. Concerning the interaction between descriptive empirical results and theory, one important point that was stressed during the conference is that theory can often rationalize procedures that work in practice. I've emphasized this point for years in teaching econometrics. The work of Cleveland and Tiao, giving conditions for rationalizing in a mean-square-error-sense use of certain well-known moving average filters for seasonal adjustment, is a beautiful example of current work that has made a great contribution to research and understanding of what is being done in applied seasonal work. The earlier rationalization of moving average filters in terms of deterministic seasonal components, I think, was extremely important, too. Further, Kuiper's work showing that different methods in use produced approximately similar results for the few series that he analyzed for historical periods but different results for recent and current values, perhaps due to the asymmetric filters used for adjusting the current values, is a very intriguing finding reported in his paper. I've been meaning to ask Estella Dagum whether empirical findings of this kind encouraged her to think of the combined X-11–ARIMA procedure described in her comment. It may be that the combined X-11–ARIMA procedure is a very promising approach to deal with the instability of current values. Shiskin mentioned to me that he's ready to experiment with the X-11–ARIMA technique. Furthermore, it was pointed out that the method utilized in the X-11–ARIMA procedure was put forward earlier in theoretical work of Cleveland, Parzen, and others as an optimal procedure. Thus, interaction between theory and application has been very strong in at least these two or three areas that have been featured at the conference.

Another consideration in terms of this interaction between theory and practice is BarOn's and Tukey's emphasis on having an expert on the phenomena being modeled and analyzed present on the scene to help the methodologist do his work. There is no question but that a person who knows the data, the way the data have been generated, the historical setting, the local nonstationarities that may be very important, major events impinging on a series, etc., can have a tremendous impact on the quality of an analysis and also may prevent the analyst from making errors of the first order of magnitude. Furthermore, I am very sympathetic regarding the point that BarOn made about local nonstationary events that may have a temporary impact on a series. In fact, in stock market work some years ago, one of our bright doctoral students at our school of business analyzed stock price data, taking account of the impact of news events, including such items as wars, presidential illnesses, strikes, etc. He got these items from going through pages of past newspapers, employing content analysis, and then analyzed stock market data following these major news events. Lo and behold, he picked up departures from the random walk model following these major events. Unfortunately, not enough of a departure was found so that one could make money from exploiting it. On the issue of local nonstationarities, I would say that Box responded to this point very knowingly by saying that intervention analysis could be used to handle effects of this kind. This means that use of generalized seasonal ARIMA models in the analysis of particular series would be of great interest to see if there is, indeed, a remarkable improvement in beating down, e.g., the mean-squared error of prediction, by taking account of local nonstationarities or interventions, or whatever you want to call them.

Another type of nonstationarity is provided by Bloomfield's example showing seasonality in the variances of monthlies. This example raises points that are extremely relevant for analyses of seasonal processes, some of which Tiao mentioned that he has encountered in analyzing air pollution problems where variances were found to be nonstationary. These examples suggest that, instead of just being concerned about the measure of location month by month, one should also be interested in other aspects of the distribution that may vary seasonally, a point also emphasized in the Cleveland, Dunn, and Terpenning paper.

Series for which current procedures do not work too well provide, I think, extremely good opportunities for theory to broaden existing models. The work of Durbin, Murphy, and Kenny on mixed models falls in this category. The work on robust, resistant techniques of Cleveland, Dunn, and Terpenning that may take account of outliers in more satisfactory ways reflects concentration of methodological work on areas of difficulty that can be helped by more structured theoretical approaches. As I stated earlier, I think that it is a good strategy to concentrate research effort on areas where difficulties are being experienced and thinking about theoretical approaches that can possibly provide improved procedures.

The next area that we covered was the development of the statistical modeling approach. Here, I think that Granger's emphasis on the need for models not purely deterministic and not purely stochastic was well reflected in the mixed deterministic stochastic models of Pierce, Wallis, and others who indicated that such models have much to recommend them. Pierce's approach is an operational approach that appears very flexible, promising, and generalizable in various dimensions. A second point on the modeling approach, which is very important, is that the decomposition into components can be done utilizing a minimum extraction principle, employed by Box, Hillmer, Tiao, earlier by Parzen, and in the work of Pierce.

Concerning statistical models for seasonal analysis, the Box-Jenkins multiplicative seasonal model certainly facilitated many analyses and is viewed by Barnard and many others as an outstanding contribution. Recently, Julius Shiskin asked me, "What does ARIMA stand for?" I told him *a*uto*r*egressive *i*ntegrated *m*oving *a*verage process, but I really should have told him something that I jotted down here—"*a*ll a*r*ise *i*n *m*onumental *a*cclamation"—the "word" has arrived. These processes are extremely useful, and you can see some evidence bearing on their predictive performance very clearly in Plosser's plots in which he compared 12-month ahead predictions for each of 10 years with actual outcomes. As he points out, his 12-month ahead predictions had an error that is rarely more than 1–2 percent. However, Lombra pointed out that 1½ percent may not be good enough. The question that then comes up is whether taking account of the innovations that BarOn mentioned or, perhaps, expanding the models in some way to become mixed models would effect any considerable improvement in predictive ability. This is a whole area of work that was suggested, I think, by the discussions and contributions at the conference. Furthermore, as you may recall, Plosser's analysis showed that, in certain cases, the restrictions required to produce a multiplicative seasonal model may not be implied, in general, by economic models. This raises issues regarding the value of broadening multiplicative seasonal ARIMA models. Will broadened models produce much better results, or will results with multiplicative seasonal ARIMA be satisfactory? Also, Sims's discussion of spectral analysis and its implications for the choice of models is very important. The restrictions we are putting on processes when we opt for multiplicative seasonal ARIMA models should be studied very carefully. It could turn out that they are good enough approximations for many, many purposes and that would be just fine. The simpler the model, in my opinion, the better.

However, some questions arise in connection with this principle. Is the minimal extraction principle, minimizing the variance of the seasonal component, general enough to be applicable to all problems? Does it put something into a series that should not be there? Should the principle be rationalized in terms of subject matter considerations? For example, from a business point of view, is it reasonable to minimize the seasonal variance? Usually minimizing something costs money. You may not get to the minimum value, because it is too costly, i.e., you may stop before you get to the minimum value. Taking account of such considerations would imply a different solution. In a very clear example, given by Pierce, application of the minimum variance principle involved setting a parameter's value equal to -1 in order to achieve identification of the components. Whether this a priori restriction on the stochastic process for an economic variable makes economic sense or sense in terms of decision making really should be examined very, very closely. I think Hillmer's remark about the somewhat arbitrary nature of the minimal extraction principle is well worth heeding. Furthermore, some have expressed great interest in having the trend-cycle component be smooth. Is this objective consistent with providing minimal variance for the seasonal component? This issue deserves further study. Closely related is the problem of determining the power of diagnostic checks using residuals to pick up departures from assumed models. This problem and other problems associated with using large-sample inference techniques in samples of the sizes with which we usually work are topics that also deserve much further work.

One theoretical development that came out of the modeling, or analytical approach, was the emphasis that Sims, Tukey, Wecker, and others placed on what I will term the "dimple problem." Dimples or dips appear in the spectral density functions at the seasonal frequencies for seasonally adjusted series. Granger, Pierce, and others pointed to this problem as being one that requires further thought. Are the dimples there because a minimum mean-square-error point estimate of the seasonal component was employed? If a broader loss function taking account of smoothness is used, will the dimples still be as prominent? That is, would another criterion that links the seasons and incorporates smoothness considerations reduce or eliminate the dimple effect, or is it something with which we have to live? This is a problem that deserves more theoretical analysis. It also figured importantly in discussions of criteria for good seasonal adjustment.

The areas of multivariate seasonal analysis, considered and presented in the Granger, Box, Hillmer, Tiao, Engle, Plosser, Geweke, and Wallis papers, and the relation of univariate and multivariate seasonal adjustment procedures in connection with aggregation and other problems are only recently opening up and seem, to me, to be of tremendous importance. Results obtained by Geweke indicate, e.g., that multivariate adjustment offers great room for improvement, but, in this connection, however, I think back on multivariate regression and how the number of parameters pile up when you get into a multivariate situation. We really have to keep down the number of parameters, particularly in the covariance structures of error processes and elsewhere. I believe that we have to find good reasons for putting patterns on covariance matrices of error processes. This and other devices can help to keep down the number of parameters in multivariate analyses and lead to better results in multivariate problems.

Regarding the econometric-statistical-causal modeling approach, Engle, Plosser, and Wallis have, in their papers, illustrated the use of causal, structural econometric models in approaching seasonal problems. This approach is still in an experimental stage, in part, because of the tentative nature of econometric models. Engle employed an unobserved component, ARIMA approach. Engineers and others are aware of the fact that one can take the engineers' state variable representation model and convert it to a restricted ARIMA representation. The question is whether the state-variable representation model plus the assumptions made about the seasonal components will be flexible enough to be useful, a topic that deserves further research. Concerning Plosser and Wallis, they exhibit the relationship between traditional causal econometric modeling techniques and statistical time series techniques that Palm and I emphasized in our earlier work. Fortunately, we in econometrics have discovered an intimate link between these two areas. Earlier, most econometricians believed that time series analysts were off by themselves, doing something completely different from what econometric modelers have been doing. In the last few years, there has been considerable recognition of the fact that these two areas are very closely related and that interaction between workers in these two areas can be most fruitful.

Regarding the use of seasonally adjusted data in constructing and analyzing econometric models, Plosser, Wallis, and others have exhibited some of the dangers of this procedure. The emphasis in Plosser's and Wallis's papers has been put on the use of seasonally unadjusted data in econometric modeling. Lombra, in his comments, remarked that this amounted to considering seasonal adjustment or seasonal analysis as part of the problem of econometric modeling. I believe that the techniques put forward by Plosser and Wallis will be studied intensively in the years ahead and will prove to be very valuable.

One point about the approach used by Plosser and Wallis, which is very basic and is embodied in earlier work by Palm and myself, is that we try to take a step-by-step approach in the econometric modeling area. First, we attempt to determine the forms of processes for individual variables. They may be found to be in the multiplicative ARIMA seasonal form. These processes are like building blocks. They can be used for certain purposes, namely for prediction and for diagnostic checks of the assumptions built into the structural equations. Then, we have another set of equations to discuss, the transfer functions. They can be used for prediction, control, and diagnostic checking. Thus, when we determine the forms and estimate the transfer functions in this approach to econometric modeling, we have a useful output in that these relationships can be used for prediction and control. Then, it may be that a structural model is obtained that is consistent with the transfer functions and processes for individual variables. If so, you may have some confidence that the structural equations of the model that you estimate are reasonably in agreement with the information in the data.

Another point that has emerged in the discussions at the conference and elsewhere is the following important methodological issue: Many time series workers have identified reasonably simple ARIMA models from the data. Now, some econometric model builders point out that, when you take a large-scale econometric model and algebraically derive the processes for individual variables, they should come out to be much more complicated than have been found by the data analysts. My feeling on this issue is that probably the data analysts are right and the econometric models are wrong. In my opinion, the models should have a simple structure that predicts what the data analysts are finding from the data. It was remarked, I think, by Plosser, that the Saint Louis model has a very nice recursive structure that will help simplify the ARIMA processes on individual variables. The early pioneering work on monthly models by T. C. Liu had the structural model completely in reduced form, i.e., a complete model in the form of a set of autoregressions with input variables. He had everything in a very simple form from the point of view of structural econometric models. Discussions at the conference and the results in the papers by Plosser and Wallis serve to emphasize further the point that the simple models discovered from the data have to be rationalized in some way, and I think it will come from rethinking the specification of the structural equations of econometric models.

I shall now turn to some prospects for the future. I shall mention a few briefly and then you can help me to finish this part of my remarks in the discussion. The list of projects that Shirley Kallek has in her paper are specific projects that need doing. I think it constitutes a fine set of research projects that are worthy of being on the agenda, and I am happy that some of the items were covered at the sessions of the conference, e.g., the problem of aggregation, and some others. Second, on the question of X-11–ARIMA, this procedure will probably come into more widespread use after considerable testing. Naturally, one doesn't want to put anything on line that hasn't been thoroughly tested. Once a procedure is on line, it is necessary to take responsibility for its output. I hope that the X-11–ARIMA procedure will be thoroughly tested, and my prediction is that this modification to X-11 will probably be found very useful. Also, it has an interesting offshoot. To use it, you have to identify a number of ARIMA processes, and that is very, very valuable, because this work will help us understand and appraise the ARIMA processes much more fully. In fact, I propose that we have a handbook of ARIMA processes, similar to handbooks of physical constants. Such a handbook would be very useful from the point of view of those wanting to make predictions, predictions that can be checked against actual outcomes. It will also be useful for those econometricians who want to take a time series approach in building their models. Thus, work with the X-11–ARIMA procedure could have a substantial impact on other parts of the seasonal analysis area, promote more beneficial interaction between theory and practice, and produce more stable current seasonal factors.

The work on evaluation of alternative models for seasonal adjustment and seasonal analysis will continue. Whether we need a broader range of models than the class of ARIMA models is certainly worthy of research. Do we have to go to mixed models rather than use purely stochastic multiplicative models? All of this work, I feel sure, will proceed rather rapidly. The strenuous testing that has to be done before the procedures are adopted for use will constitute a tremendous amount of work, and, in the process, we shall accumulate a lot of valuable research experience.

Finally, I believe that additional work and thought will be directed not only to the theory of the statistical models underlying the observations in terms of their lags and error serial correlation properties but also to the nature of error distributions. As you know, not everything is normal in the world these days. There are many cases in which Student-*t* and other nonnormal distributions of the errors are encountered in practice. Work will probably proceed by deriving traditional likelihood estimates for nonnormal models and comparing these results with robust, resistant estimates. This is a very interesting road that will be traveled.

Furthermore, one has to consider the formalization of how seasonal analyses are going to be used in practice. If you think businessmen are not concerned about seasonals, I refer you to William Wecker, who analyzed prediction problems of department store sales. Department stores have to order huge batches of items, such as girls' dresses, boys' shoes, etc., and they have to set the prices for these items at the beginning of the year. They have to forecast sales, which are highly seasonal, for the rest of the year. If they err seriously in their forecasts, they can lose a lot of money. Their criterion is not MSE; it is something much more practical. I would urge some decision theorists to get into this area and use more practical criteria, such as minimizing expected costs or maximizing expected profits, and combine this decision-theoretic-oriented approach with some of the elements Sargent brought forward in his comments on the contribution of economic theory in enhancing understanding of seasonal problems. There is a lot of work that can be done on the economic theory of seasonal problems. Combined with the data analysis emphasis that Harry Roberts and many others stressed, it appears, to me, that a decision-theoretic modeling approach can lead to fruitful results which will enhance our understanding of seasonal phenomena.

In summary, as is evident from the papers, prepared comments, and discussions presented at the conference, rapid progress is being made in the disciplines that impinge on the seasonal analysis area. Coupled with substantial progress within the field of seasonal analysis, represented by these papers, I believe that prospects for the seasonal analysis and adjustment areas in the next few years are very bright.

2.5 The Quality of Quantitative Economic Policymaking When Targets and Costs of Change Are Misspecified

1 Introduction

In a series of well-known works (Tinbergen 1954, 1955, 1956, 1964), Tinbergen has made pioneering and outstanding contributions to the theory and application of quantitative economic policymaking (QEP). Tinbergen's approach to QEP involves the following elements: (*a*) a criterion or welfare function that depends on certain economic variables, (*b*) a classification of variables into categories, target and nontarget endogenous variables and instrumental and noninstrumental exogenous variables, (*c*) an econometric model involving relationships for variables, and (*d*) boundary conditions for selected variables. Within this framework, which resembles closely the framework of modern control theory, Tinbergen provided simple, operational procedures for determining the values of policy instrument variables at a time when modern control theory was in its infancy.

In addition to structuring and providing solutions to QEP problems, Tinbergen's work importantly involves consideration of the sensitivity of policy solutions to possible errors in formulating welfare functions and economic models. He is quite aware of the many difficulties in formulating satisfactory welfare functions to be used in QEP. With regard to the relation of welfare functions of individuals and of policymakers, he writes, "there may be a certain degree of similarity between individual welfare functions and [the function] of the policymaker. The more democratic is the community, the more will the citizens be able to further this similarity" (Tinbergen 1956, p. 14). Also, he recognizes possible inconsistencies between short-run and long-run targets, mentions a possible reconciliation by instrument differentiation, and then states, "If, however, no differentiation is possible, the only possibility is a 'weighing of targets' or, in practical terms, a compromise" (ibid., p. 137). Further, in a pragmatic fashion, he writes, "For

Reprinted from *Selected Readings in Econometrics and Economic Theory: Essays in Honour of Jan Tinbergen*, Part 2 (London: Macmillan, 1973), pp. 147–64 with the kind permission of Macmillan Publishing Co.

practical purposes it will often be desirable and sometimes possible to specify the mathematical form of the utility functions in such a way as to make them workable. For modest ranges of the relevant variables simple mathematical forms will always be acceptable as approximations" (Tinbergen 1954, p. 52). He goes on to discuss the use of a quadratic approximation. As regards errors associated with econometric models, he explicitly considers errors in estimated parameter values and in functional forms of relationships (Tinbergen 1955, pp. 59–63). Taken together, these considerations constitute a remarkable contribution to the problem of assessing the *robustness* of QEP, a vital subject that has not received much attention in the literature.

In the present paper, attention is focused on several problems in which there is uncertainty about the values of parameters in a quadratic criterion function. That there may be uncertainty about the values of such parameters is emphasized by van Eijk and Sandee (1959, p. 4), who write:

> In principle, the coefficients of a welfare function can be estimated only by interviewing the policy-makers. They would have to answer a series of questions about the marginal rates of substitution for all target variables and in different situations. For the time being, however, a genuine interviewing of policy-makers is impossible. This means that interviews must be imaginary. . . . In short, the presumable outcome of a real interview must be forecast.

This quotation suggests that there may be considerable uncertainty about the values of parameters in policymakers' welfare functions, even abstracting from aggregation problems and the relation of policymakers' welfare functions to those of private citizens. Herein, for simple quadratic criterion functions, that Tinbergen has indicated may serve as useful approximations in certain instances,[1] the effects of errors in assigning target values and in assessing the cost of changing policy instruments are evaluated analytically.[2] Target values and cost of change are emphasized because it is believed that these are key considerations in QEP.[3] In fact, Tinbergen points out that "the relevant starting point to any quantitative policy . . . is the set of target values" (1956, p. 133). Some of the issues analyzed below are the following: What are some well-defined conditions in which there may be uncertainty about the parameters of simple quadratic criterion functions? Can errors in

1. See Zellner and Geisel (1968) for some results on the effects of departures from the quadratic form.

2. In particular cases, sensitivity analysis can, of course, be performed numerically.

3. In Wan (1970), the effects of departures from temporally independent preferences are analyzed in a deterministic framework with extremely interesting findings.

assigning target values be offset by errors in assessing the cost of changing policy instrument variables? Do overly ambitious policymakers who overstate target values and underestimate cost of change fare better in terms of expected utility than do more conservative policymakers who understate target values and overestimate cost of change? These questions, and others, are considered below in connection with some problems in QEP involving control of regression processes.

2 Criterion Functions and the Control of a Simple Regression Process

In this section, an example illustrating uncertainties that can arise concerning values of a criterion function's parameters is presented. Then an analysis of the effects of such uncertainties on the solution to a one-period QEP problem is reported.

Let the criterion function for individual i be the following quadratic loss function[4]

$$L_i = (y_i - a_i)^2 + c_i(x - x_0)^2 \qquad (i = 1,2,\ldots,N), \tag{1}$$

where y_i is an endogenous variable, a_i is the ith individual's target value for y_i, x is a policy instrument or control variable that a policymaker controls, x_0 is the known initial value for x, and c_i is a positive parameter. If we attach a weight,[5] w_i, to individual i's loss, L_i, with $0 \leq w_i$ and $\sum_{i=1}^{N} w_i = 1$, and assume that it is appropriate to sum individuals' weighted losses to obtain total loss, L'_T, we obtain

$$\begin{aligned} L'_T = {} & (y - \bar{a})^2 - 2(y - \bar{a})\sigma_{wa} + c(x - x_0)^2 + (1/N)\Sigma(\delta y_i - \delta a_i)^2 \\ & + \Sigma\, \delta w_i[(\delta y_i - \delta a_i)^2 + 2\,\delta y_i(y - \bar{a})], \end{aligned} \tag{2}$$

where summations extend from $i = 1$ to $i = N$, $y = \Sigma\, y_i/N$, $\bar{a} = \Sigma\, a_i/N$, $\delta y_i = y_i - y$, $\delta a_i = a_i - \bar{a}$, $\delta w_i = w_i - \bar{w}$, $\bar{w} = \Sigma\, w_i/N = 1/N$, $c = \Sigma w_i c_i$, and $\sigma_{wa} = \Sigma\, \delta w_i\, \delta a_i$. If we assume a simple regression connecting y_i and x, that is, $y_i = \beta x + u_i$ $(i = 1,2,\ldots,N)$, then

$$y = \beta x + u, \tag{3}$$

where $u = \Sigma\, u_i/N$. Since $\delta y_i = y_i - y = u_i - u$ does not depend on x, we can express (2) as follows

4. The ith individual's utility, U_i, can be regarded as given by $U_i = -L_i + K_i$, where K_i is an arbitrary constant.

5. Tinbergen writes, "Some of the controversies between communist policies and Western policies may be expressed in terms of the weight given to the interests of various social groups constituting society" (Tinbergen 1964, p. 76).

$$(4) \qquad L'_T = \left[y - \bar{a}\left(1 + \frac{\sigma_{wa}}{\bar{a}}\right)\right]^2 + c(x - x_0)^2 + \varepsilon,$$

where ε represents all other terms and is such that its mathematical expectation does not depend on the value of the control variable x. Thus we can write

$$(5) \qquad L_T = L'_T - \varepsilon = (y - a)^2 + c(x - x_0)^2,$$

where $a = \bar{a}(1 + \sigma_{wa}/\bar{a})$ and $c = \Sigma\, w_i c_i$.

In this problem, the policymaker's criterion function is assumed to be (5), and (3) is his simple economic model for y. In QEP, the policymaker must assign numerical values to the parameters a and c of (5). The value of a depends on the mean, $\bar{a}$, of individuals' targets, and the covariance σ_{wa} between individuals' weights and target values. The parameter c in (5) is a weighted average of the individual c_is. Since the policymaker generally does not know the values of the a_i's and the c_i's and since there is often considerable uncertainty about the appropriate w_i's to employ, it is to be expected that the values assigned to a and c in (5) will generally depart from 'true' values. To allow for such a departure, we write the loss function that the policymaker actually uses as follows

$$(6) \qquad L = (y - k_1 a)^2 + k_2 c(x - x_0)^2,$$

where the parameters k_1 and k_2 have been introduced to allow for errors in assigning values to a and c. Of course, if $k_1 = k_2 = 1$, there are no errors. In what follows, we shall assume $k_1, k_2 > 0$ and $a, c > 0$.

If a policymaker minimizes the mathematical expectation of L in (6) with respect to x, it is of interest to determine how his minimizing value for x, say x^*, depends on the values of k_1 and k_2 and the extent to which it departs from the optimal value of x, say x^0, obtained with $k_1 = k_2 = 1$ in (6). Also, it is relevant to determine how $E(L_T|x = x^*)$, with L_T given in (5), depends on k_1 and k_2 and the extent to which it differs from minimal expected loss, namely, $E(L_T|x = x^0)$. The analysis of these problems will be carried forward initially under the assumption that the value of β in (3) is known and positive. Then the case in which β's value is unknown will be analysed.

Analysis When Value of β Is Known ($\beta > 0$)

In (3), we assume $Eu = 0$ and $Eu^2 = \sigma^2 < \infty$. Then the mathematical expectation of the loss function in (6) is

$$(7) \qquad EL = (\beta x - k_1 a)^2 + k_2 c(x - x_0)^2 + \sigma^2.$$

The value of x, say x^*, that minimizes expected loss in (7) is given by

(8) $$x^* = (k_1 a/\beta + k_2 \nu x_0)/(1 + k_2 \nu),$$

where $\nu = c/\beta^2$. It is seen that x^* is a weighted average of $k_1 a/\beta$ and x_0 with weights 1 and $k_2 \nu$, respectively. In addition, $k_1 a/\beta$ is the value of x that provides a minimal value to $(\beta x - k_1 a)^2$, the first term on the right-hand side of (7), while x_0 is the value of x that gives a minimal value to the second term on the right-hand side of (7). Thus x^* is a weighted average of quantities, $k_1 a/\beta$ and x_0, that minimize individual components of expected loss.

For comparison with x^*, the optimal setting for x, say x^0, is the value of x that minimizes (7) when $k_1 = k_2 = 1$. When $k_1 = k_2 = 1$, (7) is identical to (5), the true loss function. The optimal value for x is given by

(9) $$x^0 = (a/\beta + \nu x_0)/(1 + \nu) = x_0 - (\beta x_0 - a)/\beta(1 + \nu).$$

From the first line of (9), it is seen that x^0 is a weighted average of a/β and x_0. Since x^* can differ from x^0, given $k_1, k_2 \neq 1$, use of $x = x^*$ can, of course, result in suboptimal QEP, except in situations in which errors in assigning the target value and the value of the cost of change parameter happen to be offsetting (see below).

With respect to x^* in (8) and x^0 in (9), the following results are of interest.

(*a*) With $a/\beta > 0$, from (8) $\partial x^*/\partial k_1 > 0$; that is, with all other quantities held constant, x^* will be greater in value the larger is k_1.

(*b*) From (8), $\partial x^*/\partial k_2 = \nu(x_0 - k_1 a/\beta)/(1 + k_2 \nu)^2$. Then $\partial x^*/\partial k_2 > 0$ if $x_0 > k_1 a/\beta$ and $\partial x^*/\partial k_2 < 0$ if $x_0 < k_1 a/\beta$. The dependence of the algebraic sign of this derivative on x_0 and $k_1 a/\beta$ can be appreciated by remembering that x^* is a weighted average of x_0 and $k_1 a/\beta$ with weights $k_2 \nu$ and 1, respectively. Thus, when $x_0 > k_1 a/\beta$, increasing k_2, an increase in the weight given to x_0, increases x^* while when $x_0 < k_1 a/\beta$, increasing k_2 results in a decrease in x^*.

(*c*) With $k_1 = 1$, no error in the target value, overstatement of the cost of change parameter, i.e. $k_2 > 1$, results in x^* being closer to x_0 than x^0, given $a/\beta \neq x_0$, while having $k_2 < 1$ results in x^* being farther from x_0 than is x^0.

(*d*) With $k_2 = 1$, no error in assessing cost of change, $x^* > x^0$ if $k_1 > 1$ and $x^* < x^0$ if $k_1 < 1$.

(*e*) With a, $\beta > 0$, if $k_2/k_1 = 1$, i.e. equally proportionate over- or understatement of target value and cost of change, then $x^* > x^0$ if $k_2, k_1 > 1$ and $x^* < x^0$ if $k_1, k_2 < 1$.

(*f*) Values of k_1 and k_2, not necessarily equal to one, can be found such that $x^* = x^0$. Such values are obtained by equating (8) and (9) to yield

(10a) $$k_1 = -k_2 \nu(\beta x_0 - a)/a(1+\nu) + \beta x^0/a$$

or

(10b) $$\delta_1 = -\delta_2 \phi \gamma,$$

where

(10c) $$\delta_1 = k_1 - 1, \qquad \delta_2 = k_2 - 1,$$
$$\phi = \nu/(1+\nu) \quad \text{and} \quad \gamma = (\beta x_0 - a)/a.$$

Since we assumed $k_1, k_2 > 0$ and $\delta_1, \delta_2 > -1$. The relations (10a) and (10b) indicate that errors in assessing the target value and cost of change can be offsetting. With $\gamma > 0$, *an overstatement of the cost of change,* $\delta_2 > 0$, *must be accompanied by an understatement of the target value,* $\delta_1 < 0$, *for* x^* *to equal* x^0. *With* $\gamma < 0$, *for minimal expected loss to be experienced, i.e.* $x^* = x^0$, δ_1 *and* δ_2 *must have the same algebraic signs which means joint over- or understatement of target value and cost of change.*[6]

Having investigated several features of the dependence of x^* on the values of k_1 and k_2, we now turn to a consideration of how the expectation of the "true" loss function in (5) depends on k_1 and k_2 when $x = x^*$ with x^* shown in (8). After some straightforward algebra, we have

(11a) $$E(L_T | x = x^*) = \frac{a^2\gamma^2}{1+\nu}\left[\left(\frac{w+z}{1+z}\right)^2 + \nu\right] + \sigma^2,$$

where $\nu = c/\beta^2$, $\gamma = (\beta x_0 - a)/a$, $w = \delta_1/\gamma$, $z = \nu\delta_2/(1+\nu)$, $\delta_1 = k_1 - 1$, and $\delta_2 = k_2 - 1$. Since $w = z = 0$ when $k_1 = k_2 = 1$ (or $\delta_1 = \delta_2 = 0$), minimal expected loss is

(11b) $$E(L_T | x = x^0) = a^2\gamma^2\nu/(1+\nu) + \sigma^2.$$

A condition on w and z in (11a) sufficient to achieve minimal expected loss shown in (11b), is $w = -z$, which is the same as (10b). Further, expected loss in (11a) will be constant for values of w and z satisfying $(w+z)/(1+z) = K$, where K is a constant; that is

(12a) $$w = K + (K-1)z$$

or

(12b) $$\delta_1 = \gamma K + (K-1)\gamma\nu\delta_2/(1+\nu)$$

6. The dependence of these results on the algebraic sign of $\gamma = (\beta x_0 - a)/a$ can be appreciated if it is noted that x^0 is a weighted average of x_0 and a/β, with weights ν and 1, respectively, while x^* is a weighted average of x_0 and $k_1 a/\beta$, with weights $k_2\nu$ and 1, respectively. Thus, for example, if $a/\beta > x_0$ ($\gamma < 0$), $k_1 > 1$, k_2 must be less than 1 for x^0 to be equal to x^*. If $a/\beta < x_0$ ($\gamma > 0$) and $k_1 > 1$, k_2 must be greater than 1 for x^0 to equal x^*.

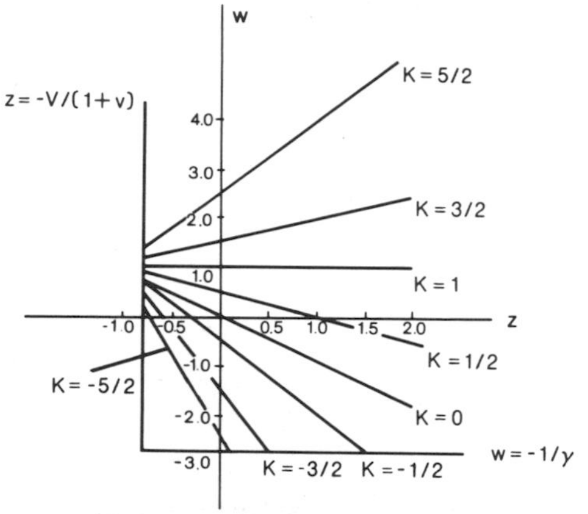

Figure 1 Contours Associated with (11a). It is assumed here that $\gamma = (\beta x_o - a)/a > 0$.

with $w > -1/\gamma$ and $z > -\nu/(1+\nu)$. The contours associated with (11a) are straight lines (see fig. 1). When $K = 0$, (12a) yields $w = -z$, the locus such that minimal expected loss is experienced. As K's absolute value increases, expected loss increases. Note that for $K < 1$, (12a) yields negatively sloped iso-loss lines while for $K > 1$ the slopes of these lines are positive. Thus the trade-off between z and w required to keep expected loss constant changes in nature as K goes through the value 1.

Next, we consider the behavior of expected loss in (11a) for values of δ_1 and δ_2 such that $|\delta_1| = |\delta_2| = \delta$. Here, equal absolute proportionate errors in the target value and in the cost-of-change parameter's value are assumed. Under this condition we wish to compare expected losses for the following four cases.

Case 1: $\delta_1, \delta_2 > 0$; target and cost of change overstated, denoted (0, 0)

Case 2: $\delta_1 < 0$ and $\delta_2 > 0$; target understated and cost of change overstated, denoted (U, 0)

Case 3: $\delta_1, \delta_2 < 0$; target and cost of change understated, denoted by (U, U)

Case 4: $\delta_1 > 0$, $\delta_2 < 0$; target overstated and the cost of change understated, denoted (0, U)

For these four cases, with $|\delta_1| = |\delta_2| = \delta$, expected losses from (11a) were compared[7] with the following results for the six distinct pairwise comparisons where P ≡ "preferred to":

7. This involves consideration of the quantity $(w + z)^2 (1 + z)^2$.

1.	Case 1 (0, 0) ν Case 3 (U, U):	(0, 0)P(U, U)
2.	Case 2 (U, 0) ν Case 4 (0, U):	(U, 0)P(0, U)
3.	Case 1 (0, 0) ν Case 2 (U, 0):	(0, 0)P(U, 0) if $\gamma < 0$
		(U, 0)P(0, 0) if $\gamma > 0$
4.	Case 1 (0,0) ν Case 4 (0, U):	(0, 0)P(0, U) if $\gamma < \delta$
		(0, U)P(0, 0) if $\gamma > \delta$
5.	Case 2 (U, 0) ν Case 3 (U, U):	(U, 0)P(U, U) if $\gamma > -\delta$
		(U, U)P(U, 0) if $\gamma < -\delta$
6.	Case 3 (U, U) ν Case 4 (0, U):	(U, U)P(0, U) if $\gamma < 0$
		(0, U)P(U, U) if $\gamma > 0$

It is seen that in the first two comparisons, unqualified results are obtained. In comparison 1 equal proportionate overstatement of target and cost of change is preferred to equal proportionate understatement of these two items. Heuristically, overstating the cost of change tends to prevent x from being varied, thereby saving on costs of change, and to prevent y from moving to an overstated target, thereby tending to keep closer to the true value. With equal proportionate understatement, x tends to be changed too much and y tends to be brought close to an understated target value. Excessive change in x and being away from the true target inflate expected loss.

In comparison 2, understating the target and overstating the cost of change, (U, 0), is preferred to overstating the target and understating the cost of change (0, U), when absolute proportionate errors are all equal in magnitude. Note that for (U, 0), understatement of the target and overstatement of cost of change tend to keep cost of change low. In the case of (0, U), an overstatement of the target and understatement of the cost of change, both errors tend to produce a large change in x, resulting in high costs of change, and to bring y close to a mistakenly high target, thereby raising the cost of being off target.

In four of the comparisons, 3–6, results depend on the initial conditions, as reflected in the value of $\gamma = (\beta x_0 - a)/a$, or the relation of the relative magnitudes of γ and δ, the absolute size of the proportionate errors. From the results in 1–6 above, we can make the following preference orderings.

Condition on $\gamma = (\beta x_0 - a)/a$	Preference ordering
$\gamma < -\delta$	(0, 0)P(U, U)P(U, 0)P(0, U)
$-\delta < \gamma < 0$	(0, 0)P(U, 0)P(U, U)P(0, U)
$0 < \gamma < \delta$	(U, 0)P(0, 0)P(0, U)P(U, U)
$\delta < \gamma$	(U, 0)P(0, U)P(0, 0)P(U, U)

We see that when $\gamma < 0$, that is $x_0 < a/\beta$, *the worst pair of errors to make is overstatement of the target and understatement of the cost of change*. When $\gamma > 0$, that is $x_0, > a/\beta$, *the worst pair of errors is understatement of the target and understatement of the cost of change*. In both these cases the error in assigning a target value involves a tendency to change the control variable too much (in the upward direction in the first instance and in the downward direction in the second). This tendency toward too much change is reinforced by the underassessment of the cost of change with the result that we end up, on average, off target and experience excessive costs of change.

For $\gamma < 0$, *the least damaging pair of errors is overstatement of the target accompanied by overstatement of the cost of change, errors that are offsetting. Similarly for* $\gamma > 0$, *that is* $x_0 > a/\beta$, *understatement of the target and overstatement of the cost of change tend to be offsetting errors and are least serious*. Note that with $\gamma > 0$, understatement of the target means adopting a target value that is farther from βx_0 than is appropriate; similarly when $\gamma < 0$ an overstated target value is farther from βx_0 than is appropriate. Both of these errors make for excessive movement of the control variable which is offset by the overstatement of the cost of change.

Analysis When Values of β and σ Are Unknown

When the values of the parameters β and σ, involved in (3), are unknown and must be estimated, it is known that such uncertainty affects the optimal setting for the control variable x (see, for example, Fisher 1962, Prescott 1967, Zellner and Geisel 1968, and Zellner 1971, chap. 11). Assume that past sample data on y and x are available that have been generated by a simple normal regression model

$$y_t = \beta x_t + u_t \qquad (t = 1, 2, \ldots, T). \tag{13}$$

We assume that the u_t's are normally and independently distributed, each with zero mean and common standard deviation, σ. If we have little information about the values of β and σ and represent this state of ignorance by the following prior pdf[8]

$$p(\beta, \sigma) \propto 1/\sigma \qquad (-\infty < \beta < \infty, 0 < \sigma < \infty), \tag{14}$$

where $\propto$ denotes proportionality, the predictive pdf for $y \equiv y_{T+1}$ is well known to be in the following univariate Student-t form (see, for example, Zellner 1971, chap. 3)

8. In (14) β and log σ are assumed independently and uniformly distributed, a representation of ignorance about the values of the parameters that has been employed extensively in the literature. The analysis presented below can be readily generalized to cases in which an informative prior pdf in the "normal-gamma" form is utilized.

$$(15)\qquad p(y\mid \mathbf{y})=\frac{\Gamma[(\nu+1)/2]}{\Gamma(\frac{1}{2})\Gamma(\nu/2)}(g/\nu)^{1/2}\{1+(g/\nu)(y-x\hat{\beta})^2\}^{-(\nu+1)/2},$$

where $\mathbf{y}'=(y_1,y_2,\ldots,y_T)$ denotes the given sample information, $x\equiv x_{T+1}$, the control variable's value in period $T+1$,

$$\nu=T-1,\ \hat{\beta}=\sum_{t=1}^{T}x_t y_t/\sum_{t=1}^{T}x_t^2,\ g^{-1}=s^2(1+x^2/\sum_{t=1}^{T}x_t^2),$$

$$\nu s^2=\sum_{t=1}^{T}(y_t-\hat{\beta}x_t)^2,\text{ and } \Gamma \text{ denotes the gamma function.}$$

The mean and variance of the pdf for y in (15) exist for $\nu>2$ and are given by

$$E(y\mid \mathbf{y},x)=x\hat{\beta}$$

and

$$(16)\qquad \operatorname{var}(y\mid \mathbf{y},x)=\nu s^2\left(1+x^2\Big/\sum_{t=1}^{T}x_t^2\right)\Big/(\nu-2).$$

It is to be noted that both the mean and variance in (16) depend on $x\equiv x_{T+1}$.

With the above results set forth, we can now use (15) and (16) to obtain the mathematical expectation of the loss function in (6), namely,

$$(17)\qquad \begin{aligned} EL&=\operatorname{var}(y\mid \mathbf{y},x)+(k_1a-\hat{\beta}x)^2+k_2c(x-x_0)^2\\ &=\bar{s}^2(1+x^2/m)+(k_1a-\hat{\beta}x)^2+k_2c(x-x_0)^2,\end{aligned}$$

where $\bar{s}^2=\nu s^2/(\nu-2)$, $m=\sum_{t=1}^{T}x_t^2$, and $x_0\equiv x_T$. In the second line of (17), the first term will be minimized if $x=0$, the second if $x=k_1a/\hat{\beta}$, and the third if $x=x_0$. The value of x that minimizes (17), say x^+, is a weighted average of these three quantities given by

$$(18)\qquad \begin{aligned} x^+&=[\hat{\beta}^2(k_1a/\hat{\beta})+k_2cx_0]/(\hat{\beta}^2+k_2c+\bar{s}^2/m)\\ &=(k_1a'/\hat{\beta}+k_2\hat{\nu}'x_0)/(1+k_2\hat{\nu}'),\end{aligned}$$

where $\hat{\nu}'=c/\hat{\beta}^2(1+h^{-1})$, $a'=a/(1+h^{-1})$ and $h^{-1}=\bar{s}^2/m\hat{\beta}^2$. $\hat{\beta}$ and $\bar{s}^2/m$ are the mean and variance, respectively, of the posterior pdf for β. Thus h is the squared coefficient of variation associated with the posterior pdf for β, a relative measure of the precision of estimation.[9]

On comparing (18), the setting for x and when β's and σ's values are unknown, with (8), the setting for x when β's value is known, it is seen that $\hat{\beta}$ replaces β and an additional term, h^{-1}, appears in the denominator of (18).

9. Note that h is of $0(T)$ and thus as T gets large $h^{-1}\rightarrow 0$.

When T is large, (18) and (8) produce identical results. Also, the second line of (18) indicates that x^+ can be viewed as a weighted average of $k_1 a'/\hat{\beta}$ and x_0 with weights 1 and $k_2 \hat{\nu}'$, respectively.

If no errors are made in assigning the target value and the cost-of-change parameter's value ($k_1 = k_2 = 1$), the optimal setting for x is, with $\hat{\nu} = c/\hat{\beta}^2$,

$$x^{\otimes} = (a/\hat{\beta} + \hat{\nu}x_0)/(1 + \hat{\nu} + h^{-1})$$

$$(19) \qquad = (a'/\hat{\beta} + \hat{\nu}'x_0)/(1 + \hat{\nu}'),$$

which is (18) with $k_1 = k_2 = 1$. Since (18) and (19) are precisely similar in form to (8) and (9), respectively, the dependence of x^+ on the values of k_1 and k_2 will be similar to that presented for x^* earlier. Also, as above, there are values of k_1 and k_2 not necessarily both equal to one, such that $x^+ = x^{\otimes}$. These are given by

$$(20) \qquad \delta_1 = -\delta_2 \hat{\phi}'\gamma',$$

where $\delta_1 = k_1 - 1$, $\delta_2 = k_2 - 1$, $\hat{\phi}' = \hat{\nu}'/(1 + \hat{\nu}')$ and $\gamma' = (\hat{\beta}x_0 - a')/a'$. The relation in (20) is precisely similar in form to that in (10b). Since this is the case, the analysis following (10b) can be utilized in the present case as well and thus will not be repeated.

3 Control of a Multiple Regression Process with a Misspecified Loss Function

A scalar endogenous policy variable y is to be generated by the following multiple regression process

$$(21) \qquad y = \mathbf{x}'\boldsymbol{\beta} + u,$$

where $\mathbf{x}' = (x_1, x_2, \ldots, x_k)$ is a $1 \times k$ vector of control variables,[10] $\boldsymbol{\beta}' = (\beta_1, \beta_2, \ldots, \beta_k)$ is a $1 \times k$ vector of regression coefficients with known values, and u is a random disturbance term with $E(u) = 0$ and $E(u^2) = \sigma^2 < \infty$. Let our loss function be

$$(22) \qquad L_T = (y - a)^2 + (\mathbf{x} - \mathbf{x}_0)'\mathbf{C}(\mathbf{x} - \mathbf{x}_0),$$

where, as above, a is given a target value for y, $\mathbf{x}_0$ is a $k \times 1$ vector of given initial values for $\mathbf{x}$, and $\mathbf{C}$ is a positive definite symmetric matrix with elements having known values. Then the mathematical expectation of L_T is

$$(23) \qquad E(L_T) = (\mathbf{x}'\boldsymbol{\beta} - a)^2 + (\mathbf{x} - \mathbf{x}_0)'\mathbf{C}(\mathbf{x} - \mathbf{x}_0) + \sigma^2.$$

10. Here we assume that all variables in $\mathbf{x}$ can be controlled. Generalization to the case in which a subset of the variables is under control is direct and will not be presented; see, e.g., Zellner (1971), chap. 11.

On differentiating (23) with respect to the elements of $\mathbf{x}$, the value of $\mathbf{x}$ that minimizes expected loss, say $\mathbf{x}^0$, is given by[11]

$$\text{(24)} \qquad \begin{aligned} \mathbf{x}^0 &= (\mathbf{C} + \boldsymbol{\beta}\boldsymbol{\beta}')^{-1}(a\boldsymbol{\beta} + \mathbf{C}\mathbf{x}_0) \\ &= \mathbf{x}_0 - (\boldsymbol{\beta}'\mathbf{x}_0 - a)\mathbf{C}^{-1}\boldsymbol{\beta}/(1 + \boldsymbol{\beta}'\mathbf{C}^{-1}\boldsymbol{\beta}). \end{aligned}$$

It is interesting to observe that the computed value of y with $\mathbf{x} = \mathbf{x}^0$ can be expressed as

$$\text{(25)} \qquad \boldsymbol{\beta}'\mathbf{x}^0 = \frac{1}{1 + \boldsymbol{\beta}'\mathbf{C}^{-1}\boldsymbol{\beta}}\boldsymbol{\beta}'\mathbf{x}_0 + \frac{\boldsymbol{\beta}'\mathbf{C}^{-2}\boldsymbol{\beta}}{1 + \boldsymbol{\beta}'\mathbf{C}^{-1}\boldsymbol{\beta}}a,$$

a weighted average of $\boldsymbol{\beta}'\mathbf{x}_0$ and a. Further, expected loss given $\mathbf{x} = \mathbf{x}^0$ is:

$$\text{(26)} \qquad E(L_T | \mathbf{x} = \mathbf{x}^0) = \sigma^2 + a^2\gamma^2/(1 + \boldsymbol{\beta}'\mathbf{C}^{-1}\boldsymbol{\beta}),$$

where $\gamma = (\boldsymbol{\beta}'\mathbf{x}_0 - a)/a$.

If, instead of (22) we employ the following loss function

$$\text{(27)} \qquad L = (y - k_1 a)^2 + (\mathbf{x} - \mathbf{x}_0)'\mathbf{G}(\mathbf{x} - \mathbf{x}_0),$$

where, just as in section 2, k_1 is a parameter introduced to allow for possible errors in specifying the target value. Also, $\mathbf{G}$ is assumed to be a positive definite symmetric matrix. If $k_1 = 1$ and $\mathbf{G} = \mathbf{C}$, (27) is identical to (22), the true loss function.

On computing the expected value of L in (27) and solving for the value of $\mathbf{x}$, say $\mathbf{x}^*$, that minimizes $E(L)$ we obtain

$$\text{(28)} \qquad \begin{aligned} \mathbf{x}^* &= (\mathbf{G} + \boldsymbol{\beta}\boldsymbol{\beta}')^{-1}(k_1 a\boldsymbol{\beta} + \mathbf{G}\mathbf{x}_0) \\ &= \mathbf{x}_0 - (\boldsymbol{\beta}'\mathbf{x}_0 - k_1 a)\mathbf{G}^{-1}\boldsymbol{\beta}/(1 + \boldsymbol{\beta}'\mathbf{G}^{-1}\boldsymbol{\beta}), \end{aligned}$$

which is similar to (24) except that $k_1 a$ replaces a and $\mathbf{G}$ replaces $\mathbf{C}$. From (28), we have

$$\text{(29)} \qquad \boldsymbol{\beta}'\mathbf{x}^* = \frac{1}{1 + \boldsymbol{\beta}'\mathbf{G}^{-1}\boldsymbol{\beta}}\boldsymbol{\beta}'\mathbf{x}_0 + \frac{\boldsymbol{\beta}'\mathbf{G}^{-1}\boldsymbol{\beta}}{1 + \boldsymbol{\beta}'\mathbf{G}^{-1}\boldsymbol{\beta}}k_1 a,$$

a weighted average of $\boldsymbol{\beta}'\mathbf{x}_0$ and $k_1 a$. On comparing (25) with (29) it is seen that there is a difference in the weights and in (29) $k_1 a$ replaces a in (25).

From (24) and (28), we can relate $\mathbf{x}^*$ and $\mathbf{x}^0$ as follows:

11. Note that

$$(C + \beta\beta')^{-1} = C^{-1} - \frac{C^{-1}\beta\beta' C^{-1}}{1 + \beta' C^{-1}\beta}.$$

$$\text{(30)}\quad \mathbf{x}^* = \mathbf{x}^0 + (\boldsymbol{\beta}'\mathbf{x}_0 - a) \times \left[\frac{1}{1+\boldsymbol{\beta}'\mathbf{C}^{-1}\boldsymbol{\beta}}\mathbf{C}^{-1} - \frac{1}{1+\boldsymbol{\beta}'\mathbf{G}^{-1}\boldsymbol{\beta}}\mathbf{G}^{-1}\right]\boldsymbol{\beta} + \frac{\delta_1 a\mathbf{G}^{-1}\boldsymbol{\beta}}{1+\boldsymbol{\beta}'\mathbf{G}^{-1}\boldsymbol{\beta}},$$

where $\delta_1 = k_1 - 1$. We see from (30) that the elements of $\mathbf{x}^*$ depend directly on the value of δ_1, the error in specifying the target value. If in (30), $\delta_1 = 0$ and $\mathbf{G} = \mathbf{C}$, then $\mathbf{x}^* = \mathbf{x}^0$; however, these are not the only conditions under which $\mathbf{x}^* = \mathbf{x}^0$. Broader sufficient conditions for $\mathbf{x}^* = \mathbf{x}^0$ are obtained by equating the last two terms on the right-hand side of (30) to zero. This yields the following sufficient condition for $\mathbf{x}^*$ to be equal to $\mathbf{x}^0$.

$$\text{(31)}\qquad \delta_1 = -\gamma\left(\frac{\boldsymbol{\beta}'\mathbf{G}^{-1}\boldsymbol{\beta} - \boldsymbol{\beta}'\mathbf{C}^{-1}\boldsymbol{\beta}}{\boldsymbol{\beta}'\mathbf{G}^{-1}\boldsymbol{\beta}}\right)\left(\frac{1}{1+\boldsymbol{\beta}'\mathbf{C}^{-1}\boldsymbol{\beta}}\right),$$

where $\delta_1 = k_1 - 1$ and $\gamma = (\boldsymbol{\beta}'\mathbf{x}_0 - a)/a$. The condition in (31) parallels that given in (30) and indicates that errors in assigning values to the true target and to the cost-of-change matrix $\mathbf{C}$ can be offsetting.

The expected loss associated with $\mathbf{x} = \mathbf{x}^*$, derived from the true loss function in (22), is

$$\text{(32)}\qquad E(L_T|\mathbf{x}=\mathbf{x}^*) = \sigma^2 + (\boldsymbol{\beta}'\mathbf{x}^* - a)^2 + (\mathbf{x}^* - \mathbf{x}_0)'\mathbf{C}(\mathbf{x}^* - \mathbf{x}_0).$$

Using $\boldsymbol{\beta}'\mathbf{x}^* - a = \boldsymbol{\beta}'\mathbf{x}^0 - a + \boldsymbol{\beta}'(\mathbf{x}^* - \mathbf{x}^0)$ and $\mathbf{x}^* - \mathbf{x}_0 = \mathbf{x}^0 - \mathbf{x}_0 + \mathbf{x}^* - \mathbf{x}^0$, we can write (32) as

$$\text{(33)}\qquad \begin{aligned} E(L_T|\mathbf{x}=\mathbf{x}^*) &= E(L_T|\mathbf{x}=\mathbf{x}^0) \\ &\quad + (\mathbf{x}^* - \mathbf{x}^0)'(\mathbf{C} + \boldsymbol{\beta}\boldsymbol{\beta}')(\mathbf{x}^* - \mathbf{x}^0) \\ &\quad + 2(\mathbf{x}^* - \mathbf{x}^0)'\{\mathbf{C}(\mathbf{x}^0 - \mathbf{x}_0) + (\boldsymbol{\beta}'\mathbf{x}_0 - a)\boldsymbol{\beta}\}, \end{aligned}$$

where $E(L_T|\mathbf{x} = \mathbf{x}^0)$, expected loss associated with the optimal setting of $\mathbf{x}$, is given in (26). The last two terms on the right-hand side of (33) represent the extent to which expected loss may be inflated if $\mathbf{x}^* \neq \mathbf{x}^0$. From (33) it is the case that $E(L_T|\mathbf{x} = \mathbf{x}^*) - E(L_T|\mathbf{x} = \mathbf{x}^0) \geq 0$.

With regard to (21), if the elements of $\boldsymbol{\beta}$ and σ have unknown values and if we have past data on y and $\mathbf{x}$, we can proceed as in section 2 to derive the predictive pdf for y and use it to evaluate the mathematical expectations of the loss functions in (22) and (27). With diffuse prior assumptions regarding $\boldsymbol{\beta}$ and σ,[12] it is well known that the predictive pdf for y in the standard linear

12. We employ a widely used diffuse prior pdf for $\boldsymbol{\beta}$ and σ, namely, $p(\boldsymbol{\beta}, \sigma) \propto 1/\sigma$ with $0 < \sigma < \infty$ and $-\infty < \beta_i < \infty$ $(i = 1, 2, \ldots, k)$. Here the elements of $\boldsymbol{\beta}$ and $\log \sigma$ are assumed uniformly and independently distributed.

normal regression model is in the univariate Student-t form with mean $\mathbf{x}'\hat{\boldsymbol{\beta}}$ and variance $\bar{s}^2(1 + \mathbf{x}'\mathbf{M}^{-1}\mathbf{x})$ where $\hat{\boldsymbol{\beta}} = (\mathbf{X}'\mathbf{X})^{-1}\mathbf{X}'\mathbf{y}$, the sample least squares quantity, $\mathbf{M} = \mathbf{X}'\mathbf{X}$ and $\bar{s}^2 = \nu s^2/(\nu - 2)$ with $\nu s^2 = (\mathbf{y} - \mathbf{X}\hat{\boldsymbol{\beta}})'(\mathbf{y} - \mathbf{X}\hat{\boldsymbol{\beta}})$, the residual sum of squares, and $\nu = T - k$, where T is the sample size.

Using the predictive pdf for y, we obtain the following expression for the expectation of L in (27)

$$(34) \qquad E(L) = \bar{s}^2(1 + \mathbf{x}'\mathbf{M}^{-1}\mathbf{x}) + (k_1 a - \mathbf{x}'\hat{\boldsymbol{\beta}})^2 + (\mathbf{x} - \mathbf{x}_0)'\mathbf{G}(\mathbf{x} - \mathbf{x}_0).$$

The value of $\mathbf{x}$ that minimizes (34), say $\mathbf{x}^+$, is given by

$$(35) \qquad \begin{aligned} \mathbf{x}^+ &= (\bar{s}^2\mathbf{M}^{-1} + \mathbf{G} + \hat{\boldsymbol{\beta}}\hat{\boldsymbol{\beta}}')^{-1}(k_1 a\hat{\boldsymbol{\beta}} + \mathbf{G}\mathbf{x}_0) \\ &= \hat{\mathbf{x}}_0 + (k_1 a - \hat{\boldsymbol{\beta}}'\hat{\mathbf{x}}_0)\bar{\mathbf{G}}^{-1}\hat{\boldsymbol{\beta}}/(1 + \hat{\boldsymbol{\beta}}'\bar{\mathbf{G}}^{-1}\hat{\boldsymbol{\beta}}), \end{aligned}$$

with $\hat{\mathbf{x}}_0 = (\mathbf{I} - \bar{s}^2\bar{\mathbf{G}}^{-1}\mathbf{M}^{-1})\mathbf{x}_0$ and $\bar{\mathbf{G}} = \mathbf{G} + \bar{s}^2\mathbf{M}^{-1}$. When $k_1 = 1$ and $\mathbf{G} = \mathbf{C}$, (35) yields the optimal setting for $\mathbf{x}$, say $\mathbf{x}^{\otimes}$, based on the true loss function in (22), namely,

$$(36) \qquad \mathbf{x}^{\otimes} = \tilde{\mathbf{x}}_0 + (a - \hat{\boldsymbol{\beta}}'\tilde{\mathbf{x}}_0)\bar{\mathbf{C}}^{-1}\hat{\boldsymbol{\beta}}/(1 + \hat{\boldsymbol{\beta}}'\bar{\mathbf{C}}^{-1}\hat{\boldsymbol{\beta}}),$$

with $\tilde{\mathbf{x}}_0 = (\mathbf{I} - \bar{s}^2\bar{\mathbf{C}}^{-1}\mathbf{M}^{-1})\mathbf{x}_0$ and $\bar{\mathbf{C}} = \mathbf{C} + \bar{s}^2\mathbf{M}^{-1}$. Since (35) and (36) are in the same forms as (24) and (28), the comparison of (35) and (36) is quite similar to that for (24) and (28) and thus will not be presented.

4 Concluding Remarks

We have examined the consequence of employing misspecified targets and costs of changing policy instrument variables within the context of one-period control of simple and multiple regression processes. As is to be expected, errors in formulating criterion functions will generally, but not always, lead to poorer, in terms of expected loss, policy decisions. In general, both for cases in which model parameters have known or unknown values, the iso-expected loss lines for misspecified quadratic loss functions were found to be linear. Also, it was found that in general errors in assessing target values and cost of change can be offsetting. However, this, of course, does not imply that errors will always be offsetting in actual problems. In each practical problem, it appears important to assess the consequences of possible errors in assigning values to parameters of a criterion function as well as the consequences of other possible errors. This conclusion is far from novel and, in fact, is reflected in much of Tinbergen's work.

References

Fisher, W. (1962). "Estimation in the Linear Decision Model." *International Economic Review*, 3:1–29.

Prescott, E. C. (1967). "Adaptive Decision Rules for Macro Economic Planning." Ph.D. diss., Graduate School of Industrial Administration, Carnegie-Mellon University.

Tinbergen, J. (1954). *Centralization and Decentralization in Economic Policy*. Amsterdam: North-Holland Publishing Co.

———. (1955). *On the Theory of Economic Policy*. 2d ed. Amsterdam: North-Holland Publishing Co.

———. (1956). *Economic Policy: Principles and Design*. Amsterdam: North-Holland Publishing Co.

———. (1964). *Central Planning*. New Haven and London: Yale University Press.

Van Eijk, C. J., and J. Sandee (1959). "Quantitative Determination of an Optimum Economic Policy." *Econometrica*, 27:1–13.

Wan, H. Y. (1970). "Optimal Saving Programs under Intertemporally Dependent Preferences." *International Economic Review*, 11:521–47.

Zellner, A., and M. S. Geisel (1968). "Sensitivity of Control to Uncertainty and Form of the Criterion Function." In D. G. Watts, ed., *The Future of Statistics*, pp. 269–89. New York: Academic Press.

Zellner, A. (1971). *An Introduction to Bayesian Inference in Econometrics*. New York: John Wiley & Sons.

Part 3

Bayesian Econometrics and Statistics

3.1 The Bayesian Approach and Alternatives in Econometrics

Introduction

The Bayesian approach and alternative approaches to the problems of inference and decision have been discussed at length in books and journals for quite a long time.[1] The subjects of these discussions are of fundamental importance for science in general since they involve consideration of conceptual frameworks and methods for analyzing data and making decisions. If, as Karl Pearson suggests, the unity of science is in the main unity in the methods employed in analyzing and learning from data, then the aforementioned discussions may have important implications for work in econometrics.[2]

Ideally, it would be desirable to have a unified set of principles for making inferences and decisions which can be readily applied in a broad range of circumstances and fields to yield good results. One of the main points of this paper, and hardly a novel one, is that the Bayesian approach approximates this ideal much more closely than do non-Bayesian approaches currently in

Reprinted from *Frontiers of Quantitative Economics*, M. D. Intriligator, ed. (Amsterdam: North-Holland Publishing Co., 1971), pp. 178–93, and also from *Studies in Bayesian Econometrics and Statistics in Honor of Leonard J. Savage*, S. E. Fienberg and A. Zellner, eds. (Amsterdam: North-Holland Publishing Co., 1975), pp. 39–54, with the kind permission of North-Holland Publishing Co.

1. See, e.g., H. Jeffreys, *Theory of Probability* (3d rev. ed.; London: Oxford University Press, 1967), esp. chaps. 1, 7, and 8; L. J. Savage et al., *The Foundations of Statistical Inference* (London: Methuen, 1962); D. V. Lindley, "The Use of Prior Probability Distributions in Statistical Inferences and Decisions," in J. Neyman, ed., *Proceedings of the Fourth Berkeley Symposium on Mathematical Statistics and Probability* (Berkeley: University of California, 1961), 1:453–68; J. W. Pratt, "Bayesian Interpretation of Standard Inference Statements," *Journal of the Royal Statistical Society* Ser. B, 27 (1965): 169–203 (with discussion); I. J. Good, "A Subjective Evaluation of Bode's Law and an 'Objective' Test for Approximate Numerical Rationality," *Journal of the American Statistical Association*, 64 (1969): 23–49 (with discussion).
2. K. Pearson, *The Grammar of Science* (London: Everyman Edition, 1938), p. 16.

use in econometrics.[3] In fact, many non-Bayesian approaches in econometrics and elsewhere are rather good examples of what has been called a collection of "ad hockeries."[4] Some examples illustrating this point will be provided below.

The plan of the paper is as follows: In section 1 several key features of the Bayesian approach will be considered with main emphasis on illustrating its unity, generality and usefulness. Section 2 provides comparisons with other approaches utilized in econometrics. Last, section 3 contains some concluding remarks.

1 Aspects of the Bayesian Approach

The following are some key points which are relevant for comparing Bayesian and non-Bayesian approaches in econometrics.[5]

(1) As Jeffreys and others have emphasized, the Bayesian approach to inference complements very nicely the activities of researchers.[6] A researcher is often concerned with the problem of how information in data modifies his beliefs about hypotheses and parameter values. In the Bayesian approach to inference, an investigator has formal and operational techniques for determining how sample information modifies his beliefs. That is, initial beliefs, represented by prior probabilities, are combined by means of Bayes's theorem with information in data, incorporated in the likelihood function, to yield posterior probabilities relating to parameters or hypotheses. In a fundamental sense, this Bayesian procedure for changing initial beliefs is a learning model of great value in accomplishing what Jeffreys and others consider to be a major objective of science, namely, learning from experience.

(2) As regards statistical estimation, Bayes's theorem (sometimes also called the principle of inverse probability) can and has been applied in analyses of all kinds of statistical models including regression models, time series models, Markov transition probability models, simultaneous equation models, errors in the variables models, etc. *In every instance*, the posterior probability density function (pdf) for parameters is proportional

3. This point has been emphasized by Jeffreys, de Finetti, and others in connection with the Bayesian approach in general vis-à-vis other approaches.

4. This phrase, used by B. de Finetti to describe non-Bayesian approaches at a meeting on statistical methods of econometrics sponsored by the Institute of Mathematics, University of Rome, Frascati, June 1968, is probably taken from I. J. Good.

5. A number of these points were put forward earlier in A. Zellner, "Bayesian Inference and Simultaneous Equation Econometric Models," invited paper presented at the First World Congress of the Econometric Society, Rome, September 1965.

6. Cf. Jeffreys, *Theory of Probability*.

to the prior pdf times the likelihood function with the factor of proportionality being a normalizing factor. That one simple principle has such wide applicability is indeed appealing. Further, it should be noted that by appropriate choice of prior pdf an investigator can introduce as much or as little prior information in his analysis as he chooses. The likelihood function in Bayes's theorem is known to incorporate all the sample information. Thus the posterior pdf for parameters of a model incorporates all the available information, prior and sample. In addition, the posterior pdf so obtained is an exact finite-sample pdf which can be used to make exact finite-sample posterior probability statements about parameters of a model. There is in general no need to rely on large-sample approximations.[7]

Since the entire posterior pdf for a model's parameters, which incorporates both prior and sample information, is generally available, posterior beliefs about parameters are fully represented. If for some reason an investigator wishes to obtain a point estimate, the Bayesian prescription, choose the point estimate which minimizes expected loss, is a general, operational principle in accord with the expected utility hypothesis. For example, if the loss function is quadratic, the mean of a posterior pdf is optimal in general. Given an absolute error loss function, the optimal estimate is the median of a posterior pdf. The Bayesian point estimate is thus tailored to the particular loss function which is deemed appropriate and is an exact finite-sample solution to the problem of point estimation. That Bayesian estimators are known to be admissible and consistent, and to minimize average risk are additional features which some point to in commending their use in practice.[8] Finally, in large samples under rather general conditions, posterior pdf's assume a normal form with mean equal to the maximum likelihood (ML) estimate. This dovetailing of Bayesian and ML results in large samples is indeed noteworthy. Jeffreys interprets this fact as providing a justification for the ML approach in large samples.[9]

(3) Bayesian methods for analyzing prediction problems are simple, operational, and generally applicable. Whatever the model, the predictive

7. Of course, if the sample size is large, large-sample approximations can be useful and are often convenient.

8. For consideration of these properties, see, e.g., T. S. Ferguson, *Mathematical Statistics: A Decision Theoretic Approach* (New York: Academic Press, 1967). Note that these results are based on the assumed use of a *proper* prior pdf for parameters.

9. See Jeffreys, *Theory of Probability*, (1967), pp. 193–94. Further work on the asymptotic properties of Bayesian procedures appears in Lindley, "The Use of Prior Probability Distributions in Statistical Inferences and Decisions," and L. Le Cam, "On Some Asymptotic Properties of Maximum Likelihood Estimates and Related Bayes Estimates," *University of California Publications in Statistics*, 1 (1953): 277–330.

pdf for future observations is obtained.[10] This predictive pdf serves as a basis for making probability statements about future observations. Also, for a given loss function involving prediction errors, it is generally possible to obtain a point prediction which minimizes expected loss. As with point estimation, the solution to the point prediction problem is in accord with the expected utility hypothesis and is tailored to be appropriate for the loss function which is employed.

(4) In the area of control theory, Bayesian methods are particularly valuable in that their application yields a combined solution to the control and estimation problems.[11] For single period control problems, a Bayesian solution incorporates both prior and sample information and involves due allowance for uncertainty about parameter values. For multiperiod control problems, Bayesian principles can and have been employed to obtain optimal, computable solutions which not only take account of prior and past sample information and uncertainty about parameter values but also take account of new information as it becomes available and how settings of control variables affect the precision of information about parameter values. Thus solutions to adaptive control problems employing Bayesian methods are solutions to the joint problems of control, estimation, and design of experiments.

(5) In the Bayesian approach, prior information about parameters or models can be flexibly and formally incorporated in analyses of estimation, prediction, control, and hypothesis testing problems. This flexibility of the Bayesian approach with respect to the incorporation of prior information in

10. If $\tilde{z}$ denotes a vector of future observations generated by a model with parameter vector $\boldsymbol{\theta}$, and the joint pdf for $\tilde{z}$ and $\boldsymbol{\theta}$, given the sample information, y, and prior information, I_0, is denoted by $p(z, \theta \mid y, I_0)$, the predictive pdf is obtained by integrating this joint pdf with respect to the elements of $\boldsymbol{\theta}$. See, e.g., Jeffreys, *Theory of Probability*; H. Raiffa and R. Schlaifer, *Applied Statistical Decision Theory* (Cambridge, Mass.: Harvard University Press, 1961); D. V. Lindley, *Introduction to Probability and Statistics from a Bayesian Viewpoint, Part 2: Inference* (Cambridge: Cambridge University Press, 1965); and A. Zellner, *Bayesian Inference in Econometrics* (New York: John Wiley & Sons, 1971), for examples of predictive pdf's for a number of models.

11. See M. Aoki, *Optimization of Stochastic Systems* (New York: Academic Press, 1967), for a valuable introduction to topics in the control area and an extensive list of references to earlier work. Some works by econometricians include W. D. Fisher, "Estimation in the Linear Decision Model," *International Economic Review*, 3 (1962): 1–29; A. Zellner and V. K. Chetty, "Prediction and Decision Problems in Regression Models from the Bayesian Point of View," *Journal of the American Statistical Association*, 60 (1965): 608–16; A. Zellner and M. S. Geisel, "Sensitivity of Control to Uncertainty and Form of the Criterion Function," in D. G. Watts, ed., *The Future of Statistics* (New York: Academic Press, 1968), pp. 269–89; E. C. Prescott, "Adaptive Decision Rules for Government and Industry" (Ph.D. diss., Graduate School of Industrial Administration, Carnegie-Mellon University, 1967).

analyses contrasts markedly with currently available non-Bayesian techniques for using prior information in econometric analyses. (See the next section for examples.) Of course non-Bayesians use prior information extensively in their work. For example, exact prior restrictions on parameters are introduced to identify parameters of simultaneous equation models. In the errors in the variables model, prior information about parameter values, say the ratio of error terms' variances, is required to identify parameters. Often in analyses of Cobb-Douglas production function models, the prior assumption of constant returns to scale is introduced in an effort to deal with multicollinearity. What should be appreciated in these and other examples is that Bayesians can introduce such required information in a flexible manner which can more accurately reflect the prior information that we may have about parameter values.[12]

(6) The problem of nuisance parameters is solved quite straightforwardly and neatly in the Bayesian approach. Parameters not of interest to an investigator, that is, nuisance parameters, can be integrated out of a posterior pdf to obtain the marginal pdf for the parameters of interest. This marginal posterior pdf can then be employed to make inferences about the parameters of interest.[13]

(7) The Bayesian approach is convenient for the analysis of effects of departures from specifying assumptions. That is, use of conditional posterior pdf's enables an investigator to determine how sensitive his inferences about a particular subset of parameters are to what is assumed about other parameters. Such an approach has been used on a variety of problems.[14]

(8) In the Bayesian approach, inferences about parameters, etc., can be made on the basis of the prior and sample information which we have. There is no need to justify inference procedures in terms of their behavior in repeated, as yet unobserved, samples. This is not to say that properties of procedures in repeated samples are not of interest and, in fact, e.g., Bayesian estimators have several good sampling properties in that they are admissible and constructed so as to minimize average risk. However, in an

12. This point has been made by J. Drèze on many occasions; see, e.g., "The Bayesian Approach to Simultaneous Equations Estimation," ONR Research Memo no. 67 (Technological Institute, Northwestern University, 1962).

13. For an example, see A. Zellner and G. C. Tiao, "Bayesian Analysis of the Regression Model with Autocorrelated Errors," *Journal of the American Statistical Association*, 59 (1964): 763–68.

14. See, e.g., G. E. P. Box and G. C. Tiao, "A Bayesian Approach to the Importance of Assumptions Applied to the Comparison of Variances," *Biometrika*, 51 (1964): 153–67; Zellner and Tiao, "Bayesian Analysis of the Regression Model with Autocorrelated Errors"; V. K. Chetty, "Bayesian Analysis of Haavelmo's Models," *Econometrica*, 36 (1968): 582–602.

inference situation, what is most relevant is the information at hand in the sample and in our prior beliefs.

(9) In the area of comparing and testing hypotheses and models, the Bayesian approach is distinguished from non-Bayesian approaches in that it associates probabilities with hypotheses and provides formal, operational techniques for modifying such probabilities in the light of new information. These posterior probabilities associated with hypotheses and models incorporate prior and sample information and are viewed by many Bayesians as representing degrees of belief. Then, too, if one has explicit losses associated with actions, such as accepting or rejecting a particular hypothesis, and posterior probabilities associated with possible states of the world, he can act so as to minimize expected loss in testing hypotheses.[15]

Having reviewed several important aspects of the Bayesian approach, a comparative review of the characteristics of some non-Bayesian approaches in econometrics will now be presented.

2 Non-Bayesian Approaches in Econometrics

Comparison of the Bayesian (B) approach with non-Bayesian (NB) approaches in econometrics is difficult since there are many formal and informal NB approaches utilized in econometrics. Some of these NB approaches are designed to handle specific types of problems and do not represent a unified set of principles which can be applied to a broad range of problems. Also, it is recognized that good researchers can sometimes obtain reasonable results even if they are not operating with an explicitly formulated set of principles. While this latter fact is recognized, what will emerge from the considerations presented below *is that there is no alternative set of principles currently being employed in econometrics which is as unified and as generally applicable as those embedded in the B approach*. To provide some structure to the discussion, a review of properties of NB approaches in econometrics to the issues and problems listed in section 1 will be presented.

(1) Above, it was pointed out that the Bayesian approach incorporates an explicit learning model which appears to complement the activities of re-

15. Some works dealing with comparing and testing hypotheses from the Bayesian point of view include Jeffreys, *Theory of Probability*; Lindley, *Introduction to Probability and Statistics from a Bayesian Viewpoint*, Part 2: *Inference*, and "A Statistical Paradox," *Biometrika*, 44 (1957): 187–92 (see also M. S. Bartlett's comment on this paper, ibid., p. 533); G. E. P. Box and W. J. Hill, "Discrimination among Mechanistic Models," *Technometrics*, 9 (1967): 57–91; H. Thornber, "Applications of Decision Theory to Econometrics" (Ph.D. diss., University of Chicago, 1966); Zellner, *Bayesian Inference in Econometrics*; M. S. Geisel, "Comparing and Choosing among Parametric Statistical Models: A Bayesian Analysis with Macroeconomic Applications" (Ph.D. diss., University of Chicago, 1970).

searchers rather nicely. As of the present writing, it is a fact that NB approaches in econometrics do not incorporate learning models as fundamentally and as explicitly as is done in the B approach. For example, in NB approaches it is usually not considered meaningful to associate probabilities with hypotheses or models. Thus in NB approaches, it is impossible to quantify a statement of the type, "The permanent income hypothesis is probably true." Further, they cannot formally allow for the modification of such probabilities in the light of new sample information. If the revision of such probabilities is regarded as a representation of the learning process in research, then, of course, NB approaches do not formally provide what is needed for this process. However, this is not to say that non-Bayesians do not engage in considerations concerning whether a particular hypothesis is probably true. They do so, but only in an informal and subjective manner.

That the B approach incorporates a formal and explicit learning model is not necessarily an advantage if, for example, by doing so the B approach could not be applied fruitfully in practice. That this latter circumstance is not the case is easily established by noting that a wide range of problems has been analyzed from the B point of view without undue difficulty and, in fact, in many instances with less difficulty, both practically and theoretically, than is the case with NB approaches.

(2) In the area of econometric estimation, it was stated above that Bayes's theorem is a simple and generally applicable principle which has been used to analyze estimation problems for a very wide range of models. In NB approaches in econometrics, the situation is quite different. There is a plethora of estimation principles, some more general than others. The following are a few principles that have been put forward: maximum likelihood, least squares, best linear unbiased estimation, generalized least squares, minimum absolute deviations, minimum chi-square, indirect least squares, instrumental variable methods, generalized classical linear estimation, two- and three-stage least squares, simultaneous equation least-squares, $\mathcal{K}$-class estimation, double $\mathcal{K}$-class estimation, minimal mean square error estimation, minimum variance unbiased estimation, best quadratic unbiased estimation, etc. While some of these methods produce satisfactory results in particular circumstances and for particular models, it is clearly the case that many are not generally applicable and are not related in any obvious way to a simple set of unified and generally applicable principles. This is one reason why many Bayesians regard current practice in econometrics and elsewhere to be rather ad hoc.

One of the more general principles listed above is the maximum likelihood (ML) method of estimation. It has been employed to produce estimates of parameters in many different kinds of econometric models. Usually in econometrics, estimators generated by ML are justified in terms of their sampling properties in large samples, for example, consistency and large-sample efficiency. As pointed out above, a ML estimate will be approximately equal to the mean of the Bayesian posterior pdf in large samples under general conditions. Thus, for many models, there is a compatibility between large-sample Bayesian and ML results, although there is an important difference in interpretation of them. However, in "small" samples the situation is fundamentally different. ML estimators do not necessarily have good small-sample sampling properties. For example, in the standard linear normal regression model, the ML estimator for the disturbance variance is usually discarded in favor of one with "better" properties. Recent work of Stein indicates that if there are three or more regression coefficients to be estimated, the ML estimator for the regression coefficients is inadmissible relative to a quadratic loss function.[16] Further, with regard to the log-normal distribution, it appears that there are estimators with better finite-sample properties than possessed by the ML estimator. Last, in connection with parameters of simultaneous equation models, it is a fact that many econometricians use other than ML estimators for a variety of reasons.

Thus while the ML method of estimation is a general one and useful in quite a few circumstances, it is a fact that for quite a few important problems in econometrics it produces unsatisfactory small-sample results according to sampling theory criteria and is often replaced by alternatives. This stands in contrast to Bayesian estimators which can be generated by simple principles and which have good sampling properties in that they are known to be admissible and minimize average risk (when it exists).

While not emphasized in much of the econometric literature, the likelihood approach of Barnard and others deserves some comment. In this approach great emphasis is placed on characterizing the shape and general features of the likelihood function without bringing in sampling properties of procedures.[17] That is, the likelihood function is considered in connection with data on hand and not with respect to other possible samples which could have arisen. The location of the mode of the likelihood function is just one feature, and perhaps not the most important feature, to be studied according to proponents of this approach. In this respect, most Bayesians

16. C. Stein, "Multiple Regression," in I. Olkin, ed., *Contributions to Probability and Statistics: Essays in Honor of Harold Hotelling* (Stanford, Calif.: Stanford University Press, 1960), pp. 424–43. See also S. L. Sclove, "Improved Estimators for Coefficients in Linear Regression," *Journal of the American Statistical Association*, 63 (1968): 596–606.

17. See, e.g., G. A. Barnard, G. M. Jenkins, and C. B. Winsten, "Likelihood Inference and Time Series," *Journal of the Royal Statistical Society*, Ser. A, 125 (1962): 321–72 (with discussion).

would agree that a thorough study of the likelihood function is desirable. However, without Bayes's theorem, it appears necessary to entertain not only the concept of probability but also the concept of likelihood. By use of Bayes's theorem the analysis can go forward in terms of the concept of probability alone which appears to be advantageous and which does not rule out the desirable practice of studying the form of the likelihood function.

While some Bayesians do not emphasize the sampling properties of B estimators, it should be recognized that B estimators have rather good sampling properties both in small and large samples. As pointed out above, the B estimator is the estimator that minimizes average risk. This is a well-known exact finite-sample property of B estimators which should be of great interest to NB's. Several Monte Carlo experiments have been performed to compare properties of B and NB estimators.[18] In all experiments to date, B estimators have performed as well or better than leading NB estimators. In one particularly outstanding study of an autoregressive model, risk functions and average risk associated with alternative B and NB estimators were estimated.[19] It was established that the properties of estimators for this "simple" model are quite different in small samples and that the B estimator's average risk is quite a bit smaller than of the ML estimator and several other popular NB estimators. Of course point estimation is just a part of the problem of inference. That the Bayesian approach provides the complete, finite sample posterior pdf for models' parameters and can be employed to make other kinds of inferences should not be overlooked.

(3) As pointed out above, the B approach provides a unified and operational approach to the problem of prediction. In NB approaches various principles are employed to generate "optimal" predictors which are not generally applicable. For example, in some situations NB econometricians use minimum variance linear unbiased predictors. It is well known that this principle cannot be applied in the case of many important models used in econometrics. Further, the restrictions that a predictor be *linear* and *unbiased* can result in suboptimal predictors in a number of cases.[20] Bayesians do

18. See, e.g., Zellner, "Bayesian Inference and Simultaneous Equation Econometric Models"; V. K. Chetty, "Bayesian Analysis of Some Simultaneous Equation Models and Specification Errors" (Ph.D. diss., University of Wisconsin, Madison, 1966); H. Thornber, "Finite Sample Monte Carlo Studies: An Autoregressive Illustration," *Journal of the American Statistical Association*, 62 (1967): 801–18; J. B. Copas, "Monte Carlo Results for Estimation in a Stable Markov Time Series," *Journal of the Royal Statistical Society*, Ser. A, 129 (1966): 110–16; T. C. Lee, G. G. Judge, and A. Zellner, "Maximum Likelihood and Bayesian Estimation of Transition Probabilities," *Journal of the American Statistical Association*, 63 (1968): 1162–79.

19. H. Thornber, "Finite Sample Monte Carlo Studies."

20. See, e.g., A. Zellner, "Decision Rules for Economic Forecasting," *Econometrica*, 31 (1963): 111–30.

not place such restrictions on their predictors and as a result can usually obtain point predictions which minimize expected loss. In addition, since the complete predictive pdf is in general available in the B approach, various probability statements about future observations can be made for a variety of models. These probability statements, made conditional upon the given sample and prior information, appear to be the kinds of statements which are of great value to economic forecasters. Needless to say, forecasters use a good deal of outside or prior information in their work. That the B approach provides a means of formally incorporating such information in forecasts and in probability statements regarding future outcomes is indeed fortunate and contrasts with what is currently available in NB approaches for accomplishing this objective.

(4) With respect to control problems in econometrics, it is probably accurate to state that approaches currently in use do not allow for uncertainty about values of parameters appearing in the equations of econometric models. This is the case in applications of "certainty equivalence" and "linear decision rule" principles which have appeared in the literature. Several studies have appeared which indicate that Bayesian solutions to control problems, which take account of uncertainty about parameter values, are different from certainty-equivalence solutions and provide lower expected loss particularly when sample information is not very extensive or precise.[21] In addition, B solutions to control problems reflect both sample and prior information (as much or as little of the latter as is judged reasonable to use). As regards multiperiod control problems with unknown model parameters which must be estimated, it appears that there is no alternative to the B adaptive control solution in the econometric literature.

(5) On the question of introducing prior information in analyses, often this is done in an informal manner in NB approaches. For example, in regression problems some use the following procedure: If an independent variable's coefficient estimate turns out to have the "wrong" algebraic sign, the variable is dropped from the regression. This ad hoc procedure can yield good results in terms of, for example, a mean square error criterion. However, it is apparent that the resulting estimator is no longer a minimum variance linear unbiased estimator. Rather it is a biased, nonlinear estimator having a mixed distribution that is part discrete (some probability piled up at zero) and part in a truncated normal form.[22] Thus, obviously, there is

21. In particular see the work of Aoki, Fisher, Geisel, Prescott, and Zellner cited in note 11 above.

22. If $\hat{\beta}$ is the unrestricted least squares estimator, then a "sign-test" estimator, denoted $\hat{\beta}^*$, is given by

$$\hat{\beta}^* = \begin{cases} \hat{\beta} \text{ for } \hat{\beta} > 0 \\ 0 \text{ for } \hat{\beta} \leq 0 \end{cases}$$

no secure basis for the usual t tests and for constructing usual confidence intervals. This is then a good example of an ad hoc procedure which departs from what some regard as a fairly general principle (minimum variance linear unbiased estimation).

Another special method for incorporating subjective prior information in NB analyses which has appeared in econometrics texts and the literature is the "mixed linear estimation" procedure for the linear regression model,[23] $\tilde{y} = X\boldsymbol{\beta} + \tilde{u}$. The subjective prior information about the nonstochastic, true parameter vector $\boldsymbol{\beta}$ is represented by $\tilde{r} = R\boldsymbol{\beta} + \tilde{v}$, where R is a matrix to be assigned by an investigator and a tilde denotes random variables. It is further assumed that $E\tilde{v} = 0$ and $E\tilde{v}\tilde{v}' = \Omega$, a matrix whose elements are assigned by an investigator. Then generalized least squares (GLS) is employed to combine the sample and prior information with the common variance of the elements of $\tilde{u}$ replaced by a sample estimate thereby getting an approximation to the GLS estimator. What appears not to have been recognized in this approach is that a rather stringent condition has been placed on the prior information. That is $E\tilde{r} = R\boldsymbol{\beta}$, or if $R = I$, $E\tilde{r} = \boldsymbol{\beta}$, the *true parameter* vector. That prior subjective information be unbiased is a severe restriction on the nature of such information, a restriction that is not imposed in the B approach. Further in analyzing the large-sample properties of the linear mixed estimator, it has been customary to assume that $R'\Omega^{-1}R$ is of order T and thus that the prior subjective information grows with the sample size, T, and is not dominated by the sample information as the sample size grows large. That the precision of the prior subjective information depends on the sample size and that the sample information does not dominate in large samples are features of this approach which appear unsatisfactory from the B point of view.

Prior information in the form of exact constraints and/or inequality constraints can, of course, be introduced in B and NB approaches. In connection with inequality constraints, the criterion function (likelihood function, sum of squared errors, etc.) can be maximized (or minimized) subject to inequality constraints.[24] The resulting point estimators often have extremely complicated, unknown distributions. Testing and interval estimation procedures for the inequality constraint case remain to be worked out. Reliance is

23. See, e.g., A. S. Goldberger, *Econometric Theory* (New York: John Wiley & Sons, 1964), p. 261, and the references cited there.

24. Examples of such an approach appear in G. G. Judge and T. Takayama, "Inequality Restrictions in Regression Analysis," *Journal of the American Statistical Association*, 61 (1966): 166–81; Lee, Judge, and Zellner, "Maximum Likelihood and Bayesian Estimation of Transition Probabilities"; A. Zellner and M. S. Geisel, Analysis of Distributed Lag Models with Applications to Consumption Function Estimation" (invited paper presented to the Econometric Society, Amsterdam, September 1968), *Econometrica*, 38 (1970): 865–88.

often placed on large-sample approximations. However, if the sample is truly a large one, the prior information incorporated in the inequality constraints will often be unimportant. In the B approach inequality constraints have been introduced via an appropriate choice of prior pdf.[25] Posterior pdf's have been obtained in the usual manner and, as always, summarize the complete information (sample and prior) about parameters. If a point estimate is desired, it can be computed and has a finite sample justification, as explained above.

NB analyses of random parameter models superficially appear to resemble B analyses of fixed parameter models in that a pdf for parameters appears in a NB analysis. However, this pdf is not given the interpretation of representing subjective prior information and, further, B analyses of random parameter models involve placing a prior pdf on the parameters of the pdf for the random parameters.[26]

(6) The problem of nuisance parameters is a particularly thorny one in NB approaches in econometrics and elsewhere. For example, an optimal estimator, say a generalized least squares estimator, may depend on a disturbance autocorrelation parameter which is not of special interest to an investigator. Often a sample estimate of the nuisance parameter (or parameters) is inserted in the expression for an optimal estimator. This procedure produces an approximation to the optimal estimator which is usually justified in terms of large-sample theory. If the sample size is not large, there is a question about how good the approximation is. As mentioned above, Bayesians handle the nuisance parameter problem quite simply: such parameters are integrated out of a posterior pdf to yield the marginal posterior pdf for the parameter (or parameters) of interest.

(7) The effects of departures from specifying assumptions have been analyzed to some extent using B and NB approaches. If, e.g., disturbance terms in a regression model are thought to be autocorrelated, the model can be broadened to include a stochastic process, say a first-order autoregressive process, for the disturbance terms. Then under alternative assumptions about the value of the autoregressive parameter, both B and NB approaches can be utilized to assess how sensitive inferences about regression coef-

25. See, e.g., Lee, Judge, and Zellner, "Maximum Likelihood and Bayesian Estimation of Transition Probabilities," and Zellner and Geisel, "Analysis of Distributed Lag Models with Applications to Consumption Function Estimation."

26. These issues have been discussed by Lindley in connection with the paper D. V. Lindley and G. M. El-Sayyad, "The Bayesian Estimation of a Linear Functional Relationship," *Journal of the Royal Statistical Society*, Ser. B, 20 (1968): 190–202. See Also P. A. V. B. Swamy, "Statistical Inference in Random Coefficient Models" (Ph.D. diss., University of Wisconsin, Madison, 1968).

ficients are to what is assumed about the autoregressive parameter. Similar calculations, involving introduction of a new parameter or two, can be performed in connection with possible departures from normality, linearity, and homoscedasticity in regression models although in these cases it is difficult to obtain the exact finite sample distributions of NB unconditional estimators.[27] Since Bayesians and some likelihood advocates take the sample as given (not random), the relevance of these sampling distributions for the problems of inference and of investigating effects of departures in a particular analysis is unclear. Bayesians, in any event, can compute conditional posterior pdf's for parameters of interest given values of a parameter (or parameters) introduced to allow for a departure from specifying assumptions. This sort of analysis can generally be carried through without a need for approximations.

(8) The relevance for inference from given data of the criterion of performance in repeated samples, which is featured in many NB approaches in econometrics and elsewhere, has not received much attention in the econometric literature. Bayesians and some likelihood advocates emphasize that inferences from given data should be based on the information that is in the given data and, for Bayesians, on given prior information. The relevance of other possible samples for the problem of analyzing a given set of data is not clear. However, as pointed out above, Bayesian estimation procedures do have good properties in repeated samples. It appears that the question of how procedures perform in connection with random data samples is an important issue before the data are drawn, for example, in designing a survey. Once the data have been obtained, the problem of inference appears to be that of bringing the information in the given data to bear on beliefs about parameter values, etc.

(9) In the area of analyzing alternative hypotheses and models, it was pointed out above that Bayesians can compute probabilities associated with alternative hypotheses or models which reflect both prior and sample information and which can be regarded as measures of belief in alternative hypotheses or models. Posterior odds relating to two mutually exclusive hypotheses or models are given *in general* by the product of prior odds times a likelihood ratio factor. Further, if a decision has to be made, namely, accept or reject, given a loss structure specifying the consequences of these acts, it is possible to act so as to minimize expected loss. NB approaches for analyzing alternative hypotheses and models do not involve introduction of probabilities associated with hypotheses or models. Rather what is involved

27. See, e.g., G. E. P. Box and D. R. Cox, "An Analysis of Transformation," *Journal of the Royal Statistical Society*, Ser. B, 26 (1964): 211–43.

in testing is the computation of a test statistic. If the test statistic assumes an "unusual" value under the null hypothesis, an investigator's view of the null hypothesis is somehow affected. The jump in logic from an unusual event under the null hypothesis to the conclusion that the null hypothesis is suspect is an issue that concerns many Bayesians. This is not to say that NB test procedures always or usually yield meaningless results. In fact under vague prior information, Lindley has provided a B rationale for usual tests (likelihood ratio, *t* tests, *F* tests, etc.).[28] On the other hand, as emphasized by Jeffreys and others, in testing situations our prior information is often not vague and it is important to take account of this fact in order to get meaningful results. Most, if not all, NB approaches to testing in econometrics do not appear at present to have the capability of formally introducing prior subjective information in testing hypotheses. Rather, such information tends to be used informally in viewing final results and, perhaps, in the choice of a significance level.

3 Conclusions

In a short paper, it is difficult to do justice to the delicate and deep issues involved in a comparison of alternative approaches in econometrics. What has been presented is an overview of some distinctive characteristics of the B approach and a comparison of NB approaches in relation to these characteristics of the B approach. Further, it must be recognized that the B approach is in a stage of rapid development with work going ahead on many new problems and applications. While this is recognized, it does not seem overly risky to conclude that the B approach, which already has had some impact on econometric work, will have a much more powerful influence in the next few years. The most important consideration underlying this prediction is the fact that the B approach rests on a unified and relatively simple set of principles which are broadly applicable and produce good results. In addition, the considerations in sections 1 and 2 of this paper point up specific features of the B approach which commend it for use in econometrics and other areas of science.

28. Lindley, *Introduction to Probability and Statistics from a Bayesian Viewpoint*, Part 2: *Inference*.

3.2 Maximal Data Information Prior Distributions

1 Introduction

In Bayesian analyses, it is often desirable to have a posterior distribution reflect mainly the information in a given sample of data. To achieve this objective, it is necessary to employ a prior distribution that adds little information to the sample information. Much work has been done to provide procedures for formulating such prior distributions, as, for example, Jeffreys (1967), Lindley (1956, 1961), Hartigan (1964), Savage (1961), Novick and Hall (1965), Box and Tiao (1973), Jaynes (1968), and Zellner (1971). In the present paper, a procedure described in Zellner (1971) is analyzed further and applied to a number of problems. Several comparisons with results produced by other procedures are reported.

The plan of the paper is as follows. In section 2, the general method and some of its properties are set forth. Section 3 reports the results of applying the method of generating maximal data information priors (MDIP's) to a number of problems. Last, some concluding remarks are presented in section 4.

2 Maximal Data Information Priors (MDIP's)

The basic idea underlying MDIP's is that they provide maximal prior average data information relative to the information in the prior distribution, with information being represented by Shannon's (1948) measure.[1] To be specific, let $\tilde{y}$ be a scalar random variable with a proper, probability density function (pdf), $p(y \mid \theta)$ defined to be positive in the region R_y, where θ is a scalar parameter such that $a \leq \theta \leq b$, with a and b finite. Then the information in the data distribution $p(y \mid \theta)$ is defined to be $I(\theta)$, given by:

Reprinted from *New Developments in the Applications of Bayesian Methods*, A. Aykac and C. Brumat, eds. (Amsterdam: North-Holland Publishing Co., 1977), pp. 211–32, with the kind permission of North-Holland Publishing Co.

1. Shannon's entropy (or uncertainty) measure is $W = -\int p(x) \log p(x) dx$, where $p(x)$ is a probability density function (pdf). In our work we use $-W$ as a measure of the information associated with $p(x)$.

(1) $$I(\theta) = \int_{R_y} p(y \mid \boldsymbol{\theta}) \log p(y \mid \theta) dy$$

The prior average information in the data pdf, denoted by $\bar{I}$, is:

(2) $$\bar{I} = \int_a^b I(\theta)\, p(\theta) d\theta\,,$$

where $p(\theta)$ is a proper prior pdf defined to be nonnegative for $\mathbf{a} \leq \boldsymbol{\theta} \leq b$ and zero elsewhere. Then the prior average information in the data pdf, $\bar{I}$, minus the information in the prior pdf, $p(\theta)$, is

(3) $$\begin{aligned} G &= \bar{I} - \int_a^b p(\theta) \log p(\theta) d\theta \\ &= \int_a^b p(\theta) I(\theta) d\theta - \int_a^b p(\theta) \log p(\theta) d\theta\,. \end{aligned}$$

As seen from (3) G is just the difference of two information measures, the first relating to the data pdf and the second to the prior pdf. An alternative view of G can be obtained by substituting for $I(\theta)$ in (3) and writing (3) as:

(4) $$G = \int_a^b \int_{R_y} \log\{p(y \mid \theta)/p(\theta)\}\, p(y, \theta) dy\, d\theta\,,$$

where $p(y, \theta) = p(\theta)p(y \mid \theta)$ is the joint pdf for θ and y. From (4) it is seen that G can be interpreted as the average log-ratio of the ordinate of the data pdf or likelihood function to the ordinate of the prior pdf.

We now present the following definition of a maximal data information prior (MDIP) pdf:

Definition: A MDIP pdf is a proper, normalized prior pdf that maximizes G, defined in (3).

The following theorem provides a simple formula for MDIP pdf's.

Theorem 1: The normalized MDIP pdf, $p_*(\theta)$ maximizing G in (3) is given by:

(5) $$p_*(\theta) = c \exp\{I(\theta)\} \qquad a \leq \theta \leq b$$

where c is a normalizing constant.

Proof: Let $g(\theta)$ be an arbitrary function with $\int_b^a g(\theta) d\theta = 0$ and consider:

$$G(\epsilon) = \int_a^b \big\{I(\theta) - \log\{p(\theta) + \epsilon g(\theta)\}\big\}\{p(\theta) + \epsilon g(\theta)\}\, d\theta\,.$$

Then, $G'(\epsilon) = \int_a^b g(\theta)\big\{I(\theta) - \log\{p(\theta) + \epsilon g(\theta)\}\big\} d\theta$, where $\int_a^b g(\theta) d\theta = 0$ has been used and the necessary condition for a maximum, $G'(0) = 0$, is satisfied for $p(\theta) = p_1(\theta)$, where $\log p_1(\theta) = I(\theta)$ or $p_1(\theta) = \exp\{I(\theta)\}$. Since $G''(0) = -\int_a^b \big\{\{g(\theta)\}^2/p_1(\theta)\big\} d\theta < 0$, $p(\theta) = p_1(\theta)$ is associated with a maximum of G. Finally, $p_*(\theta) = c \exp\{I(\theta)\}$ is the normalized, proper pdf that maximizes G where $1/c = \int_a^b \exp\{I(\theta)\} d\theta$.

Corollary: If $I(\theta)$ is a constant, independent of θ, then the MDIP pdf is the uniform pdf, $p_*(\theta) = 1/(b - a)$, $a \leq \theta \leq b$.

The following theorem provides an invariance property for MDIP pdf's.

Theorem 2: Let $\tilde{z} = d_0 + d_1\tilde{y}$, where d_0 and d_1 are given constants and the proper, normalized pdf for $\tilde{y}$ is $p(y\,|\,\theta)$, $a \le \theta \le b$ and $-\infty < y < \infty$. Then the MDIP pdf for θ associated with the data pdf $p(y\,|\,\theta)$ is identical to that for the data pdf for $\tilde{z}$, $p(z\,|\,\theta)$, $-\infty < z < \infty$.
Proof: Let $I_y(\theta) = \int_{-\infty}^{\infty} p(y\,|\,\theta)\log p(y\,|\,\theta)dy$ and $I_z(\theta) = \int_{-\infty}^{\infty} p(z\,|\,\theta)\log p(z\,|\,\theta)dz$.
Then from known properties of Shannon's information measure, $I_z(\theta) = \log|d_1| + I_y(\theta)$. Thus G defined in terms of $p(z\,|\,\theta)$ differs from G defined in terms of $p(y\,|\,\theta)$ by a constant independent of θ and maximization of G in either case will yield the same MDIP pdf.
Theorem 2, of course, provides an important invariance with respect to changes in the units of measurement.
Theorem 3: Let the random variable $\tilde{y}$ have a proper, normalized pdf $p(y\,|\,\theta) = p(y - \theta)$ with $a \le \theta \le b$ and $-\infty < y < \infty$. Now if $\theta' = k_0 + k_1\theta$, where k_0 and k_1 are given constants, the MDIP pdf's for θ and for θ' are uniform.
Proof: For $p(y\,|\,\theta) = p(y - \theta)$, $I(\theta) = \int_{-\infty}^{\infty} p(y - \theta)\log p(y - \theta)dy =$ const independent of θ since by change of variable $z = y - \theta$ the integral is $\int_{-\infty}^{\infty} p(z)\log p(z)dz$ which does not depend on θ. Similarly, $I(\theta') =$ const independent of θ'. Thus $p*(\theta) \propto \exp\{I(\theta)\} \propto$ const and $p*(\theta') \propto \exp\{I(\theta')\} \propto$ const, the MDIP pdf's, are each uniform.
Theorem 4: Let the random variable $\tilde{y}$ have a proper, normalized pdf $p(y\,|\,\theta) = (1/\theta)f(y/\theta)$, with $0 < a \le \theta \le b$ and $-\infty < y < \infty$. Now if $\theta_1 = k\theta$, where k is a given positive constant, the MDIP pdf's for θ and θ_1 are given by $p*(\theta) = c/\theta$, $a \le \theta \le b$, and $p*(\theta_1) = c_1/\theta_1$, $ka \le \theta_1 \le kb$, where c and c_1 are normalizing constants.
Proof: We have

$$\begin{aligned} I(\theta) &= \int_{-\infty}^{\infty} p(y\,|\,\theta)\log p(y\,|\,\theta)dy = \int_{-\infty}^{\infty}\{-\log\theta + \log f(y/\theta)\}p(y\,|\,\theta)dy \\ &= -\log\theta + \text{const} \end{aligned}$$

since with $\omega = y/\theta$, $\int_{-\infty}^{\infty}\{\log f(y/\theta)\}p(y\,|\,\theta)dy = \int_{-\infty}^{\infty}\{\log f(\omega)\}f(\omega)d\omega =$ const independent of θ. Similarly, $I(\theta_1) = \log\theta_1 +$ const. Thus the MDIP pdf's for θ and θ_1 have the forms $p*(\theta) = c\exp\{-\log\theta)\} = c/\theta$ and $p*(\theta_1) = c_1\exp\{-\log\theta_1\} = c_1/\theta_1$, as was to be shown.

For data pdf's involving more than one parameter, say a vector of parameters, $\boldsymbol{\theta}' = (\theta_1, \theta_2, \ldots, \theta_m)$, G is defined as follows:

$$G = \int_{R_\theta} p(\boldsymbol{\theta})I(\boldsymbol{\theta})d\boldsymbol{\theta} - \int_{R_\theta} p(\boldsymbol{\theta})\log p(\boldsymbol{\theta})d\boldsymbol{\theta}\,, \tag{6}$$

where R_θ is a finite region for $\boldsymbol{\theta}$ and

$$I(\boldsymbol{\theta}) = \int_{R_y} p(y\,|\,\boldsymbol{\theta})\log p(y\,|\,\boldsymbol{\theta})dy\,. \tag{7}$$

Proceeding as in Theorem 1, the MDIP pdf is

$$(8) \qquad p*(\boldsymbol{\theta}) = c_0 \exp\{I(\boldsymbol{\theta})\}, \qquad \boldsymbol{\theta} \subseteq R_\theta$$

where c_0 is a normalizing constant.
Last for a random vector observation, $\tilde{\mathbf{y}}' = (\tilde{y}_1, \tilde{y}_2, \ldots, \tilde{y}_p)$ with pdf $p(\mathbf{y} \mid \boldsymbol{\theta})$, where $\boldsymbol{\theta}$ is a vector of parameters, we have

$$(9) \qquad G = \int_{R_\theta} p(\boldsymbol{\theta}) I(\boldsymbol{\theta}) d\boldsymbol{\theta} - \int_{R_\theta} p(\boldsymbol{\theta}) \log p(\boldsymbol{\theta})\, d\boldsymbol{\theta},$$

with

$$(10) \qquad I(\boldsymbol{\theta}) = \int_{R_\mathbf{y}} p(\mathbf{y} \mid \boldsymbol{\theta}) \log p(\mathbf{y} \mid \boldsymbol{\theta}) d\mathbf{y},$$

and the MDIP pdf is given by:

$$p*(\boldsymbol{\theta}) = c_1 \exp\{I(\boldsymbol{\theta})\}, \qquad \boldsymbol{\theta} \subseteq R_\theta$$

with c_1 a normalizing constant.

3 Specific MDIP Pdf's and Their Properties

In table 1, we have listed a number of well-known univariate data pdf's, their data information measures, $I(\boldsymbol{\theta})$, and the associated MDIP pdf's that are proportional to $\exp\{I(\boldsymbol{\theta})\}$.

With respect to the normal data densities, the MDIP pdf's are generally those employed in Bayesian analyses and justified in various ways. With respect to the case in line 1*c*, it is well known that Jeffreys's method involving use of the square root of the determinant of the information matrix, $|\inf|^{1/2}$, yields $p(\theta, \sigma) \propto 1/\sigma^2$, a result that he deems unreasonable. By assuming θ and σ independent and evaluating $|\inf|^{1/2}$ separately for these parameters, he obtains $p(\theta, \sigma) \propto 1/\sigma$, a result that he employs in practice. Note that the normal examples in 1*a–c* of the table are special cases of 6*a–c*, respectively.

The prior pdf for the parameter θ of the rectangular pdf, $p(\theta) \propto 1/\theta$, has a form that is in accord with Jeffreys's rule for a parameter that can assume values from zero to infinity. For such a parameter, the rule is to take $\log \theta$ uniformly distributed which implies $p(\theta) \propto 1/\theta$. Also, this MDIP pdf for the parameter of the rectangular pdf is a special case of 6*b*.

The MDIP prior for the exponential pdf, $p(\theta) \propto 1/\theta$, is in accord with Jeffreys's rule mentioned in the previous paragraph.

Also, this prior pdf is a special case of 6*b*. Note that the Pareto pdf, $p(y \mid A, \beta) = (1/\beta y) \exp\{-\beta^{-1} \log(y/A)\}$, with A a given constant and $0 < A \leq y < \infty$, is a "log-exponential" pdf. Letting $x = \log y/A$, $0 \leq x < \infty$, we obtain $p(x \mid \beta) = (1/\beta) \exp\{-x/\beta\}$, the exponential pdf with parameter β for which the MDIP prior is $p(\beta) \propto 1/\beta$.

In line 4 of table 1, the MDIP prior for the location and scale parameters of the Student-*t* pdf is $p(\theta, \sigma) \propto 1/\sigma$. This is also the prior for the parameters of the Cauchy pdf, the Student-t pdf with $\nu = 1$. These results are special cases of 6c.

For the log-normal pdf in line 5 of table 1, note that θ is the median of this pdf which does not depend on σ. Since both θ and σ can range from 0 to ∞,

Table 1 Continuous Univariate Data Densities, Information Measures and Maximal Data Information Prior (MDIP) Pdf's

Data Pdf	Data Pdf Information Measure, $I(\theta)$	MDIP Pdf
1. *Normal*		
1a $p(y\|\theta) = \frac{1}{\sqrt{2\pi}} \exp\{-(y-\theta)^2/2\}$	const	$p_*(\theta) \propto \text{const}$
1b $p(y\|\sigma) = \frac{1}{\sigma\sqrt{2\pi}} \exp\{-y^2/2\sigma^2\}$	const − log σ	$p_*(\sigma) \propto 1/\sigma$
1c $p(y\|\theta,\sigma) = \frac{1}{\sigma\sqrt{2\pi}} \exp\{-(y-\theta)^2/2\sigma^2\}$	const − log σ	$p_*(\theta, \sigma) \propto 1/\sigma$
2. *Rectangular* $p(y\|\theta) = 1/\theta,\ 0 < y < \theta$	const − log θ	$p_*(\theta) \propto 1/\theta$
3. *Exponential (Pareto)* $p(y\|\theta) = \theta^{-1} \exp\{-y/\theta\}$	const − log θ	$p_*(\theta) \propto 1/\theta$
4. *Student-*t *(ν = 1, Cauchy)* $p(y\|\theta, \sigma) = \frac{k}{\sigma}\left[\nu + \left(\frac{y-\theta}{\sigma}\right)^2\right]^{-(\nu+1)/2}$	const − log σ	$p_*(\theta, \sigma) \propto 1/\sigma$
$k = \frac{\Gamma\{(\nu+1)/2\}\,\nu^{\nu/2}}{\sqrt{\pi}\,\Gamma(\nu/2)}$		
5. *Log-normal* $p(y\|\theta, \sigma) = \frac{1}{\sigma y\sqrt{2\pi}} \exp\{-(\log y - \log\theta)^2/2\sigma^2\}$	const − log σ − log θ	$p_*(\theta, \sigma) \propto 1/\theta\sigma$
6. *General forms* $(-\infty < y < \infty)$		
6a $p(y\|\theta) = f(y-\theta)$	const	$p_*(\theta) \propto \text{const}$
6b $p(y\|\sigma) = \frac{1}{\sigma} f(y/\sigma)$	const − log σ	$p_*(\sigma) \propto 1/\sigma$
6c $p(y\|\theta, \sigma) = \frac{1}{\sigma} f\left(\frac{y-\theta}{\sigma}\right)$	const − log σ	$p_*(\theta, \sigma) \propto 1/\sigma$
7. *Exponential Class* $p(y\|\theta) = \exp\{f(\theta)K(y) + S(y) + q(\theta)\}$	$f(\theta)\bar{K} + \bar{S} + q(\theta)$[a]	$p_*(\theta) \propto \exp\{f(\theta)\bar{K} + \bar{S} + q(\theta)\}$

[a]Here $\bar{K} \equiv \int K(y)p(y|\theta)\,dy$ and $\bar{S} \equiv \int S(y)p(y|\theta)\,dy$.

the form of the prior for these parameters is in accord with Jeffreys's rule. In general, if $p(y|\theta, \sigma) = (1/\sigma y) f((\log y - \log \theta)/\sigma), 0 < y < \infty$, and if $E \log y = \log \theta$, the MDIP prior for θ and σ is $p(\theta, \sigma) \propto 1/\theta\sigma$.[2]

The general forms in lines 6*a*–*c* of the table make the MDIP approach applicable to a very wide range of data pdf's. Since θ is a location parameter and σ a scale parameter, the forms of these priors are reasonable and in accord with usual prescriptions for "diffuse" or "noninformative" prior pdf's for such parameters. Note, for example, that in the case of 6*c*,

$$(11)\qquad I(\theta, \sigma) = \int p(y|\theta, \sigma) \log p(y|\theta, \sigma) dy$$
$$= -\log \sigma + \int \frac{1}{\sigma} f\left(\frac{y-\theta}{\sigma}\right) \log f\left(\frac{y-\theta}{\sigma}\right) dy$$

If the last integral on the r.h.s. of (11) we let $x = (y - \theta)/\sigma$, it becomes $\int f(x) \log f(x) dx$ which is independent of θ and σ.

Thus $I(\theta, \sigma) = \text{const} - \log \sigma$ and $p(\theta, \sigma) \propto \exp\{I(\theta, \sigma)\} \propto 1/\sigma$, as shown in table 1.

In line 7 of table 1, the MDIP prior pdf for the exponential class of pdf's is presented.[3] That this method of generating priors works not only for special cases but also for general cases is fortunate.

Above, we have obtained MDIP prior pdf's for parameters of data densities for continuous random variables. To illustrate application of the procedure to parameters of a distribution for a discrete random variable, we consider the binomial pdf. Let $Pr(\tilde{y} = 1) = \theta$ and $Pr(\tilde{y} = 0) = 1 - \theta$. Then the pdf for $\tilde{y}$ is $p(y|\theta) = \theta^y (1 - \theta)^{1-y}$, with $0 \le \theta \le 1$. The information measure $I(\theta)$ for this data pdf is[4] $I(\theta) = \theta \log \theta + (1 - \theta) \log (1 - \theta)$ and the MDIP pdf is:

$$(12)\qquad p_*(\theta) = c\theta^\theta (1 - \theta)^{1-\theta} \qquad 0 \le \theta \le 1$$

2. Note that $\log p(y|\theta, \sigma) = -\log \sigma - \log y + \log f[(\log y - \log \theta)/\sigma]$ and

$$I(\theta,\sigma) = \int_0^\infty p(y|\theta,\sigma) \log p(y|\theta,\sigma) dy = -\log \sigma - \int_0^\infty \log y p(y|\theta,\sigma) dy$$
$$+ \int_0^\infty p(y - \theta,\sigma) \log f((\log y - \log \theta)/\sigma) dy$$
$$= -\log \sigma - \log \theta + \text{const}.$$

Note that taking $x = (\log y - \log \theta)/\sigma$ in the last integral on the r.h.s. of the expression for $I(\theta, \sigma)$ reduces it to $\int_{-\infty}^{\infty} f(x) \log f(x) dx$, which is independent of θ and σ. Then $p(\theta, \sigma) \propto \exp\{I(\theta, \sigma)\} \propto 1/\theta\sigma$.

3. For some discussion of the exponential class with examples, see, e.g., Hogg and Craig (1965), pp. 223ff.

4. Note that $\log p(y|\theta) = y \log \theta + (1 - y) \log(1 - \theta)$ and its average value given that $\tilde{y} = 1$ with probability θ and $\tilde{y} = 0$ with probability $1 - \theta$ is just $I(\theta) = \theta \log \theta + (1 - \theta) \log \theta$.

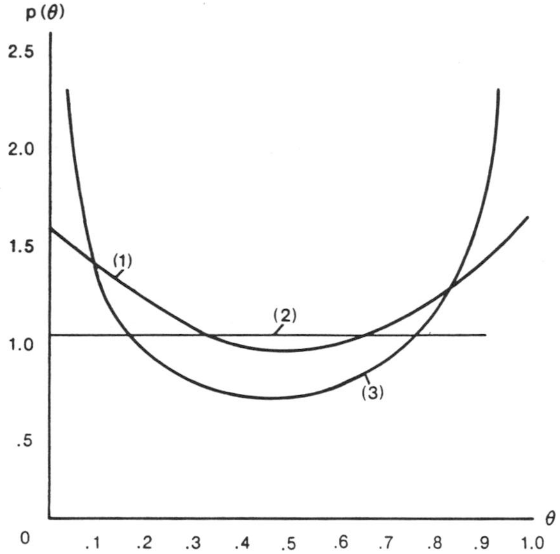

Figure 1 Prior Pdf's for Binomial Parameter θ
(1) $p_*(\theta) = 1.61856\theta^{\theta}(1-\theta)^{1-\theta}$
(2) $p(\theta) = 1$
(3) $p(\theta) = 0.3183\ \theta^{-1/2}(1-\theta)^{-1/2}$

where $c = 1.61856$ is the normalizing constant for this proper pdf[5] that is symmetric about 1/2, its mean. In figure 1 a plot of the pdf in (12) is shown along with plots of several other "diffuse" priors for the binomial parameter. It is seen that the plot of (12) lies "between" the uniform pdf $p(\theta) = 1$, $0 \leq \theta \leq 1$, and the proper beta prior $p(\theta) = \pi^{-1}\theta^{-1/2}(1-\theta)^{-1/2}$ that shoots off to ∞ as $\theta \to 0$ or $\theta \to 1$. This property is also possessed by the improper prior pdf $p(\theta) \propto \theta^{-1}(1-\theta)^{-1}$.

Jeffreys (1967, pp. 123–25) presents a cogent discussion of the problem of formulating a "diffuse" or "noninformative" prior for the binomial parameter in which he considers all of the prior pdf's presented in the preceding paragraph except that in (12). With respect to the uniform distribution, referred to as the Bayes-Laplace rule, he writes, "Certainly if we take the Bayes-Laplace rule right up to the extremes we are led to results that do not correspond to anybody's way of thinking. The rule $d\theta/\theta(1-\theta)$ goes too far the other way."[6] That the pdf in (12) lies above the uniform pdf at the

5. It is the case that $\lim_{\theta \to 0} \theta^{\theta} = 1$ and $\lim_{\theta \to 1} (1-\theta)^{1-\theta} = 1$.

6. In the quote (p. 124), Jeffreys's symbol x has been replaced by θ.

extremes, but does not shoot off to infinity, may then be a virtue associated with (12). Further, if $p(\theta) \propto 1/\theta(1 - \theta)$ is employed as a prior and if all binomial trials produce "successes," the posterior pdf will be improper whereas this problem is avoided through the use of (12).

We now consider generation of MDIP's for parameters of several continuous bivariate and multivariate data densities. Shown in table 2 are

Table 2 Continuous Bivariate and Multivariate Data Densities, Information Measures and Maximal Data Information Prior (MDIP) Pdf's

Data Pdf	Data Pdf Information Measure, $I(\theta)$	MDIP Pdf
1. *Bivariate Normal*		
1a $p(y\|\boldsymbol{\theta}) = \frac{1}{2\pi}\exp -\frac{1}{2}\{(y_1-\theta_1)^2+(y_2-\theta_2)^2\}$	const	$p_*(\boldsymbol{\theta}) \propto$ const
1b $p(y\|\sigma_1, \sigma_2, \rho) = \frac{1}{2\pi\sigma_1\sigma_2(1-\rho^2)^{1/2}}\exp\left\{-\frac{1}{2(1-\rho^2)}\left[\left(\frac{y_1}{\sigma_1}\right)^2+\left(\frac{y_2}{\sigma_2}\right)^2-2\rho\frac{y_1}{\sigma_1}\frac{y_2}{\sigma_2}\right]\right.$	const − $\log \sigma_1 \sigma_2$ − $(1/2) \log)(1-\rho^2)$	$p_*(\sigma_1, \sigma_2, \rho) \propto \frac{1}{\sigma_1\sigma_2}\frac{1}{(1-\rho^2)^{1/2}}$
1c $p(y\|\theta_1, \theta_2, \sigma_1, \sigma_2, \rho) = \frac{1}{2\pi\sigma_1\sigma_2(1-\rho^2)^{1/2}}\exp\left\{-\frac{1}{2(1-\rho^2)}\left[\left(\frac{y_1-\theta_1}{\sigma_1}\right)^2+\left(\frac{y_2-\theta_2}{\sigma_2}\right)^2-2\rho\left(\frac{y_1-\theta_1}{\sigma_1}\right)\left(\frac{y_2-\theta_2}{\sigma_2}\right)\right]\right\}$	const − $\log \sigma_1\sigma_2$ − $(1/2) \log (1-\rho^2)$	$p_*(\theta_1, \theta_2, \sigma_1, \sigma_2, \rho) \propto \frac{1}{\sigma_1\sigma_2(1-\rho^2)^{1/2}}$
2. *Multivariate Normal*		
$p(y\|\boldsymbol{\theta}, \Sigma) = \frac{\|\Sigma\|^{-1/2}}{(2\pi)^{p/2}}\exp\left\{-\frac{1}{2}(y-\boldsymbol{\theta})'\Sigma^{-1}(y-\boldsymbol{\theta})\right\}$	const − $(1/2) \log\|\Sigma\|$	$p_*(\boldsymbol{\theta}, \Sigma) \propto \|\Sigma\|^{-1/2}$
3. *General Forms*		
3a $p(y\|\theta) = f(y-\boldsymbol{\theta})$	const	$p_*(\boldsymbol{\theta}) \propto$ const
3b $p(y\|\Sigma) = \|\Sigma\|^{-1/2}f(y'\Sigma^{-1}y)$	const − $(1/2) \log\|\Sigma\|$	$p_*(\Sigma) \propto \|\Sigma\|^{-1/2}$
3c $p(y\|\boldsymbol{\theta}, \Sigma) = \|\Sigma\|^{-1/2}f\{(y-\boldsymbol{\theta})'\Sigma^{-1}(y-\boldsymbol{\theta})\}$	const − $(1/2) \log\|\Sigma\|$	$p_*(\boldsymbol{\theta}, \Sigma) \propto \|\Sigma\|^{-1/2}$

several data densities, their associated information measures, $I(\boldsymbol{\theta})$, and the MDIP's, $p*(\boldsymbol{\theta}) \propto \exp\{I(\boldsymbol{\theta})\}$. From line 1*a*, we see that the MDIP for the means θ_1 and θ_2 of a spherical bivariate normal pdf is uniform, a special case of the result in line 3*a*. In line 1*b*, the MDIP for the two standard deviations, σ_1 and σ_2, and of the correlation coefficient is $p*(\sigma_1, \sigma_2, \rho) \propto 1/\sigma_1\sigma_2(1 - \rho^2)^{1/2}$, while in line 1*c*, the MDIP for the five parameters of the bivariate normal density is given by

$$p*(\theta_1, \theta_2, \sigma_1, \sigma_2, \rho) \propto 1/\sigma_1\sigma_2(1 - \rho^2)^{1/2} \tag{13}$$

From (13), it is the case that the parameters are independent with $\log \sigma_1$ and $\log \sigma_2$ uniformly distributed. The marginal prior for ρ in (13) is $p(\rho) = c(1 - \rho)^{-1/2}(1 + \rho)^{-1/2}$, with the normalizing constant $c = 1/\pi$, a form of the beta pdf.[7] The prior for ρ, $-1 < \rho < 1$, is symmetric about $\rho = 0$ at which point the density assumes its minimal value. It is interesting to note that among other prior pdf's for ρ, Jeffreys (1967) explicitly considers $p(\rho) = 1/\pi(1 - \rho^2)^{1/2}$ that he believes is compatible with his interpretation of the correlation coefficient.[8]

With respect to the general *p*-dimensional nonsingular multivariate normal data pdf, considered in line 2 of table 2, its information measure is equal to $-(1/2)\log|\Sigma|$ plus a constant and thus the MDIP pdf is $p*(\boldsymbol{\theta}, \Sigma) \propto |\Sigma|^{-1/2}$, a form that implies that $\boldsymbol{\theta}$ and the distinct elements of Σ are independent, with the elements of $\boldsymbol{\theta}$ uniformly and independently distributed. The form of the marginal MDIP pdf for Σ, $p*(\Sigma) \propto |\Sigma|^{-1/2}$ is "close" to $|\Sigma|^{-1}$, a form leading to the Fisher-Cornish posterior pdf, but differs from the form often used,[9] namely, $p(\Sigma) \propto |\Sigma|^{-(p+1)/2}$. This latter form can be obtained by assuming $\boldsymbol{\theta}$ and Σ a priori independent and applying Jeffreys's rule, $|\text{Inf}|^{1/2}$, to the elements of Σ. For $p = 2$, this rule yields $p(\sigma_1, \sigma_2, \rho) \propto 1/\sigma_1\sigma_2(1 - \rho^2)^{3/2}$, a form discussed by Jeffreys,[10] who appears to favor

7. If we let $x = (1 + \rho)/2$, then $0 < x < 1$ for $-1 < \rho < 1$, and $p(x) = (1/\pi)x^{-1/2}(1 - x)^{-1/2}$ is a proper, normalized beta pdf.

8. He also discusses $p(\rho) \propto$ const and $p(\rho) \propto 1/(1 - \rho^2)^{3/2}$, the latter an improper pdf produced by his $|\text{Inf}|^{1/2}$ rule.

9. See, e.g., Geisser (1965), Tiao and Zellner (1964), Savage (1961), Box and Tiao (1973), and Zellner (1971). Note, however, as pointed out by S. J. Press in conversation, that if we modify (6) to read:

$$G' = q\int p(\boldsymbol{\theta})I(\boldsymbol{\theta})d\boldsymbol{\theta} - \int p(\boldsymbol{\theta})\log p(\boldsymbol{\theta})d\boldsymbol{\theta},$$

where q is a given scalar, then the MDIP in (8) is

$$p_*(\boldsymbol{\theta}) = c_0\exp\{qI(\boldsymbol{\theta})\}.$$

For $I(\boldsymbol{\theta}) = -1/2\log|\Sigma|$, $p_*(\Sigma) = c_0|\Sigma|^{-q/2}$. By taking $q = p + 1$, the "usual" diffuse prior pdf for Σ is obtained.

10. Jeffreys (1967), pp. 187 ff.

the form shown in (13) or $p(\sigma_1, \sigma_2, \rho) \propto 1/\sigma_1\sigma_2$ even though these latter priors are not yielded by his invariant rule.

The MDIP pdf's for the general forms of data densities, given in lines 3*a–c* of table 2, are relevant for a broad range of multivariate data densities. In each case, they are derived by a straightforward evaluation of the expression for the data density information measure $I(\cdot)$ and then using $p*(\cdot) \propto \exp\{I(\cdot)\}$ to obtain the MDIP pdf. That resulting MDIP pdf's are relatively simple is indeed fortunate. Also theorems 2, 3, 4 of section 2 can be generalized to relate to multivariate pdf's.

We next consider the application of the MDIP approach to yield prior pdf's for parameters of several frequently employed models. Consider the normal multiple regression model $\tilde{y} = \mathbf{x}'\boldsymbol{\beta} + \tilde{u}$, where $\mathbf{x}'$ is a $1 \times k$ given vector, $\boldsymbol{\beta}$ is a $k \times 1$ vector of parameters and $\tilde{u}$ is a normal error with zero mean and standard deviation σ. Then the information in the pdf for $\tilde{y}$ is[11] $I(\boldsymbol{\beta}, \sigma) = \text{const} - \log\sigma$ and the MDIP pdf for $\boldsymbol{\beta}$ and σ is $p*(\boldsymbol{\beta}, \sigma) \propto \exp\{I(\boldsymbol{\beta}, \sigma)\} \propto 1/\sigma$, a "diffuse" prior pdf that is usually employed.[12]

For the multivariate normal regression model, $\tilde{\mathbf{y}}' = \mathbf{x}'B + \tilde{\mathbf{u}}'$, where $\tilde{\mathbf{y}}'$ is a $1 \times p$ random vector, $\mathbf{x}'$ is a $1 \times k$ given vector, B is a $k \times p$ matrix of regression coefficients and $\tilde{\mathbf{u}}$ is a $1 \times p$ normal error vector with zero mean vector and pds covariance matrix Σ, $I(B, \Sigma) = \text{const} - (1/2)\log|\Sigma|$. Thus the MDIP pdf for B and Σ is $p*(B, \Sigma) \propto |\Sigma|^{-1/2}$ that has B and Σ independent with the elements of B uniformly and independently distributed and the distinct elements of Σ distributed in the form $p*(\Sigma) \propto |\Sigma|^{-1/2}$.

The last process that we consider is a stationary first-order normal autoregressive process with unknown mean, that is, $\tilde{y}_t = (1 - \beta)\theta + \beta\tilde{y}_{t-1} + \tilde{u}_{t'}$, with $|\beta| < 1$ and $\tilde{u}_t$ normal with zero mean and standard deviation σ.[13] The pdf for $\tilde{y}_t$ is $p(y_t|\beta, \theta, \sigma) = (\sigma\sqrt{2\pi})^{-1}(1 - \beta^2)^{1/2}\exp\{-(1 - \beta^2)(y_t - \theta)^2/2\sigma^2\}$ and $I(\beta, \theta, \sigma) = \text{const} + 1/2\log(1 - \beta^2) - \log\sigma$. Thus the MDIP pdf is:

$$(14) \qquad p*(\beta, \theta, \sigma) \propto \frac{(1 - \beta^2)^{1/2}}{\sigma} \qquad |\beta| < 1$$

11. That is, $I(\boldsymbol{\beta}, \sigma) = \int_{-\infty}^{\infty} p(y|\boldsymbol{x}, \boldsymbol{\beta}, \sigma) \log p(y|\boldsymbol{x}, \boldsymbol{\beta}, \sigma)dy$, where

$$p(y|\boldsymbol{x}, \boldsymbol{\beta}, \sigma) = (\sigma\sqrt{2\pi})^{-1}\exp\{-\frac{1}{2\sigma^2}(y - \boldsymbol{x}'\boldsymbol{\beta})^2\}.$$

12. Jeffreys obtains this prior pdf by assuming $\boldsymbol{\beta}$ and σ a priori independent and applying his rule $|\text{Inf}|^{1/2}$ separately to $\boldsymbol{\beta}$ and to σ. If $|\text{Inf}|^{1/2}$ is applied to $\boldsymbol{\beta}$ and σ jointly, the result is $p(\boldsymbol{\beta}, \sigma) \propto 1/\sigma^{k+1}$, deemed "unsatisfactory"; see Jeffreys (1967), p. 182.

13. Note if $\tilde{y}_t = \beta_1 + \beta_2\tilde{y}_{t-1} + \tilde{u}_t$, $\tilde{y}_t = \beta_1/(1 - \beta_2) + \Sigma_{i=0}^{\infty}\beta_2^i u_{t-i}$. Given that $|\beta_2| < 1$, $E\tilde{y}_t = \beta_1/(1 - \beta_2) \equiv \theta$, the mean of the process. Thus, with $\beta_2 \equiv \beta$, we write $\tilde{y}_t = (1 - \beta)\theta + \beta\tilde{y}_{t-1} + \tilde{u}_t$ in order to parameterize the process in terms of its mean, θ.

In (14), β, θ, and σ are mutually independent with θ and $\log \sigma$ uniform. The marginal prior for β, $p_*(\beta) \propto (1 - \beta^2)^{1/2}$, $|\beta| < 1$, is symmetric about $\beta = 0$, where it reaches a maximum and falls to zero as $|\beta| \rightarrow 1$.[14]

Above we have considered the MDIP approach in terms of specific parameterizations except for theorems 3 and 4 that provide invariance properties relating to linear transformations of the parameters. The problem of dealing with nonlinear transformations of parameters is a thorny one that has received considerable attention in the literature and must be considered. Our approach is to obtain the MDIP for the particular parameterization employed. By not insisting on what Hartigan (1964) calls Ω-labeling invariance, we can achieve our objective of having a posterior distribution reflect mainly the information in a data distribution for the particular parameterization employed without being restricted by broad invariance restrictions. Given that investigators use the MDIP procedure to generate priors for any given parameterization, different investigators will obtain the same posterior pdf's.

A specific nonlinear parameter transformation that has evoked much controversy is the reciprocal transformation of a location parameter. For example, let θ be the mean of a univariate normal pdf with unit variance, $p(y|\theta) = (2\pi)^{-1/2} \exp\{-(y - \theta)^2/2\}$. For this data pdf, $I(\theta) = \text{const}$ and the MDIP pdf is $p_*(\theta) \propto \text{const}$, as pointed out above. If $\eta = 1/\theta$, $p(y|\eta) = (2\pi)^{-1/2} \exp\{-(y - 1/\eta)^2/2\}$ and $I(\eta) = \text{const}$. Thus the MDIP for η is: $p_*(\eta)$ const, for $|\eta| > 0$.[15] Thus the MDIP pdf's for θ and for $\eta = 1/\theta$ are uniform since both are pure location parameters for which $I(\cdot)$ has the same constant value. It is recognized that $p(\theta)d\theta \propto d\theta$ logically implies $p(\eta) \propto d\eta/\eta^2$.[16] However, $p(\eta) \propto 1/\eta^2$ is *not* the MDIP pdf for η, that is, one that allows the information in the data pdf to be reflected most, in the sense defined above, in a posterior pdf for η. Use of the MDIP prior pdf, $p_*(\eta) \propto$ const, achieves this latter objective.

To illustrate the analysis of the reciprocal transformation, consider the simple normal regression for income change, $\tilde{y}_t = \theta x_t + \tilde{u}_t$ where x_t is the change in autonomous spending, θ is the "Keynesian multiplier" and $\tilde{u}_t$ is a normal error term with zero mean and standard deviation σ. As explained above, the MDIP pdf for θ and σ is: $p_*(\theta, \sigma) \propto 1/\sigma$. Now let $\theta = 1/\eta$, where η is the "marginal propensity to save." The MDIP pdf for η and σ is $p(\eta, \sigma) \propto$

14. As can be seen by making the change of variable $z = (1 - \beta)/2$, $p_*(\beta) \propto (1 - \beta^2)^{1/2} \propto (1 - \beta)^{1/2} (1 + \beta)^{1/2}$ is a form of a proper beta pdf. See Zellner (1971), pp. 216–20 for discussion of other diffuse priors for β, θ, and σ.

15. Note that we exclude $\eta = 0$ since $-\infty < \theta < \infty$.

16. This is the prior pdf introduced by application of Jeffreys's Ω-labeling invariant rule, $|\text{Inf}|^{1/2}$.

$1/\sigma$, that is η and $\log \sigma$ uniform and independent. On the other hand, from $\theta = 1/\eta$ and $p(\theta, \sigma) \propto 1/\sigma$, we obtain $p(\eta, \sigma) \propto 1/\eta^2\sigma$. This prior for η, defined over a finite range excluding the point $\eta = 0$, implies that small absolute values of η are more probable than large values, that is, for example, $Pr(a < \eta < a + b) > Pr(a + b < \eta < a + 2b)$ with $a, b > 0$ and the interval a to $a + 2b$ contained within the range of η. On the other hand, the MDIP pdf for η, $p*(\eta) \propto$ const, of course, implies equal prior probabilities associated with intervals of equal length for η. Thus use of the Ω-labeling invariance condition leading to priors $p(\theta) \propto$ const and $p(\eta) \propto 1/\eta^2$, both defined for a finite range, involves the implication that small absolute values of η are more probable than large values, an implication not present when MDIP pdf's for θ and η are employed. In general, if θ is a parameter of a data density for which $I(\theta) =$ const, then if $\eta = f(\theta)$ is a proper one-to-one transformation, $I(\eta) =$ const and the MDIP pdf's for θ and η are both uniform.[17]

Another important nonlinear transformation is that involving powers of a scale parameter, say the standard deviation, σ, of the normal data density, $p(y|\sigma) = (2\pi)^{-1/2} \exp\{-y^2/2\sigma\}^2$. Let $\phi_i = \sigma^i$, $i = 1, 2, 3, \ldots$. Then the MDIP for ϕ_i is given by $p*(\phi_i) \propto 1/\phi_i^{1/i}$, $i = 1, 2, 3, \ldots$. For $i = 1$, $\phi_i = \sigma$ and $p*(\phi_1) = p*(\sigma) \propto 1/\sigma$. For $i = 2$, $p*(\phi_2) = 1/(\phi_2)^{1/2}$. This latter pdf, defined for a finite range so that it is proper, is "flatter" than the Ω-labeling invariant prior, $p(\phi_2) \propto 1/\phi_2$ defined over the same finite range. As i gets large, the MDIP pdf for ϕ_i approaches a uniform pdf whereas the Ω-labeling invariant prior for ϕ_i (or the prior that is "invariant with respect to powers") $p(\phi_i) \propto 1/\phi_i$ has the same shape no matter what the value of i and is not a MDIP pdf.

In general, if $\boldsymbol{\theta}$ is a $p \times 1$ vector of parameters of a data density with information measure $I(\boldsymbol{\theta})$ and if $\theta_1 = f_1(\boldsymbol{\eta}), \theta_2 = f_2(\boldsymbol{\eta}), \ldots, \theta_p = f_p(\boldsymbol{\eta})$, is a set of proper, one-to-one transformations, denoted by $\boldsymbol{\theta} = \boldsymbol{f}(\boldsymbol{\eta})$, where $\boldsymbol{\eta}$ is a $p \times 1$ vector of parameters, the forms of the MDIP priors for $\boldsymbol{\theta}$ and for $\boldsymbol{\eta}$ are given by: $p*(\boldsymbol{\theta}) \propto \exp\{I(\boldsymbol{\theta})\}$ and $p*(\boldsymbol{\eta}) \propto \exp\{I(\boldsymbol{\eta})\}$, where $I(\boldsymbol{\eta}) = I[\boldsymbol{f}^{-1}(\boldsymbol{\theta})]$.

4 Concluding Remarks

In the present paper a procedure for generating MDIP pdf's has been presented and applied to several problems. The procedure utilizes an information measure that has been considered and employed by others, including Shannon (1948), Jeffreys (1967), Jaynes (1968), Lindley (1956, 1961), and perhaps others. What is distinctive about the present approach is

17. This is easily generalized to the cases involving a vector of p parameters, $\boldsymbol{\theta}$ and $\eta_i = f_i(\boldsymbol{\theta}), i = 1, 2, \ldots, p$. If $I(\boldsymbol{\theta}) =$ const, then $I(\boldsymbol{\eta}) =$ const and the MDIP pdf's for $\boldsymbol{\theta}$ and for $\boldsymbol{\eta}$ are each proportional to a constant.

the use of the particular function G in (3) that is used as a criterion function to be maximized by choice of a prior pdf. That use of the function G leads to simple forms for prior pdf's, some of them already in widespread use, is certainly appealing. Also, use of the MDIP approach provides a fresh view of and operational results for the problem of selecting "diffuse" prior pdf's for alternative parameterizations. That the prior pdf's yielded by the MDIP approach have been defined to be proper may appeal to some. However, if Jeffreys's (1967) arguments for the use of improper prior pdf's to represent "knowing little" or "ignorance" are considered compelling, we can take note of his remark "in the mathematical definition of an infinite integral a finite range is always considered in the first place and then allowed to tend to infinity." Thus, just as Jeffreys illustrates, we can obtain improper MDIP pdf's in many cases by allowing their ranges to tend to infinity.[18]

It is to be emphasized that it is not recommended that MDIP pdf's always be employed in Bayesian analyses. Clearly there are many circumstances in which "informative" prior pdf's will be employed. However, when an investigator knows little about parameter values or wants to proceed as if he knows little about parameter values, and wants to feature the data information in his posterior distribution,[19] it is thought that MDIP pdf's will be found useful.

Last, it is the case that prior pdf's can be found that maximize G in (3) subject not only to the condition that $\int p(\theta)d\theta = 1$ but also to one or more of the following conditions $\int \theta p(\theta)d\theta = \mu_1$, $\int \theta^2 p(\theta)d\theta = \mu_2, \ldots$, where μ_1, $\mu_2, \ldots$ are assigned values by an investigator.

Addendum (1975)

I hit on the procedure described in this paper during the summer of 1968 and included a description and some applications of it at the end of chapter 2 of Zellner (1971).[20] In recent valuable correspondence with I. J. Good, dated 8 September 1975, he drew my attention to some of his work that deals in part with related topics, in particular Good (1965, 1963). Good uses entropy measures in connection with generating null hypotheses (or prior pdf's), and writes as follows about his approach in the first reference cited above, "This method has some aesthetic appeal but is difficult to justify" (p. 75).

18. See Rényi (1970) for justification for use of Bayes's theorem with improper pdf's.

19. See Zellner and Richard (1973), where this topic is discussed in terms of a Cobb-Douglas production function estimation problem.

20. This work grew out of an investigation of a suggestion in Lindley (1956) to choose a prior to maximize the information provided by an experiment. Solutions to this latter problem proved intractable and thus I altered the criterion to the form of G in (3) or (4) that I now regard as more appropriate.

In the second reference he writes, "A possible approach, which, however, is difficult to justify, would be to maximize some linear combination of the entropy and of the log-likelihood, such as the sum." Good considers just binomial and multinomial problems for which he obtains a prior pdf in the form, $\Pi_{p_i}^{-p_i}$ with $\Sigma_{i=1}^{n} p_i = 1$, a rule that differs from my (12) for the case $n = 2$.

Another point mentioned by Good and others is that MDIP pdf's forms depend on properties of likelihood functions. This is also true of Jeffreys's $|\text{Inf}|^{-1/2}$ rule and the procedures put forward by Lindley (1956) and Box and Tiao (1973). Since the purpose of a MDIP pdf is to allow the information provided by an experiment to be featured, it seems natural that the form of a MDIP pdf that accomplished this objective be dependent on the design of an experiment.

In current work, the approach described in this paper has been extended by using what Good calls "invariantized" entropy, that is entropy expressions based on arbitrary measures. Also, in recent conversations with Edwin Jaynes, he pointed out another interpretation of my results, namely that MDIP pdf's can be interpreted as pdf's that maximize the entropy associated with a prior pdf subject to the side condition that the average entropy in the data pdf, $p(y \mid \theta)$, be constant. Last, further work to understand just how much or how little invariance is required for specific problems would be valuable.

References

Box, G. E. P., and G. C. Tiao (1973). *Bayesian Inference in Statistical Analysis*. Reading, Mass.: Addison-Wesley Publishing Co.

Geisser, S. (1965). "Bayesian Estimation in Multivariate Analysis," *Annals of Mathematical Statistics*, 36:150–59.

Good, I. J. (1965). *The Estimation of Probabilities: An Essay on Modern Bayesian Methods*. pp. 75–76. Cambridge, Mass.: MIT Press.

———. (1963). "Maximum Entropy for Hypothesis Formulation, Especially for Multinomial Contingency Tables." *Annals of Mathematical Statistics*, 34:911–34.

Hartigan, J. (1964). "Invariant Prior Distributions." *Annals of Mathematical Statistics*, 35:836–45.

Hogg, R. V., and A. T. Craig (1965). *Introduction to Mathematical Statistics*. 2d ed. New York: Macmillan Co.

Jaynes, E. T. (1968). "Prior Probabilities." *IEEE Transactions on Systems Science and Cybernetics*, SSC-4, pp. 227–41. New York: Institute of Electrical and Electronic Engineers.

Jeffreys, H. (1967). *Theory of Probability*. 3d rev. ed. London: Oxford University Press.

Lindley, D. V. (1956). "On a Measure of Information Provided by an Experiment," *Annals of Mathematical Statistics*, 27:986–1005.

———. (1961). "The Use of Prior Probability Distributions in Statistical Inference and Decisions." In J. Neyman, ed., *Proceedings of the Fourth Berkeley Symposium on Mathematical Statistics and Probability*, 1:453–68. Berkeley: University of California Press.

Novick, M., and W. Hall (1965). "A Bayesian Indifference Procedure." *Journal of the American Statistical Association*, 60:1104–17.

Rényi, A. (1970). *Foundations of Probability*. San Francisco: Holden-Day.

Savage, L. J. (1961). "The Subjective Basis of Statistical Practice." Department of Statistics, University of Michigan.

Shannon, C. E. (1948). "The Mathematical Theory of Communication." *Bell System Technical Journal*, July–October 1948. Reprinted in C. E. Shannon and W. Weaver, *The Mathematical Theory of Communication*, pp. 3–91. University of Illinois Press, 1949.

Tiao, G. C., and A. Zellner (1964). "On the Bayesian Estimation of Multivariate Regression." *Journal of the Royal Statistical Society*, Ser. B, 26:277–85.

Zellner, A. (1971). *An Introduction to Bayesian Inference in Econometrics*. New York: John Wiley & Sons.

Zellner, A., and J. F. Richard (1973). "Use of Prior Information in the Analysis and Estimation of Cobb-Douglas Production Function Models." *International Economic Review*, 14:107–19.

3.3 Bayesian and Non-Bayesian Analysis of the Log-Normal Distribution and Log-Normal Regression

1 Introduction

In this article we consider the problem of making inferences about parameters of the log-normal distribution and of log-normal regression processes. Previous work on these problems within the sampling theory framework has appeared in Aitchison and Brown (1957), Bradu and Mundlak (1968, 1970), Finney (1949), Goldberger (1968), Heien (1968), and Kendall and Stuart (1961). Some Bayesian results for the log-normal distribution have appeared in Kaufman (1963). Herein, after providing the simple analysis required to obtain posterior pdf's for parameters of interest, we present minimum mean square error (MSE) estimators for parameters and show that they are optimal Bayesian estimators when we employ a *relative* squared error loss function. Also, comparisons of several other Bayesian and non-Bayesian estimation results are provided.

2 Bayesian Analysis

Given that $z_i = \ell n y_i$ is normally distributed with mean μ and variance σ^2, then y_i has by definition a log-normal distribution. It is well known that the median and mean of y_i are given by $\phi = e^{\mu}$ and $\eta = \exp\{\mu + \sigma^2/2\}$, respectively, with $0 < \phi, \eta < \infty$. Given n independent observations $\mathbf{z}' = (z_1, z_2, \ldots, z_n)$, the likelihood function for μ and σ is $\ell(\mu, \sigma | \mathbf{z}) \propto \sigma^{-n} \exp\{-(1/2\sigma^2)[\nu s^2 + n(\mu - \bar{z})^2]\}$, where $\nu = n - 1$, $\nu s^2 = \Sigma_{i=1}^{n}(z_i - \bar{z})^2$, and $n\bar{z} = \Sigma_{i=1}^{n} z_i$. If we employ a diffuse prior pdf[1] for μ and σ, $p(\mu, \sigma) \propto 1/\sigma$, $-\infty < \mu < \infty$ and $0 < \sigma < \infty$, it is well known that:

1. The conditional posterior pdf for μ given σ is normal with mean $\bar{z}$ and variance σ^2/n and

Reprinted from the *Journal of the American Statistical Association*, 66 (June 1971): 327–30, with the kind permission of the American Statistical Association.

1. See, e.g., Jeffreys (1967) and Lindley (1965) for discussions of improper prior pdf's of this form. The analysis presented above can easily be extended to cases in which a proper natural conjugate prior pdf is utilized.

2. The marginal posterior pdf for μ is in the univariate Student-t form with mean $\bar{z}$ for, $\nu > 1$, and variance $\nu s^2/n\ (\nu - 2)$, for $\nu > 2$.

Given these facts, the following results are immediate consequences:

(A) Given σ, $\ell n\phi = \mu$, has a normal posterior pdf and thus ϕ given σ has a log-normal posterior pdf.

(B) The marginal posterior pdf for $\ell n\phi = \mu$ is in the univariate Student-t form. Thus we may say that the posterior pdf for ϕ is in the "log Student-t" form,[2] that is,

$$(2.1)\qquad p(\phi|\mathbf{z}) = \begin{cases} c/\phi\{\nu s^2 + n(\ell n\phi - \bar{z})^2\}^{-(\nu+1)/2} & \text{for } 0 < \phi < \infty \\ 0 & \text{for } \phi \leq 0 \end{cases}$$

with $c = \sqrt{2/\pi}(\nu s^2/2)^{\nu/2}\Gamma(\nu/2)$.

(C) Given σ, $\ell n\eta = \mu + \sigma^2/2$ has a normal posterior pdf with mean $\bar{z} + \sigma^2/2$ and variance σ^2/n.[3] Thus the conditional posterior pdf for η given σ is a log-normal pdf.

(D) The marginal posterior pdf for η can be obtained from the joint posterior pdf for $\theta = \ell n\eta$ and σ, $p(\theta, \sigma|\mathbf{z}) = p_1(\theta|\sigma, \mathbf{z})p_2(\sigma|\mathbf{z})$, with $p_1(\theta|\sigma,\mathbf{z}) \propto \sigma^{-1}\exp\{-n(\theta - \bar{z} - \sigma^2/2)^2/2\sigma^2\}$ and $p_2(\sigma|\mathbf{z}) \propto \sigma^{-(\nu+1)}\exp\{-\nu s^2/2\sigma^2\}$, $-\infty < \theta < \infty$ and $0 < \sigma < \infty$. That is,

$$(2.2)\qquad p(\theta|\mathbf{z}) \propto \exp(n\theta/2) \cdot \int_0^\infty \sigma^{-(\nu+2)}\exp\left\{-\left[\frac{\nu s^2 + n(\theta - \bar{z})^2}{2\sigma^2} + \frac{n\sigma^2}{8}\right]\right\}d\sigma$$

and thus

$$(2.3)\qquad p(\eta|\mathbf{z}) \propto \eta^{(n-2)/2} \cdot \int_0^\infty \sigma^{-(\nu+2)}\exp\left\{-\left[\frac{\nu s^2 + n(\ell n\eta - \bar{z})^2}{2\sigma^2} + \frac{n\sigma^2}{8}\right]\right\}d\sigma$$

for $0 < \eta < \infty$ and zero otherwise. That the integral in (2.3) can be expressed in terms of modified Bessel functions[4] may be useful in the analysis of (2.3). Alternatively, readily available bivariate numerical integration procedures

2. The posterior mean of $\phi = e^{\mu}$ does not exist.

3. This fact was pointed out in Kaufman (1963).

4. Let $t = 2/n\sigma^2$. Then the integral in (2.3) is proportional to

$$\int_0^\infty t^{\nu'-1}\exp\{-(1/4t + at)\}dt$$

with $\nu' = (\nu + 1)/2$ and $a = n[\nu s^2 + n(\ell n\eta - \bar{z})^2]/4$. The value of this integral, given in Erdélyi et al. (1954), p. 146, (29) is $2(1/4a)^{\nu'/2}K'_\nu(\sqrt{a})$, where K'_ν denotes a modified Bessel function, defined in Erdélyi et al. (1954), p. 371.

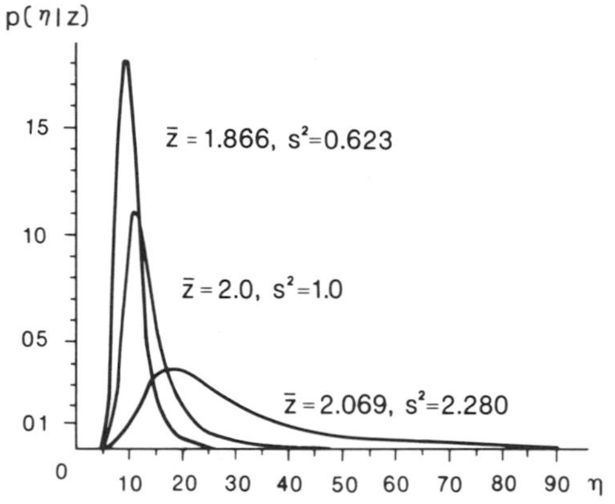

Figure 1 Posterior Pdf's for the Mean of the Log-Normal Pdf Computed from (2.3) with $n = 15$

can be employed to obtain the normalization constant for (2.3), the marginal posterior pdf for η, and to analyze other features of this pdf. It is the case that the posterior mean of η does not exist. In figure 1 several posterior pdf's for η, computed from (2.3) by numerical integration, are presented. It is seen that these pdf's are unimodal and positively skewed.

The results presented earlier for the median and mean of the log-normal distribution generalize straightforwardly to apply to log-normal regression processes. Let

$$z_i = \ell n\, y_i = \beta_1 x_{1i} + \beta_2 x_{2i} + \cdots + \beta_k x_{ki} + u_i \qquad i = 1, 2, \cdots, n \tag{2.4}$$

denote our log-normal regression process where the x's are given values of independent variables, the β's are regression coefficients with unknown values, and the u's are independent normal error terms, each with zero mean and variance σ^2. Under these assumptions, y_i has a log-normal pdf with median ϕ_i and mean η_i given by $\phi_i = exp\{\mathbf{x}_i'\boldsymbol{\beta}\}$ and $\eta_i = \exp\{\mathbf{x}_i'\boldsymbol{\beta} + \sigma^2/2\}$ where $\mathbf{x}_i' = (x_{1i}, x_{2i}, \cdots, x_{ki})$ and $\boldsymbol{\beta}' = (\beta_1, \beta_2, \cdots, \beta_k)$.

If we combine a diffuse prior pdf[5] for the elements of $\boldsymbol{\beta}$ and σ, namely, $p(\boldsymbol{\beta}, \sigma) \propto 1/\sigma$, $0 < \sigma < \infty$ and $-\infty < \beta_i < \infty$, $i = 1, 2, \cdots, k$, with the likelihood function, $\ell(\boldsymbol{\beta}, \sigma|\mathbf{z}) \propto \sigma^{-n}\exp\{-[\nu s^2 + (\boldsymbol{\beta} - \hat{\boldsymbol{\beta}})' X'X(\boldsymbol{\beta} - \hat{\boldsymbol{\beta}})]/2\sigma^2\}$, where $\nu = n - k$, $X' = (\mathbf{x}_1, \mathbf{x}_2, \cdots, \mathbf{x}_n)$, a $k \times n$ matrix with rank k, $\hat{\boldsymbol{\beta}} = (X'X)^{-1}X'\mathbf{z}$, $z' = (z_1, z_2, \cdots, z_n)$ and $\nu s^2 = (\mathbf{z} - \mathbf{X}\boldsymbol{\beta})' (\mathbf{z} - \mathbf{X}\boldsymbol{\beta})$,

5. The analysis can easily be extended to the case in which a proper natural conjugate prior pdf is employed.

then the following properties of the posterior pdf for $\boldsymbol{\beta}$ and σ are well known (see e.g., Lindley 1965 or Raiffa and Schlaifer 1961):

1. Given σ, the posterior pdf for $\boldsymbol{\beta}$ is multivariate normal with mean $\hat{\boldsymbol{\beta}}$ and covariance matrix $(X'X)^{-1}\sigma^2$ and

2. The marginal posterior pdf for $\boldsymbol{\beta}$ is in the multivariate Student-t form with mean $\hat{\boldsymbol{\beta}}$, for $\nu > 1$, and covariance matrix $(X'X)^{-1}\nu s^2/(\nu - 2)$, for $\nu > 2$.

These results lead to the following statements about the posterior pdf's for ϕ_i and η_i which parallel those in (A)–(D) above:

(A′) Given σ, $\ell n\ \phi = \mathbf{x}_i'\boldsymbol{\beta}$ has a univariate normal posterior pdf with mean $\mathbf{x}_i'\hat{\boldsymbol{\beta}}$ and variance $\mathbf{x}_i'(X'X)^{-1}\mathbf{x}_i\sigma^2$. Thus ϕ_i has a log-normal posterior pdf given σ.

(B′) The marginal posterior pdf for $\ell n\ \phi_i = \mathbf{x}_i'\boldsymbol{\beta}$ is a univariate Student-t pdf since $\mathbf{x}_i'\boldsymbol{\beta}$ is a linear combination of the elements of $\boldsymbol{\beta}$ which have a multivariate Student-t posterior pdf.[6] Thus ϕ_i has a "log Student-t" posterior pdf.

(C′) Given σ, $\ell n\ \eta_i = \mathbf{x}_i'\boldsymbol{\beta} + \sigma^2/2$ has a univariate normal posterior pdf and thus η_i has a log-normal conditional posterior pdf.

(D′) The marginal posterior pdf for η_i can be obtained from the joint posterior pdf for $\theta_i = \ell n\ \eta_i$ and σ, namely, $p(\theta_i, \sigma|\mathbf{z}) = p_1(\theta_i|\sigma, \mathbf{z})p_2(\sigma|\mathbf{z})$, where $p_2(\sigma|\mathbf{z}) \propto \sigma^{-(\nu+1)/2}\exp\{-(\nu s^2/2\sigma^2)\}$ by integrating with respect to σ and then making a change of variable using $\theta_i = \ell n\ \eta_i$. Since the analysis is quite similar to that shown under (D) above, it is not presented.

3 Comparisons of Bayesian and Non-Bayesian Results

The results in section 2 provide what is needed to make posterior inferences about parameters of the log-normal distribution and of log-normal regressions with diffuse prior pdf's. We now compare several features of these results with certain non-Bayesian results. As regards the log-normal distribution, since $\bar{z}$ and $\hat{\sigma}^2 = \Sigma_{i=1}^n (z_i - \bar{z})^2/n$ are maximum likelihood (ML) estimators for μ and σ^2, respectively, $\hat{\phi} = \exp(\bar{z})$ and $\hat{\eta} = \exp\{\bar{z} + \hat{\sigma}^2/2\}$ are ML estimators for the median and mean, respectively, of the log-normal distribution. It will be noted that if we employ the diffuse prior pdf for μ and σ shown above, $\hat{\phi} = \exp\{\bar{z}\}$ is precisely the median of the posterior pdf for ϕ which is an optimal point estimate for an absolute error loss function. Further, the mean of the ML estimator $\hat{\phi}$ is $\exp\{\mu + \sigma^2/2n\}$, which is in the same form as the mean of the conditional posterior pdf for ϕ given σ^2 (see (A) in section 2) except that μ replaces $\bar{z}$. Since $E\hat{\phi} \neq \exp\{\mu\}$,

6. See, e.g., Raiffa and Schlaifer (1961), pp. 258–59, for the derivation of the pdf of a linear combination of random variables with a multivariate Student-t pdf.

it is the case that the ML estimator for the median is biased. To obtain an unbiased estimator for $\phi = \exp\{\mu\}$, we can pursue the approach put forward by Finney (1949). An unbiased estimator for ϕ, given σ^2, is $\tilde{\phi} = \exp\{\bar{z} - \sigma^2/2n\}$. Now expand $\exp\{-\sigma^2/2n\}$ as $e^x = \Sigma_{i=0}^{\infty} x^i/i!$ and insert unbiased estimators for $\sigma^{2i}, i = 1, 2, \cdots$. Then Finney's unbiased estimator is:

$$\tilde{\tilde{\phi}} = \exp\{\bar{z}\}g(s^2) \tag{3.1}$$

where $g(s^2) = \Sigma_{i=0}^{\infty} s^{2i}/2^i n^i i! c(i)$ with $c(i) = \nu(\nu + 2) \cdots (\nu + 2i)/\nu^i(\nu + 2i)$. Since $\tilde{\tilde{\phi}}$ is a function of the sufficient statistics $\bar{z}$ and s^2 and is unbiased, it is a minimum variance unbiased estimator.

What appears to be unappreciated in the literature is that, for given σ^2, a minimum MSE estimator for ϕ can be generated as follows: Consider the class of estimators $\phi^* = k \exp\{\bar{z}\}$ where k is a constant. Then the MSE associated with ϕ^* is:

$$\begin{aligned} E(\phi^* - \phi)^2 = {} & k^2 \exp\{2(\mu + \sigma^2/n)\} \\ & - 2k \exp\{2\mu + \sigma^2/2n\} + \exp\{2\mu\}. \end{aligned} \tag{3.2}$$

Taking $k = \exp\{-3\sigma^2/2n\}$ provides a minimal value to (3.2) and thus

$$\phi^* = \exp\{\bar{z} - 3\sigma^2/2n\} \tag{3.3}$$

is a minimum MSE estimator for ϕ given σ^2 in the class $k \exp\{\bar{z}\}$.[7]

Of course, since ϕ^* in (3.3) is different from the unbiased estimator, $\tilde{\phi} = \exp\{\bar{z} - \sigma^2/2n\}$, ϕ^* is biased. However, in terms of MSE ϕ^* is decidedly superior to $\tilde{\phi}$. The ratio of MSE's associated with $\tilde{\phi}$ and ϕ^* is

$$\psi = \frac{MSE(\phi^*)}{MSE(\tilde{\phi})} = \exp\{-\sigma^2/n\}. \tag{3.4}$$

As $\sigma^2/n \to 0$, $\psi \to 1$. For a wide range of values of σ^2/n, ψ is much below one as the following table indicates:

σ^2/n	ψ
.01	.99
.10	.90
.50	.61
.70	.50
1.00	.37
2.00	.14

These results indicate that for given $\sigma^2/n \neq 0$, the unbiased estimator $\tilde{\phi}$ (and

7. Clearly, the Finney expansion approach can be applied to ϕ^*.

the ML estimator $\hat{\phi}$) are inadmissible relative to a squared error loss function.

Further, note that ϕ^* in (3.3) differs from the mean of the conditional posterior pdf for ϕ given σ^2, namely, $E(\phi \mid \sigma^2, \mathbf{z}) = \exp\{\bar{z} + \sigma^2/2n\}$, obtained using the improper diffuse prior pdf for μ and σ introduced above. For given σ^2, this conditional mean for ϕ minimizes *posterior* expected loss given that we use a quadratic loss function.[8] However, with the improper prior pdf introduced above, average risk is not finite and thus the mean of the posterior pdf cannot minimize average risk.[9] If, however, we use a relative quadratic loss function, $L = [(\phi - \check{\phi})/\phi]^2$, then, given σ^2, taking $\check{\phi} = \phi^*$, with ϕ^* given in (3.3), yields minimum posterior expected loss. That is, since $\phi = \exp\{\mu\}$, $L = [1 - \check{\phi}\exp\{-\mu\}]^2$ and

$$(3.5) \quad E_\mu(L \mid \sigma^2, \mathbf{z}) = 1 - 2\check{\phi} E_\mu(e^{-\mu} \mid \sigma^2, \mathbf{z}) + \check{\phi}^2 E_\mu(e^{-2\mu} \mid \sigma^2, \mathbf{z}).$$

The value of $\check{\phi}$ minimizing (3.5) is

$$(3.6) \qquad \check{\phi} = E_\mu(e^{-\mu} \mid \sigma^2, \mathbf{z}) / E_\mu(e^{-2\mu} \mid \sigma^2, \mathbf{z}) = \exp\{\bar{z} - 3\sigma^2/2n\}$$

which is the quantity ϕ^* shown in (3.3).

As regards estimation of the mean of the log-normal distribution, $\eta = \exp\{\mu + \sigma^2/2\}$, the ML estimator is $\check{\eta} = \exp\{\bar{z} + \hat{\sigma}^2/2\}$. For the mean of the ML estimator to exist, we must have $0 < \sigma^2/n < 1$. Under this condition, $E\check{\eta} = \exp\{\mu + \sigma^2/n\}/(1 - \sigma^2/n)^{(n-1)/2}$, a result given in Kendall and Stuart (1961, p. 68) without mention of the condition on σ^2/n. It is clear that the ML estimator can be seriously biased for large σ^2/n. Also, even under conditions insuring the existence of the MSE of the ML estimator, it is the case that for given σ^2/n, the ML estimator is inadmissible relative to a quadratic loss function.

The Finney (1949) approach has been applied to yield a minimum variance unbiased estimator for η. That is, given σ^2,

$$(3.7) \qquad \tilde{\eta} = \exp\{\bar{z} + \sigma^2/2 - \sigma^2/2n\}$$

is an unbiased estimator for η. In the Finney approach, the part of the exponential involving σ^2 is expanded in terms of powers of σ^2 and unbiased estimators of these powers of σ^2 are inserted. The resulting estimator is

8. This problem is: given σ^2, $\min_f E_\phi(\phi - f)^2$ where the expectation is taken with respect to the posterior pdf for ϕ given σ^2 and f denotes an estimate. Since $\phi = \exp\{\mu\}$, we can reformulate the problem as $\min_f E\mu(e^\mu - f)^2$ for given σ^2.

9. That is, the integral $\int\int (e^\mu - f)^2 p(\mu) p(z \mid \sigma, \mu) d\mu dz$, with $p(\mu) \propto$ const., $-\infty < \mu < \infty$, does not converge. See Stone (1967) and Thornber (1966) for further discussion of examples where the mean of posterior pdf's minimize posterior expected loss but in which average risk is not finite.

$$(3.8) \qquad \tilde{\tilde{\eta}} = \exp\{\bar{z}\}\, G(s^2),$$

where $G(s^2) = \Sigma_{i=0}^{\infty} (1 - 1/n)^i s^{2i}/2^i i! c(i)$ with $c(i) = \nu(\nu + 2) \cdots (\nu + 2i)/\nu^i(\nu + 2i)$.

It should be recognized that $\tilde{\eta}$ in (3.7) is not a minimal MSE estimator. The minimal MSE estimator in the class of estimators $k \exp\{\bar{z}\}$ can easily be shown to be

$$(3.9) \qquad \eta^* = \exp\{\bar{z} + \sigma^2/2 - 3\sigma^2/2n\}.$$

As with the minimum MSE estimator for the median, the minimal MSE estimator for η has a much smaller MSE for a broad range of conditions than that for the ML estimator $\hat{\eta}$ or for the unbiased estimator $\tilde{\eta}$ in (3.7). Also, it will be noted that the mean of the conditional posterior pdf for η given σ, based on a diffuse prior pdf, is $E(\eta \mid \sigma^2, \mathbf{z}) = \exp\{\bar{z} + \sigma^2/2 + \sigma^2/2n\}$. This quantity differs from η^* in (3.9). However, if we employ a relative squared error loss function, $L = [(\eta - \check{\eta})/\eta]^2$, it is the case that, given σ^2, taking $\check{\eta} = \eta^*$ minimizes posterior expected loss.[10]

With respect to log-normal regressions, the following are ML estimators for ϕ_i and η_i, $\hat{\phi}_i = \exp\{\mathbf{x}_i'\hat{\boldsymbol{\beta}}\}$ and $\hat{\eta}_i = \exp\{\mathbf{x}_i'\hat{\boldsymbol{\beta}} + \hat{\sigma}^2/2\}$, where $\hat{\boldsymbol{\beta}} = (X'X)^{-1}X'\mathbf{z}$ and $n\hat{\sigma}^2 = (\mathbf{z} - X\boldsymbol{\beta})'(\mathbf{z} - X\boldsymbol{\beta})$. Just as with ML estimators for the median and mean of the log-normal distribution, the ML estimators for ϕ_i and η_i are known to be biased. In Bradu and Mundlak (1968, 1970), Goldberger (1968), and Heien (1968), the Finney approach is applied to provide minimum variance unbiased estimators for ϕ_i and η_i. However, just as in the case of the parameters ϕ and η of the log-normal pdf, it is possible to construct minimum MSE estimators for ϕ_i and η_i which have much smaller MSE's than the ML estimators or Finney type estimators for these parameters. For example, given σ^2, a minimum MSE estimator for ϕ_i, in the class $\phi_i^* = k \exp\{\mathbf{x}_i'\hat{\boldsymbol{\beta}}\}$ where k is a constant, can easily be shown to be

$$(3.10) \qquad \phi_i^* = \exp\{\mathbf{x}_i'\hat{\boldsymbol{\beta}} - 3a^2\sigma^2/2\}$$

where $a^2 = \mathbf{x}_i'(X'X)^{-1}\mathbf{x}_i$, while a similar minimum MSE estimator for η_i is given by

$$(3.11) \qquad \eta_i^* = \exp\{\mathbf{x}_i'\hat{\boldsymbol{\beta}} + \sigma^2/2 - 3a^2\sigma^2/2\}.$$

It will be noted that given σ^2, ϕ_i^* and η_i^* are not equal to the means of the

10. Since $E_\eta(L|\sigma^2) = 1 - 2\check{\eta}E_\eta(1/\eta|\sigma^2) + \check{\eta}^2E_\eta(1/\eta^2|\sigma^2)$, the minimizing value for $\check{\eta}$ is: $\check{\eta} = E_\eta(1/\eta|\sigma^2)/E_\eta(1/\eta^2|\sigma^2)$. From $\eta = \exp\{\mu + \sigma^2/2\}$ and the fact that the conditional posterior pdf for μ given σ^2 is normal, we have $E_\eta(1/\eta|\sigma^2) = \exp\{-(\bar{z} + \sigma^2/2 + \sigma^2/2n)\}$ and $E_\eta(1/\eta^2|\sigma^2) = \exp\{-(2\bar{z} + \sigma^2 + 2\sigma^2/n)\}$. Thus, the minimizing value for $\check{\eta}$ is equal to $\exp\{\bar{z} + \sigma^2/2 - 3\sigma^2/2n\}$, which is just η^* as shown in (3.9).

conditional posterior pdf's for ϕ_i and η_i, respectively. However, if relative squared error loss functions, $L_1 = [(\phi_i - \check{\phi}_i)/\phi_i]^2$ and $L_2 = [(\eta_i - \check{\eta}_i)/\eta_i]^2$ are employed, then for given σ^2, ϕ_i^* in (3.10) and η_i^* in (3.11) are optimal Bayesian estimators relative to these loss functions and use of a diffuse prior pdf.[11]

4 Concluding Remarks

We have presented simple operational Bayesian results which can be applied in analyses of the log-normal distribution and of log-normal regressions. Then we reviewed several non-Bayesian results and indicated for given σ^2 certain minimum MSE estimators for parameters of interest. These estimators, which are optimal in a Bayesian sense given relative squared error loss functions and diffuse prior assumptions, depend on σ^2 whose value is often not known in practice. To circumvent this nuisance parameter problem, the Finney (1949) expansion approach, described in section 3, can be applied to obtain an approximation to the optimal minimum MSE estimators. Alternatively, for the relative squared error loss function, the value of a parameter minimizing expected loss can be found numerically after integrating out the nuisance parameter σ^2. In this way, *unconditional* optimal point estimates for the relative squared error loss function (and for others) can be obtained quite readily. Finally, while we have emphasized point estimation, it should be appreciated that in the Bayesian approach we can readily compute marginal and/or joint posterior distributions for parameters of interest. As usual, these distributions incorporate all the available prior and sample information. They can be employed not only to yield optimal point estimates but also, for example, to make probability statements about parameters' values, to perform Bayesian tests of hypotheses, and to derive predictive probability distributions for future observations.

References

Aitchison, J., and J. A. C. Brown (1957). *The Log-Normal Distribution.* Cambridge: Cambridge University Press.

11. It is also interesting to note with respect to the unknown error variance σ^2 that if we compute the MSE of an estimator $\tilde{\sigma}^2 = k\hat{\sigma}^2$, taking $k = n/(\nu + 2)$ yields a minimum MSE estimator for σ^2. In a Bayesian context, it can be shown that $\tilde{\sigma}^2 = n\hat{\sigma}^2/(\nu + 2)$ is the Bayesian estimator for σ^2 with respect to a relative squared error loss function when the posterior pdf for σ is $p(\sigma|z) \propto \sigma^{-(\nu+1)} \exp\{-(\nu s^2/2\sigma^2)\}$, where, as above, $\nu = n-k$ and $\nu s^2 = (z - X\hat{\beta})'(z - X\hat{\beta})$. This result is, of course, relevant not only for log-normal regressions but for many other problems where σ's value is unknown.

Bradu, D., and Y. Mundlak (1968). "Estimation in Linear Models with Log-Normal Dependent Variable." Paper presented to the Econometrics Workshop, University of Chicago, 1968.

———. (1970). "Estimation in Log-Normal Linear Models." *Journal of the American Statistical Association*, 65:198–211.

Erdélyi, A., W. Magnus, F. Oberhettinger, and F. G. Tricomi (1954). *Tables of Integral Transforms*, vol. 1. New York: McGraw-Hill Book Co.

Finney, D. J. (1949). "On the Distribution of a Variate Whose Logarithm Is Normally Distributed." *Supplement to the Journal of the Royal Statistical Society*, 7:155–61.

Goldberger, A. S. (1968). "The Interpretation and Estimation of Cobb-Douglas Functions." *Econometrica*, 36:464–72.

Heien, D. M. (1968). "A Note on Log-Linear Regression." *Journal of the American Statistical Association*, 63:1034–38.

Jeffreys, H. (1967). *Theory of Probability*. 3d rev. ed. London: Oxford University Press.

Kaufman, G. M. (1963). *Statistical Decision and Related Techniques in Oil and Gas Exploration*. Englewood Cliffs, N.J.: Prentice-Hall.

Kendall, M. G., and A. S. Stuart (1961). *The Advanced Theory of Statistics*, vol. 2, *Inference and Relationship*. New York: Hafner Publishing Co.

Lindley, D. V. (1965). *Introduction to Probability and Statistics from a Bayesian Viewpoint*. Part 2: *Inference*. Cambridge: Cambridge University Press.

Raiffa, H., and R. Schlaifer (1961). *Applied Statistical Decision Theory*. Boston: Harvard University, Graduate School of Business Administration.

Stone, M. (1967). "Generalized Bayes Decision Functions, Admissibility, and the Exponential Family." *Annals of Mathematical Statistics*, 38 (June):818–22.

Thornber, H. (1966). "Applications of Decision Theory to Econometrics." Ph.D. diss., University of Chicago.

3.4 Bayesian and Non-Bayesian Analysis of the Regression Model with Multivariate Student-*t* Error Terms

1 Introduction

In many applications of the univariate linear regression model, error terms are assumed normally and independently distributed, each with zero mean and common variance. In this paper, a broader assumption is employed, namely, that the error terms have a joint multivariate Student-*t* distribution with zero location vector. With this assumption, the marginal distribution of each error is univariate Student-*t*, a distribution that includes the Cauchy and normal distributions as special cases. That error terms can have nonnormal distributions in practice has been appreciated by many, including Newcomb (1886), Jeffreys (1957, pp. 64–65; 1967, pp. 214–16), Mandelbrot (1963), Wise (1966), Fama and Roll (1971), DuMouchel (1971), Box and Tiao (1962), Praetz (1972), and Blattberg and Gonedes (1972). In the work of Newcomb and Jeffreys, discrete mixtures of distributions are employed. Mandelbrot, Wise, Fama, Roll, and DuMouchel consider the class of stable Paretian distributions, while Box and Tiao analyze a class of power distributions. Last, Praetz and Blattberg and Gonedes consider continuous mixtures of normal distributions that lead to errors that are independent, each with the same univariate Student-*t* distribution. Jeffreys (1957, pp. 64–65) also reports results of analyses assuming error terms independent, each with the same univariate Student-*t* distribution.

By assuming that regression error terms have a joint multivariate Student-*t* distribution, it will be seen that inference procedures for the regression model are relatively simple. Also, certain effects of departures from normality can be readily analyzed.

The plan of this paper is as follows. In section 2, the model is specified and several situations in which it is applicable are described. Then likelihood and sampling theory inference procedures are developed. A Bayesian analysis of the regression model with multivariate Student-*t* error terms under dif-

Reprinted from *Journal of the American Statistical Association*, 71 (June 1976):400–405, with the kind permission of the American Statistical Association.

fuse and natural conjugate priors is presented in section 3 and the appendix. Last, section 4 contains a summary of results and some concluding remarks.

2 Likelihood and Sampling Theory Considerations

Let the model for n observations, $\mathbf{y}' = (y_1, y_2, \ldots, y_n)$, be

$$\mathbf{y} = X\boldsymbol{\beta} + \mathbf{u}, \tag{2.1}$$

where X is an $n \times k$ nonstochastic matrix with rank k, $\boldsymbol{\beta}$ is a $k \times 1$ vector of regression parameters with unknown values, and $\mathbf{u}$ is an $n \times 1$ random error vector. It is assumed that the joint probability density function (pdf) for the n elements of $\mathbf{u}$ is the multivariate Student-t pdf[1]

$$p(\mathbf{u} \mid \nu_o, \sigma) = \frac{g(\nu_o)}{(\sigma^2)^{n/2}} \frac{1}{\{\nu_o + \mathbf{u}'\mathbf{u}/\sigma^2\}^{(n+\nu_o)/2}} \qquad \begin{array}{l} \sigma, \nu_o > 0 \\ -\infty < u_i < \infty \\ i = 1, 2, \ldots, n \end{array} \tag{2.2}$$

where $g(\nu_o) = \nu_o^{\nu_o/2}\Gamma(\nu_o + n/2)/\pi^{n/2}\Gamma(\nu_o/2)$. As is well known, the pdf in (2.2) is symmetric about the origin, its modal value. Its mean vector and covariance matrix are given by

$$E\mathbf{u} = \mathbf{0} \quad \text{for } \nu_o > 1, \quad \text{and} \qquad E\mathbf{u}\mathbf{u}' = \nu_o\sigma^2/(\nu_o - 2)I_n \quad \text{for } \nu_o > 2; \tag{2.3}$$

while the elements of $\mathbf{u}$ are uncorrelated, it is clear from the form of their joint pdf in (2.2) that they are not independent. When $\nu_o \to \infty$, the pdf in (2.3) approaches a multivariate normal form with zero mean vector and covariance matrix $\sigma^2 I_n$. For finite ν_o, u_i/σ has a univariate Student-t pdf with ν_o degrees of freedom. For small values of ν_o, the marginal distributions of elements of $\mathbf{u}$ will have heavy tails.[2]

It is interesting and useful to recognize the well-known fact that the multivariate Student-t pdf in (2.2) is a member of the class of distributions[3]

$$p(\mathbf{u} \mid \cdot) = \int_0^\infty p_N(\mathbf{u} \mid \tau) p(\tau \mid \cdot)\, d\tau, \tag{2.4}$$

1. See, e.g., Raiffa and Schlaifer (1961), pp. 256–59 and Zellner (1971), pp. 383–89 for a review of some properties of this pdf.

2. When $\nu_0 = 1$, (2.2) is the multivariate Cauchy pdf for which no moments exist.

3. The class shown in (2.4), a "continuous mixture" of normal pdfs, can be extended to include discrete as well as continuous mixtures. Strawderman (1974) has recently considered minimax estimation of the location parameters of such mixtures of normal distributions but does not treat the range of problems considered herein.

where

$$p_N(\mathbf{u} \mid \tau) = (2\pi\tau^2)^{-n/2} \exp\{-\mathbf{u}'\mathbf{u}/2\tau^2\} \qquad -\infty < u_i < \infty \quad i = 1, 2, \ldots, n, \tag{2.5}$$

and $p(\tau \mid \cdot)$ with $0 < \tau < \infty$, is a proper pdf for τ. When $p(\tau \mid \cdot)$ is chosen to be the inverted gamma pdf,

$$p_{IG}(\tau \mid \nu_o, \sigma) = [2/\Gamma(\nu_o/2)](\nu_o\sigma^2/2)^{\nu_o/2}\tau^{-(\nu_o+1)} \cdot \exp\{-\nu_o\sigma^2/2\tau^2\}, \tag{2.6}$$

with $0 < \nu_o, \sigma, \tau < \infty$, the integration in (2.4) produces a marginal multivariate Student-*t* pdf for $\mathbf{u}$, $p(\mathbf{u} \mid \nu_o, \sigma)$ that is given in (2.2). Thus, it is possible to regard the error vector $\mathbf{u}$ in (2.1) as being randomly drawn from a multivariate normal distribution with a random standard deviation generated from (2.6).

Several situations in which the process in (2.1)–(2.2) may be useful in practice include the following. First, the observations $\mathbf{y}' = (y_1, y_2, \ldots, y_n)$ may be generated by a measuring instrument in a particular run. If the instrument's variability, represented by τ's value, has an unknown value within a run and is known to vary over runs, the model just presented in which τ is considered random can be useful. Second, if the elements of $\mathbf{y}$ are returns on particular stocks, in the "market-model" regression, $y_t = \beta_1 + \beta_2 x_t + u_t$, $t = 1, 2, \ldots, n$, where x_t is the market return, it may be reasonable to assume that the errors have a common random standard deviation τ with the inverted gamma pdf shown in (2.6). Third, in regressions for individuals or different groups of consumers or firms, common standard deviations of error terms may vary randomly across groups in accord with (2.6). If so, the regression model for a particular group would be in the form of (2.1)–(2.2).

Using (2.1) and (2.2), the likelihood function for the regression model is given by

$$p(\mathbf{y} \mid \boldsymbol{\beta}, \nu_o, \sigma) = [g(\nu_o)/\sigma^2)^{n/2}]\{\nu_o + [\nu s^2 + (\boldsymbol{\beta} - \hat{\boldsymbol{\beta}})'X'X(\boldsymbol{\beta} - \hat{\boldsymbol{\beta}})]/\sigma^2\}^{-(n+\nu_o)/2}, \tag{2.7}$$

where

$$\hat{\boldsymbol{\beta}} = (X'X)^{-1}X'\mathbf{y}, \; \nu s^2 = (\mathbf{y} - X\hat{\boldsymbol{\beta}})'(\mathbf{y} - \hat{\boldsymbol{\beta}}), \tag{2.8}$$

and $\nu = n - k$. From (2.7) it is seen that $\hat{\boldsymbol{\beta}}$ and s^2 are sufficient statistics and that the least squares estimate, $\hat{\boldsymbol{\beta}}$, is the maximum likelihood (ML) estimate for $\boldsymbol{\beta}$. The ML estimate for σ^2 is

$$(2.9) \qquad \hat{\sigma}^2 = (\mathbf{y} - X\hat{\boldsymbol{\beta}})'(\mathbf{y} - X\hat{\boldsymbol{\beta}})/n.$$

Further, $\hat{\boldsymbol{\beta}}$ is the ML estimate for $\boldsymbol{\beta}$ for all likelihood functions that are monotonically decreasing functions of $\mathbf{u}'\mathbf{u} = (\mathbf{y} - X\boldsymbol{\beta})'(\mathbf{y} - X\boldsymbol{\beta})$.[4] In addition, when $\nu_o > 2$ and (2.3) is satisfied by the error vector $\mathbf{u}$, the conditions of the Gauss-Markov theorem are met. Thus, $\hat{\boldsymbol{\beta}}$ in (2.8) is a minimum variance linear unbiased estimator[5] and also a minimum variance unbiased estimator.

From (2.8) and (2.1), $\hat{\boldsymbol{\beta}} = \boldsymbol{\beta} + (X'X)^{-1}X'\mathbf{u}$, and for $\nu_o > 1$, $E\hat{\boldsymbol{\beta}} = \boldsymbol{\beta}$, since $E\mathbf{u} = \mathbf{0}$. Also, for $\nu_o > 2$, the covariance matrix for $\hat{\boldsymbol{\beta}}$, $V(\hat{\boldsymbol{\beta}})$, is

$$(2.10) \qquad V(\hat{\boldsymbol{\beta}}) = E(\hat{\boldsymbol{\beta}} - \boldsymbol{\beta})(\hat{\boldsymbol{\beta}} - \boldsymbol{\beta})' = (X'X)^{-1}\nu_o\sigma^2/(\nu_o - 2).$$

Note that as $\nu_o \to \infty$, $\mathbf{u} \to N(\mathbf{0}, \sigma^2 I_n)$ and $V(\hat{\boldsymbol{\beta}}) \to (X'X)^{-1}\sigma^2$. Thus, for small and moderate values of ν_o, the variances of the elements of $\hat{\boldsymbol{\beta}}$ are inflated considerably, relative to those for large values of ν_o, in which case the multivariate Student-*t* distribution of $\hat{\boldsymbol{\beta}}$ is close to $N[\boldsymbol{\beta}, (X'X)^{-1}\sigma^2]$.

It is important to observe that even though the elements of $\mathbf{u}$ have the nonnormal pdf in (2.2) and are not independent, tests and intervals based on usual *t*- and *F*-statistics remain valid. That this is the case can be seen most easily by considering, for example, $t = (\hat{\beta}_i - \beta_i)/s(m^{ii})^{1/2}$, where m^{ii} is the (i, i)th element of $(X'X)^{-1}$ and $s^2 = \hat{\mathbf{u}}'\hat{\mathbf{u}}/(n - k)$. Given τ, the error vector $\mathbf{u}$ has the usual normal pdf, shown in (2.5), and, thus, t given τ has a univariate Student-*t* pdf with $n - k$ degrees of freedom. Since the joint pdf of t and τ, say, $p(t, \tau)$, can be written $p(t, \tau) = p(t|\tau)\,p_{IG}(\tau)$ and $p(t|\tau) = p(t)$, t and τ are independent. Thus, t is unconditionally univariate Student-*t* and usual probability statements based on this distribution will be appropriate. Similarly, any statistic, say, F, that has an F_{ν_1,ν_2} pdf given τ will also have a marginal F_{ν_1,ν_2} pdf, since the joint pdf for F and τ, $p(F, \tau)$, can be factored as $p(F, \tau) = p(F|\tau)p_{IG}(\tau)$. Since $p(F|\tau)$ does not depend on τ, F and τ are independent, and, thus, F has an unconditional F_{ν_1,ν_2} pdf. *This argument*

4. That $\hat{\boldsymbol{\beta}} = (X'X)^{-1}X'y$ is the ML estimate when the $\boldsymbol{u}$ vector has a nonnormal distribution might appear to be in conflict with a result of Gauss's (Jeffreys, 1967, p. 214). This result, generalized to apply to the regression model, states that if the elements of $\boldsymbol{u}$ are *independently* distributed, each with zero mean and common finite variance, and if $\hat{\boldsymbol{\beta}}$ is the ML estimate, then the elements of $\boldsymbol{u}$ are normally distributed. In this work, the independence assumption required to obtain Gauss's result is not satisfied.

5. Note that if the elements of $\boldsymbol{u}$ are independent, each with the same univariate Student-*t* pdf, as Jeffreys (1957), Praetz (1972), and Blattberg and Gonedes (1972) assume, $\hat{\boldsymbol{\beta}}$ is not the ML estimator. However, $\hat{\boldsymbol{\beta}}$ is still a minimum variance linear unbiased estimator given that its second moments exist. Further, in this case, $E(\hat{\boldsymbol{\beta}} - \boldsymbol{\beta})(\hat{\boldsymbol{\beta}} - \boldsymbol{\beta})' = (X'X)^{-1}\sigma_u^2$, where $\sigma_u^2 = \nu_c\sigma_c^2/(\nu_c - 2)$, $\nu_c > 2$ is the common variance of the elements of $\boldsymbol{u}$, and ν_c and σ_c^2 are parameters of their common univariate Student-*t* pdf.

holds not only for τ having a marginal IG pdf, $p_{IG}(\tau)$, *but also for any proper* pdf $p(\tau|\cdot)$ *for τ in* (2.4).

With respect to the ML estimator $\hat{\sigma}^2$ in (2.10), we have for $\nu_o > 2$, $E\hat{\sigma}^2 = E\mathbf{u}'[I_n - X(X'X)^{-1}X']\mathbf{u}/n = (n-k)\sigma_u^2/n$, where $\sigma_u^2 = \nu_o\sigma^2/(\nu_o - 2)$ is the common variance of the elements of $\mathbf{u}$; see (2.3). Thus, $\hat{\mathbf{u}}'\hat{\mathbf{u}}/(n-k)$ is an unbiased estimator for σ_u^2, while $(\nu_o - 2)\hat{\mathbf{u}}'\hat{\mathbf{u}}/\nu_o(n-k)$ is an unbiased estimator for σ^2. In the class of estimators $q\hat{\mathbf{u}}'\hat{\mathbf{u}}$, where q is a positive scalar, the minimal mean square error (MMSE) estimator for σ^2 is, with $\nu_o > 4$, $\tilde{\sigma}^2 = (\nu_o - 4)\hat{\mathbf{u}}'\hat{\mathbf{u}}/\nu_o(\nu + 2)$, while the MMSE estimator for σ_u^2 in this class is $\tilde{\sigma}_u^2 = (\nu_o - 4)\hat{\mathbf{u}}'\hat{\mathbf{u}}/(\nu_o - 2)(\nu + 2)$.

To test hypotheses and construct intervals for σ^2 or σ_u^2, note that given τ, $\mathbf{u}$ has the normal pdf shown in (2.7). Thus, given τ, $\hat{\mathbf{u}}'\hat{\mathbf{u}}/\tau^2 \equiv \omega/\tau^2$ has a χ^2 pdf with ν degrees of freedom. Let $x = \omega/\nu\sigma^2 = s^2/\sigma^2$, where $s^2 = \hat{\mathbf{u}}'\hat{\mathbf{u}}/\nu$. Since we know from (2.6) that $\sigma^2/\tau^2 \sim (\chi^2_{\nu_o}/\nu_o)^{-1}$, and since $x = (\omega/\nu\tau^2)/(\sigma^2/\tau^2)$, it follows that $x = s^2/\sigma^2$ has an F-distribution with ν and ν_o degrees of freedom. This fact can be used to construct confidence intervals for and test hypotheses about σ^2. Since $\sigma_u^2 = \nu_o\sigma^2/(\nu_o - 2)$, where σ_u^2 is the common variance of the elements of $\mathbf{u}$, the distribution of $x = s^2/\sigma^2$ can also be employed to set up intervals and test hypotheses relating to σ_u^2 for any given $\nu_o > 2$.

Last, on examination of the likelihood function in (2.7), a maximum of the function with respect to $\boldsymbol{\beta}$, σ^2, *and* ν_o does not exist.[6] Thus, while ML estimates of $\boldsymbol{\beta}$ and σ^2 exist for any *given* ν_o, ML estimates of $\boldsymbol{\beta}$, σ^2 *and* ν_o do not exist. Thus, to use some of the results presented before, it is necessary to assign a value to ν_o that reflects an investigator's knowledge of the distributional properties of the regression error terms. Use of the usual normal assumption for the error terms is equivalent to assigning a large value to ν_o. When a small value for ν_o is thought to be more reasonable, it can be assigned, and the results shown before are available. In section 3, it will be seen that it is possible to incorporate a prior pdf for ν_o in a Bayesian analysis.

3 Bayesian Analysis

The model in (2.1), with error terms generated by (2.2) and likelihood function shown in (2.7), will be analyzed from the Bayesian point of view with a diffuse prior pdf for the parameters. Initially, it will be assumed that ν_o's value is given. Our diffuse prior pdf for the elements of $\boldsymbol{\beta}$ and σ^2 is

6. That is, the necessary conditions on $\boldsymbol{\beta}$, σ^2, and ν_0 for maximum of the likelihood function cannot be satisfied for $\nu_0 \geq 1$. It may be possible to estimate ν_0 from the data with repeated observations.

$$(3.1)\qquad p(\boldsymbol{\beta},\sigma^2) \propto 1/\sigma^2, \quad \begin{matrix} -\infty<\beta_i<\infty, \\ 0<\sigma^2<\infty, \end{matrix} \quad i=1,2,\ldots,k.$$

In (3.1), it is assumed that the elements of $\boldsymbol{\beta}$ and log σ^2 are uniformly and independently distributed. Then the posterior pdf for the parameters is

$$(3.2)\qquad \begin{aligned} &p(\boldsymbol{\beta},\sigma^2|\mathbf{y},\nu_o) \\ &\propto (\sigma^2)^{-(n+2)/2}\{\nu_o+(\mathbf{y}-X\boldsymbol{\beta})'(\mathbf{y}-X\boldsymbol{\beta})/\sigma^2\}^{-(n+\nu_o)/2} \\ &\propto \frac{(\sigma^2)^{\nu_o/2-1}}{(\bar{\sigma}^2)^{(n+\nu_o)/2}}\{\nu_1+(\boldsymbol{\beta}-\hat{\boldsymbol{\beta}})'X'X(\boldsymbol{\beta}-\hat{\boldsymbol{\beta}})/\bar{\sigma}^2\}^{-(\nu_1+k)/2} \\ &\propto \{A(\boldsymbol{\beta})\}^{-n/2}\left\{\frac{[\nu_o\sigma^2/A(\boldsymbol{\beta})]^{\nu_o/2-1}}{A(\boldsymbol{\beta})[1+\nu_o\sigma^2/A(\boldsymbol{\beta})]^{(n+\nu_o)/2}}\right\}, \end{aligned}$$

where $A(\boldsymbol{\beta}) \equiv (\mathbf{y}-X\boldsymbol{\beta})'(\mathbf{y}-X\boldsymbol{\beta})$, $\bar{\sigma}^2 = (\nu_o\sigma^2+\nu s^2)/\nu_1$, $\nu_1=\nu+\nu_o$, $\nu = n-k$, $\hat{\boldsymbol{\beta}} = (X'X)^{-1}X'\mathbf{y}$ and $\nu s^2 = (\mathbf{y}-X\hat{\boldsymbol{\beta}})'(\mathbf{y}-X\hat{\boldsymbol{\beta}})$.

From the second line of (3.2), it is seen that the conditional posterior pdf for $\boldsymbol{\beta}$ given σ^2 and ν_o is in the form of a multivariate Student-t pdf with mean $\hat{\boldsymbol{\beta}}$, the least squares quantity and conditional posterior covariance matrix,

$$(3.3)\qquad \begin{aligned} V(\boldsymbol{\beta}|\mathbf{y},\sigma^2,\nu_o) &= (X'X)^{-1}\nu_1\bar{\sigma}^2/(\nu_1-2) \\ &= (X'X)^{-1}(\nu_o\sigma^2+\nu s^2)/(\nu_o+\nu-2), \end{aligned}$$

provided that $\nu_1>2$. As $\nu_o\rightarrow\infty$, the conditional posterior pdf for $\boldsymbol{\beta}$ given σ^2 approaches a multivariate normal pdf with mean $\hat{\boldsymbol{\beta}}$ and covariance matrix $(X'X)^{-1}\sigma^2$, the usual result for the normal regression model with our diffuse prior pdf.

To obtain the marginal posterior pdf for $\boldsymbol{\beta}$, note from the third line of (3.2) that if we let $z = n\sigma^2/A(\boldsymbol{\beta})$, $0<z<\infty$, then the joint posterior pdf for $\boldsymbol{\beta}$ and z is

$$(3.4)\qquad p(\boldsymbol{\beta},z|\mathbf{y},\nu_o) \propto \{A(\boldsymbol{\beta})\}^{-n/2}\{z^{\nu_o/2-1}/(1+z\nu_o/n)^{(n+\nu_o)/2}\}.$$

From the form of (3.4), it is seen that $z = n\sigma^2/A(\boldsymbol{\beta})$ has an $F_{\nu_o,n}$ pdf and $\boldsymbol{\beta}$ and z and independent. Thus, the marginal posterior pdf for $\boldsymbol{\beta}$ is

$$(3.5)\qquad \begin{aligned} p(\boldsymbol{\beta}|\mathbf{y},\nu_o) &\propto \{A(\boldsymbol{\beta})\}^{-n/2} \\ &\propto \{\nu s^2+(\boldsymbol{\beta}-\hat{\boldsymbol{\beta}})'X'X(\boldsymbol{\beta}-\hat{\boldsymbol{\beta}})\}^{-(\nu+k)/2}, \end{aligned}$$

which is in the form of a k-dimensional Student-t pdf and does not depend on the value given to ν_o. In fact, (3.5) is precisely the result that one obtains in the Bayesian analysis of the normal regression model with the diffuse prior for the parameters shown in (3.1). This result is the Bayesian analog of the sampling theory results reported in section 2.

The marginal posterior pdf for σ^2 can be obtained by integrating the second line of (3.2) with respect to the elements of $\boldsymbol{\beta}$ using properties of the multivariate Student-*t* pdf. The result is[7]

$$(3.6) \qquad p(\sigma^2 \mid \mathbf{y}, \nu_o) \propto (\sigma^2/s^2)^{(\nu_o/2)-1}/(1 + (\nu_o\sigma^2/\nu s^2))^{(\nu_o+\nu)/2}.$$

From the form of (3.6), it is apparent that the marginal posterior pdf for σ^2/s^2 is an F pdf with ν_o and ν degrees of freedom, a finding paralleling the sampling theory result of section 2. From properties of the F pdf, the modal value of σ^2/s^2 is $(\nu/\nu_o)(\nu_o - 2)/(\nu + 2)$, when $\nu_o > 2$, and its mean is $\nu/(\nu - 2)$ when $\nu > 2$. Also, as $\nu_o \to \infty$, the posterior distribution of $\nu s^2/\sigma^2$ approaches a χ^2 pdf with ν degrees of freedom, a distributional result that holds for Bayesian analysis of the usual normal regression model with diffuse prior assumptions. This is reasonable, since as $\nu_o \to \infty$, the error terms' pdf approaches a normal form. Last, it was noted before that the posterior pdf for $z = n\sigma^2/(\mathbf{y} - X\boldsymbol{\beta})'(\mathbf{y} - X\boldsymbol{\beta})$ is $F_{\nu_o, n}$. The effect of integrating out the elements of $\boldsymbol{\beta}$ to obtain the marginal posterior pdf for σ^2/s^2 is to change the degrees of freedom in the F pdf from ν_o and n to ν_o and $\nu = n - k$, a reasonable change, since k β's have been integrated out.

In the preceding, we have employed the diffuse prior pdf given in (3.1). It is interesting to inquire about the form of the natural conjugate prior distribution for the present model. To answer this question, note that the likelihood function in (2.7) can be expressed as

$$(3.7) \qquad p(\mathbf{y} \mid \boldsymbol{\beta}, \nu_o, \sigma^2) \propto \left\{ \frac{(\nu_o\sigma^2/\nu s^2)^{\nu_o/2}}{(1 + \nu_o\sigma^2/\nu s^2)^{(\nu_o+\nu)/2}} \right\} \cdot \left\{ \frac{1}{(\bar{\sigma}^2)^{k/2}[\nu_1 + (\boldsymbol{\beta} - \hat{\boldsymbol{\beta}})'X'X(\boldsymbol{\beta} - \hat{\boldsymbol{\beta}})/\bar{\sigma}^2]^{(\nu_1+k)/2}} \right\},$$

where $\nu_1 = \nu_o + \nu$ and $\bar{\sigma}^2 = (\nu_o\sigma^2 + \nu s^2)/\nu_1$. From the form of (3.7), the natural conjugate prior distribution for σ^2 and $\boldsymbol{\beta}$ is the product of a marginal F pdf for σ^2 times a conditional k-dimensional multivariate Student-*t* pdf for $\boldsymbol{\beta}$ given σ^2, i.e., $p(\boldsymbol{\beta}, \sigma^2 \mid \cdot) = p_F(\sigma^2 \mid \cdot)p_S(\boldsymbol{\beta} \mid \sigma^2, \cdot)$, where $p_F(\sigma^2 \mid \cdot)$ denotes an F pdf and $p_S(\boldsymbol{\beta} \mid \sigma^2, \cdot)$ a conditional multivariate Student-*t* pdf.[8] Given ν_o, the prior parameters of $p_F(\sigma^2 \mid \cdot)$ are analogs of ν and s^2 appearing in the first factor of (3.7). Similarly, the prior parameters appearing in $p_S(\boldsymbol{\beta} \mid \sigma^2, \cdot)$ are analogs of $\hat{\boldsymbol{\beta}}$ and $X'X$. Thus, explicitly, the factors of the natural conjugate prior in (3.8) for the present model are given by

7. If one has a prior pdf for ν_0, say, $p(\nu_0)$, with $0 < \nu_0 < c$ (where c is a finite constant or ∞), it can be used to average (3.6) as $p(\sigma^2|y) = \int_0^c p(\sigma^2|y,\nu_0)p(\nu_0)d\nu_0$.

8. As $\nu_0 \to \infty$, (3.8) converges to the usual normal-gamma conjugate prior distribution.

$$(3.8a)\qquad p_F(\sigma^2 \mid s_a^2, \nu_a, \nu_o) \propto \frac{(\nu_o\sigma^2/\nu_a s_a^2)^{(\nu_o-2)/2}}{(1+\nu_o\sigma^2/\nu_a s_a^2)^{(\nu_o+\nu_a)/2}} \qquad \begin{matrix} 0<\sigma<\infty \\ \nu_a, s_a > 0, \end{matrix}$$

and

$$(3.8b)\qquad p_S(\boldsymbol{\beta} \mid \sigma^2, \bar{\boldsymbol{\beta}}, A, \bar{\nu}_a) \propto (\bar{\sigma}_a^2)^{-k/2}\{\bar{\nu}_a + (\boldsymbol{\beta}-\bar{\boldsymbol{\beta}})'A(\boldsymbol{\beta}-\bar{\boldsymbol{\beta}})/\bar{\sigma}_a^2\}^{-(\bar{\nu}_a+k)/2}$$
$$A \text{ pds} \quad -\infty < \beta_i < \infty \qquad i = 1, 2, \ldots, k,$$

where $\bar{\boldsymbol{\beta}}$ is the prior mean vector, $\bar{\nu}_a = \nu_o + \nu_a$ and $\bar{\sigma}_a^2 = (\nu_a s_a^2 + \nu_o\sigma^2)/\bar{\nu}_a$.

As with the natural conjugate for the usual normal regression model, it is seen that $\boldsymbol{\beta}$ and σ^2 are not independent in the natural conjugate prior distribution in (3.8). If the natural conjugate prior distribution is thought to represent the available prior information adequately, it can be used in obtaining posterior distributions (see the appendix). Of course, if (3.8) arises from the analysis of a previous sample, the likelihood function for the previous and current samples can be formulated and used in conjunction with (3.1) to obtain posterior distributions. Finally, when the number of parameters is not large, as, for example, in simple regression, use of numerical integration techniques to analyze posterior distributions permits a rather flexible choice of informative prior distributions; see, e.g., Zellner and Geisel (1970), Zellner and Richard (1973), and Zellner and Williams (1973), where this approach was utilized in analyzing small normal models with informative prior distributions.

4 Summary and Concluding Remarks

In this paper, the traditional multiple regression model has been analyzed under the assumption that error terms have a joint multivariate Student-*t* pdf with zero mean vector and covariance matrix in the form of a scalar times a unit matrix. Thus, the errors are uncorrelated but not independent. Under these assumptions, it was shown that the maximum likelihood (ML) estimator for the regression coefficient vector is the least squares estimator and that the ML estimator is a minimum variance linear unbiased estimator when relevant moments exist. Further, given existence of relevant moments, probability statements based on usual *t*- and *F*-statistics were found to hold even though the errors were assumed nonnormal. However, to make inferences about the scale parameter, it is necessary to use an *F*-distribution rather than the usual χ^2 distribution.

In the Bayesian analysis of the model with a diffuse prior pdf for the regression coefficients and multivariate Student-*t* error terms, it was found that the joint posterior distribution for the regression coefficients is in precisely the same multivariate Student-*t* form as arises from the usual normal model. However, the posterior distribution of the scale parameter

σ^2 was found to be in the form of an F-distribution. When the degrees of freedom parameter in the error term distribution grows large, and thus the error terms' distribution approaches normality, the posterior distribution of $\nu s^2/\sigma^2$ approaches the usual χ^2 pdf with ν degrees of freedom. Last, a natural conjugate prior distribution for the "multivariate Student-t" regression model was presented.

With respect to inferences about the regression coefficients, it is relevant to appreciate that several important inference procedures for the normal regression model remain valid for the multivariate Student-t model. However, inferences about the scale parameter σ^2 will depend on the extent of the departure from normality, as measured by the value of the degrees of freedom parameter ν_o. Finally, it is conjectured that results similar to those presented before will be found for multivariate regression models with errors following a matrix Student-t distribution.

Appendix

In this appendix, the technical problems of analyzing the multivariate Student-t regression model with the natural conjugate prior distribution shown in (3.8) are considered. In particular, it will be shown how marginal posterior distributions for σ^2 and for individual regression coefficients can be computed. In this work, it is convenient to employ the joint pdf

$$\text{(A.1)} \qquad p(\mathbf{y}, \tau \mid \boldsymbol{\beta}, \sigma^2) \propto \left[\frac{1}{\tau^n} \exp\left\{-\frac{1}{2\tau^2}(\mathbf{y} - X\boldsymbol{\beta})'(\mathbf{y} - X\boldsymbol{\beta})\right\}\right] \cdot \left[\frac{(\sigma^2)^{\nu_o/2}}{\tau^{\nu_o+1}} \exp\left\{-\frac{\nu_o \sigma^2}{2\tau^2}\right\}\right].$$

When (A.1) is integrated with respect to τ, $0 < \tau < \infty$, the result is the likelihood function shown in (2.7).

As regards the natural conjugate prior distribution in (3.8), it is convenient for the present analysis to write it as

$$\text{(A.2)} \quad p(\boldsymbol{\beta}, \sigma^2, \Theta \mid \cdot) \propto p_F(\sigma^2 \mid \cdot)\left[\frac{1}{\Theta^k} \exp\left\{-\frac{1}{2\Theta^2}(\boldsymbol{\beta} - \bar{\boldsymbol{\beta}})'A(\boldsymbol{\beta} - \bar{\boldsymbol{\beta}})\right\}\right] \cdot \left[\frac{(\bar{\sigma}_a^2)^{\bar{\nu}_a/2}}{\Theta^{\bar{\nu}_a+1}} \exp\left\{-\frac{\bar{\nu}_a \bar{\sigma}_a^2}{2\Theta^2}\right\}\right],$$

where $p_F(\sigma^2 \mid \cdot)$ is given in (3.8a), $\bar{\nu}_a$ and $\bar{\sigma}_a^2$ have been defined in connection with (3.8b) and Θ is an auxiliary parameter satisfying $0 < \Theta < \infty$. When

(A.2) is integrated with respect to Θ, the resulting marginal prior pdf for $\boldsymbol{\beta}$ and σ^2 is precisely that shown in (3.8).

On multiplying (A.1) and (A.2) and performing relevant integrations, marginal posterior distributions for σ^2 and for elements of $\boldsymbol{\beta}$ can be obtained. To obtain the marginal posterior pdf for σ^2, write the product of (A.1) and (A.2) as

$$\text{(A.3)} \quad p_F(\sigma^2|\cdot)(\sigma^2)^{\nu_o/2}(\bar{\sigma}_a^2)^{\bar{\nu}_a/2}\left[\frac{1}{\tau^{n+\nu_o+1}}\exp\left\{-\frac{\nu s^2+\nu_o\sigma^2}{2\tau^2}\right\}\right]$$
$$\left[\frac{1}{\Theta^{k+\bar{\nu}_a+1}}\exp\left\{-\frac{\bar{\nu}_a\bar{\sigma}_a^2}{2\Theta^2}\right\}\right]\cdot\exp\left\{-\frac{1}{2\tau^2}[(\boldsymbol{\beta}-\hat{\boldsymbol{\beta}})'X'X(\boldsymbol{\beta}-\hat{\boldsymbol{\beta}})\right.$$
$$\left.+(\tau^2/\Theta^2)(\boldsymbol{\beta}-\bar{\boldsymbol{\beta}})'A(\boldsymbol{\beta}-\bar{\boldsymbol{\beta}})]\right\}.$$

Letting $\lambda = \tau^2/\Theta^2$, we can complete the square on $\boldsymbol{\beta}$ in the last exponential of (A.3) as

$$\text{(A.4)} \quad (\boldsymbol{\beta}-\hat{\boldsymbol{\beta}})'X'X(\boldsymbol{\beta}-\hat{\boldsymbol{\beta}})+\lambda(\boldsymbol{\beta}-\bar{\boldsymbol{\beta}})'A(\boldsymbol{\beta}-\bar{\boldsymbol{\beta}}) = (\boldsymbol{\beta}-\bar{\boldsymbol{\beta}}_\lambda)'M(\boldsymbol{\beta}-\bar{\boldsymbol{\beta}}_\lambda)$$
$$+\hat{\boldsymbol{\beta}}'X'X\hat{\boldsymbol{\beta}}+\lambda\bar{\boldsymbol{\beta}}'A\bar{\boldsymbol{\beta}}-\bar{\boldsymbol{\beta}}_\lambda'M\bar{\boldsymbol{\beta}}_\lambda,$$

where $\bar{\boldsymbol{\beta}}_\lambda = M^{-1}(X'X\hat{\boldsymbol{\beta}} + \lambda A\bar{\boldsymbol{\beta}})$ with $M = X'X + \lambda A$. With (A.4) introduced in (A.3), (A.3) can be integrated with respect to the elements of $\boldsymbol{\beta}$ to yield

$$\text{(A.5)} \quad \frac{p_F(\sigma^2|\cdot)(\sigma^2)^{\nu_o/2}(\bar{\sigma}_a^2)^{\bar{\nu}_a/2}}{\tau^{n+\nu_o+1}}\exp\left\{-\frac{\nu s^2+\nu_o\sigma^2}{2\tau^2}\right\}$$
$$\frac{1}{\Theta^{k+\bar{\nu}_a+1}}\exp\left\{-\frac{\bar{\nu}_a\bar{\sigma}_a^2}{2\Theta^2}\right\}\cdot|M/\tau^2|^{-1/2}$$
$$\exp\left\{-\frac{1}{2\tau^2}[\hat{\boldsymbol{\beta}}'X'X\hat{\boldsymbol{\beta}}+\lambda\bar{\boldsymbol{\beta}}'A\bar{\boldsymbol{\beta}}-\bar{\boldsymbol{\beta}}_\lambda'M\bar{\boldsymbol{\beta}}_\lambda]\right\}.$$

We now change parameters in (A.5) from σ^2, τ and Θ to σ^2, τ and $\lambda = \tau^2/\Theta^2$. The Jacobian of this transformation is proportional to $\tau/\lambda^{3/2}$. Thus, (A.5) expressed in terms of σ^2, τ, and λ is

$$\text{(A.6)} \quad \frac{p_F(\sigma^2|\cdot)(\sigma^2)^{\nu_o/2}(\bar{\sigma}_a^2)^{\bar{\nu}_a/2}}{\tau^{n+\nu_o+\bar{\nu}_a+1}}|M|^{-1/2}\lambda^{(k+\bar{\nu}_a-2)/2}\exp\left\{-\frac{1}{2\tau^2}[\nu s^2+\nu_o\sigma^2\right.$$
$$\left.+\bar{\nu}_a\bar{\sigma}_a^2\lambda+\hat{\boldsymbol{\beta}}'X'X\hat{\boldsymbol{\beta}}+\lambda\bar{\boldsymbol{\beta}}'A\bar{\boldsymbol{\beta}}-\bar{\boldsymbol{\beta}}_\lambda'M\bar{\boldsymbol{\beta}}_\lambda]\right\}.$$

(A.6) can be integrated with respect to τ to obtain the marginal posterior pdf for σ^2 and λ, namely,

$$\text{(A.7)}\quad \frac{p_F(\sigma^2|\cdot)(\sigma^2)^{\nu_0/2}(\bar{\sigma}_a^2)^{\bar{\nu}_a/2}|M|^{-1/2}\lambda^{(k+\bar{\nu}_a-2)/2}}{\{\nu s^2+\nu_o\sigma^2+\bar{\nu}_a\bar{\sigma}_a^2\lambda+\hat{\boldsymbol{\beta}}'X'X\hat{\boldsymbol{\beta}}+\lambda\bar{\boldsymbol{\beta}}'A\boldsymbol{\beta}-\bar{\boldsymbol{\beta}}_\lambda'M\bar{\boldsymbol{\beta}}_\lambda\}^{(n+\nu_0+\bar{\nu}_a)/2}}.$$

Using (3.8a), $\bar{\sigma}_a^2 = (\nu_a s_a^2 + \nu_o\sigma^2)/\bar{\nu}_a$ and $\bar{\nu}_a = \nu_o + \nu_a$, (A.7) can be expressed as

$$\text{(A.8a)}\qquad p(\sigma^2,\lambda|\mathbf{y},\cdot)=p_1(\sigma^2|\lambda,\mathbf{y},\cdot)p_2(\lambda|\mathbf{y},\cdot),$$

with

$$\text{(A.8b)}\qquad p_1(\sigma^2|\lambda,\mathbf{y},\cdot)\propto\left[\frac{(1+\lambda)\nu_o\sigma^2}{\nu s^2+g(\lambda)}\right]^{(2\nu_o-2)/2}\Bigg/\left[1+\frac{(1+\lambda)\nu_o\sigma^2}{\nu s^2+g(\lambda)}\right]^{(2\nu_o+n+\nu_a)/2},$$

and

$$\text{(A.8c)}\qquad p_2(\lambda|\mathbf{y},\cdot)\propto|M|^{-1/2}\lambda^{(k+\bar{\nu}_a-2)/2}/(1+\lambda)^{(2\nu_0-2)/2}[\nu s^2+g(\lambda)]^{(n+\bar{\nu}_a+\nu_0)/2},$$

where $g(\lambda) = \lambda(\nu_a s_a^2 + \bar{\boldsymbol{\beta}}'A\bar{\boldsymbol{\beta}}) - \bar{\boldsymbol{\beta}}_\lambda'M\bar{\boldsymbol{\beta}}_\lambda + \hat{\boldsymbol{\beta}}'X'X\hat{\boldsymbol{\beta}}$. It is seen that the conditional posterior pdf for σ^2 given λ is in the form of an F pdf. Bivariate numerical integration techniques can be employed to obtain the marginal posterior pdf for σ^2 from (A.8a).

To obtain the posterior pdf for $\boldsymbol{\beta}$, note that (A.3) is proportional to

$$\text{(A.9)}\quad \frac{(\sigma^2)^{\nu_0-1}}{\Theta^{k+\bar{\nu}_a+1}\tau^{n+\nu_0+1}}\exp\left\{-\frac{1}{2\tau^2}[\nu s^2+\nu_o\sigma^2+(\tau^2/\Theta^2)(\nu_a s_a^2+\nu_o\sigma^2)+c_\lambda+(\boldsymbol{\beta}-\bar{\boldsymbol{\beta}}_\lambda)'M(\boldsymbol{\beta}-\bar{\boldsymbol{\beta}}_\lambda)]\right\}$$

where $c_\lambda = \hat{\boldsymbol{\beta}}'X'X\hat{\boldsymbol{\beta}}+\lambda\bar{\boldsymbol{\beta}}'A\bar{\boldsymbol{\beta}}-\bar{\boldsymbol{\beta}}_\lambda'M\bar{\boldsymbol{\beta}}_\lambda$. In (A.9), change variables from σ^2, τ and Θ to σ^2, τ and $\lambda = \tau^2/\Theta^2$ and integrate out σ^2 and τ with the result,

$$\text{(A.10)}\quad p(\boldsymbol{\beta},\lambda|\mathbf{y},\cdot)\propto\frac{\lambda^{(k+\nu_0+4)/2}(1+\lambda)^{-\nu_0/2}}{\{\nu s^2+\lambda\nu_a s_a^2+c_\lambda+(\boldsymbol{\beta}-\bar{\boldsymbol{\beta}}_\lambda)'M(\boldsymbol{\beta}-\bar{\boldsymbol{\beta}}_\lambda)\}^{(n+k+\nu_0)/2}}.$$

From (A.10), it is seen that the conditional posterior pdf for $\boldsymbol{\beta}$ given λ is in the form of a multivariate Student-*t* pdf. Thus, (A.10) can be integrated analytically to obtain the joint posterior pdf for any element of $\boldsymbol{\beta}$, say, β_i, and λ, a bivariate pdf that can be analyzed numerically to obtain the marginal posterior pdf for β_i. For ease of numerical computation, it will be convenient to express $p(\beta_i,\lambda|\mathbf{y},\cdot)$ in terms of β_i and $\phi = \lambda/(1+\lambda)$, since the range of ϕ is given by $0<\phi<1$ given that $0<\lambda<\infty$.

References

Blattberg, R. C., and N. J. Gonedes (1972). "A Comparison of the Stable and Student Distributions as Statistical Models for Stock Prices." Graduate School of Business, University of Chicago.

Box, G. E. P., and G. C. Tiao (1962). "A Further Look at Robustness via Bayes Theorem." *Biometrika*, 49 (December):419–33.

DuMouchel, W. (1971). "Stable Distributions in Statistical Inference." Ph.D. diss., Department of Statistics, Yale University.

Fama, E. F., and R. Roll (1971). "Parameter Estimates for Symmetric Stable Distributions." *Journal of the American Statistical Association*, 66 (June):331–38.

Jeffreys, H. (1957). *Scientific Inference*. 2d ed. Cambridge: Cambridge University Press.

———. (1967). *Theory of Probability*. 3d rev. ed. London: Oxford University Press.

Mandelbrot, B. (1963). "The Variation of Certain Speculative Prices." *Journal of Business*, 36 (October):394–419.

Newcomb, S. (1886). "A Generalized Theory of the Combination of Observations So As to Obtain the Best Results." *American Journal of Mathematics*, 8 (June):343–66.

Praetz, P. D. (1972). "The Distribution of Share Price Changes." *Journal of Business*, 45 (January):49–55.

Raiffa, H., and Schlaifer, R. (1961). *Applied Statistical Decision Theory*. Boston: Graduate School of Business Administration, Harvard University.

Strawderman, W. E. (1974). "Minimax Estimation of Location Parameters for Certain Spherically Symmetric Distributions." *Journal of Multivariate Analysis*, 4 (September):255–64.

Wise, J. (1966). "Linear Estimators for Linear Regression Systems Having Infinite Residual Variances." Department of Economics, University of Hawaii.

Zellner, A. (1971). *An Introduction to Bayesian Inference in Econometrics*. New York: John Wiley & Sons.

Zellner, A., and M. S. Geisel (1970). "Analysis of Distributed Lag Models with Applications to Consumption Function Estimation." *Econometrica*, 38 (November):865–88.

Zellner, A., and J. F. Richard (1973). "Use of Prior Information in the Analysis and Estimation of Cobb-Douglas Production Function Models." *International Economic Review*, 14 (February):107–19.

Zellner, A., and A. D. Williams (1973). "Bayesian Analysis of the Federal Reserve–MIT–Penn Model's Almon Lag Consumption Function." *Journal of Econometrics* 1 (October):267–99.

3.5 Estimation of Functions of Population Means and Regression Coefficients Including Structural Coefficients: A Minimum Expected Loss (MELO) Approach

1 Introduction

In this paper, problems of estimating (a) reciprocals and ratios of population means and regression coefficients and (b) structural coefficients of linear structural econometric models are considered. For each problem in (a) and (b) formulae defining parameter estimates that minimize posterior expected loss, termed MELO estimates, are derived for specific loss functions and general forms for prior distributions and likelihood functions. Then these general results are specialized to provide explicit MELO estimates of parameters in normal likelihood functions when diffuse prior distributions are employed. When these MELO estimates are viewed as estimators, it is found that they have at least a finite second moment and thus finite risk relative to quadratic and quite a few other loss functions. In contrast, maximum likelihood (ML) estimators for the problems in (a) when likelihood functions are based on normal data distributions do not possess finite moments and have infinite risk relative to quadratic and other loss functions. With respect to problems in (b), it is well known that many widely used estimators such as 2SLS, LIML, 3SLS, FIML, etc., can fail to possess finite moments[1] and thus can have infinite risk relative to quadratic and other loss functions. Further, it is the case that for problems in (a) and (b), means of posterior distributions, based on diffuse or natural conjugate prior distributions, often fail to exist. Thus, in these cases, the usual Bayesian point estimate, the posterior mean, is not available.

The plan of the paper is as follows. In section 2, problems of estimating the reciprocal of a population mean, the reciprocal of a regression coefficient and ratios of population means and regression coefficients are analyzed. The analysis of section 3 involves deriving MELO estimators for

Reprinted from *Journal of Econometrics*, 8 (1978):127–58, with the kind permission of North-Holland Publishing Co.

1. See, e.g., Anderson and Sawa (1973), Bergstrom (1962), Hatanaka (1973), and Sawa (1972).

structural coefficients of linear structural econometric models. In section 4 further consideration is given to the properties of the MELO estimates and estimators derived in sections 2 and 3. Last, in section 5 some concluding remarks are presented.

2 MELO Estimation of Reciprocals and Ratios of Population Means and Regression Coefficients

2.1 Reciprocals of Population Means and Regression Coefficients

Let our model for the observations be

$$y_i = \mu + u_i, \quad i = 1, 2, \ldots, n, \tag{2.1}$$

where y_i is the ith observation, μ is the common mean of the observations, and u_i is the ith disturbance or error term. Our problem is to estimate $\theta = 1/\mu$.

The loss function that we shall employ is the following relative squared error loss function:[2]

$$L(\theta, \hat{\theta}) = (\theta - \hat{\theta})^2/\theta^2, \tag{2.2}$$

where $\hat{\theta} = \hat{\theta}(y)$ is an estimate of θ. Note that for the relative squared error loss function, a *given* absolute error, $|\theta - \hat{\theta}|$, is considered to be more serious when the true value of θ is small than when it is large whereas with a squared error loss function, $(\theta - \hat{\theta})^2$, the same loss is experienced for a given absolute error whatever the magnitude of the true value of θ. Further, the loss function in (2.2) can be obtained as follows. From $\theta = 1/\mu$, we have $1 - \theta\mu = 0$. Letting $\epsilon = 1 - \hat{\theta}\mu$, $\epsilon^2 = (1 - \hat{\theta}\mu)^2 = (\theta - \hat{\theta})^2/\theta^2$. The quantity ϵ measures the extent to which the relation $1 - \theta\mu = 0$ is in error when an estimate $\hat{\theta}$ is inserted for θ.

Given that we have a posterior pdf for μ, $p(\mu|y)$ that possesses finite first and second moments, we can compute posterior expected loss by expressing (2.2) as $L = (\theta - \hat{\theta})^2/\theta^2 = 1 - 2\mu\hat{\theta} + \mu^2\hat{\theta}^2$ and using the posterior pdf for μ to obtain

$$EL = 1 - 2\hat{\theta}E\mu + \hat{\theta}^2E\mu^2, \tag{2.3}$$

where $E \equiv$ posterior expectation. The value of $\hat{\theta}$ that minimizes (2.3), the MELO estimate, denoted by $\hat{\theta}^*$ is

2. Relative squared error loss functions have been previously employed and discussed in the literature; see, e.g., DeGroot (1970), p. 226, and Ferguson (1967), pp. 47, 26, 28. In Zellner and Vandaele (1975) it is shown that a Stein-like estimator for the mean of a multivariate normal pdf can be generated using a generalized relative squared error loss function and a diffuse, improper prior pdf.

$$(2.4) \qquad \hat{\theta}^* = \frac{E\mu}{E\mu^2} = \frac{\bar{\mu}}{\bar{\mu}^2 + \text{var}\,\mu} = \frac{1}{\bar{\mu}}\,\frac{1}{1 + \text{var}\,\mu/\bar{\mu}^2},$$

where $\bar{\mu} \equiv E\mu$, the posterior mean, and var $\mu \equiv$ the posterior variance of μ.[3] Thus it is seen that the MELO estimate, $\hat{\theta}^*$, is equal to the reciprocal of the posterior mean, $1/\bar{\mu}$, times a factor $1/(1 + \text{var}\,\mu/\bar{\mu}^2)$ that has a value between zero and one. This factor depends on the squared coefficient of variation of the posterior pdf for μ. When the posterior pdf for μ is very sharp, as would be the case when the sample size n is large, $\hat{\theta}^*$ is close to $1/\bar{\mu}$. However, when var $\mu/\bar{\mu}^2$ is large as would be the case when var μ is large and/or $\bar{\mu}^2$ is small, $|\hat{\theta}^*| < 1/|\bar{\mu}|$. Thus the factor $1/(1 + \text{var}\,\mu/\bar{\mu}^2)$ can be viewed as acting to "shrink" $1/\bar{\mu}$. Generally the estimate $\hat{\theta}^*$ in (2.4) will be employed when $|\bar{\mu}|/\sigma_\mu > 1$, a condition giving evidence that a value of μ in close proximity to zero is not very probable and also resulting in $\partial|\hat{\theta}^*|/\partial|\bar{\mu}| < 0$, a reasonable condition. When $|\bar{\mu}|/\sigma_\mu < 1$, the posterior pdf for θ will often show pronounced bimodality and the problem of obtaining a point estimate for θ is more complicated. In many cases prior information about the algebraic sign of μ, e.g., $\mu > 0$, is sufficient to provide a unimodal posterior pdf for θ; see the appendix for details.

We now turn to the evaluation of $\hat{\theta}^*$ in (2.4) in some special cases. Suppose that the y_i's in (2.1) are normally and independently distributed, each with mean μ and common known variance σ_0^2. Then the likelihood function is given by $l(\mu|\mathbf{y}, \sigma_0^2) \propto \exp\{-n(\mu - \bar{y})^2/2\sigma_0^2\}$, where "$\propto$" denotes proportionality and $\bar{y} = \Sigma_{i=1}^n y_i/n$, the sample mean. If we employ a diffuse prior pdf for μ, $p(\mu) \propto$ const, $-\infty < \mu < \infty$, the posterior pdf for μ is in the following normal form, $p(\mu|\mathbf{y}, \sigma_0^2) \propto \exp\{-n(\mu - \bar{y})^2/2\sigma_0^2\}$, with posterior mean, $\bar{\mu} = \bar{y}$, and posterior variance, var $\mu = \sigma_0^2/n$.[4] Thus, for this set of assumptions, the MELO estimate $\hat{\theta}^*$ in (2.4) is given by

$$(2.5) \qquad \hat{\theta}^* = \frac{1}{\bar{y}}\left(\frac{1}{1 + \sigma_0^2/n\bar{y}^2}\right),$$

which viewed as an estimator has finite moments (see section 4) and hence bounded risk relative to the loss function in (2.2). Further, $\tilde{\theta} = 1/\bar{y}$ is the ML estimator for $\theta = 1/\mu$. Since $\tilde{\theta}$ is the reciprocal of a normal variable, $\bar{y}$, its moments do not exist and it has infinite risk relative to a quadratic loss function, the loss function in (2.2), and many other loss functions.

3. For the loss functions, $L(\theta, \hat{\theta}) = (\theta - \hat{\theta})^2/\theta^{2r}$, $r = 1, 2, \ldots$, where $\theta = 1/\mu$, the MELO estimate for θ is $\hat{\theta}^* = E\mu^{2r-1}/E\mu^r$, $r = 1, 2, \ldots$, where $E \equiv$ posterior expectation operator.

4. Since μ has a normal posterior pdf, the posterior mean of $\theta = 1/\mu$ does not exist. Further, if a proper natural conjugate prior pdf for μ were employed, the posterior pdf would be normal and the posterior mean of $\theta = 1/\mu$ would still fail to exist. However, (2.4) can be readily evaluated with either a diffuse or a natural conjugate prior distribution.

When the observations in (2.1) are normally and independently distributed, each with mean μ and variance σ^2 and both μ and σ^2 have unknown values, we shall analyze the problem of estimating $\theta = 1/\mu$ under the assumption that our prior information about parameters' values is diffuse.[5] That is, we shall employ a standard diffuse prior pdf, namely, $p(\mu, \sigma) \propto 1/\sigma$, $-\infty < \mu < \infty$ and $0 < \sigma < \infty$. When this prior pdf is combined with the normal likelihood function to obtain the joint posterior pdf for μ and σ and then σ is integrated out, the marginal posterior pdf for μ is well known to be in the following univariate Student-t form,

$$p(\mu|\mathbf{y}) \propto \{\nu s^2 + n(\mu - \bar{y})^2\}^{-(\nu+1)/2},$$

where $\nu = n - 1$ and $\nu s^2 = \Sigma_{i=1}^{n}(y_i - \bar{y})^2$. For this posterior pdf, we have $E\mu = \bar{y}$ and var $\mu = \nu s^2/n(\nu - 2)$ for $\nu > 2$. Thus from (2.4), the MELO estimate for $\theta = 1/\mu$, is given by

$$(2.6) \qquad \hat{\theta}^* = \frac{1}{\bar{y}}\left(\frac{1}{1 + \nu s^2/n(\nu - 2)\bar{y}^2}\right), \qquad \nu = n - 1 > 2.$$

In (2.6), the MELO estimate $\hat{\theta}^*$ is in the form of a product of the reciprocal of the sample mean, $1/\bar{y}$, times a shrinking factor that has a value between zero and one.[6] Further (2.6) viewed as an estimator has finite moments and hence bounded risk. Additional properties of the estimators in (2.5) and (2.6) will be established in section 4. Among these is the property that these estimators have the same *large sample* normal distribution as the ML estimator and hence are consistent and asymptotically efficient.

The problem of estimating the reciprocal of a regression coefficient often arises in practice. For example, in the simple Haavelmo consumption model, the reciprocal of the "multiplier" is equal to the marginal propensity to save. Similarly in a simple quantity theory model the reciprocal of the velocity coefficient is a parameter of the money demand function. If our model for the observations is a simple regression model, $y_i = \pi x_i + u_i$, $i = 1, 2, \ldots, n$, where x_i is an independent variable and we wish to estimate $\theta = 1/\pi$ using the loss function in (2.2), we first derive the posterior pdf for π using whatever prior distribution and likelihood function that are considered appropriate. Let this posterior pdf be denoted by $p(\pi|\mathbf{y})$ and assume that it possesses finite first and second moments. Then using $\theta = 1/\pi$, the posterior expectation of the loss function in (2.2) can be expressed as $EL = 1 - 2\hat{\theta}E\pi + \hat{\theta}^2E\pi^2$ and the MELO estimate for $\theta = 1/\pi$ is given by

5. The analysis can easily be extended to the case of a proper natural conjugate prior distribution for μ and σ or to certain priors that impose restrictions on the range of μ, e.g., $0 < \mu < \infty$.

6. The condition $|\bar{\mu}|/\sigma_{\mu} > 1$, mentioned above, here specializes to $|\bar{y}|/(s/n^{1/2}) > (\nu/(\nu - 2))^{1/2}$, obviously related to a sampling theory pretest of the hypothesis $\mu = 0$.

$$(2.7)\qquad \hat{\theta}^* = \frac{1}{\bar{\pi}}\left(\frac{1}{1 + \text{var}\ \pi/\bar{\pi}^2}\right),$$

where $\bar{\pi} = E\pi$ and var π denote the posterior mean and variance of π, respectively. The MELO estimate in (2.7) is seen to be equal to the product of the reciprocal of posterior mean of π, $1/\bar{\pi}$, and a "shrinking" factor that has a value between zero and one.

To evaluate (2.7) for a particular case, assume that the data process, $y_i = \pi x_i + u_i$ is a simple normal regression, that is the u_i's are normally and independently distributed, each with zero mean and variance σ^2. If our prior information regarding the values of π and σ is vague, we can employ the following diffuse prior pdf, $p(\pi, \sigma) \propto 1/\sigma$, $-\infty < \pi < \infty$ and $0 < \sigma < \infty$.[7] The joint posterior pdf for π and σ is then given by

$$p(\pi, \sigma | \mathbf{y}) \propto \sigma^{-(n+1)} \exp\{-[\nu s^2 + (\pi - \hat{\pi})^2 m_{xx}]/2\sigma^2\},$$

where $\nu = n - 1$, $\hat{\pi} = \Sigma_{i=1}^n x_i y_i / m_{xx}$, $m_{xx} = \Sigma_{i=1}^n x_i^2$, and $\nu s^2 = \Sigma_{i=1}^n (y_i - \hat{\pi} x_i)^2$. The marginal posterior pdf for π is then

$$p(\pi | \mathbf{y}) \propto \{\nu s^2 + (\pi - \hat{\pi})^2 m_{xx}\}^{-(\nu+1)/2},$$

with posterior mean $\bar{\pi} = \hat{\pi}$ and var $\pi = \nu s^2/(\nu - 2) m_{xx}$ for $\nu > 2$. Thus for these assumptions, (2.7) becomes

$$(2.8)\qquad \hat{\theta}^* = \frac{1}{\hat{\pi}}\left(\frac{1}{1 + \nu s^2/(\nu - 2) m_{xx} \hat{\pi}^2}\right), \qquad \nu = n - 1 > 2.$$

It is seen that the MELO estimate in (2.8) is the product of $1/\hat{\pi}$, the ML estimator, and a "shrinking" factor that has a value between zero and one.[8] It is well known that the ML estimator $\tilde{\theta} = 1/\hat{\pi}$ does not possess finite moments (see, e.g., Bergstrom 1962), and has infinite risk relative to quadratic and other loss functions. On the other hand, as shown in section 4, the MELO estimator in (2.8) has finite moments and bounded risk relative to quadratic and other loss functions. Also, as the sample size gets large, the MELO estimator in (2.8) and the ML estimator have the same large-sample normal distribution.

2.2 *Ratios of Regression Coefficients and Population Means*

If our problem is to estimate the ratio of two parameters, say the ratio of two multiple regression coefficients, $\theta = \beta_1/\beta_2$, where β_1 and β_2 are multiple

7. The analysis can easily be extended to the case of a proper natural conjugate prior pdf for π and σ or to certain priors that limit the range of π, e.g., $0 < \pi < \infty$.

8. Here the condition for $\partial|\hat{\theta}^*|/\partial|\hat{\pi}| < 0$ is $|\hat{\pi}|/s m_{xx}^{-1/2} > ((\nu - 2)/\nu)^{1/2}$, obviously related to a sampling theory pretest of the hypothesis $\pi = 0$. See Zellner (1976), p. 622, for a discussion of pretesting.

regression coefficients, we have $\beta_1 - \beta_2\theta = 0$. If an estimate of θ is inserted in this last expression, $\epsilon = \beta_1 - \beta_2\hat{\theta}$, where ϵ measures the extent to which the "restriction" $\beta_1 - \beta_2\theta = 0$ fails to be satisfied. Letting our loss L be $L = \epsilon^2 = (\beta_1 - \beta_2\hat{\theta})^2$, we have

$$L = (\beta_1 - \beta_2\hat{\theta})^2 = \beta_2^2(\theta - \hat{\theta})^2. \tag{2.9}$$

In (2.9) loss is given by the product of β_2^2 and $(\theta - \hat{\theta})^2$, a generalized quadratic loss function. Note that for a *given* value of $|\theta - \hat{\theta}|$, L is larger when β_2^2 is large than when it is small. The larger β_2^2, ceteris paribus, the smaller $|\theta|$ and (2.9) provides a greater loss for a given absolute error $|\theta - \hat{\theta}|$. This contrasts with the implications of a squared error loss function, $(\theta - \hat{\theta})^2$ that provides the same loss for a given absolute error no matter what the value of θ. Thus to a large extent (2.9) behaves in a fashion similar to the relative squared error loss function introduced above.

Given that we have a posterior pdf for β_1 and β_2 that possesses finite first and second moments, we can compute posterior expected loss and obtain a MELO estimate for $\theta = \beta_1/\beta_2$ as follows:

$$EL = E(\beta_1 - \beta_2\hat{\theta})^2 = E\beta_1^2 - 2\hat{\theta}E\beta_1\beta_2 + \hat{\theta}^2E\beta_2^2, \tag{2.10}$$

where E denotes the expectation with respect to the posterior pdf for β_1 and β_2. From (2.10), the $\hat{\theta}$ that minimizes EL, denoted by $\hat{\theta}^*$, is given by

$$\begin{aligned} \hat{\theta}^* &= E\beta_1\beta_2/E\beta_2^2 \\ &= [\bar{\beta}_1\bar{\beta}_2 + \text{cov}(\beta_1, \beta_2)]/[\bar{\beta}_2^2 + \text{var}\,\beta_2] \\ &= (\bar{\beta}_1/\bar{\beta}_2)[1 + \text{cov}(\beta_1, \beta_2)/\bar{\beta}_1\bar{\beta}_2]/(1 + \text{var}\,\beta_2/\bar{\beta}_2^2), \end{aligned} \tag{2.11}$$

where $\bar{\beta}_1$ and $\bar{\beta}_2$ are posterior means, var β_2 is the posterior variance of β_2 and $\text{cov}(\beta_1, \beta_2)$ is the posterior covariance of β_1 and β_2. Given a particular posterior pdf for β_1 and β_2, the MELO estimate in (2.11) can be evaluated as shown below.[9]

If instead of the ratio of multiple regression coefficients, we consider the ratio of two population means, $\theta = \mu_1/\mu_2$, we have $\mu_1 - \mu_2\theta = 0$ and $\epsilon = \mu_1 - \mu_2\hat{\theta}$, where $\hat{\theta}$ is an estimate of θ. Then just as above we take our loss to be

$$L = \epsilon^2 = (\mu_1 - \mu_2\hat{\theta})^2 = \mu_2^2(\theta - \hat{\theta})^2.$$

Given a posterior pdf for μ_1 and μ_2 that has finite first and second moments,

9. For $\bar{\beta}_1, \bar{\beta}_2 > 0$, $\partial\hat{\theta}^*/\partial\bar{\beta}_1 > 0$ and $\partial\hat{\theta}^*/\partial\bar{\beta}_2 < 0$ if $(\bar{\beta}_1/\bar{\beta}_2)/2 < \hat{\theta}^*$, with $\hat{\theta}^*$ given in (2.11). This last inequality is equivalent to $1/2 < [1 + \text{cov}(\beta_1, \beta_2)/\bar{\beta}_1\bar{\beta}_2]/[1 + \text{var}\beta_2/\bar{\beta}_2^2]$, a condition on the factor that multiplies $\bar{\beta}_1\bar{\beta}_2$ in the second line of (2.11) and on the posterior pdf for β_1 and β_2. If $\text{cov}(\beta_1,\beta_2) = 0$, the condition reduces to $\text{var}\beta_2/\bar{\beta}_2^2 < 1$ or $\| \bar{\beta}^2 \| (\text{var}\beta_2)^{1/2} > 1$, a condition implying that β_2's value is probably not close to zero.

we have $EL = E\mu_1^2 - 2\hat{\theta}E\mu_1\mu_2 + \hat{\theta}^2E\mu_2^2$ and thus the MELO estimate, $\hat{\theta}^*$, for $\theta = \mu_1/\mu_2$ is

$$(2.12)\qquad \begin{aligned}\hat{\theta}^* &= E\mu_1\mu_2/E\mu_2^2\\ &= (\bar{\mu}_1/\bar{\mu}_2)[1 + \text{cov}(\mu_1, \mu_2)/\bar{\mu}_1\bar{\mu}_2]/(1 + \text{var}\,\mu_2/\bar{\mu}_2^2),\end{aligned}$$

where $\bar{\mu}_1$ and $\bar{\mu}_2$ are posterior means for μ_1 and μ_2, respectively, and $\text{cov}(\mu_1, \mu_2)$ and var μ_2 are the posterior covariance of μ_1 and μ_2 and the posterior variance of μ_2, respectively.

Ratios of parameters are often also encountered in analyses of simple simultaneous equation models. For example, let $y_{1t} = \gamma y_{2t} + u_{1t}$ and $y_{2t} = \beta x_t + u_{2t}$ be two structural equations. The reduced form equations for this system are $y_{1t} = \pi_1 x_t + v_{1t}$ and $y_{2t} = \pi_2 x_t + v_{2t}$ with $\pi_1 = \beta\gamma$ and $\pi_2 = \beta$. Thus the structural coefficient γ is given by $\gamma = \pi_1/\pi_2$, the ratio of two regression coefficients of a bivariate regression system, the reduced form equations. From $\gamma = \pi_1/\pi_2$, we have $\pi_1 - \pi_2\gamma = 0$, the restriction on π_1 and π_2. Let $\hat{\gamma}$ be an estimate of γ and let our loss be $L = \epsilon^2 = (\pi_1 - \pi_2\hat{\gamma})^2 = \pi_2^2(\gamma - \hat{\gamma})^2$. Then $EL = E\pi_1^2 - 2\hat{\gamma}E\pi_1\pi_2 + \hat{\gamma}^2E\pi_2^2$ and the MELO estimate for $\gamma = \pi_1/\pi_2$ is

$$(2.13)\qquad \begin{aligned}\hat{\gamma}^* &= E\pi_1\pi_2/E\pi_2^2\\ &= (\bar{\pi}_1/\bar{\pi}_2)[1 + \text{cov}(\pi_1, \pi_2)/\bar{\pi}_1\bar{\pi}_2]/(1 + \text{var}\,\pi_2/\bar{\pi}_2^2),\end{aligned}$$

where $\bar{\pi}_1$ and $\bar{\pi}_2$ are posterior means for π_1 and π_2, respectively, and $\text{cov}(\pi_1, \pi_2)$ and var π_2 are the posterior covariance of π_1 and π_2 and the posterior variance of π_2, respectively.

To illustrate applications of the above analysis, we first consider a normal multiple regression problem, $\mathbf{y} = X\boldsymbol{\beta} + \mathbf{u}$, where $\mathbf{y}$ is an $n \times 1$ vector, X is a given $n \times k$ matrix with rank k, $\boldsymbol{\beta}$ is a $k \times 1$ vector of regression coefficients with unknown values, and $\mathbf{u}$ is an $n \times 1$ disturbance vector. It is assumed that the elements of $\mathbf{u}$ have been independently drawn from a normal distribution with zero mean and variance σ^2 whose value is not known. Under these assumptions, the likelihood function is

$$l(\boldsymbol{\beta}, \sigma|\mathbf{y}, X) \propto \sigma^{-n}\exp\{-[\nu s^2 + (\boldsymbol{\beta} - \hat{\boldsymbol{\beta}})'X'X(\boldsymbol{\beta} - \hat{\boldsymbol{\beta}})]/2\sigma^2\},$$

where $\nu = n - k$, $\hat{\boldsymbol{\beta}} = (X'X)^{-1}X'\mathbf{y}$ and $\nu s^2 = (\mathbf{y} - X\hat{\boldsymbol{\beta}})'(\mathbf{y} - X\hat{\boldsymbol{\beta}})$. If our prior information about the parameters' values is vague[10] and we represent it by the usual following diffuse prior, $p(\boldsymbol{\beta}, \sigma) \propto 1/\sigma$, $0 < \sigma < \infty$ and $-\infty < \beta_i < \infty$, $i = 1, 2, \ldots, k$, the joint posterior pdf for $\boldsymbol{\beta}$ and σ is

$$p(\boldsymbol{\beta}, \sigma|\mathbf{y}, X) \propto \sigma^{-(n+1)}\exp\{-[\nu s^2 + \boldsymbol{\beta} - \hat{\boldsymbol{\beta}})'X'X(\boldsymbol{\beta} - \hat{\boldsymbol{\beta}})]/2\sigma^2\}.$$

10. The analysis can easily be extended to the case in which a proper natural conjugate prior distribution is employed.

On integrating this last expression with respect to σ, $0<\sigma<\infty$, the marginal posterior pdf for $\boldsymbol{\beta}$ is in the following well-known multivariate Student-t form,

$$p(\boldsymbol{\beta}\,|\,\mathbf{y}, X) \propto \{\nu s^2 + (\boldsymbol{\beta} - \hat{\boldsymbol{\beta}})'X'X(\boldsymbol{\beta} - \hat{\boldsymbol{\beta}})\}^{-(\nu+k)/2}.$$

Then the posterior mean and covariance matrix for $\boldsymbol{\beta}$ are $E\boldsymbol{\beta} = \hat{\boldsymbol{\beta}}$ and $V(\boldsymbol{\beta}) = (X'X)^{-1}\nu s^2/(\nu - 2)$, for $\nu > 2$. From these results we know all that is needed to evaluate the MELO estimate in (2.11) for $\theta = \beta_1/\beta_2$, where β_1 and β_2 are the first and second elements of the regression coefficient vector $\boldsymbol{\beta}$. Thus, for this problem, (2.11) specializes as follows:

$$\text{(2.14)} \quad \hat{\theta}^* = (\hat{\beta}_1/\hat{\beta}_2)[1 + m^{12}\bar{s}^2/\hat{\beta}_1\hat{\beta}_2]/(1 + m^{22}\bar{s}^2/\hat{\beta}_2^2), \qquad \nu = n - k > 2,$$

where $\hat{\beta}_1$ and $\hat{\beta}_2$ are the first two elements of $\hat{\boldsymbol{\beta}} = (X'X)^{-1}X'\mathbf{y}$, m^{ij} is the (i, j)th elements of $(X'X)^{-1}$ and

$$\bar{s}^2 = \nu s^2/(\nu - 2) = (\mathbf{y} - X\hat{\boldsymbol{\beta}})'(\mathbf{y} - X\hat{\boldsymbol{\beta}})/(\nu - 2).$$

It is seen that the MELO estimator $\hat{\theta}^*$ for $\theta = \beta_1/\beta_2$ in (2.14) is equal to $\hat{\beta}_1/\hat{\beta}_2$, the ML estimator, times a factor that depends on the relative second-order posterior moments of β_1 and β_2. It is well known that the moments of the ML estimator $\tilde{\theta} = \hat{\beta}_1/\hat{\beta}_2$ do not exist whereas the moments of the MELO estimator in (2.14) do exist. Thus the MELO and ML estimators have very different finite sample properties; however as the sample size gets large, their large-sample distributions become identical; see section 4.

The problem of estimating the ratio of two population means, $\theta = \mu_1/\mu_2$, can be solved using analysis similar to that employed above. As a specific example, let $y_{1i} = \mu_1 + u_{1i}$ and $y_{2i} = \mu_2 + u_{2i}$, $i = 1, 2, \ldots, n$, where μ_1 and μ_2 are population means, y_{1i} and y_{2i} are observations and u_{1i} and u_{2i} are disturbance terms. Here we shall assume that the u_{1i}'s and u_{2i}'s are normally and independently distributed with zero means, that the u_{1i}'s have common variance σ_1^2 and u_{2i}'s have common variance σ_2^2. Under these assumptions, the likelihood function is

$$\begin{aligned} l(\mu_1, \mu_2, \sigma_1, \sigma_2\,|\,\mathbf{y}_1, \mathbf{y}_2) \propto \sigma_1^{-n}\sigma_2^{-n}&\exp\{-[\nu s_1^2 + n(\mu_1 - \bar{y}_1)^2]/2\sigma_1^2\} \\ &\times \exp\{-[\nu s_2^2 + n(\mu_2 - \bar{y}_2)^2]/2\sigma_2^2\}, \end{aligned}$$

where $\nu = n - 1$, $\bar{y}_1 = \Sigma_{i=1}^n y_{1i}/n$, $\bar{y}_2 = \Sigma_{i=1}^n y_{2i}/n$, $\nu s_1^2 = \Sigma_{i=1}^n (y_{1i} - \bar{y}_1)^2$ and $\nu s_2^2 = \Sigma_{i=1}^n (y_{2i} - \bar{y}_2)^2$.

If we employ the following diffuse prior pdf, $p(\mu_1, \mu_2, \sigma_1, \sigma_2) \propto 1/\sigma_1\sigma_2$, $0 < \sigma_i < \infty$ and $-\infty < \mu_i < \infty$, $i = 1, 2$, the marginal posterior pdf for μ_1 and μ_2 is given by

$$p(\mu_1, \mu_2 \mid \mathbf{y}_1, \mathbf{y}_2) \propto \{\nu s_1^2 + n(\mu_1 - \bar{y}_1)^2\}^{-(\nu+1)/2} \times \{\nu s_2^2 + n(\mu_2 - \bar{y}_2)^2\}^{-(\nu+1)/2},$$

with posterior means, $E\mu_1 = \bar{y}_1$ and $E\mu_2 = \bar{y}_2$ and posterior variances, var $\mu_1 = \nu s_1^2/n(\nu - 2)$ and var $\mu_2 = \nu s_2^2/n(\nu - 2)$ for $\nu > 2$. For this problem the posterior covariance of μ_1 and μ_2 is zero. Thus the MELO estimator for $\theta = \mu_1/\mu_2$ is given from (2.12) as follows:

(2.15) $$\hat{\theta}^* = (\bar{y}_1/\bar{y}_2)\{1/(1 + \nu s_2^2/n(\nu - 2)\bar{y}_2^2)\}, \qquad \nu = n - 1 > 2.$$

It is seen that (2.15) is in the form of a product of the ML estimator, $\tilde{\theta} = \bar{y}_1/\bar{y}_2$, times a factor that depends on the coefficient of variation of the posterior pdf for μ_2. While the ML estimator $\tilde{\theta} = \bar{y}_1/\bar{y}_2$ does not possess finite moments, the MELO estimator in (2.15) has finite moments and hence bounded risk relative to quadratic and other loss functions.

As a last case, consider the simple bivariate normal regression system, $y_{1t} = \pi_1 x_t + v_{1t}$ and $y_{2t} = \pi_2 x_t + v_{2t}$, $t = 1, 2, \ldots, T$, where the pairs of error terms (v_{1t}, v_{2t}) are normally and independently distributed, each with zero mean vector and common 2×2 pds covariance matrix Ω. Given that we employ a diffuse prior pdf for π_1, π_2, and the distinct elements of Ω, $p(\pi_1, \pi_2, \Omega) \propto |\Omega|^{-1}$, it is known that the marginal posterior pdf for π_1 and π_2 is in the bivariate Student-t form with posterior mean $\hat{\boldsymbol{\pi}}' = (\hat{\pi}_1, \hat{\pi}_2)$ where

$$\hat{\pi}_i = \sum_{t=1}^{T} x_t y_{it}/\Sigma x_t^2, \qquad i = 1, 2,$$

and posterior covariance matrix $\bar{S}/m_{xx'}$ where $m_{xx} = \Sigma x_t^2$ and $\bar{S}$ is a symmetric 2×2 matrix with typical element,

$$\bar{s}_{ij} = \Sigma(y_{it} - x_t\hat{\pi}_i)(y_{jt} - x_t\hat{\pi}_j)/(\nu - 2), \qquad i, j = 1, 2,$$

with $\nu = n - 1 > 2$. On inserting these posterior moments in (2.13), the MELO estimate is

(2.16) $$\hat{\gamma}^* = (\hat{\pi}_1/\hat{\pi}_2)(1 + \bar{s}_{12}/m_{xx}\hat{\pi}_1\hat{\pi}_2)/(1 + \bar{s}_{22}/m_{xx}\hat{\pi}_2^2).$$

Again it is the case that the MELO estimate $\hat{\gamma}^*$ is the product of the ML estimate, $\hat{\pi}_1/\hat{\pi}_2$, times a "correction" factor.

For the reader's convenience, some of the results in this section are presented in tabular form in table 1.

3 MELO Estimates for Structural Coefficients

In this section we derive MELO estimates for structural coefficients of linear structural econometric models. Initially we consider a single struc-

Table 1 Tabular Summary of MELO Estimates

Problem	Loss Function	MELO Estimate[a]	Equation in Text
1. Reciprocal mean, $\theta = 1/\mu$	$L = ((\theta - \hat{\theta})/\theta)^2$	A. $\hat{\theta}^* = (1/\bar{\mu})(1/(1 + \text{var } \mu/\bar{\mu}^2))$	(2.4)
		B. $\hat{\theta}^* = (1/\bar{y})(1/[1 + vs^2/n(v-2)])$	(2.6)
2. Reciprocal of regression coefficient, $\theta = 1/\pi$	$L = ((\theta - \hat{\theta})/\theta)^2$	A. $\hat{\theta}^* = (1/\bar{\pi})(1/(1 + \text{var } \pi/\bar{\pi}^2))$	(2.7)
		B. $\hat{\theta}^* = (1/\hat{\pi})(1/[1 + vs^2/(v-2)m_{xx}\hat{\pi}^2])$	(2.8)
3. Ratio of multiple regression coefficients, $\theta = \beta_1/\beta_2$	$L = \beta_2^2(\theta - \hat{\theta})^2$	A. $\hat{\theta}^* = (\bar{\beta}_1/\bar{\beta}_2)[1 + \text{cov}(\beta_1, \beta_2)/\bar{\beta}_1, \bar{\beta}_2]/(1 + \text{var } \beta_2/\bar{\beta}_2^2)$	(2.11)
		B. $\hat{\theta}^* = (\hat{\beta}_1/\hat{\beta}_2)(1 + m^{12}\bar{s}^2/\hat{\beta}_1\hat{\beta}_2)/(1 + m^{22}\bar{s}^2/\hat{\beta}_2^2)$	(2.14)
4. Ratio of population means, $\theta = \mu_1/\mu_2$	$L = \mu_2^2(\theta - \hat{\theta})^2$	A. $\hat{\theta}^* = (\bar{\mu}_1/\bar{\mu}_2)[1 + \text{cov}(\mu_1, \mu_2)/\bar{\mu}_1\bar{\mu}_2]/(1 + \text{var } \mu_2/\bar{\mu}_2^2)$	(2.12)
		B. $\hat{\theta}^* = (\bar{y}_1/\bar{y}_2)/[1 + vs_2^2/n(v-2)\bar{y}_2^2]$	(2.15)
5. Ratio of bivariate regression coefficients, $\gamma = \pi_1/\pi_2$	$L = \pi_2^2(\gamma - \hat{\gamma})^2$	A. $\hat{\gamma}^* = (\bar{\pi}_1/\bar{\pi}_2)[1 + \text{cov}(\pi_1, \pi_2)/\bar{\pi}_1\bar{\pi}_2]/(1 + \text{var } \pi_2/\bar{\pi}_2^2)$	(2.13)
		B. $\hat{\gamma}^* = (\hat{\pi}_1/\hat{\pi}_2)(1 + \bar{s}_{12}/m_{xx}\hat{\pi}_1\hat{\pi}_2)/(1 + \bar{s}_{22}/m_{xx}\hat{\pi}_2^2)$	(2.16)

[a]Case A is the general MELO estimate expressed in terms of posterior moments. Case B is a special case of Case A in which normal data processes and diffuse prior distributions are employed.

tural equation and then go on to consider joint estimation of sets of structural equations' parameters.

3.1 "Single Equation" Analysis

Let a structural equation of a model, say the first equation that is assumed identified, be given by

$$\underset{n\times 1}{\mathbf{y}_1} = \underset{n\times m_1}{Y_1}\ \underset{m_1\times 1}{\boldsymbol{\gamma}_1} + \underset{n\times k_1}{X_1}\ \underset{k_1\times 1}{\boldsymbol{\beta}_1} + \underset{n\times 1}{\mathbf{u}_1}, \tag{3.1}$$

where $\mathbf{y}_1$ and Y_1 are an $n \times 1$ vector and an $n \times m_1$ matrix, respectively, of observations on $m = m_1 + 1$ endogenous variables, X_1 is an $n \times k_1$ matrix of rank k_1 of observations on k_1 predetermined variables, $\boldsymbol{\gamma}_1$ and $\boldsymbol{\beta}_1$ are $m_1 \times 1$ and $k_1 \times 1$ vectors of structural coefficients and $\mathbf{u}_1$ is an $n \times 1$ vector of structural disturbances. X_1 is a submatrix of the $n \times k$ matrix X of observations on all predetermined variables in the model, that is $X = (X_1 \vdots X_0)$ where X_0 is $n \times k_0$, $k = k_1 + k_0$, and it is assumed that X has rank k.

The reduced form equations for $\mathbf{y}_1$ and Y_1 are given by

$$\underset{n\times 1}{(\mathbf{y}_1} \vdots \underset{n\times m_1}{Y_1)} = \underset{n\times k}{X}\ \underset{k\times 1}{(\boldsymbol{\pi}_1} \vdots \underset{k\times m_1}{\Pi_1)} + \underset{n\times 1}{(\mathbf{v}_1} \vdots \underset{n\times m}{V_1)}, \tag{3.2}$$

where $\boldsymbol{\pi}_1$ is a $k \times 1$ vector and Π_1 is a $k \times m_1$ matrix of reduced form coefficients and $\mathbf{v}_1$ is an $n \times 1$ vector and V_1 is an $n \times m_1$ matrix of reduced form disturbances.

On multiplying both sides of (3.2) on the right by $(1 \vdots -\boldsymbol{\gamma}_1')'$ and comparing the result with (3.1), we obtain the well-known results

$$\boldsymbol{\pi}_1 = \Pi_1\boldsymbol{\gamma}_1 + \begin{pmatrix}\boldsymbol{\beta}_1\\ \mathbf{0}\end{pmatrix}, \tag{3.3a}$$

and

$$\mathbf{v}_1 - V_1\boldsymbol{\gamma}_1 = \mathbf{u}_1, \tag{3.3b}$$

where the zero vector in (3.3a) is $(k - k_1) \times 1$ with $k - k_1 \geqq m_1$ the necessary order condition for identification implied by the usual rank condition for identification of $\boldsymbol{\gamma}_1$ and $\boldsymbol{\beta}_1$. In (3.3a) we have the restrictions on the reduced form coefficients that involve the parameter vectors $\boldsymbol{\gamma}_1$ and $\boldsymbol{\beta}_1$ that we wish to estimate.

To formulate a loss function for the problem of estimating $\boldsymbol{\gamma}_1$ and $\boldsymbol{\beta}_1$ multiply both sides of (3.3a) on the left by $X = (X_1 \vdots X_0)$ to obtain $X\boldsymbol{\pi}_1 = X\Pi_1\boldsymbol{\gamma}_1 + X_1\boldsymbol{\beta}_1$, or $X\boldsymbol{\pi}_1 = \bar{Z}_1\boldsymbol{\delta}_1$, where $\bar{Z}_1 = (X\Pi_1 \vdots X_1)$ and $\boldsymbol{\delta}_1' = (\boldsymbol{\gamma}_1' \vdots \boldsymbol{\beta}_1')$. If $\hat{\boldsymbol{\delta}}_1$ is an estimate of $\boldsymbol{\delta}_1$, let $\boldsymbol{\epsilon} = X\boldsymbol{\pi}_1 - \bar{Z}_1\hat{\boldsymbol{\delta}}_1$ and define the loss function as follows:

(3.4) $$L = \boldsymbol{\epsilon}'\boldsymbol{\epsilon} = (X\boldsymbol{\pi}_1 - \bar{Z}_1\hat{\boldsymbol{\delta}}_1)'(X\boldsymbol{\pi}_1 - \bar{Z}_1\hat{\boldsymbol{\delta}}_1) = (\boldsymbol{\delta}_1 - \hat{\boldsymbol{\delta}}_1)'\bar{Z}_1'\bar{Z}_1(\boldsymbol{\delta}_1 - \hat{\boldsymbol{\delta}}_1),$$

where in going from the first to the second line of (3.4) $X\boldsymbol{\pi}_1 = \bar{Z}_1\boldsymbol{\delta}_1$ has been employed. Thus the loss function in (3.4) is quadratic in $\boldsymbol{\delta}_1 - \hat{\boldsymbol{\delta}}_1$ with a pds matrix, $\bar{Z}_1'\bar{Z}_1$, where $\bar{Z}_1 = (X\Pi_1 : X_1)$.

Given a posterior pdf for $\Pi = (\boldsymbol{\pi}_1 : \Pi_1)$ that possesses finite first and second moments, posterior expected loss, evaluated from the first line of (3.4), is

(3.5) $$EL = E\boldsymbol{\pi}_1'X'X\boldsymbol{\pi}_1 - 2\hat{\boldsymbol{\delta}}_1'E\bar{Z}_1'X\boldsymbol{\pi}_1 + \hat{\boldsymbol{\delta}}_1'E\bar{Z}_1'\bar{Z}_1\hat{\boldsymbol{\delta}}_1,$$

and the value of $\hat{\boldsymbol{\delta}}_1$, $\hat{\boldsymbol{\delta}}_1^*$ that minimizes expected loss is

(3.6) $$\hat{\boldsymbol{\delta}}_1^* = (E\bar{Z}_1'\bar{Z}_1)^{-1}E\bar{Z}_1'X\boldsymbol{\pi}_1 = \begin{bmatrix} E\Pi_1'X'X\Pi_1 & E\Pi_1'X'X_1 \\ EX_1'X\Pi_1 & X_1'X_1 \end{bmatrix}^{-1} \begin{bmatrix} E\Pi_1'X'X\boldsymbol{\pi}_1 \\ EX_1'X\boldsymbol{\pi}_1 \end{bmatrix}.$$

$\hat{\boldsymbol{\delta}}_1^*$ in (3.6) is the MELO estimate relative to the loss function in (3.4) and whatever posterior pdf is employed in evaluating the posterior moments in (3.6).[11]

As an explicit practical example illustrating application of (3.6), we write the reduced form system in (3.2) as

(3.7) $$Y = X\Pi + V,$$

where $Y = (\mathbf{y}_1 : Y_1)$, $\Pi = (\boldsymbol{\pi}_1 : \Pi_1)$ and $V = (\mathbf{v}_1 : V_1)$, and assume that the rows of V are normally and independently distributed, each with zero mean vector and common pds $m \times m$ covariance matrix Ω, with $m = m_1 + 1$. If we employ a diffuse prior pdf for Π and Ω, $p(\Pi, \Omega) \propto |\Omega|^{-(m+1)/2}$, it is well known (see, e.g., Zellner 1971*a*, p. 229) that the marginal posterior pdf for Π is in the following matrix Student-*t* form:

(3.8) $$p(\Pi | Y) \propto |S + (\Pi - \hat{\Pi})'X'X(\Pi - \hat{\Pi})|^{-n/2},$$

where $\hat{\Pi} = (X'X)^{-1}X'Y$, the posterior mean of Π, and

$$S = (Y - X\hat{\Pi})'(Y - X\hat{\Pi}) = \hat{V}'\hat{V}.$$

11. $\hat{\boldsymbol{\delta}}^*_1$ is an estimate of $\boldsymbol{\delta}_1$ that appears in $X\boldsymbol{\pi}_1 = \bar{Z}_1\boldsymbol{\delta}_1$, a set of n exact equations. In general if we are interested in estimating a vector $\boldsymbol{\theta}$ appearing in $\boldsymbol{\eta} = A\boldsymbol{\theta}$, where $\boldsymbol{\eta}$ is an $n \times 1$ vector and A is an $n \times k$ matrix of rank k, let $\hat{\boldsymbol{\theta}}$ be any estimate of $\boldsymbol{\theta}$. Then if our loss function is $L = (\boldsymbol{\eta} - A\hat{\boldsymbol{\theta}})'Q(\boldsymbol{\eta} - A\hat{\boldsymbol{\theta}}) = (\boldsymbol{\theta} - \hat{\boldsymbol{\theta}})'A'QA(\boldsymbol{\theta} - \hat{\boldsymbol{\theta}})$, where Q is an $n \times n$ pds matrix, the MELO estimate for θ is $\hat{\boldsymbol{\theta}}^* = (EA'QA)^{-1}EA'Q\boldsymbol{\eta}$, where $E \equiv$ posterior expectation operator.

Letting

$$\Pi - \hat{\Pi} = (\boldsymbol{\pi}_1 - \hat{\boldsymbol{\pi}}_1, \boldsymbol{\pi}_2 - \hat{\boldsymbol{\pi}}_2, \ldots, \boldsymbol{\pi}_m - \hat{\boldsymbol{\pi}}_m),$$

and

$$(\boldsymbol{\pi} - \hat{\boldsymbol{\pi}})' = (\boldsymbol{\pi}_1' - \hat{\boldsymbol{\pi}}_1', \boldsymbol{\pi}_2' - \hat{\boldsymbol{\pi}}_2', \ldots, \boldsymbol{\pi}_m' - \hat{\boldsymbol{\pi}}_m'),$$

the posterior covariance matrix for $\boldsymbol{\pi}$ is (see, e.g., Box and Tiao 1973, p. 477)

$$E(\boldsymbol{\pi} - \hat{\boldsymbol{\pi}})(\boldsymbol{\pi} - \hat{\boldsymbol{\pi}})' = \bar{S} \otimes (X'X)^{-1}, \tag{3.9}$$

where $\bar{S} = (Y - X\hat{\Pi})'(Y - X\hat{\Pi})/(\nu - 2)$, with $\nu = n - k - (m - 1) > 2$.

Using the above results to evaluate the posterior expectations in (3.6), we have

$$\begin{aligned} E\Pi_1' X'X\Pi_1 &= E(\Pi_1 - \hat{\Pi}_1 + \hat{\Pi}_1)'X'X(\Pi_1 - \hat{\Pi}_1 + \hat{\Pi}_1) \\ &= \hat{\Pi}_1' X'X\hat{\Pi}_1 + E(\Pi_1 - \hat{\Pi}_1)'X'X(\Pi_1 - \hat{\Pi}_1) \\ &= \hat{\Pi}_1' X'X\hat{\Pi}_1 + k\bar{S}_{22}, \end{aligned} \tag{3.10}$$

and

$$\begin{aligned} E\Pi_1' X'X\boldsymbol{\pi}_1 &= E(\Pi_1 - \hat{\Pi}_1 + \hat{\Pi}_1)'X'X(\boldsymbol{\pi}_1 - \hat{\boldsymbol{\pi}}_1 + \hat{\boldsymbol{\pi}}_1) \\ &= \hat{\Pi}_1' X'X\hat{\boldsymbol{\pi}}_1 + E(\Pi_1 - \hat{\Pi}_1)'X'X(\boldsymbol{\pi}_1 - \hat{\boldsymbol{\pi}}_1) \\ &= \hat{\Pi}_1' X'X\hat{\boldsymbol{\pi}}_1 + k\bar{\mathbf{s}}_{12}, \end{aligned} \tag{3.11}$$

where the partitionings, $\Pi = (\boldsymbol{\pi}_1 \vdots \Pi_1)$, $\hat{\Pi} = (\hat{\boldsymbol{\pi}}_1 \vdots \hat{\Pi}_1)$ and

$$\bar{S} = (Y - X\hat{\Pi})'(Y - X\hat{\Pi})/(\nu - 2) = \begin{pmatrix} \bar{s}_{11} & \bar{\mathbf{s}}_{12}' \\ \bar{\mathbf{s}}_{12} & \bar{S}_{22} \end{pmatrix}, \tag{3.12}$$

have been employed.[12] Substituting the results (3.10) and (3.11) into (3.6), we have

$$\hat{\boldsymbol{\delta}}_1^* = \begin{bmatrix} \hat{\Pi}_1' X'X\hat{\Pi}_1 + k\bar{S}_{22} & \hat{\Pi}_1' X'X_1 \\ X_1' X\hat{\Pi}_1 & X_1'X_1 \end{bmatrix}^{-1} \begin{bmatrix} \hat{\Pi}_1' X'X\hat{\boldsymbol{\pi}}_1 + k\bar{\mathbf{s}}_{12} \\ X_1' X\hat{\boldsymbol{\pi}}_1 \end{bmatrix}. \tag{3.13}$$

With $\hat{\boldsymbol{\delta}}_1^* = (\hat{\boldsymbol{\gamma}}_1'^*, \hat{\boldsymbol{\beta}}_1'^*)'$, we obtain the following expressions for $\hat{\boldsymbol{\gamma}}_1^*$ and $\hat{\boldsymbol{\beta}}_1^*$ from (3.13):

$$\hat{\boldsymbol{\gamma}}_1^* \text{ and } (M_1 + k\bar{S}_{22})^{-1}(M_1\hat{\boldsymbol{\gamma}}_1 + k\bar{S}_{22}\hat{\hat{\boldsymbol{\gamma}}}_1), \tag{3.14}$$

where $M_1 = \hat{\Pi}_1' X[I - X_1(X_1'X_1)^{-1}X_1']X\hat{\Pi}_1$, $\hat{\boldsymbol{\gamma}}_1$ is the 2SLS estimator for $\boldsymbol{\gamma}_1$, $\hat{\hat{\boldsymbol{\gamma}}} = \bar{S}_{22}^{-1}\bar{\mathbf{s}}_{12} = (\hat{V}_1' \hat{V}_1)^{-1} \hat{V}_1 \hat{\boldsymbol{v}}_1$, and

12. In the derivation reported in (3.10), note that $E(\Pi_1 - \hat{\Pi}_1)'X'X(\Pi_1 - \hat{\Pi}_1) = \{E(\boldsymbol{\pi}_i - \hat{\boldsymbol{\pi}}_i)'X'X(\boldsymbol{\pi}_j - \hat{\boldsymbol{\pi}}_j)\} = \{trX'X\text{cov}(\boldsymbol{\pi}_i, \boldsymbol{\pi}_j)\} = \{k\bar{s}_{ij}\} = k\bar{S}_{22}$. Similar operations yield $E(\Pi_1 - \hat{\Pi}_1)'X'X(\boldsymbol{\pi}_1 - \hat{\boldsymbol{\pi}}_1) = k\bar{s}_{12}$, with $\bar{S}_{22}$ and $\bar{s}_{12}$ defined in (3.12).

(3.15) $$\hat{\boldsymbol{\beta}}_1^* = (X_1'X_1)^{-1}X_1'(X\hat{\boldsymbol{\pi}}_1 - X\hat{\Pi}_1\hat{\boldsymbol{\gamma}}_1^*).$$

From (3.14), it is seen that the MELO estimate for $\boldsymbol{\gamma}_1$ is a matrix weighted average of the 2SLS estimate, $\hat{\boldsymbol{\gamma}}_1$, and the estimate $\hat{\hat{\boldsymbol{\gamma}}}_1$ formed from reduced form residuals. Also (3.14) can be expressed as a matrix weighted average of the DLS and 2SLS estimates of $\boldsymbol{\gamma}_1$ (see Zellner 1980).

Surprisingly, the estimate $\hat{\boldsymbol{\delta}}_1^*$ for $\boldsymbol{\delta}_1$ in (3.13) is in the form of a "$\mathcal{K}$-class" estimate with $\mathcal{K} = \mathcal{K}^*$ where $\mathcal{K}^* = 1 - k/(\nu - 2)$, with $\nu = n - k - (m - 1) > 2$. Hence, the present analysis yields an optimal value for $\mathcal{K}$ that is less than one, the value that yields the 2SLS estimate.[13] Hatanaka (1973, pp. 12–14) has shown that in general the first two finite-sample moments of $\mathcal{K}$-class estimators exist when $\mathcal{K} < 1$ and other conditions, satisfied above, are met.[14] Thus $\hat{\boldsymbol{\delta}}_1^*$ in (3.13) has finite first and second moments and bounded risk relative to quadratic loss functions. Further it is to be noted that $\mathcal{K}^* \rightarrow 1$ and $n^{1/2}(\mathcal{K}^* - 1) \rightarrow 0$ as $n \rightarrow \infty$. Thus $\hat{\boldsymbol{\delta}}_1^*$ is consistent and asymptotically equivalent to other consistent and asymptotically normal $\mathcal{K}$-class estimators. For the reader's benefit, the following table provides values of $\mathcal{K}^*$ for various values of k, the number of variables in X and $\nu - 2 = n - k - (m - 1) - 2$.

From the table it is interesting to observe that $\mathcal{K}^*$ is substantially below one in a variety of circumstances. Also when $k = \nu - 2$, $\mathcal{K}^* = 0$, which yields the "direct" or "ordinary" least squares estimator for $\boldsymbol{\delta}_1$. When $k > \nu - 2 = n - k - (m - 1) - 2$ or $2k + m - 1 > n$, a condition under which the number of parameters is large relative to the sample size n, $\mathcal{K}^* < 0$.

We further note that the derivation of $\hat{\boldsymbol{\delta}}_1^*$ in (3.13) is appropriate when X contains lagged endogenous variables, given that initial values of such variables are taken as given in formulating the normal likelihood function for the reduced form system, $Y = X\Pi + V$. In addition, it is possible to employ a broadened loss function $L = (\boldsymbol{\delta}_1 - \hat{\boldsymbol{\delta}}_1)'\bar{Z}_1'Q_1\bar{Z}_1(\boldsymbol{\delta}_1 - \hat{\boldsymbol{\delta}}_1)$, where Q_1 is a given pds matrix in place of (3.4).[15]

13. When $\mathcal{K} > 1$, Sawa (1972) showed that $\mathcal{K}$-class estimators for structural coefficients in an equation containing two endogenous variables do not possess finite moments of any order. See also Mariano (1973). In Nagar (1959) and Sawa (1972), "approximately optimal" values of $\mathcal{K}$ that are functions of parameters with unknown values are presented.

14. These other conditions, in terms of our notation, are: (i) $k - k_1 - m_1 \geq 0$ (order condition for identification); (ii) $n - k - m_1 \geq 0$; and (iii) $n - k_1 - m_1 \geq 2$. With the assumption $\nu = n - k - (m - 1) > 2$ satisfied, Hatanaka's conditions are also satisfied. Hatanaka further assumes that X does not contain lagged endogenous variables.

15. In Zellner and Park (1979), the MELO estimate $\hat{\boldsymbol{\delta}}_1^*$ in (3.13) is computed for equations of Klein's Model I and of the Girshick-Haavelmo demand and supply model for food and compared with DLS and 2SLS estimates. The MELO estimates tend to lie between the DLS and 2SLS estimates.

Table 2 Values of $\mathcal{H}$ for Selected Values of k and $\nu - 2$

		Values of $\nu - 2$										
		1	2	3	4	5	6	10	20	50	...	∞
Values of k	1	0	1/2	2/3	3/4	4/5	5/6	9/10	19/20	49/50	...	1
	2	−1	0	1/3	1/2	3/5	2/3	4/5	9/10	24/25	...	1
	3	−2	−1/2	0	1/4	2/5	1/2	7/10	17/20	47/50	...	1
	4	−3	−1	−1/3	0	1/5	1/3	3/5	4/5	23/25	...	1
	5	−4	−3/2	−2/3	−1/5	0	1/6	1/2	3/4	9/10	...	1

3.2 "Full-System" Analysis

We now turn to derive MELO estimates of structural coefficients, assumed identified, appearing in all equations of a linear simultaneous equation model. Let the αth structural equation be given by

$$\boldsymbol{y}_\alpha = Y_\alpha \boldsymbol{\gamma}_\alpha + X_\alpha \boldsymbol{\beta}_\alpha + \boldsymbol{u}_\alpha, \qquad \alpha = 1, 2, \ldots, g. \tag{3.16}$$

where $\boldsymbol{y}_\alpha$ is an $n \times 1$ vector of observations on an endogenous variable whose coefficient is equal to one, Y_α is an $n \times m_\alpha$ matrix of observations on m_α other endogenous variables appearing in the αth equation with $m_\alpha \times 1$ coefficient vector $\boldsymbol{\gamma}_\alpha$, X_α is an $n \times k_\alpha$ matrix of observations on k_α predetermined variables with $k_\alpha \times 1$ coefficient vector $\boldsymbol{\beta}_\alpha$ and $\boldsymbol{u}_\alpha$ is an $n \times 1$ disturbance vector. As usual, it is assumed that X_α is a submatrix of X, the $n \times k$ matrix of observations on all k predetermined variables that has rank k. Using the reduced form equations for $\boldsymbol{y}_\alpha$ and Y_α, $\boldsymbol{y}_\alpha = X\boldsymbol{\pi}_\alpha + \boldsymbol{v}_\alpha$ and $Y_\alpha = X\Pi_\alpha + V_\alpha$, it is possible to express (3.16) as

$$\boldsymbol{y}_\alpha = X\Pi_\alpha \boldsymbol{\gamma}_\alpha + X_\alpha \boldsymbol{\beta}_\alpha + \boldsymbol{v}_\alpha, \tag{3.17a}$$

or $\qquad \alpha = 1, 2, \ldots, g.$

$$X\boldsymbol{\pi}_\alpha = X\Pi_\alpha \boldsymbol{\gamma}_\alpha + X_\alpha \boldsymbol{\beta}_\alpha, \tag{3.17b}$$

From (3.17), we can write

$$\begin{pmatrix} X\boldsymbol{\pi}_1 \\ X\boldsymbol{\pi}_2 \\ \vdots \\ X\boldsymbol{\pi}_g \end{pmatrix} = \begin{pmatrix} X\Pi_1 & 0 & \cdots & 0 \\ 0 & X\Pi_2 & \cdots & 0 \\ \vdots & \vdots & \ddots & \vdots \\ 0 & 0 & \cdots & X\Pi_g \end{pmatrix} \begin{pmatrix} \boldsymbol{\gamma}_1 \\ \boldsymbol{\gamma}_2 \\ \vdots \\ \boldsymbol{\gamma}_g \end{pmatrix} + \begin{pmatrix} X_1 & 0 & \cdots & 0 \\ 0 & X_2 & \cdots & 0 \\ \vdots & \vdots & \ddots & \vdots \\ 0 & 0 & \cdots & X_g \end{pmatrix} \begin{pmatrix} \boldsymbol{\beta}_1 \\ \boldsymbol{\beta}_2 \\ \vdots \\ \boldsymbol{\beta}_g \end{pmatrix}, \tag{3.18a}$$

or

$$\bar{\boldsymbol{w}} = \bar{W}\boldsymbol{\gamma} + X\boldsymbol{\beta}, \tag{3.18b}$$

or

$$\bar{\boldsymbol{w}} = \bar{Z}\boldsymbol{\delta}. \tag{3.18c}$$

where $\bar{\boldsymbol{w}}$ denotes the partitioned vector on the l.h.s. of (3.18a), $\bar{W}$ and $\bar{X}$ the first and second block diagonal matrices on the r.h.s. of (3.18a) $\boldsymbol{\gamma}' = (\boldsymbol{\gamma}_1', \boldsymbol{\gamma}_2', \ldots, \boldsymbol{\gamma}_g')$, $\boldsymbol{\beta}' = (\boldsymbol{\beta}_1', \boldsymbol{\beta}_2', \ldots, \boldsymbol{\beta}_g')$, $\bar{Z} = (\bar{W} \vdots \bar{X})$ and $\boldsymbol{\delta}' = (\boldsymbol{\gamma}' \vdots \boldsymbol{\beta}')$.

As our loss function for estimating the parameter vector $\boldsymbol{\delta}$ in (3.18), we let $\boldsymbol{\epsilon} = \bar{\boldsymbol{w}} - \bar{Z}\hat{\boldsymbol{\delta}}$ where $\hat{\boldsymbol{\delta}}$ is an estimate of $\boldsymbol{\delta}$ and form

$$L = (\bar{\boldsymbol{w}} - \bar{Z}\hat{\boldsymbol{\delta}})'Q(\bar{\boldsymbol{w}} - \bar{Z}\hat{\boldsymbol{\delta}}) = (\boldsymbol{\delta} - \hat{\boldsymbol{\delta}})'\bar{Z}'Q\bar{Z}(\boldsymbol{\delta} - \hat{\boldsymbol{\delta}}), \tag{3.19}$$

where Q is a pds matrix that may have elements that are parameters with unknown values. Given a posterior pdf for the reduced form coefficients and elements of Q, we compute the posterior expectation of (3.19) and find the minimizing value of $\boldsymbol{\delta}$ as follows where E is the posterior expectation operator:

$$EL = E\bar{\boldsymbol{w}}'Q\bar{\boldsymbol{w}} - 2\hat{\boldsymbol{\delta}}'E\bar{Z}'Q\bar{\boldsymbol{w}} + \hat{\boldsymbol{\delta}}'\bar{Z}Q\bar{Z}\hat{\boldsymbol{\delta}}. \tag{3.20}$$

By differentiating (3.20) with respect to $\hat{\boldsymbol{\delta}}$, we find the minimum expected loss estimate to be

$$\hat{\boldsymbol{\delta}}^* = (E\bar{Z}'Q\bar{Z})^{-1}E\bar{Z}'Q\bar{\boldsymbol{w}}. \tag{3.21}$$

The MELO estimate $\hat{\boldsymbol{\delta}}^*$ is a general solution for our problem of estimating the structural coefficient vector $\boldsymbol{\delta}$ given the loss function in (3.19) and a posterior pdf for the reduced form coefficients and the elements Q. Below we shall consider the case $Q = \Omega_g^{-1} \otimes I_n$ where Ω_g is the $g \times g$ pds reduced form disturbance covariance matrix.

To evaluate (3.21) with $Q = \Omega_g^{-1} \otimes I_n$, consider the reduced form system, $Y = X\Pi + V$, where $Y = (\boldsymbol{y}_1, \boldsymbol{y}_2, \ldots, \boldsymbol{y}_g)$ is an $n \times g$ matrix of observations on all endogenous variables in the system, X is an $n \times k$ matrix of rank k of observations on all predetermined variables, Π is a $k \times g$ matrix of reduced form coefficients and V is an $n \times g$ matrix of disturbances. It is assumed that the n rows of V have been independently drawn from a g-dimensional normal distribution with zero mean vector and $g \times g$ pds covariance matrix Ω_g. If we employ the following diffuse prior pdf for Π and Ω_g, $p(\Pi, \Omega_g) \propto |\Omega_g|^{-(g+1)/2}$, the joint posterior pdf for Π and Ω_g is given by (see, e.g., Zellner 1971a, p. 227)

$$p(\Pi, \Omega_g | Y) \propto |\Omega_g|^{-(n+g+1)/2} \times \exp\{-\tfrac{1}{2}\mathrm{tr}[\hat{\Omega}_g + (\Pi - \hat{\Pi})'X'X(\Pi - \hat{\Pi})]\Omega_g^{-1}\}, \tag{3.22}$$

where $\hat{\Pi} = (X'X)^{-1}X'Y$ and $\hat{\Omega}_g = (Y - X\hat{\Pi})'(Y - X\hat{\Pi})$. From (3.22), it is seen that the conditional posterior pdf for Π given Ω_g is in the multivariate normal form with mean $\hat{\Pi}$ and covariance matrix $\Omega_g \otimes (X'X)^{-1}$. This fact will be employed to evaluate the posterior expectations in (3.16) conditional on Ω_g. That is, with respect to $E\bar{Z}'Q\bar{Z}$ on the r.h.s. of (3.16), the (α, l)th submatrix of $\bar{Z}'Q\bar{Z} = \bar{Z}'(\Omega_g^{-1} \otimes I_n)\bar{Z}$ is $\bar{Z}_\alpha'\bar{Z}_l\omega^{\alpha l}$, where $\omega^{\alpha l}$ is the (α, l)th element of Ω_g^{-1}, $\bar{Z}_\alpha = (X\Pi_\alpha : X_\alpha)$ and $\bar{Z}_1 = (X\Pi_l : X_l)$. Then the conditional posterior mean of the (α, l)th submatrix is given by

$$E\bar{Z}_\alpha'\bar{Z}_l\omega^{\alpha l} = [\hat{Z}_\alpha'\hat{Z}_l + E(\bar{Z}_\alpha - \hat{Z}_\alpha)'\,(\bar{Z}_l - \hat{Z}_l)\omega^{\alpha l}], \tag{3.23}$$

where E is the conditional (given Ω_g) posterior expectation operator, $\bar{Z}_\alpha = (X\hat{\Pi}_\alpha : X_\alpha)$ and $\hat{Z}_l = (X\hat{\Pi}_l : X_l)$ with $\hat{\Pi}_\alpha = (X'X)^{-1}X'Y_\alpha$ and $\hat{\Pi}_l = (X'X)^{-1}X'Y_l$ the posterior means of Π_α and Π_l, respectively. Further, the vector $E\bar{Z}'Q\bar{w}$ on the r.h.s. of (3.21) is

$$\begin{aligned} E\bar{Z}'(\Omega_g^{-1}\otimes I_n)\bar{w} &= E\left\{\sum_{l=1}^{g}\bar{Z}_\alpha'\bar{w}_l\omega^{\alpha l}\right\}, \qquad \alpha = 1, 2, \ldots, g, \\ &= \left\{\sum_{l=1}^{g}[\hat{Z}_\alpha'\hat{w}_l + E(\bar{Z}_\alpha - \hat{Z}_\alpha)'(\bar{w}_l - \hat{w}_l)]\omega^{\alpha l}\right\}, \end{aligned} \tag{3.24}$$

where $\hat{w}_l = X\hat{\pi}_l$, with $\hat{\pi}_l = (X'X)^{-1}X'y_l$. Thus the optimal estimate $\hat{\delta}^*$ given Ω_g is

$$\begin{aligned} \hat{\delta}^* = {} & \{[\hat{Z}_\alpha'\hat{Z}_l + E(\bar{Z}_\alpha - \hat{Z}_\alpha)'(\bar{Z}_l - \hat{Z}_l)]\omega^{\alpha l}\}^{-1} \\ & \times\left\{\sum_{l=1}^{g}[\hat{Z}_\alpha'\hat{w}_l + E(\bar{Z}_\alpha - \hat{Z}_\alpha)'(\bar{w}_l - \hat{w}_l)]\omega^{\alpha l}\right\}, \end{aligned} \tag{3.25}$$

where the entry in the first pair of curly braces is a typical submatrix, $\alpha, l = 1, 2, \ldots, g$, and in the second pair, a typical element of a vector, $\alpha = 1, 2, \ldots, g$. Given that the conditional posterior pdf for the reduced form coefficients, Π, given Ω_g is multivariate normal with mean $\hat{\Pi} = (X'X)^{-1}X'Y$ and covariance matrix $\Omega_g \otimes (X'X)^{-1}$, the conditional posterior expectations in (3.25) can be evaluated to give

$$\begin{aligned} \hat{\delta}^* = {} & \left\{\left[\begin{pmatrix} \hat{Y}_\alpha'\hat{Y}_l & Y_\alpha'X_l \\ X_\alpha'Y_l & X_\alpha'X_l \end{pmatrix} + k\begin{pmatrix} \Omega_{\alpha l} & 0 \\ 0 & 0 \end{pmatrix}\right]\omega^{\alpha l}\right\}^{-1} \\ & \times\left\{\sum_{l=1}^{g}\left[\begin{pmatrix} \hat{Y}_\alpha' \\ X_\alpha' \end{pmatrix} y_l + k\begin{pmatrix} \boldsymbol{\omega}_{\alpha l} \\ \mathbf{0} \end{pmatrix}\omega^{\alpha l}\right]\right\}, \end{aligned} \tag{3.26}$$

where $\hat{Y}_\alpha = X\hat{\Pi}_\alpha$, $\hat{Y}_l = X\hat{\Pi}_l$, $\omega^{\alpha l}$ is the (α, l)th element of Ω_g^{-1}, $\Omega_{\alpha l}$ is a submatrix of Ω_g that is equal to the sampling covariance between corresponding rows of $V_\alpha = Y_\alpha - X\Pi_\alpha$ and $V_l = Y_l - X\Pi_l$, and $\boldsymbol{\omega}_{\alpha l}$ is a vector of sampling covariances between elements of $\boldsymbol{v}_\alpha = \boldsymbol{y}_\alpha - X\boldsymbol{\pi}_\alpha$ and corresponding rows of $V_l = Y - X\Pi_l$.

From (3.22), the marginal posterior pdf for the distinct elements of Ω_g is well known to be in the form of an inverted Wishart pdf (see, e.g., Zellner

1971*a*, p. 227), and this result will be employed in future work to evaluate the following posterior expectations $E\omega^{\alpha l}$, $E\Omega_{\alpha l}$ and $E\boldsymbol{\omega}_{\alpha l}\omega^{\alpha l}$ that are needed to provide a MELO estimate of $\boldsymbol{\delta}$ that is not conditional upon Ω_g being given.[16]

4 Properties of MELO Estimates and Estimators

In this section, selected properties of MELO estimates and estimators presented above will be established. We first consider properties of MELO estimates and then go on to consider large and finite sample properties of the MELO estimators for the estimation problems considered in previous sections.[17]

4.1 Properties of MELO Estimates

For the MELO estimates presented in section 2, it is direct to establish that as the sample size grows large, each MELO estimate approaches its corresponding maximum likelihood (ML) estimate. Also, this property holds for the MELO structural coefficient estimates in section 3. Thus, when nondogmatic prior distributions are employed, as the sample size grows, the MELO estimates approach corresponding ML estimates. In this connection, it is well known that when the sample size grows, in general posterior distributions derived from nondogmatic prior distributions and well-behaved likelihood functions, approach a normal distribution's form centered at the ML estimate.[18]

In very small sample situations, it is the case that posterior distributions for the problems considered in previous sections can have more than one pronounced mode.[19] Examination of posterior distributions' shapes will indicate to an investigator whether more than one important mode is present. In such cases, it is necessary to be extremely careful and thoughtful in choosing a point estimate. In the appendix to this paper, a problem of point estimation when a posterior distribution has more than one pronounced model is analyzed.

In connection with estimation of $\theta = 1/\mu$, the reciprocal of a population mean, it is apparent from (2.5) and (2.6) that the MELO estimate, $\hat{\theta}^*$, satisfies $|\hat{\theta}^*| < |\tilde{\theta}|$ where $\tilde{\theta} = 1/\bar{y}$, the ML estimate. For (2.5) and (2.6),

16. Of course, sample estimates of $\Omega_{\alpha\ell}, \omega^{\alpha\ell}$, and $\boldsymbol{\omega}_{\alpha\ell}$ can be inserted in (3.26) to give an approximation to the unconditional MELO estimate of $\boldsymbol{\delta}$.

17. See Hill (1975) for a thoughtful discussion of the relevance of sampling properties of Bayesian estimators. In Zellner and Park (1979) further analysis of the finite sample properties of MELO estimators is presented.

18. See, e.g., Jeffreys (1967), Le Cam (1958), Lindley (1961), and Zellner (1971*a*).

19. This is also true for the sampling distributions of ML estimators, e.g., $\hat{\theta}_{\mathrm{ML}} = 1/\bar{y}$, where $\bar{y}$ is a sample mean, or $\hat{\theta}_{ML} = \hat{\beta}_1/\hat{\beta}_2$, where $\hat{\beta}_1$ and $\hat{\beta}_2$ are ML regression coefficient estimators.

$\hat{\theta}^*/\tilde{\theta} = 1/(1 + Z^2)$ where Z^2 is the square of the coefficient of variation of the posterior pdf for μ. Thus the extent to which $\tilde{\theta}^*$ differs from $\tilde{\theta}$ depends just on the relative precision of the posterior pdf for μ. Similar observations apply to (2.8), the MELO estimate for a reciprocal of a regression coefficient.

With respect to estimation of ratios of parameters, the relation of the MELO estimates in (2.12) and (2.13) to ML estimates is readily apparent. For example, for (2.12), we have $\hat{\theta}^* = \tilde{\theta}_{\mathrm{ML}}[1 + \mathrm{cov}(\beta_1, \beta_2)/\hat{\beta}_1\hat{\beta}_2]/[1 + \mathrm{var}\,\beta_2/\hat{\beta}_2^2]$, where $\tilde{\theta}_{\mathrm{ML}} = \hat{\beta}_1/\hat{\beta}_2$, the ML estimate, $\mathrm{cov}(\beta_1, \beta_2) = m^{12}\bar{s}^2$ is the posterior variance of β_1 and β_2, and $\mathrm{var}\,\beta_2 = m^{22}\bar{s}^2$ is the posterior variance of β_2. Then, with $\rho_{12} = \mathrm{cov}(\beta_1, \beta_2)/(\mathrm{var}\,\beta_1\,\mathrm{var}\,\beta_2)^{1/2}$, $\hat{\theta}^*/\tilde{\theta}_{\mathrm{ML}} = (1 + \rho_{12}\phi_1\phi_2)/(1 - \phi_2^2)$, where ϕ_1 and ϕ_2 are the posterior coefficients of variation for β_1 and β_2, respectively. Thus, depending on the values of ρ_{12}, ϕ_1 and ϕ_2, the ratio $\hat{\theta}^*/\tilde{\theta}_{\mathrm{ML}}$ can assume the values shown below:

	Condition on ρ_{12}, ϕ_1 and ϕ_2	Range of ratio $\hat{\theta}^*/\tilde{\theta}_{\mathrm{ML}}$
(a)	$\rho_{12} = 0, 0 < \phi_2^2, \phi_1^2 < \infty$	$0 < \hat{\theta}^*/\tilde{\theta}_{\mathrm{ML}} < 1$
(b)	$\phi_2^2 \leqq \rho_{12}\phi_1\phi_2 < \infty$	$1 \leqq \hat{\theta}^*/\tilde{\theta}_{\mathrm{ML}} < \infty$
(c)	$-1 < \rho_{12}\phi_1\phi_2 < \phi_2^2$	$0 < \hat{\theta}^*/\tilde{\theta}_{\mathrm{ML}} < 1$
(d)	$-\infty < \rho_{12}\phi_1\phi_2 \leqq -1$	$-\infty < \hat{\theta}^*/\tilde{\theta}_{\mathrm{Ml}} \leqq 0$

When $\rho_{12} = 0$, line (a) of the table indicates $0 < \hat{\theta}^*/\tilde{\theta}_{\mathrm{ML}} < 1$. From line (b) of the table, it is seen that $\hat{\theta}^*$ is "expanded" relative to $\tilde{\theta}_{\mathrm{ML}}$ when $\phi_2^2 < \rho_{12}\phi_1\phi_2 < \infty$. This latter condition can be satisfied when $\hat{\beta}_1$ and $\hat{\beta}_2$ have the same algebraic sign and $\rho_{12} > 0$ or $\hat{\beta}_1$ and $\hat{\beta}_2$ have opposite algebraic signs and $\rho_{12} < 0$. In either case, we have $|\phi_2| < |\rho_{12}||\phi_1|$, that is the relative variability of the posterior pdf for β_2 is less than that for β_1. Thus, heuristically, adjusting $\hat{\beta}_1$ *upward* relative to $\hat{\beta}_2$ guards against an underestimate of the ratio β_1/β_2. Under the condition of line (c), $0 < \hat{\theta}^*/\tilde{\theta}_{\mathrm{ML}} < 1$, there is a "shrinking" of the ML estimate. Last, in line (d), with $-\infty < \rho_{12}\phi_1\phi_2 < -1$, $\tilde{\theta}^*$ and $\tilde{\theta}_{\mathrm{ML}}$ can have different algebraic signs. In this case, if ϕ_1 and ϕ_2 have the same algebraic sign, then $\rho_{12} < 0$, and the coefficients of variation ϕ_1 and ϕ_2 are rather large. Thus given the negative posterior correlation of β_1 and β_2, there is a high probability of obtaining the "wrong" algebraic sign in estimating β_1/β_2 by use of the ML estimate and $\hat{\theta}^*$ has an algebraic sign different from $\hat{\theta}_{\mathrm{ML}}$. However, this will just occur for large relative variability of one or both of the marginal posterior pdf's for β_1 and β_2.

For the MELO structural coefficient estimates in (3.6), (3.13), (3.21), and (3.26), as the sample size grows these estimates approach ML estimates since they are functions of posterior means that approach ML estimates under general conditions.

In small samples, (3.14) indicates that a particular MELO estimate of the coefficient vector $\boldsymbol{\gamma}_1$ can be expressed as a matrix weighted average of the 2SLS estimate and $\hat{\hat{\boldsymbol{\gamma}}}_1 = (\hat{V}_1'\hat{V}_1)^{-1}\hat{V}_1'\hat{\boldsymbol{v}}_1$, or of the 2SLS and DLS estimates (Zellner 1980). Properties of matrix weighted averages of two vectors can be studied conveniently using the curve décolletage (Dickey 1975 and Leamer 1973). The small-sample problem of multimodal posterior distributions and point estimation for structural coefficients will not be treated herein but deserves attention.

4.2 Large-Sample Properties of MELO Estimators

When the MELO estimates presented above are viewed as estimators, it is the case that for each problem considered the MELO estimator has the same asymptotic distribution as the ML estimator.

The MELO estimator for the reciprocal of a population mean, $\theta = 1/\mu$, is given in (2.4). From (2.4), we can write

$$(4.1)\quad n^{1/2}(\hat{\theta}^* - \theta) = n^{1/2}(1/\bar{\mu} - \theta) - (n^{1/2}/\bar{\mu})(\text{var}\ \mu/\bar{\mu}^2)(1 + \text{var}\ \mu/\bar{\mu}^2),$$

where $\hat{\theta}^*$ is the MELO estimator (2.4), n is the sample size, $\bar{\mu}$ is the mean and var μ is the variance of the posterior pdf for μ. The probability limit (plim) of the second term on the r.h.s. of (4.1) is zero, given that plim $\bar{\mu} \neq 0$. Thus $n^{1/2}(\hat{\theta}^* - \theta)$ and $n^{1/2}(1/\bar{\mu} - \theta)$ have the same asymptotic distribution by use of the convergence result in Cramer (1946, p. 254). Further, with $\bar{\mu} = \bar{y} + \Delta$, where $\bar{y}$ is the sample mean and

$$\Delta = \bar{\mu} - \bar{y}, \qquad 1/\bar{\mu} = 1/\bar{y} - \Delta/\bar{y}(1 + \Delta/\bar{y}),$$

and

$$n^{1/2}(1/\bar{\mu} - \theta) = n^{1/2}(1/\bar{y} - \theta) - n^{1/2}\Delta/\bar{y}(1 + \Delta/\bar{y}).$$

Given that plim $\bar{y} \neq 0$ and plim $n^{1/2}\Delta = 0$, $n^{1/2}(1/\bar{\mu} - \theta)$, $n^{1/2}(1/\bar{y} - \theta)$, and $n^{1/2}(\hat{\theta}^* - \theta)$ all have the same asymptotic normal distribution under usual central limit theorem conditions (see, e.g., Dhrymes 1974 and Theil 1971).

For the MELO reciprocal mean estimator in (2.6), we have

$$n^{1/2}(\hat{\theta}^* - \theta) = n^{1/2}(1/\bar{y} - \theta) - (n^{1/2}/\bar{y})(\bar{s}^2/n\bar{y}^2)/(1 + \bar{s}^2/n\bar{y}^2),$$

$$\bar{s}^2 = \nu s^2/(\nu - 2), \qquad \nu s^2 = \sum_{i=1}^{n} (y_i - \bar{y})^2,$$

and

$$\nu = n - 1 > 2.$$

Then given plim $\bar{y} \neq 0$ and applying the convergence result in Cramer (1946, p. 254), $n^{1/2}(\hat{\theta}^* - \theta)$ and $n^{1/2}(1/\bar{y} - \theta)$ have the same asymptotic distribution that will be normal under usual conditions of central limit theorems. Since proofs that the asymptotic distributions of the MELO estimators in (2.7) and (2.8) and of the ML estimator $1/\hat{\pi}$ are the same follow along similar lines as those presented above, they will not be presented.

With respect to the MELO estimator for the ratio of two parameters, e.g., (2.11) that is the estimator for the ratio of two regression coefficients, we have

$$n^{1/2}(\hat{\theta}^* - \theta) = n^{1/2}(\bar{\beta}_1/\bar{\beta}_2 - \theta) + (n^{1/2}\bar{\beta}_1/\bar{\beta}_2) \times \left(\frac{\text{cov}(\beta_1, \beta_2)/\bar{\beta}_1\bar{\beta}_2 - \text{var}\,\beta_2/\bar{\beta}_2^2}{1 + \text{var}\,\beta_2/\bar{\beta}_2^2}\right), \tag{4.2}$$

where $\hat{\theta}^*$ is shown in (2.11), $\theta = \beta_1/\beta_2$, $\bar{\beta}_1$ and $\bar{\beta}_2$ are posterior means, and $\text{cov}(\beta_1, \beta_2)$ and $\text{var}\,\beta_2$ are the posterior covariance of β_1 and β_2 and the posterior variance of β_2, respectively. Given that $\text{plim}\,\bar{\beta}_2 \neq 0$ and that $\text{plim}\, n^{1/2}\text{cov}(\beta_1, \beta_2) = \text{plim}\, n^{1/2}\text{var}\,\beta_2 = 0$, $n^{1/2}(\hat{\theta}^* - \theta)$ and $n^{1/2}(\bar{\beta}_1/\bar{\beta}_2 - \theta)$ have the same asymptotic distribution that is the same as the asymptotic normal distribution for $n^{1/2}(\hat{\beta}_1/\hat{\beta}_2 - \theta)$, where $\hat{\beta}_1/\hat{\beta}_2$ is the ML estimator for θ.[20]

As regards the structural coefficient estimator $\hat{\boldsymbol{\delta}}_1^*$ in (3.6), we have

$$\begin{aligned} \hat{\boldsymbol{\delta}}_1^* &= (\hat{Z}_1'\hat{Z}_1 + \Delta_1)^{-1}(\hat{Z}_1'X\hat{\boldsymbol{\pi}}_1 + \boldsymbol{\Delta}_2) \\ &= [I + (\hat{Z}_1'\hat{Z}_1)^{-1}\Delta_1]^{-1}[(\hat{Z}_1'\hat{Z}_1)^{-1}\hat{Z}_1'X\hat{\boldsymbol{\pi}}_1 + (\hat{Z}_1'\hat{Z}_1)^{-1}\boldsymbol{\Delta}_2] \\ &= \hat{\boldsymbol{\delta}}_1 - [I + (\hat{Z}_1'\hat{Z}_1)^{-1}\Delta_1]^{-1}[(\hat{Z}_1'\hat{Z}_1)^{-1}[\Delta_1\hat{\boldsymbol{\delta}}_1 - \boldsymbol{\Delta}_2], \end{aligned} \tag{4.3}$$

where $\hat{\boldsymbol{\delta}}_1 = (\hat{Z}_1'\hat{Z}_1)^{-1}\hat{Z}_1'X\hat{\boldsymbol{\pi}}_1$ is the 2SLS estimator, $\hat{Z}_1 = (\hat{Y}_1 : X_1)$ with $\hat{Y}_1 = X\hat{\Pi}_1$ where $\hat{\Pi}_1 = (X'X)^{-1}X'Y_1$, $\Delta_1 = E\bar{Z}_1'\bar{Z}_1 - \hat{Z}_1'\hat{Z}_1$, and $\boldsymbol{\Delta}_2 = E\bar{Z}_1'X\boldsymbol{\pi}_1 - \hat{Z}_1'X\hat{\boldsymbol{\pi}}_1$, with E the posterior expectation operator and $\bar{Z}_1 = (X\Pi_1 : X_1)$. Then $n^{1/2}(\hat{\boldsymbol{\delta}}_1^* - \boldsymbol{\delta}_1) = n^{1/2}(\hat{\boldsymbol{\delta}}_1 - \boldsymbol{\delta}_1) + n^{1/2}\Delta_3$, where Δ_3 represents the second term on the r.h.s of the third line of (4.3). Since $\text{plim}\, n^{1/2}\Delta_3 = 0$,[21] $n^{1/2}(\boldsymbol{\delta}_1^* - \boldsymbol{\delta}_1)$ and $n^{1/2}(\hat{\boldsymbol{\delta}}_1 - \boldsymbol{\delta}_1)$ have the same asymptotic normal distribution.[22] Further since the 2SLS and limited-information ML estimators have the same asymptotic normal distribution, this is also the asymptotic distribution of $n^{1/2}(\hat{\boldsymbol{\delta}}_1^* - \boldsymbol{\delta}_1)$. With respect to the particular structural coefficient estimator in (3.13), note that it is a $\mathcal{K}$-class estimator with $\mathcal{K} = \mathcal{K}^* = 1 - k/(n - k - m + 1)$. Thus $\text{plim}\, n^{1/2}(\mathcal{K}^* - 1) = 0$ and under this

20. The proof that $n^{1/2}(\hat{\theta}^* - \theta)$, $n^{1/2}(\bar{\beta}_1/\bar{\beta}_2 - \theta)$, and $n^{1/2}(\hat{\beta}_1/\hat{\beta}_2 - \theta)$ all have the same asymptotic normal distribution, given $\text{plim}\,\hat{\beta}_2 = \text{plim}\,\bar{\beta}_2 \neq 0$, is direct and thus is not presented.

21. Note that $\text{plim}\, n^{1/2}(\hat{Z}_1'\hat{Z}_1)^{-1}\Delta_1\hat{\boldsymbol{\delta}}_1 = \text{plim}\, n^{1/2}(\hat{Z}_1'\hat{Z}_1)^{-1}\boldsymbol{\Delta}_2 = 0$ assuming that $\text{plim}\, \hat{Z}_1'\hat{Z}_1/n = M$, a pds matrix and since $\text{plim}\, \Delta_1/n^{1/2} = 0$ and $\text{plim}\, \boldsymbol{\Delta}_2/n^{1/2} = \mathbf{0}$.

22. For a proof that $n^{1/2}(\hat{\boldsymbol{\delta}}_1 - \boldsymbol{\delta}_1)$ has an asymptotic normal distribution, see, e.g., Dhrymes (1974) and Theil (1971).

condition it is known that $\mathcal{K}$-class estimators, including the limited information ML estimator, all have the same asymptotic normal distribution.[23]

4.3 Some Finite Sample Properties of MELO Estimators

In this section some finite sample properties of the MELO estimators, presented above, are established.[24] In particular, the existence of the moments of certain MELO estimators will be demonstrated. Also, for the reciprocal mean problem, an exact expression for the MELO estimator's average risk is derived. Finally, considerations bearing on the admissibility of certain MELO estimators are presented.

The MELO estimator (2.5) for $\theta = 1/\mu$, with the value of σ^2 assumed known, is $\hat{\theta}^* = \bar{y}/(\bar{y}^2 + \sigma_0^2/n) = (n^{1/2}/\sigma_0)Z/(1 + Z^2)$, where $Z = n^{1/2}\bar{y}/\sigma_0$. Then it is easily established that $|\hat{\theta}^*| \leqq n^{1/2}/2\sigma_0$. Thus the rth absolute moment of $\hat{\theta}^*$ is

$$E|\hat{\theta}^*|^r = \int_{-\infty}^{\infty} |\hat{\theta}^*|^r p(\bar{y}\,|\,\mu, \sigma_0/n^{1/2})d\bar{y} < n^{r/2}/(2\sigma_0)^r < \infty,$$

for $0 < \sigma_0/n^{1/2} < \infty$, where $p(\bar{y}\,|\,\mu, \sigma_0/n^{1/2})$ is the normal pdf for $\bar{y}$ with mean μ and standard deviation $\sigma_0/n^{1/2}$. Since the absolute moments of $\hat{\theta}^*$ exist and are finite, $E(\hat{\theta}^*)^r < \infty$, $r = 1, 2, \ldots$. Further, the risk of $\hat{\theta}^*$ relative to the loss function, $L = ((\theta - \hat{\theta}^*)/\theta)^2 = (1 - \mu\hat{\theta}^*)^2$ is finite for $0 < \sigma_0/n^{1/2} < \infty$ and $-\infty < \mu < \infty$.[25]

In estimating $\theta = 1/\mu$ when σ^2 has an unknown value, the MELO estimator, presented in (2.6), is $\hat{\theta}^* = \bar{y}/[\bar{y}^2 + \nu s^2/n(\nu - 2)] = (1/\bar{c})\bar{z}/(1 + \bar{z}^2)$, where $\bar{c}^2 = \nu s^2/n(\nu - 2)$, $\nu = n - 1 > 2$, and $\bar{z} = \bar{y}/\bar{c}$. Then $|\hat{\theta}^*| \leqq 1/2\bar{c}$ and

$$E|\hat{\theta}^*|^r = \int_0^{\infty}\int_{-\infty}^{\infty} |\hat{\theta}^*|^r p(\bar{y}\,|\,\mu, \sigma/n^{1/2})g(x\,|\,\nu)\,d\bar{y}\,dx$$

$$< \left(\frac{\nu - 2}{2\sigma^2/n}\right)^{r/2}\int_0^{\infty} x^{-r/2}g(x\,|\,\nu)dx < \infty,$$

for $0 < \sigma/n^{1/2} < \infty$, where $x = \nu s^2/\sigma^2$ has a χ^2 pdf with $\nu = n - 1$ degrees of freedom, denoted by $g(x\,|\,\nu)$. Thus $E|\hat{\theta}^*|^r$ and $E(\hat{\theta}^*)^r$, $r = 1, 2, \ldots$, exist and are finite. This implies that the risk of $\hat{\theta}^* = \bar{y}/[\bar{y}^2 + \nu s^2/n(\nu - 2)]$, $\nu >$

23. See, e.g., Theil (1971), pp. 505–6.

24. Further properties including exact finite sample distributions, exact and approximate risk functions, etc., are presented in Zellner and Park (1979).

25. The risk of $\hat{\theta}^*$ relative to the quadratic loss function, $L = (\hat{\theta}^* - \theta)^2$ is finite for $0 < |\mu| < \infty$ and $0 < \sigma_0/n^{1/2} < \infty$.

2, relative to $L = (\theta - \hat{\theta}^*)^2/\theta^2 = (1 - \mu\hat{\theta}^*)^2$ exists and is finite for $0 < \sigma/n^{1/2} < \infty$ and $-\infty < \mu < \infty$.

To obtain the average risk (AR) of the estimator $\hat{\theta}^* = \bar{y}/(\bar{y}^2 + \sigma_0^2/n)$, the following integral was evaluated:

$$(4.4)\quad \text{AR} = \int_{-\infty}^{\infty}\int_{-\infty}^{\infty}(1 - \mu\hat{\theta}^*)^2 p(\bar{y}\mid\mu, \sigma_0/n^{1/2})\,d\bar{y}\,d\mu = \pi\sigma_0/n^{1/2},$$

where the improper prior pdf for μ, $p(\mu)d\mu \propto d\mu$, $-\infty < \mu < \infty$ has been employed, $p(\bar{y}\mid\mu, \sigma_0/n^{1/2})$ is the normal pdf for $\bar{y}$ with mean μ and variance σ_0^2/n, and $\pi = 3.14159$.[26]

In the class of estimators for $\theta = 1/\mu$, $\hat{\theta} = \hat{\theta}(\bar{y}, \sigma/n^{1/2})$, with the value of $\sigma/n^{1/2}$ known, such that AR is finite relative to the loss function $L = (\theta - \hat{\theta})^2/\theta^2 = (1 - \mu\hat{\theta})^2$ and improper prior pdf $p(\mu)\,d\mu \propto d\mu$, $-\infty < \mu < \infty$, $\hat{\theta}^* = \bar{y}/(\bar{y}^2 + \sigma_0^2/n)$ is the estimator in this class that minimizes AR and is thus admissible. That is, there cannot be another estimator in this class that has risk below that for $\hat{\theta}^*$ over a portion (or all) of the parameter space and risk not above that for $\hat{\theta}^*$ over the remaining portion of the parameter space. If there were such an estimator, it would have smaller AR than that for $\hat{\theta}^*$ which is impossible since $\hat{\theta}^*$ is the estimator in the class that minimizes AR.

The MELO estimator for $\theta = 1/\mu$ when σ^2 has an unknown value is from (2.6), $\hat{\theta}^* = \bar{y}/(\bar{y}^2 + \bar{s}^2/n)$, where $\bar{s}^2 = \nu s^2/(\nu - 2)$, with $\nu = n - 1 > 2$ and

26. To evaluate (4.4), write $\hat{\theta}^* = \bar{y}/(\bar{y}^2 + \sigma_0^2/n) = (n^{1/2}/\sigma_0)(w + \bar{\mu})/[1 + (w\bar{\mu})^2]$, where $w = n^{1/2}(\bar{y} - \mu)/\sigma_0$ is $N(0,1)$ and $\bar{\mu} = n^{1/2}\mu/\sigma_0$. Then $L = (1 - \mu\hat{\theta}^*)^2 = \{[1 + w(w + \bar{\mu})]/[1 + (w + \bar{\mu})^2]\}^2$ and (4.4) becomes

$$\text{AR} = \sigma_0/(2\pi n)^{1/2}\int_{-\infty}^{\infty}\int_{-\infty}^{\infty}\{[1 + w(w + \bar{\mu})]/[1 + (w + \bar{\mu})^2\}^2 e^{-w^2/2}dw\,d\bar{\mu},$$

where $d\mu = (\sigma_0/n^{1/2})d\bar{\mu}$ has been employed. Now make the following change of variables, $x = w + \mu$ and $w = w$, that has Jacobian equal to one, to obtain

$$\begin{aligned}\text{AR} &= \sigma_0/(2\pi n)^{1/2}\int_{-\infty}^{\infty}\int_{-\infty}^{\infty}[(1 + wx)/(1 + x^2)]e^{-w^2/2}dw\,dx\\ &= \sigma_0/n^{1/2}\int_{-\infty}^{\infty}[1/(1 + x^2)]dx.\end{aligned}$$

In this last expression, note that $1 + x^2 = (x - i)(x + i)$, where $i = (-1)^{1/2}$, and thus there is a pole of order one in the upper half plane at $x = i$. Using a contour integration around a half circle in the upper plane of the complex domain with center at the origin, the value of the integral

$$\int_{-\infty}^{\infty}[1/(1 + x^2)]dx$$

is equal to $2\pi i$ times the residue at i, namely $\frac{1}{2}i$, that is $2\pi i/2i = \pi$ by the Cauchy residue theorem. Or more simply,

$$\int_{-\infty}^{\infty}(1 + x^2)^{-1}dx = \pi,$$

using properties of the univariate Cauchy pdf. Thus $\text{AR} = \pi\sigma_0/n^{1/2}$ as stated in (4.4).

$\nu s^2 = \Sigma_{i=1}^{n} (y_i - \bar{y})^2$. By a direct calculation, the average risk (AR) of $\hat{\theta}^*$ relative to the loss function in (2.2) is found to be[27]

$$\text{(4.5)} \qquad \text{AR} = (\pi/2n^{1/2})\left[\left(\frac{2}{\nu-2}\right)^{1/2}\Gamma\left(\frac{\nu+1}{2}\right) + \left(\frac{\nu-2}{2}\right)^{1/2}\Gamma\left(\frac{\nu-2}{2}\right)\right]\Big/\Gamma(\nu/2), \qquad \nu = n-1 > 2,$$

which is finite. Thus the MELO estimator $\hat{\theta}^* = \bar{y}/(\bar{y}^2 + \bar{s}^2/n)$ is admissible.

Some finite sample properties of MELO estimators for ratios of parameters are presented in Zellner and Park (1979). In the same paper attention is given to the properties of the MELO structural coefficient estimator $\hat{\boldsymbol{\delta}}_1^*$, shown in (3.13). Using Kadane's (1971) asymptotic small-σ approximations to the moments of $\mathcal{K}$-class estimators, it is found that the approximate risk of the MELO estimator $\hat{\boldsymbol{\delta}}_1^*$ relative to the loss function in (3.4) is smaller than that of the 2SLS estimator when the latter's moments exist under a range of conditions frequently encountered in practice.

27. To derive (4.5), write

$$\hat{\theta}^* = \bar{y}(\bar{y}^2 + \bar{s}^2)/n) = (n^{1/2}/\sigma)\,(w + \bar{\mu})^2 + z/(\nu-2)],$$

where $\bar{\mu} = n^{1/2}\mu/\sigma$, $w = (\bar{y} - \bar{\mu})/(\sigma/n^{1/2})$, and $z = (\nu-2)\bar{s}^2/\sigma^2 = \nu s^2/\sigma^2$. Note that w and z are independently distributed with w having a $N(0,1)$ pdf and z a χ^2 pdf with $\nu = n - 1$ degrees of freedom. The loss function can be expressed as follows:

$$L = \left(\frac{\hat{\theta}^* - \theta}{\theta}\right)^2 = (\hat{\theta}^*\mu - 1)^2 = \left[\frac{z/(\nu-2) + w(w+\bar{\mu})}{z/(\nu-2) + (2+\bar{\mu})^2}\right]^2.$$

From $p(\mu,\sigma) \propto 1/\sigma$, $p(\bar{\mu},\sigma) \propto 1/n^{1/2}$ and thus average risk is given by

$$\text{AR} = (1/(2\pi n)^{1/2})\int_0^{\infty}\int_{-\infty}^{\infty}\int_{-\infty}^{\infty} \text{L}e^{-w^2/2}p(z)\,dw\,d\bar{\mu}\,dz,$$

with $p(z)$ the χ_ν^2 pdf. In this last expression, let $x = w + \bar{\mu}$, $w = w$, and $z = z$, a change of variables with Jacobian equal to one, to obtain

$$\text{AR} = (1/(2\pi n)^{1/2})\int_0^{\infty}\int_{-\infty}^{\infty}\int_{-\infty}^{\infty} \frac{[z/(\nu-2) + wx]^2}{[x/(\nu-2) + x^2]^2} e^{-w^2/2}p(z)\,dw\,dx\,dz$$

$$= (1/n^{1/2})\int_0^{\infty}\left[\int_{-\infty}^{\infty} \frac{[z/(\nu-2)]^2 + x^2}{[z/(\nu-2) + x^2]^2}\,dx\right]p(z)\,dz.$$

The integral in square brackets can be evaluated using properties of the univariate Student-t pdf with three degrees of freedom to yield

$$\text{AR} = (\pi/2)\int_0^{\infty} (z/(\nu-2))^{1/2} + ((\nu-2)/z)^{1/2}p(z)\,dz.$$

This last integral can be evaluated given that $p(z)$ is a χ^2 pdf with ν d.f. to yield the expression shown in (4.5).

5 Summary and Conclusions

In this paper a minimum expected loss (MELO) approach was utilized to generate point estimates for a number of related estimation problems, including reciprocals and ratios of parameters and structural coefficients of linear structural econometric models. For these problems, well-defined and reasonable loss functions were formulated and estimates that minimize posterior expected loss were derived. These MELO estimates have relatively simple forms and thus are quite operational. In the case of "single-equation" estimation of structural coefficients, it was found that with a normal reduced form system and a diffuse prior pdf for its parameters, the MELO estimate for the structural coefficient vector is a $\mathcal{K}$-class estimate with a value of $\mathcal{K}$ less than one in finite samples. Further, a "systems" MELO estimate for structural coefficients was derived. These MELO point estimates are useful in providing information about parameters' values and can supplement other measures describing properties of posterior distributions.

When the MELO point estimates are regarded as point estimators, it was pointed out that these estimators' moments and risk exist and are finite. These properties contrast markedly with those of some other estimators for these problems that do not possess finite moments and have infinite risk relative to quadratic and other loss functions. For example, maximum likelihood estimators for reciprocals and ratios of means and of regression coefficients do not possess finite moments under a wide range of distributional assumptions relating to data processes. In the case of estimating structural coefficients, it is well known that many commonly used estimators fail to possess moments under frequently encountered conditions. That ML and some other estimators for the problems considered in this paper can or do have infinite risk relative to quadratic and other loss functions is of interest particularly in view of the widespread use of quadratic loss functions and risk considerations in choosing point estimators, for example, in the Gauss-Markov theorem, in Charles Stein's work, in Monte Carlo experiments, etc. In situations in which ML and other estimators have infinite risk whereas MELO estimators have finite risk, the former estimators are clearly inadmissible. MELO estimators based on proper-prior distributions are admissible relative to the loss functions for which they have been derived. Some MELO estimators based on improper priors are admissible while others may be only under special conditions (Hill 1975). In large samples, the sampling properties of the ML, MELO and other consistent estimators for particular problems considered in this paper are identical.

Further, it is recognized that (1) not all agree that admissibility is an overriding or even important criterion in choosing point estimates; (2) ML and perhaps other estimators might perform better relative to performance criteria that are not sensitive to the existence or nonexistence of sampling moments; and (3) while point estimates are valuable, it must be recognized that they alone are not adequate solutions to most estimation problems. Thus it is fortunate that posterior distributions are available for the problems considered in this paper that reflect the prior and sample information much better than do point estimates alone.

Appendix

A.1 Bimodality of the Posterior Pdf for $\theta = 1/\mu$[28]

To illustrate a case in which a posterior pdf is bimodal, consider $y_i = \mu + \epsilon_i$ where the ϵ_i's are NID$(0, \sigma^2)$ with the value of σ^2 assumed known. With a diffuse prior pdf for μ, $p(\mu) \propto$ const, $-\infty < \mu < \infty$, the posterior pdf for μ is $p(\mu \mid \sigma, \bar{y}) \propto \exp\{-n(\mu - \bar{y})^2/2\sigma^2\}$, a normal pdf. Making a change of variable $\theta = 1/\mu$, the posterior pdf for θ is

$$p(\theta \mid \sigma, \bar{y}) \propto \theta^{-2} \exp\left\{-\frac{z^2}{2}\left(\frac{\theta - \hat{\theta}}{\theta}\right)^2\right\}, \tag{A.1}$$

where $\hat{\theta} = 1/\bar{y}$ and $z = n^{1/2}\bar{y}/\sigma$. Note that z is the ratio of the posterior mean for μ, $\bar{y}$, to its posterior standard deviation, $\sigma/n^{1/2}$. Also z is a sampling theory test statistic for testing the hypothesis $\mu = 0$.

For convenience in analyzing the modes of (A.1), let $\eta = (\hat{\theta} - \theta)/\theta$. Then

$$\theta^{-2} \exp\left\{-\frac{z^2}{2}\left(\frac{\theta - \hat{\theta}}{\theta}\right)^2\right\} \propto (1 + \eta)^2 \exp\{-z^2\eta^2/2\}. \tag{A.2}$$

From the form of (A.2), when z^2 has a small value, it is clear from a plot of the two factors on the r.h.s. of (A.2) that there will be pronounced bimodality. On taking the logarithm of the expression on the r.h.s of (A.2) and differentiating it, the two modal values of η, η_1 and η_2, can be determined. They are $\eta_1, \eta_2 = (1/2)(-1 \pm (1 + 8/z^2)^{1/2})$. From $\eta = (\hat{\theta} - \theta)/\theta$, $\theta = \hat{\theta}/(1 + \eta)$ and thus the modal values for θ are

$$\theta_1 = \hat{\theta}\left(\frac{2}{1 + (1 + 8/z^2)^{1/2}}\right) \text{ and } \theta_2 = \hat{\theta}\left(\frac{2}{1 - (1 + 8/z^2)^{1/2}}\right). \tag{A.3}$$

28. Analysis of the bimodality of the sampling distribution of the maximum likelihood estimator for θ, $\hat{\theta} = 1/\bar{y}$, with $y \sim N(\mu, \sigma^2/n)$ is similar to that presented below.

If $\hat{\theta} > 0$, $\theta_1 > 0$ and $\theta_2 < 0$. Also, the modal values of the posterior pdf can be quite different from the ML estimate $\hat{\theta}$, particularly when $z = n^{1/2}\bar{y}/\sigma$ is small in absolute value. For example, when $z = 1$, $\theta_1 = \hat{\theta}/2$ and $\theta_2 = -\hat{\theta}$. The MELO estimate for θ is $\hat{\theta}^* = (1/\bar{y})(1 + \sigma^2/n\bar{y}^2)^{-1} = \hat{\theta}z^2/(1 + z^2)$. Thus when $z^2 = 1$, $\hat{\theta}^* = \hat{\theta}/2 = \theta_1$, a modal value. As z^2 gets large, θ_1 and $\hat{\theta}^*$ both approach $\hat{\theta}$ while θ_2 approaches $-\infty$.

On inserting the modal values for η in the expression on the r.h.s. of (A.2), denoted by $f(\eta)$, we have

$$\text{(A.4)} \quad f(\eta_1)/f(\eta_2) = \left(\frac{1 + (1 + 8/z^2)^{1/2}}{1 - (1 + 8/z^2)^{1/2}}\right)^2 \exp\left\{\frac{z^2}{2}(1 + 8/z^2)^{1/2}\right\}.$$

When $z^2 = 1$, $f(\eta_1)/f(\eta_2) = 4e^{3/2} = 17.93$, the ratio of the ordinates of the posterior pdf at the modal values, η_1 and η_2 or θ_1 and θ_2. Thus even for $z^2 = 1$, one mode is much higher than the other. When z^2 grows in value, the relative height of the modes grows. As $z^2 \to 0$, $f(\eta_1)/f(\eta_2) \to 1$.

A.2 Point Estimation of θ with Bimodal Distribution

As shown above, (A.1) is bimodal with one modal value positive and the other negative. Further, as $|\theta| \to 0$, $p(\theta|\sigma, \bar{y}) \to 0$ and the posterior probability that $\theta = 1/\mu > 0$ is

$$\int_0^\infty p(\mu|\sigma, \bar{y})d\mu.$$

Conditional upon $\mu > 0$ or $\theta > 0$, the MELO estimate of θ relative to $(\theta - \hat{\theta})^2/\theta^2$ is given by $\hat{\theta}^*_+ = E(\mu|\sigma, \mu > 0)/E(\mu^2|\sigma, \mu > 0)$ where E is the posterior expectation operator. An explicit expression for $\hat{\theta}^*_+$ is[29]

$$\text{(A.5)} \quad \hat{\theta}^*_+ = \frac{\bar{y}[1 - F(-z)] + (\sigma/n^{1/2})P(z)}{\bar{y}^2[1 - F(-z)] + 2\bar{y}(\sigma/n^{1/2})P(z) + \sigma^2/n[1 - F(-z) - zP(z)}$$

$$= \hat{\theta}^* \frac{(1 + z^2)(1 + Rz)}{(1 + z^2)(1 + Rz) - 1} = \hat{\theta}\frac{z(1 + Rz)}{z(1 + Rz) + R},$$

29. The expression for $\hat{\theta}^*_+$ in (A.5) was obtained by straightforward evaluation of the following integrals:

$$\hat{\theta}^*_+ = \int_0^\infty \mu p(\mu|\sigma, \bar{y})d\mu \Big/ \int_0^\infty \mu^2 p(\mu|\sigma, \bar{y})d\mu,$$

with

$$p(\mu|\sigma, \bar{y}) = \frac{1}{(2\pi)^{1/2}(\sigma/n^{1/2})}\exp\left\{-\frac{n}{2\sigma^2}(\mu - \bar{y})^2\right\}.$$

where $z = n^{1/2}\bar{y}/\sigma$, $P(z) = (1/(2\pi)^{1/2})\exp\{-z^2/2\}$, $F(-z) = \int_{-\infty}^{-z} P(z)\,dz$, $\hat{\theta}^* = (1/\bar{y})/(1 + \sigma^2/n\bar{y}^2)$, $\hat{\theta} = 1/\bar{y}$, and $R = [1 - F(-z)]/P(z)$ Mills's ratio. From (A.5), as $z \to \infty$, $\hat{\theta}^*_+/\hat{\theta}^* \to \hat{\theta}^*_+/\hat{\theta} \to 1$. This is reasonable since as $z \to \infty$, the mode situated over positive values of θ becomes very sharp and centered at the ML estimate $\hat{\theta} = 1/\bar{y}$. On the other hand, for $z = n^{1/2}\bar{y}/\sigma = 1$, $\hat{\theta}^*_+ = 1.4326\hat{\theta}^* = 0.7163\hat{\theta}$ from (A.5) and $\hat{\theta}^* = 0.5\hat{\theta}$. Thus with $z = 1$, introducing the conditional information that $\mu > 0$ or $\theta > 0$ results in the MELO estimate $\hat{\theta}^*_+$ being expanded relative to $\hat{\theta}^*$, the MELO estimate not incorporating the information $\mu > 0$. However, with $z = 1$, $\hat{\theta}^*_+$ is still smaller in value than the ML estimate $\hat{\theta}$. Similar calculations can be performed in the case that the conditioning information is $\mu < 0$. In this way MELO point estimates, $\hat{\theta}^*_+$ and $\hat{\theta}^*_-$ can be obtained. With a 2×2 loss structure and posterior probabilities for the hypotheses, $\mu > 0$ and $\mu < 0$, one can choose between $\hat{\theta}^*_+$ and $\hat{\theta}^*_-$ on the basis of which act has lower expected loss. In case no loss structure is available, one has posterior probabilities that $\theta > 0$ and $\theta < 0$ as well as the point estimates $\hat{\theta}^*_+$ and $\hat{\theta}^*_-$.

References

Anderson, T. W., and T. Sawa (1973). "Distributions of Estimates of a Single Equation in a Simultaneous System and Their Asymptotic Expansions." *Econometrica*, 41:683–714.

Bergstrom, A. R. (1962). "The Exact Sampling Distributions of Least Squares and Maximum Likelihood Estimators of the Marginal Propensity to Consume." *Econometrica*, 30:480–90.

Box. G. E. P., and G. C. Tiao (1973). *Bayesian Inference in Statistical Analysis*. Reading, Mass.: Addison-Wesley.

Cramer, H. (1946). *Mathematical Methods of Statistics*. Princeton, N.J.: Princeton University Press.

DeGroot, M. H. (1970). *Optimal Statistical Decisions*. New York: McGraw-Hill Book Co.

Dhrymes, P. J. (1974). *Econometrics: Statistical Foundations and Applications*. New York: Springer-Verlag.

Dickey, J. M. (1975). "Bayesian Alternatives to the F Test and Least-Squares Estimate in the Normal Linear Model." In S. E. Fienberg and A. Zellner, eds., *Studies in Bayesian Econometrics and Statistics in Honor of Leonard J. Savage*, pp. 515–54. Amsterdam: North-Holland Publishing Co.

Ferguson, T. S. (1967). *Mathematical Statistics: A Decision Theoretical Approach*. New York: Academic Press.

Goldberger, A. S. (1964). *Econometric Theory*. New York: John Wiley & Sons.

Hatanaka, M. (1973). "On the Existence and the Approximation Formulae for the Moments of the $\mathcal{K}$-Class Estimators." *Economic Studies Quarterly*, 24:1–15.

Hill, B. M. (1975). "On Coherence, Inadmissibility and Inference about Many Parameters in the Theory of Least Squares." In S. E. Fienberg and A. Zellner, eds., *Studies in Bayesian Econometrics and Statistics in Honor of Leonard J. Savage*, pp. 555–84. Amsterdam: North-Holland Publishing Co.

Jeffreys, H. (1967). *Theory of Probability*. 3d rev. ed. London: Oxford University Press.

Kadane, J. B. (1971). "Comparison of $\mathcal{K}$-Class Estimators When the Disturbances Are Small." *Econometrica*, 39:723–38.

Kappenman, R. F., and S. Geisser (1970). "Bayesian and Fiducial Solutions for the Fieller-Creasy Problem." *Sankhyā*, Ser. A 32:331–40.

Leamer, E. E. (1973). "Multicollinearity: A Bayesian Interpretation." *Review of Economics and Statistics*, 55: 371–80.

Le Cam, L. (1958). "Les Propriétés asymptotiques des solutions de Bayes," *Publications of the Institute of Statistics* 7:17–35.

Lindley, D. V. (1961). "The Use of Prior Probability Distributions in Statistical Inference and Decisions." In J. Neyman, ed., *Proceedings of the Fourth Berkeley Symposium on Mathematical Statistics and Probability*, 1:453–68. Berkeley: University of California Press.

Madansky, A. (1964). "On the Efficiency of Three-Stage Least-Squares Estimation." *Econometrica*, 32:51–56.

Mariano, R. S. (1973). "Approximations to the Distribution Functions of Theil's $\mathcal{K}$-Class Estimators." *Econometrica*, 41:715–22.

Nagar, A. L. (1959). "The Bias and Moment Matrix of the General $\mathcal{K}$-Class Estimators of the Parameters in Simultaneous Equations." *Econometrica*, 29:575–95.

Press, S. J. (1969). "The *t*-Ratio Distribution." *Journal of the American Statistical Association*, 64:242–52.

Sargan, J. D. (1964). "Three-Stage Least-Squares and Full Maximum Likelihood Estimates." *Econometrica*, 32:77–81.

Sawa, T. (1972). "Finite-Sample Properties of the $\mathcal{K}$-Class Estimators." *Econometrica*, 40:653–80.

Theil, H. (1971). *Principles of Econometrics*. New York: John Wiley & Sons.

Zellner, A. (1971*a*). *An Introduction to Bayesian Inference in Econometrics*. New York: John Wiley & Sons.

———. (1971*b*). "Bayesian and Non-Bayesian Analysis of Log-Normal Distribution and Log-Normal Regression." *Journal of the American Statistical Association*, 66:327–30.

———. (1976). "Reply." *Econometrica*, 44:619–24.

———. (1980). "A Note on the Relationship of Minimum Expected Loss (MELO) and Other Structural Coefficient Estimates." *Review of Economics and Statistics*, 62:482–84.

Zellner, A., and S. B. Park (1979). "Minimum Expected Loss (MELO) Estimators for Functions of Parameters and Structural Coefficients of Econometric Models." *Journal of the American Statistical Association*, 74:185–93.

Zellner, A., and W. Vandaele (1975). "Bayes-Stein Estimators for *k*-Means, Regression, and Simultaneous Equation Models." In S. E. Fienberg and A. Zellner, eds., *Studies in Bayesian Econometrics and Statistics in Honor of Leonard J. Savage*, pp. 627–54. Amsterdam: North-Holland Publishing Co.

3.6 Jeffreys-Bayes Posterior Odds Ratio and the Akaike Information Criterion for Discriminating between Models

Jeffreys has done pioneering work showing how posterior odds ratios can be employed to discriminate between or among alternative hypotheses or models (see in particular Jeffreys 1967, chap. 5). Applications and extensions of Jeffreys's analysis to the problem of discriminating among alternative regression models have been made by Thornber (1966), Geisel (1970), Lempers (1971), Zellner (1971), and others. In the present note, a comparison of a Jeffreys-Bayes posterior odds ratio and the Akaike information criterion (Akaike 1972, 1974, Sawa 1976), based on the Kullback-Leibler information measure, is made for the problem of discriminating between two nested regression models. It will be seen that the Akaike information criterion is a truncated version of a posterior odds ratio that omits factors that are important in discriminating between models.

Assume that we are interested in the following multiple regression equation:

$$\underset{n\times 1}{\boldsymbol{y}} = \underset{n\times k_1}{X_1}\ \underset{k_1\times 1}{\boldsymbol{\beta}_1} + \underset{n\times k_2}{X_2}\ \underset{k_2\times 1}{\boldsymbol{\beta}_2} + \underset{n\times 1}{\boldsymbol{u}}, \tag{1}$$

where $\boldsymbol{y}$ is a vector of observations on the dependent variable, X_1 and X_2 are matrices of observations on independent variables of ranks k_1 and k_2, respectively, $\boldsymbol{\beta}_1$ and $\boldsymbol{\beta}_2$ are regression coefficient vectors whose elements have unknown values and $\boldsymbol{u}$ is a vector of errors. Assume that the elements of $\boldsymbol{u}$ have been independently drawn from a normal distribution with zero mean and variance σ^2. For simplicity, we shall assume that σ^2 has a known value. (In the appendix we relax this condition.)

We are interested in the following hypotheses relating to $\boldsymbol{\beta}_2$:

$$H_0:\ \boldsymbol{\beta}_2 = \mathbf{0} \quad \text{and} \quad H_A:\ \boldsymbol{\beta}_2 \neq \mathbf{0}. \tag{2}$$

Since, in general, the posterior odds ratio relating to two mutually exclusive hypotheses is equal to the prior odds ratio times the ratio of averaged

Reprinted from *Economics Letters*, 1 (1978): 337–42, with the kind permission of North-Holland Publishing Co.

likelihood functions, where the averaging is done using the prior distributions for the parameters (see, e.g., Zellner 1971, chap. 10), we have in the present instance:

$$K_{0A} = \frac{\Pi_0}{\Pi_A} \frac{\int p(\boldsymbol{\beta}_1) l(\boldsymbol{\beta}_1 | y, \sigma) d\boldsymbol{\beta}_1}{\int p(\boldsymbol{\beta}_1, \boldsymbol{\beta}_2) l(\boldsymbol{\beta}_1, \boldsymbol{\beta}_2 | y, \sigma) d\boldsymbol{\beta}_1\, d\boldsymbol{\beta}_2}, \tag{3}$$

where Π_0/Π_A is the prior odds ratio, $p(\boldsymbol{\beta}_1)$ and $p(\boldsymbol{\beta}_1, \boldsymbol{\beta}_2)$ are prior distributions under H_0 and H_A, respectively, and

$$l(\boldsymbol{\beta}_1 | y, \sigma) = (\sqrt{2\pi})^{-n} \sigma^{-n} \exp - \{[\nu_1 s_1^2 + (\boldsymbol{\beta}_1 - \hat{\boldsymbol{\beta}}_1)' X_1' X_1 (\boldsymbol{\beta}_1 - \hat{\boldsymbol{\beta}}_1)]/2\sigma^2\}, \tag{4a}$$

$$l(\boldsymbol{\beta} | y, \sigma) = (\sqrt{2\pi})^{-n} \sigma^{-n} \exp\{-[\nu_2 s_2^2 + (\boldsymbol{\beta} - \tilde{\boldsymbol{\beta}})' Z' Z (\boldsymbol{\beta} - \tilde{\boldsymbol{\beta}})]/2\sigma^2\}, \tag{4b}$$

with $\hat{\boldsymbol{\beta}}_1 = (X_1'X_1)^{-1} X_1' y$, $\nu_1 s_1^2 = (y - X_1\hat{\boldsymbol{\beta}}_1)'(y - X_1\hat{\boldsymbol{\beta}}_1)$, $\nu_1 = n - k_1$, $\boldsymbol{\beta}' = (\boldsymbol{\beta}_1', \boldsymbol{\beta}_2')$, $Z = (X_1 \vdots X_2)$, $\tilde{\boldsymbol{\beta}} = (Z'Z)^{-1} Z'y$, $\nu_2 s_2^2 = (y - Z\tilde{\boldsymbol{\beta}})'(y - Z\tilde{\boldsymbol{\beta}})$, and $\nu_2 = n - k_1 - k_2$.

On substituting from (4) in (3),

$$K_{0A} = (\Pi_0/\Pi_A) \exp\{-(\nu_1 s_1^2 - \nu_2 s_2^2)/2\sigma^2\} \cdot \times \frac{\int p(\boldsymbol{\beta}_1) \exp\{-(\boldsymbol{\beta}_1 - \hat{\boldsymbol{\beta}}_1)' X_1' X_1 (\boldsymbol{\beta}_1 - \hat{\boldsymbol{\beta}}_1)/2\sigma^2\}\, d\boldsymbol{\beta}_1}{\int p(\boldsymbol{\beta}) \exp\{-(\boldsymbol{\beta} - \tilde{\boldsymbol{\beta}})' Z'Z (\boldsymbol{\beta} - \tilde{\boldsymbol{\beta}})/2\sigma^2\}\, d\boldsymbol{\beta}}. \tag{5}$$

Given the prior distributions $p(\boldsymbol{\beta}_1)$ and $p(\boldsymbol{\beta})$, (5) can be evaluated to yield a value for K_{0A} (for one example, see Zellner 1971, p. 309). If our prior distributions are relatively flat over the regions in which the exponential factors in the integrands assume appreciable values, we can approximate the integrals' values by expanding $p(\boldsymbol{\beta}_1)$ around $\hat{\boldsymbol{\beta}}_1$ and $p(\boldsymbol{\beta})$ around $\tilde{\boldsymbol{\beta}}$ to linear terms, that is, $p(\boldsymbol{\beta}_1) \doteq p(\hat{\boldsymbol{\beta}}_1) + (\boldsymbol{\beta}_1 - \hat{\boldsymbol{\beta}}_1)' f(\hat{\boldsymbol{\beta}}_1)$ and $p(\boldsymbol{\beta}) \doteq p(\tilde{\boldsymbol{\beta}}) + (\boldsymbol{\beta} - \tilde{\boldsymbol{\beta}})' g(\tilde{\boldsymbol{\beta}})$, where $f(\hat{\boldsymbol{\beta}}_1)$ and $\boldsymbol{g}(\tilde{\boldsymbol{\beta}})$ are vectors of first derivatives of $p(\boldsymbol{\beta}_1)$ and $p(\boldsymbol{\beta})$, evaluated at $\hat{\boldsymbol{\beta}}_1$ and $\tilde{\boldsymbol{\beta}}$, respectively. On inserting these approximations in the integrals in (5) and performing the integrations over the elements of $\boldsymbol{\beta}_1$ and $\boldsymbol{\beta}$ from $-\infty$ to ∞, the result is

$$K_{0A} \doteq \frac{\Pi_0}{\Pi_A} \exp\{-(\nu_1 s_1^2 - \nu_2 s_2^2)/2\sigma^2\} \frac{p(\hat{\boldsymbol{\beta}}_1)}{p(\tilde{\boldsymbol{\beta}})} \cdot \frac{|X_1'X_1/\sigma^2|^{-1/2}}{|Z'Z/\sigma^2|^{-1/2}} \frac{(\sqrt{2\pi})^{k_1}}{(\sqrt{2\pi})^{k}} \doteq \frac{\Pi_0}{\Pi_A} \frac{p(\hat{\boldsymbol{\beta}}_1)}{p(\tilde{\boldsymbol{\beta}})} \left| \frac{\hat{V}_{12}' \hat{V}_{12}}{n\sigma^2} \right|^{1/2} \cdot \left(\frac{n}{2\pi}\right)^{k_2/2} \exp\{-(\nu_1 s_1^2 - \nu_2 s_2^2)/2\sigma^2\}, \tag{6a}$$

where $\hat{V}_{12}'\hat{V}_{12} = X_2'X_2 - X_2'X_1(X_1'X_1)^{-1}X_1'X_2$ and $|Z'Z| = |X_1'X_1||\hat{V}_{12}'\hat{V}_{12}|$ have been employed, or

$$\text{(6b)}\quad K_{0A} \doteq \frac{\Pi_0 p(\hat{\boldsymbol\beta}_1)}{\Pi_A p(\tilde{\boldsymbol\beta})}\left(\frac{|X_1'X_1|}{|Z'Z|}\right)^{-1/2}(1/2\pi\sigma^2)^{k_2/2}\exp\{-(\nu_1 s_1^2 - \nu_2 s_2^2)/2\sigma^2\}.$$

It is seen that K_{0A} in (6b) depends on the following factors:

(i) Π_0/Π_A, the prior odds ratio,
(ii) $p(\hat{\boldsymbol\beta}_1)/p(\tilde{\boldsymbol\beta})$, the prior pdfs evaluated at the maximum likelihood estimates $\hat{\boldsymbol\beta}_1$ and $\tilde{\boldsymbol\beta}$,
(iii) $(|X_1'X_1|/|Z'Z|)^{-1/2}$, a factor involving the determinants of the design matrices,
(iv) $(1/2\pi\sigma^2)^{k_2/2}$, and
(v) $\exp\{-(\nu_1 s_1^2 - \nu_2 s_2^2)/\sigma^2\}$, the likelihood ratio.

While much could be said about each of the factors (i)–(v), just brief comments will be presented. Factor (ii) reflects the extent to which prior information is in agreement with sample information in the sense that $p(\hat{\boldsymbol\beta}_1)$ will have a small value if $\hat{\boldsymbol\beta}_1$ is far from the modal value of the prior pdf for $\boldsymbol\beta_1$ and similar considerations relate to $p(\tilde{\boldsymbol\beta})$. Thus K_{0A}'s value depends on the extent to which sample estimates agree with prior information. Factor (iii) reflects relative design considerations. If $X_1'X_2 = 0$ and if $X_1'X_1 = I$ and $X_2'X_2 = I$, $|X_1'X_1|/|Z'Z| = 1$. Otherwise properties of the design matrices under H_0 and H_A generally affect the value of K_{0A}. Factor (iv) shows a partial dependence of K_{0A} on σ^2's value with the remaining dependence in the last factor of (6b). Since

$$\partial \ln K_{0A}/\partial\sigma^2 = [(\nu_1 s_1^2 - \nu_2 s_2^2)/\sigma^2 - k_2]/2\sigma^2,$$
$$\partial \ln K_{0A}/\partial\sigma^2 > 0 \quad \text{if} \quad (\nu_1 s_1^2 - \nu_2 s_2^2)/k_2\sigma^2 > 1,$$

and

$$\partial \ln K_{0A}/\partial\sigma^2 < 0 \quad \text{if} \quad (\nu_1 s_1^2 - \nu_2 s_2^2)/k_2\sigma^2 < 1.$$

Last factor (v), the likelihood ratio reflects goodness of fit considerations; note that $\nu_1 s_1^2 - \nu_2 s_2^2 \geqslant 0$. Thus if H_0 leads to a poor fit relative to H_A, the value of K_{0A} will diminish.

From (6a), we have

$$\text{(7)}\qquad -2\ln K_{0A} \doteq -2\ln[\Pi_0 p(\hat{\boldsymbol\beta}_1)/\Pi_A p(\tilde{\boldsymbol\beta})] + (\nu_1 s_1^2 - \nu_2 s_2^2)/\sigma^2 - k_2[\ln n/2\pi + \ln|\hat{V}_{12}'\hat{V}_{12}/n\sigma^2|^{1/k_2}].$$

The Akaike information criterion (AIC) for the present problem, with σ^2's value assumed known, is (see Sawa 1976, eq. 2.10)

$$\text{(8)} \qquad \begin{aligned} \text{AIC} &= -2[\ln p_0(y\,|\,\hat{\beta}_1) - \ln p_A(y\,|\,\tilde{\beta})] + 2(k_1 - k) \\ &= -2[-(\nu_1 s_1^2 - \nu_2 s_2^2)/2\sigma^2] - 2k_2 \\ &= (\nu_1 s_1^2 - \nu_2 s_2^2)/\sigma^2 - 2k_2, \end{aligned}$$

where $p_0(y\,|\,\hat{\beta}_1)$ and $p_A(y\,|\,\tilde{\beta})$ are the likelihood functions in (4a) and (4b) evaluated at the ML estimates, $\beta_1 = \hat{\beta}_1$ and $\beta = \tilde{\beta}$. If AIC < 0, one chooses the simpler model, H_0 while if AIC > 0, one chooses the more complex model, H_A.

On comparing (7) and (8), it is seen that the last two terms in (7) are in the form of the AIC except that k_2 has a different coefficient. However the AIC in (8) does not include the first term on the right-hand side of (7). If $(\Pi_0/\Pi_A)[p(\hat{\beta}_1)/p(\tilde{\beta})] = 1$ and $\ln|\hat{V}_{21}'\hat{V}_{21}/n\sigma^2| + \ln n/2\pi = 2$ very special conditions, (7) and (8) become identical.

As is well known, the posterior odds ratio K_{0A} is a measure of relative strength of beliefs in the competing hypotheses H_0 and H_A. If we have a two-state–two-action loss structure that is symmetric (see, e.g., table 1), then acting so as to minimize expected loss results in choosing the hypothesis with the higher posterior probability. That is, if $K_{0A} = p_0/p_A > 1$, one chooses H_0, and if $K_{0A} < 1$, one chooses H_A. When $K_{0A} = 1$, one is indifferent in terms of expected loss. Applying these well-known considerations to (7), the posterior odds criterion (POC) under the loss structure shown above reduces to: if $-2 \ln K_{0A} < 0$, choose H_0; if $-2 \ln K_{0A} > 0$, choose H_A; and if $-2 \ln K_{0A} = 0$, both hypotheses are equivalent in terms of expected loss since $p_0 = p_A$. Generalization to asymmetric loss structures is direct.

From (7) and (8), the relation of the posterior odds criterion (POC) and the AIC has been made explicit. It is seen that the AIC is a truncated version of the POC. The analysis above has been performed using an approximate POC and under the assumption that σ^2 has a known value. In practice, it is not necessary to employ the approximate POC as long as one has explicit

Table 1

		State of World		Expected
		H_0 true	H_A true	Loss
Actions	State H_0 true	0	L	$p_A L$
	State H_A true	L	0	$p_0 L$
	Posterior probabilities $K_{0A} = p_0/p_A$	p_0	p_A	

prior pdf's, $p(\boldsymbol{\beta}_1)$ and $p(\boldsymbol{\beta})$ and can evaluate (3) analytically or numerically. Also, as shown in the appendix the assumption that σ^2 has a known value can be relaxed without much difficulty. Last, the POC can be computed for variants of the above problem and for many other problems.

Appendix

In the case that σ has an unknown value and we have just vague or diffuse prior information, we shall assume that σ and the regression coefficients are independently distributed and the prior pdf for σ under H_0 and H_A is in the usual diffuse form, $p(\sigma) \propto 1/\sigma$, $0 < \sigma < \infty$. Then (3) becomes,

$$K_{0A} = \frac{\Pi_0}{\Pi_A} \frac{\iint p(\boldsymbol{\beta}_1) l(\boldsymbol{\beta}_1, \sigma | y) d\boldsymbol{\beta}_1 \, d\sigma/\sigma}{\iiint p(\boldsymbol{\beta}_1, \boldsymbol{\beta}_2) l(\boldsymbol{\beta}_1, \boldsymbol{\beta}_2, \sigma | y) d\boldsymbol{\beta}_1 \, d\boldsymbol{\beta}_2 \, d\sigma/\sigma}. \tag{9}$$

Using the likelihood functions (4a) and (4b) and the linearizations of the prior pdf's for the regression coefficients, integration over the β's in (9) yields

$$K_{0A} \doteq \frac{\Pi_0}{\Pi_A} \frac{p(\hat{\boldsymbol{\beta}}_1)}{p(\tilde{\boldsymbol{\beta}})} \left(\frac{|X_1' X_1|}{|Z'Z|} \right)^{-1/2} \frac{1}{(\sqrt{2\pi})^{k_2}} \times \frac{\int_0^\infty \sigma^{-(k_1+1)} \exp\{-\nu_1 s_1^2/2\sigma^2\} \, d\sigma}{\int_0^\infty \sigma^{-(k+1)} \exp\{-\nu_2 s_2^2/2\sigma^2\} \, d\sigma} \tag{10}$$

The integrals on the right-hand side of (10) can be evaluated using the results in Zellner (1971, p. 371) to yield

$$\begin{aligned} K_{0A} &\doteq \frac{\Pi_0}{\Pi_A} \frac{p(\hat{\boldsymbol{\beta}}_1)}{p(\tilde{\boldsymbol{\beta}})} \left(\frac{|X_1' X_1|}{|Z'Z|} \right)^{-1/2} \frac{1}{(\sqrt{2\pi})^{k_2}} \cdot \frac{\Gamma(\nu_1/2)(2/\nu_1 s_1^2)^{\nu_1/2}}{\Gamma(\nu_2/2)(2/\nu_2 s_2^2)^{\nu_2/2}} \\ &\doteq \frac{\Pi_0}{\Pi_A} \frac{p(\hat{\boldsymbol{\beta}}_1)}{p(\tilde{\boldsymbol{\beta}})} \left(\frac{n}{2\pi} \right)^{k_2/2} \left| \frac{\hat{V}_{12}' \hat{V}_{12}}{n s_2^2} \right|^{1/2} \left(\frac{\nu_2 s_2^2}{\nu_1 s_1^2} \right)^{\nu_1/2} \frac{\Gamma[(\nu_2 + k_2)/2]}{\nu_2^{k_2/2} \Gamma(\nu_2/2)}, \end{aligned} \tag{11}$$

where $\Gamma(\cdot)$ is the gamma function. From (11), we have

$$\begin{aligned} -2 \ln K_{0A} \doteq & -2 \ln[\Pi_0 p(\hat{\boldsymbol{\beta}}_1)/\Pi_A p(\tilde{\boldsymbol{\beta}})] - \nu_1 \ln(\nu_2 s_2^2/\nu_1 s_1^2) \\ & - k_2[\ln n/2\pi + |\hat{V}_{21}' \hat{V}_{21}/n s_2^2|^{1/k_2}] \\ & - 2 \ln\{\Gamma(\nu_1/2)/\nu_2^{k_2/2} \Gamma(\nu_2)\}, \end{aligned} \tag{12}$$

where $(\nu_2 + k_2)/2 = \nu_1/2$ has been employed. Note that the likelihood ratio for this problem with σ's value unknown is $(\nu_2 s_2^2/\nu_1 s_1^2)^{n/2}$, and thus the second term on the right-hand side of (12) is related to the likelihood ratio and reflects relative goodness of fit. The first and third terms on the right-hand side of (12) are identical in form to the corresponding terms in (7) in the text except that the sample quantity s_2^2, rather than σ^2, appears. The last term on the right-hand side of (12) is an additional term not appearing in (7).

References

Akaike, H. (1972). "Information Theory and the Extension of the Maximum Likelihood Principle." In B. N. Petrov and F. Csaki, eds., *Proceedings of the Second International Symposium on Information Theory*, pp. 267–81.

———. (1974). "A New Look at Statistical Model Identification." *IEEE Transactions on Automatic Control*, AC-19, pp. 716–23.

Geisel, M. S. (1970). "Comparing and Choosing among Parametric Statistical Models: A Bayesian Analysis with Macroeconomic Applications." Ph.D. diss., Graduate School of Business, University of Chicago.

Jeffreys, H. (1967). *Theory of Probability*. London: Oxford University Press.

Lempers, F. B. (1971). *Posterior Probabilities of Alternative Linear Models*. Rotterdam: University of Rotterdam Press.

Sawa, T. (1976). "Information Criterion for the Choice of Regressions." Paper presented to Econometric Society meeting, September 1976, and to the 14th Meeting of the NBER-NSF Seminar on Bayesian Inference in Econometrics, June 1977.

Thornber, H. (1966). "Applications of Decision Theory to Econometrics." Ph.D. diss., Department of Economics, University of Chicago.

Zellner, A. (1971). *An Introduction to Bayesian Inference in Econometrics*, New York: John Wiley & Sons.

3.7 Posterior Odds Ratios for Regression Hypotheses: General Considerations and Some Specific Results

1 Introduction

Much work reported in the econometric literature has been directed at comparing Bayesian and non-Bayesian *estimation* results while much less work has been devoted to comparing Bayesian and non-Bayesian *analyses of alternative hypotheses*. This is not to say that the latter topic has been entirely neglected in the literature; see, for example, the references at the end of this paper, which include important works by Jeffreys, DeGroot, Dickey, Geisel, Good, Jaynes, Leamer, Lempers, Lindley, Raiffa, Schlaifer, Schwarz, Whittle, and others.[1] However, I believe it fruitful to open up discussion of some issues which appear relevant and important for practical analyses of hypotheses because they are not treated well and/or systematically in most statistics and econometric textbooks and in other portions of the literature.

What are some of the issues regarding analyses of hypotheses? First, there is the basic issue of whether to associate probabilities with hypotheses, that is, whether it is meaningful in a theory for analyzing hypotheses to quantify a statement like, "The parameter's value is probably zero." Most sampling theory analyses of hypotheses do not or cannot quantify such a statement. Second, the issue of what concept of probability is to be employed in quantifying such a statement arises. Most Bayesians regard probability as a measure of a degree of reasonable belief and not a frequency concept utilized widely in non-Bayesian analyses of hypotheses (see Jeffreys 1967, chap. 7 for a cogent discussion of this issue). Third, there is the issue of whether a separate theory of testing is needed; perhaps it is possible "to roll together significance testing and estimation in a single process," as sug-

Some minor changes have been made in the article, "Posterior Odds Ratios for Regression Hypotheses: General Considerations and Some Specific Results," which was an invited paper presented at the Econometric Society meeting, December 28–30, 1979, Atlanta, Georgia.

1. Jeffreys's name is placed first in this list because of his pioneering work on the philosophy, development, and applications of posterior odds ratios; see Jeffreys (1957, 1967).

gested by Good (1980). This suggestion seems questionable and fails to take account of a fundamental difference between estimation and significance testing problems. In the former, no particular value or values of the parameters are singled out for special attention, whereas in the latter, particular values, often zero, are given special attention. This is not to deny that estimation problems are often erroneously treated as testing problems.[2] However, as Jeffreys (1963) states, "Every quantitative law in physics implies a series of significance tests that have rejected numerous possible modifications of the law" (p. 403). In econometrics, too, most economic theories such as Friedman's theory of the consumption function imply hypotheses which can and have been tested. For example, is the elasticity of permanent consumption with respect to permanent income equal to one? Fourth, there is the issue of sharp nulls versus nonsharp nulls, that is, with respect to a regression coefficient $\beta = 0$, a sharp null hypothesis or $-\epsilon < \beta < \epsilon$, with $\epsilon > 0$ and small, a nonsharp null hypothesis. Good theories of testing should be able to provide results for both types of null hypotheses. Fifth, there is the issue of the use of prior information in testing. Use of one-tailed rather than two-tailed tests involves use of some prior information about the parameter space. Good testing procedures should be able to accommodate this kind and other kinds of prior information about parameters' possible values in analyzing hypotheses. Sixth, the use of power functions for tests requires prior information regarding parameters' values under the alternative hypothesis which is usually summarized poorly, if at all in practice. Seventh, choices of significance levels when the sample size is large and the use of "*P*-values" or "tail-areas" have to be more clearly explained.[3] Eighth, in some problems, asymptotically equivalent sampling theory tests yield conflicting results in finite samples (see Berndt and Savin

2. Some years ago, a student who estimated a demand function for tin was shocked by the finding that his estimate of the price elasticity was "not significantly different from zero at the 5% significance level." Since there was no special reason for concentrating attention on the zero value, his problem was an estimation and not a testing problem. His negative point estimate, accompanied by a broad confidence interval, showed that his estimate was not very precise, not that the parameter's value is necessarily equal to zero.

3. In conversation with the author, Dennis Lindley has pointed out that very few, if any, statistics textbooks explain how the significance level for a given test is to be changed as the sample size changes. The same can be said about econometrics textbooks. For large sample sizes, say 5,000, as encountered in survey data, empirical workers usually lament that use of usual t-statistics and the 5% significance level shows that parameters' values are usually significantly different from zero. Many of them sense that they should not be using the 5% level but do not know how to obtain a more appropriate significance level. On this point of large t-values when the sample size is large, see Jeffreys's (1967, pp. 435–36) cogent discussion which suggests that they may be caused by departures from assumptions, particularly independence assumptions, associated with hypotheses when the sample size is large.

1977 and Savin 1976), an issue which deserves attention. Ninth, the rationale for the 5% "accept-reject syndrome" which afflicts econometrics and other areas requires immediate attention. If a test statistics' value is just a shade larger than a 5% critical value, does it make sense to reject the null hypothesis or is it better practice to be able to calculate a result which says that the data information does not convincingly support either of the hypotheses? Tenth, does it make sense to test a null hypothesis with no alternative hypothesis present? Jeffreys (1967) and others point out that this is not good practice since there will always be some functions of the observations, that is, test statistics, which will assume unusual values under the null hypothesis.[4] Eleventh, there is the issue of how to combine analyses of hypotheses with estimation and prediction procedures.

The above are just some of the issues and problems which arise in analyzing hypotheses in econometrics and other areas. While not all of these issues can be thoroughly treated in one paper, what will be done is first, in section 2, to provide some information on what kinds of hypotheses are considered by economists and econometricians and how they are analyzed. In section 3, Bayesian methods for analyzing hypotheses will be described along with some applied simple examples. Several regression hypotheses are analyzed in section 4, while in section 5 some concluding remarks are provided.

2 Hypotheses and Procedures for Analyzing Them in Economics and Econometrics

Since there is much controversy about the kinds of hypotheses and procedures for analyzing them actually used by economists and econometricians, it was decided to attempt to get some facts relating to these issues by conducting a small survey of a portion of the 1978 economic and econometric literature. For each of the following five journals, *American Economic Review*, *Journal of Political Economy*, *International Economic Review*, *Journal of Econometrics*, and *Econometrica*, a 1978 issue was randomly selected. In the issues so selected, 22 full-length articles which

4. Jeffreys remarks, "The fundamental idea, and one that I should naturally accept, is that a law [or model] should not be accepted on data that themselves show large departures from its predictions. But this requires a quantitative criterion of what is to be considered a large departure. The probability of getting the whole of an actual set of observations, given the law [or model], is ridiculously small. . . . If mere improbability of the observations, given the hypothesis, was the criterion, any hypothesis would be rejected. Everybody rejects the conclusion, but this can mean only that improbability of the observations, given the hypothesis, is not the criterion, and some other must be provided. The principle of inverse probability [Bayes's theorem] does this at once" (1967, pp. 384–85).

contained analyses of quantitative data were studied with results summarized in table 1.

As can be seen in table 1, of the 22 quantitative articles appearing in 1978 issues of the journals listed above, 18 or 82 percent included analyses of hypotheses. Thus, analysis of hypotheses is a central activity in current applied economic and econometric research, hardly a surprising result. Apparently, applied workers do not regard (rightly or wrongly) their problems as amenable to analysis in just an estimation framework.

Of the 18 quantitative articles involving analyses of hypotheses, standard sampling theory hypothesis testing and/or *P*-value techniques were employed. In 7 of the 18 articles, or 39 percent, the 5% level of significance was employed throughout. In 2 articles both the 5% and 1% levels of signifi-

Table 1 Survey of 22 Quantitative Articles in Leading Economic Journals in 1978 with Respect to Hypothesis Testing

Item	Number of Articles	Proportion
1. Includes hypothesis testing	18	.82[a]
2. Significance level employed		
5%	7	.39
5% and 1%	2	.11
1%	1	.06
Various levels[b]	6	.33
Not applicable	2	.11
3. Includes discussion of power	1	.06
4. Types of hypotheses[c]		
Sharp	7	.39
Nonsharp	9	.50[d]
Both	2	.11

NOTE: Only full-length articles which contained analyses of quantitative data were included. From each of the five journals, *American Economic Review*, *Journal of Political Economy*, *International Economic Review*, *Journal of Econometrics*, and *Econometrica*, we randomly selected an issue in 1978 and categorized the quantitative articles in those issues.

[a]Proportion calculated with respect to 22 articles. The other proportions are calculated with respect to 18 articles.

[b]Either report of *P*-values or various significance levels were used within the same article.

[c]A sharp hypothesis involves assigning a specific value to a parameter, e.g., H_0: $\mu = 0$.

A nonsharp hypothesis does not involve assigning a specific value to a parameter, e.g., H_0: $\mu \geq 0$.

[d]The high proportion of nonsharp null hypotheses is due to (i) theories that only specify the algebraic sign of a coefficient and (ii) testing of nonnested models. An example of (ii) is testing which of two different nonnested theoretical distributions better fits the data.

cance were employed. In 6 articles various significance levels and/or *P*-values were used in the same article. An explicitly stated significance level was not mentioned in 2 of the 18 articles. In none of the papers was there a discussion of the relation between choice of significance levels and sample sizes which varied considerably both within and across studies; nor was there any discussion of the meaning of *P*-values.

Of the 18 articles in which hypotheses were analyzed and tested, there was just *one* which included a discussion of power. This is surprising in view of the fact that statistics and econometrics textbooks emphasize the importance of errors of the first and second kind and power considerations in general and in choice of a level of significance. Also, in almost all 18 papers, the usual accept-reject procedure was followed without attention given to the actual values of test statistics. For example, in one leading study, a *t*-statistic's value just barely exceeded the 5% critical value and the null hypothesis was rejected with no discussion of the "strength of the evidence."

Finally, the results in table 1 indicate that both sharp and nonsharp null hypotheses are considered in current applied economic and econometric research. The high proportion of nonsharp null hypotheses encountered is due to use of economic theories which specify only the algebraic signs of coefficients and not their exact values and to analyses involving comparisons of nonnested alternative models. An example of the latter analyses is an effort to determine which of two different distributions is better supported by the data.

To summarize, this small survey has uncovered the following points:

1. There is widespread use of the 5% and 1% levels of significance in testing with no systematic relation between choice of significance level and sample size.

2. Where *P*-values were employed, their meaning and rationale were not explained.

3. Power considerations are not generally discussed in empirical studies involving tests of hypotheses.

4. Both sharp and nonsharp hypotheses are utilized in empirical work, with the former generally being analyzed by use of Neyman-Pearson testing theory. Nonsharp null hypotheses were not analyzed very well in general.

5. There was very little formal or informal use of prior information regarding the values of parameters involved in the testing problems considered in these 18 articles.

6. Practically no attention was given in these 18 articles to the effects of tests or pretests on the properties of subsequent tests and/or computed

coefficient estimates. That is, the problems of pretest biases and lack of independence of various test statistics were not mentioned in most of the studies under review.

The results of this small survey, probably not surprising to many, suggest that there is room for improvement in analyses of hypotheses in economics and econometrics. In the following sections Bayesian results, which may be helpful in this regard, will be presented.[5]

3 Bayesian Analyses of Hypotheses

In the Bayesian approach to comparing and testing hypotheses, it is considered meaningful and useful to employ probabilities to represent degrees of reasonable belief associated with alternative hypotheses. The inductive calculus, primarily Bayes's theorem, is utilized to calculate the effects of the information in new data on initial or prior probabilities associated with alternative hypotheses in a logically consistent and operational manner. It should be appreciated that such calculations can in certain circumstances yield surprising and dramatic changes in initial probabilities. Also, while not discussed herein, Bayesian principles can be employed to design experiments to provide maximal discrimination between or among alternative hypotheses (see, e.g., Box and Hill 1967).

In the case in which a parameter θ, $-\infty < \theta < \infty$, is being considered and hypotheses do not specify a particular value for θ but rather just a range of possible values, for example, $\theta > 0$ versus $\theta < 0$ or $\theta > 1.0$ versus $\theta < 1.0$, examples of nonsharp hypotheses, Bayesians employ the following "Laplacian" approach, to use Jaynes's (1980) terminology in using data to modify initial probabilities associated with alternative hypotheses. Let $p(\theta \mid I_0)$ be the prior probability density function (pdf), where I_0 denotes the prior information. Then *before* observing the data, denoted by $\boldsymbol{y}$, the initial probabilities associated with, for example, $H_1: \theta > 0$ and $H_2: \theta < 0$ are obviously given by $p_1^{(0)} = \int_0^\infty p(\theta \mid I_0)d\theta$ and $p_2^{(0)} = 1 - p_1^{(0)} = \int_{-\infty}^0 p(\theta \mid I_0)d\theta$ for H_1 and H_2, respectively. The prior odds ratio for H_1 and H_2 is, by definition, $K_{12}^{(0)} = p_1^{(0)}/p_2^{(0)}$. Above, we have assumed that $p(\theta \mid I_0)$ is a proper prior pdf. If we have little prior information regarding θ's possible values and employ Jeffreys's prior for representing knowing little, $p_J(\theta \mid I_0)d\theta \propto d\theta$, $-\infty < \theta < \infty$, an improper prior,[6] then, as Jeffreys (1967,

5. In view of the controversies about alternative testing procedures in the statistical literature, it is surprising that there were no discussions of alternative testing methodologies in the papers surveyed.

6. See A. Rényi (1970) for an axiom system for probability theory, a generalization of Kolmogorov's, which accommodates unbounded measures and improper prior pdf's used in quantum theory, statistical mechanics, and mathematical statistics. In particular, Rényi's theory, as well as other results, shows that Bayes's theorem is valid when improper prior pdf's are employed.

pp. 117 ff.) points out, $K_{12}^{(0)}$ is indeterminate in value, his representation of the assumed state of ignorance. Whether the prior is proper or improper, Bayes's theorem can be employed to obtain the posterior pdf for θ, $p(\theta \mid D)$ where $D \equiv (I_0, y)$ as follows

$$p(\theta \mid D) = cp(\theta \mid I_0)\ell(\theta \mid y) \qquad -\infty < \theta < \infty \tag{3.1}$$

where the normalization constant c is given by $1/c = \int_{-\infty}^{\infty} p(\theta \mid I_0)\ell(\theta \mid y)d\theta$, with $\ell(\theta \mid y)$ being the likelihood function. As is well known, the posterior pdf $p(\theta \mid D)$ incorporates both the information in the prior pdf and in the data y. Given that we have the posterior pdf in (3.1), it is possible to calculate the following posterior probabilities, p_1 associated with $H_1: \theta > 0$ and p_2 associated with $H_2: \theta < 0$:

$$p_1 = Pr(\theta > 0 \mid D) = \int_0^{\infty} p(\theta \mid D)d\theta \tag{3.2a}$$

and

$$p_2 = Pr(\theta < 0 \mid D) = \int_{-\infty}^{0} p(\theta \mid D)d\theta \tag{3.2b}$$

and the posterior odds ratio, K_{12} for H_1 relative to H_2 is just $K_{12} = p_1/p_2$, or

$$\begin{aligned} K_{12} &= Pr(\theta > 0 \mid D)/Pr(\theta < 0 \mid D) \\ &= \int_0^{\infty} p(\theta \mid D)d\theta \Big/ \int_{-\infty}^{0} p(\theta \mid D)d\theta . \end{aligned} \tag{3.3}$$

Some simple but important examples illustrating uses of (3.3) and related odds ratios will now be presented. First, consider the usual linear normal regression model $y = X\beta + u$, where y is $n \times 1$, X is a given $n \times k$ matrix of rank k, β is a $k \times 1$ vector of regression coefficients, and u is an $n \times 1$ disturbance vector. It is assumed that the elements of u have been independently drawn from a normal distribution with zero mean and variance σ^2. The likelihood function is

$$\begin{aligned} \ell(\beta, \sigma \mid D) &\propto \sigma^{-n}\exp\{-(y - X\beta)'(y - X\beta)/2\sigma^2\} \\ &\propto \sigma^{-n}\exp\{-[\nu s^2 + (\beta - \hat{\beta})'X'X(\beta - \hat{\beta})]/2\sigma^2\}, \end{aligned} \tag{3.4}$$

where $\hat{\beta} = (X'X)^{-1}X'y$, $\nu s^2 = (y - X\hat{\beta})'(y - X\hat{\beta})$, and $\nu = n - k$. If we employ a standard diffuse prior pdf for β and σ, $p(\beta, \sigma) \propto 1/\sigma$, $0 < \sigma < \infty$ and $-\infty < \beta_i < \infty$, $i = 1, 2, \ldots, k$, then it is well known that the marginal posterior pdf for β_i is in the univariate Student-t form, that is,

$$(\beta_i - \hat{\beta}_i)/s_{\hat{\beta}_i} = t, \tag{3.5}$$

where β_i and $\hat{\beta}_i$ are the i'th elements of β and $\hat{\beta}$, respectively, $s^2_{\hat{\beta}_i} = m^{ii}s^2$, with m^{ii} the i–ith element of $(X'X)^{-1}$, and t is a random variable with a univariate Student-t pdf with $\nu = n - k$ degrees of freedom. Suppose that we are interested in the following hypotheses, $H_1: \beta_i > 0$ and $H_2: \beta_i < 0$. From (3.5), $\beta_i = \hat{\beta}_i + s_{\hat{\beta}_i} t$ and thus $\beta_i > 0$ is equivalent to $\hat{\beta}_i + s_{\hat{\beta}_i} t > 0$ or $t > -\hat{\beta}_i/s_{\hat{\beta}_i}$. Thus the posterior probability that $\beta_i > 0$ is $Pr(\beta_i > 0 \mid D) = Pr\{t > -\hat{\beta}_i/s_{\hat{\beta}_i} \mid D\}$, a probability which can be evaluated using tables of the Student-t distribution with ν degrees of freedom. Similarly, the hypothesis $\beta_i < 0$ is equivalent to $\beta_i = \hat{\beta}_i + s_{\hat{\beta}_i} t < 0$ or $t < -\hat{\beta}_i/s_{\hat{\beta}_i}$ and its posterior probability is $Pr(\beta_i < 0 \mid D) = Pr(t < -\hat{\beta}_i/s_{\hat{\beta}_i} \mid D)$. Then the posterior odds ratio for $H_1: \beta_i > 0$ and $H_2: \beta_i < 0$ is

$$K_{12} = \frac{Pr(\beta_i > 0 \mid D)}{Pr(\beta_i < 0 \mid D)} = \frac{Pr(t > -\hat{\beta}_i/s_{\hat{\beta}_i} \mid D)}{Pr(t < -\hat{\beta}_i/s_{\hat{\beta}_i} \mid D)}, \tag{3.6}$$

where, it should be noted $\hat{\beta}_i/s_{\hat{\beta}_i}$ is the usual sample t-statistic. Shown in table 2 are values of K_{12} and $Pr(\beta_i > 0 \mid D)$ for selected values of $\hat{\beta}_i/s_{\hat{\beta}_i}$ using a value of $\nu = n - k = 20$.

From table 2, it is seen that when $\hat{\beta}_i/s_{\hat{\beta}_i} = 0$, $Pr(\beta_i > 0 \mid D) = .5000$ and $K_{12} = 1.00$ while when $\hat{\beta}_i/s_{\hat{\beta}_i} = 2.00$, $Pr(\beta_i > 0 \mid D) = 0.9704$ and $K_{12} = 32.8$. These results are useful in appraising the implications of sample evidence for the algebraic sign of a regression coefficient. It should be appreciated that the above analysis can also be carried through using informative prior pdf's for $\boldsymbol{\beta}$ and σ, for the regression model with multivariate Student-t disturbance terms (see Zellner 1976), and other models. In addition, it is possible to compute $Pr\{\beta_i > 0$ and $\beta_j > 0 \mid D\}$ from the bivariate posterior distribution for β_i and β_j; see, for example, Davis (1978) for this and more general results. Last, below it is shown how to analyze three hypotheses, namely, $\beta_i > 0$, $\beta_i < 0$ and the sharp null hypothesis $\beta_i = 0$.

A second example of nonsharp null hypotheses involves study of the properties of solutions to a second-order autoregressive process, $y_t = \alpha_1 y_{t-1} + \alpha_2 y_{t-2} + \epsilon_t$, $t = 1, 2, \ldots, T$ where the ϵ_t's are assumed independently drawn from a normal distribution with zero mean and variance σ^2. Given two initial values of y_t and a diffuse prior for α_1, α_2, and σ, it is shown in Zellner (1971, pp. 194 ff.) that the marginal posterior pdf for α_1 and α_2 is

Table 2

	Values of $\hat{\beta}_i/s_{\hat{\beta}_i}$, $\nu = 20$					
	0.00	0.50	1.00	1.50	2.00	2.50
$Pr(\beta_i > 0 \mid D)$	0.5000	0.6887	0.8354	0.9254	0.9704	0.9894
K_{12}[a]	1.00	2.20	5.06	12.4	32.8	93.3

[a] $K_{12} = Pr(\beta_i > 0 \mid D)/Pr(\beta_i < 0 \mid D)$.

in the bivariate Student-t form and how numerical integration techniques can be employed to compute posterior probabilities that the solution to the model is (i) explosive and nonoscillatory, or (ii) nonexplosive and nonoscillatory, or (iii) nonexplosive and oscillatory or (iv) explosive and oscillatory. These posterior probabilities are just volumes under the posterior pdf, $p(\alpha_1, \alpha_2 | D)$ over regions in the $\alpha_1 - \alpha_2$ plane associated with solution properties (i)–(iv). This analysis can be performed using not only a diffuse prior pdf but also informative prior pdf's.

The next example, presented and analyzed by Jaynes (1976, pp. 181 ff.), involves study of two independent samples of data to determine whether the population mean for the first is larger than that of the second. That is, we have n_1 independent observations drawn from $N(\mu_1, \sigma^2)$ and n_2 independent observations drawn from $N(\mu_2, \sigma^2)$, and the nonsharp hypotheses are $H_1 : \mu_1 > \mu_2$ and $H_2 : \mu_1 < \mu_2$. Using a diffuse prior pdf for μ_1, μ_2 and σ, $p(\mu_1, \mu_2, \sigma) \propto 1/\sigma$, Jaynes derived the marginal posterior pdf for μ_1 and μ_2, $p(\mu_1, \mu_2 | D)$ which is in the bivariate Student-t form. From this posterior pdf, he computed the posterior probability that $\mu_1 > \mu_2$, that is, $Pr(\mu_1 > \mu_2 | D) = \int_{-\infty}^{\infty} \int_{\mu_2}^{\infty} p(\mu_1, \mu_2 | D) d\mu_1, d\mu_2$, and contrasted this solution to the problem with a sampling theory analysis involving a test of $\mu_1 = \mu_2$ versus $\mu_1 \neq \mu_2$, which appeared in a leading engineering statistics textbook. This example illustrates the importance of obtaining the solution to the question asked, $\mu_1 > \mu_2$ versus $\mu_1 < \mu_2$ rather than the solution to some other question, for example, $\mu_1 = \mu_2$ versus $\mu_1 \neq \mu_2$.[7]

Another example of nonsharp hypotheses involves the comparison of two hypothesized distributions for a set of independent observations, x_1, $x_2, \ldots, x_n$. Under H_1, the pdf for the observations is $f_1[(x - \mu)/\sigma]$, where μ is a location parameter and σ is a scale parameter, while under H_2 it is $f_2[(x - \mu)/\sigma]$. For example, $f_1(\cdot)$ might be a normal pdf while $f_2(\cdot)$ might be a double-exponential distribution. Using Bayes's theorem, it is well known that the posterior odds ratio K_{12} for this problem is given by:

$$K_{12} = \frac{\Pi_1 \int\int \ell_1(\mu, \sigma | \boldsymbol{x}) p_1(\mu, \sigma) d\mu d\sigma}{\Pi_2 \int\int \ell_2(\mu, \sigma | \boldsymbol{x}) p_2(\mu, \sigma) d\mu d\sigma}, \tag{3.7}$$

7. Jaynes (1976) analyzes several other specific, important problems from Bayesian and non-Bayesian points of view and presents an interesting review of historical developments in statistics and physics. He comments, "In most real applications, it is just the specific case at hand that is of concern to us; and it is hard to see how frequency statements about a mythical population or an imaginary experiment can be considered any more 'objective' than the Bayesian statements. Finally, no statistical method which fails to provide any way of taking prior information into account can be considered a full treatment of the problem [of comparing and testing alternative hypotheses]" (pp. 193–94).

where Π_1/Π_2 is the prior odds ratio, $x' = (x_1, x_2, \ldots, x_n)$, $p_1(\mu, \sigma)$ and $p_2(\mu, \sigma)$ are the prior pdf's, and $\ell_1(\mu, \sigma | x) = \Pi_{i=1}^n f_1[(x_i - \mu)/\sigma]$ and $\ell_2(\mu, \sigma | x) = \Pi_{i=1}^n f_2[(x_i - \mu)/\sigma]$ are the likelihood functions under H_1 and H_2, respectively. Among others, Dyer (1972, 1973) has studied the use of (3.7) with $\Pi_1/\Pi_2 = 1$ and, for $i = 1, 2, p_i(\mu, \sigma) = c/\sigma$, with c a positive constant, $-\infty < \mu < \infty$ and $0 < \sigma < \infty$ for discriminating between alternative distributions. Under these assumptions, he pointed out that a theorem from Zidek (1969) shows that K_{12} is a uniformly most powerful invariant test statistic for discriminating between $f_1(\cdot)$ and $f_2(\cdot)$. Also, he and others have reported Monte Carlo results showing that K_{12} performs well or better than other test statistics for discriminating between various $f_1(\cdot)$ and $f_2(\cdot)$. See also Blattberg and Gonedes (1974), who have applied (3.7) to discriminate between various hypothesized distributions for stock returns.

In Thornber (1966), Geisel (1970, 1973), Gaver and Geisel (1974), Lempers (1971), Zellner (1971), and Leamer (1978), odds ratios for nonnested normal linear regression models have been studied and applied. For example, Geisel computed posterior odds ratios to evaluate variants of money-multiplier and Keynesian-multiplier models studied earlier by Friedman and Meiselman. Zellner (1971, pp. 306 ff.) derived and studied the posterior odds ratio for two nonnested linear normal multiple regression models, $y = X_1\beta_1 + u_1$ and $y = X_2\beta_2 + u_2$ employing natural conjugate prior distributions for regression coefficients and disturbance terms' variances. It was found that the posterior odds ratio's value reflects (*a*) the prior odds ratio's value, (*b*) relative precision of prior and posterior distributions for parameters, (*c*) relative goodness of fit of the two models, and (*d*) extent to which prior and sample information regarding parameters' values are in agreement. It is thus seen that the value of the posterior odds ratio for the two models is conditioned by a range of relevant considerations and not just by relative goodness of fit.[8]

In summary, posterior probabilities can be computed for a number of nonsharp hypotheses frequently encountered in applied work. The posterior probabilities so computed reflect sample and prior information, as little or as much of the latter as an investigator decides to use. Further, posterior probabilities for investigators with different prior pdf's can be computed and compared; see, for example, Leamer (1978), Zellner and Geisel (1970), Zellner and Richard (1973), and Zellner and Williams (1973) for illustrations of this point. In addition, if an investigator has a loss structure giving the consequences of errors in choosing between or among hypotheses, it is well known that posterior probabilities can be employed to

8. See also Zellner (1978), where these points are made in another context.

evaluate expected losses associated with different choices of hypotheses and to choose among them in such a way as to minimize expected loss; see, for example, Blackwell and Girshick (1954), Chernoff and Moses (1959), DeGroot (1970), Zellner (1971) and Leamer (1978).

Having discussed various examples of nonsharp hypotheses, we now turn our attention to a consideration of sharp hypotheses.

As indicated by the results of the survey discussed in section 2, economists often consider sharp null hypotheses, for example, $\beta_i = 0$ versus $\beta_i \neq 0$, where β_i is a regression coefficient or $\eta = 1$ versus $\eta \neq 1$, where η is a returns-to-scale parameter, or $\boldsymbol{\beta} = \mathbf{0}$ versus $\boldsymbol{\beta} \neq \mathbf{0}$ where $\boldsymbol{\beta}$ is a vector of slope coefficients in a regression. Much work has been done to derive posterior odds ratios for sharp null hypotheses and alternative hypotheses, either sharp or nonsharp; see, for example, Jeffreys (1957, 1967, 1980), who is a pioneer in this area, Dickey (1971, 1975, 1977, 1980), Geisel (1970), Good (1950, 1965), Griffiths and Dao (1980), Leamer (1978), Lempers (1971), Lindley (1957), Mayer (1979), Reynolds (1982), Smith and Spiegelhalter (1980), Thornber (1966), Whittle (1951), Zellner (1971, 1978), and Zellner and Siow (1979, 1980).

First, it has been generally noted that in comparing two sharp, *simple* hypotheses, say $H_1 : \boldsymbol{\theta} = \boldsymbol{a}$ and $H_2 : \boldsymbol{\theta} = \boldsymbol{b}$, where $\boldsymbol{a}$ and $\boldsymbol{b}$ are given vectors, the posterior odds ratio is given by:

$$K_{12} = (\Pi_1/\Pi_2) f(\boldsymbol{y} \mid \boldsymbol{\theta} = \boldsymbol{a})/g(\boldsymbol{y} \mid \boldsymbol{\theta} = \boldsymbol{b}), \tag{3.8}$$

where Π_1/Π_2 is the prior odds ratio, $f(\boldsymbol{y} \mid \boldsymbol{\theta} = \boldsymbol{a})$ is the pdf for $\boldsymbol{y}$, the data under H_1 and $g(\boldsymbol{y} \mid \boldsymbol{\theta} = \boldsymbol{b})$ is the pdf for $\boldsymbol{y}$ under H_2. In many problems, $f(\cdot)$ and $g(\cdot)$ have the same form. From (3.8) it is seen that the so-called Bayes factor is just the likelihood ratio, $f(\boldsymbol{y} \mid \boldsymbol{\theta} = \boldsymbol{a})/g(\boldsymbol{y} \mid \boldsymbol{\theta} = \boldsymbol{b})$, and thus well-known optimal properties of likelihood ratio tests for simple hypotheses (see, e.g., Silvey 1970, pp. 97 ff.) are enjoyed by posterior odds ratios.

In many situations, the hypotheses do not specify all values of the parameters. For example, if $\boldsymbol{\theta}' = (\boldsymbol{\theta}_1', \boldsymbol{\theta}_2')$ and the hypotheses are $H_1 : \boldsymbol{\theta}_1 = \boldsymbol{a}_1$ and $\boldsymbol{\theta}_2$ unrestricted, where $\boldsymbol{a}_1$ is a given vector and $H_2 : \boldsymbol{\theta}_1$ and $\boldsymbol{\theta}_2$ unrestricted, the posterior odds ratio, based on data $\boldsymbol{y}$, is

$$K_{12} = (\Pi_1/\Pi_2) \int p_1(\boldsymbol{y} \mid \boldsymbol{\theta}_1 = \boldsymbol{a}_1, \boldsymbol{\theta}_2) p(\boldsymbol{\theta}_2 \mid \boldsymbol{\theta}_1 = \boldsymbol{a}_1) d\boldsymbol{\theta}_2 / \int p_2(\boldsymbol{y} \mid \boldsymbol{\theta}_1, \boldsymbol{\theta}_2) p(\boldsymbol{\theta}_1, \boldsymbol{\theta}_2) d\boldsymbol{\theta}_1 d\boldsymbol{\theta}_2 . \tag{3.9}$$

In (3.9) for $i = 1, 2$, $p_i(\boldsymbol{y} \mid \cdot)$ is the likelihood function, $p(\boldsymbol{\theta}_2 \mid \boldsymbol{\theta}_1 = \boldsymbol{a}_1)$ is the conditional prior pdf for $\boldsymbol{\theta}_2$ given $\boldsymbol{\theta}_1 = \boldsymbol{a}_1$, $p(\boldsymbol{\theta}_1, \boldsymbol{\theta}_2)$ is the joint prior pdf for $\boldsymbol{\theta}_1$ and $\boldsymbol{\theta}_2$ under H_2 and the integrations are performed over the region of $\boldsymbol{\theta}_2$ in the numerator and over the region of $\boldsymbol{\theta}_1$ and $\boldsymbol{\theta}_2$ in the denominator. K_{12} in (3.9) is seen to be a product of the prior odds ratio, Π_1/Π_2 and the Bayes factor, which here is the ratio of averaged likelihood functions with prior pdf's serving as the weight functions. To appreciate how (3.9) relates to problems encountered in practice, some specific examples will be provided.

Among many analyses of sharp null hypotheses frequently encountered in practice, Jeffreys (1967, pp. 268 ff.) considers hypotheses relating to a mean θ, $H_1: \theta = 0$ and $H_2: \theta \neq 0$ under the assumption that normal independent observations are available, each with a common standard deviation with unknown value. That is, $y_i = \theta + \epsilon_i$, $i = 1, 2, \ldots, n$ with the ϵ_i's assumed independently drawn from a normal distribution with zero mean and variance σ^2 with unknown value. For this and similar problems, Jeffreys noted that old-line physicists and astronomers usually computed something like $t = \bar{y}/s_{\bar{y}}$, where $\bar{y}$ is the sample mean, $\Sigma_{i=1}^n y_i/n$ and $s_{\bar{y}}$ is the standard error of the mean, where $s_{\bar{y}}^2 = \Sigma_{i=1}^n (y_i - \bar{y})^2/n(n-1)$. If $|t| < 2$, usually the measurements were taken as supporting $H_1: \theta = 0$; if $2 < |t| < 3$, some limited support for $H_2: \theta \neq 0$ is provided by the data; if $|t| > 3$, then strong support for $H_2: \theta \neq 0$ is provided by the data. All of this was done without use of formal statistical theory and thus Jeffreys (1979) mentioned that years ago he saw a need to produce a connected theory which would rationalize these rough rules used in applied work. In approaching this problem, Jeffreys (1967, p. 252) recognized that there might be little or much prior information available. He decided to develop his theory of significance testing for cases in which there is little prior information, as in "early stages of a subject." (p. 252). Herein, this course will also be followed because it leads to results which can be used in practice and which can be readily compared with non-Bayesian testing procedures. However, as Jeffreys recognized, if more prior information is available, it can be used in formulating and computing posterior odds ratios, as shown in work by Dickey (1971, 1975, 1977, 1980), Zellner (1971, pp. 307 ff.) and others.

For hypotheses $H_1: \theta = 0$ and $0 < \sigma < \infty$ and $H_2: \theta \neq 0$ and $0 < \sigma < \infty$ about a normal mean and standard deviation, Jeffreys takes the prior odds ratio Π_1/Π_2 equal to one and considers the following posterior odds ratio

$$(3.10) \qquad K_{12} = \int_0^\infty p(y \mid \theta = 0, \sigma) g(\sigma) d\sigma \Big/ \int_{-\infty}^{\infty} \int_0^\infty p(y \mid \theta, \sigma) f(\theta \mid \sigma) g(\sigma) d\sigma d\theta .$$

In (3.10), the likelihood functions are $p(y \mid \theta = 0, \sigma) = (2\pi\sigma^2)^{-n/2} \exp\{-n(\bar{y}^2 + \hat{\sigma}^2)/2\sigma^2\}$ and $p(y \mid \theta, \sigma) = (2\pi\sigma^2)^{-n/2} \exp\{-n[(\theta - \bar{y})^2 + \hat{\sigma}^2]/2\sigma^2\}$, where $\bar{y}$ is the sample mean and $n\hat{\sigma}^2 = \Sigma_{i=1}^n (y_i - \bar{y})^2$, $g(\sigma) \propto 1/\sigma$, the diffuse prior on σ, and $f(\theta/\sigma)$ is the prior on θ/σ. Jeffreys (1967, p. 268)

Table 3 Values of t^2 Associated with Corresponding Values of K_{12} and $\nu = n-1$ from (3.11)

	K_{12}				
ν	1	$10^{-1/2}$	10^{-1}	$10^{-3/2}$	10^{-2}
9[a]	3.5	7.7	13.3	...	...
15	3.8	7.1	11.1	15.9	21.5
20	4.0	7.0	10.6	14.5	18.9
50	4.6	7.4	10.0	12.8	16.0
100	5.2	7.7	10.3	12.8	15.5
200	5.7	8.2	10.7	13.1	15.6
500	6.8	9.1	11.4	13.8	16.2
1,000	7.4	9.7	12.0	14.3	16.6
2,000	8.1	10.4	12.7	15.0	17.3
5,000	9.0	11.3	13.6	15.9	18.2
10,000	9.7	12.0	14.3	16.6	18.9
50,000	11.3	13.6	15.9	18.2	20.5
100,000	12.0	14.3	16.6	18.9	21.2

[a]For $\nu = 9$, Jeffreys has used his exact result for K_{12} to compute the following t^2 values: 3.8 for $K_{12} = 1$, 7.7 for $K_{12} = 10^{-1/2}$, and 13.1 for $K_{12} = 10^{-1}$. It is seen that the exact results are in good agreement with the approximate results even though $\nu = 9$ is small. Jeffreys (1967, p. 439) tabulates exact values for $\nu = 1,2,3, \ldots, 9$.

presents several ingenious arguments for using $f(\theta \mid \sigma) = 1/\pi\sigma(1 + \theta^2/\sigma^2)$, a Cauchy prior for θ given σ which is centered at zero, the value suggested by H_1 when there is little prior information, other than that θ's value may be zero.[9] If these likelihood functions and prior pdf's are substituted in (3.10) and the integrations are performed, exactly in terms of the numerator and approximately in terms of the denominator, the result is:

$$K_{12} \doteq (\pi\nu/2)^{1/2}/(1 + t^2/\nu)^{(\nu-1)/2}, \tag{3.11}$$

where $\nu = n - 1$, $t = \sqrt{n}\,\bar{y}/s$, the usual t-statistic with $\bar{y} = \Sigma_{i=1}^{n} y_i/n$ and $s^2 = \Sigma_{i=1}^{n} (y_i - \bar{y})^2/\nu$ and the error of the approximation is of order $1/n$ of the whole expression.

In table 3 values of K_{12} from (3.11) for selected values of ν and t^2 from Jeffreys's (1967, p. 439) table are presented. From table 3, it is seen that

9. Use of the Cauchy prior results in $K_{12} \doteq 1$ when $n = 1$ and $K_{12} \doteq 0$ when $\bar{y} \neq 0$ and $\hat{\sigma} \doteq 0$ when $n \geq 2$. Also, use of the Cauchy prior avoids some difficulties associated with the use of a normal prior when the sample size is small, see Jeffreys (1967), p. 273. Jeffreys (1967, p. 251) points out that use of $p(\theta) \propto$ const, $-\infty < \theta < \infty$ is in conflict with the prior information that θ's value is probably small, as suggested by the null hypothesis and leads to $K_{12} = \infty$, an unsatisfactory result. On the other hand, when the Cauchy prior is employed and $\bar{y} \gg 0$, the posterior pdf under $\theta \neq 0$ is very similar to what is obtained in estimation using a diffuse prior pdf for θ.

with $\nu = 20$, $K_{12} \doteq 1.0$ when $t^2 = 4.0$ or $t = \pm 2$. Thus a value of $t = \pm 2$ when $\nu = 20$ does not provide convincing support for either $\theta = 0$ or $\theta \neq 0$. On the other hand when $\nu = 20$ and $t^2 = 10.6$ or $t = \pm 3.26$, $K_{12} \doteq 10^{-1}$; that is, the posterior odds ratio is 10:1 against $\theta = 0$. Further as ν grows in value, the value of t^2 associated with $K_{12} = 1$ grows in value. For example, when $\nu = 5{,}000$, $K_{12} \doteq 1$ when $t^2 = 9.0$ or $t = \pm 3.0$, which corresponds to many sample theorists' usual informal lowering of the significance level as the sample size grows in order to maintain a balance between probabilities of errors of the first and second kind. Also, this result is related to Lindley's (1957) paradox.

Jeffreys points out that for moderately large ν, K_{12} in (3.11) can be further approximated by $K_{12} \doteq (\pi\nu/2)^{1/2}\exp\{-t^2/2\}$ from which the dependence of K_{12} on ν and t is clearly seen. Further, as is evident from (3.11), for given ν, K_{12} is a monotonically decreasing function of t^2 and hence a monotonically increasing function of the P-value associated with $t = \sqrt{n}\,\bar{y}/s$, $t \geq 0$. From a numerical analysis of (3.11) for $\nu = 20$, the empirical relation connecting $\ell n K_{12}$ and $\ell n P$, where $P \equiv P$-value is:

$$\text{(3.12)} \quad \ell n K_{12} = \underset{(.0162)}{2.52} + \underset{(.00284)}{0.877}\ell n P + \hat{u}, \qquad r^2 = 0.9998,$$

based on 21 pairs of values of P and K_{12}, the latter ranging from 0.01 to 1.0. From (3.12), it is seen that the elasticity of the odds ratio K_{12} with respect to the P-value is 0.877 and thus high P-values are associated with high values for K_{12}. This may account for the widespread use of P-values in practice. That is, they can often be justified in terms of their relation to posterior odds ratios based on particular priors. However, since posterior odds ratios have a direct interpretation, their use is favored.

Jeffreys (1967, pp. 384 ff.) provides strong criticism[10] of the usual sampling interpretation of P-values, denoted by P in the following words,

> If P is small, that means that there have been unexpectedly large departures from prediction [under the null hypothesis]. But why should these be stated in terms of P? The latter gives the probability of departures, measured in a particular way, equal to *or greater than* the observed set, and the contribution from the actual value [of the test statistic] is nearly always negligible. *What the use of* P *implies, therefore, is that a hypothesis that may be true may be rejected because it has not predicted observable results that have not occurred.* This seems a remarkable procedure. On the face of it the fact that such results have not occurred might more reasonably be taken as evidence for the law [or null hypothesis], not against it. The same applies to all the current significance tests based on P integrals. [P. 385]

10. See also Jaynes (1976) and note 7, above.

Jeffreys (1967, pp. 395 ff.) is also critical of Neyman-Pearson testing procedures. While he lauds Neyman and Pearson for their giving attention to explicitly formulated alternative hypotheses and their detailed analysis of errors of the first and second kind, he remarks,

> Now Pearson and Neyman proceed by working out the above risks [of errors] for different values of the new parameter, and call the result the power function of the test, the test itself being in terms of the *P* integral. But if the actual value [of the parameter or parameters] is unknown the value of the power function is also unknown; the total risk of errors of the second kind must be compounded of the power functions over the possible values, with regard to their risk of occurrence. [Pp. 395–96]

Thus problems associated with use of *P*-values and in assessing "total risk of errors of the second kind" without a prior distribution are considered by Jeffreys to be critical defects of Neyman-Pearson testing theory. In addition, Jeffreys (1967, pp. 396–97) shows that for two hypotheses, regarding a scalar parameter α, $H_1: \alpha = 0$ and $H_2: \alpha \neq 0$, if it is known that both hypotheses have probability 1/2 and if under H_2, α is known to be uniformly distributed over its range, then the expectation of the total fraction of mistakes of the first and second kind will be made a minimum by use of the critical value $K_{12} = 1$; that is, if $K_{12} > 1$, choose H_1 and if $K_{12} < 1$ choose H_2. This is an early statement of a Bayesian decision theoretic result relevant for choosing hypotheses.

Above, two hypotheses were considered, namely, $\theta = 0$ and $\theta \neq 0$. In Zellner and Siow (1979) attention is given to the following three hypotheses: $H_1: \theta = 0$, $H_2: \theta > 0$, and $H_3: \theta < 0$, with prior probabilities Π_1 Π_2, and Π_3, respectively, and $\Pi_1 + \Pi_2 + \Pi_3 = 1$. The odds ratios for these three hypotheses are:[11]

$$K_{12} = (\Pi_1/\Pi_2)p(y\,|\,\theta = 0)/\int_0^\infty p(y\,|\,\theta)p_2(\theta)d\theta, \tag{3.13}$$

$$K_{13} = (\Pi_1/\Pi_3)p(y\,|\,\theta = 0)/\int_{-\infty}^0 p(y\,|\,\theta)p_3(\theta)d\theta, \tag{3.14}$$

and

$$K_{23} = (\Pi_2/\Pi_3)\int_0^\infty p(y\,|\,\theta)p_2(\theta)d\theta/\int_{-\infty}^0 p(y\,|\,\theta)p_3(\theta)d\theta, \tag{3.15}$$

11. Similar odds ratios can be obtained for three hypotheses relating to a regression coefficient's value, namely, $\beta_i = 0$, $\beta_i > 0$, and $\beta_i < 0$.

where y is a vector of observations, $p(y\,|\,\theta)$ is the likelihood function and $p_2(\theta)$ and $p_3(\theta)$ are the prior pdf's for θ under H_2 and H_3, respectively. Given values of the Π's, the prior pdf's and likelihood functions (3.13)–(3.15) can readily be computed as shown in the Zellner and Siow (1979) analysis of the normal mean problem with σ's value known and unknown. In this paper, Jeffreys's Cauchy priors for θ/σ, defined over $\theta > 0$ and $\theta < 0$, were employed along with a diffuse prior for σ and the following approximate odds ratios were derived.

$$K_{12} \doteq (\Pi_1/\Pi_2)(1/2)(\pi\nu/2)^{1/2}/(1+t^2/\nu)^{(\nu-1)/2}F(t), \tag{3.16}$$

$$K_{13} \doteq (\Pi_1/\Pi_3)(1/2)(\pi\nu/2)^{1/2}/(1+t^2/\nu)^{(\nu-1)/2}F(-t), \tag{3.17}$$

and

$$K_{23} \doteq (\Pi_2/\Pi_3)F(t)/F(-t), \tag{3.18}$$

where $t = \sqrt{n}\,\bar{y}/s$, the usual t-statistic, $\nu = n - 1$, and $F(\cdot)$ is the cumulative normal distribution. Tabulation of the odds ratio in (3.16) in table 4 reveals that by taking $\Pi_1 = .50$, $\Pi_2 = .40$, and $\Pi_3 = .10$, $K_{12} \doteq 1$ when $\nu = 20$ and $t = \sqrt{n}\,\bar{y}/s$ is slightly larger than 1.70, not far from the one-tailed 5% critical value, 1.725 used in non-Bayesian one-tailed testing of $H_1: \theta = 0$ versus $H_2: \theta > 0$ when $\nu = 20$. Of course other values of the prior probabilities Π_1, Π_2, and Π_3 and different prior pdf's can be employed if they are thought to be more appropriate.

In table 5, taken from Zellner and Siow (1979), values of $K_{23} \div \Pi_2/\Pi_3$ for various values of $t = n^{1/2}\bar{y}/s$ are shown. For example, it is seen that when $t = 1.00$, Bayes's factor in favor of $H_2: \theta > 0$ versus $H_3: \theta < 0$ is 5.30. Appropriate choice of the value of Π_2/Π_3 can be made to reflect initial information about H_2 and H_3.

In addition to the hypotheses considered above, Jeffreys (1967) has developed and applied Bayesian posterior odds ratios for hypotheses relating to a binomial parameter, contingency tables, Poisson parameters, equality of normal means with standard deviations assumed equal or unequal, standard deviations and correlations of normal populations, and other problems. In addition, he has provided a large sample approximation to the odds ratio for two hypotheses, namely, $-2\ell n K_{12} \doteq \chi_q^2 - q\ell n\, n$ where q is the number of restrictions implied by the null hypotheses H_1 relative to the alternative hypothesis, H_2, n = sample size, and $\chi_q^2 = -2\ell n\mathrm{LR}$, where LR denotes the usual likelihood ratio test statistic. Similar large-sample approximations were developed later and independently by Lindley (1961) and Schwarz (1978). Thus, it may be concluded that not only has the theory of Bayesian analyses of hypotheses been developed, but also applications of it

Table 4 Approximate Values of K_{12} Computed from Equation (3.16) with Prior Odds Ratio $\pi_1/\pi_2 = 1.25$

Degrees of freedom,	Values of $t = n^{1/2}\bar{y}/s$										
$\nu = n-1$	1.20	1.40	1.50	1.60	1.70	1.80	1.90	2.00	2.50	3.00	3.50	4.00
15	1.80	1.40	1.22	1.07	.925	.801	.690	.593	.267	.113	.0465	.0188
20	2.05	1.57	1.36	1.18	1.02	.873	.746	.634	.266	.103	.0374	.0132
50	3.12	2.35	2.02	1.72	1.46	1.23	1.03	.860	.311	.096	.0258	.0062
100	4.36	3.26	2.79	2.37	2.00	1.68	1.39	1.15	.392	.110	.0257	.0050
200	6.13	4.57	3.90	3.31	2.78	2.32	1.92	1.58	.522	.139	.0299	.0052
500	9.66	7.18	6.12	5.18	4.35	3.63	3.00	2.46	.795	.205	.0418	.0068
1000	13.6	10.1	8.64	7.31	6.14	5.11	4.22	3.45	1.11	.282	.0566	.0089
2000	19.3	14.3	12.2	10.3	8.66	7.21	5.95	4.87	1.56	.395	.0784	.0122
5000	30.6	22.6	19.3	16.3	13.7	11.4	9.39	7.70	2.46	.620	.122	.0189

NOTE: K_{12} is the posterior odds ratio relating to hypotheses H_1: $\theta = 0$ and H_2: $\theta > 0$, where θ is the mean of normal distribution with variance σ^2. Under H_1 the prior pdf employed is $p(\sigma) \propto 1/\sigma$ while under H_2 the prior pdf $p(\theta|\sigma) = (2/\pi)/(1+\theta^2/\sigma^2)$, $0 < \theta < \infty$, multiplied by $1/\sigma$ was used.

Table 5 Approximate Values of $K_{23} \div \Pi_2/\Pi_3 \doteq F(t)/F(-t)$

Values of	Values of $t = n^{1/2}\bar{y}/s$								
	0	.25	.50	.75	1.00	1.25	1.50	1.75	2.00
$F(t)/F(-t)$	1.00	1.49	2.24	3.41	5.30	8.47	14.0	24.0	43.0

NOTE: K_{23} is the posterior odds ratio in favor of H_2: $\theta > 0$ relative to H_3: $\theta < 0$, Π_2/Π_3 is the prior odds ratio, and $F(\cdot)$ denotes the cumulative normal distribution function.

to a number of important small-sample and large-sample problems have been developed.

In the next section some recent extensions of Jeffreys's analyses to selected regression hypotheses will be described.

4 Analyses of Selected Regression Hypotheses

Let the regression model for the $n \times 1$ observation vector $\boldsymbol{y}$ be:

(4.1) $$\boldsymbol{y} = \boldsymbol{\iota}\alpha + X\boldsymbol{\beta} + \boldsymbol{u},$$

where $\boldsymbol{\iota}$ is an $n \times 1$ vector with all elements equal to one, α and $\boldsymbol{\beta}$ are a scalar parameter and a $k \times 1$ vector of regression coefficients, respectively, $(\boldsymbol{\iota} \vdots X)$ is an $n \times (k + 1)$ given matrix of rank $k + 1$, and $\boldsymbol{u}$ is an n $\times$ 1 vector of disturbance terms. It is assumed that the variables in X are measured in terms of deviations from their respective sample means and thus $\boldsymbol{\iota}'X = \boldsymbol{0}'$. Further, the elements of $\boldsymbol{u}$ are assumed independently drawn from a normal population with zero mean and finite variance σ^2 with an unknown value.

In Zellner and Siow (1980), the following two hypotheses are considered:

(4.2) $$H_1 : \boldsymbol{\beta} = \boldsymbol{0}, \quad -\infty < \alpha < \infty \text{ and } 0 < \sigma < \infty$$

(4.3) $$H_2 : \boldsymbol{\beta} \neq 0, \quad -\infty < \alpha < \infty \text{ and } 0 < \sigma < \infty.$$

The likelihood functions under these two hypotheses are:

(4.4) $$p(\boldsymbol{y}\,|\,\alpha, \sigma, H_1) \propto \sigma^{-n}\exp\{-(\boldsymbol{y} - \alpha\boldsymbol{\iota})'(\boldsymbol{y} - \alpha\boldsymbol{\iota})/2\sigma^2\} \\ \propto \sigma^{-n}\exp\{-[\nu_1 s_1^2 + n(\alpha - \bar{y})^2]/2\sigma^2\}$$

and

(4.5) $$p(\boldsymbol{y}\,|\,\alpha, \boldsymbol{\beta}, \sigma, H_2) \propto \sigma^{-n}\exp\{-(\boldsymbol{y} - \alpha\boldsymbol{\iota} - X\boldsymbol{\beta})' \\ (\boldsymbol{y} - \alpha\boldsymbol{\iota} - X\boldsymbol{\beta})/2\sigma^2\} \\ \propto \sigma^{-n}\exp\{-[\nu_2 s_2^2 + n(\alpha - \bar{y})^2 \\ + (\boldsymbol{\beta} - \hat{\boldsymbol{\beta}})'X'X(\boldsymbol{\beta} - \hat{\boldsymbol{\beta}})]/2\sigma^2\}$$

where the proportionality constant is $(2\pi)^{-n/2}$ in each case,

$$\bar{y} = \sum_{i=1}^{n} y_i/n,\ \nu_1 s_1^2 = \sum_{i=1}^{n} (y_i - \bar{y})^2,\ \nu_1 = n - 1,$$
$$\hat{\boldsymbol\beta} = (X'X)^{-1}X'\mathbf{y},\ \nu_2 s_2^2 = (\mathbf{y} - \bar{y}\boldsymbol\iota - X\hat{\boldsymbol\beta})'(\mathbf{y} - \bar{y}\boldsymbol\iota - X\hat{\boldsymbol\beta}),$$
$$\text{and } \nu_2 = n - k - 1.$$

With prior odds ratio equal to one, the posterior odds ratio for H_1 and H_2, denoted by K_{12} is

$$K_{12} = \frac{\int\int p(\mathbf{y}\,|\,\alpha, \sigma, H_1)p(\alpha, \sigma\,|\,H_1)d\alpha\, d\sigma}{\int \cdots \int p(\mathbf{y}\,|\,\alpha, \boldsymbol\beta, \sigma, H_2)p(\alpha, \boldsymbol\beta, \sigma\,|\,H_2)d\alpha\, d\boldsymbol\beta\, d\sigma} \tag{4.6}$$

where the integrations for α and the elements of $\boldsymbol\beta$ are to be performed over the range $-\infty$ to $+\infty$ while those for σ are over the range $0 < \sigma < \infty$. As regards the prior pdf's in (4.6), Zellner and Siow (1980) employed the following Jeffreys-like priors:

$$p(\alpha, \sigma\,|\,H_1) \propto 1/\sigma \qquad -\infty < \alpha < \infty \text{ and } 0 < \sigma < \infty \tag{4.7}$$

and

$$p(\alpha, \boldsymbol\beta, \sigma) \propto f(\boldsymbol\beta\,|\,\sigma)/\sigma \quad -\infty < \alpha < \infty \text{ and } 0 < \sigma < \infty \tag{4.8a}$$

with

$$f(\boldsymbol\beta\,|\,\sigma) = c\,|X'X/n\sigma^2|^{1/2}/(1 + \boldsymbol\beta'X'X\boldsymbol\beta/n\sigma^2)^{(k+1)/2} \qquad -\infty < \beta_i < \infty \quad i = 1, 2, \ldots, k \tag{4.8b}$$

where the proportionality constants in (4.7) and (4.8a) are the same, $c = \Gamma[(k + 1)/2]/\pi^{(k+1)/2}$ is the normalizing constant for the proper k-dimensional Cauchy pdf for $\boldsymbol\beta$ given σ which is centered at $\mathbf{0}$, the value suggested by the null hypothesis H_1. The matrix of the pdf in (4.8b), $X'X/n\sigma^2$ is suggested by the form of the information matrix and/or by consideration of standardized coefficients for the regression model.

When (4.7) and (4.8) are inserted in (4.6) and the integrations are performed, exactly in terms of the numerator and approximately in terms of the denominator (see Zellner and Siow 1980 for details), the result is:

$$\begin{aligned} K_{12} &\doteq a(\nu_2/2)^{k/2}(\nu_2 s_2^2/\nu_1 s_1^2)^{(\nu_2-1)/2} \\ &= a(\nu_2/2)^{k/2}/[1 + (k/\nu_2)F_{k,\nu_2}]^{(\nu_2-1)/2} \\ &= a(\nu_2/2)^{k/2}(1 - R^2)^{(\nu_2-1)/2}, \end{aligned} \tag{4.9}$$

where $a = \pi^{1/2}/\Gamma[(k + 1)/2]$, $F_{k,\nu_2} = \hat{\boldsymbol\beta}'X'X\hat{\boldsymbol\beta}/ks_2^2$, $R^2 = \hat{\boldsymbol\beta}'X'X\hat{\boldsymbol\beta}/(\nu_2 s_2^2 + \hat{\boldsymbol\beta}'X'X\hat{\boldsymbol\beta})$, and $\nu_2 s_2^2 + \hat{\boldsymbol\beta}'X'X\hat{\boldsymbol\beta} = \nu_1 s_1^2$ have been employed in going from the first to the second line of (4.9). As shown in Zellner and Siow (1980), the error of the approximation in (4.9) is of order $1/n$ of the whole expression. In the first line of (4.9) K_{12} has been expressed in terms of $\nu_2 s_2^2/\nu_1 s_1^2$, the ratio of the sum of squared least squares residuals under H_1 and H_2 while in the second and third lines, K_{12} has been expressed in terms of the usual F-statistic, F_{k,ν_2}, and the sample squared multiple correlation coefficient, respectively. Also, from (4.9), the following large-sample Jeffreys-like approximation can be obtained:

$$-2\ell n K_{12} \doteq \chi_k^2 - k \ell n \nu_2, \tag{4.10}$$

where $\chi_k^2 = \hat{\boldsymbol{\beta}}' X' X \hat{\boldsymbol{\beta}}/s_2^2$.

Shown in table 6, taken from Zellner and Siow (1980), is a tabulation of K_{12} values from (4.9) for various values of k and R^2 and the associated values of F_{k,ν_2} for $\nu_2 = 20$ and $\nu_2 = 100$. Also shown in the table are .05 and .01 critical values of F_{k,ν_2} and associated values of R^2. For example, when $\nu_2 = 20$ and $k = 1$, $K_{12} \doteq 1$ when $F_{1,20} = t_{20}^2 = 4.0$ or $R^2 = .16$. Under these conditions as R^2 or $F_{1,20}$ grows in value, K_{12} declines in value. For $R^2 = .49$ or $F_{1,20} = 18.9$, the associated value of K_{12} is 10^{-2}, strong evidence against $H_1 : \boldsymbol{\beta} = 0$. With $\nu_2 = 20$, as k, the number of regression coefficients, grows, a higher value of R^2 is needed to have $K_{12} = 1$. When $k = 6$, an $R^2 = .48$ or $F_{6,20} = 3.1$ provides $K_{12} \doteq 1$. Generally, the R^2 values associated with $K_{12} = 1$ for $\nu_2 = 20$ are not far different from the .05 critical values of R^2 provided in the last column of the table. However, when $\nu_2 = 100$, part B of the table shows that the values of R^2 associated with $K_{12} = 1$ when $k > 1$ are larger than the R^2 values corresponding to the .01 critical values of the F-statistic. Thus for large ν_2 values, the .05 critical values of F and their associated R^2 values are poor approximations to indifference values ($K_{12} = 1$) of these posterior odds ratios. Further, for $\nu_2 = 100$, (4.10) provides results similar to those in table 6 in terms of indifference values for R^2. For example, with $\nu_2 = 100$, $k = 6$, and $\chi_6^2 = 27.6$ or $R^2 = .22$, (4.10) yields $K_{12} \doteq 1$, which is precisely the value of R^2 yielding $K_{12} \doteq 1$ in table 6. However, for $\nu_2 = 20$, the approximation in (4.10), while not far off, is not as accurate; see table 7 for more details.

Now let (4.1) be rewritten as

$$\underset{n\times 1}{\boldsymbol{y}} = \underset{n\times 1}{\boldsymbol{\iota}}\underset{1\times 1}{\alpha} + \underset{n\times k_1}{X_1}\underset{k_1\times 1}{\boldsymbol{\beta}_1} + \underset{n\times k_2}{X_2}\underset{k_2\times 1}{\boldsymbol{\beta}_2} + \underset{n\times 1}{\boldsymbol{u}} \tag{4.11}$$

with $k = k_1 + k_2$, $X = (X_1 : X_2)$, and $\boldsymbol{\beta}' = (\boldsymbol{\beta}_1', \boldsymbol{\beta}_2')$. Consider the hypotheses

$$H_A : \boldsymbol{\beta}_2 = \mathbf{0} \tag{4.12}$$

$$H_B : \boldsymbol{\beta}_2 \neq \mathbf{0} \tag{4.13}$$

with α, the elements of $\boldsymbol{\beta}_1$, and σ unrestricted under H_A and H_B. Using prior assumptions similar to those presented above, Zellner and Siow (1980) derived the following posterior odds ratio, K_{AB} for H_A and H_B with their prior odds ratio assumed equal to one:

$$(4.14)\quad \begin{aligned} K_{AB} &\doteq b(\nu_B/2)^{k_2/2}(\nu_B s_B^2/\nu_A s_A^2)^{(\nu_B-1)/2} \\ &= b(\nu_B/2)^{k_2/2}[(1-R_B^2)/(1-R_A^2)]^{(\nu_B-1)/2} \\ &= b(\nu_B/2)^{k_2/2}/[1+(k_2/\nu_B)F_{k_2,\nu_B}]^{(\nu_B-1)/2} \end{aligned}$$

Table 6 Values of R^2 and F_{k,ν_2} Associated with Particular Values of K_{12} and k in (4.9) for $\nu_2 = 20$ and $\nu_2 = 100$

k	Value of:	K_{12}: 1	$10^{-1/2}$	10^{-1}	$10^{-3/2}$	10^{-2}	.01 and .05 Critical Values of F and Associated R^2s: .01	.05
				A. $\nu_2 = 20$				
1	R^2	.16	.26	.35	.42	.49	.29	.18
	$F_{1,20}$	4.0	7.0	10.6	14.5	18.9	8.10	4.35
2	R^2	.27	.35	.43	.49	.55	.37	.26
	$F_{2,20}$	3.7	5.5	7.5	9.7	12.3	5.85	3.49
3	R^2	.35	.42	.48	.54	.60	.43	.32
	$F_{3,20}$	3.5	4.8	6.3	8.0	9.9	4.94	3.10
4	R^2	.40	.47	.53	.58	.63	.47	.36
	$F_{4,20}$	3.4	4.4	5.7	7.0	8.6	4.43	2.87
5	R^2	.45	.51	.57	.61	.66	.51	.40
	$F_{5,20}$	3.2	4.2	5.2	6.4	7.7	4.10	2.71
6	R^2	.48	.54	.59	.64	.68	.54	.44
	$F_{6,20}$	3.1	3.9	4.9	5.9	7.1	3.87	2.60
				B. $\nu_2 = 100$				
1	R^2	.050	.072	.093	.11	.13	.065	.380
	$F_{1,100}$	5.2	7.7	10.3	12.8	15.5	6.90	3.94
2	R^2	.089	.11	.13	.15	.17	.088	.058
	$F_{2,100}$	4.9	6.2	7.5	8.8	10.3	4.82	3.09
3	R^2	.12	.14	.16	.18	.20	.11	.075
	$F_{3,100}$	4.6	5.5	6.4	7.4	8.3	3.98	2.70
4	R^2	.15	.17	.19	.21	.23	.12	.090
	$F_{4,100}$	4.4	5.1	5.9	6.6	7.3	3.51	2.46
5	R^2	.18	.20	.21	.23	.25	.14	.10
	$F_{5,100}$	4.3	4.9	5.5	6.1	6.7	3.20	2.30
6	R^2	.20	.22	.24	.25	.27	.15	.12
	$F_{6,100}$	4.2	4.7	5.2	5.7	6.2	2.99	2.19

NOTE: $F_{k,\nu_2} = (\nu_2/k)R^2/(1-R^2)$, with $\nu_2 = n-k-1$.

where $b = \pi^{1/2}/\Gamma[(k_2 + 1)/2]$, R_A^2 and R_B^2 are the squared sample multiple correlation coefficients under H_A and H_B, respectively, $F_{k_2, \nu_B} = \hat{\boldsymbol{\beta}}_2' V'V\hat{\boldsymbol{\beta}}_2/k_2 s_B^2$, the usual F-statistic with k_2 the number of elements in $\boldsymbol{\beta}_2$, $V = [I - X_1(X_1'X_1)^{-1}X_1']X_2$, $\nu_A = n - k_1 - 1$, $\nu_B = n - k_1 - k_2 - 1 = n - k - 1$, and $\nu_A s_A^2$ and $\nu_B s_B^2$ the sum of squared least squares residuals under H_A and H_B, respectively. It is seen that the third line of (4.14) is in a form exactly similar to that of the second line of (4.9). Thus table 6 can be employed to obtain values of K_{AB} associated with values of F_{k_2, ν_B} if in using the table, ν_B is identified with ν_2 and k_2 is identified with k.

To illustrate application of the above analysis, the Hald data, 13 observations on a dependent variable and four independent variables given in Draper and Smith (1966, App. B) and Geisser and Eddy (1979, p. 158) have been analyzed. The problem is to compare all possible regression models, that is, the model with a constant term and all four independent variables and models including any three variables, any two variables, any one variable, and none of the four variables. In toto, there are 16 possible models, each assumed to be linear in the independent variables. By use of the posterior odds ratio in (4.14), the results in table 6, from Zellner and Siow (1980), were obtained.

In the second column of table 7, values of K_{AB}, the posterior odds ratio for a particular subset regression (H_A), relative to the regression including all four independent variables and a constant (H_B) are presented. The largest value of K_{AB}, 3.9 is encountered for model (1,2,c) while the next largest values are 3.3 for (1,2,3,c) and (1,2,4,c), 2.8 for (1,3,4,c), 1.8 for (1,4,c) and .90 for (2,3,4,c). That overwhelming evidence in favor of a particular subset regression is not obtained is not surprising with just 13 observations. On the other hand, a number of subset regressions have very small values for their posterior odds ratios.

Also shown in table 7 are the results of applying several other criteria to the Hald data. As is well known, use of R^2 results in choice of the model with the largest number of free parameters here (1,2,3,4,c), for which $R^2 = .9824$, considered by most to be a defect of R^2. Interestingly, the six models other than (1,2,3,4,c) with the highest posterior odds ratios are the ones with the highest R^2 values, undoubtedly a reflection of the fact that K_{AB} can be expressed as a function of R^2; see (4.14). However, note that model (3,4,c) has a posterior odds ratio of only .14 while its $R^2 = .9353$. Use of the standard error of regression and the Geisser-Eddy predictive sample reuse (PSR) criterion leads to about the same set of preferred models as does use of the posterior odds ratios. Similarly Aitken's R^2-adequate criterion at the 5% significance level also selects about the same set of preferred subset regressions. In this last approach, a significance level must be chosen; see

Table 7 Posterior Odds Ratios, K_{AB}, and Other Model Selection Criteria Computed Using the Hald Data ($n = 13$)

Independent Variables, H_A	Posterior Odds Ratio, K_{AB}[b]	R^2	Standard Error of Regression	Geisser-Eddy PSR Criterion[c]	Aitken's R^2 Adequate Criterion (.05)[d]
1,2,3,c[a]	3.3	.9823	2.312	−33.50	adequate
1,2,4,c	3.3	.9823	2.309	−33.22	adequate
1,3,4,c	2.8	.9813	2.377	−33.64	adequate
2,3,4,c	0.90	.9728	2.864	−36.26	adequate
1,2,c	3.9	.9787	2.406	−33.18	adequate
1,3,c	4.1×10^{-4}	.5482	11.077	−53.23	—
1,4,c	1.8	.9725	2.734	−35.08	adequate
2,3,c	1.1×10^{-2}	.8470	6.445	−46.86	—
2,4,c	1.2×10^{-3}	.6800	9.321	−51.62	—
3,4,c	1.4×10^{-1}	.9353	4.192	−40.95	—
1,c	3.2×10^{-4}	.5339	10.727	−51.93	—
2,c	8.5×10^{-4}	.6663	9.077	−50.58	—
3,c	8.7×10^{-5}	.2859	13.278	−54.83	—
4,c	9.2×10^{-4}	.6745	8.964	−49.84	—
c	8.9×10^{-5}	0	15.044	—	—
1,2,3,4,c	1.0	.9824	2.446	−34.84	adequate

[a] 1,2,3,c indicates that H_A in this case is a linear regression involving the independent variables x_1, x_2, x_3 and a constant term.

[b] In each case, K_{AB} is the posterior odds ratio for H_A, as shown in the first column, relative to H_B: 1,2,3,4,c, the model with all four independent variables and a constant term, and the prior odds ratio's value has been taken equal to one.

[c] W. F. Eddy provided these to the author; reported values in Geisser and Eddy (1979), table 4, are erroneous.

[d] Reported in Aitken (1974). Models indicated to be "adequate" passed the 5% R^2-adequate criterion while the others did not.

Aitken (1974, p. 226) for discussion of the effects of varying the significance level.

While the results of applying various criteria to the Hald data are not qualitatively very different, except for use of R^2, it appears that the posterior odds ratio metric seems preferable for the problem of reflecting the effects of both sample and prior information as it impinges on the evaluation of alternative subset regressions. Also, posterior odds ratios provide posterior probabilities associated with alternative subset regressions which can be employed to average parameter estimates and forecasts from alternative models as pointed out in the literature. Finally, it is not suggested that posterior odds ratios be used mechanically in variable selection problems.

The present approach can be elaborated to take account of more subject matter information through use of more informative priors; see Dickey (1975, 1980), of possible autocorrelation, and Gaver and Geisel (1974), Griffiths and Dao (1980), Fomby and Guilkey (1978), and Mayer (1979) and of other possible departures from standard assumptions regarding error terms' properties. In addition, posterior odds ratios can be formulated and computed for a wide range of problems, as mentioned earlier and not just for linear regression problems.

Some results presented by Zellner and Siow (1978) for a two-equation regression system will now be reviewed. The model for the observations is:

$$y_1 = X_1 \beta_1 + u_1 \tag{4.15a}$$

$$y_2 = X_2 \beta_2 + u_2, \tag{4.15b}$$

where for $i = 1, 2$, y_i is an $n_i \times 1$ vector, X_i is an $n_i \times k$ given matrix of rank k, β_i is a $k \times 1$ vector of regression parameters, u_i is an $n_i \times 1$ vector of disturbance terms. It is assumed that the elements of u_1 and u_2 have been independently drawn from normal populations with zero means and variances σ_1^2 and σ_2^2, respectively. The likelihood function is then,

$$p(y_1, y_2 \mid \beta_1, \beta_2, \sigma_1 \sigma_2) \propto \sigma_1^{-n_1}\sigma_2^{-n_2}\exp\{-[(y_1 - X_1\beta_1)'(y_1 - X_1\beta_1)/2\sigma_1^2 + (y_2 - X_2\beta_2)'(y_2 - X_2\beta_2)/2\sigma_2^2]\}. \tag{4.16}$$

Given a prior pdf for the parameters of (4.16), the associated posterior distribution can be obtained and used to investigate nonsharp null hypotheses about parameters' values, for example, $H: c_1 < \phi < c_2$ and its negation $\bar{H}: 0 < \phi < c_1$ or $c_2 < \phi < \infty$, where c_1 and c_2 are given positive numbers and $\phi = \sigma_2^2/\sigma_1^2$.

With a diffuse prior pdf for the parameters of (4.16),

$$p(\beta_1, \beta_2, \sigma_1, \sigma_2) \propto 1/\sigma_1\sigma_2, \tag{4.17}$$

where, for $i = 1, 2$, $0 < \sigma_i < \infty$ and $-\infty < \beta_{ij} < \infty$, $j = 1, 2, \ldots, k$,

$$p(\beta_1, \beta_2, \sigma_1, \sigma_2 \mid D) \propto \prod_{i=1}^{2} \sigma_i^{-(n_i+1)} \times \exp\{-[\nu_i s_i^2 + (\beta_i - \hat{\beta}_i)'X_i'X_i(\beta_i - \hat{\beta}_i)]/2\sigma_i^2\}, \tag{4.18}$$

where $D = (y_1, y_2, I)$, the data and prior information, $\hat{\beta}_i = (X_i'X_i)^{-1}X_i'y_i$, $\nu_i s_i^2 = (y_i - X_i\hat{\beta}_i)'(y_i - X_i\hat{\beta}_i)$, and $\nu_i = n_i - k$ for $i = 1, 2$. On integrating (4.18) with respect to β_1 and β_2, the result is:

$$p(\sigma_1, \sigma_2 \mid D) \propto \prod_{i=1}^{2} \sigma_i^{-(\nu_i+1)}\exp\{-\nu_i s_i^2/2\sigma_i^2\}, \tag{4.19}$$

the product of two inverted gamma pdf's for σ_1 and σ_2. As shown in Zellner (1971, p. 378), (4.19) implies that

$$F = (\sigma_2^2/s_2^2)/(\sigma_1^2/s_1^2) \tag{4.20}$$

has an F_{ν_1,ν_2} posterior pdf.[12] Then

$$Pr\{c_1 < \sigma_2^2/\sigma_1^2 < c_2 \mid D\} = Pr\{(s_1^2/s_2^2)c_1 < F < (s_1^2/s_2^2)c_2 \mid D\} \tag{4.21}$$

which can be evaluated using tables of the F-distribution or by univariate numerical integration. Also, $F' = (\sigma_1^2/s_1^2)/(\sigma_2^2/s_2^2)$ has an F_{ν_2,ν_1} posterior pdf and thus inferences about $\lambda = \sigma_1^2/\sigma_2^2$ can also be made easily.

If $(\boldsymbol{\beta}_1, \sigma_1)$ and $(\boldsymbol{\beta}_2, \sigma_2)$ are independently distributed, each with a natural conjugate prior pdf, then it is straightforward to show that $\lambda = \sigma_1^2/\sigma_2^2$ has a posterior pdf in the F-form and thus posterior probabilities such as $Pr(a_1 < \lambda < a_2 \mid D)$ can be easily evaluated. If in (4.15), $\boldsymbol{\beta}_1 = \boldsymbol{\beta}_2 = \boldsymbol{\beta}$ and a diffuse prior pdf $p(\boldsymbol{\beta}, \sigma_1, \sigma_2) \propto 1/\sigma_1\sigma_2$ is employed, Zellner (1971, p. 107) has derived the posterior pdf for $\lambda = \sigma_1^2/\sigma_2^2$. Also, Zellner and Siow (1978) show how to obtain the posterior pdf for λ when the model in (4.15) is parameterized in terms of $\boldsymbol{\beta}_1$, $\boldsymbol{\delta} = \boldsymbol{\beta}_2 - \boldsymbol{\beta}_1$, σ_1, and σ_2 and an informative prior pdf for $\boldsymbol{\delta}$ is employed.

If interest centers on $\boldsymbol{\delta} = \boldsymbol{\beta}_1 - \boldsymbol{\beta}_2$, its marginal posterior pdf can be derived using several different prior pdf's. For example, with respect to the system in (4.15), if it is assumed that $\sigma_1 = \sigma_2 = \sigma$ and the diffuse prior pdf $p(\boldsymbol{\beta}_1, \boldsymbol{\beta}_2, \sigma) \propto 1/\sigma$ is employed, it is shown in Zellner and Siow (1978) that F, given by

$$F = (\boldsymbol{\delta} - \hat{\boldsymbol{\delta}})'M(\boldsymbol{\delta} - \hat{\boldsymbol{\delta}})/ks^2, \tag{4.22}$$

where $\hat{\boldsymbol{\delta}} = \hat{\boldsymbol{\beta}}_1 - \hat{\boldsymbol{\beta}}_2$, $M^{-1} = (X_1'X_1)^{-1} + (X_2'X_2)^{-1}$, and $\nu s^2 = (\mathbf{y}_1 - X_1\hat{\boldsymbol{\beta}}_1)'(\mathbf{y}_1 - X_1\hat{\boldsymbol{\beta}}_1)$ with $\nu = n - 2k$ has an $F_{k,\nu}$ posterior pdf, the Bayesian version of what has come to be known as the Chow (1960) test statistic. Using (4.22), various posterior probabilities relating to $\boldsymbol{\delta}$'s possible values can be evaluated. Also, this analysis is easily generalizable to the case in which the prior pdf for $\boldsymbol{\beta}_1$, $\boldsymbol{\beta}_2$, and σ is in the natural conjugate form. Further, in the case $\boldsymbol{\delta} = \boldsymbol{\beta}_2 - \boldsymbol{\beta}_1$ and $\sigma_1 \neq \sigma_2$, the posterior pdf for $\boldsymbol{\delta}$ can also be obtained.

In the case of sharp hypotheses regarding parameters of the system in (4.15), Zellner and Siow (1978) considered the hypotheses shown in the following table:

12. This result is Bayesian analogue of the Goldfeld and Quandt (1965) sampling theory test for the equality of disturbance variances.

	$\beta_1 = \beta_2$	$\beta_1 \neq \beta_2$
$\sigma_1 = \sigma_2$	H_A	H_B
$\sigma_1 \neq \sigma_2$	H_C	H_D

For example, employing Jeffreys-like prior pdf's for the parameters under H_A and H_B and a prior odds ratio of one, the following approximate posterior odds ratio was obtained:

$$K_{AB} \doteq a(\nu_B/2)^{k/2}/[1 + (k/\nu_B)F_{k,\nu_B}]^{(\nu_B-1)/2}, \tag{4.23}$$

where $a = \pi^{1/2}/\Gamma[(k+1)/2]$, $\nu_B = n - 2k$, $F_{k,\nu_B} = \hat{\delta}'A\hat{\delta}/ks_B^2$, the usual F-statistic with $\hat{\delta} = \hat{\beta}_1 - \hat{\beta}_2$, $A = V'V$, with $V = Z - XP$, where $Z' = (0' \vdots X_2')$, $X' = (X_1' \vdots X_2')$, and $P = (X'X)^{-1}X'Z$, and $\nu_B s_B^2 = (y_1 - X_1\hat{\beta}_1)'(y_1 - X_1\hat{\beta}_1) + (y_2 - X_2\hat{\beta}_2)'(y_2 - X_2\hat{\beta}_2)$, the sum of squared least squares residuals under H_B.

It is seen that (4.23) is in the form of the second line of (4.9) and thus table 5 can be utilized to obtain values of K_{AB} associated with particular values of F_{k,ν_B}, k, and ν_B given that one takes $\nu_B = \nu_2$ in using the table. Additional odds ratios pertaining to other pairs of hypotheses, for example, H_C versus H_D have been derived.

In connection with (4.23), and other posterior odds ratios in this form, for given k and ν_B, K_{AB} is a monotonic function of F_{k,ν_B}. This fact makes it easy to obtain the cumulative sampling distribution of K_{AB} under the null hypothesis $H_A: \beta_1 = \beta_2$ and $\sigma_1 = \sigma_2$. That is, under the null hypothesis, F_{k,ν_B} has a well-known sampling distribution which permits evaluation of $Pr(c_1 < F_{k,\nu_B} < c_2)$ with c_1 and c_2 given positive constants. Let b_1 and b_2 be the values of K_{AB} associated with $F_{k,\nu_B} = c_1$ and $F_{k,\nu_B} = c_2$, respectively. Then $Pr(b_2 < K_{AB} < b_1) = Pr(c_1 < F_{k,\nu_B} < c_2)$, and probability statements can be made regarding the sampling properties of K_{AB} by use of the cumulative F-distribution with k and ν_B degrees of freedom. Further, any test procedure in the form reject H_A if $F_{k,\nu_B} > F_c$, where F_c is a critical value, is equivalent to reject H_A if $K_{AB} < K_c$, where K_c is the value of K_{AB} associated with $F_{k,\nu_B} = F_c$. Thus any "optimal" sampling properties of such F-tests will be enjoyed by use of the posterior odds ratio K_{AB} in the way described above. However, as pointed out above, the sampling theory rationalization of testing procedures has some controversial aspects and is not needed to justify the computation of posterior odds ratios for a given sample of data. For a given sample of data, the inductive probability calculus, in particular Bayes's theorem, provides a justification for computing logically consistent posterior probabilities and odds ratios.

5 Concluding Remarks

In what has been presented, some Bayesian results for comparing and testing both sharp and nonsharp hypotheses have been reviewed. Bayesian posterior odds ratios have been derived for a number of hypotheses encountered in econometrics and other sciences. Their use permits investigators to incorporate prior information formally and flexibly in appraising alternative hypotheses. Moreover, if an explicit loss structure is available, it is well known that it is possible to use posterior probabilities to choose among alternative hypotheses in such a way as to minimize posterior expected loss and average risk. Further, as has been pointed out in the literature, posterior probabilities can be employed to obtain Bayesian pretest estimates and combined predictions from alternative models.[13] In addition, several optimal sampling properties associated with use of posterior odds ratios in testing have been mentioned.

As regards sampling theory test procedures, some controversial points regarding their use and justification have been reviewed. In particular, Jeffreys's critiques of the use of *P*-values and sampling theory power functions were presented. It is thought that these issues merit further consideration by sampling theorists and others.

The results of the survey of testing procedures in use, presented in section 2, revealed that there is much room for improvement in analyzing alternative hypotheses in applied studies. Further development and use of posterior odds ratios will be helpful in producing improved analyses of alternative hypotheses and models in econometrics and other sciences.

References

Aitken, M. A. (1974). "Simultaneous Inference and the Choice of Variable Subsets in Multiple Regression." *Technometrics*, 16:221–27.

Berndt, E. R., and N. E. Savin (1977). "Conflict among Criteria for Testing Hypotheses in the Multivariate Linear Regression Model." *Econometrica*, 45:1263–77.

Blackwell, D., and M. A. Girshick (1954). *Theory of Games and Statistical Decisions*. New York: John Wiley & Sons.

Blattberg, R. C., and N. J. Gonedes (1974). "A Comparison of the Stable and Student Distributions as Statistical Models for Stock Prices." *Journal of Business*, 47:244–80.

13. See, e.g., Geisel (1970, 1973), Griffiths and Dao (1980), Zellner (1979), and Zellner and Vandaele (1975).

Box, G. E. P., and W. J. Hill (1967). "Discrimination among Mechanistic Models." *Technometrics*, 9:57–71.

Chernoff, H., and L. E. Moses (1959). *Elementary Decision Theory*. New York: John Wiley & Sons.

Chow, G. C. (1960). "Tests of Equality between Sets of Coefficients in Two Linear Regressions." *Econometrica*, 28:591–605.

Davis, W. M. (1978). "Bayesian Analysis of the Linear Model Subject to Linear Inequality Constraints." *Journal of the American Statistical Association*, 73:573–79.

DeGroot, M. H. (1970). *Optimal Statistical Decisions*. New York: McGraw-Hill Book Co.

Dickey, J. M. (1971). "The Weighted Likelihood Ratio, Linear Hypotheses on Normal Location Parameters." *Annals of Mathematical Statistics*, 42:204–23.

———. (1975). "Bayesian Alternatives to the *F*-test and Least-Squares Estimates in the Normal Linear Model." In S. E. Fienberg and A. Zellner, eds., *Studies in Bayesian Econometrics and Statistics in Honor of Leonard J. Savage*, pp. 515–54. Amsterdam: North-Holland Publishing Co.

———. (1977). "Is the Tail Area Useful as an Approximate Bayes Factor?" *Journal of the American Statistical Association*, 72:138–42.

———. (1980). "Approximate Coherence for Regression Model Inference with a New Analysis of Fisher's Broadbalk Wheatfield Example." In A. Zellner, ed., *Bayesian Analysis in Econometrics and Statistics: Essays in Honor of Harold Jeffreys*, pp. 333–54. Amsterdam: North-Holland Publishing Co.

Draper, N. R., and H. Smith (1966). *Applied Regression Analysis*. New York: John Wiley & Sons.

Dyer, A. R. (1972). "A Comparison of Classification and Hypothesis Testing Procedures for Separate Families of Hypotheses." Ph.D. diss., Department of Statistics, University of Chicago.

———. (1973). "Discrimination Procedures for Separate Families of Hypotheses." *Journal of the American Statistical Association*, 68:970–74.

Fomby, T. B., and D. K. Guilkey (1978). "On Choosing the Optimal Level of Significance for the Durbin-Watson Test and the Bayesian Alternative." *Journal of Econometrics*, 8:203–13.

Gaver, K. M., and M. S. Geisel (1974). "Discriminating among Alternative Models: Bayesian and Non-Bayesian Methods." In P. Zarembka, ed., *Frontiers of Econometrics*, pp. 49–77. New York: Academic Press.

Geisel, M. S. (1970). "Comparing and Choosing among Parametric Statistical Models: A Bayesian Analysis with Macroeconomic Applications." Ph.D. diss., Graduate School of Business, University of Chicago.

———. (1973). "Bayesian Comparisons of Simple Macroeconomic Models." *Journal of Money, Credit and Banking*, 5:751–72. Reprinted in S. E. Fienberg and A. Zellner, eds., *Studies in Bayesian Econometrics and Statistics in Honor of Leonard J. Savage*, pp. 227–56. Amsterdam: North-Holland Publishing Co., 1975.

Geisser, S., and W. F. Eddy (1979). "A Predictive Approach to Model Selection." *Journal of the American Statistical Association*, 74:153–60.

Goldfeld, S. M., and R. E. Quandt (1965). "Some Tests for Homoscedasticity." *Journal of the American Statistical Association*, 60:539–47.

Good, I. J. (1950). *Probability and the Weighing of Evidence*. New York: Hafner Publishing Co.

———. (1965). *The Estimation of Probabilities*. Research Monograph no. 30. Cambridge, Mass.: MIT Press.

———. (1980). Comment presented at the International Meeting on Bayesian Statistics, Valencia, Spain, May 28–June 2, 1979. In J. M. Bernardo, M. H. DeGroot, D. V. Lindley, and A. F. M. Smith, eds., *Bayesian Statistics: Proceedings of the First International Meeting Held in Valencia (Spain), May 28 to June 2, 1979*, pp. 636–37. Valencia, Spain: University Press.

Griffiths, W., and D. Dao (1980). "A Note on a Bayesian Estimator in an Autocorrelated Error Model." *Journal of Econometrics*, 12: 389–92.

Jaynes, E. T. (1976). "Confidence Intervals Vs. Bayesian Intervals." In W. L. Harper and C. A. Hooker, eds., *Foundations of Probability Theory, Statistical Inference, and Statistical Theories*, pp. 175–213, followed by discussion. Dordrecht, Holland: D. Reidel Publishing Co.

———. (1980). Comment presented at the International Meeting on Bayesian Statistics, Valencia, Spain, May 28–June 2, 1979. In J. M. Bernardo, M. H. DeGroot, D. V. Lindley, and A. F. M. Smith, eds., *Bayesian Statistics: Proceedings of the First International Meeting Held in Valencia (Spain), May 28 to June 2, 1979*, pp. 618–29. Valencia, Spain: University Press.

Jeffreys, H. (1957). *Scientific Inference*. 2d ed.; 1st ed. 1931, Cambridge, England: University Press.

———. (1963). "Review of L. J. Savage et al., *The Foundations of Statistical Inference (1962)*." *Technometrics*, 5:407–10.

———. (1967). *Theory of Probability*. 3d rev. ed.; 1st ed. 1939. London: Oxford University Press.

———. (1979). Personal communication to author.

———. (1980). "Some General Points in Probability Theory." In A. Zellner, ed., *Bayesian Analysis in Econometrics and Statistics: Essays in Honor of Harold Jeffreys*, pp. 451–53. Amsterdam: North-Holland Publishing Co.

Leamer, E. E. (1978). *Specification Searches: Ad Hoc Inference with Nonexperimental Data*. New York: John Wiley & Sons.

Lempers, F. B. (1971). *Posterior Probabilities of Alternative Linear Models*. Rotterdam: University of Rotterdam Press.

Lindley, D. V. (1957). "A Statistical Paradox." *Biometrika*, 44:187–92. See also M. S. Bartlett's comment on Lindley's paper in *Biometrika*, 44:533–34.

———. (1961). "The Use of Prior Probability Distributions in Statistical Inference and Decision." In J. Neyman, ed., *Proceedings of the Fourth Berkeley Symposium on Mathematical Statistics and Probability*, 1:453–68. Berkeley: University of California Press.

Mayer, F. (1979). "Sur l'Utilisation du critere de decision MELO dans le choix d'un seuil de signification optimal." Department of Economics, University of Montreal.

Raiffa, H., and R. Schlaifer (1961). *Applied Statistical Decision Theory*. Boston: Graduate School of Business Administration, Harvard University.

Rényi, A. (1970). *Foundations of Probability*. San Francisco: Holden-Day.

Reynolds, R. A. (1982). "Posterior Odds for the Hypothesis of Independence between Stochastic Regressors and Disturbances." *International Economic Review*, 23:479–90.

Savin, N. E. (1976). "Conflict among Testing Procedures in a Linear Regression Model with Autoregressive Disturbances." *Econometrica*, 40:1303–15.

Schwarz, G. (1978). "Estimating the Dimension of a Model." *Annals of Statistics*, 6: 461–64.

Silvey, S. D. (1970). *Statistical Inference*. Baltimore: Penguin Books.

Smith, A. F. M., and D. J. Spiegelhalter (1980). "Bayes Factors and Choice Criteria for Linear Models." *Journal of the Royal Statistical Society*, Ser. B, 42: 213–20.

Thornber, E. H. (1966). "Applications of Decision Theory to Econometrics." Ph.D. diss., Department of Economics, University of Chicago.

Whittle, P. (1951). *Hypothesis Testing in Time Series Analysis*. Uppsala: Almqvist and Wiksells Boktryckeri AB.

Zellner, A. (1971). *An Introduction to Bayesian Inference in Econometrics*. New York: John Wiley & Sons.

———. (1976). "Bayesian and Non-Bayesian Analysis of the Regression Model with Multivariate Student-*t* Errors." *Journal of the American Statistical Association*, 71:400–405.

———. (1978). "Jeffreys-Bayes Posterior Odds Ratio and the Akaike Information Criterion for Discriminating between Models." *Economics Letters*, 1:337–42.

———. (1979). "Statistical Analysis of Econometric Models." *Journal of the American Statistical Association*, 74:628–43, followed by discussion.

Zellner, A., and M. S. Geisel (1970). "Analysis of Distributed Lag Models with Applications to Consumption Function Estimation." *Econometrica*, 38:865–88.

Zellner, A., and J. F. Richard (1973). "Use of Prior Information in the Analysis and Estimation of Cobb-Douglas Production Function Models." *International Economic Review*, 14:107–19.

Zellner, A., and A. Siow (1978). "Uses of Posterior Odds Ratios in Econometrics with Applications to Hypotheses in Regression Analysis." Paper presented at the 16th meeting of the NBER-NSF Seminar on Bayesian Inference in Econometrics, University of Chicago, June 2–3, 1978; see A. Zellner, ed., *Reports of the NBER-NSF Seminar on Bayesian Inference in Econometrics*, pp. 227–28. H. G. B. Alexander Research Foundation, Graduate School of Business, University of Chicago, 1979.

———. (1979). "On Posterior Odds Ratios for Sharp Null Hypotheses and One-Sided Alternatives." H. G. B. Alexander Research Foundation, Graduate School of Business, University of Chicago.

———. (1980). "Posterior Odds Ratios for Selected Regression Hypotheses." Paper presented at the International Meeting on Bayesian Statistics, Valencia, Spain, May 28–June 2, 1979. In J. M. Bernardo, M. H. DeGroot, D. V. Lindley, and A. F. M. Smith, eds. *Bayesian Statistics: Proceedings of the First International Meeting Held in Valencia (Spain), May 28 to June 2, 1979*, pp. 585–603. Valencia, Spain: University Press.

Zellner, A., and W. H. Vandaele (1975). "Bayes-Stein Estimators for *k*-Means, Regression, and Simultaneous Equation Models." In S. E. Fienberg and A. Zellner, eds., *Studies in Bayesian Econometrics and Statistics in Honor of Leonard J. Savage*, pp. 627–53. Amsterdam: North-Holland Publishing Co.

Zellner, A., and A. Williams (1973). "Bayesian Analysis of the Federal Reserve–MIT–Penn Model's Almon Lag Consumption Function." *Journal of Econometrics*, 1:267–99.

Zidek, J. V. (1969). "A Representation of Bayes Invariant Procedures in Terms of Haar Measure." *Annals of the Institute of Statistical Mathematics*, 21:291–308.

3.8 The Current State of Bayesian Econometrics

1 Introduction

Since the word "econometrics" may be unfamiliar to some statisticians, I believe that a definition of it may be helpful. Econometrics is the field of study in which economic theory, statistical methods, and economic data are combined in the investigation of economic problems. Some of the problems considered and analyzed in econometrics include: measurement and forecasting problems; formulation and testing of economic theories that enhance understanding of economic behavior and provide a basis for prediction; decision and control problems of individuals, households, firms, unions, governments, and other economic agents; and design and execution of surveys and experiments involving humans and/or animals to shed light on scientific and practical policy problems.

As is evident from this listing of problems in econometrics, many of them have important statistical components. That is, statistical procedures are employed to help solve model selection, testing, parameter estimation, prediction, decision, control, and design problems that arise in econometrics. Since Bayesian techniques are available for analyzing most, if not all, of these problems, it is of interest to consider the current state of Bayesian analysis in econometrics.

Given that the present is just a point in time between the past and the future, it is fruitful to consider the past in order to obtain appropriate perspective with respect to the present and future. Thus, in section 2, I shall try to summarize the role of Bayesian analysis in econometrics in the early 1960s, when work in modern Bayesian econometrics commenced. Section 3 is devoted to my observations on the current state of Bayesian analysis in econometrics, and section 4 to factors in its growth, while in section 5, I briefly consider prospects for the future.

Invited address presented at the Canadian Conference on Applied Statistics, Concordia University, Montreal, April 29–May 1, 1981, and reprinted from *Topics in Applied Statistics*, T. D. Dwivedi, ed. (New York: Marcel Dekker, 1983), by courtesy of Marcel Dekker, Inc.

2 Econometrics and Bayesian Analysis in the Early 1960s

In the early 1960s, there was practically no formal Bayesian analysis in econometrics. Econometrics textbooks and Cowles Commission Monograph numbers 10 and 14, two key contributions to econometric methodology, made almost no mention of Bayesian techniques. As far as I know, courses in econometrics did not consider Bayesian analysis. The leading quantitative economic journals published few, if any, articles on the development and application of Bayesian analysis. There was very little Bayesian econometric research.

Perhaps the extremely low or practically nonexistent level of activity in Bayesian econometrics in the early 1960s reflected a similarly low level of activity in Bayesian statistics in the 1940s and 1950s, when many econometricians of the early 1960s were trained. Also, it is highly probable that the impact of well-known anti-Bayesian views of some prominent statisticians and the negative pronouncements on Bayesianism in some leading statistics textbooks spilled over to affect econometricians' views. In addition, the Fisher and Neyman-Pearson systems of inference had a great influence in econometrics. Maximum likelihood estimation, Neyman-Pearson testing and general sampling theory principles dominated the econometrics textbooks and courses of the period. The early Bayesian statistical research of the economist and statistician F. Y. Edgeworth,[1] which was prominent in the opening decades of this century, was apparently forgotten by econometricians in the early 1960s.

What gave rise to the early work in Bayesian econometrics in the early 1960s? While it is difficult to answer this question precisely, I believe that the following factors played a role. First, L. J. Savage's book *The Foundations of Statistics* (1954), his other writings, and his interactions with economists certainly were influential. In particular, Savage's friendship with the economist and statistician Milton Friedman and their important joint papers, "The Utility Analysis of Choices Involving Risk" (1948) and the "The Expected-Utility Hypothesis and the Measurability of Utility" (1952), helped to introduce Bayesian ideas and principles to economists and econometricians.[2] Second, the publication in 1961 of *Applied Statistical Decision Theory* by H. Raiffa and R. Schlaifer had a substantial impact on some researchers in econometrics and many more in business statistics. Third, the work of H. Jeffreys, particularly his books *Theory of Probability* and *Scientific Inference*, was a key factor in spurring the interest of some

1. See, e.g., Bowley (1928) and Stigler (1978).

2. These articles are reprinted in *The Writings of Leonard Jimmie Savage: A Memorial Selection* (Washington, D.C.: American Statistical Association, 1981).

econometricians in Bayesian analysis. Fourth, the 1962 paper "Likelihood Inference and Time Series," by G. A. Barnard, G. M. Jenkins, and C. B. Winsten, which emphasized exact "weighted" likelihood inferences in time series analysis suggested to some that these weighting functions could be interpreted as prior distributions and thus exact Bayesian inferences for time series problems could be made. Finally, the early Bayesian research of the statisticians I. J. Good, D. V. Lindley, G. E. P. Box, S. Geisser, G. C. Tiao, and others influenced some econometricians.

These then are some of the influences that played a role in connection with early contributions to Bayesian econometrics, namely, Drèze (1962), Fisher (1962), Rothenberg (1963), Ando and Kaufman (1964), Tiao and Zellner (1964), and Zellner and Tiao (1964), and possibly also, in unusual attempts to utilize subjective prior information in a frequentist framework, Goldberger and Theil (1961) and Theil (1962).

In summary, in the early 1960s there was very little Bayesian analysis in econometrics. The early works, cited above, constituted a beginning of modern research on Bayesian analysis in econometrics that has been increasing in volume. Some of the research following the early 1960s is reported in Zellner (1971), Fienberg and Zellner (1975), Leamer (1978) and Zellner (1980*b*). In these works many central statistical problems of econometrics are analyzed from the Bayesian point of view and some examples of Bayesian analysis in decision-making and economic theory are presented. To an important degree, interaction between statisticians and econometricians has been a key element in the history of Bayesian analysis in econometrics. Since 1970, such interaction has been a distinguishing feature of semiannual meetings of thc NBER-NSF Seminar on Bayesian Inference in Econometrics.

3 The Current State of Bayesian Analysis in Econometrics

Bayesian econometrics in the early 1980s is very different from its practically nonexistent state in the early 1960s. Just as is the case with many present statistics texts, almost all recent and current econometrics textbooks include sections on Bayesian analysis. In addition, a number of universities have instituted specialized courses in Bayesian econometrics and statistics. The teaching of Bayesian decision theory and statistics in business schools is widespread. Some instructors devote special sections of their general econometrics courses to Bayesian topics. While the Bayesian approach has not as yet "swept the field," it is accurate to state that a Bayesian component of growing importance is present in econometrics textbooks and teaching.

As regards research in Bayesian econometrics, work is currently being pursued on methods, applications, and computer programs. With respect to

methods, Bayesian research has been focused on producing improved analyses of univariate and multivariate statistical models employed in econometrics; see Drèze (1972), Fienberg and Zellner (1975), Rothenberg (1975*b*), Leamer (1978), Zellner (1971, 1979*a*, 1980*b*), and Zellner and Vandaele (1975) for a review of results and references to the literature. With respect to estimation, Bayesian research has shown that many sampling theory estimates in use in econometrics can be produced by Bayesian methods. That is, many sampling theory estimates are often equivalent to means, modes, or conditional means of posterior distributions based on diffuse prior distributions. Of course, means of conditional posterior distributions are not optimal and can differ markedly from means of marginal posterior distributions. In Zellner (1978) and Zellner and Park (1979), it is shown that a Bayesian estimate of coefficients of a linear structural econometric model that is optimal relative to a generalized quadratic loss function is a member of the $\mathcal{K}$-class with a value of $\mathcal{K}$ less than one in finite samples. While point estimation has been emphasized, or overemphasized, in the literature, many have come to appreciate the fact that the Bayesian approach provides complete, finite-sample posterior distributions of models' parameters as well as optimal estimates. These results have been important in enhancing understanding of the relationship of Bayesian and non-Bayesian estimation results.

Currently, much Bayesian research is focused on the formulation of informative prior distributions and study of the impact of their use on estimation results; see, for example, Leamer (1978) and Swamy (1980). Just as "reference" diffuse prior distributions have been found to be useful, it is probable that the development of operational and convenient "reference" informative prior distributions for use with standard statistical models will be found useful; see, for example, Zellner (1980*a*).

Bayesian research on testing problems has been pursued by a number of researchers. This work includes analyses of model selection problems in the work of Thornber (1966), Geisel (1970, 1975), Gaver and Geisel (1974), Leamer (1978), Lempers (1971), Poirier and Klepper (1981), Zellner (1971), and others. Reynolds (1982) has derived posterior odds ratios for the hypotheses of independence and dependence of stochastic regressors and error terms, the Bayesian analogue of the Wu-Hausman tests for exogeneity. Posterior odds ratios for linear hypotheses in multiple regression models have been derived and studied by Mayer (1980), Leamer (1978), Zellner and Siow (1980), and Zellner (1979*b*) and in multivariate regression models by Rossi (1980).

This work on Bayesian posterior odds ratios has been very useful in showing the relations between Bayesian and non-Bayesian testing approaches, much in the spirit of earlier work by Jeffreys (1967) and Lindley (1957). In a number of cases, Bayesian posterior odds ratios have been found to be monotonic functions of usual sampling theory test statistics' values and of tail areas or "*P*-values." In such cases, it is relatively easy to see what the use of a particular critical value for a test statistic in a non-Bayesian framework implies in terms of a "critical" value for a posterior odds ratio. These interpretations of Bayesian and non-Bayesian results, including their relative sampling properties, have been of great interest to general econometricians.

On other econometric problems, Prescott (1971), Harkema (1975) and Bowman and Laporte (1975) have compared Bayesian and non-Bayesian solutions to several economic control problems and found that Bayesian solutions are superior. Bawa, Brown, and Klein (1979) have developed Bayesian methods for analyzing portfolio problems. The statisticians Abrahams and Dempster (1979) and Hillmer and Tiao (1980) have reported work on Bayesian approaches to seasonal analysis; also Akaike and his colleagues have developed a Bayesian approach and computer program for seasonal adjustment. Ohtani (1981) has developed Bayesian estimation techniques for the switching regression model with autocorrelated errors and Dagenais (1975) has analyzed missing observation problems in regression. With respect to forecasting, Litterman (1980) has developed and applied an innovative Bayesian vector autoregression approach for forecasting important macroeconomic variables such as GNP, unemployment, and the like. In this work, he employs a rather ingenious informative prior distribution. Earlier, Chow (1973) derived optimal multiple-step-ahead forecasts for a multivariate autoregressive model with a diffuse prior distribution and Richard (1973) has studied predictive densities for structural econometric models.

The works cited above are just a part of the work that is being pursued on Bayesian methods in econometrics. In addition, there has been a growing number of applications of Bayesian methods in econometrics although progress in this area has been slower than in work on methods. Some works in the area of Bayesian applications include Geisel (1970, 1975), who used posterior odds ratios to compare the performance of simple Keynesian and quantity theory models. Peck (1974) utilized Bayesian estimation techniques in analyzing investment behavior of firms in the electric utility industry. Varian (1975) developed and applied Bayesian methods for real estate tax assessment problems. Flood and Garber (1980*a*, *b*) applied Bayesian methods in their study of monetary reforms using data from the German and several other hyperinflations. Evans (1978) employed posterior odds ratios in a study to determine which of several models best explains the data from the German hyperinflation. Shiller (1973), Zellner and Geisel (1970), and Zellner and Williams (1973) used Bayesian analysis in the study of time series models for U.S. investment and personal consumption expenditures. Production function models have been analyzed from the Bayesian point of view in Sankar (1969), Zellner and Richard (1973), and Rossi (1980). Tsurumi (1976) and Tsurumi and Tsurumi (1981) analyzed structural change problems employing Bayesian techniques. Reynolds (1980) used Bayesian estimation and testing techniques in an analysis of extensive survey data relating to health status, income, and other variables. As mentioned above, Litterman (1980) has developed a Bayesian vector autoregressive model that he is employing to generate quarterly forecasts of major economic variables for the U.S. with results that compare very favorably with those of alternative forecasting procedures. In an interesting paper Merton (1980) utilized Bayesian techniques in a study of the market rate of return.

In economic theory there has been considerable work that utilizes the Bayesian learning model; see, for example, DeGroot and Cyert (1975), Grossman (1975), Holt (1977), Milgrom (1978), and papers in Fienberg and Zellner (1975) and Zellner (1980*b*) for works in this area and references to this substantial literature.

This partial listing of some recent Bayesian econometric research indicates that the volume of such work has grown considerably since the early 1960s. There is now a fairly substantial number of econometricians who are familiar with the Bayesian approach and a much larger number of researchers in Bayesian econometrics than in the early 1960s. A brief review of factors possibly explaining this upswing in Bayesian econometric activity will now be reviewed.

4 Major Factors in the Growth of Bayesian Analysis in Econometrics

The following seem to me to be some of the factors accounting for the burst of activity in the area of Bayesian econometrics since the 1960s:

1. The contributions to Bayesian statistics by Jeffreys, Savage, de Finetti, Good, Lindley, Box, Geisser, Hill, Tiao, Dempster, Blackwell, DeGroot, Kadane, Pratt, Raiffa, Schlaifer, Press, and others had a continuing and growing influence in promoting Bayesian econometric research. Key contributions, in addition to those mentioned above, are Lindley (1965, 1971), DeGroot (1970), and Box and Tiao (1973).

2. The often emphasized sophisticated simplicity and unity of the Bayesian approach to inference and decision problems has come to be appreciated by a growing number of econometricians.

3. Comparative Bayesian and non-Bayesian analyses of estimation, testing, decision, and control problems have yielded results in the main favor-

able to the Bayesian approach. Both analytical and Monte Carlo experimental studies have shown that Bayesian estimation and testing techniques have very good sampling properties. In all Monte Carlo studies, Bayesian estimators have performed as well or better than non-Bayesian estimators; see, for example, Thornber (1967), Chetty (1966), Zellner (1971), Fomby and Guilkey (1978), Lee, Judge, and Zellner (1977), and Park (1982). As mentioned earlier, in comparative analyses of control problems, Bayesian results were found superior to non-Bayesian results. A growing number of econometricians have come to be impressed by these results.

4. There has been a considerable increase in the number of Bayesian courses and publications, and this increase has had a stimulating effect on the number of Bayesian researchers and the volume of Bayesian research in econometrics.

5. In recent years there has been progress in developing Bayesian computer programs; see Press (1980) for a listing and description of a number of Bayesian computer programs. This work is in its early stages and further progress can be expected.

6. Perhaps most fundamentally, there has been a growing awareness among econometricians that prior information plays an important role in econometric analyses and that the Bayesian approach provides formal, operational procedures for incorporating such information in analyses.

With respect to this last point, in many situations in econometrics data are limited and thus prior information plays an extremely important role; see Swamy (1980) for analysis of an extreme case. For example, consider a vector autoregressive model for a $p \times 1$ vector of variables, z_t, $z_t = A_1 z_{t-1} +$ $1\ A_2 z_{t-2} + \cdots + A_q z_{t-q} + \epsilon_t$, $t = 1, 2, \ldots, T$, where the A's are $p \times p$ matrices of coefficients and ϵ_t is a zero-mean, white noise error vector with $p \times p$ covariance matrix Σ. This system contains $qp^2 + p(p + 1)/2$ free parameters. For a "small" system in which $p = 6$ and $q = 10$, there are 381 free parameters. If twenty years of quarterly data are available, $T = 80$ and the total number of observations is $pT = 6 \times 80 = 480$. Thus, the observation-parameter ratio, 480/381 is abysmally low. To cope with such problems, strong prior information is frequently employed that involves setting coefficients and/or elements of Σ equal to zero. In the Bayesian approach, prior information can be represented more flexibly and utilized in obtaining estimates and predictions as in the work of Litterman (1980). Similar considerations apply to more complicated, structural econometric time series models in which many restrictions associated with the assumption that some of the variables in z_t are exogenous and those needed for parameter identification are often introduced quite casually. Such prior information requires careful treatment in order to obtain satisfactory results.

Similarly, in work with unobservable random components or random parameter models, prior information plays a critical role. Let y denote the sample information and θ the random components and/or parameters. Then the joint distribution, $p(y,\theta) = f(y \mid \theta)\, g(\theta)$ is the model. It has two components, $f(y \mid \theta)$, the conditional density of the observations given θ, and the marginal distribution, $g(\theta)$. The likelihood function $h(y \mid \cdot) = \int f(y \mid \theta)\, g(\theta)\, d\theta$ clearly depends on how both $f(y \mid \theta)$ and $g(\theta)$ are formulated. That considerable prior information is employed in this connection has been recognized by many. Such considerations are extremely important in use of random coefficient regression models where the form of $g(\theta)$ must be very carefully specified and is very close to being part of a prior distribution. Also in seasonal analysis work, it is often assumed that $y_t = T_t + S_t + N_t$, where T_t, S_t, and N_t are random trend-cycle, seasonal and noise components, respectively. Often T_t and S_t are carelessly assumed to be independent and processes are hypothesized for T_t and S_t with very little subject matter justification. Clearly, inappropriate assumptions can vitally affect seasonal analyses and adjustment procedures. In these cases, and many more, careful treatment of prior information is required in order to obtain good results. The Bayesian framework is one in which these problems can be approached most fruitfully.

While the factors mentioned above have been in part responsible for considerable growth in Bayesian econometrics, some limiting factors must be noted to round out the picture. They are:

1. More convenient and effective methods for assessing prior distributions for use in Bayesian econometrics are needed. Work by Winkler (1977), Kadane (1980), Zellner (1972), and others is helping to overcome this range of problems for regression models. Perhaps the concept and development of reference informative prior distributions will be helpful too; see Zellner (1980*a*) for an example.

2. Since many econometric models tend to be complicated (too complicated in my opinion) and involve many parameters, formulating appropriate prior distributions for them has been difficult. In this regard, it should be noted that non-Bayesians have difficulty in determining what are "reasonable" estimation results. Formalizing the concept of "reasonableness" in this context is very similar to formulating a prior distribution. Perhaps what is needed in this area is a clever use of prior information (or economic theory) to simplify these complicated models.

3. While some Bayesian computer programs have been developed in recent years (see Press 1980), there is a need for more work in this area. The work of Kloek and van Dijk (1980), Stewart (1977), and Friedman and Wright (1980) on Monte Carlo numerical multivariate integration has not as yet been integrated into Bayesian econometric computer packages. This

work is important in terms of permitting more flexibility in the choice of prior distributions and models for observations.

4. More work remains to be done on the Bayesian analysis of nonnormal and nonlinear models, models for mixtures of continuous and discrete random variables and models for time series data. Of course, Bayesians can rely on large-sample results just as non-Bayesians do, and indeed the work of Heyde and Johnstone (1979) suggests that Bayesian large-sample or asymptotic results for stochastic processes are simpler and more robust than non-Bayesian asymptotic results. However, a real challenge is to produce useful and operational finite-sample posterior distributions and predictive density functions for such models.

5. Most important, further work on Bayesian procedures for diagnostic checking of models is required. Previous Bayesian work on analyses of autocorrelation, heteroscedasticity and other departures from standard conditions has to be extended to other kinds of departures and incorporated in Bayesian computer programs.

Further Bayesian research to lessen the effects of these limiting factors will be important in enhancing the effectiveness of the Bayesian approach in econometrics.

5 Conclusions and Prospects for the Future

From what has been presented, it is apparent that Bayesian analysis in econometrics is now much more important than it was in the early 1960s. Several possible reasons for this change have been reviewed. Basically, the progress of Bayesian econometrics is closely linked to the quality of the results it produces in practice, a pragmatic dictum that is weighted heavily by most econometricians. So far, Bayesian results appear to be satisfactory according to this criterion. The probable accumulation of further results of this kind and the removal of the limiting factors, mentioned above, will contribute to the further growth of Bayesian econometrics.

In closing, I believe that there are strong similarities between the roles of Bayesian analysis in econometrics and Bayesian analysis in statistics. At the twenty-first meeting of the NBER-NSF Seminar on Bayesian Inference in Econometrics, I. J. Good (1980) described his bet with Bartlett in his prepared address as follows: "In about 1946 I had a long argument about Bayesian Statistics with Maurice Bartlett in the Faculty Lounge at Manchester University. At the end of our argument Bartlett proposed the bet or test of waiting for a hundred years to see which was dominant, a classical or a neo-Bayesian one. After a third of a century I think Bartlett is losing the bet." I agree with Good's conclusion and believe that it also applies to the future state of Bayesian analysis in econometrics.

References

Abrahams, D. M. and A. P. Dempster (1979). "Research on Seasonal Analysis." Department of Statistics, Harvard University, Cambridge, Mass.

Ando, A., and G. Kaufman (1964). "Bayesian Analysis of Reduced Form Systems." MIT, Cambridge, Mass.

Barnard, G. A., G. M. Jenkins, and C. B. Winsten (1962). "Likelihood Inference and Time Series." *Journal of the Royal Statistical Society*, Ser. A, 125:321–72.

Bawa, V. S., S. J. Brown, and R. W. Klein (1979). *Estimation Risk and Optimal Portfolio Choice*. Amsterdam: North-Holland Publishing Co.

Bowley, A. L. (1928). *F. Y. Edgeworth's Contributions to Mathematical Statistics*. London: Royal Statistical Society. Reprinted in 1972 by Augustus M. Kelley Publishers, Clifton, N.J.

Bowman, H. W., and A. M. Laporte (1975). "Stochastic Optimization in Recursive Equation Systems with Random Parameters with an Application to Control of the Money Supply." In S. E. Fienberg and A. Zellner, eds., *Studies in Bayesian Econometrics and Statistics in Honor of Leonard J. Savage*, pp. 441–62. Amsterdam: North-Holland Publishing Co.

Box, G. E. P., and G. C. Tiao (1973). *Bayesian Inference in Statistical Analysis*. Reading, Mass.: Addison-Wesley.

Chetty, V. K. (1966). "Bayesian Analysis of Some Simultaneous Equation Models and Specification Errors." Ph.D. diss., Department of Economics, University of Wisconsin, Madison, Wis.

Chow, G. (1973). "Multiperiod Predictions from Stochastic Difference Equations by Bayesian Methods." *Econometrica*, 41: 109–18.

Dagenais, M. (1975). "Multiple Regression Analysis with Incomplete Observations from a Bayesian Viewpoint." In S. E. Fienberg and A. Zellner, eds., *Studies in Bayesian Econometrics and Statistics: Essays in Honor of Leonard J. Savage*, pp. 259–72. Amsterdam: North-Holland Publishing Co.

DeGroot, M. H. (1970). *Optimal Statistical Decisions*. New York: McGraw-Hill Book Co.

DeGroot, M. H., and R. Cyert (1975). "Bayesian Analysis and Duopoly Theory." In S. E. Fienberg and A. Zellner, eds., *Studies in Bayesian Econometrics and Statistics in Honor of Leonard J. Savage*, pp. 79–97. Amsterdam: North-Holland Publishing Co.

Drèze, J. H. (1962). "The Bayesian Approach to Simultaneous Equations Systems." ONR Research Monograph no. 67, Technological Research Institute, Northwestern University.

———. (1972). "Econometrics and Decision Theory." *Econometrica*, 40:1–17.

Evans, P. (1978). "Time Series Analysis of the German Hyperinflation." *International Economic Review*, 19:195–209.

Fienberg, S. E., and A. Zellner, eds. (1975). *Studies in Bayesian Econometrics and Statistics in Honor of Leonard J. Savage*. Amsterdam: North-Holland Publishing Co.

Fisher, W. D. (1962). "Estimation in the Linear Decision Model." *International Economic Review*, 3:1–29.

Flood, R., and P. Garber (1980*a*). "An Economic Theory of Monetary Reform." *Journal of Political Economy*, 88:24–58.

———. (1980*b*). "Process Consistency and Monetary Reform: Further Evidence and Implications." Department of Economics, University of Rochester and University of Virginia.

Fomby, T. B., and D. K. Guilkey (1978). "On Choosing the Optimal Level of Significance for the Durbin-Watson Test and the Bayesian Alternative." *Journal of Econometrics*, 8:203–13.

Friedman, J. H., and M. H. Wright (1980). "A Nested Partitioning Procedure for Numerical Multiple Integration." Computation Research Group, Linear Accelerator Center, Stanford, Calif.

Gaver, K. M., and M. S. Geisel (1974). "Discriminating among Alternative Models: Bayesian and Non-Bayesian Methods." In P. Zarembka, ed., *Frontiers of Econometrics*, pp. 49–77. New York: Academic Press.

Geisel, M. S. (1970). "Comparing and Choosing among Parametric Statistical Models." Ph.D. diss., Graduate School of Business, University of Chicago.

———. (1975). "Bayesian Comparison of Simple Macroeconomic Models." In S. E. Fienberg and A. Zellner, eds., *Studies in Bayesian Econometrics and Statistics in Honor of Leonard J. Savage*, pp. 227–56. Amsterdam: North-Holland Publishing Co.

Goldberger, A. S., and H. Theil (1961). "On Pure and Mixed Statistical Estimation in Economics." *International Economic Review*, 2:65–78.

Good, I. J. (1980). Invited address, presented at the 21st Meeting of the NBER-NSF Seminar on Bayesian Inference in Econometrics, October 31–November 1, 1980, University of Chicago and included in the report of the meeting.

Grossman, S. (1975). "Rational Expectations and the Econometric Modeling of Markets Subject to Uncertainty: A Bayesian Approach." *Journal of Econometrics*, 3:255–72.

Harkema, R. (1975). "An Analytical Comparison of Certainty Equivalence and Sequential Updating." *Journal of the American Statistical Association*, 70:348–50.

Heyde, C. C., and I. M. Johnstone (1979). "On Asymptotic Posterior Normality for Stochastic Processes." *Journal of the Royal Statistical Society*, Ser. B, 41:184–89.

Hillmer, S. C., and G. C. Tiao (1980). "Smoothing of Time Series from a Bayesian Viewpoint." In A. Zellner, ed., *Bayesian Analysis in Econometrics and Statistics: Essays in Honor of Harold Jeffreys*, pp. 271–80. Amsterdam: North-Holland Publishing Co.

Holt, C. A, (1977). "Bidding for Contracts." In C. A. Holt and R. W. Shore, *Bayesian Analysis in Economic Theory and Time Series Analysis*, pp. 1–82. Amsterdam: North-Holland Publishing Co.

Jeffreys, H. (1967). *Theory of Probability*. 3d rev. ed.; 1st ed. 1939. London: Oxford University Press.

———. (1973). *Scientific Inference*. 3d ed.; 1st ed. 1931. Cambridge: Cambridge University Press.

Kadane, J. B. (1980). "Predictive and Structural Methods for Eliciting Prior Distributions." In A. Zellner, ed., *Bayesian Analysis in Econometrics and Statistics in Honor of Harold Jeffreys*, pp. 89–93. Amsterdam: North-Holland Publishing Co.

Kloek, T., and H. K. van Dijk (1980). "Bayesian Estimates of Equation System Parameters: An Application of Integration by Monte Carlo." In A. Zellner, ed., *Bayesian Analysis in Econometrics and Statistics: Essays in Honor of Harold Jeffreys*, pp. 311–30. Amsterdam: North-Holland Publishing Co.

Leamer, E. E. (1978). *Specification Searches*. New York: John Wiley & Sons.

Lee, T. C., G. G. Judge, and A. Zellner (1977). *Estimating the Parameters of the Markov Probability Model from Aggregate Time Series Data*, 2d ed. Amsterdam: North-Holland Publishing Co.

Lempers, F. B. (1971). *Posterior Probabilities of Alternative Linear Models*. Rotterdam: Rotterdam University Press.

Lindley, D. V. (1957). "A Statistical Paradox." *Biometrika*, 44:187–92.

———. (1965). *Introduction to Probability and Statistics from a Bayesian Viewpoint*. 2 vols. Cambridge: Cambridge University Press.

———. (1971). *Bayesian Statistics: A Review*. Philadelphia: Society for Industrial and Applied Mathematics.

Litterman, R. (1980). "A Bayesian Procedure for Forecasting with Vector Autoregressions." Department of Economics, MIT, Cambridge, Mass.

Mayer, F. (1980). "Specification et choix d'un seuil de signification optimal: Une approche Bayesienne." Ph.D. diss., Department of Economics, University of Montreal.

Merton, R. (1980). "On Estimating the Expected Return on the Market." *Journal of Financial Economics*, 8:323–61.

Milgrom, P. (1978). *The Structure of Information in Competitive Bidding*. New York: Garland Publishing.

Ohtani, K. (1981). "Bayesian Estimation of the Switching Regression Model with Autocorrelated Errors." Working Paper no. 55. Institute of Economic Research, Kobe University of Commerce.

Park, S. B. (1982). "Some Sampling Properties of Minimum Expected Loss (MELO) Estimators of Structural Coefficients." *Journal of Econometrics*, 18:295–311.

Peck, S. C. (1974). "Alternative Investment Models for Firms in the Electric Utilities Industry." *Bell Journal of Economics and Management Science*, 5:420–58.

Poirier, D. J., and S. Klepper (1981). "Model Occurrence and Model Selection in Panel Data Sets." *Journal of Econometrics*, 17:333–50.

Prescott. E. C. (1971). "Adaptive Decision Rules for Macroeconomic Planning." *Western Economic Journal*, 9:369–78.

Press, S. J. (1980). "Bayesian Computer Programs." In A. Zellner, ed., *Bayesian Analysis in Econometrics and Statistics: Essays in Honor of Harold Jeffreys*, pp. 429–42. Amsterdam: North-Holland Publishing Co.

Raiffa, H., and R. Schlaifer (1961). *Applied Statistical Decision Theory*. Boston: Graduate School of Business Administration, Harvard University.

Reynolds, R. A. (1980). "A Study of the Relationship between Health and Income." Ph.D. diss., Department of Economics, University of Chicago.

———. (1982). "Posterior Odds for the Hypothesis of Independence between Stochastic Regressors and Disturbances." *International Economic Review*, 23:479–90.

Richard, J. F. (1973). *Posterior and Predictive Densities for Simultaneous Equation Models*. Berlin: Springer-Verlag.

Rossi, P. E. (1980). "Testing Hypotheses in Multivariate Regression: Bayes vs. Non-Bayes Procedures." H. G. B. Alexander Research Foundation, Graduate School of Business, University of Chicago. Paper presented at Econometric Society Meeting, September 1980, Denver, Colo.

Rothenberg, T. J. (1963). "A Bayesian Analysis of Simultaneous Equation Systems." Econometric Institute, Netherlands School of Economics, Rotterdam.

———. (1975*a*). "The Bayesian Approach and Alternatives in Econometrics." In S. E. Fienberg and A. Zellner, eds., *Studies in Bayesian Econometrics and Statistics in Honor of Leonard J. Savage*, pp. 55–67. Amsterdam: North-Holland Publishing Co.

———. (1975*b*). "Bayesian Analysis of Simultaneous Equations Models."

In S. E. Fienberg and A. Zellner, eds., *Studies in Bayesian Econometrics and Statistics in Honor of Leonard J. Savage*, pp. 405–24. Amsterdam: North-Holland Publishing Co.

Sankar, U. (1969). "Elasticities of Substitution and Returns to Scale in Indian Manufacturing Industries." Ph. D. diss., Department of Economics, University of Wisconsin, Madison.

Shiller, R. J. (1973). "A Distributed Lag Estimator Derived from Smoothness Priors." *Econometrica*, 41:775–88.

Stewart, L. (1977). "Bayesian Analysis Using Monte Carlo Integration." Lockheed Palo Alto Research Laboratory, Palo Alto, Calif.

Stigler, S. M. (1978). "Francis Ysidro Edgeworth, Statistician." *Journal of the Royal Statistical Society*, Ser. A, 141:287–313.

Swamy, P. A. V. B. (1980). "A Comparison of Estimators for Undersized Samples." *Journal of Econometrics*, 14:161–82.

Theil, H. (1962). "On the Use of Incomplete Prior Information in Regression Analysis." *Journal of the American Statistical Association*, 58:401–14.

Thornber, E. H. (1966). "Applications of Decision Theory to Econometrics." Ph.D. diss., Department of Economics, University of Chicago.

———. (1967). "Finite Sample Monte Carlo Studies: An Autoregressive Illustration." *Journal of the American Statistical Association*, 62:801–18.

Tiao, G. C., and A. Zellner (1964). "Bayes' Theorem and the Use of Prior Information in Regression Analysis." *Biometrika*, 51:219–30.

Tsurumi, H. (1976). "A Bayesian Test of the Product Life Cycle Hypothesis Applied to Japanese Crude Steel Production." *Journal of Econometrics*, 4:371–92.

Tsurumi, H., and Y. Tsurumi (1981). "U.S.–Japanese Automobile Trade: A Bayesian Test of a Product Life Cycle." Bureau of Economic Research, Rutgers University, New Brunswick, N.J.; published in *Journal of Econometrics*, 23 (1983):193–210.

Varian, H. R. (1975). "A Bayesian Approach to Real Estate Assessment." In S. E. Fienberg and A. Zellner, eds., *Studies in Bayesian Econometrics and Statistics in Honor of Leonard J. Savage*, pp. 195–208. Amsterdam: North-Holland Publishing Co.

Winkler, R. (1977). "Prior Distributions and Model-Building in Regression Analysis." In A. Aykac and C. Brumat, eds., *New Developments in the Applications of Bayesian Methods*, pp. 233–42. Amsterdam: North-Holland Publishing Co.

Zellner, A. (1971). *An Introduction to Bayesian Inference in Econometrics*. New York: John Wiley & Sons.

———. (1972). "On Assessing Informative Prior Distributions for Regression Coefficients." H. G. B. Alexander Research Foundation, Graduate School of Business, University of Chicago.

———. (1975). "The Bayesian Approach and Alternatives in Econometrics." In S. E. Fienberg and A. Zellner, eds., *Studies in Bayesian Econometrics and Statistics in Honor of Leonard J. Savage*, pp. 39–54. Amsterdam: North-Holland Publishing Co.

———. (1978). "Estimation of Functions of Population Means and Regression Coefficients Including Structural Coefficients: A Minimum Expected Loss (MELO) Approach." *Journal of Econometrics*, 8:125–58.

———. (1979*a*). "Statistical Analysis of Econometric Models." *Journal of the American Statistical Association*, 74:628–43.

———. (1979*b*). "Posterior Odds Ratios for Regression Hypotheses: General Considerations and Some Specific Results." Paper presented at Econometric Society Meeting, December 28–30, 1979. Atlanta, Georgia.

———. (1980*a*). "On Bayesian Regression Analysis with *g*-Prior Distributions." Paper presented at Econometric Society Meeting, September 1980, Denver, Colo.

Zellner, A., ed. (1980*b*). *Bayesian Analysis in Econometrics and Statistics: Essays in Honor of Harold Jeffreys*. Amsterdam: North-Holland Publishing Co.

Zellner, A., and M. S. Geisel (1970). "Analysis of Distributed Lag Models with Applications to Consumption Function Estimation." *Econometrica*, 38:865–88.

Zellner, A., and S. B. Park (1979). "Minimum Expected Loss (MELO) Estimators for Functions of Parameters and Structural Coefficients of Econometric Models." *Journal of the American Statistical Association*, 74:185–93.

Zellner, A., and J. F. Richard (1973). "Use of Prior Information in the Analysis and Estimation of Cobb-Douglas Production Function Models." *International Economic Review*, 14:107–19.

Zellner, A., and A. Siow (1980). "Posterior Odds Ratios for Selected Regression Hypotheses." In J. M. Bernardo, M. H. DeGroot, D. V. Lindley, and A. F. M. Smith, eds., *Bayesian Statistics, Proceedings of the First International Meeting Held in Valencia, (Spain), May 28–June 2, 1979*, pp. 586–603. Valencia, Spain: University Press.

Zellner, A., and G. C. Tiao (1964). "Bayesian Analysis of the Regression Model with Autocorrelated Errors." *Journal of the American Statistical Association*, 59:763–78.

Zellner, A., and W. Vandaele (1975). "Bayes-Stein Estimators for *k*-Means, Regression and Simultaneous Equation Models." In S. E. Fienberg and A. Zellner, eds., *Studies in Bayesian Econometrics and Statistics in Honor of Leonard J. Savage*, pp. 627–53. Amsterdam: North-Holland Publishing Co.

Zellner, A., and A. Williams (1973). "Bayesian Analysis of the Federal Reserve–MIT–Penn Model's Almon Lag Consumption Function." *Journal of Econometrics*, 1:267–99.

Author Index

Numbers followed by *n* refer to footnotes and those followed by *r* to references.

Abrahams, D. M., 310, 315r
Adelman, F. L., 24n
Adelman, I., 24n
Aigner, D. J., 106, 112r
Aitchison, J., 216, 223r
Aitken, M. A., 296–97, 301r
Akaike, H., xx, 269, 274r, 310
Allais, M., 45, 72r
Anderson, T. W., 18, 90, 112r, 238n, 266r
Ando, A., 8, 143n, 157r, 308, 315r
Ansley, C. F., 36–37, 72r
Aoki, M., 190n, 196n
Arrow, K. J., 8, 29
Aykac, A., 201n

Barnard, G. A., xix, 163, 194n, 308, 315r
BarOn, R. R. V., 162–63
Bartlett, M. S., 192n
Basmann, R. L., 22n, 28, 36, 50–54, 57, 70, 72r
Bawa, V. S., 310, 315r
Bayes, T., 3, 76
Belsley, D. A., xivn, 27n
Bergstrom, A. R., 238n, 242, 266r
Bernardo, J. M., 303r, 320r
Berndt, E., 98, 112r, 276, 301r
Bhalla, S. S., 10r
Blackwell, D., 285, 301r, 311
Blattberg, R. C., 225, 228, 236r, 284, 301r
Bloomfield, P., 162
Boltzmann, H., 45
Boot, J. C. G., 24n
Bowley, A. L., 307n, 315r
Bowman, H. W., 310, 315
Box, G. E. P., xivn, xv, xvin, 7, 10r, 30n, 33n, 44, 63, 92, 102, 105–7, 112r, 114r, 118r, 123n, 126n, 135–36n, 137n–38r, 161–63, 165, 191n–92n, 199n, 201, 209n, 214r, 225, 236r, 250, 266r, 280, 302r, 308, 311, 315r
Bradu, D., 216, 222, 224r
Brown, J. A. C., 216, 223r
Brown, S. J., 310, 315r
Brumat, C., 201n
Brumberg, R., 8
Brunner, K., xii, 11r, 28n, 35n
Burks, A. W., 43, 46, 57, 72r
Burns, A. R., 4, 27, 161

Chenery, H. B., 8, 29
Chernoff, H., 285, 302r
Chetty, V. K., 60, 72r, 190n–91n, 195n, 312, 315r
Chow, G. C., 100, 112r, 299, 302r, 310, 315r
Christ, C. F., xivn, 27n, 101, 110–12r
Clemence, R. V., 27n
Cleveland, W. S., xv, 161–63
Commons, J. R., 26
Cooper, R. L., 101, 113r

Copas, J. B., 195n
Cournot, A., 16
Cox, D. R., 199n
Craig, A. T., 206n, 214r
Cramer, H., 258, 266r
Crutchfield, J., xvi, 23
Currie, D., 3n, 29n
Cyert, R., 311, 315r

Dagenais, M., 310, 315r
Dagum, E., xv, 162
Dao, D., 285, 298, 301n, 303r
Davis, W. M., 282, 302r
de Finetti, B., 188n, 311
DeGroot, M. H., 10r, 239n, 266r, 275, 285, 302r–3r, 311, 315r, 320r
de Leeuw, F., 143n, 157r
Dempster, A. P., 310–11, 315
Dhrymes, P. J., 100, 106, 113r, 138rn, 258, 259n, 266r
Dickey, J. M., 258, 266r, 275, 285–86, 298, 302r
Draper, N. R., 296, 302r
Drèze, J., 22n, 93, 95–96, 113r, 191n, 308–9, 315r–16r
Duesenberry, J. S., 8
DuMouchel, W., 225, 236r
Dunn, D. M., xv, 237
Durbin, J., 163
Dwivedi, T. D., 29n, 306n
Dyer, A. R., 284, 302r

Eaton, M., 91
Eddy, W. F., 296–97, 303r
Edgeworth, F. Y., 3, 16, 307
Einstein, A., 43–44
El-Sayyad, G. M., 198n
Engle, R. F., 165
Erdélyi, A., 217n, 224r
Evans, P., 102, 106, 109, 113r, 310, 316r

Fama, E. F., 34n, 110, 113r, 225, 236r
Feige, E. L., 61–62, 64, 67–69, 71, 73r
Feigl, H., 28, 38, 40, 42–48, 50–54, 57–58, 61–62, 69–73r
Ferguson, T. S., 189n, 239n, 266r
Fienberg, S. E., 10r, 28n, 73r, 112r–14r, 117r–19r, 187n, 302r–3r, 308–9, 311, 315–16r, 319r, 320r
Finney, D. J., 216, 220–24r
Fisher, R. A., 3, 7, 17n, 44, 98
Fisher, W. D., 177, 183r, 190n, 196n, 308, 316r
Flood, R. P., 109, 113r, 310, 316r
Fomby, T. B., 298, 302r, 312, 316r
Forrester, J., xin
Fox, K. A., 23n
Frank, P., x
Friedman, J. H., 313, 316r
Friedman, M., xiv, 6–10r, 16n, 30n, 44, 63–64, 73r, 101, 130, 138r, 284, 307
Fromm, G., 160
Fuller, W. A., 91, 113r

Garber, P. M., 109, 113r, 310, 316r
Gaver, K. M., 284, 298, 302r, 309, 316r
Geisel, M. S., 106, 113r, 170n, 177, 183r, 190n, 192n, 196n–198n, 236r, 269, 274r–75, 284–85, 298, 301n–2r, 305r, 309–11, 316r, 320r
Geisser, S., xx, 31n, 75n, 79r, 209n, 214r, 296–97, 303r, 308, 311
Geweke, J., 108, 113r, 165
Ghiselin, B., ixn
Gibbs, W., 45
Girshick, M. A., 285, 301r
Goldberger, A. S., 22n, 24n, 197n, 216, 222, 224r, 267r, 308, 316r
Goldfeld, S. M., 299n, 303r
Goldstone, S. E., xn, 12n, 114r, 139r, 157r
Gonedes, N. J., 225, 228n, 234r, 284, 301r
Good, I. J., 75n, 78n–79r, 187n–88n,

213–14r, 275–76, 285, 303r, 308, 311, 314, 316r
Gordon, R. J., 141, 157r
Gramlich, E. M., 143n, 157r
Granger, C. W. J., xii, 28, 36–37, 54–57, 61–62, 64–65, 70, 73r, 101, 106, 110, 113r, 160, 163, 165
Griffiths, W., 285, 298, 301n, 303r
Griliches, Z., 106, 114r, 141, 157r
Grossman, S., 109, 114r, 311, 316r
Guilkey, D. K., 298, 302r, 312, 316r
Gupta, R. P., 119r, 120n

Haavelmo, T., 18n–19, 58–60, 73r
Hadamard, J., 8, 11r
Hale, C., 89, 114r
Hall, W., 201, 215r
Hamilton, H. R., xn, 12n, 85n, 114r, 120n, 139r, 142n, 157r
Hannan, E. J., 104, 114r, 126n, 137, 139r
Hansen, A. H., 27n
Hanson, N. R., 11r
Harkema, R., 95, 114r, 310, 316r
Harper, W. L., 303r
Hartigan, J. A., 30n, 201, 211, 214r
Hatanaka, M., 238n, 251n, 267r
Haugh, L. D., 106, 114r, 116r
Heien, D. M., 216, 222, 224r
Hendry, D. F., 63, 73r, 109, 114r
Hernández-Iglesias, C., xiin, 28n
Hernández-Iglesias, F., xiin, 28n
Heyde, C. C., 314, 317r
Hickman, B. N., 101, 114r, 120, 127n, 157r
Hickman, G. B., 120n, 139r
Hill, B. M., 256n, 263, 267r, 311
Hill, W. J., 192n, 280, 302r
Hillmer, S., xv, 107, 118r, 161, 163–65, 310, 317r
Hogg, R. V., 206n, 214r
Holt, C. A., 311, 317r
Hood, W. C., 18n–19n, 36
Hooker, C. A., 303r
Hotelling, H., 194
Huang, D. S., 137n, 140r
Hume, D., 5, 40–42, 47
Hurwicz, L., 18
Huzurbazar, V. S., 78

Intrilligator, M., xvii, 187n

Jaynes, E. T., xviiin, 201, 212, 214r, 275, 280, 283n, 288n, 303r
Jeffreys, H., xiiin, xx, 3–5, 7, 11r, 17n, 22n, 28n, 31n, 38, 40–44, 46, 49, 51, 53–54, 56–57, 70–71, 73r, 75–76n, 77–78, 79rn, 87, 114r, 135n, 139r, 187n–190n, 192n, 200–201, 204, 207, 209, 210n, 211–14r, 216, 224r–225, 228, 236r, 256, 267r, 269, 274–77n, 280, 285–87n, 288–89, 303r, 307, 310–11, 317r
Jenkins, G. M., xivn, 30n, 63, 102, 105–7, 112r, 123n, 126n, 135n–36, 138r, 163, 194n, 308, 315r
Johnstone, I. M., 314, 317r
Johnstone, J., 22n
Judge, G. G., 195n, 197n–98n, 312, 317r

Kabe, D. G., 22n
Kadane, J. B., 93, 114r, 262, 267r, 311, 313, 317
Kaitz, H. B., xvin
Kallek, S., xvi, 159–60, 167
Kant, I., 40
Kappenman, R. F., 267r
Kaufman, G. M., 216–17n, 224r, 308, 315r
Kendall, M. G., 216, 221, 224r
Kenny, P. B., 163
Keynes, J. M., xi, 3, 17, 18n–19n, 26–27n, 38–40, 73r
Klein, L. R., 19n, 27, 160
Klein, R. W., 310, 315r
Klepper, S., 309, 318r
Kloek, T., 96, 115r, 313, 317r
Knight, J. L., 100
Knight, M. M., 115r, 158

Koopmans, T. C., 18–19n, 36
Kruskal, W. H., xiin
Kuh, xivn, 27n
Kuiper, J., 161
Kuznets, S., 8, 29, 161

Laporte, A. M., 310, 315
Laub, P. M., 108, 115r
Leamer, E. E., 258, 267r, 275, 284–85, 304r, 308–9, 317r
LeCam, L., 189n, 256n, 267r
Lee, T. C., 195n, 197n–98n, 312, 317r
Leibniz, G., 44
Lempers, F. B., 269, 274r–75, 284–85, 304r, 309, 317r
Leuthold, R. M., 101, 109, 115r, 127n, 139r
Levedahl, J. M., 108, 115r
Lindley, D. V., 22n, 75n, 79r, 135n, 139r, 187n, 189n–90n, 192n, 198n, 200n–201, 212–13n, 214–15r, 216n, 219, 224r, 256n, 267r, 275–76n, 285, 288, 290, 303r–4r, 308, 310–11, 317r, 320r
Litterman, R., xivn, 29n, 33n–34n, 310–12, 317r
Liu, T. C., 22n, 24n, 166
Lombra, R. E., 163, 166
Lucas, R. E., 108, 115r

MacCormick, A. J. A., 115r, 139r
Mach, E., 5, 79n
Madansky, A., 267r
Magnus, W., 224r
Malinvaud, E., 27n
Mandelbrot, B., 225, 236r
Mariano, R. S., 89, 114r, 251n, 267r
Marshall, A., 3, 16–17n
Mason, J. M., 126n, 140r
Maxwell, C., 44
Mayer, F., 285, 298, 304r, 309, 317r
McCallum, B. T., 109, 115r
McCarthy, M. D., 138n–39r
McDonald, J., 34n
Mehta, J. S., 95, 97, 115r
Meiselman, D., 141, 157r, 284
Meltzer, A. H., xii, 11r, 28n, 35n
Merton, R., 311, 317
Milgrom, P., 311, 318r
Milliman, J. W., xn, 12n, 114r, 139r, 157r
Minhas, B. S., 8, 29
Mitchell, W. C., 4, 27, 161
Modigliani, F., 8, 143n, 157r
Moore, G. H., xvin
Moore, H., ixn, 17
Morales, J. A., 95–96, 113r, 115r
Morgan, A., 98, 115r
Moses, L. E., 285, 302r
Mundlak, Y., xviii, 216, 222, 224r
Murphy, M. J., 163
Muth, J., 34n, 115r, 109

Nagar, A. L., 91, 115r, 251n, 267r
Nelson, C. R., 34n, 101, 109, 115r, 124n, 127n, 139r
Nerlove, M., 19n, 120n, 139r
Newbold, P., 37, 54, 57, 62, 73r, 101, 106–7, 110, 113r, 116r, 136n, 139r
Newcomb, S., 225, 236r
Neyman, J., 17n, 187n
Nicholls, D. F., 106, 116r
Nobay, R., 3n, 29n
Novick, D., 13n
Novick, M., 201, 215r

Oberhettinger, R., 224r
Ohtani, K., 310, 318r
Olkin, I., 194n
Orcutt, G., 28

Pagan, A. R., 106, 116r
Palm, F., xiv, 102, 104–5, 116r, 119r, 122–24n, 130n, 133–35n, 137, 139r–140r, 165–66
Park, S. B., xxn, 97, 119r, 251n, 256n, 260n, 262, 268r, 309, 312, 318r, 320r
Parks, R. W., 137n, 139r
Parzen, E., 162

Pearce, D. K., 61–62, 64, 67–69, 71, 73r
Pearson, E. S., 17n
Pearson, K., 3–4, 11r, 13n, 77, 187n
Peck, S. C., xv, 11r, 108, 116r, 141n, 310, 318r
Peel, D., 3n, 29n
Perlman, M. D., 91
Pierce, C. S., 8
Pierce, D. A., xv, xvin, 61–65, 67–71, 73r, 106, 116r, 126n, 140r, 163–65
Plosser, C., xvi, 101–2, 107, 116r, 163, 165–67
Poirier, D. J., 309, 318r
Powell, A. A., 141n
Praetz, P. D., 225, 228n, 236r
Pratt, J. W., 187n, 311
Prescott, E. C., 30n, 177, 183r, 190n, 196n, 310, 318r
Press, S. J., xivn, 209n, 267r, 312–13, 318r
Prothero, D. L., 102, 109, 116r
Pugh, A. L., xn, xi, 12n, 114r, 139r, 157r

Quandt, R. E., 299n, 303r
Quenouille, M. H., 66, 73r, 102, 105, 116r, 123, 136n, 140r

Raiffa, H., 190n, 219n, 224r, 226n, 236r, 275, 304r, 307, 311, 318r
Ramage, J. G., 89, 114r
Ramsey, J., 3, 76
Ranson, R. D., xix, 109, 116r
Reichenbach, H., 5, 11r
Rényi, A., 213n, 215r, 280n, 304r
Reynolds, R. A., 96, 99, 116r, 285, 304r, 309, 311, 318r
Ricardo, D., 3
Richard, J. F., 95, 100, 117r, 213n, 215r, 232, 236r, 284, 305r, 310–11, 318r, 320r
Roberts, E. R., xn, xi, 12n, 114r, 139r, 157r
Roberts, H. V., 168
Robinson, P. M., xivn, 27n
Roll, R., 225, 236r
Rose, D. E., 108, 117r
Rossi, P. E., 309, 311, 318r
Rothenberg, T. J., xivn, 22n, 27n–28n, 96, 117r, 308–9, 318r
Rubin, H., 18

Samuelson, P. A., 34n
Sandee, J., 23n, 170, 183r
Sankar, U., 311, 319r
Sargan, J. D., 90, 117r, 267r
Sargent, T., 36, 73r, 109, 117r, 168
Savage, L. J., 75, 77–78, 80r, 187n, 201, 209n, 215r, 307, 311
Savin, N. E., 98, 112r, 117r, 276–77, 301r, 304r
Sawa, T., 91, 97, 117r, 238n, 251n, 266r–67r, 269, 271, 274r
Schlaifer, R., 190n, 219n, 224r, 226n, 236r, 275, 304r, 307, 311
Schmidt, P., 100, 117r
Schmitz, A., 115r, 139r
Schultz, H., 17
Schwarz, G., 275, 290, 304r
Sclove, S. L., 194
Sengupta, J. K., 23n
Shannon, C. E., 201, 203, 212, 215r
Shiller, R. J., 106, 117r, 136n, 140r, 310, 319r
Shiskin, J., xvi, 159, 162–63
Shore, R. W., 317r
Silvey, S. D., 285, 304r
Simon, H. A., xiin, 19n, 23n, 28, 36–37, 46–49n, 53–54, 70–71, 74r
Sims, C. A., 27n–28, 36, 46, 61–62, 64–69, 73r, 106, 117r, 160, 164
Siow, A., 285, 289–90, 292–96, 298–99, 305r, 309, 320r
Skoog, G. R., 106, 117r
Smith, A. F. M., 3, 285, 303r–304r, 320r
Smith, H., 296, 302r
Solow, R., 8, 29
Sowey, E. R., 90, 117r
Spiegelhalter, D. J., 285, 304r

Stein, C., 56, 194n
Stephenson, J. A., xvin
Stewart, L., 313, 319r
Stigler, G. J., 35
Stigler, S. M., 74r, 307n, 319r
Stone, M., 221n, 224r
Strawderman, W. E., 226n, 236r
Strotz, R. H., 28, 36, 50–51, 53–54, 70–71, 74r
Stuart, A. S., 216, 221, 224r
Suits, D. B., 23n
Swamy, P. A. V. B., 95, 97, 115r, 198n, 309, 312, 319r

Takayama, T., 197n
Tanur, J. M., xiin
Telser, L. G., 137n, 140r
Terpenning, I. J., xv, 163
Terrell, R. D., 106, 116r
Theil, H., 22n–24n, 258–59n, 260n, 267r, 308, 316r, 319r
Thorbecke, E., 23n
Thornber, H., 91, 117r, 192n, 195n, 221n, 224r, 269, 274r, 284–85, 304r, 309, 312, 319r
Tiao, G. C., xv, 10r, 22n, 30n, 33n, 92, 107–8, 118r, 137n–38r, 140r, 161, 163, 165, 191n, 201, 209n, 214r–15r, 225, 236r, 250, 266r, 308, 310–11, 315r, 317r, 319r–20r
Tinbergen, J., xi, xvi, xvii, 17n–18n, 19, 23n, 26–27n, 169–71n, 182–83r
Townsend, R. M., 30n
Tricomi, N. G., 224r
Trivedi, P. K., 102, 118r
Tse, E., 136, 140r
Tsurumi, H., 311, 319r
Tsurumi, Y., 311, 319r
Tukey, J. W., 7, 30n, 98, 118r, 159–60, 162, 164

Vandaele, W., 95, 98, 115r, 119r, 239n, 268r, 301n, 305r, 309, 320r
van den Bogaard, P. J. M., 23n
van Dijk, H. K., 96, 115r, 313, 317r
van Eijk, C. J., 23n, 170, 183r
Varian, H. R., 310, 319r
von Neumann, J., 43

Wald, A., 17n
Wallace, N., 109, 117r
Wallis, K. F., xvi, 102, 107, 109, 116r, 118r, 163, 165–67
Walras, L., 17
Wan, H. Y., 170n, 183r
Watts, D. G., 115r, 139r, 183r, 190n
Wecker, W. E., 164, 168
Wei, W. S., 108, 118r
Whittle, P., 106, 118r, 275, 285, 304r
Wickens, M. R., 109, 118r
Wiener, N., 37, 54, 58, 70–71
Williams, A. D., 232, 237r, 284, 305r, 311, 321r
Williams, R. A., 141n
Winkler, R., 313, 319r
Winsten, C. B., 194n, 308, 315r
Wise, J., 225, 236r
Wold, H. O. A., 28, 36, 50–51, 53–54, 70–71, 74r
Wright, M. H., 313, 316r
Wu, D. M., 106, 118r

Zarembka, P., 302r
Zarnowitz, V., 142, 157r
Zellner, A., xn, xi, xvin, xxn, 10r–11r, 12n, 22n, 27n–31n, 73r, 78, 79r–80r, 85n, 94–97, 101–2, 104–5, 108–9, 112r–14r, 117r–18r, 122–24n, 130, 133–34, 135n–37n, 139r–40r, 144n, 157r–58n, 170n, 177, 179n, 183r, 187n–88n, 190n–92n, 195n–98n, 201, 209n, 211n, 213n, 215r, 226n, 232, 236r, 239n, 242n, 249, 251n, 254, 255–56n, 258, 260n, 262, 267r, 269–70, 273–74r, 282, 284n, 285–86, 289–90, 292–96, 298–99, 301n–2r, 303r–4r, 308–13, 315r–21r
Zidek, J. V., 284, 305r

Subject Index

aggregation problems, 20–21, 108
Akaike information criterion (AIC), xx, 269–74
applications of Bayesian methods, xxi, 29, 188–89, 310–11

Bayesian computer programs, xxi, 312–14
Bayesian econometrics, xvii, 187
—applications of, xxi, 29, 188–89, 310–11
—current state of, xxi, 29, 306–21
—factors in development of, 307–8, 311–12
—limiting factors, 313–14
—pragmatic approach, xvii
—prospects for future, 314
—teaching of, 308
Bayesian forecasting, 310
Bayesian methods
—and alternatives, 187–99
—control, 169–83, 190–91, 310
—estimation, 92–98, 188–91
—hypothesis testing, 98–99, 190–92, 269–74, 275–305
—prediction, 100–101, 189–91
Bayesian vector autoregression model, 310
Bell Labs seasonal adjustment (SABL), xv, 163
bottom-up approach, 32–33
Box-Jenkins ARIMA schemes, 34, 101, 112, 166–67
—seasonality and, 162–64, 166–67
British contributions to economics and statistics, 3
business cycle analysis, 27

causal econometric model-building
—traditional approach to, 60–61
causality, ix, xii
—and hypothesis testing, 58–70
—animistic conception, 40
—Basmann-Strotz-Wold discussion, 50–54
—controversies regarding, 36
—definitions of, xii, 28, 35–58
—econometrics and, 35ff.
—economic theory and, xii, 28, 35ff.
—final causes, 39–40
—forms of econometric models and, 53–54
—instantaneous, 45, 55
—Jeffreys's concept, 49
—philosophers' concept, 37–46
—rationalistic conception, 40–41
—Simon's concept, 46–49
—tests of, xii, xx, 4, 28, 36, 58–72
—Wiener-Granger concept, 36–37, 54–58
causal orderings, 36, 46–49
Chicago quantity theory of money, 5
complexity, index of, 31, 44
computer techniques, xi, 17
—Bayesian computer programs, xxi, 312–14

constant elasticity of substitution (CES) production function, 8, 29
consumption, theories of, 6, 8–9, 29
control policies, 23, 108, 120, 169–83
—Bayesian analysis of, 169–83, 190–91, 310
—Tinbergen's contributions, 169–70, 182
—with misspecifications, 169–83
Cowles Commission contributions, 18

data bases, xi, 17, 21, 83
deductive inference, x, 10
—definition of, 4
description, 4, 14, 27–30
—exploratory data analysis, 30
determinism, 42–43, 47

econometric model-building, 84–87, 120
—complicated models, 7
—concept of sophisticated simplicity and, 7, 31, 86
—macroeconometric modeling, xvi, 17–21
—model size, 7, 31
—seasonality and, 107, 166
econometric model-building industry, 120, 141
econometric models
—accuracy of forecasts, 23–24, 110–11, 142
—aggregation problems, 20–21
—causality and, 35ff.
—criteria for evaluation, 141–42
—criticisms of, 87
—dynamic properties, 19–20, 24
—formulation of, xii–xiii, 24, 32–33, 60–61, 84–87, 120–22
—measurement problems, 14, 20–21, 83–84
—organization of model-building efforts, 24–25
—simulation experiments, xv, 141–57
—size and complexity, x, 7, 15, 19–20, 31–32, 86–87
—statistical analysis of, xiii–xiv, 83ff.
—statistical estimation, 22, 87–98
econometric pioneers, 17
economic policymaking, xvi, 169–83
—econometric methods for, 23
—Lucas effect, 23, 108, 120
—robustness of, xvii, 169–83
—tests of causality and, 64–65
—Tinbergen's contributions to, 169–70, 182
economic theory, x–xii, xxi
—Bayesian methods and, 311
—causality and, xii, 28, 35ff.
—empirical econometrics and, xi, xv, 26, 29, 34, 72, 87
—prediction and, 30–31
—seasonality and, 107, 168
—statistical models and, 30, 86–87
—unusual facts and, x, 8–10, 29
efficient market models, 30
Einstein's laws, 6, 31
empirical econometrics
—and causation, xii, 35ff.
—interaction with theory, xi, xv, 26, 34
—overfitting, 31
entropy, 201
—invariantized, 214
epistemological problems, 49, 78
estimation of structural econometric models
—asymptotically justified procedures, 18, 22, 88–89
—Bayesian estimation, 92–98, 136
—classical least squares, 88, 90, 97
—effects of pretesting, 91–92
—finite sample procedures, 89–91
—$\mathcal{K}$-class estimates, 88, 91, 97
—maximum likelihood estimation, 88–91
—MELO estimation, xx, 97, 246–56
—sampling theory criteria, 92

—Steinian issues, 91
—two- and three-stage least squares estimation, 88, 96–97
experimentation in econometrics, xxi, 14–15
—and unusual facts, 10

Federal Reserve–MIT–Penn macroeconometric model, xv, 143–45
feedback effects, 21
—causality and, 45, 55
Feigl's definition of causality, 38ff.
filtering time series
—tests of causality and, 62–64
final equations, 33, 104–6, 124–27
—estimation of, 136–37
forecast errors of macromodels, 110–11
forecasting, 101, 110–11, 142, 163
—accuracy of, 23–24, 110–11
Friedman's consumption theory, 6, 9, 30–31
Friedman's monetary model, 130–34

Good's bet, 314

Haavelmo's consumption models, xix, 58–61
Handbook of ARIMA processes, 167
Heisenberg uncertainty principle, 15
Hendry UK model, 109
hog market model, 127–29
human behavior, 16
hypothesis testing
—AR(2) process, 282–83
—Bayesian pretest estimate, 99
—causality and, 58–70
—equality of means, 283
—Laplacian approach, 280
—normal mean, 286–91
—P-values, 276, 279
—pre-tests, 99, 279–80
—regression hypotheses, 282, 292–300
—survey of methods used, 277–80

identification problem, 18, 26
induction, ix–x, 10
—definitions of, 4–5
—Jeffreys's contributions to, 5
inductive generalizations, 5–6
—starting point, 6
inductive logic, 6, 10
—causality, relation to, 46
industrial dynamics approach, xi
IS-LM analysis, 153, 156

Jeffreys's concept of probability, 75–79
Jeffreys's theory of scientific method, 6
Jeffreys-Wrinch simplicity postulate, 7, 31, 71, 87
—ordering of laws according to, 44

laws
—causality and, 35, 38ff., 57–58, 60–62
—characteristics of, 42–46
—domains of, 44–46
—forms of, 43–44
—probabilistic, 43, 47
linearity measures, 151
log-normal distribution, 216–24
—Bayesian approach, 216–19
—Finney approach, 220
—maximum likelihood approach, 219–21
—minimum MSE approach, 220–22
log-normal regression, xviii, 216–24
—Bayesian approach, 218–19, 222–23
—Finney approach, 222
—maximum likelihood approach, 222
—minimum MSE approach, 222–23
loss functions
—bounded, xix
—generalized quadratic, xix–xx
—relative squared error, xviii–xix
—squared error, xix
Lucas effect, 23, 108

macroeconometric modeling, xvi, 17–18
—accuracy of forecasts, 23–24
—aggregation problems, 20–21
—and economic knowledge, 19–20
—dynamic properties, xv, 19–20, 24
—economics profession's reactions to, 19–21
—Federal Reserve–MIT–Penn model, xv
—Keynes-Tinbergen discussion, 18, 27
—Klein's contributions, 19
—measurement problems, 14, 20–21
—organization of model-building efforts, 24–25
—size and complexity of models, x, 7, 15, 19–20, 31–32, 86–87
—statistical problems, 20
—Tinbergen's models, 17–18
mathematical models
—in social sciences, x, xvi, 12–25
maximal data information prior distributions, xvii, 201–15
maximum likelihood estimation
—Cowles Commission methods, 18, 22
—log-normal distribution, 219, 221
—log-normal regression, 222
—ratio of regression coefficients, xix
—regression model with *t*-errors, 227–29
—structural econometric models and, 88–90, 92, 96
measurement
—and mathematical models, 14, 20–21
—and theory, xi, 4, 14, 27–28, 72
—error, 14, 20–21, 107–8
minimum expected loss (MELO) estimates, 97, 238–68
—properties of, 256–64
—ratios of parameters, 242–46
—reciprocals of parameters, xix, 239–42, 264–66
—structural coefficients, xx, 97, 246–56
missing observation problems, 310
model identification, 106, 112, 135–36
multiple regression model
—linear hypotheses, xx
—log-normal, 218–19, 222
—multivariate Student-*t* errors, xviii, 225–37
multiple time series process, 102, 123
multivariate statistical methods, 17, 22
Muth's rational expectations hypothesis, 23, 30, 133

NBER-Census Conference on Seasonal Analysis of Economic Time Series, xv, 158–67
NBER-NSF Seminar on Bayesian Inference in Econometrics, 308
Newton's laws, 5, 12, 31
non-Bayesian methods, 192–200
—control, 196
—criterion of performance in repeated samples, 199
—departures from specifying assumptions, 198
—estimation, 87–92, 193–95, 219–23
—hypothesis testing, 98–99, 199–200
—nuisance parameters and, 198
—prediction, 99–100, 195–96
—prior information and, 196–98
normative social science, 16
nuisance parameter problem, 198, 223

Ockham's razor, 7, 31, 87
outlying observations, 8

Pacific halibut conservation program, xvi
—effects of policies, 23
philosophical idealism, 76
philosophical realism, 76
philosophy and objectives of econometrics, 3–11.
philosophy of science, ix, 3ff.

portfolio problem, 310
positive social science, 16
posterior odds ratios, xx, 78–79, 269–74, 275–305, 309–10
—and Akaike information criterion (AIC), xx, 269–74
—and regression hypotheses, xx, 282, 292–300
prediction, 12, 137–38
—causation and, xii, 28, 35, 38ff.
—economic theories and, 30, 35
—empirical econometrics and, 31, 120, 137–38
—final equations and, 137–38
—Friedman's predictions, 6, 30
—human behavior and, 16
—induction and, 4–5, 79
—Jeffreys-Wrinch simplicity postulate and, 44
—Newton's predictions, 13
—transfer functions and, 137–38
pretest biases, 280
principle of parsimony, 7, 31, 71, 87
prior distributions, xvii–xviii
—for binomial process, 206–8
—for bivariate and multivariate processes, 208–10
—for stationary AR(1) process, 210–11
—for univariate processes, 205
—invariance properties, 202–3
—Jeffreys's rule for, 204
—maximal data, xvii, 201–15
—reference, 309
—uninformative, 79
prior information, xviii, 201–14
probability
—as degree of reasonable belief, 6, 28, 75
—definitions of, ix, xiii, 6, 28, 75ff., 275
—frequency concept, 275
—necessarist view, xiii, 77
—personal subjective view, 76, 78
progress of science, xvii
P-values, 276, 288–89, 301

random walk processes, 6, 33
reduced form equations, 100
reductive inference, ix–x, 10
—definition of, 8
regression model
—control of, 171–83
—forward and backward, 66–67, 71–72
—hypotheses, xx
—hypothesis-testing and, 232, 269–74, 275–305
—log-normal, xviii, 216–24
—multiple with Student-*t* errors, xviii, 225–37
robustness
—of policymaking, xvii
—of statistical techniques, xxi, 8

savings rate, constancy of, 8, 29
seasonal analysis, xv, 158–68
—Bayesian adjustment, 310
—Bell Labs seasonal adjustment (SABL), xv, 163
—conceptual issues, xvi, 160–61
—definition of, 160
—descriptive approach, xvi, 161
—dips in spectrum, 164–65
—econometric modeling and, 166
—economic theory and, 168
—minimal extraction principle, 163–64
—multivariate, 165
—objectives of, 160
—practical uses of, 168
—SEMTSA approach and, 107, 165–66
—signal extraction ARIMA procedure, xv, 163–64, 167
—statistical modeling approach, xvi, 161, 163–64
—structural econometric approach, xvi, 107, 161, 165–66

seasonal analysis (cont.)
—X-11–ARIMA procedure, xv, 162, 167
—X-11 procedure, xvi, 158, 167
SEMTSA approach, xiv, 33, 101–9
—applications of, 106–7, 127–34
—seasonal modeling and, 107
signal extraction ARIMA approach, xv
Simon's causal orderings, 46–49
simulation experiments, xv, 7, 86–87, 141–57
—and unusual facts, 9
—linearity and symmetry experiments, 145–51, 156
—macroeconometric, 141–57
—major depression experiments, 152–56
simultaneous equation model, 19
—estimation methods for, 18, 22, 87–98
—hypothesis-testing, 98–99
—prediction procedures, 99–101, 310
solipsism, 76–77
Strotz-Wold definitions of causality, 50–54
supply and demand models, 7, 26, 31, 127–29
survey methods, xxi
—and unusual facts, 10
survey of hypothesis-testing procedures, xx, 277–80
Susquehanna River basin model, x–xi
switching regression model, 310
symmetry measures, 146–47

teaching, ix–x, 10
three-stage least squares, 22, 88, 96
top-down approach, 32–33
transfer functions, 33, 103–6, 126–27
—estimation of, 136–37
two-stage least squares, 22, 88, 90–91, 96–97

unity of science principle, 3–4, 13
unusual facts, x, 8, 29
—production of, 9–10
unusual historical periods, 9

value judgments, 16
vector autoregressive model, 32
—Bayesian vector autoregressive model, 29, 34

welfare functions
—policymakers', 170–71
Wiener-Granger causality concept, 36–37, 54–58

X-11–ARIMA seasonal adjustment procedure, xv, 162, 167
X-11 seasonal adjustment procedure, xvi, 158, 167